ZAGAT
2014

Washington, DC
Baltimore
Restaurants

LOCAL EDITORS
Olga Boikess and Martha Thomas
with Senior Consulting Editor Marty Katz

STAFF EDITOR
Josh Rogers

Published and distributed by
Zagat Survey, LLC
76 Ninth Avenue
New York, NY 10011
T: 212.977.6000
E: feedback@zagat.com
www.zagat.com

ACKNOWLEDGMENTS

We're grateful to our local editors, Olga Boikess, a Washington lawyer and avid diner who has edited this Survey since 1987; Martha Thomas, a Baltimore-based freelance writer who contributes to numerous local and national publications and worked on Zagat's *New York City Restaurants* guide more than a decade ago; and Marty Katz, a Baltimore writer, photographer and barbecue researcher who has worked with us since 1995. We also sincerely thank the thousands of people who participated in this survey – this guide is really "theirs."

We also thank Kara Freewind (editor), Julie Alvin, American Institute of Wine and Food-DC Chapter, Jennifer Barger, Dan Boward, Jody Brady, Kathryn Carroll, Elizabeth Daleske, Corrie Davidson, Mike Evitts, Bill and Lorraine Fitzsimmons, Dina Gan, Barbara Johnson, Natasha Lesser, Miranda Levenstein, Mike Lima, Emily Parsons, Simon Spelling and Stefanie Tuder, as well as the following members of our staff: Brian Albert, Sean Beachell, Maryanne Bertollo, Reni Chin, Larry Cohn, John Deiner, Andrew Dolan, Nicole Diaz, Kelly Dobkin, Jeff Freier, Alison Gainor, Michelle Golden, Justin Hartung, Marc Henson, Anna Hyclak, Ryutaro Ishikane, Aynsley Karps, Natalie Lebert, Mike Liao, Vivian Ma, Molly Moker, James Mulcahy, Andrew Murphy, Polina Paley, Josh Siegel, Albry Smither, Amanda Spurlock, Chris Walsh, Jacqueline Wasilczyk, Art Yagci, Sharon Yates, Anna Zappia and Kyle Zolner.

ABOUT ZAGAT

In 1979, we asked friends to rate and review restaurants purely for fun. The term "user-generated content" had yet to be coined. That hobby grew into Zagat Survey; 34 years later, we have loyal surveyors around the globe and our content now includes nightlife, shopping, tourist attractions, golf and more. Along the way, we evolved from being a print publisher to a digital content provider. We also produce marketing tools for a wide range of corporate clients, and you can find us on Google+ and just about any other social media network.

Our reviews are based on public opinion surveys. The ratings reflect the average scores given by the survey participants who voted on each establishment. The text is based on quotes from, or paraphrasings of, the surveyors' comments. Phone numbers, addresses and other factual data were correct to the best of our knowledge when published in this guide.

JOIN IN

To improve our guides, we solicit your comments – positive or negative; it's vital that we hear your opinions. Just contact us at **nina-tim@zagat.com**.

Contents

Ratings & Symbols

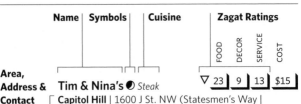

	Name	Symbols		Cuisine		Zagat Ratings			
						FOOD	DECOR	SERVICE	COST

Area, Address & Contact
Tim & Nina's ◑ *Steak* ▽ 23 | 9 | 13 | $15
Capitol Hill | 1600 J St. NW (Statesmen's Way |
202-555-6000 | www.zagat.com

Review, surveyor comments in quotes
This "meat-and-greet mecca" boasts the ultimate "see-or-avoid-being-seen" experience, with one-way glass booths ("you can look out but others can't look in") and a "hot line to the family quarters at the White House"; in the absence of waiters, you "pick your own salad" from the hydroponic planters, but the "real attraction" is the low price since "lobbyists pay for most meals."

Ratings   **Food, Decor** & **Service** are rated on a 30-point scale.

26 - 30   extraordinary to perfection

21 - 25   very good to excellent

16 - 20   good to very good

11 - 15   fair to good

0 - 10   poor to fair

▽   low response | less reliable

Cost   The price of dinner with a drink and tip; lunch is usually 25% to 30% less. For unrated **newcomers,** the price range is as follows:

I $25 and below   E $41 to $65

M $26 to $40   VE $66 or above

Symbols   ◑   serves after 11 PM
              Ⓢ   closed on Sunday
              Ⓜ   closed on Monday
              ⊅   cash only

Maps   Index maps show the restaurants with the highest Food ratings and other notable places in those areas.

What's New

This **2014 Washington, DC/Baltimore Restaurants Survey** is an update covering 1,600 restaurants in the area, including 108 important additions that have helped fire up the local dining scenes over the past year.

BIG NAMES: The most recent crop of farm-to-table dining options yielded notable entries by Bryan Voltaggio, who planted the American **Range** in Chevy Chase, and Frederik de Pue, whose European **Table** graced Shaw. Blue-chip chefs also helped kick hip 14th Street NW into overdrive with the debuts of Stephen Starr's picture-postcard French brasserie **Le Diplomate,** Peter Pastan's artisanal wine bar **Etto** and Ann Cashion's transporting **Taqueria Nacional.**

GUILTY PLEASURES: Fried chicken and donuts, an of-the-moment 'it' cuisine, spawned fry shops like **Astro Doughnuts & Fried Chicken** Downtown and **GBD** below Dupont Circle. And the Philly cheesesteak, another indulgence, now has a dedicated purveyor in **Taylor Charles Steak & Ice** in the Atlas District.

SMOKE: High-tech grills and smokers infused all manner of foodstuffs with woodsy flavor, most notably at Belgian **B Too** near Logan Circle, Pan-Latin **Del Campo** in the Penn Quarter and **The Red Hen,** a wine-focused Italian in Bloomingdale.

DRINK-CENTRIC DINING: Artisanal beverages and food paired up at hip haunts like **Black Whiskey,** the American carvery and bourbon specialist just west of Logan Circle, and **Beuchert's Saloon** on Capitol Hill, which infuses cocktails with housemade mixers. Japanese bar culture arrived in Chinatown via **Daikaya Izakaya**; Russian vodka with a chaser of kitsch hit the Golden Triangle at **Mari Vanna**; and **Ambar** on Capitol Hill features uncommon Balkan wines and spirits along with small plates.

CASUAL SOPHISTICATES: Classy design sets the stage for casual, if not always inexpensive, evenings out at chic, airy American brasserie **NoPa Kitchen + Bar** and contemporary, multilevel seafooder **Azur,** both in Penn Quarter, plus Downtown's mod American **Woodward Table** and Bethesda's winkingly woodsy Mediterranean **Wildwood Kitchen.**

MEANWHILE IN BALTIMORE: Charm City is witnessing the rebirth of some iconic names and spaces, including **McFaul's IronHorse Tavern,** bringing new life to the old Sanders' Corners home in Parkville, plus **The Chesapeake** and the about-to-open **Martick's** Downtown, rejiggered to indulge contemporary tastes for locally sourced fare. Serious pizza efforts continue apace, with newcomer **Verde Pizza Napolitano** slinging authentic Neapolitan pies, **Birroteca** sprinkling on the bacon and figs and the about-to-open **Paulie Gee's** (a well-regarded Brooklyn transplant) refurbishing an old Hampden drinking club. And local restaurant groups keep adding options, like **Johnny's,** from Foreman Wolf, and **Fleet Street Kitchen** plus the forthcoming **Cunningham's** from the Bagby Restaurant Group.

Washington, DC
Baltimore, MD
August 22, 2013

Olga Boikess
Martha Thomas

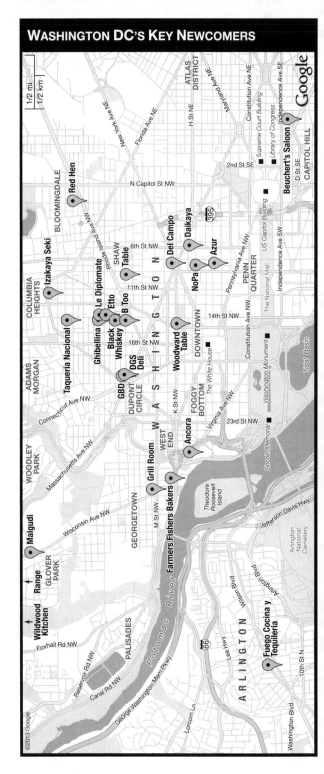

Key Newcomers

Our editors' picks among this year's arrivals. See full list at p. 186

Ancora | *Italian* | Bob Kinkead's latest act near Kennedy Center

Azur | *Seafood* | Sophisticated seafood and setting in Penn Quarter

Beuchert's Saloon | *Amer.* | Capitol Hill farm-to-table with chef's table

Black Whiskey | *Amer.* | Meat and whiskey meet on hip 14th St. NW

B Too | *Belgian* | Smoky bivalves in bi-level bistro near Logan Circle

Dakaiya | *Japanese* | Ramen and sake bring Japan to Chinatown

Del Campo | *Pan-Latin* | Elegant Penn Quarter grilled-meat showcase

DGS | *Jewish* | Updated deli fare meets chic Dupont digs

Etto | *Italian/Pizza* | Artisanal pizza, tapas and wine on 14th St. NW

Farmer Fishers Bakers | *Amer.* | Stylish Washington Harbour American

Fuego Cocina | *Mexican* | Classy Clarendon cantina and tequileria

GBD | *Bakery/Chicken* | Donuts and fried chicken tempt Dupont

Ghibellina | *Italian* | Ambitious 14th St. NW Florentine resto-lounge

Grill Room | *Amer.* | High-end steak rendezvous in Georgetown

Izakaya Seki | *Japanese* | Low-key Japanese authenticity on U St. NW

Le Diplomate | *French* | 14th St. NW channels the Champs-Élysées

Malgudi | *Indian* | Uncommon southern Indian fare in Glover Park

NoPa | *Amer.* | Industrial brasserie hosts chic Penn Quarter scene

Range | *Amer.* | Bryan Voltaggio's inside-the-Beltway hit in Chevy Chase

Red Hen | *Italian* | Bloomingdale Italian wine-and-dine spot

Table | *European* | Minimalist foodie destination in Shaw

Taqueria Nacional | *Mex.* | Cheap eats in transporting 14th St. NW digs

Wildwood Kitchen | *Med.* | Bethesda's upscale scene spot

Woodward Table | *Amer.* | Upscale regional classics Downtown

---

WHAT'S NEXT

NYC's Michael White will step up to the plate near Nationals Park this summer with outlets of his Italian **Osteria Morini** and **Nicoletta Pizzeria** concepts. Also in the lineup, **Bluejacket,** a state-of-the-art brewery, bar and restaurant from the **Churchkey** talents, will be batting nearby in The Yards. Elsewhere, look for Southeast Asian **Doi Moi** from the Proof/Estadio team on the sizzling 14th Street NW strip, along with Mike Isabella's Greek **Kapnos** and the Italian sandwich shop **G.** In late fall, José Andrés plans to bring his **America Eats Tavern** concept to the posh Ritz-Carlton Tysons Corner. And NYC top toque Daniel Boulud will establish an outpost of his vibrant French bistro **DBGB** Downtown in 2014.

Washington, DC's Most Popular

This list is plotted on the map at the back of this book.

1. Clyde's | *American*
2. 2 Amys | *Pizza*
3. Zaytinya | *Med./Mideast.*
4. Rasika | *Indian*
5. 1789 | *American*
6. Jaleo | *Spanish*
7. Inn at Little Washington | *Amer.*
8. Founding Farmers | *American*
9. 2941 Restaurant | *American*
10. Blue Duck Tavern | *American*
11. Old Ebbitt Grill | *American*
12. Busboys/Poets | *Amer./Eclectic*
13. L'Auberge François* | *French*
14. Matchbox | *American*
15. Sweetwater Tavern | *SW*
16. Volt | *American*
17. Central M. Richard | *Amer./Fr.*
18. Dogfish Head | *Pub Food*
19. Coastal Flats | *Seafood*
20. Acadiana | *Cajun/Creole*
21. Artie's | *American*
22. Brasserie Beck | *Belgian/French*
23. Mike's "American"* | *American*
24. 100° Chinese | *Chinese*
25. Chef Geoff's | *American*
26. Ben's Chili Bowl | *Diner*
27. Carlyle | *American*
28. Komi | *American/Mediterranean*
29. 8407 Kitchen Bar | *American*
30. Ray's The Steaks | *Steak*
31. BlackSalt | *American/Seafood*
32. Lebanese Taverna | *Lebanese*
33. Oyamel | *Mexican*
34. CityZen | *American*
35. Marcel's | *Belgian/French*
36. La Tasca | *Spanish*
37. Dutch's Daughter | *American*
38. Austin Grill | *Tex-Mex*
39. Mon Ami Gabi* | *French*
40. Addie's | *American*

MOST POPULAR CHAINS

1. Five Guys | *Burgers*
2. Cheesecake Factory | *American*
3. Capital Grille | *Steak*
4. Ledo Pizza | *Pizza*
5. Uncle Julio's | *Tex-Mex*
6. Ruth's Chris | *Steak*
7. Maggiano's Little Italy | *Italian*
8. Legal Sea Foods | *Seafood*
9. P.F. Chang's | *Chinese*
10. McCormick/Schmick | *Seafood*

MOST SEARCHED ON ZAGAT.COM

1. Jaleo
2. Clyde's
3. Central Michel Richard
4. Hank's Oyster Bar
5. Capital Grille
6. 701
7. Inn at Little Washington
8. Hamilton
9. Mintwood Place
10. District Commons

---

* Indicates a tie with restaurant above

Top Food

<u>29</u> Inn at Little Washington | *Amer.*

<u>28</u> Rasika | *Indian*
L'Auberge François | *French*
Komi | *Amer./Med.*
Marcel's | *Belgian/French*
Prime Rib | *Steak*
Volt | *American*
Corduroy | *American*
Lucky Corner | *Vietnamese*
Minibar | *Eclectic*
Obelisk | *Italian*
Little Serow | *Thai*
Monocacy Crossing | *American*
Peking Duck Rest.* | *Chinese*

<u>27</u> CityZen | *American*
Tasting Room | *American*
Restaurant Eve | *American*
Makoto | *Japanese*
Russia House Rest. | *Russian*
Foti's | *American*

Palena | *American*
Ray's The Steaks | *Steak*
Blue Duck Tavern | *American*
Ashby Inn | *American*
Tosca | *Italian*
BlackSalt | *American/Seafood*
Fiola | *Italian*
Ruan Thai | *Thai*
2941 Restaurant | *American*
Fogo de Chão | *Braz./Steak*
Hong Kong Palace | *Chinese*
Il Pizzico | *Italian*
Source | *Asian*

<u>26</u> Thai Square | *Thai*
Capital Grille | *Steak*
Niwano Hana | *Japanese*
Pasta Mia* | *Italian*
Sushi Taro | *Japanese*
Bistro Provence | *French*
Pupatella Pizzeria | *Pizza*

Top Decor

<u>29</u> Inn at Little Washington

<u>28</u> Plume
Grace's Mandarin

<u>27</u> Lightfoot
L'Auberge François
Oya
Magnolias at the Mill
CityZen
2941 Restaurant

<u>26</u> Cafe Renaissance

Prime Rib*
Marcel's
Volt
Charlie Palmer Steak
Eventide
Bistro L'Hermitage
Trummer's On Main

<u>25</u> Bombay Club
Bourbon Steak
Sei

Top Service

<u>29</u> Inn at Little Washington
Plume

<u>28</u> Komi
Cafe Renaissance
L'Auberge François
Prime Rib
Marcel's
Volt

<u>27</u> Minibar
CityZen

Little Serow
Bistro L'Hermitage
Fogo de Chão

<u>26</u> Obelisk
Restaurant Eve
Tasting Room
Corduroy
Ashby Inn
Tosca
Capital Grille

Excludes places with low votes, unless otherwise indicated

TOPS BY CUISINE

AMERICAN (NEW)

<u>29</u> Inn at Little Washington
<u>28</u> Komi
    Volt
    Corduroy
    Monocacy Crossing
<u>27</u> CityZen
    Tasting Room
    Restaurant Eve
    Foti's
    Palena
    Blue Duck Tavern

AMERICAN (TRAD.)

<u>26</u> Mike's "American"
<u>25</u> Dutch's Daughter
    Ray's/Third
    Artie's
<u>24</u> Majestic

BURGERS

<u>25</u> Ray's/Third
    Black & Orange
<u>24</u> Five Guys
    Thunder Burger & Bar
<u>23</u> Good Stuff Eatery

CHINESE

<u>28</u> Peking Duck Rest.
<u>27</u> Hong Kong Palace
<u>25</u> China Jade
    Peking Gourmet
    Mark's Duck Hse.

FRENCH (BISTRO)

<u>26</u> Bistro L'Hermitage
    Central Michel Richard
    Le Refuge
<u>25</u> Yves Bistro
    Montmartre

FRENCH (CLASSIC)

<u>28</u> L'Auberge François
<u>26</u> La Bergerie
    Brabo by Robert Wiedmaier
    La Chaumière
<u>25</u> Et Voila

FRENCH (NEW)

<u>28</u> Marcel's
<u>26</u> Bistro Provence
    Bistro Bis
<u>24</u> Bezu
<u>23</u> Matisse

GREEK/MED.

<u>28</u> Komi
<u>26</u> Zaytinya
    Nostos
    Athens Grill
    Vaso's Kit.

INDIAN

<u>28</u> Rasika
<u>26</u> Bombay Tandoor
<u>25</u> Masala Art
    Jaipur
    Bombay Club

ITALIAN

<u>28</u> Obelisk
<u>27</u> Tosca
    Fiola
    Il Pizzico
<u>26</u> Pasta Mia

JAPANESE

<u>27</u> Makoto
<u>26</u> Niwano Hana
    Sushi Taro
<u>25</u> Kaz Sushi
    Kotobuki

MEXICAN

<u>25</u> Oyamel
<u>24</u> Cacique
    Azucar
<u>23</u> Rosa Mexicano
<u>22</u> Taqueria Poblano

MIDDLE EASTERN

<u>26</u> Zaytinya
    Kabob Palace
    Bamian
<u>25</u> Afghan Kabob Rest.
    Kabob Bazaar

PAN-ASIAN

<u>27</u> Source
<u>25</u> Sweet Ginger
<u>23</u> Asian Spice
    Raku
<u>22</u> Batik

PIZZA

<u>26</u> Pupatella Pizzeria
<u>25</u> 2 Amys
    Seventh Hill Pizza
    Mia's Pizzas
    Mellow Mushroom

SEAFOOD

27 BlackSalt
26 Pesce
   PassionFish
   Ford's Fish Shack
   Pearl Dive Oyster

SOUTH AMERICAN

27 Fogo de Chão
26 Chima
24 Grill from Ipanema
23 La Canela
22 El Chalan

SOUTHERN

26 Vidalia
25 Carolina Kitchen
24 Acadiana
23 Evening Star
   Art & Soul

SPANISH

26 Isabella's
   La Taberna del Alabardero
25 Estadio
24 Cacique
   Jaleo

STEAKHOUSES

28 Prime Rib
27 Ray's The Steaks
26 Capital Grille
   Ruth's Chris
   Morton's

TEX-MEX

25 El Mariachi
22 Mi Rancho
   Guapo's
   Calif. Tortilla
21 Uncle Julio's

THAI

28 Little Serow
27 Ruan Thai
26 Thai Square
   Thai Basil
   Nava Thai

VIETNAMESE

28 Lucky Corner Vietnamese
26 Present
25 Pho 14
   Huong Viet
   Four Sisters

TOPS BY SPECIAL FEATURE

BREAKFAST

24 Pho 75
23 Bread Line
   Old Ebbitt Grill
22 Bayou Bakery
21 Café du Parc

BRUNCH

27 Palena
   Blue Duck Tavern
   BlackSalt
26 Pearl Dive Oyster
25 Bombay Club

CHILD-FRIENDLY

25 2 Amys
24 Majestic
22 Pete's Apizza
21 Cactus Cantina
20 Comet Ping Pong

CRAB CAKES

26 PassionFish
24 Oceanaire
   Hank's Oyster Bar
22 Clyde's
21 Johnny's Half Shell

DC HOTEL DINING

27 CityZen (Mandarin Oriental)
   Blue Duck (Park Hyatt)
26 Plume (The Jefferson)
   Bistro Bis (Hotel George)
25 Bourbon Steak (Four Seasons)

DINING ALONE

27 Palena
26 Pesce
   Zaytinya
   Central Michel Richard
   Vidalia

LIVE ENTERTAINMENT

24 Dukem
22 Perrys
21 Hill Country
20 Hamilton
   Bayou

OUTDOORS

28 L'Auberge François
25 Tabard Inn
21 Café du Parc
20 Old Angler's
   Poste Moderne

POWER SCENES

27 Tosca
26 Capital Grille
Charlie Palmer Steak
Central Michel Richard
Bistro Bis

PRIVATE ROOMS

28 Rasika
Marcel's
Corduroy
27 CityZen
Fiola

RAW BARS

27 BlackSalt
26 Pearl Dive Oyster
24 Hank's Oyster Bar
23 Old Ebbitt Grill
- Range

ROMANTIC

25 Cork
24 Co Co. Sala
23 Eventide
Marvin
Firefly

SMALL PLATES/TAPAS

28 Rasika
27 Fiola
Source
26 Zaytinya
La Taberna del Alabardero

TRENDY

28 Rasika
Komi
27 Fiola
26 Zaytinya
Pearl Dive Oyster

VIEWS

27 2941 Restaurant
Source
26 Charlie Palmer Steak
22 Perrys
17 Sequoia

WORTH A TRIP

29 Inn at Little Washington (VA)
28 Volt (Frederick, MD)
27 Foti's (Culpeper, VA)
Ashby Inn (Paris, VA)
26 Isabella's (Frederick, MD)

TOPS BY OCCASION

Some best bets – in a range of prices and cuisines – for these occasions

ANNIVERSARY

29 Inn at Little Washington
28 Komi
Marcel's
27 CityZen
Restaurant Eve

BRIDAL SHOWER

27 Blue Duck Tavern
25 Tabard Inn
24 Trummer's On Main
21 Ping Pong Dim Sum
20 Teaism

BUSINESS CELEBRATION

28 Rasika
Marcel's
27 CityZen
Tosca
Fiola

DISCREET RENDEZVOUS

26 Pesce
Plume
22 Il Canale
New Heights
21 1905

GRADUATION DINNER

28 Rasika West End (GW)
26 1789 (GU)
25 Bourbon Steak (GW/GU)
22 District Commons (GW)
- Al Dente (AU)

GROUP BIRTHDAY

26 Zaytinya
25 Cava Mezze
24 Birch & Barley
22 Zengo
Ardeo + Bardeo

MEET FOR A DRINK

28 Rasika
26 Central Michel Richard
Vidalia
Plume
21 Johnny's Half Shell

POST-WORK HAPPY HOUR

27 Fiola
Source
26 Zaytinya
Central Michel Richard
24 Proof

TOPS BY LOCATION

ADAMS MORGAN

26 Pasta Mia
25 Amsterdam Falafel
   Cashion's Eat Place
   Mellow Mushroom
24 Grill from Ipanema

ALEXANDRIA (OLD TOWN)

27 Restaurant Eve
26 La Bergerie
   Le Refuge
   Vaso's Kitchen
   Brabo by Robert Wiedmaier

ATLAS DISTRICT

26 Toki Underground
25 Atlas Room
24 Granville Moore's
   Ethiopic
23 Sticky Rice

BETHESDA

26 Bistro Provence
25 Kabob Bazaar
   Mia's Pizzas
24 Faryab
   Tako Grill

CAPITOL HILL

26 Charlie Palmer Steak
   Bistro Bis
25 Montmartre
   Belga Café
   Seventh Hill Pizza*

CHINATOWN

24 Graffiato
   Five Guys
23 Chinatown Express
   Asian Spice
   Matchbox

CLARENDON

25 Kabob Bazaar
   Cava Mezze
24 Pho 75
   Delhi Club
   Lyon Hall

CLEVELAND PARK

27 Palena
25 2 Amys
24 Dino
23 Ripple
   Indique

DOWNTOWN

26 Plume
   Mio
25 Bibiana Osteria
   Brasserie Beck
24 Oceanaire

DUPONT CIRCLE

28 Komi
   Obelisk
   Little Serow
26 Sushi Taro
   Pesce

FALLS CHURCH

27 2941 Restaurant
   Hong Kong Palace
26 Present Restaurant
   Bamian
   Elephant Jumps

FREDERICK

28 Volt
   Lucky Corner Vietnamese
   Monocacy Crossing
27 Tasting Room
26 Firestone's

GEORGETOWN

26 1789
   La Chaumière
25 Bourbon Steak
24 Filomena Ristorante
   Neyla

GOLDEN TRIANGLE

28 Prime Rib
26 Morton's
   Vidalia
   Oval Room
25 BLT Steak

LOGAN CIRCLE

26 Pearl Dive Oyster
25 Cork
   Estadio
24 Birch & Barley
23 Posto

PENN QUARTER

28 Rasika
   Minibar
27 Tosca
   Fiola
   Fogo de Chão

ROCKVILLE

- 27 Il Pizzico
- 26 Niwano Hana
- 25 China Jade
- Sushi Damo
- Yuan Fu

SILVER SPRING

- 25 Ray's The Classics
- 24 Samantha's
- Crisp & Juicy
- 8407 Kitchen Bar
- Thai at Silver Spring

TYSONS CORNER

- 26 Capital Grille
- Nostos
- Bombay Tandoor
- Chima*
- 25 Palm

U STREET CORRIDOR

- 25 Black & Orange
- 24 Etete
- Dukem
- Negril*
- 23 Al Crostino

WEST END

- 28 Rasika
- Marcel's
- 27 Blue Duck Tavern
- 25 Ris
- 22 Westend Bistro

WORLD BANK

- 26 La Taberna del Alabardero
- 25 Kaz Sushi
- 24 Founding Farmers
- 23 Bread Line
- Aroma Indian Cuisine

TOPS BY DESTINATION

Some best bets – in a range of prices and cuisines – near these points of interest

AFRICAN AMERICAN CIVIL WAR MEMORIAL

- 24 Dukem
- 23 Marvin
- Eatonville
- 22 Ben's Chili Bowl
- Busboys & Poets

CAPITOL (HOUSE SIDE)

- 23 Good Stuff Eatery
- 22 Sweetgreen
- We the Pizza
- 21 Sonoma
- 20 Hunan Dynasty▽

CAPITOL (SENATE SIDE)

- 26 Bistro Bis
- 23 Bistro Cacao
- Art & Soul
- 21 Monocle
- Johnny's Half Shell

CONVENTION CENTER

- 28 Corduroy
- 25 Kushi
- 24 Acadiana
- 23 Mandu
- 22 Busboys & Poets

EASTERN MARKET

- 25 Montmartre
- Belga Café
- 24 Acqua al 2
- Hank's Oyster Bar
- 23 Ted's Bulletin

KENNEDY CENTER

- 28 Rasika
- Marcel's
- 22 Westend Bistro
- District Commons
- _ Ancora

NATIONAL GALLERY OF ART

- 28 Rasika
- 27 Fiola
- Source
- 26 Capital Grille
- 23 701

NATIONAL PORTRAIT GALLERY

- 26 Zaytinya
- Sei
- 24 Proof
- Graffiato
- _ NoPa

NATIONAL THEATRE

26 Central Michel Richard
24 J&G Steakhouse
23 Occidental Grill
21 Chef Geoff's
   Café du Parc

NATIONAL ZOO

24 Dino
22 Sorriso▽
   California Tortilla
21 Nam-Viet
   Open City

VERIZON CENTER

25 Oyamel
24 Jaleo
23 Matchbox
21 Hill Country
20 Carmine's

THE WHITE HOUSE

26 Oval Room
25 BLT Steak
   Equinox
   Bombay Club
23 Old Ebbitt Grill

Best Buys

BAR MENU LUNCHES

27 Restaurant Eve ($15)
   Fiola ($19)
25 Bourbon Steak ($21)
   Bibiana Osteria ($17)
24 Proof ($14)

CHICKEN ROASTERS

26 El Pollo Rico
24 Crisp & Juicy
   Chicken on the Run
23 La Limeña
   Don Pollo

DINERS

22 Ben's Chili Bowl
   Florida Ave. Grill
21 Open City
   Diner
20 Double T Diner

NOODLE SHOPS

26 Toki Underground
25 Full Key
21 Nooshi
⌐ Daikaya Ramen
   Sakuramen

PRE-THEATER MENUS

28 Rasika ($35)
27 Tosca ($38)
26 Oval Room ($39)
24 J&G Steakhouse ($39)
23 701 ($32)

PUB FOOD

24 Liberty Tavern
23 Lost Dog Cafe
22 Brewer's Alley
   Clyde's
21 Dogfish Head

QUICK BITES

25 Ravi Kabob
24 C.F. Folks
   Fishnet▽
23 Juice Joint Cafe▽
22 Cava Mezze Grill

SANDWICHES

23 Bread Line
   Chutzpah
22 Paul
   Buzz
   Taylor Gourmet

BANG FOR THE BUCK

In order of rating.

1. Buzz
2. CapMac
3. Lunchbox
4. Calif. Tortilla
5. Five Guys
6. Banh Mi DC
7. Amsterdam Falafel
8. DC-3
9. Shophouse
10. Black & Orange
11. El Pollo Rico
12. Chop't Creative Salad
13. Roti Mediterranean
14. Pollo Campero
15. Elevation Burger
16. Sweetgreen
17. Pho 14
18. Horace & Dickie's Seafood
19. Ben's Chili Bowl
20. Crisp & Juicy

21. Chicken on the Run
22. Negril
23. Taylor Gourmet
24. Bobby's Burger Palace
25. Bob & Edith's Diner
26. Tryst
27. Pho 75
28. Good Stuff Eatery
29. Food Corner Kabob House
30. Cava Mezze Grill
31. Burger, Tap & Shake
32. Sunflower Vegetarian
33. Northside Social
34. BGR, The Burger Joint
35. Bread Line
36. Shake Shack
37. Pret A Manger
38. Nando's Peri-Peri
39. Dangerously Delicious Pies
40. Moby Dick

OTHER GOOD VALUES

Amma Vegetarian
&pizza
Athens Grill
Bangkok Golden
Bar Pilar
Bayou Bakery
Burma Road
Carolina Kitchen
Daikaya Ramen
Don Pollo
Eamonn's
Eatonville
Ethiopic
Family Meal
Fast Gourmet
Fishnet
Florida Ave.
Four Sisters
Hard Times Cafe
Haven
Honey Pig
India Palace
Izakaya Seki
Juice Joint Cafe
Kabob Bazaar

Kabob Palace
Kangaroo Boxing Club
Lost Dog Cafe
Luke's Lobster
Malgudi
Medium Rare
Merzi
Mothership
Oohh's & Aahh's
Original Ledo
Palena
Pete's Apizza
Pizzeria Paradiso
Pupatella Pizzeria
Ray's/Third
Ren's Ramen
Room 11
Ruan Thai
Standard
Surfside
Taqueria Distrito Federal
Taqueria Nacional
Ted's Bulletin
Toki Underground
We the Pizza

WASHINGTON, DC
RESTAURANT
DIRECTORY

	FOOD	DECOR	SERVICE	COST

A&J ⊄ *Chinese* | 25 | 13 | 19 | $19 |

Rockville | Woodmont Station | 1319 Rockville Pike (Wootton Pkwy.), MD | 301-251-7878

Annandale | 4316 Markham St. (Little River Tpke.), VA | 703-813-8181

"Authentic" Chinese dim sum "shines brightly" at these "well-run machines" in Annandale and Rockville, where "fantastic", "freshly made" noodles and "dishes you rarely see" are delivered with "nononsense bustle" in "'80s cafeteria" premises; yes, they're "short on charm", but "who cares" when the lack of ambiance translates into "rock-bottom prices" – just be sure to "bring cash" since they don't take plastic.

Acacia Bistro Ⓜ *American* | 24 | 22 | 24 | $40 |

Frederick | 129 N. Market St. (bet. Church & 2nd Sts.), MD | 301-694-3015 | www.acacia129.com

This New American "foodie find" in Downtown Frederick puts the focus on "local, fresh and seasonal" ingredients – indeed, you may even see the chef "picking herbs" if you sit in the "wonderful" "secret garden" in back (otherwise, the long, narrow interior has several "tasteful", "cozy" dining rooms); the staff's "cheerful" demeanor goes hand in hand with friendly tabs; P.S. accommodates vegan and gluten-free diners.

Acacia Bistro Ⓩ *Mediterranean* | 20 | 18 | 21 | $40 |

Upper NW | 4340 Connecticut Ave. NW (Yuma St.) | 202-537-1040 | www.acaciabistro.com

Mediterranean small plates feature at this "light, bright" Upper Northwest "shoebox-sized bistro" that's prized for its "thoughtful cooking", "pleasant service" and relatively "reasonable pricing"; add in a "charming patio" and a wine list that offers "a ton of variety" and, in an area with "lackluster" dining options, it "stands far above the crowd."

Acadiana *Cajun/Creole* | 24 | 23 | 23 | $45 |

Mt. Vernon Square/Convention Center | 901 New York Ave. NW (9th St.) | 202-408-8848 | www.acadianarestaurant.com

"Bayou showstoppers" rule at this "classy" Mt. Vernon Square "power spot" with "consistently excellent", "progressive takes" on Cajun-Creole cooking, "genteel" manners and a "beautifully simple" multilevel setting decorated with tasteful nods to New Orleans; it's "a bit pricey", but admirers find "great value" in the Sunday jazz brunch prix fixe; P.S. the restaurant is getting a makeover in summer 2013.

Acqua al 2 *Italian* | 24 | 21 | 22 | $47 |

Capitol Hill | 212 Seventh St. SE (North Carolina Ave.) | 202-525-4375 | www.acquaal2dc.com

"This is what pasta is supposed to taste like" say fans of the "dazzling array" on offer at this "charming", "cozy" brick-walled space across from Eastern Market on Capitol Hill (the steaks are also "fabulous", especially with blueberry sauce); the menu is "priced appropriately", i.e. it's "not cheap", but there's always the potential of spotting "a senator wander in."

	FOOD	DECOR	SERVICE	COST

Acre 121 *BBQ/Southern* `21` `20` `20` `$29`

Columbia Heights | 1400 Irving St. NW (14th St.) | 202-328-0121 | www.acre121.com

"Surprisingly good" barbecue for a joint that's "smack in the middle" of Columbia Heights is the judgment on the Southern fare (including "some delicious vegetarian options") at this "friendly" spot with a bit of an upscale wine bar look; middling prices, an outdoor patio and a calendar of countrified live music add appeal.

Adam Express 🗷🅼 *Asian/Seafood* `25` `18` `22` `I`

Mt. Pleasant | 3211 Mount Pleasant St. NW (Lamont St.) | 202-328-0010

"Good catch" Korean, Chinese and Japanese dishes like "great noo-dles", dumplings and sushi lure Mt. Pleasant urbanites to this tiny yet "appealing" hole-in-the-wall with exposed brick and views of the surrounding neighborhood; fin fans note that the "price isn't too high", either, for the "freshest fish going"; P.S. irregular hours and a small, counter-only room make takeout a good bet.

Addie's *American* `25` `19` `23` `$44`

White Flint | 11120 Rockville Pike (Edson Ln.) | Rockville, MD | 301-881-0081 | www.addiesrestaurant.com

"Wonderful", "thoughtfully prepared" New American fare from the Black Restaurant Group (BlackSalt, etc.) is served with "care" at this "little old house" across from the White Flint Mall, with a "quaint", "1930s cottage ambiance"; somewhat "high" prices may be un-avoidable, but diners can escape "close quarters" inside if they "snag a table on the lawn" in front or in the "backyard retreat."

Aditi *Indian* `23` `20` `20` `$25`

Greater Alexandria | 5926 Kingstowne Ctr. (Kingstowne Blvd.) | Alexandria, VA | 703-922-6111 | www.myaditi.com

Aditi Indian Kitchen *Indian*

Capitol Hill | Union Station | 50 Massachusetts Ave. NE (Capitol St.) | 202-682-0304

Sense-travel to "Delhi" at this Indian duo via their "well-made and -served" "authentic" specialties, which come cafeteria-style in white-tiled digs at Union Station or in Alexandria's comparatively "cool setting", with its curvy banquettes and room dividers, plus a dramatic crackled wall; the staff at both locations is "friendly", and the tabs are "reasonable."

Afghan *Afghan* `23` `14` `20` `$25`

Greater Alexandria | 2700 Jefferson Davis Hwy. (Raymond Ave.) | Alexandria, VA | 703-548-0022 | www.afghanrestaurantva.com

"Overlook" the "less than elegant" setting, and enjoy the "excel-lent" chow at this Alexandria Afghan where "great kebabs" and other traditional "homestyle" dishes in "ample quantities" keep it "full of Afghani families", some of whom come for music-filled parties in the banquet hall; it's all "inexpensive", but the lunch buffet is the biggest "bargain."

	FOOD	DECOR	SERVICE	COST

Afghan Kabob House *Afghan* | 23 | 14 | 18 | $18

Courthouse | 2045 Wilson Blvd. (Courthouse Rd.) | Arlington, VA |
703-294-9999 | www.afghankabobhouse.org

"Honest food" at an "honest price" is the deal at this Arlington Afghani
"quick-service" eatery where "wonderful" kebabs, "interesting rice
options" and other "excellent" eats trump its "hole-in-the-wall" appearance; night owls note that "it's one of the few late-night spots in
the [Courthouse] area" on Friday and Saturday (till 3 AM).

Afghan Kabob Restaurant *Afghan* | 25 | 19 | 24 | $20

Springfield | West Springfield Plaza | 6357 Rolling Rd. (Old Keene Mill Rd.),
VA | 703-913-7008 | www.afghankabobrestaurant.com

Start newbies on Afghan cuisine in this "well-appointed" white-
tablecloth Springfielder with "delicious-tasting and -smelling"
food and a staff that "willingly explains dishes" and is "kid-
friendly" too; don't let the budget prices or "shabby" shopping-
center surroundings "fool you" – this is a step or two "above
typical kebab places."

NEW AGB *American* | – | – | – | E

Georgetown | The Graham Georgetown Hotel |
1075 Thomas Jefferson St. NW (M St.) | 202-337-0900 |
www.thegrahamgeorgetown.com

This hotel hideaway restaurant/bar in the recently reopened Graham
Georgetown features an upscale New American menu that can
accommodate anything from a cocktail snack to a serious meal; its
below-the-lobby space is done up in handsome, contemporary style
with gleaming wood floors, exposed brick and chic chocolate accents; P.S. the Observatory rooftop lounge boasts killer views and a
bar bites menu courtesy of AGB.

Agora *Turkish* | 23 | 19 | 21 | $37

Dupont Circle | 1527 17th St. NW (bet. Church & Q Sts.) |
202-332-6767 | www.agoradc.net

"Istanbul" in Dupont Circle East offers a "delicious" "tapas-
inspired twist" on Turkish and Mediterranean meze delivered by
folks who "take real pride" in their work; a meal in the "trendy"
low-lit and brick-walled lounge "feels fancy without being overly
expensive", or "watch the world go by" on 17th Street from the patio; P.S. there's also an "active bar scene" fueled by "inventive" cocktails and "serious" wines.

Agrodolce *Italian* | 23 | 20 | 22 | $30

Germantown | Milestone Shopping Ctr. | 21030 Frederick Ave.
(bet. Ridge Rd. & Shakespeare Blvd.), MD | 301-528-6150 |
www.agrodolcerestaurant.com

MoCo diners are sweet on the "fresh and flavorful" pastas, "strong"
wood-fired pizzas and other "good food for the price" served in
"sunny" Mediterranean digs at this "bit of Italy" in a Germantown
strip mall; the vibe is *molto* "casual", especially at lunch, when you
"order at the counter", but the staff is always "friendly", plus there's
a "nice" wine selection and a "delightful" patio.

	FOOD	DECOR	SERVICE	COST

A La Lucia *Italian*

23 | 18 | 22 | $36

Old Town | 315 Madison St. (bet. Fairfax & Royal Sts.) | Alexandria, VA | 703-836-5123 | www.alalucia.com

"Well off the much-traveled" Old Town tourist itinerary is this "much appreciated" "neighborhood favorite", an Italian trattoria that treats its guests like "family" and is prized for "well-prepared" classics and year-round, restaurant week–like deals (e.g. nightly prix fixe, discount wines Sunday–Tuesday); hence, most shrug off the "garage"-y space's "noisy" echo and "funky" look as adding to the "fun vibe."

Al Crostino *Italian*

23 | 18 | 23 | $38

U Street Corridor | 1324 U St. NW (bet. 13th & 14th Sts.) | 202-797-0523 | www.alcrostino.com

"Custom pastas, delicious sauces" and a varied selection of wines by the glass are the lure at this "cute" lemon-colored Italian "tucked into the hustle and bustle of U Street"; further signs that it's a keeper are the "decent" tabs and "hands-on" mother-daughter management, who treat customers "(cliché, but) like family."

Al Dente *Italian/Pizza*
(fka La Forchetta)

- | - | - | M

Upper NW | 3201 New Mexico Ave. NW (Lowell St.) | 202-244-2223 | www.aldentedc.com

Roberto Donna is cooking up a storm at restaupreneur Hakan Ilhan's sleek, contemporary modern Italian in Wesley Heights, offering a broad, midpriced menu that features trattoria-style small bites, pastas and entrees, as well as Donna's popular Neapolitan-style pizza; there's a molded concrete bar for nibbling and sipping and lots of table-seating for families and duos beneath elaborate chandeliers; P.S. on select evenings, the chef also offers a 12-or-more-course tasting menu (with optional wine add-on) to four prime seats at the bar.

Alegria *Mexican*

- | - | - | M

Vienna | 111 Church St. NW (Dominion Rd.), VA | 703-261-6575 | www.alegriaonchurch.com

Chef-owner Patrick Bazin's small-plates Mexican cantina, next door to his eponymous New American in Vienna, offers a wallet-friendly taste of his creative takes on south-of-the-border staples, plus margaritas and sangria, *por supuesto*; the Spanish-styled setting features wood furniture, patterned walls and deco-style chandeliers, along with a brick-walled seasonal patio.

Al Tiramisu *Italian*

25 | 20 | 24 | $53

Dupont Circle | 2014 P St. NW (bet. Hopkins & 20th Sts.) | 202-467-4466 | www.altiramisu.com

There's "terrific seafood" and "housemade pasta" like you might find at "superb spots in Rome" at "friendly" chef-owner Luigi Diotaiuti's "small" step-down off Dupont Circle, which, though "cramped", retains a "dimly lit, romantic vibe"; the menu's a bit "expensive", but be sure to ask the "very professional waiters" about the "prices for the specials", because those "can be over the top."

	FOOD	DECOR	SERVICE	COST

NEW **Ambar** *E European* | - | - | - | M |

Capitol Hill | 523 8th St. SE (bet. E & G Sts.) | 202-813-3039 | www.ambarrestaurant.com

Balkan cuisine arrives on Capitol Hill via this midpriced entry offering small shared plates complemented by a colorful assortment of *rakia* (Eastern European fruit liqueurs) and regional wines; inspired by the traditional Serbian farm building for which it's named, the stylish, two-story space combines rustic details, like rough-wood slats, with a modern sensibility.

American Ice Co. *BBQ* | 19 | 23 | 18 | $21 |

U Street Corridor | 917 V St. NW (bet. 10th St. & Vermont Ave.) | 202-758-3562 | www.amicodc.com

A "Brooklyn dive" on V Street NW, this reclaimed "industrial setting (garage door and chalkboard included)" chills out with a "superb canned beer selection" and "decent" BBQ at "bargain-basement" prices; yes, it's "where the hipsters roam", but the staff is "far from pretentious", meaning it's a great place to "grab a beer" and some 'cue "before a show at the 9:30 Club" nearby.

Amici Miei *Italian* | 21 | 18 | 20 | $40 |

Potomac | 1093 Seven Locks Rd. (Wootton Pkwy.), MD | 301-545-0966 | www.amicimieiristorante.com

Potomac's "go-to" Italian for "solid" pizza, "fresh pasta" and the like at "midrange prices" can easily "swing from a romantic dinner to a kid-friendly place", offering something for "everyone"; "charming" owners preside over an "attractive" dining room lined with tasteful artwork, but many skip the "bustle" inside, preferring to sit outdoors.

Amma Vegetarian Kitchen *Indian* | 22 | 11 | 17 | $16 |

Vienna | 344 Maple Ave. E. (bet. Beulah Rd. & Glyndon St.), VA | 703-938-5328 | www.ammavegkitchen.com

"Dosas are the star" on the "delicious vegetarian" menu at this easy-on-the-wallet South Indian in Vienna; it can be "hard to know what to order" at the counter (no descriptions), and decor is "spartan, with Formica tables", but just sit back and enjoy the "fireworks."

Amsterdam Falafelshop ● *Mideastern* | 25 | 11 | 17 | $11 |

Adams Morgan | 2425 18th St. NW (Columbia Rd.) | 202-234-1969 | www.falafelshop.com

"Eat big and cheap" at this "edgy", always "packed" Adams Morgan late-night "institution" where "amazing, crisp" Belgian-style fries and "gold-standard" falafel in pitas, piled high with "myriad" toppings, "absorb the alcohol in the most wonderful way" for the throngs of clubgoers "in line"; for most, the lack of decor, service and utensils is "irrelevant" – they take their nosh in "all its messy glory" to go.

NEW **Ancora** ●⑤ *Italian* | - | - | - | M |

Foggy Bottom | Watergate | 600 New Hampshire Ave. NW (F St.) | 202-333-1600 | www.ancoradc.com

Venerable DC chef-owner Bob Kinkead (of the erstwhile Kinkead's) unveils a midpriced Italian slate at his new act in the Watergate complex directly across from Kennedy Center; the muted setting is scheduled for a complete overhaul later in 2013, but the space already boasts an attractive happy-hour crowd in its expansive bar.

NEW &pizza *Pizza* — | — | — | I

U Street Corridor | 1250 U St. NW (bet. 12th & 13th Sts.) | 202-733-1286
Atlas District | 1118 H St. NE (bet. 11th & 12th Sts.) | 202-733-1285
www.andpizza.com

Customizable pizzas are made on an assembly line at this hip Atlas District and U Street duo, where diners choose their dough, sauce and upmarket toppings, then watch as their pies are fired to order; the spaces have whitewashed brick walls and reclaimed-wood tables, and stay open late on weekends to catch the bar crowds.

Angeethi *Indian* 23 | 20 | 21 | $25

Herndon | 645 Elden St. (bet. Jackson & Monroe Sts.), VA | 703-796-1527
Leesburg | 1500 E. Market St. (bet. Battlefield & River Creek Pkwys.), VA | 703-777-6785
www.angeethiva.com

"Indian friends" recommend these Herndon and Leesburg subcontinentals for their deft "blend of spices" ("try the vindaloo") and "reasonably priced" lunch buffets stocked with "stuff that Americanized-Indian-food eaters won't recognize"; so maybe the "decor is minimal", but it's "better than many buffets", and besides, these establishments are "calm and quiet" and graced by "good, solid" service.

Ardeo + Bardeo *American/Wine Bar* 22 | 21 | 21 | $44

Cleveland Park | 3311 Connecticut Ave. NW (bet. Macomb & Ordway Sts.) | 202-244-6750 | www.ardeobardeo.com

"Stylish", "sleek and inviting", this Cleveland Park New American offers a dinner menu full of "zest and zing", as well as "breakfastified versions" of dinner menu favorites at its "amazing" weekend brunch; an "attentive" staff easily contends with the "lively setting", which includes a "busy" bar scene, all of which adds up to a "great date place without being insanely expensive" – just don't overdo those "spendy adult beverages."

Argia's *Italian* 21 | 18 | 21 | $31

Falls Church | 124 N. Washington St. (bet. Broad St. & Park Ave.), VA | 703-534-1033 | www.argias.com

A "solid choice" for an "affordable, family-friendly" night out is this Falls Church Italian dishing up "[more] than just pasta and red sauce" in "hearty and satisfying" portions; the "pleasant" staff keeps an even keel in the "convivial", if "close" and "noisy", main dining area, which brings to life the accompanying murals of "happy Italian townspeople"; P.S. "enjoy a bottle of wine" on the back patio or in the wine bar.

NEW Aroma Espresso Bar *Coffeehouse* — | — | — | I

Bethesda | Westfield Montgomery | 7101 Democracy Blvd. (Westlake Dr.), MD | 301-312-6376 | www.aroma.us

Wafting into bright, modern quarters in Bethesda's Westfield Montgomery Mall is this Israeli chain cafe, whose budget-friendly

	FOOD	DECOR	SERVICE	COST

espresso drinks, salads, soups and sandwiches attract the latte-and-lunch bunch; although the menu is mostly American, Middle Eastern standouts include a halloumi sandwich and salad, regional pastries and drinks like Turkish coffee and *sachlav,* a warm beverage made with orchids.

Aroma Indian Cuisine *Indian*

23 | 18 | 21 | $26

World Bank | 1919 I St. NW (bet. 19th & 20th Sts.) | 202-833-4700 ☒
Shirlington | 4052 Campbell Ave. (Randolph St.) | Arlington, VA | 703-575-8800
www.aromarestaurant.com

Curry's "seductive scent" sharpens World Bank and Shirlington appetites for the "flavorful" subcontinental fare at these Indian "gems"; "attentive" service is the rule at both locations, but Shirlington excels with its "well-stocked", "good-value" lunch buffet and "nicely decorated" digs.

Art & Soul *Southern*

23 | 22 | 22 | $47

Capitol Hill | Liaison Capitol Hill | 415 New Jersey Ave. NW (bet. D & E Sts.) | 202-393-7777 | www.artandsouldc.com

"Artfully crafted" "haute" Southern and New American food is on display at chef-owner Art Smith's hotel venue hard by the Capitol, and though tabs are "pricey", they're not museum quality; lobbyists "feel cool" in the gallerylike dining, recently redone with hardwood floors and rustic touches (possibly outdating the Decor rating), while its bar/lounge offers "unique cocktails" and the "best mix of Capitol Hill and hipster action."

Artie's *American*

25 | 23 | 25 | $31

Fairfax | Fairfax Circle Shopping Ctr. | 3260 Old Lee Hwy. (Fairfax Blvd.), VA | 703-273-7600 | www.greatamericanrestaurants.com

All aboard this "comfortable", "classic yacht"–themed Fairfax "treasure" for "always delightful" American fare at "excellent-value" prices; repeat visitors "wish all restaurants had servers this good" (if "something doesn't float your boat", "they'll make it right") and recommend using the "call-ahead" service on weekends, when there's often a "long wait."

Arucola *Italian*

20 | 17 | 21 | $36

Chevy Chase | 5534 Connecticut Ave. NW (bet. McKinley & Morrison Sts.) | 202-244-1555 | www.arucola.com

The "dedicated, long-standing staff" at this "convenient", "reliable" Italian "haunt" in Chevy Chase strives to be "gracious and efficient" in the face of "frantic" hordes, some discharged from the nearby cinema; but any concerns about the "limited", faux-rustic space are overcome by the "moderate prices."

Ashby Inn Ⓜ *American*

27 | 25 | 26 | $59

Paris | The Ashby Inn | 692 Federal St. (Rte. 50), VA | 540-592-3900 | www.ashbyinn.com

"Think of heaven" – "rolling hills, green as far as the eye can see" and "sophisticated" New American cuisine that's "a thrill" for "real foodies" – and it's "worth the drive" (and expense) to dine at this "romantic" wine country getaway set in a "charming" inn in Paris, VA; "gracious" servers and an "accomplished sommelier" enhance "special occasions", which are even more special if you can "tumble into bed at the end of the night"; P.S. closed Monday and Tuesday.

Asia Bistro *Asian* 21 | 20 | 21 | $24

Pentagon City | Pentagon Row | 1301 S. Joyce St. (Army Navy Dr.) | Arlington, VA | 703-413-2002 | www.asia-bistro.com

Zen Bistro & Wine Bar *Asian*

Pentagon City | Pentagon Row | 1301 S. Joyce St. (Army Navy Dr.) | Arlington, VA | 703-413-2002 | www.zen-bistro.com

The "tasty" Asian fare, including sushi, is "good for the price" at this "conveniently" located Pentagon Row pair; creative thinkers can channel a "chic restaurant in the Pacific Rim" by "grabbing a glass of vino" and some apps in the separate but connected mod-Eastern spaces; P.S. look for "large crowds" on "speed-dating nights" in the wine bar.

Asian Bistro *Asian* 25 | 20 | 22 | $26

Old Town | 809 King St. (bet. Columbus & Alfred Sts.) | Alexandria, VA | 703-836-1515

Fairfax | 3950 University Dr. (North St.), VA | 703-865-4937 www.abistro.com

There's no need to "fight about" whether to have "sushi, Chinese or Thai", since there are "lots of options" (even Malaysian and Indonesian) at this Pan-Asian in Old Town and Fairfax; its "prompt service", "reasonably" priced lunch specials and "classy-enough-for-the-middle-class" atmosphere especially suit midday meetings, but it's also favored for "high-quality" delivery/takeout.

Asian Spice *Asian* 23 | 21 | 22 | $30

Chinatown | 717 H St. NW (bet. 7th & 8th Sts.) | 202-589-0900 | www.asianspice.us

"Multiple Asian cuisines" are prepared with "delicacy and knowl-edge" at this Chinatown spot known for its sizable "selection for vegetarians" and "unfailingly warm" staff; the "lovely, modern" setting in a turreted 19th-century building, along with "sexy cock-tails", creates a "romantic" ambiance, and "inexpensive" tabs sweeten the deal.

Assaggi Mozzarella Bar *Italian* 23 | 21 | 20 | $46

Bethesda | 4838 Bethesda Ave. (bet. Arlington Rd. & Woodmont Ave.), MD | 301-951-1988 | www.assaggirestaurant.com

Assaggi Osteria *Italian*

McLean | 6641 Old Dominion Dr. (Holmes Pl.), VA | 703-918-0080 | www.assaggiosteria.com

This Italian duo in Bethesda and McLean features "convivial" bars for "wine and apps" (e.g. "fabulous mozzarella") along with "somewhat costly" but "delicious pastas, meat and fish" in "urbane", "white-tablecloth" surroundings; they're "relaxed" at lunch, with "atten-tive" service, but if "you can't hear yourself eat" on busy nights in Bethesda, try sitting on its "people-watching" patio.

	FOOD	DECOR	SERVICE	COST

NEW Astro Doughnuts & Fried Chicken Ⓑ *Bakery/Chicken*

-	-	-	I

Downtown | 1308 G St. NW (bet. 13th & 14th Sts.) | 202-809-5565 | www.astrodoughnuts.com

Dieters beware the twin temptations – donuts and fried chicken – at this inexpensive, mod-looking Metro Center grab-and-go stop; the racks of sinkers always include a few unique rotating flavors (e.g. 'creamsicle') for the breakfast and dessert crowd, while several types of fried chicken (including Korean-style) work for a quick lunch or a late-afternoon snack.

Athens Grill Ⓑ *Greek*

26	13	21	$19

Gaithersburg | Goshen Plaza | 9124 Rothbury Dr. (Goshen Rd.), MD | 301-975-0757 | www.athensgrill.com

At this "tiny", "family-owned" storefront Gaithersburg Greek, Hellenic-hunters find "excellent food for the price", including some of the "biggest, best gyros in Greater Washington"; the "nice", "welcoming" staff takes orders at the counter, but "don't expect fast food", as "good food takes time", and given the "cafeteria" ambiance (and no booze), many "do takeaway."

Atlas Room Ⓜ *Eclectic*

25	20	23	$41

Atlas District | 1015 H St. NE (bet. 10th & 11th Sts.) | 202-388-4020 | www.theatlasroom.com

On the rapidly "changing" H Street corridor, this "ambitious" Eclectic stands out with its "adventurous" yet "approachable" cooking and "fancy cocktails"; the menu is arranged in an "offbeat" layout (with apps and small and large plates grouped by main ingredient), but the "engaging" staff is there to help diners find their bearings in the dark, "warm" and "cozy" room – decorated, appropriately, with colorful old maps.

Austin Grill *Tex-Mex*

18	17	19	$23

Penn Quarter | 750 E St. NW (bet. 7th & 8th Sts.) | 202-393-3776
Silver Spring | 919 Ellsworth Dr. (bet. Fenton St. & Georgia Ave.), MD | 240-247-8969
Old Town | 801 King St. (Columbus St.) | Alexandria, VA | 703-684-8969
Springfield | 8430 Old Keene Mill Rd. (Rolling Rd.), VA | 703-644-3111
www.austingrill.com

A "home away from home" for "displaced Texans", this "Tex-Mex to the max" chainlet with "huge", "irresistible" margaritas and "laid-back", "colorful" decor is appreciated by "frat boys" and "families" alike (if "you like noise and kids, this is your place"); some say the eats are "pretty commonplace", but "portions are large", "prices are cheap" and the varied menu, with vegetarian and gluten-free options, "satisfies" most.

Azucar *Mexican/Pan-Latin*

24	21	22	$28

Silver Spring | Layhill Shopping Ctr. | 14418 Layhill Rd. (Bel Pre Rd.), MD | 301-438-3293 | www.azucarrestaurantmd.com

"Superb" Mexican and Pan-Latin fare – from the complimentary salsa and "deliciously thin" chips, "right down to dessert and drinks" –

makes this "festively" colored, "candlelit" Silver Spring venue a neighborhood "standout"; add "diligent, unobtrusive" servers to the equation, and it's an all-around "good value."

NEW Azur ◑Ⓜ *Seafood* — | — | — | E

Penn Quarter | 405 Eighth St. NW (D St.) | 202-347-7491 | www.azurdc.com

Frederik de Pue's Penn Quarter seafood sophisticate offers diners artfully composed fish dishes plus European meat and vegetarian selections at prices befitting the upscale setting; a central staircase swirls around sculptural light fixtures that simulate seafoam bubbling up through the multilevel, marine-accented space, which also hosts a showcase raw bar and a ground-floor bar pouring cocktails named after famous boats.

Bamian *Afghan* 26 | 20 | 22 | $27

Falls Church | 5634 Leesburg Pike (Carlin Springs Rd.), VA | 703-820-7880 | www.bamianrestaurant.com

"The price is right" at this Falls Church "perennial favorite", where "exceptional" Afghani fare is distinguished by "delightful depth of flavor" and "amazing" vegetarian choices ("don't miss the pumpkin!") and is delivered by an "attentive" staff; though set "amid a sea of aging strip malls", the spacious and "surprisingly upscale" space makes a "great place for a party."

Banana Café & 19 | 17 | 19 | $27
Piano Bar *Cuban/Puerto Rican*

Capitol Hill | 500 Eighth St. SE (E St.) | 202-543-5906 | www.bananacafedc.com

Peel into this "festive" "Barracks Row hangout", serving "bountiful" heaps of solid, midpriced Puerto Rican and Cuban favorites delivered by an "attentive" staff amid a "predictably yellow"-and-green interior or out on the "popular" patio; the few who find the fare "so-so" or the decor "cheesy" may still enjoy downing *muy bien margaritas*" and "singing along" in the upstairs piano bar.

Banana Leaves *Asian* — | — | — | I

Dupont Circle | 2020 Florida Ave. NW (Connecticut Ave.) | 202-986-1333 | www.mybananaleaves.com

This casual Dupont Circle Pan-Asian has split appeal: the main room serves Southeast Asian comfort food while downstairs does sushi; the spiffy setting has exposed brick, colorful art and wainscoting, plus a handful of second-story window tables overlooking a vibrant street scene.

Bandolero *Mexican* — | — | — | M

Georgetown | 3241 M St. NW (bet. Potomac St. & Wisconsin Ave.) | 202-625-4488 | www.bandolerodc.com

Mike Isabella (Graffiato) goes modern Mexican at this trendy Georgetown spot serving midpriced small plates and fancified versions of traditional *comida*, all washed down with crafty cocktails and margaritas; just don't bring *abuela* to the loud, rollicking dimly lit space decorated with bleached skulls and mismatched furniture.

Bangkok 54 *Thai*

| 25 | 21 | 22 | $26 |

Arlington | 2919 Columbia Pike (Walter Reed Dr.), VA |
703-521-4070 | www.bangkok54restaurant.com
At this "hip Thai" eatery on Columbia Pike, "well-spiced", "affordable" curries and other specialties "shine with rich flavors" and are delivered with "panache" by a "fresh-faced" crew in "modern" Eastern surroundings that are "easy on your eyes", if not always your ears (it's often "noisy" at night); "sit in the lounge for the coolest experience", and sample the "creative" drinks during happy hour.

Bangkok Golden *Thai*

| 24 | 16 | 21 | $26 |

Fort Washington | 9503 Livingston Rd. (Oxon Hill Rd.), MD |
301-248-8810 | www.bangkokgoldenrestaurant.com
Fairfax | University Mall | 10621 W. Braddock Rd. (bet. County & Ox Rds.), VA | 703-691-0700 | www.bangkokgoldenrestaurant.com
Falls Church | Seven Corners Ctr. | 6395 Seven Corners Ctr. (bet. Arlington Blvd. & Leesburg Pike), VA | 703-533-9480 |
www.bangkokgolden7corners.com
"Everyone talks about" the "no-longer-secret" Laotian menu at the Falls Church branch of this "inexpensive" trio (not served at the other outlets in Fairfax and Fort Washington), but true fans caution "don't sell the Thai dishes short" – they're "excellent" too; either way, nobody talks about the basic decor at these strip-mall spots, though they do speak up for the "earnest" staff that is always ready with "good advice" for the "adventurous eater."

Bangkok Joe's *Thai*

| 23 | 22 | 21 | $29 |

Georgetown | Washington Harbour | 3000 K St. NW (Thomas Jefferson St.) | 202-333-4422 | www.bangkokjoes.com
Dumplings "to die for" with "great cocktails to boot" draw a "lively" crowd to this "modern" Thai lounge in Georgetown's Washington Harbour, by the Potomac; its "fast, friendly" service, relative "value" and location near the AMC cinema make it a natural "dinner-and-a-movie" spot.

Banh Mi DC *Vietnamese*

| 21 | 10 | 16 | $9 |

Falls Church | 3103 Graham Rd. (Woodley Ln.), VA | 703-205-9300
When your "teeth crackle into the sublime baguette" at this "fast", "cheap" no-frills Falls Church Vietnamese market, you've found a "classic" Vietnamese sandwich "worth going out of your way for" enthuse its devotees; there are also other "authentic" prepared snacks on display, and a handful of tables, but most take things "to go."

Bar Pilar ◗ *American*

| 23 | 19 | 19 | $20 |

U Street Corridor | 1833 14th St. NW (bet. S & T Sts.) |
202-265-1751 | www.barpilar.com
This "trendy" 14th Street NW gastropub dishes "delicious" contemporary American "nose-to-tail cuisine" in small- and large-plate formats, which are considered some of the "best bangs for the buck" on the local scene; hipster foodies also recommend the "dark", "arty" bar for a "romantic" date, and a post-Survey expansion should alleviate waits, thus outdating the Decor rating.

	FOOD	DECOR	SERVICE	COST

Bastille *French*
24 | 19 | 22 | $52

Old Town | 1201 N. Royal St. (3rd St.) | Alexandria, VA | 703-519-3776 | www.bastillerestaurant.com

Those "homesick for France" swear this bistro in North Old Town takes them back with its "terrific" "modernized takes" on Gallic classics; "efficient but not intrusive service" helps guests "have a romantic time" in the "intimate" dining room (which was warmed up by a recent renovation) or on the patio that's "fabulous in belle weather"; P.S. prices are "high", so sou-savers take advantage of the many prix fixe offers as well as value vino courtesy of wine director Mark Slater.

Batik ☒ *Asian*
22 | 21 | 19 | $21

Gaithersburg | 200 Main St. (Kentlands Blvd.), MD | 301-869-8661 | www.batikasiancuisine.com

"Top-shelf food on a pauper's budget" sums up this Kentlands Pan-Asian street-fare specialist that's a "terrific treat" for families and foodies who dig its "unique" dumpling menu (e.g. American BBQ pork); "friendly smiles" greet visitors to the tiki bar–gone-upscale premises, sealing the deal.

Bayou Ⓜ *Cajun/Creole*
20 | 17 | 21 | $26

West End | 2519 Pennsylvania Ave. NW (bet. 25th & 26th Sts.) | 202-223-6941 | www.bayouonpenn.com

"Finger-lickin'" eats "capture the true flavors of N'Awlins" in an "atmosphere as funky as the bayou" at this "value"-priced West End Cajun-Creole eatery; "cool" (but not "hipper than thou") servers navigate the "lively" scene, which often includes jazz musicians "wailing" upstairs.

Bayou Bakery, Coffee
Bar & Eatery *Southern*
22 | 18 | 19 | $17

Courthouse | 1515 N. Courthouse Rd. (15th St.) | Arlington, VA | 703-243-2410 | www.bayoubakeryva.com

A "New Orleans sensibility" pervades this "friendly" Courthouse counter-serve bakery/cafe where "terrific" Southern standards, "delicious" beignets, "OMG" desserts and "awesome" coffee keep it humming from breakfast till dinner; in fact, some folks "never want to leave" the "comfy couch" in the corner of the "cute" room, "whimsically decorated" with mason jar lights and salvaged artifacts.

Bazin's on Church Ⓜ *American*
26 | 22 | 23 | $48

Vienna | 111 Church St. NW (bet. Center St. & Lawyers Rd.), VA | 703-255-7212 | www.bazinsonchurch.com

"NoVa foodies" hit this "upscale" "Vienna power spot" for "exciting" New American cooking and "killer" wines; the staff "makes you feel at home" in the "lovely" brick-wall-and-exposed-beam space that's always "happily noisy", thanks in part to the hopping bar, and though it's "pricey", you "get what you pay for: a great dinner"; P.S. Alegria, a Mexican tapas venture from the same owners, is next door.

	FOOD	DECOR	SERVICE	COST

🆕 Beau Thai *Thai*

-	-	-	M

Mt. Pleasant | 3162 Mt. Pleasant St. NW (bet. Kenyon St. & Kilbourne Pl.) | 202-450-5317
Shaw | 1700 New Jersey Ave. NW (bet. Rhode Island Ave. & R St.) | 202-536-5636
www.beauthaidc.com
Fairly new but already popular, this Thai eatery with branches in Shaw and Mt. Pleasant serves neighborhood up-and-comers who need a reasonably priced pad Thai pick-me-up (or a soothing alcoholic beverage) on the way home from work; a change of pace from typical Thai restaurant decor, the look here is hip and industrial, with open ductwork and the like.

Belga Café *Belgian*

25	20	21	$39

Capitol Hill | 514 Eighth St. SE (bet. E & G Sts.) | 202-544-0100 | www.belgacafe.com
"Handsome" with "great mussels" sums up why legions "love, love, love" chef-owner Bart Vandaele's "real taste of Belgium" on an "edgy" stretch of Capitol Hill; "outstanding" midpriced eats aside, it's also a "beer destination", which along with the "tight", brick-walled art-"gallery"-like quarters, produces a "notable din", cut through ably by "competent" servers.

🆕 The Bench *American*

-	-	-	M

Gaithersburg | Marriott Gaithersburg Washingtonian Ctr. | 9751 Washingtonian Blvd. (bet. Boardwalk Pl. & Fields Rd.), MD | 301-590-0044 | www.marriott.com
In Gaithersburg's sprawling Washingtonian Center shopping/dining/entertainment complex, this Marriott American kitchen and lounge sports a spiffy, modern interior, a large patio overlooking the lake and a midpriced menu that suits everything from a workday bite to a celebration; regional influences and beer culture are evident in signature dishes like roasted pepper and crab soup and beer-battered fish 'n' chips and, of course, local craft brews on tap.

Benjarong *Thai*

23	20	21	$25

Rockville | Wintergreen Plaza | 885 Rockville Pike (bet. Edmonston Dr. & Wootton Pkwy.), MD | 301-424-5533 | www.benjarongthairestaurant.com
"Blessedly quiet", with "consistently excellent" Thai fare at "reasonable prices" served by an "attentive" crew – it should come as no surprise that this Rockville stalwart has been "popular" for so many years; longtime loyalists appreciate the "spaciousness" of the Siamese-art-filled digs and remind first-timers that the dishes can "have some serious heat."

Ben's Chili Bowl ●⊅ *Diner*

22	14	19	$14

U Street Corridor | 1213 U St. NW (bet. 12th & 13th Sts.) | 202-667-0909 | www.benschilibowl.com
"Junk-food heaven" is a "mouthwatering" 'half-smoke' (spicy hot dog), "drenched chili-cheese fries" and a "creamy" milkshake at this "venerable" DC "icon" with long lines full of blue-collar "workers, college students, U Street partygoers and the tux- and ball-gown–

clad" (the POTUS never has to wait); sure, the "'50s diner"-style digs are a bit "dumpy" and "crowded", but the counter staff is "always cheerful", and it's awfully "cheap" for a "piece of history"; P.S. an H Street NE outlet is expected soon.

NEW Beuchert's Saloon *American*

| - | - | - | E |

Capitol Hill | 623 Pennsylvania Ave. SE (bet. 6th & 7th Sts.) | 202-733-1384 | www.beuchertssaloon.com

Bison heads above a marble bar are a nod to the past life of this onetime Capitol Hill saloon recently reinvented as a restaurant serving upscale farm-to-table American fare washed down with plenty of craft beer, wine and spirits; there's a small dining room at the rear, but adventurous types will want to reserve seats at the chef's table facing the open kitchen; P.S. chef Andrew Markert will work with diners to tailor a special tasting menu at the chef's table (Tuesday-Thursday evenings and with at least 72 hours notice).

Bezu ⊠ *American/French*

| 24 | 21 | 23 | $58 |

Potomac | Potomac Promenade Shopping Ctr. | 9812 Falls Rd. (River Rd.), MD | 301-299-3000 | www.bezurestaurant.com

The Potomac strip-mall locale "belies the treasure inside" this "small storefront": an "upscale eatery" turning out "surprisingly sophisticated" French–New American cuisine, albeit at "downtown prices"; nonetheless, its "passionate" chef and "helpful" sommelier enhance the "warm and comfortable atmosphere" in the white-and-gold, Eastern-accented space.

BGR, The Burger Joint *Burgers*

| 22 | 15 | 17 | $15 |

Dupont Circle | 1514 Connecticut Ave. NW (Q St.) | 202-299-1071
Bethesda | 4827 Fairmont Ave. (Woodmont Ave.), MD | 301-358-6137
Old Town | 106 N. Washington St. (bet. Cameron & King Sts.) | Alexandria, VA | 703-299-9791
Arlington | Lyon Vill. | 3129 Fairfax Blvd. (Spout Run Pkwy.), VA | 703-812-4705
Clarendon | 3024 Wilson Blvd. (bet. Garfield & Highland Sts.), VA | 703-566-1446
Springfield | 8420 Old Keene Mill Rd. (bet. Bauer Dr. & Rolling Rd.), VA | 703-451-4651
www.bgrtheburgerjoint.com

Chomp a "fancy burger cooked right" and "sweet potato fries to die for" at this inexpensive chain specializing in "juicy goodness on a bun" plus "thick", "yummy" shakes; service veers between "prompt" and "slow" at its varied locations, but the "create-your-own-soda" machines and "'80s flashback" digs (e.g. giant LP covers on the walls) keep most occupied when it gets "crowded."

Bibiana Osteria-Enoteca ⊠ *Italian*

| 25 | 24 | 24 | $56 |

Downtown | 1100 New York Ave. NW (entrance on H St. at 12th St.) | 202-216-9550 | www.bibianadc.com

"When Tuscany is too far away", "boldface names" and others head to this Downtown Italian that has "everything going for it": "delightful" cooking that acknowledges the "old country, but for today", a wine list that "would get Bacchus excited" and "impeccable" service; so despite the "expense", it's always a "scene" in the "light, airy" loungelike space.

Biergarten Haus ❶ *German* | 17 | 22 | 18 | $25 |

Atlas District | 1355 H St. NE (bet. 14th St. & Linden Ct.) | 202-388-4053 | www.biergartenhaus.com

"Navigate through the sea of hipsters" at this "Germany-meets–H Street NE" beer hall/garden featuring a 4,000-sq.-ft. outdoor "wonderland" with "rustic wooden tables" and a permanent "Oktoberfest atmosphere" that puts extra oompah into a menu of "great, big beers" and "decent" German grub; *ja*, "service can be slow when it's extremely busy", but staffers "make up for" occasional lapses with "charm and humor."

Big Bear Cafe *American* | - | - | - | M |

Bloomingdale | 1700 First St. NW (R St.) | 202-643-9222 | www.bigbearcafe-dc.com

A coffeehouse by day, this oasis for Bloomingdale gentrifiers becomes a full-fledged restaurant at night; its college-hangout-esque interior and greenery-swathed patio get dressed up with candles and table service for midpriced New American dinners that put locally sourced ingredients at the center of the plate; P.S. light breakfast and lunch also served.

Big Board *Burgers* | - | - | - | I |

Atlas District | 421 H St. NE (bet. 4th & 5th Sts. NE) | 202-543-3630 | www.thebigboarddc.com

Reverse supply and demand is the law governing the beverages at this hot H Street NE burger and beer joint where the price of each brew goes down as its sales increase (the cost of its gussied-up burgers and salads, while affordable, is fixed); customers can follow the draft brew price action on a monitor in the narrow brick-and-wood-trimmed space lined with big windows.

Birch & Barley Ⓜ *American* | 24 | 23 | 24 | $41 |

Logan Circle | 1337 14th St. NW (bet. P St. & Rhode Island Ave.) | 202-567-2576 | www.birchandbarley.com

Pairing "super-creative" New American food with beer is the mission of this somewhat spendy Logan Circle gastropub, whose "chipper" servers are "great guides" to the "tremendous" brew list (50 on tap, 500 bottles); it's easy to "impress a date" in the "beautiful" "dark" and distressed digs that are "cool" "without being obnoxious about it", and its "indulgent" Sunday brunch is also popular; P.S. sister bar/lounge Churchkey is upstairs.

Bistro Bis *French* | 26 | 23 | 24 | $55 |

Capitol Hill | Hotel George | 15 E St. NW (bet. Capitol St. & New Jersey Ave.) | 202-661-2700 | www.bistrobis.com

The "see-and-be-seen" crowd at this "sophisticated" French rendezvous on Capitol Hill often includes "a senator" or two munching "skillfully served", "modern takes on classic" dishes; "expensive" *oui*, but the "stylish" cherry-wood–paneled room is a "classy" venue for a "power breakfast", "expense-account lunch" or "date night", and what's more, its "bar scene is great."

Bistro Bohem ❍Ⓜ *Czech/European* | - | - | - | M |

Shaw | 600 Florida Ave. NW (6th St.) | 202-735-5895 | www.bistrobohem.com

Folks are Czech-ing out this trendy, midpriced spot that brings Prague to Shaw with Slavic specialties like pierogi and schnitzel updated in a small-plates format, all washed down with absinthe-based cocktails and (of course) beer; the compact space sports a spiffy look, its gray walls brightened with gilded mirrors and eye-popping art, plus there's an outdoor patio; P.S. there's a next-door bakery/cafe from the same owner.

Bistro Cacao *French* | 23 | 22 | 23 | $45 |

Capitol Hill | 320 Massachusetts Ave. NE (bet. 3rd & 4th Sts.) | 202-546-4737 | www.bistrocacao.com

At this Capitol Hill townhouse (by way of the "Right Bank"), "authentic" French bistro dishes and "attentive" service back up the "*complètement charmant*" "date-night" setting decorated with antiques and "cozy" curtained booths, while its "lovely" patio is the "place to be spotted" for lunch; it's a bit "expensive" but "worth the coin" say friends (and lovers).

Bistro D'Oc *French* | 23 | 18 | 22 | $40 |

Penn Quarter | 518 10th St. NW (bet. E & F Sts.) | 202-393-5444 | www.bistrodoc.com

Seemingly "plucked right out of Southern France" and transplanted to a "touristy" Penn Quarter location opposite Ford's Theatre, this bistro turns out "well-crafted" classics, like the "amazing cassoulet", at relatively moderate prices; "servers who know each dish" patrol the "homey" bi-level space that's warmed by the bright red and yellow colors of Languedoc's flag.

Bistro Français ❍ *French* | 21 | 20 | 20 | $41 |

Georgetown | 3124 M St. NW (bet. 31st St. & Wisconsin Ave.) | 202-338-3830 | www.bistrofrancaisdc.com

Francophiles count on this "prototypical bistro" (it's "perfectly named") in Georgetown that "hasn't changed in years" for "well-prepared" Gallic fare that's "reasonably priced" for the area, especially the "excellent-value" prix fixe; a suitably Parisian look and "professional" service are pluses, and it also has the "virtue of staying open later than just about anyone" (till 3 AM weekdays, 4 AM weekends).

Bistro La Bonne ❍ *French* | 21 | 17 | 19 | $31 |

U Street Corridor | 1340 U St. NW (bet. 13th & 14th Sts.) | 202-758-3413 | www.bistrolabonne.com

"A shot of Paris" in "the middle of the" U Street scene, this "neighborhood spot" specializes in "classic, hearty" French fare that's "*bonne*" if "not *merveilleux*"; the "cute", "simple" decor (vintage posters plus blue, white and red banners) and "friendly" service are nice enough, but the real draw is the "great value", including a "spectacular happy hour."

Bistro LaZeez ☒ *Mideastern* · 22 | 16 | 21 | $26

Bethesda | 8009 Norfolk Ave. (bet. Auburn & Del Ray Aves.), MD |
301-652-8222 | www.bistrolazeez.com

"Tasty", "authentic" Syrian and Lebanese specialties at "rock-bottom
prices" make this "friendly" "family-owned" Mideasterner in
Bethesda "worth visiting"; the food can be eaten in the "simple"
black, gray and olive "postage stamp" of a dining room, on the patio
under umbrellas or taken home.

Bistro L'Hermitage ☒ *French* · 26 | 26 | 27 | $54

Woodbridge | 12724 Occoquan Rd. (Old Bridge Rd.), VA |
703-499-9550 | www.bistrolhermitage.com

Upon entering this "hidden treasure" in Woodbridge's historic
Occoquan area, guests are transported to a "quaint French village"
auberge, where one can "dine in decadence" on "wonderful" Gallic
cuisine or while away an hour over "pâté and a great wine" at the
"warm"-feeling bar; under the eye of owner Youssef Essakl, the
"exceptional" staff "never fails to accommodate", so though it's
"pricey", "you actually get your money's worth."

Bistro Provence *French* · 26 | 22 | 21 | $66

Bethesda | 4933 Fairmont Ave. (bet. Norfolk Ave. &
Old Georgetown Rd.), MD | 301-656-7373 |
www.bistroprovence.org

What a "treat" to watch the "artist" (chef Yannick Cam) in the
"open kitchen" whipping together "superb", "expertly" crafted
contemporary French repasts at his Bethesda bistro; comparatively, "service can leave something to be desired", and being
"squeezed" into the "tiny", Provençal-themed dining room tem-
pers an otherwise "exquisite dining" experience that's, all-in-all,
"not to be missed if you've got the bucks"; P.S. the stone-walled patio is a "gorgeous" seating alternative.

Bistrot du Coin ❶ *French* · 22 | 20 | 18 | $36

Dupont Circle | 1738 Connecticut Ave. NW (bet. R & S Sts.) |
202-234-6969 | www.bistrotducoin.com

It's "all about the mussels", with "plump" mollusks "available by the
bucket" alongside other midpriced "classic bistro" fare at this "*très*
noisy" "endless party" in Dupont Circle with a "*vieux* Paris" look;
"traditionally 'French'" service rubs some the wrong way, but legions of fans ask what's not to "love" about "any place where people
drink wine before noon"?

Bistrot Lepic & Wine Bar ❶ *French* · 24 | 19 | 22 | $49

Georgetown | 1736 Wisconsin Ave. NW (S St.) | 202-333-0111 |
www.bistrotlepic.com

"Worthy of the proximity" to the French embassy is this "authentically" Gallic haven in Upper Georgetown dishing out "expensive"
but "high-quality" bistro "classics" "à la the 1950s", including offal;
"use your inside voice" when placing orders with the "knowledgeable" servers because it can be "loud" in the "charmingly" "rustic"
dining room, though "the upstairs wine bar is a quiet oasis."

FOOD | DECOR | SERVICE | COST

Bistro Vivant *French*

| - | - | - | M |

McLean | 1394 Chain Bridge Rd. (Old Dominion Dr.), VA |
703-356-1700 | www.bistrovivant.com

A venture from industry vets Domenico Cornacchia (Assagi) and
Aykan Demiroglu (the erstwhile Locanda), this midpriced French
bistro in McLean is where well-heeled locals go to reminisce about
their last trip to Paris while sharing regional classics, small plates
and vin; natural light filters through lace curtains into the oak-and-
burgundy-bedecked dining room, which also boasts a full bar poshly
appointed with granite and golden faux-ostrich-covered stools.

Black & Orange ● *Burgers*

| 25 | 18 | 20 | $13 |

Dupont Circle | 1300 Connecticut Ave. NW (N St.) | 202-296-2242
U Street Corridor | 1931 14th St. NW (bet. U St. & Wallach Pl.) |
202-450-5365
www.blackandorangeburger.com

"Juicy hand-formed patties" helped by "interesting spices", "creative"
toppings and "fresh brioche buns" have meatheads piling into these
"spare but stylish", industrial-looking fast-casual joints in Dupont
and the U Street area; patty partisans also dig the "reasonable" prices
and "late-night" hours on weekends.

Blackfinn American Saloon ● *American*

| 18 | 17 | 18 | $26 |

Downtown | 1620 I St. NW (bet. Connecticut Ave. & 16th St.) |
202-429-4350 | www.blackfinndc.com
Bethesda | 4901 Fairmont Ave. (Norfolk Ave.), MD |
301-951-5681 | www.blackfinnbethesda.com

"Young professionals" congregate at these "sleek and stylized" pubs
in Downtown DC and Bethesda, where "affable" crews serve a "diverse" range of American "comfort" eats that are "a step above normal bar food" at everyday prices; however, they're mainly known for
their "booming bar scenes", which morph from "great spots to catch
a game" to having a "loud" "club feel" geared toward "singles who
do not want to engage in conversation."

Black Market Bistro *American*

| 26 | 23 | 24 | $40 |

Garrett Park | 4600 Waverly Ave. (Strathmore Ave.), MD |
301-933-3000 | www.blackmarketrestaurant.com

"Like Brigadoon", this "quaint", "old" clapboard house appears to
be set in a "place out of time" – Garrett Park, a relic of "small-town
beauty" – yet its "incredible" American menu reveals a contemporary, "energetic approach to old favorites" (it's part of the Black restaurant "empire"); also reminiscent of "a quieter day and age" is its
"staff that loves to serve", relatively "reasonable prices" and a
"dreamy" front porch where you can watch the trains "rattling" by.

BlackSalt *American/Seafood*

| 27 | 21 | 23 | $55 |

Palisades | 4883 MacArthur Blvd. NW (U St.) | 202-342-9101 |
www.blacksaltrestaurant.com

"Inventive, gorgeous and impeccably executed" New American seafood at "not-quite lobbyist prices" is served with "care" at the Black
Restaurant Group's "popular" Palisades flagship; if the "decor is not

up to the quality of the food", it's not apparent from the "sit-and-be-seen" hordes always packing the "fun bar", "lively" main dining room and somewhat more "intimate" and "elegant" back room; P.S. it's "hard to resist" the "terrific" on-site market for "fresh, fresh, fresh" fish "on your way out."

Black's Bar & Kitchen *American*   24 | 22 | 22 | $49

Bethesda | 7750 Woodmont Ave. (bet. Norfolk Ave. & Old Georgetown Rd.), MD | 301-652-5525 | www.blacksbarandkitchen.com

Happy-hour crowds mob this "wonderful" Bethesda New American seafooder "like salmon swimming upstream" ("single or not") to "oyster up" with "fabulous mojitos" or sit down to "phenomenal mussels" and "fish specials" in the "comfy, fashionable" dining room; insiders note one can "go upscale and spend a lot" or have a "great experience" with lighter fare, and suggest arriving "early" to snag an outdoor table and "watch Bethesda walk by."

NEW Black Whiskey ● *American*   - | - | - | M

Logan Circle | 1410 14th St. NW (P St.) | 202-800-8103 | www.blackwhiskeydc.com

A hip vibe pervades this newly distilled 14th Street NW watering hole, with an upstairs barroom where (mostly American) whiskey bottles reach to the rafters and a pool table declares its lack of pretension (the ground floor is more of an art gallery and live music space); a chalkboard gastropub menu reveals each evening's artisanal carving plates and veggie sides, and there are intriguing whiskey-based cocktails, beer and wine.

BLT Steak ⧅ *Steak*   25 | 23 | 23 | $65

Golden Triangle | 1625 I St. NW (bet. 16th & 17th Sts.) | 202-689-8999 | www.bltsteak.com

At this "classy but not stuffy steak palace", an NYC import near the White House, "beautiful", "big slabs of meat" and signature "huge popovers" star in a "power-laden setting" with a "swanky, French bistro kind of feel" (with a few French menu selections, added post-Survey); such "great quality and service" "don't come cheap", but for those who "want to dine with politicians" it's worth the "big bucks."

Blue Duck Tavern *American*   27 | 25 | 26 | $64

West End | Park Hyatt | 1201 24th St. NW (bet. M & N Sts.) | 202-419-6755 | www.blueducktavern.com

Birds of a feather are "wowed every time" by the elevated, "beautifully crafted" "comfort food" at this "elegant" West End New American; just as ducky: it's "high on style and low on pretension", with an "extremely gracious" staff that "knows how to show you a good time" in "modern", "Shaker-inspired" environs that are often graced by "famous" faces; P.S. should the bill "make you 'blue'", there are "lower prices" at lunch, and in the bar/lounge.

Blue Ridge Grill *American*   24 | 21 | 23 | $28

Leesburg | 955 Edwards Ferry Rd. NE (Leesburg Bypass), VA | 703-669-5505

(continued)

Blue Ridge Grill

Ashburn | Brambleton Towne Ctr. | 22865 Brambleton Plaza
(bet. Regal Wood & Soave Drs.), VA | 703-327-1047
www.brgrill.com

It's "hard to choose" among all the "excellent" "culinary comfort food" at these Virginia-based all-Americans, "dependable" "down-home" spots with a "casual" vibe and "friendly" service; families fancying "value for the dollar" keep things "busy" and "a bit noisy", so consider "sitting outside" on the "awesome" patio (Leesburg) or moving quickly on to an after-dinner "movie" (Ashburn).

Blue Rock Inn Restaurant ▣ *American* ∇ 24 | 25 | 25 | $49

Sperryville | Blue Rock Inn | 12567 Fairfax Blvd. (5 mi. west of Hwy. 522 N.), VA | 540-987-3388 | www.thebluerockinn.com

"Picturesque country dining" that combines "wonderful food and views" of the Blue Ridge Mountains is the thing at this "lovely rural" retreat in a Sperryville inn; the "upmarket", "white-tablecloth" dining room features an "expensive" New American menu, while the casual pub and "comfy" patio offer cheaper eats – either way, service is deft and plenty of "local" wines flow.

Bob & Edith's Diner ◑ *Diner* 20 | 12 | 19 | $14

Arlington | 2310 Columbia Pike (Wayne St.), VA | 703-920-6103 | www.bobandediths.com

"Beloved" by everyone from "disheveled hipsters" to "families", this "friendly", "classic dive diner" in Arlington slings "kitschy, greasy goodness" at "affordable" tabs; don't let "tough parking", "nothing-fancy" decor or "waits on weekends" deter you – it "scratches the itch", especially for "after-hours partyers" thanks to its 24/7 schedule.

Bobby's Burger Palace *Burgers* 22 | 19 | 19 | $16

West End | George Washington University | 2121 K St. NW (21st St.) | 202-974-6260
College Park | Varsity | 8150 Baltimore Ave. (Campus Dr.), MD | 240-542-4702
NEW **Woodbridge** | Potomac Mills Outlet Mall |
2712 Potomac Mills Circle (Worth Ave.), VA | 703-490-2121
www.bobbysburgerpalace.com

Celeb chef Bobby Flay "knows how to cook a burger", as proven by his "funky", "futuristic"-looking chain outposts, where "innovative" "twists on the tried-and-true" include regionally inspired "gourmet" creations washed down by "adult shakes" that are "worth the calories"; perhaps it's "overpriced" for a "joint" where you "order at the counter", but where else can you get "your burger 'crunchified'"?

Bobby Van's Grill ▣ *Steak* 23 | 21 | 23 | $57

Downtown | 1201 New York Ave. NW (12th St.) | 202-589-1504

Bobby Van's Steakhouse *Steak*

Downtown | 809 15th St. NW (bet. H & I Sts.) | 202-589-0060
www.bobbyvans.com

"Administration folks having dinner" and "business-lunch" crowds affirm it's "always a quality experience" at these "reliable, friendly"

	FOOD	DECOR	SERVICE	COST

Downtown steakhouses where you'll need "your wallet and your appetite" for the "man-sized beef"; "dark wood" and "traditional" trappings signify an "old boys' club" atmosphere near the White House, while the New York Avenue address is brighter and airier.

Bob's Noodle 66 ⊄ *Taiwanese* | 22 | 10 | 18 | $17 |

Rockville | 305 N. Washington St. (bet. Beall Ave. & Hungerford Dr.), MD | 301-315-6668

Come "as close to Taiwan as you'll get in the States", or at least the DC area, with "real-deal" offerings "not for the faint of heart" ("like pig's ear or stomach or stinky tofu") in this "no-frills" Rockville stripmaller; "quick service" may make some "feel rushed", but fans appreciate how "cheap" it is; P.S. cash only.

Bodega Spanish | 23 | 23 | 22 | $34 |
Tapas & Lounge *Spanish*

Georgetown | 3116 M St. NW (bet. 31st St. & Wisconsin Ave.) | 202-333-4733 | www.bodegadc.com

You may "want to stick a rose in [your] mouth and tango" after a romantic rendezvous at this Spanish "date spot" in Georgetown with a bullfighting theme to its "dark" black, red and cow-accented interior; the "great ambiance" is backed by "delicious tapas", "stellar sangria" and "original" drinks, all at attractive prices and delivered by a professional crew.

Bombay Bistro *Indian* | 24 | 17 | 22 | $26 |

Rockville | Bell's Corner | 98 W. Montgomery Ave. (Adams St.), MD | 301-762-8798 | www.bombaybistro.com

There's "great bang for your rupee" at the "cheap", "tasty" lunch buffet of this Rockville strip-mall "gem", where "food like your Indian mother would make" satisfies "cravings" for subcontinental "standards"; the "1970s"-style dining room can get "crowded", but the "comfy" "neighborhood atmosphere" offers "a certain warmth" and the staff is a model of "efficiency."

Bombay Club *Indian* | 25 | 25 | 25 | $49 |

Golden Triangle | 815 Connecticut Ave. NW (bet. H & I Sts.) | 202-659-3727 | www.bombayclubdc.com

"Refinement pervades" this "sophisticated Indian" a few "steps from the White House", where "delightful" dishes are served "with style" in "serene", "British raj" environs "tinkling" with live piano – no wonder "Washington-type celebrities abound" at its "luxuriously big tables"; tabs are "upscale but won't break the bank", especially for the "amazing" Sunday brunch.

Bombay Tandoor *Indian* | 26 | 21 | 23 | $30 |

Tysons Corner | 8603 Westwood Center Dr. (Leesburg Pike) | Vienna, VA | 703-734-2202 | www.bombaytandoor.com

Indian-food devotees are "mesmerized" by the "outstanding-quality" cuisine coming out of the kitchen at this subcontinental "hidden" in a Tysons Corner office building; "kudos" extend to its "great" service and "good value", especially at its "amazing" lunch buffet, while the formal-feeling dining room is a "great place for parties."

	FOOD	DECOR	SERVICE	COST

BonChon Chicken *Korean* — 26 | 14 | 15 | $19

Fairfax | 3242 Old Pickett Rd. (Old Lee Hwy.), VA | 703-865-5688 ●
Centreville | 14215 Centreville Sq. (Machen Rd.), VA | 703-825-7711
www.bonchon.co.kr

"How do they get the skin so crispy?" on the "incredible" double-fried chicken cluck fans of these Fairfax County outposts of the Korean chain where the "addictive" wings compensate for often "scattered service"; some advise skip the "sports-bar atmosphere" and lines that can be "sooo long", and "call in way ahead" to score your birds to go.

Bond 45 *Italian* — 22 | 24 | 24 | $61

National Harbor | National Harbor | 149 Waterfront St.
(National Plaza), MD | 301-839-1445 | www.bond45.com

It's "all about the view" – an "absolutely incredible" Potomac River panorama – wax couples celebrating "memorable evenings" at this "romantic" Italian steak-and-seafood place in National Harbor (an offshoot of the NYC original); "accommodating" servers deliver "great steaks" and "some of the best" housemade burrata to "date night"–worthy dining alcoves in the handsome old-world digs, but it's not for the faint of wallet.

Boqueria *Spanish* — - | - | - | E

Dupont Circle | 1837 M St. NW (19th St.) | 202-558-9545 |
www.boqueriarestaurant.com

A hot spot straight out of the gate, Marc Vidal's pricey *bar de tapas* newly arrived in Dupont Circle repeats the successful formula of its NYC siblings, plying a trendy crowd with plenty of vino and a battery of classic tapas, cheese and charcuterie; watching the small-plate assembly adds more buzz to the energetic, contemporary space, outfitted with blond-wood and sand-colored tiles, and its outdoor patio is a people-watching perch.

Boulevard Woodgrill *American* — 20 | 18 | 19 | $26

Clarendon | 2901 Wilson Blvd. (Fillmore St.), VA | 703-875-9663 |
www.boulevardwoodgrill.com

The "smell of the wood-burning grill" whets the appetite for "fall-off-the-bone ribs" and other "tasty" bites on the "wide-ranging menu" at this "friendly", "value"-priced Clarendon American standby; the simple "upscale"-"casual" setting is bathed in sunlight, though many prefer to "people-watch" at the sidewalk tables, especially during its popular weekend brunch, lubricated by "great Bloody Marys."

Boundary Road ● *Eclectic* — - | - | - | M

Atlas District | 414 H St. NE (bet. 4th & 5th Sts.) | 202-450-3265 |
www.boundaryrd.com

Edgy Atlas District coordinates haven't kept politicians and foodies from swarming this midpriced Eclectic tavern for fancified eats – like a foie gras torchon PB&J with housemade peanut butter – which can be paired with draft brews, artisanal cocktails or wine; the rustic, exposed-brick-and-wood-beam environs include a roomy bar area for getting together with pals.

Boundary Stone *Pub Food*   ▽ 24 | 26 | 25 | $21

Bloomingdale | 116 Rhode Island Ave. NW (bet. 1st & 2nd Sts.) |
202-621-6635 | www.boundarystonedc.com

Bloomingdale's young strivers welcome this "awesome" watering hole
for its "above-par" pub fare served by a pro crew to wooden booths
in the "lovely" reclaimed-everything setting; discerning drinkers note
that the "beautiful" bar is stocked with a "well-curated selection of
whiskeys and beers", and tame tariffs seal the deal.

Bourbon ❶ *Pub Food*   21 | 19 | 19 | $27

Adams Morgan | 2321 18th St. NW (bet. Columbia & Kalorama Rds.) |
202-332-0800
Glover Park | 2348 Wisconsin Ave. NW (bet. Calvert St. & Hall Pl.) |
202-625-7770
www.bourbondc.com

"Bourbon converts" are born at these "friendly" sour-mash specialists in Adams Morgan and Glover Park, where the "extensive collec-
tions" of brown spirits are ballasted by "glorified bar food" on the
cheap (e.g. "fantastic" tater tots); both locations sport a "classy"
and contemporary (i.e. non-tavernlike) look, but the AdMo branch
particularly stands out as a "grown-up" spot "in a sea of college bars."

Bourbon Steak *Steak*   25 | 25 | 25 | $70

Georgetown | Four Seasons Hotel Washington DC |
2800 Pennsylvania Ave. NW (28th St.) | 202-944-2026 |
www.bourbonsteakdc.com

"Of course the steaks are superb" at Michael Mina's DC chophouse,
but "trust the chefs" to take you on an "amazing adventure" via the
rest of the "inventive" New American menu at this "popular" Four
Seasons venue – "the place to see, be seen and spend money in
Georgetown"; "impeccable service" is de rigueur and "celebrity
sightings" are common in the "modern and polished" dining room,
as well as the bar that's "rife with power-sippers (and those looking
to get attached to them)."

NEW Bóveda ❶ *Pan-Latin*   - | - | - | M

West End | Westin Georgetown | 2350 M St. NW (bet. 23rd & 24th Sts.) |
202-448-1000 | www.boveda-dc.com

Rusticity rules at this Pan-Latin tapas bar located in the newly refurbished Westin Georgetown Hotel and decorated with reclaimed
wood and stone walls; prices are moderate for the decent-sized
small plates (ceviche, tacos, etc.), which are paired with classic
south-of-the-border cocktails plus wine and beer.

Boxcar Tavern *American*   21 | 21 | 19 | $30

Capitol Hill | 224 Seventh St. SE (bet. C St. & Independence Ave.) |
202-544-0518 | www.boxcardc.com

Despite a Victorian London look, this moderately priced freshman
Barracks Row tavern is living in the here and now with its relatively
"imaginative" (and mostly American) pub fare and "well-done" beer
and wine lists; solid service and a "great vibe" in the "narrow" space
mean "seating can be hard to come by on a busy night."

	FOOD	DECOR	SERVICE	COST

Brabo by
Robert Wiedmaier *Belgian/French*

| 26 | 22 | 24 | $55 |

Old Town | Lorien Hotel & Spa | 1600 King St. (bet. Diagonal Rd. & West St.) | Alexandria, VA | 703-894-3440 | www.braborestaurant.com

An Old Town "favorite", this "upscale", "modern" hotel "respite" offers "fantastic" Belgian-French fare from chef Robert Wiedmaier (Marcel's, Brasserie Beck) with "wine to match"; it's "costly", but you can expect "remarkable" service for a truly "luxe evening"; P.S. next door is Tasting Room, Wiedmaier's "more casual (and affordable)" concept, known for its "can't-be-beat" mussels.

Brasserie Beck *Belgian/French*

| 25 | 22 | 22 | $49 |

Downtown | JBG Bldg. | 1101 K St. NW (11th St.) | 202-408-1717 | www.beckdc.com

"Amazing mussels", a "tremendous beer list" and "relatively moderate" tabs keep Robert Wiedmaier's (of Marcel's) "lusty", "authentic" Belgian brasserie Downtown "crowded" and "boisterous"; since its "power bar" seems to attract "more young lobbyists per square inch" than most, those seeking a quieter "business lunch" or "intimate dinner" should sit in back and enjoy the old-fashioned "European train station" motif.

Brasserie Monte Carlo *French/Mediterranean*

| 22 | 18 | 21 | $43 |

Bethesda | 7929 Norfolk Ave. (Cordell Ave.), MD | 301-656-9225 | www.bethesdarestaurant.com

"Far less risky than the casino" is a meal at this French-Med spot with a "solid menu that has stood the test of time" from a chef-owner who "works tirelessly" to deliver "a touch of the Riviera in Downtown Bethesda"; rendering outdoor tables "a big plus" is "close" seating in the "small" saffron- and orange-hued dining room that's dominated by a mural of Monte Carlo in its heyday.

Bread Line 🖂 *Bakery/Sandwiches*

| 23 | 12 | 17 | $15 |

World Bank | 1751 Pennsylvania Ave. NW (bet. 17th & 18th Sts.) | 202-822-8900 | www.breadline.com

"It's the bread, stupid", say fans who find the way this gently priced bakery/cafe "down the block" from the White House and World Bank can "pack so many flavors and textures" into one "delicious" sandwich makes for an "unmatched" lunch; at midday, an "efficient" crew moves the "long" queue "fast", though many leave the "stark" industrial premises to sit outside or go "picnicking"; P.S. it's line-free at breakfast, or go for "fine pastry and coffee" in the afternoon.

Brewer's Alley �● *Pub Food*

| 22 | 21 | 22 | $25 |

Frederick | 124 N. Market St. (bet. Church & 2nd Sts.), MD | 301-631-0089 | www.brewers-alley.com

"Upscale pub grub" and "terrific" house-label microbrews make this "family-friendly" "fixture" in Downtown Frederick a "go-to" spot whether you "dress up or dress down"; the staff is "passionate about their food and drinks", and the airy, stained-glass-trimmed digs (it's located in an old municipal building/opera house) further the "great value."

FOOD | DECOR | SERVICE | COST

NEW Brickside
Food & Drink ❶ *American*   — | — | — | M

Bethesda | 4866 Cordell Ave. (bet. Norfolk & Woodmont Aves.), MD | 301-312-6160 | www.bricksidebethesda.com

'Vote Against Prohibition' is prominently painted on the distressed brick wall of this appropriately booze-fueled gastropub in Bethesda, which features relaxed American cooking plus upscale takes on bar-fare staples from chef Andrea Pace (Villa Mozart); the popular happy hour (4–7 PM daily in the bar area) features deals on beer, wine, cocktails and apps.

The Brixton ❶ *American/British*   — | — | — | M

U Street Corridor | 901 U St. NW (Florida Ave.) | 202-560-5045 | www.brixtondc.com

Young, cosmopolitan types hobnob at this midpriced U Streeter from the Marvin talents where the action takes place on three levels; a replica English pub on the ground floor serves British and American fare, the upstairs bar/lounge offers a short menu and brews (plus cocktails and wine) in an ornate hunting-lodge setting and the roof deck is fitted out with two more bars and affords DC monument views.

B. Smith's *Southern*   22 | 24 | 22 | $42

Capitol Hill | Union Station | 50 Massachusetts Ave. NE (1st St.) | 202-289-6188 | www.bsmith.com

A "beautiful" beaux arts setting from the "heyday of passenger trains" (Union Station's former 'Presidential Suite') provides a "stately" backdrop to enjoy a "stylish" yet "timeless take on Southern food" from the eponymous lifestyle TV personality; critics contend it's a bit "overpriced", but most appreciate the staff's "Southern charm" in this "soothing" "respite from the hectic real world"; P.S. check out the "legendary" Sunday brunch buffet.

NEW B Too *Belgian*   — | — | — | E

Logan Circle | 1324 14th St. NW (bet. N St. & Rhode Island Ave.) | 202-627-2800 | www.btoo.com

Bart Vandaele (Belga Café) is behind this bi-level Belgian on happening 14th Street NW, which showcases upscale contemporary cooking backed by craft beer and clever cocktails; the playful decor mixes blond wood and cowhide, while a high-temperature charcoal oven gives moules and the like a smoky twist; P.S. look for waffles and frites from a sidewalk bar.

NEW Bub & Pops 🍴 *Sandwiches*   — | — | — | I

Dupont Circle | 1815 M St. NW (bet. 18th & 19th Sts.) | 202-457-1111 | www.bubandpops.com

Philly sandwich fans give the nod to this new, warmly decorated Dupont storefront for its handcrafted hoagies, which star on a menu that also includes a smattering of other sandwiches plus soups, salads, housemade chips and a variety of interesting pickles; additional perks are its down-to-earth prices and late-night weekend hours (till 3 AM on Friday and Saturday).

	FOOD	DECOR	SERVICE	COST

Buck's Fishing & Camping Ⓜ *American*

20 | 19 | 18 | $46

Upper NW | 5031 Connecticut Ave. NW (bet. Fessenden St. & Nebraska Ave.) | 202-364-0777 | www.bucksfishingandcamping.com

A campfirelike "glow" flickers on the "canoes in the rafters" and other countrified trappings at this rustic retreat in the Upper NW backcountry that's known for its "tasty" but "limited" American menu ("perfectly charred" wood-grilled steak, "never-fail" burgers); "inconsistent" service ranges from "helpful" to "rude", but most are willing to make the hike – even though it's "pricier than you might expect given the camping theme."

NEW Bungalow Lakehouse ◑ *American*

- | - | - | M

Sterling | Lake Center Plaza | 46116 Lake Center Plaza (bet. Cascades Pkwy. & Rte 7), VA | 703-430-7625 | www.bungalowlakehouse.com

Chef Jason Maddens (ex Central Michel Richard) brings culinary cred and an appreciation for local ingredients to the midpriced modern American bistro menu at this sprawling new Sterling complex; the nouveaux-rustic environs feature a range of options that include (get ready for it) a mahogany-paneled dining room, a bright and airy skylit 'porch' room, a saloonlike bar with billiards and darts, a lounge, a cigar bar and an oversized outdoor terrace overlooking the water.

Burger Tap & Shake *Burgers*

21 | 15 | 19 | $15

Foggy Bottom | 2200 Pennsylvania Ave. NW (bet. 22nd & 23rd Sts.) | 202-587-6258 | www.burgertapshake.com

"Not pretentious, just darn good burgers" accessorized with "crisp" Boardwalk-style fries are the hallmark of this counter-serve patty haven and bar near George Washington U. that lets folks eat in "Foggy Bottom for cheap"; its staff "seems to like working" in the spiffy space wrapped with reclaimed wood and floor-to-ceiling windows looking out on Washington Circle; P.S. the "spiked shakes are a dream."

Burma *Burmese*

22 | 11 | 20 | $23

Chinatown | 740 Sixth St. NW (bet. G & H Sts.) | 202-638-1280

"Out of sight" – both literally and figuratively – say fans of this "unassuming gem" with a "slightly obscure" second-story location in Chinatown that serves "well-prepared" "classic Burmese" fare like "hauntingly addictive" tea-leaf salad; decor is at "a minimum", but "kindly" service and "decent" tabs make up for the "plain" digs.

Burma Road *Burmese/Chinese*

22 | 14 | 21 | $23

Gaithersburg | 617 S. Frederick Ave. (bet. Central Ave. & Westland Dr.), MD | 301-963-1429 | www.burmaroad.biz

Adventuresome eaters enjoy the "best of both worlds" at this Burmese-Chinese "match-up" in Gaithersburg, though most "order from the Burmese menu", judging the dishes "unique" and "authentic"; while its Asian-influenced decor and "ambiance could be improved", a "cordial" staff helps make this place one "to return to", especially since the "value is outstanding."

Busara *Thai* | 22 | 19 | 19 | $25 |

Reston | Reston Town Ctr. | 11964 Market St. (Library St.), VA |
703-435-4188
Tysons Corner | 8142 Watson St. (bet. Chain Bridge Rd. &
International Dr.) | McLean, VA | 703-356-2288
www.busara.com

"Aromatic and flavorful" plates "presented well" in Tysons Corner
and Reston business/shopping hubs make these tandem Thais a
"good bet" for "business lunches" or an affordable "night out";
there's nary a straight line in Tysons' "glitzy" brightly colored space,
while Reston's earth tones and right angles are more staid – expect
"expeditious" service at both.

Busboys & Poets *American/Eclectic* | 22 | 22 | 21 | $23 |

Mt. Vernon Square/Convention Center | City Vista | 1025 Fifth St. NW
(K St.) | 202-789-2227 ●
U Street Corridor | 2021 14th St. NW (V St.) | 202-387-7638 ●
Hyattsville | 5331 Baltimore Ave. (Jefferson St.), MD | 301-779-2787
Shirlington | Village at Shirlington | 4251 S. Campbell Ave.
(Arlington Mill Dr.) | Arlington, VA | 703-379-9756 ●
www.busboysandpoets.com

"Is it a bookstore, a coffee shop, a restaurant or a space for activists
to gather?" – it's "all of the above", and there's "never a dull moment" in these "friendly" and "happening" "polyglot hangouts" in
the DC area; you can "surf the web" while enjoying "affordable"
American-Eclectic fare to suit "pretty much any appetite", "grab
drinks" at the bar (full range of caffeine and alcohol), "take in some
poetry" or sink into one of the "comfy" chairs in the "funky" settings
and talk "politics, books or movies."

Buzz *Coffeehouse* | 22 | 20 | 21 | $11 |

Greater Alexandria | 901 Slaters Ln. (Potomac Greens Dr.) |
Alexandria, VA | 703-600-2899 | www.buzzonslaters.com
Ballston | 818 N. Quincy St. (Wilson Blvd.) | Arlington, VA |
703-650-9676 | www.buzzbakery.com

"Wonderful" "snack options" – from "real food" like quiche and
sammies to "creative" desserts – at everyday prices make these
"friendly" Alexandria and Ballston bakery/cafes the DC area's No. 1
value; you can keep your "laptop blazing" while sipping "good coffee", perhaps with one of their signature cupcakes with "lick-your-
fingers-good frosting", plus there's wine and beer at night to kindle
a "nice 'buzz'" in the "cute", "retro" spaces.

Cacique *Mexican/Spanish* | 24 | 20 | 23 | $28 |

Frederick | 26 N. Market St. (Patrick St.), MD | 301-695-2756 |
www.caciquefrederick.com

The "*muy bueno*" "mix of Spanish and Mexican" dishes is "full of flavor" and "reasonably priced", while the "excellent" margaritas and
sangrias pack a punch at this "friendly" *posada* "in the heart of
Frederick"; there may be more seating in the white-tablecloth interior, but the prime perches are in the "cramped" sidewalk area, "one
of the best places to people-watch on Market Street."

	FOOD	DECOR	SERVICE	COST

Cactus Cantina *Tex-Mex*   21 | 17 | 19 | $25

Cleveland Park | 3300 Wisconsin Ave. NW (Macomb St.) | 202-686-7222 | www.cactuscantina.com

"Never leave hungry and never leave broke" could be the motto of this "reliable" Cleveland Park Tex-Mex known for "enormous" helpings at "starving-artist prices" served by a "genuinely nice" staff; the sidewalk patio is huge, while the interior is "festive" but "different than one might expect" (airy and relatively free of kitsch), and though it's "always packed" with "rowdy college kids" and those with "strollers", "somehow you always leave happy – it may be the margaritas."

Cafe Asia *Asian*   21 | 16 | 18 | $24

Golden Triangle | 1720 I St. (bet. 17th & 18th Sts.) | 202-659-2696 | www.cafeasiadc.com 🖂
Rosslyn | 1550 Wilson Blvd. (Pierce St.), VA | 703-741-0870 | www.cafeasia.com

The "ultimate happy-hour places" for "twentysomethings", these clublike Pan-Asian purveyors in the Golden Triangle and Rosslyn are "always buzzing" at night, though they're "solid" "lunch spots" too, offering "consistently good" sushi plus a "vast" assortment of Asian staples; service is "so-so" and the "modern" interiors strike some as "sterile" and "cold", but hearts warm to the "affordable" tabs.

Café Bonaparte *French*   23 | 20 | 18 | $29

Georgetown | 1522 Wisconsin Ave. NW (bet. P St. & Volta Pl.) | 202-333-8830 | www.cafebonaparte.com

Georgetown's "jewel box" of a French cafe "shines" with its "superb" crêpes, "steady" bistro fare plus "great" coffee and wine; while "service can be spotty" and "there's very little 'Elba' room" in this *très* "cozy corner of Paris", at least "they won't rush you", so *"bon appétit!"*

Cafe Deluxe *American*   20 | 18 | 20 | $29

Cleveland Park | 3228 Wisconsin Ave. NW (bet. Macomb St. & Woodley Rd.) | 202-686-2233
Bethesda | 4910 Elm St. (bet. Arlington Rd. & Woodmont Ave.), MD | 301-656-3131
Gaithersburg | Rio Entertainment Ctr. | 9811 Washingtonian Blvd. (Rio Blvd.), MD | 240-403-7082
Tysons Corner | 1800 International Dr. (Shoptysons Blvd.) | McLean, VA | 703-761-0600
www.cafedeluxe.com

"Classic American" "diner" meets "slightly upscale", "European"-feeling cafe at this "friendly" chainlet "popular" with "mixed age groups" for "reasonably priced" "comfort food" of the kind "you wish your mom used to make"; lest the "decibel count" (beware the "screaming kids") detract, head outside and "linger awhile" on the "lovely" patios; P.S. it's a "favorite weekend brunch destination."

Cafe Divan *Turkish*   24 | 20 | 20 | $32

Glover Park | Georgetown Hill Inn | 1834 Wisconsin Ave. NW (34th St.) | 202-338-1747 | www.cafedivan.com

The "refined" Turkish cuisine is "terrific" and "well priced" to boot, at this Ottoman outpost in Glover Park, one of the "few places" serving "Turkish wine" in the area; the "staff greets everyone with a smile", but "the shape of the restaurant's the most fun thing about it", since it's housed in the tip of a flatiron building (ergo you're almost "always near a window" in the "modern", almost sculptural space).

Café du Parc   *French*

21 | 20 | 19 | $48

Downtown | Willard InterContinental Hotel | 1401 Pennsylvania Ave. NW (bet. 14th & 15th Sts.) | 202-942-7000 | www.cafeduparc.com

It's "so Parisian" to breakfast *en plein air* on the "pleasant" terrace at this Downtown French brasserie in the Willard InterContinental or dig into "inventive takes" on the classics in its blue-and-white dining room (there's also a separate sidewalk cafe where one can "see the White House" and "maybe even a politician or two"); sure, it's "crowded", "overpriced" and, being "French, how warm could the servers really be?", but Francophiles insist it's "very much the real thing."

Café Dupont   *French*

21 | 21 | 20 | $44

Dupont Circle | Dupont Circle Hotel | 1500 New Hampshire Ave. NW (Dupont Circle) | 202-483-6000 | www.doylecollection.com

For professional "people-watchers" it's all about "location" – and this French bistro in the Dupont Circle Hotel delivers with front-row seats on a "nice" patio, plus a bank of floor-to-ceiling windows lining the "cool, contemporary" dining room; though "a little pricey", the Gallic offerings are quite "respectable", the "drinks are generous" and the staff is "professional."

Cafe Milano   *Italian*

22 | 21 | 20 | $59

Georgetown | 3251 Prospect St. NW (bet. Potomac St. & Wisconsin Ave.) | 202-333-6183 | www.cafemilano.com

"Get your fabulous on before going" to DC's "'it' place": this high-end Italian in Georgetown frequented by "pro athletes, politicians" and other "celebrities" who cavort in various "fancy" dining nooks, some with zany ceiling frescoes (Milan Metro map, Plácido Domingo); one can certainly "eat well" here (witness "fantastic" risotto, fish "cooked perfectly"), but "people-watching" is the main event – just "don't expect the best service if you aren't one of the watched."

Cafe Nola   ❶ *American*

24 | 20 | 22 | $25

Frederick | 4 E. Patrick St. (Market St.), MD | 301-694-6652 | www.cafe-nola.com

"Expect quality" organic ingredients and "plenty" of "vegetarian choices" on the New American menu of this all-purpose coffeehouse/cafe where "local food and music" (and art) "come together" in Frederick; the "laid-back", "granola" vibe pulses from the "best" cappuccinos in the morning to "awesome infused" spirits late at night.

Café Olé   ▣ *Mediterranean*

20 | 14 | 17 | $27

Upper NW | 4000 Wisconsin Ave. NW (Upton St.) | 202-244-1330 | www.cafeoledc.com

Tenleytown regulars remark "you can't go wrong" sampling the "fresh and flavorful" Mediterranean meze at this "simple", peach-colored Upper NW cafe that's "less pricey and more homey" than many other DC tapas bars; service is solid, and it has a "pleasant" patio that's a "relaxing" place to "sit around with friends."

Cafe Pizzaiolo *Italian/Pizza*　　24 | 17 | 21 | $20

Greater Alexandria | 1623 Fern St. (Kenwood Ave.) | Alexandria, VA | 703-717-9324

Greater Alexandria | Cameron Station | 4906 Brenman Park Dr. (Somervelle St.) | Alexandria, VA | 703-894-2250 Ⓜ

Arlington | 2800 S. Randolph St. (Walter Reed Dr.), VA | 703-894-2250

www.cafepizzaiolo.com

"Kids and parents are at ease" at these "friendly" Italian "neighborhood knockouts" where a low-stress, "no-fuss atmosphere" complete with "board games and puzzles" sets the stage for "off-the-hook" pies crafted from "simple, fresh ingredients" (the other menu items are "good too"); decor may be "lacking", but takeout is always an option and, hey, the "price is right."

Café Renaissance *Continental*　　26 | 26 | 28 | $49

Vienna | 163 Glyndon St. SE (bet. Locust St. & Maple Ave.), VA | 703-938-3311 | www.caferenaissance.com

"Without a GPS", finding this "elegant, old-world" destination in a Vienna strip mall takes some doing, but the "consistently outstanding" Continental menu and "fine choice of wines" served by "cordial", "snappily dressed" waiters make it a "gem" worth hunting for; its intimate, "ornate and gilded" rooms are "romantic", furthering its status as a "top choice in Vienna" for a "special", if pricey, meal.

Café Saint-Ex ● *Eclectic*　　20 | 17 | 18 | $33

Logan Circle | 1847 14th St. NW (T St.) | 202-265-7839 | www.saint-ex.com

"Space is really tight" at this 14th Street "hangout", but an "interesting crowd" squeezes in for "comforting", midpriced Eclectic eats and "amazing" brews doled out by a sometimes-"cooler-than-thou" crew; on the ground floor a "clever aviation theme" flies below a pretty tin ceiling, downstairs "doubles as a club" with a DJ Tuesday-Saturday nights and sidewalk seating is "icing on the cake."

Cajun Experience *Cajun/Creole*　　▽ 23 | 16 | 19 | $23

Leesburg | 14 Loudoun St. SE (bet. Church & King Sts.), VA | 703-777-6580 | www.cajunexperience.biz

"Displaced Cajuns" rage about their 'experience' at this affordable Leesburg Louisianan, musing that the food must be "transported magically" from a kitchen in "Baton Rouge"; "real nice folks" patrol the "simple" houselike digs, creating a down-home feel that's like "being back in NO."

California Tortilla *Tex-Mex*　　22 | 16 | 21 | $11

Chinatown | Gallery Pl. | 728 Seventh St. NW (bet. G & H Sts.) | 202-638-2233 ●

Cleveland Park | 3501 Connecticut Ave. NW (bet. Ordway & Porter Sts.) | 202-244-2447

(continued)

(continued)

California Tortilla

Bethesda | 4871 Cordell Ave. (bet. Norfolk & Woodmont Aves.), MD | 301-654-8226

Olney | Olney Village Ctr. | 18101 Village Center Dr. (Olney Sandy Spring Rd.), MD | 301-570-2522

Potomac | Cabin John Shopping Ctr. | 7727 Tuckerman Ln. (Seven Locks Rd.), MD | 301-765-3600

Rockville | Rockville Town Sq. | 199 E. Montgomery Ave. (Maryland Ave.), MD | 301-610-6500

Silver Spring | Burnt Mills Shopping Ctr. | 10721 Columbia Pike (Hillwood Dr.), MD | 301-593-3955

Greater Alexandria | Hoffman Town Ctr. | 301 Swamp Fox Rd. (bet. Eisenhower Ave. & Mandeville Ln.) | Alexandria, VA | 703-329-3333

Courthouse | 2057 Wilson Blvd. (bet. Troy & Veitch Sts.) | Arlington, VA | 703-243-4151

Fairfax | Fair Lakes Promenade Shopping Ctr. | 12239 Fair Lakes Pkwy. (bet. Monument Dr. & Ox Rd.), VA | 703-278-0007
www.californiatortilla.com
Additional locations throughout the DC area

In "the fast-casual burrito wars" this homegrown chain defends its turf with "some of the best burritos for the money", but its secret weapon is a "sense of humor" extending from "friendly cashiers" to events like Jungle Noise Day to its colorful settings, each sporting a wall filled with "a stunning collection of piquant condiments" (some locations also have mix-your-own-soda stations); even if they're "not places you'd go to propose", they're a "first choice for a dinner with kids."

The Capital Grille *Steak*   26 | 25 | 26 | $62

Penn Quarter | 601 Pennsylvania Ave. NW (6th St.) | 202-737-6200

Chevy Chase | Wisconsin Pl. | 5310 Western Ave. (Wisconsin Ave.), MD | 301-718-7812

Tysons Corner | 1861 International Dr. (Leesburg Pike) | McLean, VA | 703-448-3900
www.thecapitalgrille.com

At these "clubby" steakhouses oozing "sophistication" and "swagger", "toothsome" slabs of beef are matched with "phenomenal" wine by "snazzy"-looking servers who "remember who you are"; "you never know who you'll run into" ("members of Congress?") at Penn Quarter, though all locations are "fine incarnations" of the genre, so expect "prices that reflect the quality."

CapMac ⓩ *American*   23 | 13 | 21 | $10

Location varies; see website | 914-489-2897 | www.capmacdc.com

"Ooey-gooey" mac 'n' cheese topped with a "crunchy Cheez-It" crumble has tailgaters "chasing" this orange-and-yellow truck all over DC for what fans claim is a "delicacy more fit to be eaten from a porcelain bowl than a cardboard box"; the el cheapo elbows can be topped with meat and veggies for a small up-charge, while atmosphere is in the form of service "with a smile"; P.S. check online for schedule.

	FOOD	DECOR	SERVICE	COST

Capri *Italian* ▽ 23 | 20 | 25 | $41

McLean | Giant Shopping Ctr. | 6825 Redmond Dr. (bet. Beverly & Chain Bridge Rds.), VA | 703-288-4601 | www.caprimcleanva.com
"Old-school" waiters "work very hard" at this McLean "neighborhood joint" starring seafood "at its finest" and pastas "clearly cooked by someone in the know" (there's a "mama" in the kitchen) and served in a fairly "pleasing", sunny setting; though prices match the area's high-income demographics, it does offer a "true taste of Italy."

Carlyle *American* 25 | 23 | 24 | $36

Shirlington | 4000 Campbell Ave. (Quincy St.) | Arlington, VA | 703-931-0777 | www.greatamericanrestaurants.com
Diners are "greeted with smiles and fed with kindness" – and "unchallenging", "well-executed" New American eats – at this cavernous and "classy" deco-esque brasserie in Shirlington that's priced for "everyday" but "good enough for special occasions"; hit the "noisy bar scene" or head upstairs to dine where it's "more conducive to conversation."

Carmine's *Italian* 20 | 18 | 20 | $36

Penn Quarter | 425 Seventh St. NW (bet. D & E Sts.) | 202-737-7770 | www.carminesnyc.com
"Hungry" *paesani* tie on "old-world feedbags" at this "family-style tomato palace" in the Penn Quarter, feasting on "ginormous portions" ("meatballs like "baseballs"") in a woody, 1930s-style "barracks-sized dining hall" that rings with "loud" "conversation" and "laughter"; servers are "always there" when needed, and most leave sighing "money well spent", though a minority calls the "assembly-line" experience "a bit stressful"; P.S. the bar menu is a "best deal" for a twosome.

Carolina Kitchen *Southern* 25 | 23 | 23 | $24

Hyattsville | 6501 America Blvd. (East-West Hwy.), MD | 301-927-2929 | www.thecarolinakitchen.com
See review in the Baltimore Directory.

NEW Carving Room ◑ *Sandwiches* – | – | – | I

Chinatown | 300 Massachusetts Ave. NW (H St.) | 202-525-2116 | www.carvingroom.com
Slicing into a recent trend – artisanal sandwich shops with serious bars – this gently priced Chinatown entry serves up hearty sammies and small plates composed of house-cured meats, pickled veggies and a few Middle Eastern dishes complemented by fancy cocktails and craft drafts; the industrial-mod premises feature a big bar, wood tables and counter seating near large windows plus amenities like table service after 4 PM and on weekends.

Casa Oaxaca Ⓜ *Mexican* 22 | 16 | 17 | $32

Adams Morgan | 2106 18th St. NW (bet. California St. & Wyoming Ave.) | 202-387-2272 | www.oaxacaindc.com
"Holy mole!" it feels like "eating in a restaurant off the Zócalo" at this "loud", "festive" Adams Morgan townhouse where the midpriced

"authentic Mexican regional" menu includes a "variety" of "incredible" mole and "exotic" treats that make you "forget cheap Tex-Mex"; service is only "decent" but may seem better after sampling the mojitos and caipirinhas "muddled to supremacy."

Cashion's Eat Place Ⓜ *American*
| 25 | 21 | 24 | $53 |

Adams Morgan | 1819 Columbia Rd. NW (bet. Biltmore St. & Mintwood Pl.) | 202-797-1819 | www.cashionseatplace.com
"Expect to find something very special" at chef/co-owner John Manolatos' Adams Morgan New American "neighborhood destination" with a "grown-up, slightly glam vibe", whose "informed" staff delivers seasonal, local dishes full of "delicious surprises"; "eclectic in every sense of the word", it's just as "perfect for date night" or "eating alone" at the central bar as for "people-watching" from its sidewalk patio or enjoying an "upscale brunch at not-upscale prices" (it's more costly but still "worth the money" at night).

Cassatt's Café *New Zealand*
| 20 | 17 | 17 | $23 |

Arlington | 4536 Fairfax Blvd. (Woodrow & Woodstock Sts.), VA | 703-527-3330 | www.cassattscafe.com
With "the best flat white this side of Wellington", kiwi coffee clutchers also praise Arlington's native New Zealander for its "awesome brunch", "great" desserts and other-hemisphere "noshes" at budget prices; the staff is "efficient" and the "pleasant, "arty" decor – featuring rotating works by local artists – would make the cafe's namesake Impressionist proud.

Cava Mezze *Greek*
| 25 | 20 | 21 | $34 |

Capitol Hill | 527 Eighth St. SE (Pennsylvania Ave.) | 202-543-9090
Rockville | 9713 Traville Gateway Dr. (Shady Grove Rd.), MD | 301-309-9090
Clarendon | 2940 Clarendon Blvd. (Fillmore St.), VA | 703-276-9090
www.cavamezze.com
The "flaming cheese" will "light up your palate" as well as the "dark" "caverns" that house this moderately priced Greek chainlet that also wows with "diptastic" spreads and "bold" small plates; "generous" staffers ferry "potent" cocktails that help fuel the "high decibel levels."

Cava Mezze Grill *Greek*
| 22 | 15 | 18 | $15 |

Columbia Heights | 3105 14th St. NW (bet. Irving St. & Park Rd.) | 202-695-8100
Upper NW | 4237 Wisconsin Ave. NW (bet. Veazey & Warren Sts.) | 202-695-8115
Bethesda | 4832 Bethesda Ave. (bet. Arlington Rd. & Woodmont Ave.), MD | 301-656-1772
Tysons Corner | Tysons Corner Ctr. | 8048 Tysons Corner Ctr. (Shoptysons Blvd.) | McLean, VA | 703-288-0005
NEW **Merrifield** | Mosiac Shopping Ctr. | 2905 District Ave. (Strawberry Ln.), VA | 703-988-4313
www.cavagrill.com
At these "in-and-out" Greek spots (a spin-off concept from sit-down parent Cava Mezze), "delicious" pitas, bowls or salads are assembled "Chipotle-style" in a "pick-what-you-like"-for-toppings line by

"fast", "friendly" crews; "fast-food prices" and raw-industrial settings that are "nicer than similar" spots draw a cava-lcade of fans.

Cedar Restaurant *American*　　23 | 19 | 22 | $46

Penn Quarter | 822 E St. NW (bet. 8th & 9th Sts.) | 202-637-0012 | www.cedardc.com

This "chic basement hideout" with "fine", if pricey, New American fare is an "appealing stop on the Penn Quarter circuit" for "first dates", "pre-theater dinners" and "post-work drinks"; a "tall wall of mirrors" and "tree murals well disguise" the fact that it's "below ground", and the "engaging" staff lends a *Cheers* quality to it."

Ceiba *Nuevo Latino*　　24 | 22 | 23 | $45

Downtown | 701 14th St. NW (G St.) | 202-393-3983 | www.ceibarestaurant.com

"Different and delightful" Nuevo Latino fare awakens the "passion in your palate" in an "exuberant" and "elegant" Downtown setting where "singles" often meet over "creative cocktails" at the bar or in the low-lit, modern lounge area; it's a Goldilocks kind of place, with "not too much, not too little" service, and though not cheap (except for the "competitively priced" happy hour), you can go "with confidence."

Central Michel Richard ⊠ *American/French*　26 | 21 | 23 | $54

Penn Quarter | 1001 Pennsylvania Ave. NW (11th St.) | 202-626-0015 | www.centralmichelrichard.com

"Proving Michel Richard doesn't need beaucoup bucks to be brilliant", his "high-energy brasserie" in Penn Quarter dazzles with its "outstanding" riffs on tradition that run from New American (fried chicken that "slaps the Colonel in the face") to French ("I'm going to marry their faux gras"); a "welcoming" staff and a "casual" vibe let ordinary folk feel like the "movers and shakers" that line the "striking" "modern" dining room and "hopping" bar – in short, a "winner."

Cesco Osteria *Italian*　　19 | 21 | 18 | $46

Bethesda | Bethesda Metro | 7401 Woodmont Ave. (bet. Edgemoor & Montgomery Lns.), MD | 301-654-8333 | www.cesco-osteria.com

Longtime followers of "real Tuscan chef" Francesco Ricchi praise his Italian menu that "does not disappoint" at his "cavernous" quarters in Bethesda where there's an extra dash of "fun" (happy hour at the huge bar, live music); prices are high, and it gets mixed service marks, but the "beautiful" wood-lined interior and huge patio with "flaming torches" are "enjoyable."

C.F. Folks ⊠ *Eclectic*　　24 | 10 | 20 | $19

Dupont Circle | 1225 19th St. NW (Jefferson Pl.) | 202-293-0162 | www.cffolksrestaurant.com

"It's time someone declared" this Eclectic luncheonette below Dupont Circle "a national treasure" say longtime loyalists who depend daily on its "gourmet" "homestyle" eats like "can't-go-wrong" sandwiches, some of DC's "best" crab cakes and "delicious" specials; its "counter is packed with Washington power" and regulars who swear the staff's "friendly/edgy attitude grows on you"; P.S. if it's too "cramped", "eat outside", or take it to go.

	FOOD	DECOR	SERVICE	COST

Charlie Palmer Steak 🗷 *Steak* — 26 | 26 | 25 | $69

Capitol Hill | 101 Constitution Ave. NW (bet. 1st St. & Louisiana Ave.) |
202-547-8100 | www.charliepalmer.com

You might "find your congressman" at this "top-end" Capitol Hill
chophouse, where lobbyists get "whiplash" scanning the "sleek, sophisticated" room, and tourists are awed by "wonderful views of the
Capitol" from the window tables; it's "pricey", of course, but the
steaks are "cooked to perfection" (there's "excellent" fish too) and
complemented by "fabulous" American wines, and "even if you're
not a VIP", you'll be treated like one.

Chart House *Seafood* — 23 | 25 | 23 | $45

Old Town | 1 Cameron St. (Union St.) | Alexandria, VA | 703-684-5080 |
www.chart-house.com

A "wonderful view" of the Potomac and an "especially nice" outdoor
patio are the main reasons to chart course to this "classic"-looking
dockside seafooder in Old Town, but bolstering the case are the
"fantastic" fin fare and prime rib, plus a "fabulous" salad bar; aye,
cap'n, it's priced for "once-in-a-while" dining, but "attentive" service and the "incredible" location make it a popular "place to take
visitors" or mark a "special occasion."

Chasin' Tails *Cajun/Creole* — - | - | - | I

Arlington | 2200 N. Westmoreland St. (Washington St.), VA |
703-538-2565 | www.chasintailscrawfish.com

The main event at this sporty, brick-walled watering hole in
Greater Arlington (near Falls Church) takes place when robustly
seasoned crawfish, boiled in a bag, are dumped on the table, and
folks roll up their sleeves and dig in; for those diners not up for
messy, hands-on eating, the menu offers other easy-on-the-wallet
Cajun-Creole specialties.

Cheesecake Factory *American* — 24 | 22 | 22 | $30

Chevy Chase | Chevy Chase Pavilion | 5345 Wisconsin Ave. NW
(bet. Jenifer St. & Western Ave.), MD | 202-364-0500
White Flint | White Flint Mall | 11301 Rockville Pike (bet. Flanders Ave. &
Nicholson Ln.) | Rockville, MD | 301-770-0999
Clarendon | Market Common Clarendon | 2900 Clarendon Blvd.
(Fillmore St.), VA | 703-294-9966
Fairfax | Fair Oaks Mall | 11778 Fair Oaks Mall (Fair Lakes Pkwy.), VA |
703-273-6600
Tysons Corner | Tysons Galleria | 1796 International Dr.
(bet. Galleria Dr. & Tysons Blvd.) | McLean, VA | 703-506-9311
Woodbridge | Potomac Mills Outlet Mall | 2708 Potomac Mills Circle
(Nazarine Way), VA | 703-490-8155
Sterling | Dulles Town Ctr. | 21076 Dulles Town Circle (Nokes Blvd.), VA |
703-444-9002
www.thecheesecakefactory.com
See review in the Baltimore Directory.

Chef Geoff's *American* — 21 | 19 | 20 | $36

Downtown | 1301 Pennsylvania Ave. NW (bet. E & F Sts.) |
202-464-4461 ◗

(continued)
Chef Geoff's

Upper NW | 3201 New Mexico Ave. NW (bet. Embassy Park Dr. & Sutton Pl.) | 202-237-7800 ●

NEW **Rockville** | 12256 Rockville Pike (Bet. Bou & Rollins Aves.), MD | 240-621-3090

Tysons Corner | Fairfax Sq. | 8045 Leesburg Pike (Aline Ave.) | Vienna, VA | 571-282-6003 ●

www.chefgeoff.com

"Solid American food with some tasty twists" that's "fairly priced" and dished up in "vibrant" environs is the format at Geoff Tracy's bistros in the DC area; they all have "active" bar scenes, with "two-fisted" happy hours, yet they're "surprisingly kid-friendly", which can make them "cacophonous" – still, adept service and "great gluten-free offerings" help keep them "busy."

Chesapeake Room *American/Seafood*   20 | 21 | 19 | $38

Capitol Hill | 501 Eighth St. SE (E St.) | 202-543-1445 | www.thechesapeakeroom.com

Arguably DC's "coolest" 350-gallon fish tank hovers over the bar in this Barracks Row bistro, handsomely decorated with maple trim, leather seats and oil paintings, and serving "reliably good" American fare that sources local surf 'n' turf; service is solid, and the prices are right, giving it "lots of potential", though it may be "best enjoyed in warm weather, when you can sit on the large", luxe patio.

Chez Billy ⓜ *French*   - | - | - | M

Petworth | 3815 Georgia Ave. NW (bet. Quincy & Randolph Sts.) | 202-506-2080 | www.chezbilly.com

At this French bistro in Petworth's landmarked Billy Simpson's building, flickering candles and ornate chandeliers cast a glow over its bi-level bar, while the separate dining room sparkles with verve and class with its wood-backed booths, vintage lighting and tiled floor; in both settings, moderately priced favorites like mussels, steak frites and duck confit are enjoyed with classic cocktails, French wines and international beers by its cosmopolitan clientele.

Chicken on the Run *Chicken/Peruvian*   24 | 11 | 19 | $14

Bethesda | 4933 St. Elmo Ave. (bet. Norfolk Ave. & Old Georgetown Rd.), MD | 301-652-9004 | www.chickenbethesda.com

"Fabulous Peruvian spit-roasted chicken" and deep-fried yuca have Bethesdans racing to this counter-serve joint where "cheap" prices and "huge portions" add up to a big "bang for your buck"; there's "no decor" and minimal seating, so "takeout" may be the way to go – just be warned that your car may "smell so good you can hardly wait to get your order home."

Chima *Brazilian*   26 | 24 | 25 | $58

Tysons Corner | 8010 Towers Crescent Dr. (Leesburg Pike) | Vienna, VA | 703-639-3080 | www.chimasteakhouse.com

"You'll never want to eat again, but in a good way" after a trip to this "high-class rodizio" in Tysons Corner, with its "never-ending" parade of meat backed by a "salad bar the length of a bus" ("get your money's worth"); the waiters running around with "swords" are "a hoot", yet the "chic", "contemporary", Brazilian wood-accented environs make for a "classy night" out.

China Bistro *Chinese*
24 | 9 | 17 | $15

Rockville | 755 Hungerford Dr. (Martins Ln.), MD | 301-294-0808
"Dumplings, dumplings, dumplings" are the draw at this "casual" Rockville Asian turning out "luscious" packets of "homemade goodness" (along with other "authentic" eats) at "attractive" prices; prime-time "lines" and sometimes "not friendly" service don't deter fans, and while a post-Survey remodel spruced it up a bit, it's still not ritzy.

China Garden *Chinese*
22 | 16 | 18 | $29

Rosslyn | Twin Towers | 1100 Wilson Blvd. (bet. Kent & Lynn Sts.), VA | 703-525-5317 | www.chinagardenva.com
"Chinese tour buses disgorge" loads of tourists for the "yum yum" dim sum (weekends only) at this "reliable", "reasonably priced" Rosslynite that's "efficient at moving large crowds through"; the "huge" office tower venue has uninspiring "standard Chinese restaurant" decor, but locals say it works for a "super-fast lunch" during the week, when it offers a "varied menu" of Cantonese cuisine.

China Jade *Chinese*
25 | 18 | 22 | $21

Rockville | 16805 Crabbs Branch Way (Shady Grove Rd.), MD | 301-963-1570 | www.chinajaderockville.com
This "authentic" Chinese in a Rockville shopping center may feel "halfway to China" for some, but is "worth" a drive on account of its "complex yet well-balanced" Sichuan and Cantonese specialties; the typical digs are pleasant enough, and patrons appreciate the cheap tabs and "friendly", "helpful" staffers.

China Star *Chinese*
24 | 14 | 16 | $19

Fairfax | Fair City Mall | 9600 Main St. (Pickett Rd.), VA | 703-323-8822
"There is no need to ask for extra-spicy" at this Fairfax strip-mall spot: the "authentic" Sichuan cuisine "tortures" the tongues of the biggest heat-seekers (for those who cower at the low end of the Scoville heat scale, there's Americanized Chinese fare); service is "not the greatest", and there's "zero atmosphere", but it's still a "wonderful buy."

Chinatown Express *Chinese*
23 | 8 | 15 | $17

Chinatown | 746 Sixth St. NW (H St.) | 202-638-0424
"C'mon, you didn't come here for the decor" say those who stand "transfixed at the entrance ogling" the "guy making noodles and dumplings in the window" before descending into Chinatown's "dirt-cheap" den for noodles "tasty and chewy" enough to ensure you "steer clear of the rest" of the standard eats; service is so "quick" here, "they practically throw the food at you."

Ching Ching Cha *Tearoom*
∇ 20 | 25 | 25 | $21

Georgetown | 1063 Wisconsin Ave. NW (M St.) | 202-333-8288 | www.chingchingcha.com
"Cheaper than a massage but almost as effective" coo visitors to this "tranquil" Chinese tearoom in Georgetown, where lounging on plush

pillows and being treated by serene servers provides "a cool, quiet getaway" from busy lives; more than 70 freshly brewed teas dominate a menu with a modest selection of "snacks" like dumplings and cookies that perhaps work "better for relaxing than [as] a full meal."

Chop't Creative Salad *American*

| 21 | 14 | 19 | $12 |

Chinatown | Jemal's Chinatown | 730 Seventh St. NW (bet. G & H Sts.) | 202-347-3225

Downtown | Metro Ctr. | 618 12th St. NW (G St.) | 202-783-0007

Dupont Circle | 1300 Connecticut Ave. NW (N St.) | 202-327-2255

Golden Triangle | 1629 K St. NW (bet. 16th & 17th Sts.) | 202-688-0333 🖪

Golden Triangle | 1105 19th St. NW (bet. L & M Sts.) | 202-955-0665 🖪

Capitol Hill | Union Station | 50 Massachusetts Ave. NE (1st St.) | 202-688-0330

NEW Bethesda | Wildwood Shopping Ctr. | 10307 Old Georgetown Rd. (Democracy Blvd.), MD | 240-752-9942

Rosslyn | 1735 N. Lynn St. (bet. 19th St. & Wilson Blvd.), VA | 703-875-2888

www.choptsalad.com

The mixmasters behind the counters "keep things moving at a fast clip" – er, chop – at these "high-volume", "assembly-line" lunch spots that offer a "bewildering variety of salad" fixin's for "customizable" bowls (they also have wraps); wilted wallets worry they're paying "too much green for the greens", but most health-seekers find the "gigantic" "end products" "worth" the mild "splurge."

NEW Chupacabra *Pan-Latin*

| – | – | – | I |

Atlas District | 822 H St. NE (9th St.) | 202-505-4628 | www.chupacabradc.com

Spun off from a popular food truck, this new Atlas District storefront slings traditional (barbacoa) and not-so-traditional (vegan) tacos on the cheap along with other Latin specialties like Venezuelan arepas and Cuban sandwiches; with the brick-and-mortar location also comes later hours and a sidewalk patio; P.S. it plans to serve Mexican beer and Latin-leaning cocktails too.

Chutzpah *Deli*

| 23 | 12 | 18 | $18 |

Fairfax | Fairfax Towne Ctr. | 12214 Fairfax Towne Ctr. (bet. Monument Ct. & Ox Rd.), VA | 703-385-8883 | www.chutzpahdeli.com

"Sandwiches too big to finish in one sitting" plus "delicious" breakfast items and other "authentic" deli favorites answer the "craving" for "Jewish soul food" at this Fairfax shopping-center noshery; some say oy vey about the authentically "surly" service and "NYC-style" check, but even if "you'll never confuse this with a real NY deli", it's "not a bad start for Northern Virginia."

Circa *American*

| 20 | 21 | 20 | $32 |

Dupont Circle | 1601 Connecticut Ave. NW (Q St.) | 202-667-1601 | www.circaatdupont.com ◗

Foggy Bottom | 2221 I St. NW (23rd St.) | 202-506-5589 | www.circaatfoggybottom.com ◗

(continued)

(continued)
Circa

Clarendon | 3010 Clarendon Blvd. (Garfield St.), VA | 703-522-3010 | www.circaatclarendon.com

These "sleek, trendy" New American bistros in Dupont Circle, Foggy Bottom and Clarendon are "hopping" meet-up spots, where "consistently solid" food with the "right level of creative flair" anchors "vibrant bar" scenes chock-full of "twentysomethings"; staff members are generally "helpful" and the prices "fair", but you have to be "lucky to snag" a table in one of the "lovely" outdoor areas.

Circle Bistro *American*   20 | 17 | 19 | $46

West End | One Washington Circle Hotel | 1 Washington Circle NW (bet. New Hampshire Ave. & 23rd St.) | 202-293-5390 | www.thecirclehotel.com

At this West Ender "hidden" in a hotel, a "small but well-balanced menu" of "fine" New American dishes is ferried to tables by "attentive" help; its "quiet, simply decorated" earth-toned dining room, bar/lounge with fireplace and "sweet", secret-feeling patio are so "convenient to the Kennedy Center" that "more people should know about" it – and its "bargain" pre-theater menu.

City Lights of China *Chinese*   19 | 13 | 18 | $26

Dupont Circle | 1731 Connecticut Ave. NW (bet. R & S Sts.) | 202-265-6688 | www.citylightsofchina.com

Bethesda | 4820 Bethesda Ave. (bet. Arlington Rd. & Woodmont Ave.), MD | 301-913-9501 | www.bethesdacitylightsofchina.com

"Large portions" of "cheap", "classic" Chinese "standards" ("crispy beef" is the "standout") have kept these "friendly" and "reliable" Dupont Circle and Bethesda joints going for years; given their "hole-in-the-wall" looks, happily they're known for "fast delivery."

CityZen ⓈⓂ *American*   27 | 27 | 27 | $115

SW | Mandarin Oriental | 1330 Maryland Ave. SW (12th St.) | 202-787-6006 | www.mandarinoriental.com

Chef Eric Ziebold "delivers taste, imagination and fun" via a multicourse menu that adds up to a "fabulous meal full of pleasant surprises" at this "stunningly beautiful" "Nouvelle American" "destination" in the Mandarin Oriental; a "personal touch from the minute you walk in the door" enhances the experience, which leads flush foodies to exult "fine dining is still alive and worth every cent"; P.S. the "very hip" bar offers a "real-bargain" tasting menu.

Clyde's ● *American*   22 | 23 | 22 | $33

Chinatown | 707 Seventh St. NW (G St.) | 202-349-3700

Georgetown | Georgetown Park Mall | 3236 M St. NW (bet. Potomac St. & Wisconsin Ave.) | 202-333-9180

Chevy Chase | 5441 Wisconsin Ave. (Wisconsin Circle), MD | 301-951-9600

Rockville | 2 Preserve Pkwy. (bet. Tower Oaks Blvd. & Wootton Pkwy.), MD | 301-294-0200

Greater Alexandria | Mark Ctr. | 1700 N. Beauregard St. (Highview Ln.) | Alexandria, VA | 703-820-8300

(continued)

Clyde's

Reston | Reston Town Ctr. | 11905 Market St. (bet. Library & Presidents Sts.), VA | 703-787-6601

Tysons Corner | 8332 Leesburg Pike (Pinnacle Dr.) | Vienna, VA | 703-734-1901

Broadlands | Willow Creek Farm | 42920 Broadlands Blvd. (Chickacoan Trail Dr.), VA | 571-209-1200

www.clydes.com

"Nostalgic" themes (old farmhouse, Adirondack lodge, the Golden Age of Travel) make each location of this homegrown American saloon feel like a "unique" "adventure", so it's no wonder they're "popular" stops for everyone from "kids" to "grandma" – indeed, they're Greater DC's Most Popular places to dine; "upbeat" service also plays a role, along with the fact that diners are sure to "get their money's worth" via a "value"-packed menu of "solidly appealing", "honest" eats.

Coal Fire *Pizza* 22 | 18 | 20 | $21

Frederick | 7820 Wormans Mill Rd. (bet. Catoctin Mountain Hwy. & Liberty Rd.), MD | 301-631-2625

Gaithersburg | 116 Main St. (Kentlands Blvd.), MD | 301-519-2625

www.coalfireonline.com

See review in the Baltimore Directory.

Coastal Flats *Seafood* 24 | 22 | 23 | $30

Fairfax | Fairfax Corner | 11901 Grand Commons Ave. (Fairfax Corner Ave.), VA | 571-522-6300

Tysons Corner | Tysons Corner Ctr. | 7860 Tysons Corner Ctr. (bet. Fashion Blvd. & International Dr.) | McLean, VA | 703-356-1440

www.greatamericanrestaurants.com

"To-die-for" crab cakes, "overflowing" lobster rolls and other "plate-licking" fin fare reel in Tysons Corner and Fairfax mall shoppers to these midpriced "islandy" "theme parks" (colorful decor, sculptures of underwater critters hanging overhead) sporting "lively bar scenes"; the resulting "madhouse" crowds are "well managed" by "Johnny-on-the-spot" serving teams – still, to avoid waits, "go early or call ahead."

Co Co. Sala ❷ *Eclectic* 24 | 24 | 21 | $41

Penn Quarter | 929 F St. NW (bet. 9th & 10th Sts.) | 202-347-4265 | www.cocosala.com

"Chocoholics'" "dreams are answered" at this "sexy" Penn Quarter Eclectic lounge, where "snazzy" decor (curvy ceilings, shimmering walls) and staffers who "enjoy" themselves set the stage for "clever sweet and savory takes" on the cocoa bean – "decadent" desserts, sure, but "even the salad" is chocolaty; "small plates meant for savoring, not devouring" may leave big eaters "hungry" and with an "emptier wallet", but "sweet tooths" swear it's "worth the investment."

Columbia Firehouse ❷ *American* 23 | 23 | 22 | $35

Old Town | 109 S. St. Asaph St. (bet. King & Prince Sts.) | Alexandria, VA | 703-683-1776 | www.columbiafirehouse.com

Old Town's "cool remake of an old firehouse" offers a "moderately" priced American menu alight with "interesting twists", served by an "attentive" crew amid "lots of seating options": an "airy" exposed-brick atrium, a "classy" upstairs salon and a "charming" patio; but it's at its best, perhaps, when one is sipping "tasty, old-fashioned drinks" with the "power brokers" in the "beautiful" barroom.

Comet Ping Pong *Pizza*   20 | 15 | 16 | $25

Upper NW | 5037 Connecticut Ave. NW (Nebraska Ave.) | 202-364-0404 | www.cometpingpong.com

When this Upper Northwest "pizza, Ping-Pong and live music" venue is on its game, it's a "fun place" for "cheap" "family outings" or an "unusual date", with "crunchy" New Haven–style pies and "addictive" wings; it loses points for its warehouse decor, "uncomfortable" bench seating and a half-hearted serve from the "so-so" staff, but paddle partisans call it a winner, citing, duh, free "Ping-Pong!"

Commissary *American*   19 | 17 | 18 | $24

Logan Circle | 1443 P St. NW (bet. 14th & 15th Sts.) | 202-299-0018 | www.commissarydc.com

All-in-one bar/coffeehouse/restaurant, Logan Circle's "refreshingly inexpensive", "cozy" "neighborhood dive" does it all with a "solid" American menu "broad enough to suit just about anyone", "comfortable" armchairs and "free WiFi"; locals "doing some work" or "meeting up" for happy hour appreciate a "welcoming" vibe from the staff.

Comus Inn Ⓜ *American*   20 | 24 | 22 | $46

Dickerson | 23900 Old Hundred Rd. (Comus Rd.), MD | 301-349-5100 | www.thecomusinn.com

Dining "out in the middle of nowhere" has its charms when "magnificent" views of Sugarloaf Mountain set the stage for "romantic" dinners, "lovely" receptions or a scenic brunch at this historic Montgomery County farmhouse; its "perfectly good" New American fare strikes some as "overpriced" – still, the staff makes everyone "feel like a celebrity"; P.S. reservations are "a must"; closed Monday and Tuesday.

Corduroy Ⓩ *American*   28 | 25 | 26 | $68

Mt. Vernon Square/Convention Center | 1122 Ninth St. NW (bet. L & M Sts.) | 202-589-0699 | www.corduroydc.com

"Every morsel from the kitchen is a thing of beauty", and matched by "excellent" wines, at Tom Power's "civilized" New American in a townhouse opposite the Convention Center; service that's "polished yet the antithesis of stuffy" and "clean-lined", "modern" decor both strike a balance between "elegant" and "casual", adding up to an "expensive-but-worth-it" experience; P.S. the "hideaway upstairs bar" offers what may be the "best" three-course "bar bargain" in town.

Cork Ⓜ *American*   25 | 22 | 23 | $44

Logan Circle | 1720 14th St. NW (bet. R & S Sts.) | 202-265-2675 | www.corkdc.com

At this über-trendy Logan Circle wine bar, "a huge array of wines by the glass without an outrageous markup" is paired with "delightful" New American small plates with an "extra edge of creativity"; the "well-informed" staff doubles as "eye candy" in the "stylish", brick-walled, "dimly lit" space that gets "loud" and "crowded" late, so best come "early."

Cosmopolitan Grill ⓜ *E European*

▽ 27 | 17 | 24 | $31

Greater Alexandria | 7770 Richmond Hwy. (Belford Dr.) | Alexandria, VA | 703-360-3660 | www.restaurant-cosmopolitan.com

"Great goulash", "Wiener schnitzel like your mother used to make" and other "wonderful" Balkan specialties at "reasonable prices" make this "hidden gem" a nice alternative in Alexandria; "high standards of hospitality" are upheld, and the "no-frills" decor leaves guests to focus on "food not found everywhere."

The Counter *Burgers*

21 | 15 | 18 | $17

Reston | Reston Town Ctr. | 11922 Democracy Dr. (bet. Explorer & Library Sts.), VA | 703-796-1008 | www.thecounterburger.com

"Bring your appetite and creative spirit" to this "friendly" Reston branch of a West Coast chain for the "drool-worthy" burgers "made to your liking" with near-"endless" options for customization; supporters cite a "stylish" industrial setting and low cost, and wonder "who can resist" the 'adult' milkshakes that make good use of the full bar.

Crème *Southern*

21 | 16 | 19 | $31

U Street Corridor | 1322 U St. NW (bet. 13th & 14th Sts.) | 202-234-1884 | www.cremedc.com

"Brunch!" is the word on this "cool" Southern belle on U Street (there's also a newer Baltimore branch), where folks are "willing to wait" on weekends for "delicious every-which-way Benedicts" and hearty fare like chicken and waffles; the "tiny", industrial digs serve as a reliable "date" or "meeting spot" for dinner too, bolstered by solid service and everyday tabs.

Crisp & Juicy *Chicken/Peruvian*

24 | 10 | 17 | $13

Upper NW | 4533 Wisconsin Ave. (River Rd.) | 202-966-1222
Gaithersburg | 18312 Contour Rd. (Lost Knife Rd.), MD | 301-355-7377
Rockville | Sunshine Sq. | 1331 Rockville Pike (Templeton Pl.), MD | 301-251-8833
Silver Spring | 1314 E. West Hwy. (Colesville Rd.), MD | 301-563-6666
Silver Spring | Leisure World Plaza | 3800 International Dr. (Georgia Ave.), MD | 301-598-3333
Wheaton | Westfield Wheaton | 11160 Veirs Mill Rd. (University Blvd. W.), MD | 301-962-6666
Arlington | 4540 Fairfax Blvd. (Woodstock St.), VA | 703-243-4222
Falls Church | 913 W. Broad St. (bet. Spring & West Sts.), VA | 703-241-9091
www.crispjuicy.com

"Lip-smacking" rotisserie chicken "falls off the bone" at these Peruvian counter joints where fried yuca and other "tasty" sides "complete the feast" – still, their real "secret" is a dipping sauce so addictive some wonder if they "mix crack in"; bar cooking at home, it may be one of the "cheapest ways to feed a family", but "nonexistent" service and decor leave some squawking "takeout preferred."

	FOOD	DECOR	SERVICE	COST

NEW Crossroads *Eclectic*

| - | - | - | M |

World Bank | 1901 Pennsylvania Ave. NW (bet. 19th & 20th Sts.) | 202-331-2112 | www.crossroadswashingtondc.com

A 500-lb. Buddha statute greets visitors to a newly launched hybrid space located below street level near World Bank, which houses a branch of Heritage India as well as this globally accented concept known as Crossroads; internationally inspired small plates and cocktails are served in a cosmopolitan bar/lounge/bistro warmed by curry-toned walls and colorful native masks, while traditional subcontinental fare is served past the carved doorposts – though, if desired, food from both menus can be ordered wherever you sit.

Crystal Thai *Thai*

| 23 | 18 | 20 | $25 |

Arlington | Arlington Forest Shopping Ctr. | 4819 First St. N. (Columbus St.), VA | 703-522-1311 | www.crystalthai.com

"An early standout" on the Thai restaurant scene is this aging Arlingtonian, whose "loyal patrons" keep coming back to its "pleasant" Eastern-accented dining room, dressed up by "friendly" servers in traditional attire; classic dishes, like its "dream-come-true" crispy fish, and "reasonable" prices, especially at lunch, seal the deal.

Cuba de Ayer Ⓜ *Cuban*

| 25 | 17 | 23 | $24 |

Burtonsville | 15446 Old Columbia Pike (Spencerville Rd.), MD | 301-476-9622 | www.cubadeayerrestaurant.com

A real "asset to Burtonsville" is this "unassuming" Cuban "gem" where "authentic", "*muy rico*" benchmarks of its native cuisine come to the table at prices reflecting its "down-home sensibility"; despite "unremarkable" dinerlike decor, the "lively" salsa soundtrack and "gracious" staff "welcome" make a visit feel like a "vacation"; P.S. reservations recommended; plans to add a bar and more seating are in the works.

Cuba Libre Restaurant & Rum Bar *Cuban*

| 20 | 24 | 20 | $38 |

Penn Quarter | 801 Ninth St. NW (bet. H & I Sts.) | 202-408-1600 | www.cubalibrerestaurant.com

Leave Penn Quarter behind via this "over-the-top", "Disney"-esque nuevo Cubano where an "Old Havana" town "plaza" – complete with wrought-iron balconies, lush plants and street lamps – offers "plenty of room to rumba" when not partaking of the comparatively "toned-down" fare; still, the "reasonably priced" plates "come quickly", and "inspiring" rum drinks ("grilled pineapple" mojito, anyone?) complete the "transporting" affair.

Cubano's *Cuban*

| 23 | 19 | 21 | $32 |

Silver Spring | 1201 Fidler Ln. (Ramsey Ave.), MD | 301-563-4020 | www.cubanosrestaurant.com

No "government license to travel" is needed to partake of "authentic" ropa vieja or lechón asado at this "relaxed" Cuban joint "hidden away" in Silver Spring; its mojitos "will light up your experience" and, along with "friendly" servers, lend an "upbeat" vibe to the already "colorful" space, making the "pricey"-for-the-genre ticket price "worth it."

Curious Grape Wine, Dine & Shop *Eclectic* — | — | — | M

Shirlington | Shirlington Vill. | 2900 S. Quincy St. (bet. Campbell Ave. & Randolph St.) | Arlington, VA | 703-671-8700 | www.curiousgrape.com
The name says it all at Shirlington's all-in-one bastion of Bacchus: part wine shop and part spiffy wine bar/restaurant serving a full Eclectic dinner menu (with budget-friendly half-size options), as well as cheese and charcuterie, to pair with vino at a circular bar or at tables in the urbane dining room; as if that weren't enough, there's also an all-day cafe and specialty market.

Curry Mantra *Indian* ▽ 23 | 20 | 22 | $27

Fairfax | Main Street Ctr. | 9984 Main St. (bet. Fairfax Sq. & Tedrich Blvd.) | Fairfax City, VA | 703-218-8128 | www.dccurrymantra.com
NEW **Falls Church** | 1077 W. Broad St. (bet. Falls Ave. & West St.), VA | 703-992-0077 | www.currymantra2.com
Indian-food lovers praise this Fairfax standard bearer's "fresh and pungent and very authentic" regional specialties, featuring many vegetarian dishes, served with aplomb in a dining room that recently doubled in size, warmed by "memorable" curry-colored decor; its lunch buffet is a "great-value" way to try lots of "different foods" at once; P.S. there's a newer Falls Church branch.

Da Domenico 🗷 *Italian* 23 | 19 | 24 | $40

Tysons Corner | 1992 Chain Bridge Rd. (bet. International Dr. & Leesburg Pike) | McLean, VA | 703-790-9000 | www.dadomenicova.com
There's a "campy", "old-school feel" (nonna and nonno "would have loved this place in 1950") to this fancy, candlelit Tysons Corner "staple" where "roaming" singers occasionally break into "arias" as "attentive" servers deliver "tasty" Southern Italian fare; regulars insist it has the "world's best veal chop", while the opera-adverse note the live performances are Friday and Saturday nights only.

NEW **Daikaya Izakaya** *Japanese* — | — | — | I

Chinatown | 705 Sixth St. NW (bet. G & H Sts.) | 202-589-1600 | www.daikaya.com
This celebration of Japanese bar culture, installed above its Chinatown sibling, Daikaya Ramen, replicates a traditional izakaya's settle-in-and-stay-awhile vibe with its roomy bar and intimate wood booths framed by posters of Japanese bands and movies; an extensive selection of sake, shochu, whiskey, beer and cocktails is backed by inexpensive snack food (e.g. rice balls, sashimi, fermented vegetables), just as in Tokyo.

NEW **Daikaya Ramen** *Noodle Shop* — | — | — | I

Chinatown | 705 Sixth St. NW (bet. G & H Sts.) | 202-589-1600 | www.daikaya.com
Slurping is encouraged at this long-awaited Chinatown Japanese ramen bar from restaurateur Daisuke Utagawa (Sushiko) and chef Katsuya Fukushima (formerly on José Andrés' team) that has been drawing crowds since day one with its inexpensive, traditional noodles; the sleek setting uses textural elements like raw wood and

raked plaster walls to achieve a hip vibe; P.S. upstairs sister Daikaya Izakaya offers Tokyo-style drinking and noshing.

Dangerously Delicious Pies *American/Bakery*

`21` `13` `18` `$15`

Atlas District | 1339 H St. NE (bet. 14th St. & Linden Ct.) | 202-398-7437 ●
NEW **Chinatown** | 675 I St. NW (bet. 6th & 7th Sts.) | 202-450-1292 ⌧
NEW **Capitol Hill** | Union Station | 50 Massachusetts Ave. NE (First St.) | 202-289-1600 ⌧
www.dangerouspies.com

"Tempting treats" lure ardent calorie-counters to these "hip" but "tiny" separately owned bakeries in DC and Baltimore selling "scratch"-made "slices of heaven" in the form of sweet and savory pies; skeptics scoff it's best known for "being on the Food Network" (maybe that explains "premium" prices), but crust-cravers parry it "ain't pretty, but it sure is good"; P.S. DC denizens should keep an eye out for the food truck.

Daniel O'Connell's ● *Pub Food*

`20` `23` `20` `$29`

Old Town | 112 King St. (bet. Lee & Union Sts.) | Alexandria, VA | 703-739-1124 | www.danieloconnells.com

This "rambling" tavern (it's "like four pubs in one") may be the "classiest" spot in Old Town to savor "a good pint" while "sitting by the fireplace" thanks to "quaint" Emerald Isle decor with plenty o' "old-world style"; the "slightly upscale" pub grub may be "an afterthought", but it's perfectly "fine", moderately priced and served by an amenable staff.

DC Coast *American*

`23` `22` `23` `$52`

Downtown | 1401 K St. NW (14th St.) | 202-216-5988 | www.dccoast.com

"K Street types" gravitate to this "steady" seafood-strong New American spot on account of its "consistently performing" kitchen and "professional" staff that delivers a "value-oriented" "power lunch" in a "very DC" atmosphere; the art deco, former bank space is "stylish and architecturally distinct", so "sit upstairs and enjoy the view", though some prefer "hanging at the bar" downstairs with the "lobbyists."

DC-3 *Hot Dogs*

`18` `18` `19` `$12`

Capitol Hill | 423 Eighth St. SE (bet. D & E Sts.) | 202-546-1935 | www.eatdc3.com

Buckle up for a trip around the U.S. wiener scene via this airplane-themed "hot dog heaven" on Capitol Hill, where an "interesting" range of "regionally" themed franks – e.g. Philly (Whiz wit), California (veggie dog, avocado) – arrives "fast" at the gate; a "friendly" crew runs the counter-serve setup, and you fly at "non-DC prices (i.e. affordable)."

Dean & DeLuca *Eclectic*

`23` `16` `18` `$27`

Georgetown | 3276 M St. NW (Potomac St.) | 202-342-2500 | www.deandeluca.com

"Terrific" sandwiches and "tasty" Eclectic "snacks" from DC's outpost of the "fancy" NYC gourmet grocer come with people-watching perks at Georgetown's "foodie mecca"; decor is "n/a", but the shelves themselves offer a "feast for the eyes", so cruise the "mile-long display case" of prepared foods before heading to the outdoor cafe area – all in all, it's "a splurge that's worth it."

🆕 Decanter *Mediterranean*

- | - | - | VE

Downtown | St. Regis | 923 16th St. NW (K St.) | 202-509-8000 | www.stregiswashingtondc.com/decanter

Special occasions and power meals continue on in this historic room, just steps from the White House, after the St. Regis Hotel replaced Adour with a new fine-dining concept: high-end Mediterranean fare from longtime executive chef Sébastien Rondier; as with its previous incaruation, expect sophisticated service and an elegant backdrop (crystal everywhere) at breakfast, lunch and dinner.

Degrees *French*

▽ 22 | 19 | 24 | $47

Georgetown | Ritz-Carlton Georgetown | 3100 South St. NW (bet. 31st St. & Wisconsin Ave.) | 202-912-4100 | www.ritzcarlton.com

Paris in Georgetown describes this rebranded Ritz-Carlton venue that serves expensive Gallic fare from breakfast through the late evening; the contemporary space sports exposed brick and plush red curtains, and its inviting bar pours cocktails, craft beers and wine (*bien sûr*) to pair with internationally inspired bar bites.

🆕 Del Campo *Pan-Latin*

- | - | - | E

Penn Quarter | 777 I St. NW (8th St.) | 202-289-7377 | www.delcampodc.com

Chef-owner Victor Albisu mines his South American heritage at this new, upscale carne-y-vino-centric Penn Quarter gathering spot that features wood-grilled and smoked meats plus Pan-Latin specialties including Peruvian ceviche and house-baked Argentinian bread; its two bars pour Latin drinks, while the spacious, light-filled dining room features showstopping chandeliers and restrained earth tones.

Del Frisco's Grille ◗ *Steak*

- | - | - | VE

Penn Quarter | 1201 Pennsylvania Ave. NW (12th St.) | 202-450-4686 | www.delfriscosgrille.com

Power players, desk jockeys and tourists can tuck into the signature steaks and seafood, along with comfort classics and lighter fare, at this Penn Quarter steakhouse that's part of a national chainlet; bills can be high, in keeping with the handsome, modern setting that features a wall of wine at the entrance and a classy island bar with windows opening to a spacious, canopied terrace.

Delhi Club *Indian*

24 | 13 | 21 | $23

Clarendon | 1135 N. Highland St. (Clarendon Blvd.), VA | 703-527-5666 | www.delhiclub.com

"Look no further" than this "friendly" subcontinental "holding down the fort for Indian food in Clarendon" say locals who love its "authentic", "correctly prepared" cuisine; true, it's a tiny bastion with "just a few tables" near its big windows, but if decor is not an "issue", go for "consistently good food" at a "reasonable price."

	FOOD	DECOR	SERVICE	COST

Delhi Dhaba *Indian*
20 | 11 | 17 | $19

Courthouse | 2424 Wilson Blvd. (Barton St.) | Arlington, VA |
703-524-0008 | www.delhidhaba.com

This "down-market but downright tasty" Punjabi stands as "one
of the few remaining bits of old Arlington", and locals have long
counted on its "good, basic curries" and "mix-and-match platters"
at "almost giveaway prices"; the red and yellow no-frills setting and
"cafeteria-style" service suggest "takeout" may be "best", though
the patio is also a good bet.

NEW DGS Delicatessen *Jewish*
- | - | - | M

Dupont Circle | 1317 Connecticut Ave. NW (bet. Dupont Circle &
18th St.) | 202-293-4400 | www.dgsdelicatessen.com

Not your typical old-school deli, this midpriced Dupont Circle sit-
down restaurant updates Jewish classics like pastrami sandwiches,
smoked fish and matzo ball soup with contemporary touches; more-
over, its smart-looking, two-tier setting has stylish exposed brick
and an inviting bar that stirs up chocolate egg creams as well as craft
cocktails; P.S. at lunchtime, a limited menu of sandwiches and sides
is also available for takeout from a counter.

Dickson Wine Bar *Eclectic*
∇ 21 | 22 | 18 | $33

U Street Corridor | 903 U St. NW (9th St.) | 202-332-1779 |
www.dicksonwinebar.com

A "smart", "sexy" design makes this midpriced Eclectic wine bar on
U Street seem "more NYC than DC", with its "extensive" wine collection displayed on three open floors, and young folks catching
views of the action around them; "enjoyable" small plates (foodies
"recommend" the banh mi) are designed to match the vino and fancy
cocktails ferried by the "caring" staff.

The Diner ● *Diner*
21 | 16 | 20 | $20

Adams Morgan | 2453 18th St. NW (bet. Columbia & Kalorama Rds.) |
202-232-8800 | www.dinerdc.com

"When everywhere else is closed", this 24/7 Adams Morgan diner
just keeps on slinging its "consistently tasty", "reasonably priced"
grub served "with a smile" in deco-esque premises that are "a bit
classy" for the genre; still, it feels like home – whether you're digging
into an "early-morning" breakfast when "strollers take over", waiting in line for an "amazing brunch" or satisfying post-"wild-night-
on-the-town" "munchies."

Dino *Italian*
24 | 19 | 22 | $42

Cleveland Park | 3435 Connecticut Ave. NW (Ordway St.) |
202-686-2966 | www.dino-dc.com

Cleveland Park's "great little restaurant with the big heart" is a real
"keeper" for its "off-the-beaten-track Italian" fare, an "encyclo-
pedic yet reasonably priced wine list" and "best of all, Dino himself",
aka Dean Gold, the "charming" chef-owner; the contempo-Euro
furnishings are "comfortable", and the staff treats diners with "genuine warmth", so "take advantage" – "if this place were situated
Downtown", "prices would be double."

	FOOD	DECOR	SERVICE	COST

Dish + Drinks *American*

▽ 21 | 18 | 21 | $44

Foggy Bottom | The River Inn | 924 25th St. NW (bet. I & K Sts.) | 202-338-8707 | www.dishanddrinks.com

At this Foggy Bottom New American, dishes with "familiar foundations" are given fresh appeal with "interesting" flavor combinations in a "little" "modern" dining room that puts on the dog with large William Wegman prints; although it's near Kennedy Center and "suitable for pre-theater dining", an "obscure" address keeps it more a spot for neighborhood "regulars" and "hotel guests" who get "attentive" treatment.

District ChopHouse & Brewery *Steak*

21 | 20 | 20 | $39

Penn Quarter | 509 Seventh St. NW (bet. E & F Sts.) | 202-347-3434 | www.districtchophouse.com

A "wonderful cross between upscale steakhouse and comfortable sports bar", this Penn Quarter venue serves "good-value" chops along with "tasty" sides and a "nice selection" of its own "artisanal beers" in "casual, crowded and noisy" environs; though some say the fare "rarely knocks your socks off", it also "rarely disappoints", and "efficient" servers get guests to nearby Verizon Center events on time.

District Commons *American*

22 | 22 | 22 | $43

Foggy Bottom | 2200 Pennsylvania Ave. NW (22nd St.) | 202-587-8277 | www.districtcommonsdc.com

This "posh, sassy" Foggy Bottom spot (from the Passion Food group) updates the tavern concept with a "cool", "modern" look featuring huge windows, plus a "cheeky" menu that "reimagines" American comfort food; service "hits the mark", and though some find the tabs "pricey for what it is", the real issue is that when it gets "busy" it can really "put the 'din' in dinner."

District Kitchen ◗ *American*

▽ 24 | 20 | 26 | $48

Woodley Park | 2606 Connecticut Ave. NW (bet. Calvert & 24th Sts.) | 202-238-9408 | www.districtkitchen.com

Chef-owner Drew Trautmann's "clever use of interesting", locally sourced ingredients distinguishes the "outstanding" New American plates that emerge from his Woodley Park kitchen, to be served in a rustic dining room with brick walls and engaging artifacts; it's a bit expensive, but imbued with a warm "neighborhood feel" that "encourages folks to return."

District of Pi *Pizza*

23 | 20 | 20 | $22

Penn Quarter | 910 F St. NW (bet. 9th & 10th Sts.) | 202-681-3141 | www.pi-dc.com

"Carb up before a Caps game" with "fabulous" deep-dish Chicago pizza and St. Louis–style pies (featuring super-thin crust) at this chain outpost close to Verizon Center, where "delicious" gluten-free and vegan options make it a "game-changer when it comes to team outings"; its "deft" staffers sling the dough in a "huge", "fancier"-than-expected space full of reclaimed wood and exposed brick.

	FOOD	DECOR	SERVICE	COST

Dogfish Head Alehouse *Pub Food*   21 | 20 | 22 | $24

Gaithersburg | 800 W. Diamond Ave. (Bureau Dr.), MD | 301-963-4847
Fairfax | 13041 Lee Jackson Memorial Hwy. (bet. Majestic & Plaza Lns.), VA | 703-961-1140
Falls Church | Seven Corners Shopping Ctr. | 6363 Leesburg Pike (bet. Patrick Henry Dr. & Thorne Rd.), VA | 703-534-3342
www.dogfishalehouse.com

"Knock-you-on-your-backside" craft beers on a "seasonally changing" slate take "center stage" at these "popular" suburban showcases for the famed Delaware brewer; the "reasonably priced" bar food may be "secondary" but it's "solid" and staffers are "cheerfully attentive", so if some say the "simple" "pub-style" environs are "too loud, even for bars", most toast the "warm, inviting atmosphere."

Dolce Veloce   – | – | – | M
Cicchetti Wine Bar ⑤ *Italian*

Fairfax | 10826 Fairfax Blvd. (Fairchester Dr.), VA | 703-385-1226 | www.dolceveloce.com

At chef-owner Giuseppe 'Joe' Ricciardi's intimate osteria next to his Dolce Vita restaurant in Fairfax, Italian-style tapas (cicchetti) are paired with vino by the glass or bottle in a relaxed, informal setting wrapped with shelves of wine; pizza cones (filled wraps shaped for handheld eating) are among the many inexpensive small dishes that can serve as a snack or add up to a full meal.

Dolce Vita *Italian*   25 | 20 | 23 | $33

Fairfax | 10824 Fairfax Blvd. (Main St.), VA | 703-385-1530 | www.dolcevitafairfax.com

They're "eager to please" at this Fairfax trattoria whose "amazing" Italian fare, graced with "homemade touches", has *paesani* clamoring for seats in its "small" "old-world" room; it's "well priced" to boot, has a "nice wine list" and "you won't be rushed out the door"; P.S. its wine bar next door, Dolce Veloce Cicchetti, can ease waits.

Domku   ∇ 22 | 19 | 16 | $23
Bar & Café Ⓜ *E European/Scandinavian*

Petworth | 821 Upshur St. NW (bet. 8th & 9th Sts.) | 202-722-7475 | www.domkucafe.com

Where else in DC can one "order pickled herring without getting weird looks" than at this Petworth purveyor with a menu of "rib-sticking" Scandinavian and Eastern European fare that notably includes "varied vegetarian offerings", plus "refreshing" aquavits; "hipsters" say the "thrift-store" finds give it a "homey feel", but many sniff that "slow" service leaves them "colder than a night in Warsaw."

Don Pollo *Chicken/Peruvian*   23 | 12 | 19 | $18

Chevy Chase | 7007 Wisconsin Ave. (bet. Leland & Walsh Sts.), MD | 301-652-0001
Rockville | Twinbrooke Shopping Ctr. | 2206 Veirs Mill Rd. (Meadow Hall Dr.), MD | 301-309-1608

Feathered friends "looove" the "fabulous", "well-seasoned" Peruvian spit-roasted chicken served with "spicy, flavorful traditional sauces" and "excellent" sides at "rock-bottom" prices at this Maryland mini-chain; there is "no decor" to speak of, so some surveyors opt for "fast" takeout, but most don't mind the "casual" feel.

Double T Diner *Diner*

| 20 | 16 | 21 | $18 |

Frederick | 5617 Spectrum Dr. (bet. Holiday Dr. & Lowes Ln.), MD | 301-620-8797 | www.doubletdiner.com

See review in the Baltimore Directory.

Duangrat's *Thai*

| 26 | 20 | 22 | $30 |

Falls Church | 5878 Leesburg Pike (Glen Forest Dr.), VA | 703-820-5775 | www.duangrats.com

"Dishes not normally seen in standard Thai restaurants" can make ordering at this "white-linen-tablecloth" Falls Church venue "seem overwhelming"; but not to worry since its "attentive" staff in traditional dress can help diners choose a specialty from an "extensive" menu that offers "excellent quality and value"; P.S. there's a popular Thai-style dim sum menu on weekends.

Dukem ● *Ethiopian*

| 24 | 15 | 19 | $25 |

U Street Corridor | 1114-1118 U St. NW (12th St.) | 202-667-8735 | www.dukemrestaurant.com

"Look ma, no utensils!", just "perfect spongy, tangy injera bread" to scoop up "tasty" Ethiopian kitfo, tibs (the lamb's "amazing") and the like, including many veggie options, at these "traditional" outposts in DC and Baltimore; "ho-hum" decor afflicts both locales, but "attentive" service and "reasonable" tabs make them handsome choices for most; P.S. there's an "elaborate" coffee ceremony on Sunday at both branches, and live music in DC Wednesday–Sunday.

Dutch's Daughter *American*

| 25 | 24 | 25 | $41 |

Frederick | 581 Himes Ave. (Rte. 40), MD | 301-668-9500 | www.dutchsdaughter.com

This "class act" in Frederick is a "special-occasion" magnet thanks to a "beautiful" facility that feels like a "hunter's mansion", plus a "consistently excellent" upmarket American menu ("crab cakes reign supreme") and "impeccable" service; though some say it's a place your "grandmother" would love, it's also a hit with the prom squad and brunchers, as well as locals who gather downstairs in the comparatively "cool" bar.

Eamonn's *Irish*

| 23 | 16 | 18 | $18 |

Old Town | 728 King St. (Columbus St.) | Alexandria, VA | 703-299-8384

NEW **Arlington** | 2413 Columbia Pike (Barton St.), VA | 703-920-0315 www.eamonnsdublinchipper.com

"Grease stains on the brown paper bags" signify that "something good lies within" – namely "perfectly crisp, piping hot" fish and spuds – at this "easy"-on-the-wallet fish 'n' chips counter from Eve's Cathal Armstrong in Old Town (there's a newer branch with a large bar in Arlington); the publike space is often "crowded" with "nowhere to linger" at the few communal tables, so just "grab and go"; P.S. the "speakeasy"-style lounge upstairs, PX, mixes "unique" cocktails.

	FOOD	DECOR	SERVICE	COST

NEW East Dumpling House *Chinese* — | — | — | I

Rockville | 12 N. Washington St. (bet. Middle Ln. & Montgomery Ave.), MD | 301-762-6200

Buzzing at lunchtime, this inexpensive arrival near Rockville Town Square specializes in Northeast Chinese cuisine, including a broad range of dumplings and kebabs, and also offers housemade drinks like soy milk and milk tea; the small storefront has a casual modern feel with a few traditional decorative touches; P.S. remember to get your parking ticket validated.

East Pearl *Chinese* — | — | — | M

Rockville | 838 Rockville Pike (bet. Edmonston Dr. & Wootton Pkwy.), MD | 301-838-8663

This midpriced Rockville Chinese distinguishes itself from the fray with two separate kitchens that each handle a different side of the menu – the small kitchen up front preps noodle dishes, while the main one in back handles all the other Hong Kong–style fare; also setting it apart is the bright, contemporary space that displays upscale touches.

Eat First ● *Chinese* 22 | 8 | 20 | $21

Chinatown | 609 H St. NW (bet. 6th & 7th Sts.) | 202-289-1703

Check out "what Chinatown used to be" like at this subterranean "treasure" that "rewards" intrepid eaters with "incredible" Cantonese "specials marked on the mirrored walls", plus "extremely well-prepared" standards on "the American menu"; should the "joint" look "tired", focus on "hospitable and quick" service and "good food for the price."

Eatonville *Southern* 23 | 24 | 22 | $35

U Street Corridor | 2121 14th St. NW (V St.) | 202-332-9672 | www.eatonvillerestaurant.com

At this culinary tribute to Zora Neale Hurston, one of the "greats of the Harlem Renaissance", "down-home" touches like "drinks served in mason jars" and an "indoor porch with rocking chairs" set a twangy scene for "terrific" Southern cuisine "with a modern twist" just off U Street; everyday prices and "energetic, knowledgeable servers" complete the picture-perfect "Southern charm."

NEW Edgar *American* — | — | — | M

Golden Triangle | Mayflower Renaissance Hotel | 1127 Connecticut Ave. NW (bet. Desales & L Sts.) | 202-347-2233 | www.edgarbarandkitchen.com

In the legendary Mayflower Renaissance Hotel, in what was an old haunt of former FBI director J. Edgar Hoover (its namesake), this American brasserie features several dining areas decked out with polished wood and capacious booths; the moderately priced menu skews modern in its small plates, flatbreads and trendy entrees, and there's a strong after-work drinks scene at the bar.

Eggspectation *American* 21 | 20 | 21 | $22

Silver Spring | 923 Ellsworth Dr. (bet. Fenton St. & Georgia Ave.), MD | 301-585-1700

(continued)

Eggspectation

Chantilly | Westone Plaza | 5009 Westone Plaza Dr. (Stonecroft Blvd.), VA | 703-263-7444

Leesburg | Village at Leesburg | 1609 Village Market Blvd. SE (Tupper Way), VA | 703-777-4127

www.eggspectations.com

"Eggs any way you like them" star at these "upscale diners" that also offer a "quirky menu" of "to-swoon-for" pancakes, "freshly squeezed" juices and "anything you can imagine doing to a bagel", and even some lunch and dinner options; some say it's "expensive for breakfast food" and the "brightly lit" venues are "too loud", but most egg-heads leave feeling "well cared for" and "satiated."

8407 Kitchen Bar *American*   24 | 23 | 23 | $42

Silver Spring | 8407 Ramsey Ave. (bet. Bonifant St. & Wayne Ave.), MD | 301-587-8407 | www.8407kb.com

"Silver Spring has sprung" onto the food scene via this "innovative" New American "destination" ("shockingly hip" for the area) with an "industrial" dining room full of "exposed beams and rafters", and a similarly neo-rustic bar/lounge downstairs serving the likes of "creative" charcuterie and martinis with a "kick"; if some find it "a little pricey for a regular night", it's still a "go-to spot for dates", complete with a "welcoming" crew.

El Centro D.F. ◑ *Mexican*   21 | 20 | 20 | $32

Logan Circle | 1819 14th St. NW (bet. S & T Sts.) | 202-328-3131 | www.elcentrodf.com

A "super-sexy vibe" permeates Richard Sandoval's "always crowded" 14th Street Mexican triplex (near his Masa 14) serving moderately priced, "innovative" takes on Mexican "street eats" backed by a "beyond-amazing selection of tequila" poured by folks who "know about the stuff"; "trendy" types "get the night started" at the rooftop bar before descending to the "dungeonesque" basement tequileria that pulses like an "underground club in Mexico City."

El Chalan ⊠ *Peruvian*   22 | 14 | 19 | $33

Foggy Bottom | 1924 I St. NW (bet. 19th & 20th Sts.) | 202-293-2765 | www.elchalandc.com

"Step down and arrive in South America" at this Foggy Bottom Peruvian serving "zesty ceviche" and "ever-reliable lomo saltado" to "World Bank, IMF and embassy crowds"; the "small" subterranean digs, decorated simply with regional paintings, may "need the help they get from the bar's pisco sours", but the food is the reason why it's "still a favorite" after so many years.

El Chucho Cocina Superior ◑ *Mexican*   – | – | – | I

Columbia Heights | 3313 11th St. NW (Park Rd.) | 202-290-3313

Named for a legendary 19th-century bandit, this sun-washed Columbia Heights Mexican (from the Jackie's team in Silver Spring) slings inexpensive, upgraded takes on classic taqueria fare, plus margaritas on tap and 60-plus types of tequila; the downstairs bar boasts a colorful industrial-mod look, while the partially enclosed roof deck has picnic tables and vintage wrought-iron decorations.

Elephant Jumps *Thai* | 26 | 18 | 23 | $25 |

Falls Church | 8110 Arlington Blvd. (Gallows Rd.), VA | 703-942-6600 | www.elephantjumps.com

"Worth the trip from DC", this "bargain" Falls Church favorite offers "imaginative" Thai cuisine via a "creative" menu with "elements of fusion" – check out the 'East Meets West' section for items "unseen elsewhere" (e.g. drunken spaghetti chicken); with a "friendly" owner who will "offer a detailed tour" of the options, and the whimsical if bare-bones decor, regulars "can't recommend it enough."

Elevation Burger *Burgers* | 21 | 13 | 18 | $12 |

NEW **Frederick** | 7810 Wormans Mill Rd. (Liberty Rd.), MD | 301-644-3314

National Harbor | 108 Waterfront St. (National Harbor Blvd.), MD | 301-749-4014

Hyattsville | 5501 Baltimore Ave. (Jefferson St.), MD | 301-985-6869

Rockville | 12525 Park Potomac Ave. (bet. Cadbury Ave. & Fortune Terr.), MD | 301-838-4010

Wheaton | Westfield Wheaton Mall | 11160 Veirs Mill Rd. (University Blvd.), MD | 301-933-0333

Arlington | Lee Harrison Shopping Ctr. | 2447 N. Harrison St. (bet. Lee Hwy. & 26th St.), VA | 703-300-9467

NEW **Fairfax** | Fair Oaks Shopping Ctr. | 11943 Fair Oaks Mall (Fair Lakes Pkwy.), VA | 703-364-5154

NEW **Fairfax** | Turnpike Shopping Ctr. | 9518 Main St. (Pickett Rd.), VA | 703-426-2017

Falls Church | 442 S. Washington St. (Tinner Hill), VA | 703-237-4343

McLean | Tysons Corner Ctr. | 7827 Tysons Corner Ctr. (Chain Bridge Rd.), VA | 703-288-0020

www.elevationburger.com

Additional locations throughout the DC area

Burgers get the "organic" treatment at these bright, airy "natural-fast-food" counter-serves slinging "high-quality" grass-fed, free-range beef along with vegetarian options and "crispy" fries cooked in olive oil; some judge it "a little pricey" for its milieu, and the "friendly" service can seem "a bit slow", but remember, "they cook your food to order."

El Golfo *Pan-Latin*   ▽ | 23 | 15 | 24 | $23 |

Silver Spring | 8739 Flower Ave. (bet. Arliss St. & Piney Branch Rd.), MD | 301-608-2121 | www.elgolforestaurant.com

"Family-friendly" describes this "welcoming" Silver Springer with its "cheerful" crew ferrying "full" plates of "delicious" Pan-Latin fare to all ages; while it's "not big on decor" (a few South American textiles on yellow walls plus a small stage for live music) fans rely on this "trusty" performer for "excellent-value", "low-maintenance" meals.

Ella's Wood-Fired Pizza *Pizza* | 21 | 17 | 19 | $24 |

Penn Quarter | The Gallup | 610 9th St. (F St.) | 202-638-3434 | www.ellaspizza.com

"Tasty" wood-fired pizza with "crisp", "chewy" crust and "fantastic" craft beers come at a "bargain in a high-cost neighborhood", ensuring this Penn Quarter pie shop is always "busy"; the "casual" stone-wall-accented setting turns into a "madhouse" during events at nearby Verizon Center, but the "prompt", "efficient" crew keeps its cool.

El Manantial *Mediterranean* 24 | 23 | 24 | $41

Reston | Toll Oaks Village Ctr. | 12050 N. Shore Dr. (Wiehle Ave.), VA | 703-742-6466 | www.elmanantialrestaurant.com

"They will make any occasion a special one" at this "out-of-the-way" Reston "gem" whose "outstanding" seafood-centric Mediterranean menu sparkles like the storied inland sea pictured on the trompe l'oeil murals; best of all, it comes without the "hassle" of "more crowded Reston Town Center" venues, so very few quibble about the tab.

El Mariachi *S American/Tex-Mex* 25 | 18 | 24 | $23

Rockville | Ritchie Ctr. | 765 Rockville Pike (Wootton Pkwy.), MD | 301-738-7177 | www.elmariachirockville.com

"You can't go wrong" with this "popular neighborhood" Tex-Mex (and South American) cantina in Rockville say loyalists who laud its "tasty homemade salsa" and "authentically flavored" entrees served by an "outstanding" staff; the space is "plain but pleasant", with white tablecloths, and prices are "quite reasonable", so it "stays busy."

El Pollo Rico *Chicken/Peruvian* 26 | 10 | 19 | $12

NEW **Gaithersburg** | 211 N. Frederick Ave. (bet. Maryland & Walker Aves.), MD | 301-977-7760

Wheaton | 2517 University Blvd. (bet. Georgia & Grandview Aves.), MD | 301-942-4419

Arlington | 932 N. Kenmore St. (bet. Fairfax Dr. & Wilson Blvd.), VA | 703-522-3220

Woodbridge | 13470 Minnieville Rd. (Smoketown Rd.), VA | 703-590-3160 www.welovethischicken.com

The Peruvian chicken is so "finger-lickin' good" that folks are eating it "before they're done paying" at these "bare-bones" counter-serve roasters; indeed, everyone from "Anthony Bourdain" to "three-piece suits to day laborers" raves about the "delicious greasiness" that can be had for just a "few bucks", and since service is "quick", nobody clucks too much about occasional "lines out the door."

El Tamarindo ❶ *Mexican* 21 | 14 | 20 | $24

Adams Morgan | 1785 Florida Ave. NW (U St.) | 202-328-3660 | www.eltamarindodc.com

One can "satisfy a Mexican-food craving", a yen for "*auténtico*" Salvadoran specialties like "hot and melty" pupusas or a thirst for "knee-knocking margaritas" at this long-running, late-night Adams Morgan standby; "affordable" tabs, "easy seating" and a "nice" staff compensate for festive "hole-in-the-wall" decor that leaves something "to be desired" – and really, "after a night of drinking", who cares?

Eola 🅂Ⓜ *American* ▽ 25 | 18 | 20 | $85

Dupont Circle | 2020 P St. NW (Hopkins St.) | 202-466-4441 | www.eoladc.com

"Expect to spend the evening" dining "on the cutting-edge" at this "innovative" Dupont Circle New American, where a $75 five-course prix fixe menu (no à la carte) is served at a "leisurely pace" in a "quiet" townhouse "sparsely" decorated with exposed bricks and ochre walls; its "smart" wine list is parsed by "knowledgeable" servers, though the staff "isn't as polished" as "such an ambitious menu" would suggest.

Equinox *American*
25 | 22 | 24 | $68

Golden Triangle | 818 Connecticut Ave. NW (bet. H & I Sts.) | 202-331-8118 | www.equinoxrestaurant.com

The folks in the kitchen "can just plain cook", using "locally sourced" ingredients in "creative" ways in the "outstanding" New American dishes that grace the tables at chef/co-owner Todd Gray's "pricey" fine-dining spot steps from the White House; "polished" service is "worthy of that special night" out but "also establishment enough for business lunches", when one spots famous faces in the "sleek", contemporary rooms.

Estadio *Spanish*
25 | 23 | 21 | $44

Logan Circle | 1520 14th St. NW (Church St.) | 202-319-1404 | www.estadio-dc.com

"Bustling with energy", this "spirited" Logan Circle Spanish tapas destination is "big on creative flavors", with an "ever-changing" menu of "earthy", "sometimes daring" delights (take care: the bill "can add up"); however, it's "small on space", so come early to avoid "painful waits" for a table in the "playful" "Moorish-meets-Almodóvar" space – or if you must wait, the "knowledgeable" bartenders can mix you a "fancy drink", like the "famous slushito."

Etete ● *Ethiopian*
24 | 14 | 18 | $26

U Street Corridor | 1942 Ninth St. NW (U St.) | 202-232-7600 | www.eteterestaurant.com

This "sparse" but "modern" nook in DC's 'Little Ethiopia' (in the U Street Corridor) is like being in "Addis Ababa", where diners scoop up "spicy" and "filling" stews with spongy injera bread; service is "friendly if not super-quick", but for those looking for "something different" (e.g. eating with your hands), it's a "great alternative" in "a sea of sameness", and cheap too.

Ethiopic ⓜ *Ethiopian*
24 | 21 | 21 | $31

Atlas District | 401 H St. NE (4th St.) | 202-675-2066 | www.ethiopicrestaurant.com

Ethiopian food is staged for "cosmopolitans" at this "upscale" West African in the burgeoning Atlas District, where basketweave tables and homeland art provide a "lovely" backdrop for "very flavorful" cuisine, served "graciously"; while it lacks the "raw feel of similar joints on Ninth Street", this slightly "pricier" version is "very popular", ergo reservations are "a must."

NEW Etto ⓜ *Italian/Pizza*
- | - | - | M

Logan Circle | 1541 14th St. NW (Q St.) | 202-232-0920 | www.ettodc.com

Defining artisanal, this buzzing Italian newcomer near Logan Circle pours wine from chef-owner Peter Pastan's winery and grinds its own flour for its country breads and wood-fired pizza (check out the wooden hand-operated mill); beyond that, the sunny space has a chalkboard listing salumi and other specials as well as some small plates similar to those offered at sibling 2 Amys.

Et Voila *Belgian/French*

| 25 | 17 | 21 | $45 |

Palisades | 5120 MacArthur Blvd. NW (bet. Arizona Ave. & Dana Pl.) | 202-237-2300 | www.etvoiladc.com

"Cramped but delicious" describes this "charming European-style bistro tucked away" in the Palisades, where "hearty" French-Belgian fare "elevated with just enough elegance and finesse" is delivered by waiters from "central casting", who adroitly navigate the "runway" of its long, narrow room; "outstanding moules frites" matched with "very good" wine and "even better" Belgian beer – it's all "well worth the price."

Evening Star Cafe *Southern*

| 23 | 20 | 21 | $38 |

Del Ray | 2000 Mt. Vernon Ave. (Howell Ave.) | Alexandria, VA | 703-549-5051 | www.eveningstarcafe.net

Del Rey's "upscale Southern" lodestar and its chef, Jim Jeffords, puts "updated twists" on Dixie favorites in a diner-esque dining room sporting "clever fixtures" and artwork repurposed from vintage finds (there's also a back bar and upstairs lounge with live music); further points of light include solid service, "reasonable" tabs and "amazing" wines from its next-door shop, Planet Wine.

Eventide ●Ⓜ *American*

| 23 | 26 | 23 | $45 |

Clarendon | 3165 Wilson Blvd. (Hudson St.), VA | 703-276-3165 | www.eventiderestaurant.com

"Guests dressed to the nines" live up to the "soaring", "sumptuous" surroundings ("love those velvet curtains"), lingering over "well-executed" New American dishes and "indulgent" treatment at Clarendon's "date-night destination"; "inventive" cocktails (and tamer tariffs for food) can be had at the "sophisticated" yet casual street-level bar or "divine" rooftop patio.

Evo Bistro *Mediterranean*

| 22 | 18 | 20 | $44 |

McLean | Salona Shopping Ctr. | 1313 Old Chain Bridge Rd. (Dolley Madison Blvd.), VA | 703-288-4422 | www.evobistro.com

"Meet friends and share small plates" at McLean's restaurant for "wine lovers" that offers a "well-done" variety of Mediterranean bites and entrees to pair with "terrific" vino from self-serve vending machines (the bartenders are "helpful" too) in a "low-key", earth-toned space flooded with "natural light"; just be wary since "it's easy to rack up quite a bill", or stick to the $5 pours and plates during happy hour.

Ezmè *Turkish*

| 22 | 21 | 24 | $34 |

Dupont Circle | 2016 P St. NW (Hopkins St.) | 202-223-4304 | www.ezmedc.com

Fans say this Dupont Circle spot "competes with Istanbul" when it comes to Turkish meze, offering "authentic" dishes served on "the prettiest plates" paired with flights of vino; "responsive" servers tend to the "relaxing", loungelike room that's lined with wine racks, a solid venue for a "romantic" date that won't empty the wallet.

Faccia Luna Trattoria *Pizza* | 23 | 17 | 21 | $24 |

Old Town | 823 S. Washington St. (bet. Green & Jefferson Sts.) | Alexandria, VA | 703-838-5998

Clarendon | 2909 Wilson Blvd. (bet. Fillmore & Garfield Sts.), VA | 703-276-3099

www.faccialuna.com

"Craveable" "gourmet pizzas" and pastas at "reasonable" prices, including "awesome lunch deals", make these Clarendon and Old Town trattorias "longtime favorites" of local folks, some of whom have "been there a couple hundred times"; "helpful" staffers and "casual", "comfortable" settings with booth seating make them especially "friendly to families."

Family Meal *American/Diner* | - | - | - | M |

Frederick | 880 N. East St. (8th St.), MD | 301-378-2895 | www.voltfamilymeal.com

Bryan Voltaggio's (Volt) modern American diner offers easy-on-the-wallet all-day meals in a former Frederick car dealership transformed by clever design and raw, natural materials into an open, airy space, with a long counter fronting an open kitchen; its menu elevates the comfort-food canon, while adult beverages include boozy milkshakes as well as wine, beer and cocktails.

NEW Farmers Fishers Bakers *American* | - | - | - | M |

Georgetown | Washington Harbour | 3000 K St. NW (30th St.) | 202-298-8783 | www.farmersfishersbakers.com

Relaunched with a new name, this Washington Harbour American (formerly Farmers & Fishers) serves a diverse menu ranging from flatbreads to grilled meats to sushi made with local seafood along with treats from an open bakery and pastry studio; reclaimed materials abound throughout the LEED-certified space that's a mix of whimsical and chic (think farmyard meets marina), plus there's a patio overlooking the Potomac and the ice rink in winter.

Farrah Olivia   *American* | ▽ 23 | 15 | 20 | $65 |

Crystal City | Crystal City Shops | 2250 Crystal Dr. (23rd St.) | Arlington, VA | 703-445-6571 | www.farraholiviarestaurant.com

One "must do a little searching" for this "restaurant within a restaurant" hidden in the small purple-hued back room of Kora in Crystal City, but seekers are rewarded by "clever", "inventive" New American repasts; prices are high, and a few say it "doesn't always work", but when it does, it's "amazing"; P.S. open Wednesday–Saturday for dinner only.

Faryab Ⓜ *Afghan* | 24 | 16 | 22 | $33 |

Bethesda | 4917 Cordell Ave. (bet. Norfolk Ave. & Old Georgetown Rd.), MD | 301-951-3484

Diners are invariably "impressed" by this "moderate" Bethesda Afghan serving "excellent" Mideastern fare, including "delicious" kebabs, "savory" aushak and "distractingly good" pumpkin dishes; service is "prompt", and the "simple" environs hung with native tapestries are "pleasant", so bring guests and "harvest the compliments."

	FOOD	DECOR	SERVICE	COST

Fast Gourmet *Pan-Latin* ▽ 27 | 10 | 18 | $13

U Street Corridor | 1400 W St. NW (14th St.) | 202-448-9217 |
www.fast-gourmet.com

"Fill up both tanks" at this U Street Corridor "gourmet gas station"
(seriously, the pumps work) where a "friendly" counter crew slaps
together Latin sandwiches that are "meaty masterpieces", like the
"monumental" Uruguayan *chivito* stuffed with various meats, mozzarella, egg and olives; the decor is upscale Mobil Mart (a few tables
and chairs next to a rack of Slim Jims), but "don't let it put you off" –
it's cheap, and open way-late on weekends.

NEW Fat Shorty's *Belgian* - | - | - | I

Clarendon | 3035 Clarendon Blvd. (Garfield St.), VA | 703-243-5660 |
www.fatshortys.com

Steins of Belgian and German brews wash down mussels and sausages
(in many varieties including traditional brats plus alligator, rattle-
snake, andouille and veggie links) at this affordable new Clarendon
counter-serve; a modern, miniaturized take on the beer hall, the interior is outfitted with communal picnic tables, string lights and vintage sausage grinders, and there's a small patio to boot.

15 Ria *American* 22 | 20 | 21 | $39

Scott Circle | DoubleTree by Hilton Hotel Washington DC |
1515 Rhode Island Ave. NW (15th St.) | 202-742-0015 |
www.15ria.com

"Cozy" club chairs and "attractive place settings" contribute to an
"inviting", "upscale" ambiance that belies this New American spot's
setting "off the lobby of a chain hotel" – a DoubleTree near Scott Circle;
chef changes put the Food rating in question, but the "good values"
and "well-trained staff" remain, making it "great for a date" or a
"post-work happy hour, especially if you can nab a patio seat."

Filomena Ristorante *Italian* 24 | 21 | 23 | $44

Georgetown | 1063 Wisconsin Ave. NW (M St.) | 202-338-8800 |
www.filomena.com

With "pasta mamas" making noodles in the front window, one might
think this "bustling" Georgetown trattoria would be like "your Italian
grandmother's kitchen" – but it's "cavernous" inside, and even nonna
never had so much "kitsch" or "gaudy" ("yet somehow fabulous")
holiday decor; still, the "thoughtful" staff makes it feel like "home" to
legions of locals, "tourists" and "celebrities" who've stuffed themselves for years on the "rich", "massive" red-sauce plates; P.S. the
weekend buffet is a way around "high prices."

Finemondo Ⓩ *Italian* 20 | 19 | 20 | $44

Downtown | 1319 F St. NW (bet. 13th & 14th Sts.) | 202-737-3100 |
www.finemondo.com

"Simple" "Italian country meals" are served under a vaulted ceiling
in the "romantic", "relaxed" old-word dining room of this expensive
Downtown spot; while thespians count it as a "nice pre-theater option", citing "efficient" service, tipplers get comfortable in "overstuffed
chairs" amid the warm, woody surroundings of its "humming" bar.

Fiola 🅂 *Italian*

27 | 25 | 26 | $68

Penn Quarter | 601 Pennsylvania Ave. NW (entrance on Indiana Ave. bet. 6th & 7th Sts.) | 202-628-2888 | www.fioladc.com

"Wow", Fabio Trabocchi's "sensational" Penn Quarter venue offers the "complete package" – "his elegant magic touch" with contemporary Italian cuisine, a "fabulous" (and "unstuffy") villalike ambiance plus "extremely engaging" help; aim for a table in the rear to "ogle" the objets d'art and the "lively crowd", and though it's not cheap, tabs are an "unbelievable" value given the "truly wonderful dining experience."

Firefly *American*

23 | 23 | 21 | $42

Dupont Circle | 1310 New Hampshire Ave. NW (N St.) | 202-861-1310 | www.firefly-dc.com

At this Dupont Circle "hideaway", chef Daniel Bortnick's New American "funked-up comfort food" is displayed in an "engaging" setting that's both "romantic" and "kid-friendly" as it's built around an "enormous indoor tree" (a recent renovation added a tree swing, cottagelike details and more bar seats, possibly outdating the Decor rating); the staff is "great", and if the bill is big, at least it's cute – it "comes in a mason jar" flickering with light.

Firestone's 🅼 *American*

26 | 24 | 25 | $34

Frederick | 105 N. Market St. (Church St.), MD | 301-663-0330 | www.firestonesrestaurant.com

There's a "fantastic, lively energy" humming at this Downtown Frederick brick-and-wood tavern where the "phenomenal" New American fare may come as a "happy shock" given the "casual" environment and moderate prices; the mezzanine is quieter and affords stellar "people-watching" of the "active" bar scene below, but up or down, the service is "exceptional"; P.S. its adjacent shop offers prepared foods and gourmet gadgetry.

Fire Works Pizza *Pizza*

24 | 20 | 21 | $23

Courthouse | 2350 Clarendon Blvd. (Adams St.) | Arlington, VA | 703-527-8700 ◑

Leesburg | 201 Harrison St. SE (bet. Loudoun & South Sts.), VA | 703-779-8400

www.fireworkspizza.com

"Rock-star" pizza sporting "flavorful" crusts and "locally sourced ingredients" whets the appetite for the "fantastic" beers at this "casual" Courthouse and Leesburg "wood-fired" duo with "reasonable" checks and "snappy" service; inside they're "industrial" and "noisy", while outside large patios provide "primo" seating in nice weather.

First Watch *American*

21 | 16 | 22 | $14

Rockville | 100 Gibbs St. (Middle Ln.), MD | 301-762-0621

Fairfax | 9600 Main St. (Pickett Rd.), VA | 703-978-3421

NEW Chantilly | 13027 Lee Jackson Memorial Hwy. (Majestic Ln.), VA | 703-263-2344

www.firstwatch.com

As a "consistently good" breakfast-and-lunch option (no dinner), this chain cafe pleases with its "varied" menu (you can be "healthy" or "bad") and "can't-beat" prices; the brand's "bright, happy colors" go well with the "friendly" service, leading the families and business folks who frequent it to lament "too bad" the hours are "so short."

Fishnet ☒ *Seafood*　∇ 24 | 16 | 20 | $17

College Park | 5010 Berwyn Rd. (College Park Trolley Trail), MD | 301-220-1070 | www.eatfishnet.com

Inspired by the grilled fish sandwiches sold as street food in his native Istanbul, Ferhat Yalcin replicates them at this "bare-bones" College Park counter-serve; the "carefully prepared" catch, topped with a "special Turkish sauce" and accompanied by fries you "can't pass up", makes for "a blessed relief from fast-food chains."

Five Guys *Burgers*　24 | 14 | 21 | $12

Chinatown | 808 H St. NW (bet. 8th & 9th Sts.) | 202-393-2900
Georgetown | 1335 Wisconsin Ave. NW (Dumbarton St.) | 202-337-0400
Bethesda | 4829 Bethesda Ave. (Arlington Rd.), MD | 301-657-0007
Frederick | 1700 Kingfisher Dr. (Monocacy Blvd.), MD | 301-668-1500
Greater Alexandria | 4626 King St. (bet. Beauregard & 28th Sts.) | Alexandria, VA | 703-671-1606
Greater Alexandria | 7622 Richmond Hwy. (Outlet Rd.) | Alexandria, VA | 703-717-0090
Old Town | 107 N. Fayette St. (bet. Cameron & King Sts.) | Alexandria, VA | 703-549-7991
Herndon | Fox Mill Ctr. | 2521 John Milton Dr. (Fox Mill Rd.), VA | 703-860-9100
Springfield | 6541 Backlick Rd. (Springfield Blvd.), VA | 703-913-1337
Manassas | Manassas Corner | 9221 Sudley Rd. (Centerville Rd.), VA | 703-368-8080
www.fiveguys.com
Additional locations throughout the DC area

"Hot, juicy and smothered in whatever your heart desires", this is "the way a burger should be" say fans of these ubiquitous counters, rated the DC area's Most Popular chain; while the "sparse" white-and-red-tiled settings earn few raves, "who cares" when "the prices are right" and there are free peanuts to shell while you wait – which won't be long since the "hard-working" crews fill orders "fast."

Fleming's Prime Steakhouse & Wine Bar *Steak*　25 | 24 | 25 | $61

Tysons Corner | 1960 Chain Bridge Rd. (International Dr.) | McLean, VA | 703-442-8384 | www.flemingssteakhouse.com

"Quality" cuts of "properly prepared" steak bring beef-eaters to the Tysons Corner and Harbor East links of this "expense-account" chophouse chain; adding to the "excellent" experience are the "top-notch" servers who ably tend the "crowded" dining rooms and "busy" bar with "dark and woody", "men's club" decor.

Floriana Restaurant *Italian*　24 | 22 | 23 | $40

Dupont Circle | 1602 17th St. NW (Q St.) | 202-667-5937 | www.florianarestaurant.com

In the diadem of "reasonably priced Italians", this Dupont townhouse "gem" shines, with a "brilliant" staff dishing up "lasagna just as good as it was 30 years ago" (at a prior location) along with more recent innovations; its "intimate" "Victorian" charm works for a "celebration meal" or for casual drinks with friends on "half-price wine nights."

Florida Ave. Grill Ⓜ *Diner*　　　22 | 12 | 20 | $17

Shaw | 1100 Florida Ave. NW (11th St.) | 202-265-1586 | www.floridaavenuegrill.com

A "true DC vibe" flavors the "down-home" soul food "cooked with experience and served up hot" and "greasy" at this old-time Shaw diner lined with "pictures of famous diners" and not much else; the staff is "friendly", and its customers get "plenty of food for the price", especially if they come Tuesday–Friday for the early-bird deal.

Fogo de Chão *Brazilian/Steak*　　27 | 24 | 27 | $61

Penn Quarter | 1101 Pennsylvania Ave. NW (11th St.) | 202-347-4668 | www.fogodechao.com

"It's all about the meat" at this "well-appointed" Brazilian steak-house chain (with outposts in DC's Penn Quarter and Baltimore's Inner Harbor), "a carnivore's version of paradise" thanks to "gaucho"-attired servers who "cruise the floor" doling out "familiar" and "un-usual" cuts of skewered beef, pork and poultry "until you beg them to stop"; it may be "spendy", but with the "all-you-can-eat" policy, guests leave "stuffed"; P.S. there's a "well-stocked salad bar" too.

Fontaine Caffe & Creperie *French*　　▽ 25 | 20 | 22 | $31

Old Town | 119 S. Royal St. (bet. King & Prince Sts.) | Alexandria, VA | 703-535-8151 | www.fontainecaffe.com

This "adorably cute" French cafe "in the heart of" Old Town's historic district fills affordable sweet and savory crêpes "for every taste" and pairs them with "surprisingly good wines" and European ciders; its blue-walled dining room or a table outside makes a "darling" rendez-vous for a "fantastic brunch", "spur-of-the-moment" nosh or "not-too-formal date"; P.S. the buckwheat crêpes are naturally gluten-free.

Fontina Grille *Italian*　　　　20 | 18 | 18 | $28

Rockville | King Farm Village Ctr. | 801 Pleasant Dr. (Redland Blvd.), MD | 301-947-5400 | www.fontinagrille.com

"There's always a crowd" at this "reliable" Rockville ristorante where the "tasty" Italian entrees and brick-oven pizza earn fans; "reasonable" tabs, a "smiling" staff and "cozy", wood-trimmed digs make it a "decent neighborhood joint to take the family."

Food Corner Kabob House *Afghan*　　25 | 15 | 21 | $16

Dupont Circle | 2029 P St. NW (21st St.) | 202-331-3777
Annandale | 7031 Little River Tpke. (bet. Carrico & John Marr Drs.), VA | 703-750-2185
Springfield | 7031 Brookfield Plaza (Backlick Rd.), VA | 703-866-7834
Tysons Corner | 8315 Leesburg Pike (bet. Chain Bridge & Gosnell Rd.) | Vienna, VA | 703-893-2333
Centreville | 14220 Centreville Sq. (Lee Hwy.), VA | 703-543-7166
www.foodcornerkabob.com

For "a lot of healthy food for very little money", frugal foodies rec-ommend these Afghan "grab"-and-eat joints serving "superb" kebab platters, "freshly baked" breads and "melt-in-your-mouth" meats; "average" decor is overlooked thanks to "flexible", "friendly" counter staffers who can "make combinations upon request."

Food Wine & Co. *American* 22 20 20 $40

Bethesda | 7272 Wisconsin Ave. (bet. Bethesda Ave. & Elm St.), MD | 301-652-8008 | www.foodwineandco.com

A "versatile venue", this midpriced Bethesda New American appeals to "all generations" as a place to "grab a drink" with friends in the dark-wood bar or partake of a "nice sit-down dinner" of artisanal, farm-to-table fare in its high-ceilinged, tall-windowed dining area; service is "relaxed" but "professional", and "wine prices are sane", so locals say it's a "perfect way to end a long day at the office."

Ford's Fish Shack *New England/Seafood* 26 21 23 $30

NEW **Chantilly** | South Riding Market Sq. | 25031 Riding Plaza (Loudoun County Pkwy.), VA | 703-542-7520
Ashburn | Ice Rink Plaza | 44260 Ice Rink Plaza (Farmwell Rd.), VA | 571-918-4092
www.fordsfishshack.com

Folks feel like they're in Maine when chowing down on the "authentic" specialties (lobster rolls, whoopie pies) at this casual, maritime-themed fishouse in Ashburn's Ice Rink Plaza (with a newer Chantilly location); it's "always busy", but the staff makes everyone "feel special" and doesn't charge much for the pleasure.

Fortune *Chinese* 22 14 18 $22

Falls Church | Seven Corners Ctr. | 6249 Arlington Blvd. (Thorne Rd.), VA | 703-538-3333

Dim sum devotees praise the "amazing" offerings at this massive Seven Corners banquet hall; of course, it's "always chaotic" and "rushed", and "the only ambiance is provided by the clientele (so many people)", but folks who "come hungry leave sated – with leftovers!"; P.S. there's also a Cantonese seafood menu at dinner.

Foti's ⓜ *American* 27 23 25 $52

Culpeper | 219 E. Davis St. (East St.), VA | 540-829-8400 | www.fotisrestaurant.com

It's "worth the drive" to Frank and Sue Maragos' "charming" Downtown Culpeper foodie "haven", where the former Inn at Little Washington talents serve "sophisticated", "imaginative" New American fare that "holds its own when compared with more expensive places", especially now that it has lowered prices on the regular menu, possibly outdating the Cost rating (it has more spendy tasting menus for high rollers); what's more, you "never feel rushed" by the "earnest" staff while savoring "perfect wine pairings" in the glowing, brick-and-dark-wood storefront; P.S. closed Monday and Tuesday.

Founding Farmers *American* 24 22 20 $35

World Bank | IMF Bldg. | 1924 Pennsylvania Ave. NW (20th St.) | 202-822-8783

(continued)

(continued)

Founding Farmers

Potomac | Fortune Terrace Shopping Ctr. | 12505 Park Potomac Ave. (Fortune Terr.), MD | 301-340-8783
www.wearefoundingfarmers.com

These "buzzing", cooperative-grower-owned all-Americans have planted their "farm-to-table"–themed comfort cuisine in "rustic-chic" digs in DC's IMF Building and Potomac, MD, where "homey" vittles like "awesome cornbread" and "bacon lollies" are ferried by "youthful" farmhands, while "artisanal" drinks are swilled at the "packed bars"; service is "solid but nothing stellar", and though many complain about the "unbearable" noise, most are "impressed with how affordable" it is.

Four Sisters *Vietnamese*
25 | 20 | 21 | $28

Merrifield | Merrifield Town Ctr. | 8190 Strawberry Ln. (bet. Gallows Rd. & Lee Hwy.), VA | 703-539-8566 | www.foursistersrestaurant.com

A "huge selection" of "authentic", "consistently excellent" dishes brings diners to this "bargain-priced" Vietnamese spot, a "subdued" space decorated with "beautiful flower displays" in Merrifield Town Center; "gracious", "helpful" servers further explain why this "family-friendly" place is a "popular" pick.

Franklin's *Pub Food*
21 | 22 | 23 | $24

Hyattsville | 5123 Baltimore Ave. (Gallatin St.), MD | 301-927-2740 | www.franklinsbrewery.com

For "affordable" "good old American standards" like burgers and ribs and "distinctive" "proprietary brews", Hyattsville residents visit this "airy", industrial bi-level brew pub with an adjacent general store selling "quirky" and "nostalgic" gifts; "pleasant" staffers lend to the "casual", "irreverent" vibe, though a few shout it can be "so loud it's hard to talk."

Freddy's Lobster & Clams ☒ *Seafood*
19 | 14 | 18 | $26

Bethesda | 4867 Cordell Ave. (Norfolk Ave.), MD | 240-743-4257 | www.freddyslobster.com

It feels "very summer-at-the shore" at this "casual" Bethesda seafood shack where New England specialties like fried whole-belly clams, peel-and-eat shrimp and "fab" lobster rolls are eaten at "wood picnic tables", with vintage boating gear adding to the "nostalgic" vibe; still, critics carp that it's "a bit underwhelming for the price", though the service is "fast" and "friendly", and the beer list is "phenomenal."

🆕 Fuego Cocina y Tequileria *Mexican*
– | – | – | M

Clarendon | 2800 Clarendon Blvd. (Fillmore St.), VA | 571-970-2180 | www.fuegova.com

The Passion Food team (Ceiba, PassionFish) expanded its reach into trendy Clarendon with this modern Mexican kitchen and tequila specialist that takes an artisanal, made-from-scratch approach to its food; the colorful, high-gloss setting sprawls over two floors, with an upstairs dining room outfitted with booths and a giant fireplace, while downstairs, a TV-lined bar and lounge tempts drinkers with over 100 tequilas.

Fuel Pizza Cafe *American/Pizza*
| - | - | - | I |

Penn Quarter | 600 F St. NW (bet. 6th & 7th Sts.) | 202-547-3835
Downtown | 1606 K St. NW (bet. 16th & 17th Sts.) | 202-659-3835
www.fuelpizza.com

NY-style pizza pulls up at these gas station–themed refueling spots where pies and slices with every conceivable topping are doled out at the counter, and spicy wings (plus subs at K Street) fly out the door too; cheap tabs, delivery service and late weekend hours are powerful attractions for the young and hungry, while grease monkeys get revved scoping out the automotive memorabilia.

Fujimar ●🕾 *Asian/Pan-Latin*
| - | - | - | E |

Downtown | 1401 K St. NW (14th St.) | 202-789-2800 |
www.fujimarrestaurant.com

At this dazzling second-floor Downtown venue, high-end sushi, ceviche and other seafood dishes – all given Asian-Latin twists – glisten against an ultramod backdrop comprising two loungey dining areas, several bars and a futuristic sushi counter; diners dressed to kill knock back fancy cocktails and terroir-driven wines at commensurate prices.

Full Kee Restaurant ● *Chinese*
| 23 | 8 | 16 | $20 |

Chinatown | 509 H St. NW (bet. 5th & 6th Sts.) | 202-371-2233 |
www.fullkeedc.com

"Dead ducks" in the window and a "Formica-filled" interior ID this Chinese eatery as a "hard-core, real-deal" Chinatown spot where the "amazingly long menu" (much of it posted on the wall) ranges from Hong Kong's "traditional soups" to "rare and interesting delicacies" that come at "rock-bottom" prices; the "ornery" service just "makes the experience more genuine"; P.S. the same-named Falls Church operation is separately owned.

Full Kee Restaurant ● *Chinese*
| 22 | 13 | 16 | $21 |

Falls Church | 5830 Columbia Pike (Leesburg Pike), VA | 703-575-8232
The kee to this "no-frills" (but late-night) Falls Church Chinese is to "go with a group" so you can order lots of bargain-priced, "not-Americanized" Cantonese food to share (don't miss the "heavenly" shrimp dumplings or "must-have" oyster casserole); while its "menu looks similar" to some other local Chinese eateries, fans swear that the "taste is a cut above."

Full Key ● *Chinese*
| 25 | 12 | 19 | $20 |

Wheaton | Wheaton Manor Shopping Ctr. | 2227 University Blvd. W. (bet. Amherst & Georgia Aves.), MD | 301-933-8388
"Authentic Hong Kong–style" specialties, like "outstanding noodle soups" and "rich roast meats", are the keys to ordering at this "unassuming" Wheaton Chinese where there's "not much decor" but there is "great congee" (it also serves "American-Chinese" standards); the staff is "nice", and it's "one of the cheapest places in town", which means it's often full.

	FOOD	DECOR	SERVICE	COST

Fu Shing Cafe *Chinese*   22 | 14 | 20 | $19

Bethesda | 10315 Westlake Dr. (Lakeview Dr.), MD | 301-469-8878 | www.fushingcafebethesda.com

An "oldie but goodie", this strip-mall "hole-in-the-wall" in Bethesda is the "neighborhood Chinese go-to" spot for a "cheap", "flavorful" fill-up; service is "fast" and "friendly", and if the "tight quarters" are "no place to 'dine'" (you "order at the counter", and food's "brought to the table"), there's always "carryout and delivery."

Fyve *American*   ▽ 24 | 22 | 23 | $54

Pentagon City | The Ritz-Carlton Pentagon City | 1250 S. Hayes St. (bet. Army Navy Dr. & 15th St.) | Arlington, VA | 703-412-2762 | www.ritzcarlton.com

"Super service", always expected from the Ritz-Carlton brand, highlights this Pentagon City resto-lounge where "delicious" albeit "pricey" American bistro fare and "martinis served in your own personal shaker" are found in "quiet", elegant surroundings that work well for "sitting by the fireplace with friends"; bonus: formal tea is served on weekends.

Gadsby's Tavern *American*   21 | 25 | 21 | $34

Old Town | 138 N. Royal St. (Cameron St.) | Alexandria, VA | 703-548-1288 | www.gadsbystavernrestaurant.com

"A true Revolutionary experience" awaits at this "historical" Alexandria tavern space that once hosted our first president, and where "Colonial characters" now provide "excellent entertainment" while you sup on midpriced Traditional American fare that's "nicely done"; while some say it's "not for those looking for a culinary experience", the historically minded argue you do have the opportunity to try George Washington's "favorite duck recipe" – and hey, "maybe James Madison" will talk to you!

NEW GBD ● *Bakery/Chicken*   - | - | - | I

Dupont Circle | 1323 Connecticut Ave. NW (bet. Dupont Circle & N St.) | 202-524-5210 | www.gbdchickendoughnuts.com

Donuts and fried chicken (the name is short for 'golden, brown, delicious') bring crowds to this buzzy brick-walled Dupont storefront decked out with bold graphics and church pews, the new budget effort from the owners of Birch & Barley; morning coffee and sinker selections are augmented by chicken at lunch, while more robust dishes are added at dinner, when there's table service; P.S. craft beer, mixed drinks and snacks keep things going late, and there's brunch on the weekends.

Georgia Brown's *Southern*   22 | 22 | 22 | $42

Downtown | 950 15th St. NW (bet. I & K Sts.) | 202-393-4499 | www.georgiabrowns.com

At this "Lowcountry" "magnet for high-powered regulars" just "blocks from the White House", you never know who you'll see "digging into the fried tomatoes" and other "high-end comfort food" ferried by "down-home, Southern-friendly" folk in its "packed-beyond-reason" room; even if the "classy", "Clinton-era decor" could stand an "update", it's got "staying power", and there "ain't nothin' like" its "amazing" Sunday jazz brunch.

Geranio *Italian*   25 | 22 | 23 | $46

Old Town | 722 King St. (bet. Columbus & Washington Sts.) | Alexandria, VA | 703-548-0088 | www.geranio.net

A "perennial favorite" since 1976, this pretty, rustic Old Town Italophiles' haunt is home to "pleasant" servers who present "not-to-be-missed" lobster risotto and seasonal specials that are "relatively pricey" but "delicious"; flush wallets favor it for "special-occasion dinners" or a "romantic evening", while thinner wads find cheaper prices at lunch.

NEW Ghibellina Restaurant Ⓜ *Italian*   - | - | - | M

Logan Circle | 1610 14th St. NW (Corcoran St.) | 202-803-2389 | www.ghibellina.com

At this ambitious new Tuscan trattoria on 14th Street NW from the Acqua al 2 crew, small plates, including a large selection of salumi and cheese, plus pasta, meats and wood-fired pizza are washed down by craft cocktails, wine and beer; the rustic-industrial setting offers diners (and drinkers) a variety of seating options, including at a long marble-topped bar, perches by the window, brick-enclosed nooks or tables by the open kitchen.

Good Fortune *Chinese*   ▽ 22 | 13 | 16 | $24

Wheaton | 2646 University Blvd. W. (bet. Grandview Ave. & Veirs Mill Rd.), MD | 301-929-8818

Perhaps "best for weekend dim sum", when the rolling carts make it "fun", this affordable Chinese eatery near the Westfield Wheaton shopping complex also serves the "terrific" bites off its regular menu all week long; the "large" dining area may be low on frills, but first-timers especially count themselves fortunate that the staff is so "patient and helpful."

Good Stuff Eatery Ⓢ *Burgers*   23 | 15 | 17 | $15

Capitol Hill | 303 Pennsylvania Ave. SE (bet. 3rd & 4th Sts.) | 202-543-8222
Crystal City | 2110 Crystal Dr. (bet. 20th & 23rd Sts.) | Arlington, VA | 703-415-4663
www.goodstuffeatery.com

Former *Top Chef* contender Spike Mendelsohn is behind this "popular" Capitol Hill counter serve (and newer Crystal City sibling) wooing "celebrities", "pols" and "policy wonks" with "creative", "juicy" burgers, "perfectly seasoned" fries and "unbelievably decadent" milkshakes ("heaven in a plastic cup"), all doled out "fast" in upscale-industrial "fast-food" digs; despite "limited" seating, occasional "long" waits and tabs some consider "pricey" for the genre, it's still usually "jam packed."

Grace's Mandarin *Asian*   25 | 28 | 25 | $41

National Harbor | 188 Waterfront St. (Fleet St.), MD | 301-839-3788 | www.gracesrestaurants.com

"Delightful" Asian fare, including "so good" sushi, is backed by "superior" service at Grace Tang's waterfront spot, and though it's "pricey, that's National Harbor for ya"; making it further worth the while is an "awesome" view of the Potomac, though the exuberant Eastern decor is also "intriguing" ("love the huge Buddha").

Graffiato ◐ *Italian/Pizza* 24 | 18 | 21 | $43

Chinatown | 707 6th St. NW (bet. G & H Sts.) | 202-289-3600 | www.graffiatodc.com

Top Chef's Mike Isabella delivers "Italian comfort food like none other" at this somewhat "pricey" Chinatown spot where the pizzas are "creative", the "tapas-style" plates "pack a punch" and, yes, the famous pepperoni sauce is indeed "worth bathing in"; service is "efficient" and the bi-level "industrial-chic" setting has a "high-energy", "rock 'n' roll" vibe (read: "loud") that provides a "fun way to dine on a date" or "with friends."

Granville Moore's *American/Belgian* 24 | 19 | 21 | $30

Atlas District | 1238 H St. NE (bet. 12th & 13th Sts.) | 202-399-2546 | www.granvillemoores.com

"Even Popeye would be jealous" of the "phenomenal" mussels at this affordable Belgian-American gastropub in the Atlas District, which "packs a lot" of "hipsters" scarfing "gourmet bar food" into its rough-hewn, "pocket-sized" space; you may "have to wait for a seat", but glass-half-full types see it as a perfect time to flag down one of the amenable staffers and dive into the "deep, rich and wide beer list."

Grapeseed ☒ *American* 23 | 19 | 21 | $49

Bethesda | 4865 Cordell Ave. (bet. Norfolk & Woodmont Aves.), MD | 301-986-9592 | www.grapeseedbistro.com

The staff will "steer you right" for "imaginative food with tasteful wine pairings" at this vine-centric Bethesda New American whose contemporary space includes "romantic" two-person booths for "date night", private "wine cellar" rooms for small groups and a chef's table overlooking the kitchen that keeps kids "occupied"; a few sour grapes say it's "noisy" and "pricey" but they're crushed by great bunches of folks who "love this place."

Green Pig Bistro *American* - | - | - | M

Clarendon | 1025 N. Fillmore St. (11th St.), VA | 703-888-1920 | www.greenpigbistro.com

This mod-rustic, moderately priced Clarendon American arrival reflects chef Scot Harlan's passion for nose-to-tail cooking - watch him craft 'redneck' charcuterie in the open kitchen - and for giving French classics a decidedly American push; the bar and dining rooms, decorated with vintage kitchen collectibles, offer both intimate and communal seating arrangements.

The Grille *American/French* ▽ 25 | 23 | 27 | $63

Old Town | Morrison Hse. | 116 S. Alfred St. (bet. King & Prince Sts.) | Alexandria, VA | 703-838-8000 | www.thegrillealexandria.com

"Feeling far from the madding crowd" in an Old Town hotel, this "understated yet elegant" American-French place treats diners like "honored guests", pampering them with "wonderful" service and "very carefully" prepared food; it's "expensive", but also a "perfect spot for a celebration" given its "charm and sophistication."

Grillfish *Seafood*   20 | 18 | 20 | $37

West End | 1200 New Hampshire Ave. NW (bet. M St. & Ward Pl.) | 202-331-7310 | www.grillfishdc.com
"Simply prepared seafood" "lets the fish do the talking" at this West End eatery serving "fresh" aquatica at prices "you don't have to take out a second mortgage to afford"; "friendly" servers put diners at ease in the "comfy", "unpretentious" dining room with columns and faux-stone walls and out on the "pleasant" sidewalk.

Grill from Ipanema *Brazilian*   24 | 20 | 23 | $41

Adams Morgan | 1858 Columbia Rd. NW (Belmont Rd.) | 202-986-0757 | www.thegrillfromipanema.com
This "little piece of Brazil in Adams Morgan" proffers "classic" Carioca cooking like moqueca (fish stew) that "makes the mouth mambo" served by an "attentive" staff in tropical-themed environs; it's not cheap, but its "hearty" weekend brunch is a "deal" for under $20, and evokes a "relaxing day in Rio" – especially after one or two caipirinhas.

Grillmarx Steakhouse &   22 | 22 | 20 | $41
Raw Bar *Steak*

Olney | Fairhill Shopping Ctr. | 18149 Town Center Dr. (Olney Sandy Spring Rd.), MD | 301-570-1111 | www.grillmarxsteakhouse.com
A "great" "upmarket" addition to Olney say locals who welcome this steakhouse and raw bar serving "smoky" ribs, tasty chowders and "well-prepared" entrees in a "noisy" bar area or a "more spacious, quieter" dining room trimmed with exposed brick, wood beams and leather banquettes; if some say it's "a bit pricey", others point to a "fairly priced" wine list.

NEW The Grill Room *American*   - | - | - | E

Georgetown | Capella Hotel | 1050 31st St. NW (Waters Alley) | 202-617-2400 | www.thegrillroomdc.com
Arresting modern design and luxurious appointments (e.g. embroidered upholstery, floors from a French castle) provide an air of relaxed refinement at the Capella Hotel's new high-end American serving grilled artisanal meats and seafood; large windows afford sweeping views of the C&O Canal, while a glass-enclosed private room (curtained if one chooses) is further enticement for power breakfasts and lunches or celebratory dinner parties; P.S. be sure to check out the soigné and intimate Rye Bar for a drink.

NEW The Gryphon ●🗷Ⓜ *American*   - | - | - | M

Dupont Circle | 1337 Connecticut Ave. NW (bet. Dupont Circle & N St.) | 202-827-8980 | www.thegryphondc.com
Part sports bar, part gastropub, this new Dupont Circle behemoth boasts two bars, a full array of TVs and an ambitious kitchen turning out midpriced American fare plus fancified pub food; plenty of beer, wine and jazz-age cocktails fuel the action in the polished-wood-and-leather interior and out on the see-and-be-seen patio.

Guajillo *Mexican*

21 | 16 | 19 | $25

Courthouse | 1727 Wilson Blvd. (bet. Quinn & Rhodes Sts.) | Arlington, VA | 703-807-0840

"Savor the smoky flavors of Mexico" at this "authentic", affordable Arlington Courthouse–area cantina known for its "no-competition" moles, "clever" tacos and "complex" margaritas; it's "crowded but fun" in the brightly painted nook stuffed with traditional leather chairs handcrafted in Mexico, and "quick" service gives it a boost.

Guapo's *Tex-Mex*

22 | 18 | 21 | $25

Upper NW | 4515 Wisconsin Ave. NW (Albemarle St.) | 202-686-3588

Bethesda | 8130 Wisconsin Ave. (bet. Battery Ln. & Cordell Ave.), MD | 301-656-0888

Gaithersburg | Rio | 9811 Washingtonian Blvd. (Rio Blvd.), MD | 301-977-5655

Shirlington | 4028 Campbell Ave. (bet. Quincy & Randolph Sts.) | Arlington, VA | 703-671-1701

Fairfax | Fairlakes Shopping Ctr. | 13050 Fairlakes Shopping Ctr. (Fair Lakes Blvd.), VA | 703-818-0022

www.guaposrestaurant.com

Guests "never leave hungry" at this "good, basic" multilocation "Tex-Mex machine", a "kids' favorite" on account of "tasty" tacos and fajitas – while many adults may gravitate to the "feel-good margarita pitchers"; festive, "informal surroundings" are further "brightened by a happy, helpful staff", adding up to a "great value" that "holds its own" against similar chains.

Guardado's 🅼 *Pan-Latin/Spanish*

23 | 14 | 21 | $32

Bethesda | 4918 Del Ray Ave. (bet. Norfolk Ave. & Old Georgetown Rd.), MD | 301-986-4920 | www.guardadosnico.com

"Tantalizing tapas minus all the glam and glitz" of other area tapas joints is the draw at this "homey", "good-value" Bethesda Spanish-Latin "mom-and-pop" co-owned by chef Nicolas José Guardado and his wife, Reyna; together, they oversee a "cheerful" staff that sets a "comfortable, pleasurable" mood for an "informal meal."

Haad Thai *Thai*

▽ 21 | 15 | 20 | $28

Downtown | 1100 New York Ave. NW (bet. 11th & 12th Sts.) | 202-682-1111 | www.haadthairestaurant.com

"For a quick Thai fix", Downtown denizens duck into this "dependable" "neighborhood standby" for midpriced Southeast Asian "comfort food"; a large mural depicting the silhouette of a Thai long-tail boat sets a "soothing" tone in the casual space, one that's furthered by the "accommodating", "warm" service.

Haandi *Indian*

24 | 17 | 21 | $29

Falls Church | Falls Plaza Shopping Ctr. | 1222 W. Broad St. (Gordon Rd.), VA | 703-533-3501 | www.haandi.com

"Standard-setting Indian food" has long been the draw at this "unwaveringly steady" Falls Church subcontinental with waiters who are "helpful, approachable" and "ready to share their culture"; it's "reasonably" priced too, especially the "impressive" lunch buffet that "attracts a crowd" daily to the "pleasant" setting.

	FOOD	DECOR	SERVICE	COST

Hama Sushi *Japanese*

▽ 25 | 18 | 22 | $32

Herndon | Village Center at Dulles | 2415 Centreville Rd.
(Sunrise Valley Dr.), VA | 703-713-0088 | www.hama-sushi.com
"You would never know it from the outside", but this traditional-looking Japanese in Herndon is a winner among local "sushi lovers" thanks to "very creative" rolls and "interesting" specials; solid service, a midsized sake selection and moderate prices further its appeal.

The Hamilton ● *American*

20 | 25 | 18 | $36

Downtown | 600 14th St. NW (F St.) | 202-787-1000 |
www.thehamiltondc.com
This "massive" late-night eatery/performance venue (from the Clyde's folks), in a "prime" spot near the White House, will "blow you away" with its "high-ceilinged hunting lodge" look featuring stately, "active" bars and private booths, plus its downstairs live-music area; the "something-for-everyone" American menu leaves diners "with enough money to pay the mortgage" – and though some call the service "indifferent", glass-half-full fans see it as "still getting the hang of it."

Hank's Oyster Bar *American/Seafood*

24 | 17 | 21 | $38

Capitol Hill | 633 Pennsylvania Ave. SE (bet. 6th & 7th Sts.) | 202-733-1971
Dupont Circle | 1624 Q St. NW (bet. 16th & 17th Sts.) | 202-462-4265
Old Town | 1026 King St. (bet. Henry & Patrick Sts.) | Alexandria, VA |
703-739-4265 Ⓜ
www.hanksrestaurants.com
"Oysters and clams and lobster rolls, oh my" trill fans of these "classic" raw bars in Dupont Circle, Old Town and Capitol Hill, the latter of which showcases popular mixologist Gina Chersevani; "congeniality" and "fair value" inspire some happy shuckers to say they "could slurp oysters all day" in the "comfortable" New England (by way of *Martha Stewart Living*) digs.

Hard Times Cafe *American*

22 | 17 | 21 | $18

Bethesda | 4920 Del Ray Ave. (bet. Norfolk Ave. &
Old Georgetown Rd.), MD | 301-951-3300
Germantown | 13032 Middlebrook Rd. (bet. Father Hurley Blvd. &
Germantown Rd.), MD | 240-686-0150
College Park | 4738 Cherry Hill Rd. (Baltimore Ave.), MD | 301-474-8880
Rockville | Woodley Gdns. | 1117 Nelson St. (Azalea Dr.), MD |
301-294-9720
Old Town | 1404 King St. (West St.) | Alexandria, VA | 703-837-0050
Clarendon | 3028 Wilson Blvd. (Highland St.), VA | 703-528-2233 ●
Fairfax | 4069 Chain Bridge Rd. (Sager Ave.), VA | 703-267-9590 ●
Springfield | Springfield Plaza | 6362 Springfield Plaza (Old Keene
Mill Rd.), VA | 703-913-5600 ●
Manassas | 7753 Sudley Rd. (Sudley Manor Dr.), VA | 703-365-8400 ●
Woodbridge | Potomac Festival Plaza | 14389 Potomac Mills Rd.
(Opitz Blvd.), VA | 703-492-2950 ●
www.hardtimes.com
Additional locations throughout the DC area
"God said 'let there be chili'" before creating this regional chain "staple" say fans of the "superb" variations (Texas, Cincinnati, spicy,

vegetarian) available by the bowl or in many of its less-lauded pubby menu items – though some say those are "surprisingly good" too; "prompt" service, "value" and a "honky-tonk" atmosphere with "sports bar leanings" that includes a "decent" beer selection make them great places to "catch a game."

Harry's Smokehouse *BBQ/Burgers*   ▽ 21 | 22 | 22 | $23

Pentagon City | The Fashion Centre at Pentagon City | 1100 S. Hayes St. (Army Navy Dr.) | Arlington, VA | 703-416-7070 | www.harryssmokehouse.com

Inside Pentagon City's Fashion Centre, this "good ol' American BBQ" spot serves "melt-in-your-mouth" brisket, solid burgers and other eats at "great prices"; TVs, craft beers and a large open kitchen anchoring the raw-wood-and-stone space provide an "escape" from shopping.

Härth *American*   ▽ 23 | 27 | 23 | $58

Tysons Corner | Hilton McLean Tysons Corner | 7920 Jones Branch Dr. (Westpark Dr.) | McLean, VA | 703-847-5000 | www.harthrestaurant.com

"Fabulously chic and sexy decor" meshing woodsy elements with fiery accents (including the wood-burning oven it's named for) imparts a "cool atmosphere" to this pricey Tysons Corner Hilton New American; the "not-your-average-hotel-restaurant" feel extends to the "delicious" comfort food, fancy drinks and "courteous" service that make it "worth fighting traffic" to dine here.

Haven *Pizza*   - | - | - | I

Bethesda | 7137 Wisconsin Ave. (bet. Leland St. & Willow Ln.), MD | 301-664-9412 | www.havenpizzeria.com

New Haven–style pizzas fired in two 2,200-degree coal ovens – most notably the tribute to Connecticut's famed 'white-clam tomato pie' – have been drawing crowds to this new Bethesda pie shop since day one; its handsome, brick-trimmed setting is family-friendly and casual with roomy booths and a granite bar dispensing wine and beer, and it's priced friendly too; P.S. leave room for homemade gelato for dessert.

Hee Been *Korean*   23 | 18 | 19 | $29

Greater Alexandria | 6231 Little River Tpke. (Oasis Dr.) | Alexandria, VA | 703-941-3737 | www.heebeen.com

Those who "can't decide between Korean barbecue and Japanese" find an affordable fix at this Asian "feast" in Alexandria and Arlington, where "fun tabletop grilling" rubs shoulders with "enormous" "all-you-can-eat" buffet spreads that leave guests full for "days"; "industrial" decor suits the largely self-serve model, with diners focused on chowing "to their heart's delight."

Heritage India *Indian*   22 | 20 | 20 | $34

NEW **Dupont Circle** | 1633 P St. NW (bet. Dupont Circle & 18th St.) | 202-387-7400

NEW **World Bank** | 1901 Pennsylvania Ave. (19th St.) | 202-331-2112

Glover Park | 2400 Wisconsin Ave. NW (Calvert St.) | 202-333-3120 www.heritageindiausa.com

Go "upscale Indian" "without losing authenticity" at this Glover Park subcontinental serving "rich" and "spicy" classics plus Indian street food–inspired tapas; considering the "pleasant" ambiance that flows from the "friendly" staff and "beautiful" heritage on display, it's reasonably priced; P.S. there are two newer branches in Dupont Circle and World Bank (the latter shares its space with Eclectic small-plates concept Crossroads).

NEW Hikari Sushi & Saki Bar *Japanese* — | — | — | M

Atlas District | 644 H St. NE (bet. First & N. Capitol Sts.) | 202-546-0523 | www.hikarirestaurant.com

This modern two-story Japanese entry on the Atlas District's Restaurant Row offers midpriced traditional fare plus some clever sushi selections at its sleek sushi counter and cozy tables; there's also a street-level bar serving cocktails, beer and wine.

Hill Country ● *BBQ* 21 | 19 | 16 | $28

Penn Quarter | 410 Seventh St. NW (D St.) | 202-556-2050 | www.hillcountrywdc.com

You'll find a "li'l bit of Texas" (via NYC, and with "Manhattan" prices) in the "finger-lickin'" ribs and "moist" brisket at this "barn"-sized "Disney-did-Lockhart" BBQ spot in Penn Quarter; its "meal-ticket"-based, "cafeterialike service" is "fun", "kitschy", "confusing" or perhaps all three – but most agree that "cold beer" and "great live music" in the downstairs club add to an "awesome concept."

Himalayan Heritage *Indian/Nepalese* 21 | 19 | 20 | $27

Adams Morgan | 2305 18th St. NW (Kalorama Rd.) | 202-483-9300
NEW Bethesda | 4925 Bethesda Ave. (Arlington Rd.), MD | 301-654-1858
www.himalayanheritagedc.com

"Spicy", "complex" Nepalese-Indian fare is "served with love" via "friendly" sherpas who guide diners through the "adventurous menu" at this eatery "right in the thick of things" in Adams Morgan (with a new Bethesda branch); the "cozy" space has a Himalayan lodge feel, which, with "reasonable" tabs, brings folks back "over and over."

Hinode *Japanese* 20 | 16 | 19 | $28

Bethesda | The Shoppes of Bethesda | 4914 Hampden Ln. (bet. Arlington Rd. & Woodmont Ave.), MD | 301-654-0908
Frederick | 50 Carroll Creek Way (Market St.), MD | 301-620-2943
Rockville | 134 Congressional Ln. (bet. Jefferson St. & Rockville Pike), MD | 301-816-2190
www.hinode-frederick.com

Locals depend on these "friendly" Maryland Japanese joints for a "wide variety" of "competently done" sushi; at the spartan Bethesda and Rockville links it's all about the "bargain" lunch buffet, and though Frederick lacks the buffet, it boasts a "charming" creekside setting.

Hollywood East Cafe *Chinese* 24 | 15 | 18 | $24
(aka Hollywood East on the Boulevard)

Wheaton | Westfield Wheaton | 11160 Veirs Mill Rd. (University Blvd. W.), MD | 240-290-9988 | www.hollywoodeastcafe.com

It's "worth getting up early" and heading to this Wheaton Chinese on weekends, to dig your chopsticks into its "fantastic" Cantonese

| | FOOD | DECOR | SERVICE | COST |

dim sum the "friendly" staff brings around on carts (weekdays, it's available à la carte); there's also a large "authentic" menu "ranging from the common to the extraordinary" served in a modern space that some say is "hard to find" inside a shopping mall.

Honey Pig Gooldaegee

| 23 | 13 | 17 | $24 |

Korean BBQ ● *Korean*
(aka Seoul Gool Dae Gee)
Annandale | 7220 Columbia Pike (Maple Pl.), VA | 703-256-5229
Centreville | 13818 Braddock Rd. (Old Centreville Rd.), VA | 703-830-5959
www.eathoneypig.com

"Prepare to smell like" the "wonderful" barbecue meats grilling "right in front" of you at the table at these "hip", "lively" Seoul sisters in Annandale, Centreville and Ellicott City, which are popular "after-clubbing" destinations since they're open 24/7 (except Monday, when it's closed from 2–10 AM) and blare "upbeat K-pop music" "as loud as a club" with the simple "industrial" "decor to match"; most non-Korean speakers can work around the staff's "minimal English" to seek out the strong "price-to-flavor ratio."

Hong Kong Palace *Chinese*

| 27 | 11 | 16 | $21 |

Falls Church | 6387 Seven Corners Ctr. (Leesburg Pike), VA |
703-532-0940 | www.hkpalace.webs.com

"Long lines" don't lie at this "friendly", "real Sichuan" "hole-in-the-wall", a "favorite" of the "local Asian" community and others in the know for "amazing, authentic Chinese" so "well done" it leaves folks wondering "what did Falls Church do to deserve this place?"; you don't need to bring much money, but "be prepared for spicy."

Hooked *Seafood*

| 20 | 21 | 16 | $42 |

Sterling | Potomac Run Plaza | 46240 Potomac Run Plaza
(Bartholomew Fair Dr.), VA | 703-421-0404 | www.hookedonseafood.com

A "swanky, cool vibe" filled with glitz provides an "upscale" "change of pace" for Sterling say fans of this Potomac Run venue that proffers "well-prepared" seafood and sushi; some detractors note "unreliable" service and "steep" tabs, though most locals are reeled in by the "reliably tasty" eats and attractive bait like a "nice", huge "outdoor patio."

Horace & Dickie's Seafood

| 22 | 6 | 20 | $12 |

Carryout ● *Seafood*
Atlas District | 809 12th St. NE (bet. H & Wylie Sts.) | 202-397-6040
Horace & Dickie's Seafood 🚫Ⓜ *Seafood*
Takoma | 6912 Fourth St. (bet. Blair Rd. & Butternut St.) |
202-248-4265
www.horaceanddickies.com

It's a little late to "not tell anyone" about this Atlas District "land-mark" carryout (and its more polished Takoma spin-off) and its "dy-namite", "good-eating" seafood and soulful sides that have been giving folks their "money's worth" for years; occasional "lines out the door" prove that "lack of decor and ambiance" is no deterrent to business when they "give you plenty of fish" in your sandwich.

	FOOD	DECOR	SERVICE	COST

Hot 'N Juicy Crawfish *Cajun/Creole* ▽ 20 | 17 | 20 | $24

Woodley Park | 2651 Connecticut Ave. NW (Woodley Rd.) | 202-299-9448 | www.hotandjuicycrawfish.com

Pick a "spice level", grab "plenty of napkins" and indulge in "crawfish-sucking, shrimp-peeling, crab-cracking madness" at this Cajun-Creole chain outpost in Woodley Park where "friendly and prompt" servers keep the cold beer coming; yes, it's a "very casual" atmosphere (plastic-covered tables, bibs) but the good times roll "in the summer when you can sit outside."

Howard Theatre *Southern* - | - | - | M

Shaw | Howard Theatre | 620 T St. NW (7th St.) | 202-803-2899 | www.thehowardtheatre.com

This storied African-American theater in Shaw, where the likes of Duke Ellington came to fame, now serves a sophisticated, moderately priced Southern-accented American supper-club menu designed by consulting chef Marcus Samuelsson (Harlem's Red Rooster) on performance nights; the weekly Sunday gospel buffet brunch is also worthy of the limelight.

Hunan Dynasty *Chinese* ▽ 20 | 16 | 21 | $36

Capitol Hill | 215 Pennsylvania Ave. SE (bet. 2nd & 3rd Sts.) | 202-546-6161

"Longtime staff members are friendly and warmly welcome" regulars, like "members of Congress", who bipartisanly approve the "solid", "flavorful" Chinese fare at this Capitol Hill "mainstay" that does sushi and Thai too; typical restaurant chinoiserie is par for the course, as are "reasonable" tabs.

Hunter's Head Tavern *British* ▽ 23 | 23 | 20 | $30

Upperville | 9048 John Mosby Hwy./Rte. 50 (Parker St.), VA | 540-592-9020 | www.huntersheadtavern.com

It's "worth the drive" to scenic Upperville to visit this "ersatz British pub" housed in a historic 18th-century home, where guests dine inside the "cozy" "country tavern" or on the "beautiful outdoor patio"; after placing initial orders at the bar, the "efficient" staff delivers the "very good", midpriced grub (bangers 'n' mash, Welsh rarebit), much of it made from local meats and produce from nearby Ayrshire Farm.

Huong Viet ⊄ *Vietnamese* 25 | 14 | 20 | $23

Falls Church | Eden Ctr. | 6785 Wilson Blvd. (bet. Arlington & Roosevelt Blvds.), VA | 703-538-7110 | www.huong-viet.com

This "no-contest" pick in Falls Church's Eden Center epitomizes "true Vietnamese cuisine" swear fans, citing its "great noodle dishes", "excellent" bun, indeed, pretty much everything on its looong menu; with "willing, friendly service", most "don't care about" the "no-frills" decor or that one must "bring cash" to pay the "cheap" bill.

Il Canale *Italian/Pizza* 22 | 18 | 20 | $33

Georgetown | 1063 31st St. NW (M St.) | 202-337-4444 | www.ilcanaledc.com

Taste buds are "transported to Italy" via "genuine, wood-fired" Neapolitan pizza (plus "delicate" pasta and other "authentic" fare)

at this "friendly" Georgetowner "romantically" "tucked away" near the C&O Canal; the good value is bolstered by a "peerless wine list" with a "fair corkage policy" and a plethora of distinctive seating options: "lovely" sidewalk, "modern" "industrial" ground floor, "quaint rooftop" or by a "magical" window upstairs.

Il Fornaio *Italian*

25 | 23 | 23 | $43

Reston | Reston Town Ctr. | 11990 Market St. (bet. Reston & St. Francis Pkwys.), VA | 703-437-5544 | www.ilfornaio.com
"Remarkable" house-baked breads presage a "sumptuous" Italian meal at Reston's "terrific, classy trattoria" chain place, where a "really nice staff" ferries plates through a Tuscan "movie set"; a few penne-pinchers say it's "pricey", but everyone loves happy hour when there's $5 pizza at the bar.

Il Pizzico 🗷 *Italian*

27 | 20 | 24 | $41

Rockville | Suburban Park | 15209 Frederick Rd. (Gude Dr.), MD | 301-309-0610 | www.ilpizzico.com
You'd think that "more than two decades" of dishing up "beautiful homemade pastas" and other simply "amazing food for the price" would have put this Rockville Italian on the foodie radar screen, but its "unassuming strip-mall" location has kept it something of a local "find"; that doesn't mean you won't "wait" for a prime-time table in the contemporary setting – so go "early", "inhale the atmosphere", "salute the wines" and banter with the "helpful", "talkative" waiters.

Il Porto Ristorante *Italian*

24 | 22 | 23 | $36

Greater Alexandria | 121 King St. (S. Lee St.) | Alexandria, VA | 703-836-8833 | www.ilportoristorante.com
Yes, it's "been there forever", and this midpriced Alexandria Italian remains a "favorite" of fans who swear by its sauces, both "light and complex" and so "rich" and "meaty" they taste as if they'd "been cooking for hours", proffered by "polite" servers; "retro in a good way", the plaster-and-beam construction lends it an "old-world charm."

India Palace Bar & Tandoor *Indian*

∇ 26 | 23 | 26 | $23

Germantown | Fox Chapel Shopping Ctr. | 19743 Frederick Rd. (Gunners Branch Rd.), MD | 301-540-3000 | www.indiapalacegermantown.com
This Germantown shopping-center subcontinental offers "appealing", affordable Indian fare (including a "great buffet selection" at lunch) in a simple, traditionally decorated setting that works for "date night" or a meal with "the whole family"; the service is as "exceptional" as the food, with "inviting" staffers tending to every need.

Indique *Indian*

23 | 21 | 21 | $37

Cleveland Park | 3512-14 Connecticut Ave. NW (bet. Ordway & Porter Sts.) | 202-244-6600 | www.indique.com

Indique Heights *Indian*

Chevy Chase | 2 Wisconsin Circle (Western Ave.), MD | 301-656-4822 | www.indiqueheights.com
"Exciting, high-end" riffs on Indian "street food" at these "upperend" Cleveland Park and Chevy Chase subcontinentals raise them to

"Himalayan heights" say supporters who also give high marks to "pleasant" service; "mezzanine seating" at DC's "beautiful" bi-level space strikes a "romantic" note, while "casbahlike" dining on "cushions" lends a "relaxing" vibe just over the district line in Maryland.

Inn at Little Washington
Restaurant *American*

29	29	29	$205

Washington | Inn at Little Washington | 309 Middle St. (Main St.), VA | 540-675-3800 | www.theinnatlittlewashington.com

"Simply the best", Patrick O'Connell's hunt-country New American "citadel" earns the No. 1 ratings for Food, Decor and Service in the Greater DC area for what amounts to a "life-altering experience" as guests get "pampered" in an "intimate", richly embroidered setting, where "revelatory" multicourse repasts are "prepared with extraordinary skill" and seasoned with a "touch of whimsy"; in short, it's "worth every penny . . . and that's a lot of pennies!"; P.S. "spend the night for the ultimate indulgence."

I Ricchi ☒ *Italian*

24	23	24	$65

Dupont Circle | 1220 19th St. NW (bet. M & N Sts.) | 202-835-0459 | www.iricchi.net

"Power brokers unite" at this "old-world" Dupont Circle Italian, whose "divine" classics and "professional" service have "stood the test of time"; regulars who "feel pampered" in its "lovely", villaesque room counter protests that "you have to be one of the ricchi indeed to afford to eat here", by conceding that, yes, prices are "high" but so is the "quality."

Irish Inn at Glen Echo *Irish*

20	19	22	$36

Glen Echo | 6119 Tulane Ave. (MacArthur Blvd.), MD | 301-229-6600 | www.irishinnglenecho.com

"Genuine Irish hospitality" powers this "charming" Glen Echo pub where "familiar" Irish (and American) "comfort food" is "well represented" and is bolstered by fancier items from further afield; choose from several "adorable", "conversation"-friendly rooms or "skip the food" to down a "pint" in the bar or on the outdoor deck.

Irish Whiskey
Public House ◗ *Pub Food*

-	-	-	M

Dupont Circle | 1207 19th St. NW (bet. M & N Sts.) | 202-463-3010 | www.irishwhiskeydc.com

Serious tipplers drink to this Irish pub near Dupont Circle, where bars on three floors pour an impressive roster of whiskeys and noteworthy beers, and are backed by a midpriced menu of spirited Auld Sod classics (e.g. beer-battered fish 'n' chips, shepherd's pie with Guinness gravy); the modern-Dublin-in-DC setting features gleaming dark wood, barrel-and-brick-lined walls, fireplace seating and an outdoor patio.

Iron Bridge Wine Company *American*

25	23	23	$41

Warrenton | 29 Main St. (1st St.), VA | 540-349-9339 | www.ironbridgewines.com
See review in the Baltimore Directory.

	FOOD	DECOR	SERVICE	COST

Isabella's *Spanish*

26 | 22 | 23 | $32

Frederick | 44 N. Market St. (Rte. 144), MD | 301-698-8922 | www.isabellas-tavern.com

At this "popular" midpriced Spanish in Frederick, "helpful" staffers "guide diners through the amazing array" of tapas that are designed to "share" but which are so "fantastic" you "may not want to"; a "super" happy hour enlivens the "casual" setting with exposed-brick walls.

It's About Thyme 🗷🅼 *American/European*

25 | 21 | 23 | $38

Culpeper | Thyme In Culpeper | 128 E. Davis St. (Main St.), VA | 540-825-4264 | www.thymeinfo.com

"Outstanding", reasonably priced European and American food is "beautifully prepared and happily served" by a "knowledgeable" staff at this Culpeper "destination" with a "small town feel"; the "distinctive" interior, with its tin ceiling and European landscape murals, can get "a bit crowded", but it's definitely "worth the squeeze."

ⓃⒺⓌ Izakaya Seki *Japanese*

‒ | ‒ | ‒ | M

U Street Corridor | 1117 V St. NW (bet. 11th & 12th Sts.) | 202-588-5841 | www.sekidc.com

It didn't take long for this unmarked spot in the U Street NW corridor to hit the foodie radar screen thanks to its authentic, as-in-Japan small plates, tempura and noodles (no sushi), plus sake and rare-in-DC Japanese microbrews; the minimalist digs fill up quickly, and there are no reservations, so go early to grab a seat at the chef's counter downstairs or at one of the upstairs tables.

Jackie's *American*

23 | 20 | 20 | $38

Silver Spring | 8081 Georgia Ave. (Sligo Ave.), MD | 301-565-9700 | www.jackiesrestaurant.com

What used to be an "old" auto-parts garage hides Silver Spring's "nifty", "funky '60s"-looking resto-lounge with "inventive" American "cuisine that doesn't take itself too seriously" and "won't break the bank" that's "delivered in style" by an "unfailingly friendly" crew; "crafty cocktails" are also poured at its next-door sibling, Sidebar.

Jack Rose Dining Saloon ⓓ *American*

∇ 20 | 24 | 18 | $45

Adams Morgan | 2007 18th St. NW (bet. California & U Sts.) | 202-588-7388 | www.jackrosediningsaloon.com

"There are few cooler spaces" than this spirits-centric saloon in Adams Morgan with its "walls of bourbon and whiskey", "a glorious sight to behold" while partaking of the non-liquid accompaniments, i.e. the "decent" if "slightly expensive" American food; it's also "worth a trip to sip" (and nosh on tasty "bar nibbles" in warm weather) on the upstairs terrace.

Jackson's Mighty Fine Food & Lucky Lounge ⓓ *American*

23 | 21 | 23 | $31

Reston | Reston Town Ctr. | 11927 Democracy Dr. (Library St.), VA | 703-437-0800 | www.greatamericanrestaurants.com

Folks flock to Reston Town Center's "never-miss", "family-friendly" American saloon for its "broad menu" of "great-tasting" "familiar" favorites served in "hearty" portions at "moderate" prices; the "thoughtful" staff caters to the "littlest needs" in an "expansive" sea of "comfortable", "roomy booths" surrounded by 1940s-inspired decor, and though a few complain it's "hard to have a conversation", most enjoy the "energetic" atmosphere, especially the "hopping bar scene" with its many "upscale singles."

Jackson 20 ● *American* 21 | 21 | 21 | $39

Old Town | Hotel Monaco Alexandria | 480 King St. (Pitt St.) | Alexandria, VA | 703-842-2790 | www.jackson20.com

The kitchen takes "old Southern dishes you remember and gives them" a New American "kick" at this Old Town Alexandria hotel spot with a look that's both "chic" (dark and modern with an open kitchen) and "quirky" ("an unusual amount of pigs"); "crazy-busy" brunches are handled with an "efficient approach" – at other times it's a nice place to "relax and unwind" with one of the 20 bottles of wine under $20.

Jaipur *Indian* 25 | 22 | 25 | $27

Fairfax | 9401 Fairfax Blvd. (Circle Woods Dr.), VA | 703-766-1111 | www.jaipurcuisine.com

"Intoxicating", "exotic aromas" hint at the "amazing" traditional food found at this "colorfully" decorated Fairfax Indian, where the curries "dance in your mouth"; a "popular" and affordable lunch buffet and staffers who "go out of their way" put it "heads and tails above" many other nearby options.

Jaleo *Spanish* 24 | 20 | 21 | $39

Penn Quarter | 480 Seventh St. NW (E St.) | 202-628-7949
Bethesda | 7271 Woodmont Ave. (Elm St.), MD | 301-913-0003
Crystal City | 2250 Crystal Dr. (23rd St.) | Arlington, VA | 703-413-8181
www.jaleo.com

A "pitcher of sangria" and a "steady stream" of "delicious", "witty" tapas at this local chainlet overseen by "rock-star" Spanish chef José Andrés are the answer to a "bruising work week", "out-of-town guests" or a "date-night" dilemma; "terrific" crews deftly handle the "racket and bustle" in "festively" decorated settings that feel as "fresh and exciting as ever", though costs can "add up quickly" – especially if you "have to try everything"; P.S. Penn Quarter boasts a bold, avant-garde designer look.

J&G Steakhouse *American/Steak* 24 | 24 | 23 | $68

Downtown | W Hotel | 515 15th St. NW (bet. F St. & Pennsylvania Ave.) | 202-661-2440 | www.jgsteakhousewashingtondc.com

Jean-Georges Vongerichten's "modern take" on the steakhouse genre brings some of the "best" "juicy" cuts to Downtown, though often the "stars of the meal" are his "transcendent" New American dishes; the soaring dining room, located just off the W Hotel's lobby, is about to undergo a major redo at press time (which could outdate the Decor rating); P.S. the less pricey "hidden wine bar" downstairs is "perfect for an illicit tryst."

NEW Jardenea *American*

— | — | — | **E**

West End | The Melrose Georgetown Hotel | 2430 Pennsylvania Ave. NW (bet. 24th & 25th Sts.) | 202-955-6400 | www.melrosehoteldc.com

This upscale farm-to-fork New American in the West End Melrose Hotel serves three square organic, locally sourced meals a day, while a full bar in the adjacent lounge offers guiltier pleasures; not just for hotel guests, the spacious and subdued setting – with cool colors, clean lines and bold patterns – is ideal for special occasions.

Joe's Noodle House *Chinese*

23 | 9 | 14 | $18

Rockville | 1488 Rockville Pike (bet. Edmonston Dr. & Halpine Rd.), MD | 301-881-5518 | www.joesnoodlehouse.com

"Adventurous palates" find "authentic" Sichuan "kick and flavor" ("experience the burn") and "amazing value for money" at this "crowded", "divey" Rockville spot; the "vast" menu with "hundreds of dishes" can seem "overwhelming", but the counter staff is "willing to help" before you sit down and "wait" for your picks to arrive.

Johnny's Half Shell ☒ *American/Seafood*

21 | 20 | 20 | $47

Capitol Hill | 400 N. Capitol St. NW (Louisiana Ave.) | 202-737-0400 | www.johnnyshalfshell.net

Super-"fresh" seafood, seasoned with the "Congressional or Supreme Court gossip" that can be overheard at this Capitol Hill New American's "active bar" or in its "more reserved" dark-wood dining room, powers Ann Cashion and John Fulchino's "tightly run ship"; time-honored Gulf and Chesapeake recipes are "prepared with skill and served with speed", live jazz enlivens Saturdays and there's a contemporary new look to its spacious courtyard terrace.

Juice Joint Cafe ☒ *Health Food*

∇ 23 | 13 | 21 | $11

Downtown | 1025 Vermont Ave. NW (L St.) | 202-347-6783 | www.juicejointcafe.com

The "rare" combo of "healthy and delicious" keeps a "daily lunch crowd coming back" to this Downtown canteen with a "huge" list of "inventive" salads, stir-fries, sandwiches and other casual fare; there can be a "long line" at lunchtime, despite an expansion, but the "friendly" team takes "great care of their customers."

Juniper *American*

∇ 24 | 24 | 26 | $55

West End | Fairmont Hotel | 2401 M St. NW (24th St.) | 202-457-5020 | www.fairmont.com

A true sleeper, this "quiet" West Ender in the Fairmont is "not your typical hotel restaurant", providing "exquisite" New American meals; you'll pay a premium for the "elegant" service and "luxurious" setting overlooking a "beautiful courtyard" that qualify it as "romantic."

Kabob Bazaar *Persian*

25 | 17 | 21 | $20

Bethesda | 7710 Wisconsin Ave. (Old Georgetown Rd.), MD | 301-652-5814

Clarendon | 3133 Wilson Blvd. (N. Herndon St.), VA | 703-522-8999 www.kabobbazaar.com

"Authentic" Persian as well as Lebanese and other Middle Eastern dishes make for "balanced", "virtuous" and "reasonably priced" meals at these Bethesda and Clarendon "neighborhood gems" serving "delightful" kebabs, stews and "exotic specials"; "simple" brick-lined surrounds are tended by "helpful servers", though some folks just grab a seat at the bar for a quick spot of "Persian tea."

Kabob N Karahi ● *Indian/Pakistani*   ▽ 26 | 8 | 23 | $15

Silver Spring | 15521 New Hampshire Ave. (Briggs Chaney Rd.), MD | 301-879-0044 | www.kabobnkarahi.com

It may be "just a [disposable] plate and fluorescent light kind of place" but this Silver Spring strip-mall "hole-in-the-wall" serves "expertly done" kebabs and other Pakistani and Indian treats at prices "you won't even blink at"; what's more, "courteous" servers make patrons feel "like visitors in someone's home."

Kabob Palace
Family Restaurant *Mideastern*   26 | 12 | 20 | $18

Crystal City | 2333 S. Eads St. (bet. 23rd & 24th Sts.) | Arlington, VA | 703-979-3000 | www.kabobpalaceusa.com

"People in the know" come to this Arlington Mideasterner for "authentic" kebabs of "unfailing" quality plus an "excellent" lunch buffet at affordable prices; it's "always busy" despite "no decor" and "informal" service, bringing "all ages, races and creeds together in pursuit of awesome food."

NEW Kadhai *Indian*   - | - | - | M

Bethesda | 7907 Norfolk Ave. (St. Elmo Ave.), MD | 301-718-0121 | www.kadhaimd.com

This Indian entry in Bethesda offers a long menu that includes all your standard subcontinental faves at moderate prices (it also serves a lunch buffet daily); the dining room features warm wood paneling, salmon-colored walls and white-linen-draped tables.

Kangaroo Boxing Club ● *BBQ*   - | - | - | I

Columbia Heights | 3410 11th St. NW (bet. Monroe St. & Park Rd.) | 202-505-4522 | www.kangaroodc.com

PORC *BBQ*

Location varies; see website | no phone | www.porcmobile.com

An offspring of the PORC food truck, this Columbia Heights brick-and-mortar venue offers inexpensive, house-smoked BBQ (and some veggie options); the space has a rustic, been-there-forever quality with a cozy window nook, bar topped with an ornate fireplace mantel, classic jukebox and vintage photos of DC; P.S. the food truck is still rolling, so check its website for locations and times.

Kazan ⬚ *Turkish*   25 | 20 | 25 | $40

McLean | Chain Bridge Corner Shopping Ctr. | 6813 Redmond Dr. (Chain Bridge Rd.), VA | 703-734-1960 | www.kazanrestaurant.com

After several decades, this McLean Turk sure "knows how to serve flavorful food", most notably its "out-of-this-world" doner kebab – and at "reasonable prices for the quality"; what's more, chef-owner Zeynel Uzun is almost "always on-site" overseeing an "accommodating" staff, and while "sophisticated Turkish decor" doesn't quite transcend the "strip-mall" locale, it at least feels like a strip mall in Istanbul.

	FOOD	DECOR	SERVICE	COST

Kaz Sushi Bistro ⚅ *Japanese* — 25 | 17 | 21 | $47

World Bank | 1915 I St. NW (bet. 19th & 20th Sts.) | 202-530-5500 | www.kazsushi.com

Japanophiles give props to the "classical and innovative" sushi and "creative" small plates at Kaz Okochi's World Bank bistro; "yes, it is pricey" – except at lunch, when "hearty" bento boxes offer "terrific value" – and sure, the "sterile" decor could use an "upgrade", but most feel the "pristine" fish and "great" service more than "compensate."

Kellari Taverna *Greek* — 23 | 21 | 21 | $62

Golden Triangle | 1700 K St. NW (17th St.) | 202-535-5274 | www.kellaridc.com

"Swim" to this "elegant Greek" seafooder in the Golden Triangle "that can rival any in Athens" with its "beautifully done" fish and tasty meze in a "bright", airy room that will "impress a business associate"; although it "can get expensive", there's a "steal" of a three-course lunch, a pre-theater prix fixe and "free cheese and olives at the bar" that expresses its Hellenic hospitality.

Kobe Japanese Steak & Seafood House *Japanese* — 27 | 24 | 25 | $41

Leesburg | Leesburg Plaza | 514 E. Market St. (Plaza St.), VA | 703-443-8300 | www.kobejs.com

See review in the Baltimore Directory.

Komi ⚅Ⓜ *American/Mediterranean* — 28 | 22 | 28 | $176

Dupont Circle | 1509 17th St. NW (P St.) | 202-332-9200 | www.komirestaurant.com

Johnny Monis leads diners on a "gastro-adventure" at his Dupont Circle American-Med "temple" offering a "dazzling variety of dishes beautifully prepared and executed" in a "subdued", "understated" setting, made more "relaxing" by a staff that's "detail-oriented without being uptight"; "expect to spend the evening" as they "serve and serve and serve" a fixed-price "parade" of plates along with "witty wine pairings" – and while the "high price" and "hard-to-get reservations" give "mere eaters" pause, food fanatics chant "just go."

Kora ⚅ *Italian* — 17 | 20 | 17 | $34

Crystal City | 2250 Crystal Dr. (23rd St.) | Arlington, VA | 571-431-7090 | www.korarestaurant.com

A "soaring", "modern" dining room lined with floor-to-ceiling windows and eggplant hues is the backdrop for "casual" Italian meals, including pizza, at this Crystal City eatery catering to "office" workers and "families"; a few say it's "unmemorable"' but most find it "solid" with decent service and middling tabs; P.S. the owners' American restaurant within a restaurant, Farrah Olivia, is located in the back room.

Kotobuki *Japanese* — 25 | 10 | 18 | $27

Palisades | 4822 MacArthur Blvd. NW (U St.) | 202-281-6679 | www.kotobukiusa.com

"Good things come in small packages" at this "quirky" Palisades Japanese where a "focused selection" of "high-quality" sushi plus *kamameshi,* a rice-based hot pot, come at "very reasonable prices"; the "tiny", "square box" of a space (above Makoto, on the second story) is made more fab by a "Beatles-heavy play list" and "prompt and courteous" service; P.S. it's also a "favorite" take-out spot.

Kramerbooks & Afterwords Cafe ● *American*

19 | 18 | 18 | $27

Dupont Circle | 1517 Connecticut Ave. NW (Q St.) | 202-387-1462 | www.kramers.com

"Eating surrounded by books is such a treat" at this bookstore cafe "institution" in Dupont Circle with an American menu of "casual" fare served up in a "lively", "cosmopolitan" setting that "makes you feel smarter" just being there; prices are "fair", service is "friendly" and the "always-packed" weekend brunch is "one of the best" around ("browse the fantastic" reading selection while you wait); P.S. open 24 hours on the weekend.

Kushi *Japanese*

25 | 21 | 21 | $44

Mt. Vernon Square/Convention Center | City Vista | 465 K St. NW (bet. 4th & 5th Sts.) | 202-682-3123 | www.eatkushi.com

"The best seats are at the bar" watching the "fascinating" chefs in action at this "hip" Mt. Vernon Square Japanese izakaya that goes "beyond the usual sushi" (though that's "beautifully" prepared) with "tasty" kushiyaki and robata selections, plus small-batch sake and microbrews; its lofty, "minimalist" quarters exude a "contemporary Tokyo vibe" as do the "accompanying prices", but you pay for the "privilege of authenticity."

La Bergerie *French*

26 | 24 | 24 | $58

Old Town | Crilley Warehse. | 218 N. Lee St. (bet. Cameron & Queen Sts.) | Alexandria, VA | 703-683-1007 | www.labergerie.com

"Fantastic" French "classics" – like "superb" sole meunière and "heavenly" soufflés – continue to "exceed the highest expectations" at this "old-style" Old Towner; "sublime" service and a "quiet", "elegant" dining room with brick walls, crystal chandeliers and "well-spaced" booths make it excellent for "special occasions", leading most to deem it "worth the cost."

La Canela *Peruvian*

23 | 22 | 21 | $37

Rockville | Rockville Town Sq. | 141 Gibbs St. (Beall Ave.), MD | 301-251-1550 | www.lacanelaperu.com

"Want to visit Peru? start here" say fans of this Rockville "charmer" that "elevates" the country's cuisine with "superb" takes on regional specialties washed down with "so-good" pisco sours; considering the "not particularly expensive" prices, "attentive" service and "nicely appointed" interior (wrought-iron accents, "larger-than-life mirrors"), it's a "real gem."

La Caraqueña *S American*

▽ 25 | 15 | 22 | $25

Falls Church | 300 W. Broad St. (Little Falls St.), VA | 703-533-0076 | www.lacaraquena.com

"Holy cow" – "the arepas are incredible" at this "charmer" that dishes up "some of the best South American food this side of the equator" according to fans; connected to a "nothing" motor lodge in Falls Church, it's got a "motel-chic" vibe that's definitely "not fancy", but "friendly service" and prices that please the crowds "jammed" into the "teeny-tiny" space make reservations "essential."

La Chaumière 🔲 *French*   26 | 24 | 24 | $58

Georgetown | 2813 M St. NW (bet. 28th & 29th Sts.) | 202-338-1784 | www.lachaumieredc.com

One can "almost imagine Julia [Child] and Jacques [Pepin] sharing a cozy meal" of "excellent" classics at this "long-lived, much-loved" Georgetown "country French" *auberge,* with its "rustic stone fireplace", proper tablecloths and a sound level that would have allowed them "to converse"; "been-there-forever" pros ensure that there are "not many empty chairs at peak times", especially since it's a "wonderful value" (if "not cheap").

LacoMelza Ethio
Cafe & Gallery *Ethiopian*   - | - | - | I

Silver Spring | 7912 Georgia Ave. (Eastern Ave.), MD | 301-326-2435

Ethiopian culture pervades this affordable Silver Spring spot, from the colorful art for sale on the walls to the brilliantly hued food on the plates; that's right, many of the stews and such are piled on plates (though some are on spongy bread as at many other Ethiopian venues), which may make for an easy intro to this cuisine for newbies.

La Côte d'Or Café *French*   24 | 22 | 23 | $45

Arlington | 6876 Fairfax Blvd. (Westmoreland St.), VA | 703-538-3033 | www.lacotedorcafe.com

Francophiles find a "little bit of France in the Arlington suburbs" thanks to the "consistently excellent" classics served up in "unpretentious" country-cafe digs at this long-running "neighborhood" bistro with "welcoming owners"; locals judge the considerable prices "fair" for a "romantic rendezvous" or "special occasion."

Lafayette Room *American*   ▽ 27 | 28 | 26 | $80

Golden Triangle | The Hay-Adams | 800 16th St. NW (bet. H & I Sts.) | 202-638-2570 | www.hayadams.com

You might be too busy rubbernecking the "familiar faces at breakfast and lunch" to notice the "superb execution of the classics" and "professional" service at this "beautiful, formal" American hotel dining room with a view across to the White House; you'll pay a pretty penny, but as "one of the last" of its kind, it's an "experience not to be missed"; P.S. no dinner Saturday or Sunday.

La Ferme *French*   24 | 25 | 23 | $51

Chevy Chase | 7101 Brookville Rd. (Taylor St.), MD | 301-986-5255 | www.lafermerestaurant.com

This "long-standing" Chevy Chase French bastion's "elegant" farmhouse ambiance along with its "expensive" repertoire of "classic" dishes "prepared to perfection" unite for a "visual and culinary escape" for its largely "older, established" clientele who appreciate the "professional" level of service; regulars' advice to young 'uns: don't dismiss it as "a little passé" because "this old chestnut seems [even] tastier today."

La Fourchette *French*

| 23 | 20 | 23 | $41 |

Adams Morgan | 2429 18th St. NW (bet. Columbia & Kalorama Rds.) | 202-332-3077 | www.lafourchettedc.com

"Providing a calm center" in the "heart of Adams Morgan", this "sweet, little" French old-timer is "just what a bistro should be", proffering "simple" "classics" in an "unpretentious" atmosphere; decorated with an oversized mural, the "cozy" space is "charming" and the service is "fantastic", all adding up to a "terrific value."

La Limeña *Cuban/Peruvian*

| 23 | 14 | 20 | $22 |

Rockville | 765 Rockville Pike (Wootton Pkwy.), MD | 301-424-8066

"Packed" at lunch and weekends, this "unpretentious" Rockville strip-maller is "deservedly popular" for "amazing" Peruvian (and some Cuban) dishes like "outstanding" anticuchos, "exceptional" tamales and "dream"-worthy ceviche; a "family-friendly" atmosphere pervades the simple space decorated with paintings and roof tiles that evoke old Lima, and with "courteous" service and "excellent prices", regulars reckon it's "a grand bargain."

Landini Brothers *Italian*

| 25 | 22 | 23 | $48 |

Old Town | 115 King St. (bet. Lee & Union Sts.) | Alexandria, VA | 703-836-8404 | www.landinibrothers.com

Old Town's "brassy Italian with an established clientele" that includes local notables delivers the kind of "mouthwatering" and "hearty" "old-fashioned" food that leaves you with a "stuffed feeling", even if it costs "much money"; it's "see and be seen" in the "dimly lit", "clubby" interior while its *bellíssimo* patio delights romantics.

Las Canteras Ⓜ *Peruvian*

| ▽ 24 | 22 | 24 | $40 |

Adams Morgan | 2307 18th St. NW (Kalorama Rd.) | 202-265-1780 | www.lascanterasdc.com

Decked with handcrafted artwork and a "cozy" red color palette, this two-story Adams Morgan Andean retaurant/bar offers a "chic" environment for enjoying "flavorful" Peruvian standards – lomo saltado, ceviche, "not-to-be-missed" *parihuela* (seafood soup) – alongside some "interesting" nuevo notions; service is "proficient", and though it's not cheap, there are weekday early-bird specials and half-priced wine on Tuesdays.

Las Tapas *Spanish*

| 24 | 23 | 23 | $39 |

Old Town | 710 King St. (bet. Columbus & Washington Sts.) | Alexandria, VA | 703-836-4000 | www.lastapas.us

It pays to "be adventurous" at this brick-walled Spaniard that "transposes you right into Seville" from Old Town with a "wonderful selection" of "scrumptious", midpriced small plates; "very good" sangria and "quick and friendly" service add to the vibrant atmosphere – and to really get "immersed in the culture", come on Tuesday, Wednesday or Thursday evenings for live flamenco performances.

| | FOOD | DECOR | SERVICE | COST |

La Taberna del Alabardero *Spanish*   26 | 24 | 25 | $62

World Bank | 1776 I St. NW (18th St.) | 202-429-2200 |
www.alabardero.com

The "Rolls-Royce of Spanish" restaurants, this venerable World
Banker takes diners on an "atmospheric mini-trip to Spain" via "opulent" decoration (elaborate chandeliers, lace, gilt accents), "exquisite", "refined" food and a "magnificent" Iberian wine collection, all
of it made "memorable" by a "professional and friendly" staff; yet
it's "open to informality" too: happy-hour "tapas at the bar are a
wonderful bargain", and "sangria on the patio" is a summer delight.

NEW La Tagliatella *Italian*   - | - | - | M

Clarendon | 2950 Clarendon Blvd. (Garfield St.), VA | 571-257-4600 |
www.latagliatella.us

This European chain outpost in Clarendon offers a swank backdrop –
ornate chandeliers, dramatic ceiling, polished wood – for enjoying
thin-crust pizzas with toppings ranging from foie gras to fried eggplant, seemingly endless pasta choices, unique salads and other
Italian entrees; there's also a lively bar scene fueled by cocktails as
well as lots of wine by the glass and beer.

La Tasca *Spanish*   21 | 22 | 20 | $32

Chinatown | 722 Seventh St. NW (bet. G & H Sts.) | 202-347-9190
Rockville | Rockville Town Sq. | 141 Gibbs St. (bet. Beall Ave. &
Middle Ln.), MD | 301-279-7011
Old Town | 607 King St. (St. Asaph St.) | Alexandria, VA | 703-299-9810
Clarendon | 2900 Wilson Blvd. (Fillmore St.), VA | 703-812-9120
www.latascausa.com

"Over-the-top" Iberian decor – stucco walls, mosaics, wrought iron –
plus "deadly" sangria and "fantastic" happy-hour deals make this
"spicy" Spanish chainlet "best enjoyed with groups" who don't mind
it "loud" and "crowded"; a "vast" menu of "reasonably" priced small
plates "offers something for everyone", though some say "sampling
is an adventure" with eats ranging from just "ok" to "excellent."

La Tomate *Italian*   19 | 17 | 19 | $41

Dupont Circle | 1701 Connecticut Ave. NW (R St.) | 202-667-5505 |
www.latomatebistro.com

Early birds at this "wedge-shaped", light-filled Dupont Circle eatery
"get a window corner seat" and "watch the throngs" stroll by or, if
those are taken, snag a table on the "pleasant patio" of this neighborhood Italian "standby"; cheap? no, but its "old favorites" and "interesting new dishes" are "reliably" "well prepared" and served by
an "attentive" crew.

L'Auberge Chez François ⓜ *French*   28 | 27 | 28 | $81

Great Falls | 332 Springvale Rd. (Beach Mill Rd.), VA | 703-759-3800
Jacques' Brasserie ⓜ *French*
Great Falls | 332 Springvale Rd. (Beach Mill Rd.), VA | 703-759-3800
www.laubergechezfrancois.com

This "fairy-tale destination" in Great Falls, VA, is "like a fine wine
that ages beautifully", eternally providing visitors with "wonderful",

"gemütlich" Alsatian cuisine that's in perfect harmony with its "charming", "rustic" farmhouse setting; the "unstuffy" staff "pampers" diners during "long and leisurely" multicourse repasts, and though the air is "rarefied", the prix fixe menu means there's "no wincing" over surprises on the bill; P.S. thrifty types may prefer the more "casual ambiance" of the garden-level brasserie, whose à la carte menu has "less impact on your wallet."

L'Auberge Provençale Restaurant *French*

▽ 26 | 25 | 26 | $86

Boyce | L'Auberge Provençale | 13630 Lord Fairfax Hwy. (Rte. 50), VA | 540-837-1375 | www.laubergeprovencale.com

After touring Virginia's wine country, oenophiles can "come 'home'" to this "beautiful" Boyce retreat for a "magnificent" meal amid "authentic French country style" – there's even a fireplace to warm "chilly nights"; expect a "sophisticated" (and "pricey") prix fixe menu accompanied by "world-class" service in a "comfortable", antiques-filled setting, and, if you "spend the night" (and you should), the "breakfasts are superb."

Lauriol Plaza *Mexican*

21 | 19 | 20 | $28

Dupont Circle | 1835 18th St. NW (T St.) | 202-387-0035 | www.lauriolplaza.com

Relax, "sip a margarita and socialize" because it often "takes awhile to get a table" at this "sprawling", light-filled multilevel Dupont Circle East Mexican – after all, you're competing with "an army of twentysomethings" who down "overflowing pitchers" and some of the "best bang-for-the-peso" chow of its class, all "served with smiles"; purists call it a "factory", but with its "gorgeous roof deck" and ample "people-watching", "no wonder it's mobbed constantly."

Lavandou *French*

23 | 20 | 22 | $45

Cleveland Park | 3321 Connecticut Ave. NW (Macomb St.) | 202-966-3002 | www.lavandoudc.com

"Year after year", this "wonderful neighborhood bistro" brings "joie de vivre" to a "devoted" Cleveland Park clientele with "tasty" French fare (including "tremendous" mussels) bolstered by "charming" service and "excellent" nightly deals like corkage-free Mondays; the "rustic" setting feels like "spending an evening in the countryside in Provence", and if it's "perhaps too cozy" for some – "hope for friendly neighbors."

Layalina *Lebanese/Syrian*

24 | 22 | 22 | $33

Arlington | 5216 Wilson Blvd. (bet. Florida & Greenbrier Sts.), VA | 703-525-1170

"Stupendous" Syrian and Lebanese specialties – like "the freshest meze" and a signature lamb shank dish – are served up in this "atmospheric" Arlington eatery crowded with "celebrating families" and crammed with rugs and artwork that "transport you to Beirut"; it's a warm", "friendly" place, and fans note you'd "pay twice as much elsewhere" for food this good.

Lebanese Taverna *Lebanese* | 23 | 20 | 21 | $29 |

Woodley Park | 2641 Connecticut Ave. NW (bet. Calvert St. & Woodley Rd.) | 202-265-8681
Bethesda | 7141 Arlington Rd. (Elm St.), MD | 301-951-8681
Rockville | Rockville Town Sq. | 115 Gibbs St. (bet. Beall Ave. & Middle Ln.), MD | 301-309-8681
Rockville | Congressional Plaza | 1605 Rockville Pike (Congressional Ln.), MD | 301-468-9086
Silver Spring | 933 Ellsworth Dr. (Georgia Ave.), MD | 301-588-1192
Arlington | 5900 Washington Blvd. (McKinley Rd.), VA | 703-241-8681
Pentagon City | Pentagon Row | 1101 S. Joyce St. (Army Navy Dr.) | Arlington, VA | 703-415-8681
Tysons Corner | Tysons Galleria | 1840 International Dr. (Greensboro Dr.) | McLean, VA | 703-847-5244
www.lebanesetaverna.com

"The hummus will ruin you for all other hummus" at this "small, casual" chain ("that never feels like one") where "the multiple joys of Lebanese cuisine" include "excellent" vegetarian options and "wonderful" meze platters perfect for groups; the "family-friendly" settings are "modern" with "traditional" touches that "don't overdo it", and there's the added attraction of a "great price-to-quality ratio."

Le Chat Noir *French* | 20 | 18 | 20 | $42 |

Upper NW | 4907 Wisconsin Ave. NW (42nd St.) | 202-244-2044 | www.lechatnoirrestaurant.com

"If you have a hankering for crêpes" and other "reliable" bistro fare, this "touch of France" in Upper NW is "a must-try", catering to a "mostly neighborhood" crowd with its simple, "comfortable and low-key" setting and "cordial" service; there's also a "very good" selection of wines, some of which thrifty types point out are offered at half-price on Tuesday and Wednesday (as well as on weekends in the upstairs lounge).

NEW Le Diplomate *French* | - | - | - | M |

Logan Circle | 1601 14th St. NW (Q St.) | 202-332-3333 | www.lediplomatedc.com

Trendy 14th Street NW feels a bit like the Champs-Élysées at Stephen Starr's movie set of a French brasserie, with its zinc bar, tile floors and vintage fittings plus a sidewalk cafe; a menu of Gallic classics completes the scene, along with cocktails, apéritifs, beer and wine, *bien sûr*; P.S. it's been a hit from the get-go, so reserve or go early to nab an outdoor seat.

Ledo Pizza *Pizza* | 23 | 15 | 20 | $17 |

Georgetown | 1721 Wisconsin Ave. NW (S St.) | 202-342-0091
Capitol Hill | 7435 Georgia Ave. NW (Hemlock St.) | 202-726-5336
Bethesda | 10301 Westlake Dr. (Lakeview Dr.), MD | 301-469-6700
Bethesda | Kenwood Station | 5245 River Rd. (Brookside Dr.), MD | 301-656-5336
Wheaton | 2638 W. University Blvd. (Grandview Ave.), MD | 301-929-6111
Arlington | 1035 S. Edgewood St. (bet. Columbia Pike & 11th St.), VA | 703-521-5336

(continued)

Ledo Pizza

Courthouse | 1501 Arlington Blvd. (Fairfax Dr.) | Arlington, VA | 703-528-3570

Falls Church | 7510 Leesburg Pike (Pimmit Dr.), VA | 703-847-5336

Reston | 2254 Hunters Woods Plaza (Colts Neck Rd.), VA | 703-758-9800
www.ledopizza.com

This "cheap-and-cheerful", "tried-and-true" local pizza chain eschews the circular standard in favor of cheesy "squares of pure delight" with "flaky", "buttery", "French pastry dough–quality" crusts, a "tart but sweet" sauce and toppings "piled high"; aside from "nonexistent decor" ("who needs it?"), each location "maintains a single-store atmosphere fairly well" with a "nice family" feel and "quick" service.

Legal Sea Foods *Seafood* | 23 | 20 | 22 | $39 |

Chinatown | 704 Seventh St. NW (G St.) | 202-347-0007

Bethesda | Westfield Montgomery | 7101 Democracy Blvd. (Westlake Dr.), MD | 301-469-5900

Crystal City | 2301 Jefferson Davis Hwy. (23rd St.) | Arlington, VA | 703-415-1200

Tysons Corner | Tysons Galleria | 2001 International Dr. (Greensboro Dr.) | McLean, VA | 703-827-8900
www.legalseafoods.com

"Always a safe choice for a fine meal", this Boston-based piscine purveyor "looks like a chain" but "tastes much better" with "swimmingly delicious" standards, like its "famous" New England clam chowder; "attractive", contemporary settings and "upbeat", "well-trained" staffs make the tabs "reasonable" for the overall "quality."

NEW Le Grenier ● Ⓜ *French* | – | – | – | M |

Atlas District | 502 H St. NE (5th St.) | 202-544-4999 |
www.legrenierdc.com

Part of the Atlas District's growing Restaurant Row, this French bistro from the Le Chat Noir team adds to the scene its midpriced menu of Gallic staples and au courant cocktails; the street-level marble bar plays it sleek, while the second-floor dining room is scattered with thrift-shop finds and attic-sourced treasures.

Leopold's Kafe & Konditorei *Austrian* | 23 | 21 | 18 | $29 |

Georgetown | 3315 M St. NW (33rd St.) | 202-965-6005 |
www.kafeleopolds.com

"You'd think you were in Vienna" when sipping Austrian wines by the "fountain" at this Georgetown cafe/bistro's back alley patio – or ensconced at a window table in its "sleek", "stylish" Euro interior; further "transporting" is the "hearty" fare like bratwurst for lunch and a pastry case for "sophisticated adults" to "salivate over", not to mention the Germanic "efficiency" of the service.

Le Pain Quotidien *Bakery/Belgian* | 21 | 18 | 17 | $22 |

Capitol Hill | 660 Pennsylvania Ave. SE (7th St.) | 202-459-9148

Dupont Circle | Blaine Mansion | 2000 P St. NW (20th St.) | 202-459-9176

(continued)

(continued)

Le Pain Quotidien

Georgetown | 2815 M St. NW (bet. 28th & 29th Sts.) | 202-315-5420
Upper NW | 4874 Massachusetts Ave. NW (49th St.) | 202-459-9141
NEW **Chevy Chase** | 5310 Western Ave. NW (Wisconsin Ave.), MD | 202-499-6785
Bethesda | Bethesda Row | 7140 Bethesda Ln. (Elm St.), MD | 301-913-2902
Old Town | 701 King St. (Washington St.) | Alexandria, VA | 703-683-2273
Clarendon | 2900 Clarendon Blvd. (Fillmore St.), VA | 703-465-0970
www.lepainquotidien.com

"Phenomenal" bread with a "crunchy crust" and "delicate crumb", "fabulous" pastries, "heavenly" chocolate spreads and other "imaginative" bites "perfect for a quick lunch" make these Belgian bakery/cafes "hard not to like"; communal tables and "rustic" decor are "very Euro" – likewise what some call "touch-and-go" service and somewhat "steep" tabs, though many say the "yummy carbs just lift you up and away."

Le Refuge ☒ *French*

26 | 21 | 25 | $47

Old Town | 127 N. Washington St. (bet. Cameron & King Sts.) | Alexandria, VA | 703-548-4661 | www.lerefugealexandria.com
It's "the restaurant that time forgot (and that's not so bad)" say supporters of this family-run Old Towner that's been cooking up "superb" French standards that "warm the soul" for roughly three decades; the "country French"–style dining room may be a "little cramped", but the "cozy atmosphere" is enhanced by "wonderful" service, leading admirers to deem it "worth the splurge."

Levante's *Mideastern*

21 | 19 | 20 | $33

Dupont Circle | 1320 19th St. NW (Sunderland Pl.) | 202-293-3244 | www.levantes.com
"Large portions" and "quality ingredients" make the "reliable" "traditional dishes" like baba ghanoush, dolma and falafel a "good value" at this Middle Eastern oasis near Dupont Circle; service is "cordial", and the sleek, Mediterranean-looking dining room is "vivifying" – throw in a "nice" outdoor terrace and most say it's a "great lunch spot."

Le Zinc Ⓜ *French*

▽ 22 | 21 | 21 | $51

Cleveland Park | 3714 Macomb St. NW (bet. 38th St. & Wisconsin Ave.) | 202-686-2015 | www.lezincdc.com
At this "friendly" Cleveland Park affair, a French menu "with a modern touch" goes hand in hand with the "lively", tin-ceilinged "bistro" setting lined with "wonderful" photos that reflect the proprietor's music-industry roots (as does the "great" playlist); it's "expensive for the neighborhood", but even so most call it a "great new addition."

Lia's ◑ *American/Italian*

21 | 20 | 20 | $39

Chevy Chase | 4435 Willard Ave. (Wisconsin Ave.), MD | 240-223-5427 | www.liasrestaurant.com
Hitting the sweet spot between "neighborhood hang" and "fine dining", Geoff Tracy's Chevy Chase restaurant satisfies all comers with a "great variety" of "consistently tasty" contemporary American-

	FOOD	DECOR	SERVICE	COST

Italian fare served by a "personable" staff in a "sleek", almost "Scandinavian"-looking space; its generally "good price point" is further improved by a "screaming deal" early-bird dinner and some of the "best" happy-hour specials around.

Liberty Tavern ◐ American

| 24 | 20 | 21 | $36 |

Clarendon | 3195 Wilson Blvd. (Irving St.), VA | 703-465-9360 | www.thelibertytavern.com

At this split-level Clarendon New American, an "interesting", "ever-changing" menu and a "wonderful" brunch please folks dining in the "quiet but never dull" Arts and Crafts–style dining room upstairs, while downstairs there's a "happening bar scene of twenty- and thirty-somethings" drinking their way through an "awesome" beer collection and noshing "very serious" pub grub; a "well-trained staff" and "good prices" keep both floors "packed."

Liberty Tree American/Pizza

| ▽ 23 | 17 | 22 | $27 |

Atlas District | 1016 H St. NE (bet. 10th & 11th Sts.) | 202-396-8733 | www.libertytreedc.com

"Keep this place a secret" smile supporters of this "small" Atlas District room with a "cozy" "New England vibe" that may "not [get] a lot of buzz" but does "do nicely with fish", "cracker-thin"-crusted pizza and other American eats; add "above-average" beers and "personal service" to its recommendations for a "quiet" meal "on a street more known for its rowdy bar scene."

Lightfoot American

| 26 | 27 | 23 | $42 |

Leesburg | 11 N. King St. (Market St.), VA | 703-771-2233 | www.lightfootrestaurant.com

There's an "enduring" "sense of history" at this New American in Downtown Leesburg housed in a "beautiful" Romanesque Revival former bank building "gloriously appointed" with cozy fireplaces and Venetian chandeliers – and yet for all its "elegance", there's a "relaxed" atmosphere; satisfied surveyors say the "creative", "delicious" dishes (e.g. "dream"-inducing fried green tomatoes) and "strong service" make it an "excellent place to celebrate", concluding it's "not cheap" but "you get what you pay for."

Lighthouse Tofu Korean

| ▽ 24 | 14 | 18 | $19 |

Rockville | 12710 Twinbrook Pkwy. (bet. Ardennes Ave. & Halpine Rd.), MD | 301-881-1178

"Talk about your great finds", this Korean "comfort-food" kitchen in Rockville pumps out "top-notch" "cheap eats" including "amazing" seafood, meat and veggie tofu stews (they "can't be beat in chilly weather"), "delish" BBQ ribs and other traditional favorites; it "isn't a fancy place", but service is "kind and attentive enough" and the "price is right."

Lincoln ◐ American

| 20 | 23 | 20 | $40 |

Downtown | 1110 Vermont Ave. NW (L St.) | 202-386-9200 | www.lincolnrestaurant-dc.com

The "young, trendy and loud" hit this Downtown New American's bar for "creative and perfectly made" cocktails, then head to the dining room for "conversation" and a "wide variety of decent-tasting" small plates at "great-for-the-waistline" prices that "inhibit" ordering too many; service is "professional", and the decor's "homage" to Honest Abe ("pennied floor", "big white chair") is "fun" if "a bit odd."

Little Fountain Cafe ⓜ *Eclectic* ▽ 23 | 22 | 22 | $42
Adams Morgan | 2339 18th St. NW (Belmont Rd.) | 202-462-8100 | www.littlefountaincafe.com

A "refuge from the glitz and squalor of 18th Street NW" is this "quaint and romantic" subterranean spot where "love and care" go into each "imaginative" Eclectic dish served by the "nice people" who work here; a "decent" wine list (half-price Wednesday nights) and a prix fixe deal seal its "date-night" appeal; P.S. the menu is also available at its upstairs bar, Angles.

NEW Little Ricky's ⓜ *Cuban* - | - | - | M
Brookland | 3522 12th St. NE (bet. Monroe & Newton Sts.) | 202-525-2120 | www.littlerickysdc.com

Energizing the slowly developing Brookland dining scene, this Cuban *paladar* (informal family-run restaurant) offers traditional dishes in a funky setting filled with huge art posters and repurposed fittings; lunch and dinner are served Thursday through Saturday, and there's a Sunday brunch featuring Eclectic fare.

Little Serow ⓢⓜ *Thai* 28 | 19 | 27 | $60
Dupont Circle | 1511 17th St. NW (P St.) | no phone | www.littleserow.com

"Small in size but packed with flavor and flair", chef-owner Johnny Monis' Issan-style Thai in Dupont Circle "transports" taste buds with "intense and unusual", "kick-your-ass spicy" fare; it's "easier on the pocket" than his celebrated Komi (upstairs next door), and you should "check your control freak at the door" of this "superdark" cave and let the "incredibly knowledgeable" staff guide you through the "delicious" set-menu journey.

Local 16 ◐ *American/Pizza* ▽ 17 | 19 | 19 | $27
U Street Corridor | 1602 U St. NW (16th St.) | 202-265-2828 | www.localsixteen.com

An "awesome rooftop bar" and "good music" make this "nightclubby" U Street "hot spot" a meeting ground for "attractive singles"; but food fans say it "deserves a visit before 11 PM too" thanks to "surprisingly good pizza" and its "mission to use local ingredients" in its American fare, backed by dependable service (brunch is popular too).

Logan Tavern *American* 20 | 17 | 18 | $31
Logan Circle | 1423 P St. NW (bet. 14th & 15th Sts.) | 202-332-3710 | www.logantavern.com

There's "nothing too exotic" about this Logan Circle "neighborhood favorite", but the airy, industrial space is "always full of locals" enjoying "hearty" American comfort food in a "friendly, relaxed" atmosphere; it's a "first choice" for pre–Studio Theatre dining and Sunday brunch ("you can't beat the Bloody Marys") – throw in "pretty peoplewatching" and reasonable prices and "what's not to love?"

	FOOD	DECOR	SERVICE	COST

Lost Dog Cafe *Pub Food* | 23 | 18 | 21 | $18 |

Arlington | 2920 Columbia Pike (Walter Reed Dr.), VA | 703-553-7770
Arlington | 5876 Washington Blvd. (McKinley Rd.), VA | 703-237-1552
NEW **Fairfax** | 2729 Merrilee Dr. (Merrifield Ave.), VA | 703-205-9001
McLean | The Commons Shopping Ctr. | 1690 Anderson Rd.
(Magarity Rd.), VA | 703-356-5678
www.lostdogcafe.com

"Every taste" is accounted for at these "funky" eateries with a huge
menu of "darned good" pizza, a "refreshing diversity of sandwiches"
and an "enormous" craft beer selection; pet-lovers "applaud" its "soft
spot for our four-legged friends" (a portion of profits go to dog and cat
rescue), "kids" are "entertained" by the "colorful", "adorable" animal
murals – and everyone else digs the "affordable" tabs and "nicest
staff on earth"; P.S. Washington Boulevard is separately owned.

Lost Society ●▨Ⓜ *American/Steak* | ▽ 18 | 21 | 17 | $41 |

U Street Corridor | 2001 14th St. NW (U St.) | 202-618-8868 |
www.lostsociety-dc.com

"Urban and sexy", this New American steakhouse on U Street is a
"place to see and be seen" – whether imbibing "handcrafted" cocktails
at the rooftop or second-story bars, or in its "romantic-yet-funky" dining room; "interesting" entrees skew comforting, though pricey.

Lucky Corner Vietnamese | 28 | 19 | 23 | $21 |
Cuisine *Vietnamese*

Frederick | 700 N. Market St. (7th St.), MD | 301-624-1005 |
www.luckycornerrestaurant.com

"Pho-get about getting Vietnamese anywhere else in Frederick" de-
clare devotees of this under-the-wire place serving "mouthwatering"
hot pots, noodle dishes and seafood specialties at a "great value";
an "attentive" staff tends to the "cute", simply decorated dining
room that nonetheless is "very small" (it's "great for takeout").

Luke's Lobster *Seafood* | 23 | 14 | 17 | $23 |

Penn Quarter | 624 E St. NW (bet. 6th & 7th Sts.) | 202-347-3355
NEW **Georgetown** | 1211 Potomac St. NW (bet. M & Prospect Sts.) |
202-333-4863
Bethesda | Bethesda Row | 7129 Bethesda Ln. (Arlington Rd.), MD |
301-718-1005
www.lukeslobster.com

"No need to go to Maine" (or to the NYC original) say claw-noisseurs
of the "fresh", "meaty" rolls with "subtle seasoning" at these "mock
lobster shacks" in DC; "lobster costs what lobster costs", which
makes it "pricey" for a counter-serve with "basic" amenities, but
New England rusticators sigh "the only thing missing is the ocean."

Luna Grill & Diner *Diner/Vegetarian* | 19 | 16 | 19 | $22 |

Dupont Circle | 1301 Connecticut Ave. NW (N St.) | 202-835-2280
Shirlington | The Village at Shirlington | 4024 Campbell Ave.
(Quincy St.) | Arlington, VA | 703-379-7173
www.lunagrillanddiner.com

Folks "know what to expect" at this "reliable" Dupont and Shirlington
diner duo: "cheap", "tasty" "comfort food" from a "varied" menu

that offers "something for everyone", vegetarians and "picky eaters" included; "low-pressure" service and "homey", "comfortable" surroundings make them "good for relaxing and talking."

Lunchbox *American*   24 | 19 | 23 | $12

Frederick | 50 Carroll Creek Way (Market St.), MD | 301-360-0580 | www.voltlunchbox.com

Bryan Voltaggio has "struck gold again" with this counter-service luncheonette sporting a posh-"high-school-cafeteria" look near Frederick's "picturesque" Carroll Creek, a few blocks from his flagship Volt; a "nostalgic"-leaning menu of "yummy", "high-quality" sandwiches, salads and soups, plus cookies for dessert, incorporates the owner's considerable "culinary talents", hence your "lunch money is well spent."

Lyon Hall ❶ *French/German*   24 | 19 | 22 | $38

Clarendon | 3100 N. Washington Blvd. (Highland Ave.), VA | 703-741-7636 | www.lyonhallarlington.com

"Meat-heavy" Alsatian "treasures" chased by "unique" beers, all at "reasonable prices", have Clarendon's "trendy who's who" thronging this French-German brasserie, causing its *Midnight in Paris*-like space" to get "crowded and loud" on weekends; "divine" homemade donuts at brunch and "thoughtful" servers are among the touches that attract a "late-thirties set who have enough pride to avoid chain dining."

Mad Fox Brewing Company *American*   20 | 20 | 20 | $25

Falls Church | 444 W. Broad St. (bet. Pennsylvania & Virginia Aves.), VA | 703-942-6840 | www.madfoxbrewing.com

"Foxy for sure", this affordable Falls Church brew-'n'-eatery "lives up to the 'gastropub' moniker" with "made-from-scratch" nosh like "wonderful" pizza and fried pickles that "are a taste of foodie heaven" – still, "beer is obviously the name of the game", with "fantastic" seasonal selections; the "contemporary" space with a 60-ft. bar is "casual", "fun" and ably served by a "personable" staff.

Madhatter ❶ *American/Pub Food*   18 | 20 | 18 | $24

Dupont Circle | 1319 Connecticut Ave. NW (bet. Dupont Circle & N St.) | 202-833-1495 | www.madhatterdc.com

"More of a mad keg party than tea party", this "popular" Dupont Circle American tavern approximates "Alice's Wonderland" with themed decor like white-rabbit prints and a giant floating top hat; "young, hip individuals flock here" for "solid chow" that's just "a step above pub fare" at "reasonable prices" and "great beer", so "go early or get trampled by the post-collegiate meet-market crowd."

Maggiano's Little Italy *Italian*   23 | 22 | 23 | $34

Upper NW | 5333 Wisconsin Ave. NW (Jenifer St.) | 202-966-5500
Tysons Corner | Tysons Galleria | 2001 International Dr. (Galleria Dr.) | McLean, VA | 703-356-9000
www.maggianos.com

"Always good for celebrating", especially with "large groups", these Upper NW and Tysons chain links "never waiver" in providing "full-flavored" "red-sauce" "classics" in portions suitable for "King Kong" at a "fair price"; if the "checkered-tablecloth", wood-paneled rooms seem "noisy" to some, most say they're a "wonderful environment" for a "family-style" meal on account of "smooth" service that makes everyone "feel special."

Magnolias at the Mill *American*   25 | 27 | 25 | $35

Purcellville | 198 N. 21st St. (Main St.), VA | 540-338-9800 | www.magnoliasmill.com

In a "beautiful", "rustic mill" that "reflects its heritage" with "quilts", farming implements and "worn wood", this midpriced New American enclave in Purcellville is an "attractive" stop "after a day in wine country" (or "go cycling first" since it's just off the W&OD Trail); with "excellent" choices that run the gamut "from burgers to steaks and some traditional Southern dishes", all ferried by "friendly" help, most "leave with a smile."

Mai Thai *Thai*   23 | 20 | 20 | $26

Dupont Circle | 1200 19th St. NW (Jefferson Pl.) | 202-452-6870
Georgetown | 3251 Prospect St. NW (bet. Potomac St. & Wisconsin Ave.) | 202-337-2424
Old Town | 6 King St. (Strand St.) | Alexandria, VA | 703-548-0600
www.maithai.us

There are "no real surprises" on the menu at these "bit-more-upscale"-than-the-norm Thai places that turn out "consistently tasty" "standards" delivered "fast" by "accommodating" servers at prices that "won't break the bank" – though there is an "interesting and affordable wine list"; all boast colorful, modern interiors, while the Old Town original has "beautiful views" of the Potomac.

The Majestic *American*   24 | 19 | 23 | $44

Old Town | 911 King St. (bet. Alfred & Patrick Sts.) | Alexandria, VA | 703-837-9117 | www.majesticcafe.com

"Home cookin' like your mama wished" she made (including a kids' menu with a healthy bent) stars at this "casual" Old Town American from the Restaurant Eve team – and for "much less money" than a meal at its fancier big sister; while this venue looks more like a "diner", the "same quality and attention to detail" that marks the brand means that "meatloaf can rise to a gourmet experience", service is "as it should be" and "reservations can be hard to come by" (try the bar).

Makoto ⓜ *Japanese*   27 | 19 | 23 | $78

Palisades | 4822 MacArthur Blvd. NW (U St.) | 202-298-6866

"Leave your shoes – and your ego – at the door" of this tiny Palisades Japanese temple where the "exquisite jewel-box plates" on its multicourse omakase menu come to the table the "chef's way"; the setting is simple and traditional, with "hard" bench seating, but it's "unparalleled in DC" say those who "know the difference", so a little patience and a thick wallet will transport you "half a world away."

Mala Tang *Chinese* | 22 | 18 | 19 | $30 |

Arlington | 3434 Washington Blvd. (Kirkwood Rd.), VA | 703-243-2381 |
www.mala-tang.com

Named for the hot and "numbing" sensation that distinguishes
Sichuan food, this "fun" Arlington eatery is outfitted with special tables for individual hot pots that allows everyone to cook "in their
own style and level of spiciness"; there are also other dishes that
would be found in the Chengdu street stalls depicted in the back wall
mural, all of them offering a "good value for the money."

Malaysia Kopitiam *Malaysian* | 23 | 11 | 18 | $24 |

Dupont Circle | 1827 M St. NW (bet. 18th & 19th Sts.) |
202-833-6232 | www.malaysiakopitiam.com

A "giant" picture menu makes it easy to envision the "tasty", "no-
compromise" Malaysian dishes at this Dupont Circle "jewel" that
connoisseurs claim is the "only place in town that comes close to the
real thing"; there is "no pretense" and "nothing to look at" in the
subterranean digs, but it's still a "bargain."

NEW Malgudi Ⓜ *Indian* | – | – | – | M |

Glover Park | 2400 Wisconsin Ave. NW (bet. Calvert St. &
Observatory Ln.) | 202-333-3120 | www.heritageindiausa.com

The Heritage India talents recently made space in their Glover Park
complex for this midpriced southern Indian concept featuring regional meat and fish dishes as well as plenty of vegetarian choices;
the big-windowed bistro setting on the ground floor offers both restaurants' menus at lunchtime, while at dinnertime it's reserved ex-
clusively for Malgudi patrons (Heritage India diners head upstairs).

NEW Malmaison Ⓜ *French* | – | – | – | E |

Georgetown | 3401 K St. NW (Wisconsin Ave.) | 202-817-3340 |
www.malmaisondc.com

Directly across from Georgetown's waterfront park is this trendy,
modern French dining salon whose rough edges (it's in an old warehouse under an elevated freeway) are smoothed with elegant touches
(lilac-hued settees, huge mirrors); well-regarded DC chef Gerard
Pangaud designed the upscale dining room menu, though wallet-
watchers can grab pastries and light fare in the adjoining cafe area –
and a bar and event space complete the oeuvre.

Mamma Lucia *Italian* | 22 | 16 | 21 | $23 |

Bethesda | 4916 Elm St. (bet. Arlington Rd. & Woodmont Ave.), MD |
301-907-3399

Frederick | Shops of Monocacy | 1700 Kingfisher Dr. (Liberty Rd.), MD |
301-694-2600

Olney | Olney Village Ctr. | 18224 Village Center Dr. (Hillcrest Ave.), MD |
301-570-9500

College Park | College Park Plaza | 4734 Cherry Hill Rd.
(Baltimore Ave.), MD | 301-513-0605

Rockville | Federal Plaza | 12274 Rockville Pike (Rollins Ave.), MD |
301-770-4894

Rockville | Fallsgrove Village Shopping Ctr. | 14921 Shady Grove Rd.
(Fallsgrove Blvd.), MD | 301-762-8805

(continued)

Mamma Lucia

Silver Spring | Blair Shops | 1302 E. West Hwy. (Colesville Rd.), MD |
301-562-0693
www.mammaluciarestaurants.com

Neighborhood folks visit these "reliable" eateries for "generous portions" of "solid standby Italian" and "mmm" "NY-style" pizza served in "very casual" environs or via "quick" takeout; service "varies by location", but the staff generally "makes you feel at home", so if some dissenters deem the food merely "decent", most ask "at these prices, who cares?"

Mandalay *Burmese*

23 | 13 | 19 | $25

Silver Spring | 930 Bonifant St. (bet. Fenton St. & Georgia Ave.), MD |
301-585-0500 | www.mandalayrestaurantcafe.com

This "friendly", "family-run" Burmese in Downtown Silver Spring "artfully combines" "simple ingredients" and "tantalizing spices" for "complex flavors" – and "when they say spicy, they really mean it" (though "wimps" note they can "turn down the heat"); "un-fancy" decor doesn't deter those who dub it "a value eatery"; P.S. there are "tons" of vegetarian and vegan options.

M&S Grill *Seafood/Steak*

22 | 21 | 21 | $38

Downtown | 600 13th St. NW (F St.) | 202-347-1500
Reston | Reston Town Ctr. | 11901 Democracy Dr. (Bluemont Way), VA |
703-787-7766
www.mandsgrill.com

"Less stuffy" little brothers of McCormick & Schmick's, these "reliable" American grills offer "something for everyone" with "consistently" "tasty" if "not inventive" seafood and steaks that "don't cost an arm or leg"; if a few call them "typical businessman's lunch" places, a passel of partisans praise the "comfortable" clubby decor, "effective" service and happy hours with "wonderful selections."

Mandu ● *Korean*

23 | 16 | 20 | $28

Dupont Circle | 1805 18th St. NW (bet. S & Swann Sts.) | 202-588-1540
Mt. Vernon Square/Convention Center | City Vista | 453 K St. NW
(bet. 4th & 5th Sts.) | 202-289-6899
www.mandudc.com

Seoul searchers satisfy Korean "cravings" with "wonderful" dumplings, "sizzling" bibimbop and "dangerous" sojutinis, "all priced right" in a "21st-century hip-hop setting" (Mt. Vernon Square) or in "warmth and intimacy" (Dupont Circle); "efficient yet relaxed" service and happy-hour deals make most want to "man-do it again"; P.S. Mt. Vernon serves a late-night bar menu that includes Asian tacos.

Mannequin Pis *Belgian*

23 | 17 | 19 | $45

Olney | 18064 Georgia Ave. (Olney Laytonsville Rd.), MD |
301-570-4800 | www.mannequinpis.com

This "out-of-the-way" Olney "mussel paradise" offers over a dozen "divine" bivalve preparations (an "art form" they have "perfected") along with other Belgian standbys and, *naturellement,* a "great" selection of imported brews; a few call the service "erratic", but the mellow, wood-paneled dining room is "cozy", which helps make it "worth a visit."

Maple ● Ⓜ *Italian*

| - | - | - | M |

Columbia Heights | 3418 11th S. NW (bet. Monore St. & Park Rd.) | 202-588-7442 | www.dc-maple.com

Light, midpriced Italian fare – bruschetta, panini, pasta and such – soaks up the drinks at this cool 'n' casual Columbia Heights watering hole; as for the liquid refreshment, expect a focus on well-chosen Italian vino (some on tap), craft beers and digestives poured at a gleaming tiger-maple-wood bar.

Maple Ave Restaurant Ⓜ *Eclectic*

| - | - | - | M |

Vienna | 147 Maple Ave. W. (bet. Center St. & Courthouse Rd.), VA | 703-319-2177 | www.mapleaverestaurant.com

This midpriced Eclectic on Vienna's main drag turns out farm-fresh small and large plates (and exciting cocktails) that reflect chef-owner Tim Ma's Asian-Latin sensibility and time at NYC's Momofuku; though it flew under the foodie radar for the first years of its life, now the few tables in its simple, earth-toned room often require reservations; P.S. don't miss the funnel cakes for dessert.

Marcel's *Belgian/French*

| 28 | 26 | 28 | $95 |

West End | 2401 Pennsylvania Ave. NW (24th St.) | 202-296-1166 | www.marcelsdc.com

"Build your own feast" at this "refined" West End modern French-Belgian by choosing from its "expansive" prix fixe menu selections, all of which showcase the "intricacy" and "subtlety" of Robert Wiedmaier's "brilliant" cuisine; factor in "pampering" service and an "elegant", "special-occasion" atmosphere and you get "full value" for the "expensive" tab – for a real deal, there's a pre-theater option that includes shuttle service to the Kennedy Center.

🆕 Mari Vanna ● *Russian*

| - | - | - | E |

Golden Triangle | 1141 Connecticut Ave. NW (bet. Desales & M Sts.) | 202-783-7777 | www.marivanna.ru

A transporting Slavic vibe – courtesy of chandeliers, antique-looking wallpaper, costumed servers and occasional live accordion music – is the hallmark of this themed chain born in St. Petersburg, which recently landed in the Golden Triangle; expensive Russian fare (including caviar) and vodka is on tap in the main dining area on the second floor, which features a balcony overlooking the action in the bar.

Mark's Duck House *Chinese*

| 25 | 11 | 18 | $24 |

Falls Church | Willston Ctr. | 6184 Arlington Blvd. (Patrick Henry Dr.), VA | 703-532-2125 | www.marksduckhouse.com

"Succulent Peking duck" hits a "home run" at this Falls Church Cantonese joint, but it's hardly the only star in a lineup that includes Hong Kong–style dim sum that'll "rock your socks off"; the simple, "bustling" storefront "can get cramped" at times, but just consider the "looong" lines "confirmation that the food is very good"; P.S. duck and pork roasts are sold by the pound for takeout.

	FOOD	DECOR	SERVICE	COST

Mark's Kitchen *Eclectic*

21 | 9 | 18 | $18

Takoma Park | 7006 Carroll Ave. (bet. Tulip & Willow Aves.), MD | 301-270-1884 | www.markskitchen.com

It may "look ordinary", but "there's a reason" this Takoma Park storefront is "packed day and night": it has "a little bit of everything" from "reliable hipster diner food" to Korean fare to "interesting" vegetarian choices and "great" desserts – all at "good value"; the "hip, friendly" staff will keep things "laid-back" amid the "hustle and bustle."

Marrakesh P Street *Moroccan*

▽ 23 | 24 | 21 | $35

Dupont Circle | 2147 P St. NW (bet. 21st & 22nd Sts.) | 202-775-1882

"Fantastic" traditional decor of intricate mosaic tiles, fountains and a souklike scattering of rugs and pillows at this Dupont Circle Moroccan creates a "welcoming" backdrop for "excellent" standards like tagines, couscous and kebabs at "great prices"; it can get "busy", but service is "good", and the nightly belly-dancing performances are "cool."

Martin's Tavern ● *American*

20 | 21 | 21 | $37

Georgetown | 1264 Wisconsin Ave. NW (N St.) | 202-333-7370 | www.martins-tavern.com

"Ghosts of administrations past" haunt this "historic" Georgetown tavern that's been hosting locals, pols and presidents in the "narrow" wooden booths in its "cozy" confines since the New Deal; the "reliably good" American menu, which includes items not found elsewhere (e.g. the signature "hot brown" sandwich), has "endured the test of time", and prices remain "reasonable."

Marvin ● *American/Belgian*

23 | 22 | 20 | $36

U Street Corridor | 2007 14th St. NW (bet. U & V Sts.) | 202-797-7171 | www.marvindc.com

What's going on at this "friendly", midpriced U Street bistro (and homage to Marvin Gaye) is a "delicious" mix of flavors from Belgium and the American South, like "must"-have moules frites and "fantastic" chicken and waffles washed down by a "nice choice of beers"; dine downstairs in a "dark", "cool" setting featuring a mural of its namesake crooner, or "head upstairs" to the "awesome" rooftop for a drink and a bite from the bar menu.

Masa 14 ● *Asian/Pan-Latin*

23 | 22 | 20 | $40

Logan Circle | 1825 14th St. NW (Swann St.) | 202-328-1414 | www.masa14.com

"Creative Latin-Asian fusion" and tapas collide in the little dishes "bursting with flavor" served by a "knowledgeable" crew at this "trendy" late-night Logan Circle "hot spot" from Richard Sandoval (Zengo) and Kaz Okochi (Kaz Sushi); the airy industrial space features a "long concrete bar stocked with plenty of eye candy" in the form of a "spirited, young" crowd; P.S. prices are moderate, but the $35 all-you-can-eat-and-drink brunch is such a "deal", it's almost a "community service."

	FOOD	DECOR	SERVICE	COST

Masala Art *Indian*
25 | 17 | 19 | $34

Upper NW | 4441 Wisconsin Ave. NW (Albemarle St.) | 202-362-4441 | www.masalaartdc.com

The "superb", "authentic" Indian menu at this Upper NW subcontinental includes some regional specialties "not commonly found", piquing purists' interest; its compact storefront space, decorated with native art, is a "modest" backdrop for such "exciting" fare, and while a few say service is "slow" at times, the staff is "pleasant", and there's "great value" to be had, especially at the "bargain" lunch buffet.

NEW Masala Express *Indian*
- | - | - | I

Arlington | 2622 N. Pershing Dr. (bet. Cleveland & Danville Sts.), VA | 703-567-1067 | www.masalaexpress2622.com

This simple storefront cafe/carryout in Arlington dishes up Indian classics with a bit more spice than most; factor in cheap tabs, and its tangy cooking has quickly developed a local following.

Matchbox *American*
23 | 22 | 21 | $29

Capitol Hill | 521 Eighth St. SE (bet. E & G Sts.) | 202-548-0369 ●

Chinatown | 713 H St. NW (bet. 7th & 8th Sts.) | 202-289-4441 ●
NEW U Street Corridor | 1901 14th St. NW (T St.) | 202-328-0369
Rockville | Congressional Plaza | 1699 Rockville Pike (bet. Congressional Ln. & Halpine Rd.), MD | 301-816-0369
NEW Fairfax | 2911 District Ave. (bet. Merrifield Town Ctr. & Strawberry Ln.), VA | 571-395-4869
www.matchboxchinatown.com

"Awesome" wood-fired pizzas with "high-quality" toppings, and "nasty-good" sliders "piled high" with onion straws kindle a blaze of praise for these "go-to" New American "hangouts" – and a "very nice" selection of beer and wine fans the flames; add in "kind" service, chic "industrial"-designer digs and "great prices", and it's no surprise there's often a "wait."

Matisse *French/Mediterranean*
23 | 21 | 22 | $54

Upper NW | 4934 Wisconsin Ave. NW (bet. Ellicott & Fessenden Sts.) | 202-244-5222 | www.matisserestaurantdc.com

"Delightful" French-Med fare is "prepared in a contemporary manner" (i.e. "without a lot of sauces") at this "higher-end" Upper NW retreat, whose "open", "airy" dining room, managed by a "nice" staff, is graced with "soft lighting, copious mirrors and muted decor"; hence, it draws a clientele that skews "a little old", and who enjoy a "quiet dinner" and can afford the "expensive" tabs.

Matuba *Japanese*
23 | 15 | 21 | $32

Bethesda | 4918 Cordell Ave. (bet. Norfolk Ave. & Old Georgetown Rd.), MD | 301-652-7449 | www.matuba-sushi.com
At this Bethesda Japanese "institution" it's easy for regulars to "embarrass themselves" by gobbling so much of the "reliable, classic" fin fare – especially at the "fun" conveyor-belt lunch buffet (the price is "awesome for all-you-can-eat"); the dining area is "plain", but service is "friendly" and "kids" are welcome.

FOOD | DECOR | SERVICE | COST

McCormick & Schmick's *Seafood* | 23 | 22 | 23 | $45

Penn Quarter | 901 F St. NW (9th St.) | 202-639-9330
Golden Triangle | 1652 K St. NW (17th St.) | 202-861-2233
Crystal City | 2010 Crystal Dr. (20th St.) | Arlington, VA | 703-413-6400
Reston | Reston Town Ctr. | 11920 Democracy Dr. (Library St.), VA |
703-481-6600 ◗
Tysons Corner | Ernst & Young | 8484 Westpark Dr. (Leesburg Pike) |
McLean, VA | 703-848-8000
www.mccormickandschmicks.com

"Trusted" by legions for its "wide selection" of "fresh" and "delicious"
seafood dishes, this "quasi-fine-dining" chain wins over fin fans
with a "refined-without-being-snooty" atmosphere and a "hopping
happy hour with good specials"; "very attentive" service and "clubby"
dining rooms create a "relaxing" vibe, leading most patrons to de-
clare the sizable bills "money well spent."

Medium Rare *Steak* | 22 | 18 | 21 | $32

Cleveland Park | 3500 Connecticut Ave. NW (Ordway St.) |
202-237-1432 | www.mediumrarerestaurant.com

This Cleveland Parker "keeps it simple and does it well" with a single
"no-choices" set menu for $19.50, consisting of bread, salad,
"crispy fries" and a dry-aged sirloin cap "done perfectly", plus a "big
surprise: second helpings"; the "friendly" staff herds dishes through
the "noisy" modern bistro or to a patio with "terrific people-watching",
and while add-ons like "smartly selected wines and beers" and "huge"
desserts drive up costs, it's still an "excellent value."

Meiwah *Chinese* | 21 | 17 | 19 | $28

West End | 1200 New Hampshire Ave. NW (M St.) | 202-833-2888
Chevy Chase | Chase Tower | 4457 Willard Ave. (The Hills Plaza), MD |
301-652-9882
www.meiwahrestaurant.com

"Reliable, repeatable results" that "always please" make these
"Americanized Chinese" twins in the West End and Chevy Chase
"hugely popular" – and it doesn't hurt that they're "fairly priced";
floor-to-ceiling windows lend a bright feel to the simple, contemporary spaces, and "speedy" service "will give you whiplash."

Me Jana *Lebanese* | 24 | 21 | 24 | $36

Courthouse | Navy League Bldg. | 2300 Wilson Blvd. (Adams St.) |
Arlington, VA | 703-465-4440 | www.me-jana.com

"Warm", "attentive" staffers go "out of their way to make you feel at
home" at this affordable Arlington Courthouse purveyor of "authentic"
Lebanese specialties and "excellent meze" ("order anything and everything") that make it a perfect "destination for a group"; the contemporary interior, with large windows, is "inviting", and the "nice
atmosphere" continues on the umbrella-shaded sidewalk patio.

Mellow Mushroom *Pizza* | 25 | 20 | 22 | $20

Adams Morgan | 2436 18th St. NW (Columbia Rd.) | 202-290-2778 |
www.mellowmushroom.com

"You'd never know it" was a chain given the location-specific "funky
decor" and calendar of events at this Adams Morgan link in the

psychedelic-themed pizzeria empire; servers aiming to "please without being fawning" sling "excellent" pizzas with "unique, chewy crusts" and "satisfying" piled-high toppings, as well as calzones, salads and an "admirable" draft beer selection.

Menomale *Pizza*

| - | - | - | l |

Brookland | 2711 12th St. NE (Evarts St.) | 202-248-3946 | www.menomale.us

Real-deal Neapolitan pizza, calzones and panuozzos come to restaurant-starved Brookland courtesy of Ettore Rusciano, a Naples-certified maestro pizzaiolo who crafts gourmet pies and more using a wood-fired oven imported from Italy; pair the cheap bites with a smart list of craft brews in the tidy, white-walled bistro with tomato-red accents brightened by a charming picture window.

Meridian Pint ● *Pub Food*

| 20 | 19 | 21 | $24 |

Columbia Heights | 3400 11th St. NW (Park Rd.) | 202-588-1075 | www.meridianpint.com

The "friendly" "bartenders know their brews" at this inexpensive tavern in Columbia Heights, where "rotating" drafts "quench your thirst" in a modern-rustic dining room or a basement den equipped with "draw-your-own-pint" machines; while "mostly known for its beer", it cooks up a full slate of "better-than-average" pub grub.

Merzi *Indian*

| ∇ 20 | 14 | 16 | $12 |

Penn Quarter | 415 Seventh St. NW (bet. D & E Sts.) | 202-656-3794 | www.merzi.com

A "choose-your-own-adventure" approach that's "good, cheap and fast" governs this Penn Quarter counter-serve, where guests choose naan, chaat, rice or salad as a base for "yum" "mix 'n' match" meats, veggies and sauces; its simple modern storefront is a "convenient" stop after visiting nearby museums and the Mall.

Meskerem *Ethiopian*

| 22 | 18 | 20 | $26 |

Adams Morgan | 2434 18th St. NW (bet. Belmont & Columbia Rds.) | 202-462-4100 | www.meskeremethiopianrestaurantdc.com

This "granddaddy of Ethiopian cuisine in Adams Morgan" remains "a good intro" to the "classics" of this affordable genre – sopping up "delicious" meat or vegetarian samplers with "tasty" injera bread is "a fun break to the monotony" of fork-and-knife dining; likewise the traditional hassock seating in the spice-colored triplex, so even if a few sigh that the service seems occasionally "overwhelmed", most are happy to return "again and again."

Mezè ● *Mideastern*

| 24 | 20 | 22 | $39 |

Adams Morgan | 2437 18th St. NW (bet. Belmont & Columbia Rds.) | 202-797-0017 | www.mezedc.com

Adams Morgan's "exotic getaway" is this stylish bi-level Middle Eastern offering a "wide selection" of "delicious" small plates (and a few entrees) washed down by "extraordinary" mojitos that taste even better when they're half-price during the weekday happy hour; a "great late-night menu" plus "open-air" seating and smooth service make for a "reasonably priced", "romantic night out."

Mia's Pizzas *Pizza*

25 | 17 | 20 | $25

Bethesda | 4926 Cordell Ave. (bet. Norfolk Ave. & Old Georgetown Rd.),
MD | 301-718-6427 | www.miaspizzasbethesda.com

"Love the 'za!" say fans of the "wonderful" wood-fired pies with
"beautifully charred" thin crusts and "tangy-sweet tomato sauce" at
this Bethesda "favorite" with solid service; if some say the "small",
airy interior can get "hectic" with "noisy kids", most note that it's
"easy on the wallet", and there's always the patio (and takeout).

Michael's Noodles *Chinese*

22 | 11 | 18 | $19

Rockville | Travilah Sq. | 10038 Darnestown Rd. (bet. Travilah Rd. &
Traville Gateway Dr.), MD | 301-738-0370 | www.michaelsnoodles.com
There are many Taiwanese "dishes you can't find anywhere else" on
the broad-ranging Chinese menu of this simple Rockville storefront,
so foodies skip the General Tso's and "order something unusual" off
the 250-item list; seating is "limited" at this "genuinely delicious
place" with "decent prices", so "come early" or opt for takeout.

NEW Mi Cocina *Mexican*

- | - | - | M

Chevy Chase | The Shops at Wisconsin Place | 5471 Wisconsin Ave.
(bet. Montgomery St. & Wisconsin Circle), MD | 301-652-1195 |
www.micocinarestaurants.com

This Texas-bred Mexican hacienda in Chevy Chase's Wisconsin Place
dishes up traditional eats like tacos and enchiladas at moderate prices;
the contemporary space – with sparkling chandeliers and lots of natural light spilling through the glass-walled bar area – provides a stylish
backdrop for anything from a shopping break to a celebration.

NEW Mi Cuba Cafe *Cuban*

- | - | - | I

Columbia Heights | 1424 Park Rd. NW (bet. Hiatt Pl. & Kenyon St.) |
202-813-3489 | www.micubacafe.com

Havana comes to Columbia Heights at this cheery new storefront
cafe turning out traditional plates – empanadas, ropa vieja, Cuban
sandwiches – at affordable prices; tropical-colored walls and windows painted with palm trees add a Caribbean vibe.

Mike's "American" *American*

26 | 24 | 26 | $31

Springfield | 6210 Backlick Rd. (Commerce St.), VA | 703-644-7100 |
www.greatamericanrestaurants.com

Credit this "classy" Springfield mainstay's "attraction" to its "super-
solid" American fare – be it a "fresh, colorful salad, a tender grilled fish
or a large, juicy steak" – and moderate tabs (you can "eat a lot for a little"); "eager", young servers make it work as well for "family" outings
as for "meeting business associates or just an after-work get-together"
in the "happening" bar, but given its near-universal appeal, there's
nearly "always a wait, so call ahead" to be placed on the list.

Minerva *Indian*

23 | 14 | 18 | $20

Gaithersburg | Grove Plaza | 16240 Frederick Rd. (Shady Grove Rd.), MD |
301-948-9898 | www.minervacuisine.com
Fairfax | 10364 Fairfax Blvd. (University Dr.), VA | 703-383-9200 |
www.minervafairfax.com

(continued)

(continued)

Minerva

Herndon | Village Center at Dulles | 2443 Centreville Rd. (Sunrise Valley Dr.), VA | 703-793-3223 | www.minervacuisine.com

Chantilly | Chantilly Park | 14513 Lee Jackson Memorial Hwy. (bet. Avion Pkwy. & Lee Rd.), VA | 703-378-7778 | www.minervacuisine.com

Especially if you like it "spicy", it's "hard to beat" this Indian chainlet for "authentic" dishes, some of which you "can't find elsewhere", plus a weekday buffet with a "wide variety" of "affordable" options; service reviews are mixed, and interior decoration is "lacking", but large flat-screen TVs make it easy "to catch up on Bollywood movies."

Minh's Restaurant ⓜ *Vietnamese* | 24 | 16 | 18 | $27 |

Courthouse | 2500 Wilson Blvd. (Cleveland St.) | Arlington, VA | 703-525-2828

Its location in an Arlington Courthouse office building "isn't special, but the food is" assert fans of this Vietnamese venue offering a "tremendous variety" of "outstanding" dishes, representing "both Northern and Southern styles"; it "usually isn't too crowded" in the "relaxing", white-tablecloth room, and though a few say service is like "rolling dice", most find it "friendly" and "reasonably" priced.

Minibar by José Andrés ⓜ *Eclectic* | 28 | 21 | 27 | VE |

Penn Quarter | 855 E St. NW (bet. 8th & 9th Sts.) | 202-393-0812 | www.minibarbyjoseandres.com

José Andrés' "rock-my-world" Eclectic "culinary adventure" is now firmly transplanted into new svelte, modernist Penn Quarter digs, which are studded with playful Gaudí-esque touches (thus outdating the Decor rating); the "mind-bending" multicourse meals, prepared by "engaging" chefs, provide an "expensive" "treat of a lifetime", and though it now hosts a whopping 12 people per seating (double its old location), and has a lounge and bar area for dessert, it's still "nearly impossible" to score a reservation.

Mintwood Place ⓜ *American* | - | - | - | M |

Adams Morgan | 1813 Columbia Rd. NW (Biltmore St.) | 202-234-6732 | www.mintwoodplace.com

There's a been-here-forever feel about this convivial, midpriced sophomore in Adams Morgan, showcasing Cedric Maupillier's (ex Central Michel Richard) French-accented American cooking, much of it done in a wood-burning oven; the farmhouse-moderne look (pale wainscoting, antique implements) instills an easygoing ambiance, and there's a sidewalk patio for watching the neighborhood pass by.

Mio Ⓢ *Nuevo Latino* | 26 | 24 | 24 | $41 |

Downtown | 1110 Vermont Ave. NW (L St.) | 202-955-0075 | www.miorestaurant.com

"Creativity and addictive flavors permeate" this high-end Downtown Nuevo Latino thanks to its chef, Giovanna Huyke, who puts an "emphasis on Puerto Rican food"; a "friendly atmosphere" pervades the "stylish" interior accessorized with modern art plus an "active bar scene" fueled by some of "the best mojitos in town."

Mi Rancho *Tex-Mex* | 22 | 18 | 21 | $25 |

Germantown | 19725 Germantown Rd. (bet. Crystal Rock Dr. & Middlebrook Rd.), MD | 301-515-7480
Rockville | Congressional Plaza | 1488 Rockville Pike (bet. Congressional Ln. & Templeton Pl.), MD | 240-221-2636
Silver Spring | 8701 Ramsey Ave. (Fidler Ln.), MD | 301-588-4872
www.miranchotexmexrestaurant.com

The "simple and great-tasting" Tex-Mex at this "comfortable", "un-assuming" chainlet may not blow away anyone who "comes from west of the Mississippi", but portions are "plentiful", margaritas are "fabulous" and "homemade" tortillas are a nice touch; "vibrant colors", "festive" lighting and servers with "constant smiles" are "good for families" – and you "won't go broke" or "go away hungry."

Mitsitam Café *American* | ▽ 23 | 13 | 13 | $24 |

SW | National Museum of the American Indian | 950 Independence Ave. SW (4th St.) | 202-633-7039 | www.mitsitamcafe.com

This "honest-to-goodness gourmet" oasis in the National Museum of the American Indian offers "delicious" seasonal specialties of indigenous peoples (think cedar-planked salmon from the Pacific Northwest and "fantastic" soft tacos from Mesoamerica); it's a "typical cafeteria" ("crowded", you "buss your own trays"), but pros profess it's "the best place to eat on the Mall", only "wishing it stayed open" after museum hours.

Moby Dick *Persian* | 23 | 11 | 17 | $15 |

Dupont Circle | 1300 Connecticut Ave. NW (N St.) | 202-833-9788 ⑤
Georgetown | 1070 31st St. NW (M St.) | 202-333-4400
Bethesda | 7027 Wisconsin Ave. (Leland St.), MD | 301-654-1838
Gaithersburg | Kent Land Ctr. | 105 Market St. (Kentlands Blvd.), MD | 301-987-7770
Germantown | Century Plaza | 12844 Pinnacle Dr. (Century Blvd.), MD | 301-916-1555
Rockville | Fallsgrove Village Shopping Ctr. | 14929 Shady Grove Rd. (Fallsgrove Blvd.), MD | 301-738-0005
Silver Spring | 909 Ellsworth Dr. (Fenton St.), MD | 301-578-8777
Arlington | 3000 Washington Blvd. (Highland St.), VA | 703-465-1600
Fairfax | Fairfax Towne Ctr. | 12154 Fairfax Towne Ctr. (Ox Rd.), VA | 703-352-6226
McLean | 6854 Old Dominion Dr. (bet. Beverly Rd. & Ingleside Ave.), VA | 703-448-8448
www.mobysonline.com
Additional locations throughout the DC area

"Go straight for" the "juicy, flavorful" kebabs (the lamb is "to die for") at this local Persian-style street-eats chain that "never fails" in its quest to produce "off-the-charts-good" faves like "tangy" grape leaves, "delicious" hummus and "melt-in-your-mouth" baklava, all served up in portions "big enough for Ahab and his men"; "no-frills" surroundings may call for carryout, but with this much "bang for the buck", you will "forget about the decor."

Mon Ami Gabi *French*
22 | 21 | 21 | $40

Bethesda | 7239 Woodmont Ave. (bet. Bethesda Ave. & Elm St.), MD | 301-654-1234
Reston | Reston Town Ctr. | 11950 Democracy Dr. (bet. Explorer & Library Sts.), VA | 703-707-0233
www.monamigabi.com

You "may not be in Paris" – just Bethesda or Reston – "but you can pretend for a few hours" at this "lively" and "cute" art deco-esque Gallic chain where the French onion soup is "mouthwatering" and you "can't beat" the steak frites and "excellent wines by the glass"; it's "not inexpensive" – and a few say *non* to a "cacophonous", "Disney-like" atmosphere – but service is "American" (read: "friendly"), and a "loyal following" means "reservations are a must."

Monocacy Crossing ☒ *American*
28 | 21 | 26 | $43

Frederick | 4424 Urbana Pike (bet. Araby Church & Ball Rds.), MD | 301-846-4204 | www.monocacycrossing.com

"Don't let the outside appearance fool you" say Frederick denizens who laud the "fabulous", "innovative" American cuisine (whiskey duck nachos are "out of this world") "elegantly" served at this "unassuming"-looking "farmhouse" on a "country road"; "strong" drinks and somewhat "expensive" tabs make this "simply" decorated "rustic gem" worthy of an "adult-only date night."

The Monocle ☒ *American*
21 | 22 | 24 | $49

Capitol Hill | 107 D St. NE (1st St.) | 202-546-4488 | www.themonocle.com

Peek "behind the curtain" of government at this "old-school" American establishment in the "shadow of the Capitol", where politicians and other powerful faces are "greeted by name", and tourists in its clubby booths feel that they're "sitting in the heartbeat of the USA"; the traditional fare is "darn good" too, but it's the "power" and the "history" that keep this "landmark" humming, especially at lunch; P.S. closed weekends.

Montmartre ☒ *French*
25 | 20 | 23 | $45

Capitol Hill | 327 Seventh St. SE (Pennsylvania Ave.) | 202-544-1244 | www.montmartredc.com

"Which arrondissement are we in?" ask *amis* of this "charmingly French" "sanctuary" on Capitol Hill, where "remarkable", "real-deal" bistro eats like "braised rabbit and escargot" are well "worth" the "not-cheap" price; the "attentive" staff treats guests "like family", albeit in a "small and crowded" room, so in *bonne* weather, many prefer to sit on the patio and "watch passersby."

🆕 Monty's Steakhouse *Steakhouse*
– | – | – | E

Springfield | 8426 Old Keene Mill Rd. (Rolling Rd.), VA | 703-942-8676 | www.montyssteakhouse.com

With its white and airy decor, bistro-esque vibe and diminutive size, this Springfield newcomer dispenses with a host of old-school steakhouse traditions; however, the prime cuts should look familiar to carnivores, as will the hefty price tags.

	FOOD	DECOR	SERVICE	COST

Morrison-Clark Restaurant *American* ▽ 24 | 25 | 24 | $51

Downtown | Morrison-Clark Inn | 1015 L St. NW (11th St.) |
202-898-1200 | www.morrisonclark.com

Set in a "stately" "historic" inn, this Downtown vet remains a "well-kept secret" with "wonderful architecture" – including marble fire-places and crystal chandeliers – that creates a "grand old atmosphere" for enjoying "memorable" New American cuisine served by a solicitous staff; prix fixe dinner options prevent wallet shock.

Morton's The Steakhouse *Steak* 26 | 24 | 26 | $71

Georgetown | 3251 Prospect St. NW (bet. Potomac St. & Wisconsin Ave.) |
202-342-6258
Golden Triangle | Washington Sq. | 1050 Connecticut Ave. NW
(bet. K & L Sts.) | 202-955-5997
Bethesda | Hyatt Regency | 7400 Wisconsin Ave.
(Old Georgetown Rd.), MD | 301-657-2650
Crystal City | Crystal City Shops | 1750 Crystal Dr. (bet. 15th & 18th Sts.) |
Arlington, VA | 703-418-1444
Reston | Reston Town Ctr. | 11956 Market St. (Freedom Sq.), VA |
703-796-0128
www.mortons.com

Sure it's a chain, but this "quintessential" steakhouse has "distin-guished itself" time and again with "power steaks" that "melt in your mouth" and "superb" seafood in "comfortable" traditional digs; with always "impeccable" service, it's perfect for "cutting a deal" – just put it on the "expense account."

Mosaic Cuisine & Café *Eclectic* 23 | 18 | 22 | $25

White Flint | Congressional Shopping Ctr. | 186 Halpine Rd. (Rockville Pike) |
Rockville, MD | 301-468-0682 | www.mosaiccuisine.com

There's no waffling about the focus of this "refreshing" Rockville "concept place" – what with multiple breakfast variations, "sand-wiches on waffles", dessert waffles, etc. – but the affordable menu also includes "divine" soups, salads and "creative" entrees, many with a French accent; "incredibly friendly" servers work a "crowded" dining room of "soothing hues" and "tasteful wall art"; P.S. Wicked Waffle, its counter-serve spin-off Downtown, offers breakfast and lunch items to go.

NEW Mothership Ⓜ *American* - | - | - | I

Columbia Heights | 3301 Georgia Ave. NW (bet. Lamont & Morton Sts.) |
202-629-3034

El Floridano ⓧ *Sandwiches*
Location varies; see website | 202-286-0643 |
www.elfloridanodc.com

The El Floridano food truck recently gave birth to a brick-and-mortar mothership on Georgia Avenue NW, allowing owner Stephan Boillon to expand his offerings with an affordable full menu of French-, Caribbean- and Latin-inspired New American small plates and family-style entrees; the brick-walled, tin-ceilinged space also make a casual setting for downing some craft beer and cocktails; P.S. the sandwich truck is still rolling.

Mourayo *Greek* 25 | 18 | 23 | $45

Dupont Circle | 1732 Connecticut Ave. NW (bet. R & S Sts.) | 202-667-2100 | www.mourayous.com

"Inventive" Greek fare makes this pricey Dupont Circle "culinary find" not "your regular gyro place" – rather, it excels with "fresh fish", "refined" classics and interesting Hellenic wines; "available but unobtrusive" servers keep an even keel in the "unpretentious", "nautically themed" space, resulting in a "simply delightful dining experience."

Mrs. K's Toll House Ⓜ *American* 23 | 24 | 24 | $42

Silver Spring | 9201 Colesville Rd. (Dale Dr.), MD | 301-589-3500 | www.mrsks.com

"One of a kind", this sprawling Silver Spring "institution" has a Tudor "inn"–like setting that's "quaintly elegant" and just right for "highly civilized" (though "pricey") repasts of "interesting" contemporary American cuisine; it's been a "family favorite" with "fabulous" service since the '30s, but these days the winepress room attracts a "younger crowd" that prefers not to "dine with their grandmothers' friends."

Murasaki *Japanese* ▽ 23 | 15 | 20 | $30

Upper NW | 4620 Wisconsin Ave. NW (bet. Brandywine & Chesapeake Sts.) | 202-966-0023 | www.murasakidc.com

"Appearance matters to the chefs" behind the sushi counter at this "well-priced" Upper NW Japanese "neighborhood" spot, which is why the "creative" rolls are not only "tasty" but "good looking"; solid service contributes to its "reliable" reputation, and a "comfortable" patio is a warm-weather alternative to the typical blond-wood interior.

Mussel Bar & Grille ◗ *Belgian* 20 | 17 | 18 | $34

Bethesda | 7262 Woodmont Ave. (Elm St.), MD | 301-215-7817 | www.musselbar.com

"The name says it all" at Robert Wiedmaier's tribute to his Belgian heritage in Bethesda, where "great" mussels flex their stuff alongside a "huge, well-thought-out beer selection" that lubricates a "hopping" bar scene; a few critics plead "they've got to do something about the acoustics" (it's "all hard wood and metal"), but service is solid, and if you dig mussels, "this is the place to go in the 'burbs."

NEW MXDC *Mexican* – | – | – | M

Downtown | 600 14th St. NW (F St.) | 202-393-1900 | www.mxdcrestaurant.com

Texas-born celebrity chef Todd English explores Mexican food and drink at his new, rustic-mod bi-level Downtown venue; tequila tastings at the bar (there are about 100 labels plus high-end salts) prime guests for upscale takes on traditional items like guacamole with lobster, whole grilled fish and housemade tortillas and sauces.

Myanmar Ⓜ *Burmese* ▽ 24 | 11 | 14 | $22

Falls Church | Merrifalls Plaza | 7810 Fairfax Blvd. (Hyson Ln.), VA | 703-289-0013

"Authentic" and "reliably terrific" curries et al attract a following to this "tiny, out-of-the-way" Falls Church Burmese joint; "modest trappings" and service snags that bother some don't deter "adventurous eaters", who assert it's well worth the cheap tabs for this "unique" ethnic food.

Mykonos Grill Ⓜ *Greek* 23 | 22 | 23 | $35

Rockville | 121 Congressional Ln. (bet. Jefferson St. & Rockville Pike), MD | 301-770-5999 | www.mykonosgrill.com

"The warm breeze of the Mediterranean wafts through" this "reliable", "moderately priced" veteran Greek in Rockville, where "wonderful seafood" and "flavorful" specialties are served by "polite", "professional" waiters; dining in the "bright" white-and-blue room is "always a pleasure", though it can get "busy", so "make reservations or come early."

Nage *American/Seafood* 21 | 16 | 18 | $37

Scott Circle | Marriott Courtyard Embassy Row | 1600 Rhode Island Ave. NW (16th St.) | 202-448-8005 | www.nagerestaurant.com

Net "creative seafood dishes" at dinner and "great snacks and drinks for happy hour" (or a "terrific" "bottomless brunch") at this "lively" Scott Circle New American that provides "service with a smile"; the contemporary corporate decor "reminds you that it's a hotel restaurant", but supporters say it offers "better fare than most" such venues.

Nam-Viet *Vietnamese* 21 | 12 | 20 | $24

Cleveland Park | 3419 Connecticut Ave. NW (bet. Macomb & Ordway Sts.) | 202-237-1015

Clarendon | 1127 N. Hudson St. (bet. 13th St. & Wilson Blvd.), VA | 703-522-7110

www.namviet1.com

Standouts like "fabulous" lemongrass chicken and "fantastic" pho that really "hit the spot" star on an otherwise "reliable", "well-done" Vietnamese menu at these long-running "neighborhood gems" in Clarendon and Cleveland Park; a "sincere" staff adds warmth to the "simple", "unassuming" settings, and prices are "more than fair."

Nando's Peri-Peri *Chicken* 22 | 19 | 19 | $17

Chinatown | 819 Seventh St. NW (bet. H & I Sts.) | 202-898-1225

Dupont Circle | 1210 18th St. NW (bet. Jefferson Pl. & M St.) | 202-621-8603

Bethesda | 4839 Bethesda Ave. (bet. Arlington Rd. & Hager Ln.), MD | 301-500-2182

Gaithersburg | Washingtonian Ctr. | 224 Boardwalk Pl. (Washingtonian Blvd.), MD | 240-408-7146

National Harbor | Aloft Washington National Harbor | 191 American Way (bet. Fleet St. & St George Blvd.), MD | 301-686-8388

Silver Spring | 924 Ellsworth Dr. (bet. Fenton St. & Georgia Ave.), MD | 301-588-7280

🆕 **Old Town** | 702 King St. (Washington St.) | Alexandria, VA | 571-858-9945

Pentagon City | 1301 S. Joyce St. (bet. Army Navy Dr. & Hayes St.) | Arlington, VA | 571-858-9953

🆕 **Woodbridge** | 15001 Potomac Town Pl. (Dale Blvd.), VA | 571-659-6340

www.nandosperiperi.com

"Addictive" flame-grilled chicken brings "repeat" customers to this Portuguese–South African chain where "unique" sauces (including

| | FOOD | DECOR | SERVICE | COST |

"fiery" ones "from the depths of hell") and "amazing" sides play able wingmen to the big bird; you "wait in line to order", then the "food is brought to your table" in "pleasant", woody digs – it's an "ingenious fast-food concept" that's "quick, cheap and fun."

Napoleon Bistro *French*   ▽ 24 | 24 | 19 | $36

Adams Morgan | 1847 Columbia Rd. NW (bet. Biltmore St. & Mintwood Pl.) | 202-299-9630 | www.napoleondc.com

This "very French" Adams Morgan spot serving "delicious" mid-priced bistro fare, most notably "excellent" crêpes, features dark walls, black velvet and glowing candles, which help make it a perfect place "for hand-holding and eye-gazing"; if a few are less enamored of the service ("not so great"), most say it's "friendly", and the popular brunch "never disappoints."

Nava Thai *Thai*   26 | 16 | 20 | $25

Wheaton | 11301 Fern St. (Price Ave.), MD | 240-430-0495

"Sublime", "big and bold" curries exemplify the "interestingly un-routine" dining possibilities at this Thai eatery that, along with "real value", make it "well worth the trek to Wheaton"; so worth it, indeed, that there's often a "wait" for a table in its basic, yellow-hued dining rooms where "friendly" servers create a "warm and inviting" feel.

Negril 🗷 *Jamaican*   24 | 13 | 20 | $15

U Street Corridor | 2301 Georgia Ave. NW (Bryant St.) | 202-332-3737
Silver Spring | 965 Thayer Ave. (bet. Fenton & Georgia Aves.), MD | 301-585-3000
www.negrileats.com

"Yeah mon", the "awesome" "homestyle" meals at this Jamaican chainlet bring island flavor to Greater DC and Baltimore via "delicious" beef patties, roti and more; some locations are counter service only, and overall a few suggest the "colorful" decor "could use some help", but staffers are "friendly", and the price "cannot be beat."

New Fortune *Chinese*   23 | 13 | 19 | $21

Gaithersburg | Walnut Hill Shopping Ctr. | 16515 S. Frederick Ave. (Westland Dr.), MD | 301-548-8886 | www.newfortunedimsum.com

"Never-ending carts" of "wonderful" dim sum rush by at a "frenetic pace" at this "huge" Gaithersburg Cantonese during lunchtime hours; the authenticity of its "traditional" dishes is "confirmed" by "lots of Asian diners" at its family-style round tables, and "reasonable" prices won't dent your personal fortune.

New Heights 🗷 *American*   22 | 20 | 20 | $59

Woodley Park | 2317 Calvert St. NW (bet. Connecticut Ave. & 24th St.) | 202-234-4110 | www.newheightsrestaurant.com

Longtime loyalists joke "every time you turn around, there's a new chef" at this "high-end" Woodley Park New American, most recently, the well-regarded Takeshi Nishikawa (ex Volt); service is solid upstairs in the "contemporary Arts and Crafts" dining room, while at the downstairs bar "knowledgeable" mixologists make full use of the "unsurpassed array of gin."

New Kam Fong ● *Chinese*
▽ 25 | 11 | 18 | $28

Wheaton | 2400 University Blvd. (Elkin St.), MD | 301-933-6388

For "excellent" Cantonese fare, including some "exotic dishes", this "friendly" Wheaton storefront is considered "one of the best" and as "authentic" as the "ducks and pigs hanging" in the display case suggest; the simple setup is "brightly" lit, illuminating budget-worthy bills.

Newton's Table *American*
22 | 18 | 21 | $54

Bethesda | 4917 Elm St. (bet. Arlington Rd. & Woodmont Ave.), MD | 301-718-0550 | www.newtonstable.com

The "attractively plated, inventive" New American food "tastes as good as it looks" at chef-owner Dennis Friedman's place in Bethesda; maybe it's "pricey for the 'burbs", and a few find the contemporary ambiance "bland", but with "polished" service and "delicious" food, it's considered by most a "nice addition" to the local scene.

Neyla *Lebanese*
24 | 21 | 21 | $46

Georgetown | 3206 N St. NW (bet. Potomac St. & Wisconsin Ave.) | 202-333-6353 | www.neyla.com

"Sense-tingling" dishes are "designed to be shared" at this "high-end" Lebanese lounge some consider the "best-kept secret in Georgetown"; though a few say it's "overpriced", most are happy to place themselves in the hands of the "accommodating" staff and relax in the "exotic" environs, which include a room "draped like an Arab tent."

Nick's Chophouse *Steak*
21 | 22 | 21 | $44

Rockville | 700 King Farm Blvd. (bet. Gaither Rd. & Piccard Dr.), MD | 301-926-8869 | www.nickschophouserockville.com

Rockville's carnivores gather at this "dependable", "suburban" steakhouse to relish "simple", if expensive, meaty fare served professionally; the light, airy dining room is formal but not fussy, the lounge bar is spacious and, as both are "never very crowded", locals relish it as a "quiet" place for "happy-hour eats" or dinner "at the last minute."

1905 Ⓜ *American*
21 | 22 | 19 | $35

Shaw | 1905 Ninth St. NW (bet. T & U Sts.) | 202-332-1905 | www.1905dc.com

"Get your green fairy on" with the "hot crowd" sipping absinthe at this "hip", "friendly" Shaw "speakeasy" "hidden" upstairs, where you can also sup on upscale Southern-tinged American comfort fare, a switch from French courtesy of a new chef (which may outdate the Food rating); the "dark, cozy" setting, furnished with an "eclectic" mix of fittings and curios (and the happening rooftop space) is "great for a date that you hope will last way past dinner."

NEW Ninnella Ⓜ *Italian*
- | - | - | M

Capitol Hill | 106 13th St. SE (bet. Capitol St. & Massachusetts Ave.) | 202-543-0184

Set in a cozy space with white tablecloths, a fireplace and modern art, this sophisticated Capitol Hill Italian is a romantic spot for a moderately priced meal; it's also unassuming enough for the neighborhood's dog and stroller sets to gather here, especially on the patio.

	FOOD	DECOR	SERVICE	COST

Niwano Hana *Japanese*

Niwano Hana *Japanese*   26 | 16 | 23 | $26

Rockville | Wintergreen Plaza | 887 Rockville Pike (Edmonston Dr.), MD | 301-294-0553 | www.niwanohana.com

No wonder this Rockville Japanese has been a local "favorite" for decades – its "incredible" sushi (both "classic" and "edgy" rolls) always includes "generous, well-proportioned pieces" of "so-fresh" fish; there's "not much maneuvering room" in the "crowded" traditional-looking digs, but that just makes it "feel more like Japan" – besides, the "polite" staff always keeps your teacup "full", and best of all is the "very reasonable price."

Nooshi *Asian*   21 | 15 | 17 | $21

NEW Capitol Hill | 524 Eighth St. SE (bet. E & G Sts.) | 202-827-8832
Golden Triangle | 1120 19th St. NW (bet. L St. & Lingers Ct.) | 202-293-3138
www.nooshidc.com

"All things noodles and sushi" ferried by "rushed but efficient" servers makes this cheap, "consistently good" Golden Triangle Pan-Asian a "crowded" "work-lunch" spot (there's also a newer Capitol Hill location); during the "super-affordable happy hour", however, the "tight" quarters are ceded to a "young, loud" GW crowd bent on "having a good time"; P.S. there's a newer branch upstairs from Capitol Hill's Tash House of Kabob.

NEW NoPa Kitchen + Bar *American*   – | – | – | E

Penn Quarter | 800 F St. NW (bet. 8th & 9th Sts.) | 202-347-4667 | www.nopadc.com

Smart and sophisticated, this new Penn Quarter American brasserie (from the owners of Rasika) boasts an airy, light-filled bar/lounge and chic dining rooms with whitewashed brick walls, which are conducive to casual, business and celebratory meals; the somewhat pricey menu offers a range of options (raw bar, fish, steaks, salads, sandwiches), and there are several private rooms suitable for large groups and events.

Nora ⓩ *American*   26 | 23 | 24 | $65

Dupont Circle | 2132 Florida Ave. NW (R St.) | 202-462-5143 | www.noras.com

"Farm-to-table before it was fashionable" (more than 30 years ago), Nora Pouillon's Dupont Circle New American standard-bearer remains "eternally new" by always treating the "freshest" "local" ingredients with "sophistication" yet "without fuss"; the "adorable" and "intimate" environs, complete with "eavesdropping opportunities", are tended by a staff that "makes you feel like a millionaire", which makes sense given the tab.

Northside Social *Coffeehouse*   22 | 18 | 18 | $16

Clarendon | 3211 Wilson Blvd. (Fairfax Dr.), VA | 703-465-0145 | www.northsidesocialarlington.com

It's "like my own living room" say folks who "camp out on laptops" while sipping "froufrou" java and noshing "great" baked goods and sandwiches at this "hip" "hangout" in Clarendon; those who find it "overpopulated" can ascend to the more "intimate" second-floor wine bar for small plates and vino, but up or down, the vibe is "friendly" and the tabs low.

Nostos ☒ *Greek* | 26 | 24 | 25 | $47 |

Tysons Corner | 8100 Boone Blvd. (bet. Aline Ave. & Gallows Rd.) | Vienna, VA | 703-760-0690 | www.nostosrestaurant.com
This "sparkling" gem in Tysons Corner (a sibling of Mykonos Grill) offers "too many" "tempting" choices for just one meal – from "incredible" lollipop lamb chops to "delightful" fish – claim fans who "go back again and again"; sure, the prices are high, but "even the restrooms are posh" in this "beautifully" designed "modern" setting (light-gray stone walls, interesting art) that's warmed by skilled waiters who can help "navigate the extensive Greek wine list."

Notti Bianche *Italian* | 22 | 17 | 22 | $43 |

Foggy Bottom | George Washington University Inn | 824 New Hampshire Ave. NW (bet. H & I Sts.) | 202-298-8085 | www.nottibianche.com
"What's not to like" about this "intimate" Italian in Foggy Bottom, with a "small" but "pricey" menu that's "well chosen", "well prepared" and well served by a "hospitable" staff in the "quiet", film-poster-bedecked room; the pre-theater prix fixe makes it a "wonderful" go-to "before a Kennedy Center performance."

Oakville Grille & Wine Bar *American* | 21 | 19 | 21 | $44 |

Bethesda | Wildwood Shopping Ctr. | 10257 Old Georgetown Rd. (Cheshire Dr.), MD | 301-897-9100 | www.oakvillewinebar.com
A "quiet, classy neighborhood spot", this Bethesda bistro has a "varied" American menu that strikes some as "old-fashioned" but appeals to the "mix of suits and plaid shirts" and "ladies who lunch", who don't blink at the "premium prices" and appreciate the "lovely" California-heavy wine list; staffers are "unobtrusive" and want to "please diners", making this a "dependable" destination "for stopping after shopping."

Obelisk ☒Ⓜ *Italian* | 28 | 20 | 26 | $98 |

Dupont Circle | 2029 P St. NW (bet. 20th & 21st Sts.) | 202-872-1180
From the antipasto "spectrum of delights" to sweet endings, a "stellar" prix fixe dinner (no à la carte) at Peter Pastan's Dupont Circle Italian soars to "heights taller than the Washington Monument", DC's other obelisk; the "intimate", "informal" townhouse setting allows diners to focus on "what Italian cooking is really about": "simple but expertly prepared food served by pros", which, along with "superb" wines, is "worth every euro."

Occidental Grill & Seafood *Seafood/Steak* | 23 | 24 | 24 | $65 |

Downtown | Willard Plaza | 1475 Pennsylvania Ave. NW (bet. 14th & 15th Sts.) | 202-783-1475 | www.occidentaldc.com
"Washington powers" have been tucking into the "reliably" "terrific" surf 'n' turf for years at this "touch of old-time DC" just steps from the White House, and lined with "portraits of statesmen" peering down from on high; sure, it's "expensive" (as is the small-plates

menu in the attached wine room), but "good service will never go out of style", and "establishment" types affirm it's important "to dine here at least once a year."

Oceanaire Seafood Room *Seafood*   24 | 23 | 24 | $58

Downtown | 1201 F St. NW (bet. 12th & 13th Sts.) | 202-347-2277 | www.theoceanaire.com

Essentially a "steakhouse for fish", this "upper-end" chain seafooder, with links in DC and Baltimore, attracts a "power" crowd with its "invariably delicious and fresh" fish "prepared to perfection" and suited to "business dinners" and "special occasions"; you'll need to "bring your gold card", but it's "money well spent", especially given the "sleek", "elegant" setting (think 1930s steamliner) and "fabulous" happy hour.

Olazzo *Italian*   24 | 19 | 22 | $29

Bethesda | 7921 Norfolk Ave. (bet. Cordell & St. Elmo Aves.), MD | 301-654-9496
Silver Spring | 8235 Georgia Ave. (bet. Silver Spring & Thayer Aves.), MD | 301-588-2540
www.olazzo.com

"Terrific lasagna" is the highlight of the menu at this Bethesda–Silver Spring duo owned by a pair of brothers who serve up "delicious" Italian fare and "jump in" to help out with the "delightful" service; with such rustic, flatteringly lit digs, plus "spectacular" martinis, it's perfect for "date night" and "reasonably priced" to boot.

Old Angler's Inn *American*   20 | 24 | 20 | $58

Potomac | 10801 MacArthur Blvd. (Stable Ln.), MD | 301-365-2425 | www.oldanglersinn.com

An "incomparable" setting near the C&O Canal in Potomac sets a "romantic" mood throughout this old favorite – out on the "divine" terrace or informal beer garden, inside for drinks by the "roaring fire" or up narrow stairs in the dining rooms; though "expensive", the "well-served", "quality" New American fare keeps it a great "special-occasion" (or any occasion) place.

Old Ebbitt Grill ◗ *American*   23 | 24 | 23 | $42

Downtown | 675 15th St. NW (bet. F & G Sts.) | 202-347-4800 | www.ebbitt.com

Imagine if the "walls could talk" at this "iconic" DC tavern "convenient" to the White House, since day and night its vast space "bustles" with an "interesting" mix of "tourists" and "politicos" seated in the "rich, paneled" "Victorian"-style rooms or perched at the "long, stately bars"; happily, the "tasty" American menu "fits all budgets" – on the low end, check out the "excellent" burgers and "one of the best happy-hour deals for oyster-lovers" around.

Old Glory All-American BBQ ◗ *BBQ*   19 | 15 | 18 | $28

Georgetown | 3139 M St. NW (bet. 31st St. & Wisconsin Ave.) | 202-337-3406 | www.oldglorybbq.com

"At the crossroads of crowded and delicious" lies this Georgetown BBQ joint beloved by "coeds and tourists", where the "old-fashioned" ribs and such, "multiple" sauces and standard sides sometimes take a backseat to the "college scene" and "watching a game"; while the ephemera-filled space is "nothing fancy", it's been around for over two decades – and the rooftop seating is mighty appealing.

Old Hickory Steakhouse *Steak*   ∇ 26 | 26 | 24 | $111

National Harbor | Gaylord National Hotel | 201 Waterfront St. (St. George Blvd.), MD | 301-965-4000 | www.gaylordhotels.com
"Superb steaks and wonderful, imaginative sides", together with "excellent cheeses" cared for and served by a dedicated "cheese sommelier", make this lesser-known steakhouse in the Gaylord National Hotel something of a destination dinner spot; the light and elegant environs evoke a Georgetown mansion, so the "expensive" bill should not come as a surprise (it's "worth it"); P.S. "get a window seat" to enjoy views of the Potomac.

100 Degree Chinese Cuisine *Chinese*   24 | 21 | 22 | $30

Fairfax | Fair Ridge Ctr. | 3903 Fair Ridge Dr. (bet. Fairfax County Pkwy. & Ox Rd.), VA | 703-537-0788 | www.100degreehot.com
"As the name implies, the spicy specialties are the best" at this Hunan standard-bearer in Fairfax, where a roomful of people enjoying family-style meals is a testament to the menu's "authenticity"; "reasonable" prices, a staff that "really cares" and a "modern" "minimalist Asian" setting featuring multicolored lanterns and a wall sculpture add up to a real "neighborhood find."

Oohh's & Aahh's ∌ *Southern*   ∇ 23 | 7 | 17 | $21

U Street Corridor | 1005 U St. NW (bet. 10th & 11th Sts.) | 202-667-7142 | www.oohhsnaahhs.com
At this U Street soul food "pit stop", "down-home" Southern fare in helpings that would "easily serve two" "make up" for its "nothing-to-write-home-about" decor; some moan that it's "overpriced", but BYO helps compensate, and the staff is "nice and friendly."

Open City ⦿ *Diner*   21 | 17 | 20 | $21

Woodley Park | 2331 Calvert St. NW (24th St.) | 202-332-2331 | www.opencitydc.com
"Quality" diner fare at a "decent price" – from "pizza to all-day breakfast" seasoned with "just the right amount of funk" – has a mix of "zoo tourists", "locals" and "conventioneers" "crowding" into this eatery in Woodley Park; despite its "bustling" nature, the service is generally "attentive" in the airy, tin-ceilinged interior and out on the "lovely" patio.

The Orchard ⊠Ⓜ *Eclectic*   25 | 22 | 25 | $24

Frederick | 45 N. Market St. (Church St.), MD | 301-663-4912 | www.theorchardrestaurant.com
An "oasis" in Downtown Frederick for its "lighter-than-most" menu of "organic and local" eats (stir-fries, salads, veggie/vegan choices), this Eclectic eatery works for a casual "first date" or a "girls' night out"; the "homey" storefront has a "charming" atmosphere, "always great" service and budget prices that speak to a "real find."

Oriental East *Chinese*
23 | 14 | 16 | $23

Silver Spring | 1312 East-West Hwy. (Colesville Rd.), MD | 301-608-0030 | www.orientaleast.com

"Crowds stretch out the door and down the sidewalk on weekends" for the "delicious" "value"-priced dim sum at this Silver Spring Chinese, which fans claim is worth braving the "zoo" for; there's "not much decor", and the staff "isn't there to exchange pleasantries", but the food arrives "rapidly" and "piping hot", so really the "hardest part is deciding when to stop"; P.S. pros show up well before opening time on weekends.

Original Ledo Restaurant *Italian/Pizza*
24 | 15 | 20 | $18

College Park | 4509 Knox Rd. (Yale Ave.), MD | 301-422-8122 | www.ledorestaurant.com

A "local favorite" since 1955, this pizza joint in College Park maintains a devoted following thanks to pies that are "unique from the cheese to the crust", which is rich, flaky and "rectangular"; it's still priced like yesteryear and family-owned, and though in a newer, "nondescript" location, that doesn't stop "loyalists" from returning for "slices you don't have to fold" and "Italian-American food too."

Oro Pomodoro *Italian/Pizza*
21 | 18 | 20 | $29

Rockville | Rockville Town Sq. | 33 Maryland Ave. (bet. Beall Ave. & Middle Ln.), MD | 301-251-1111 | www.oropomodoro.com

"Delicious" pizza, certified by the Verace Pizza Napoletana Association, "is the star", though the other Italian "selections are worth considering" too at this Rockville Town Square spot that reminds guests of a "sophisticated city pizzeria in Roma", especially on the "pleasant" patio in the venue's central piazza; inside, an "impressive" bar dominates a glitzy gold-toned room where "timely" service and "reasonable" tabs please most.

Osteria Elisir ⑤ *Italian* (fka Elisir)
▽ 26 | 24 | 23 | E

Penn Quarter | 427 11th St. NW (bet. E St. & Pennsylvania Ave.) | 202-546-0088 | www.elisirrestaurant.com

Enzo Fargione's Penn Quarter Italian showcase was recently tweaked, expanding its menu to offer many more affordable options in addition to its higher-end items; along with this change, the setting now has a somewhat more casual, rustic feel (out with the white tablecloths, in with wine barrels and agricultural artifacts).

Oval Room ⑤ *American*
26 | 23 | 25 | $69

Golden Triangle | 800 Connecticut Ave. NW (bet. H & I Sts.) | 202-463-8700 | www.ovalroom.com

Deep "in lobbyist territory" close to the White House, this "sophisticated" New American trades in "inventive" dishes served with "panache and style", at prices that may "not be for the 99%"; still, it's a "great experience" dining among "power" in the "quiet and understated" green-and-red (but not oval) room, with tables spread "far enough apart for good conversation."

	FOOD	DECOR	SERVICE	COST

Oya *Asian*   24 | 27 | 22 | $45

Penn Quarter | 777 Ninth St. NW (H St.) | 202-393-1400 |
www.oyadc.com

"Fireplaces, mirrors, glass and white leather" give a "Vegas" vibe to
this "gorgeous" resto-lounge in Penn Quarter pairing "creative sushi" and Asian fusion fare "done right" with an "off-the-wall" wine
list; such a combo of "hip and chic" means it's *"très cher"*, but it's
also a "great first-date" location, with service that provides "attention without hovering"; P.S. the lunch and dinner prix fixe deals
"can't be beat."

Oyamel ● *Mexican*   25 | 22 | 21 | $42

Penn Quarter | 401 Seventh St. NW (D St.) | 202-628-1005 |
www.oyamel.com

"No burritos or chimichangas here!" cheer fans of the "delightful,
creative" tapas and street food given "a typical José Andrés twist"
(e.g. grasshopper tacos "you'll jump for") at this high-end Penn
Quarter Mexican with a "funky", "loud" atmosphere; some say that
service, while "friendly", "doesn't match the quality of the food", but
for most, niceties like "super-strong" margaritas and the "edible entertainment" of guacamole made tableside extend the fiesta feeling;
P.S. it recently expanded next door, doubling the size of its bar and
adding an avant-garde lounge area plus more tables, possibly
outdating the Decor rating.

Ozzie's Corner Italian ● *Italian*   24 | 24 | 24 | $31

Fairfax | Fairfax Corner | 11880 Grand Commons Ave.
(Monument Wall Way), VA | 571-321-8000 |
www.greatamericanrestaurants.com

"Fresh housemade pasta" is a favorite of the "delicious" fare that
comes in "plentiful" portions at this Fairfax Corner "Italian with a
twist", where the "price is right"; the "big" space feels "cozy" on
account of comfy red-leather booths and "welcoming" staff that
"makes you feel at home"; P.S. there are no reservations at busy
times, but "phone ahead to get on the seating list."

Pacci's Neapolitan Pizzeria *Pizza*   23 | 19 | 21 | $24

Silver Spring | 8113 Georgia Ave. (Sligo Ave.), MD | 301-588-1011 |
www.paccispizzeria.com

In the "wasteland" of Maryland pizza, the "soupy, yummy tomato-
and-cheese goodness" atop a "delicious thin crust" produced by this
Silver Spring pie-maker is regarded as "top of the line", and is supported by a "very passable" wine selection; add in "friendly" service
and a "warm", "cozy" brick-lined setting, and one can make an "inexpensive date happen" here.

Pacci's Trattoria & Pasticceria Ⓜ *Italian*   ▽ 23 | 17 | 19 | $24

Silver Spring | 6 Post Office Rd. (Seminary Rd.), MD | 301-588-0867
Housed in Forest Glen's historic old Post Office & General Store
building, this "neighborhood Italian" (a sibling of Pacci's Neapolitan
Pizzeria) remains somewhat "undiscovered"; but locals report a
"limited" menu featuring "very nice pastas" plus "beautiful, inexpen-

sive treats to quench your wine palate", all for an affordable price in rustic, wood-beamed digs.

Palena *American*   27 | 22 | 24 | $98

Cleveland Park | 3529 Connecticut Ave. NW (bet. Ordway & Porter Sts.) | 202-537-9250 | www.palenarestaurant.com

"Ambrosia fit for the gods" is on the menus at Frank Ruta's Cleveland Park New American, and fans swear the "quiet", "dimly lit" back room's prix fixe (no à la carte) is "worth" the "expense", while noting the "casual" front cafe is "one of the best bargains in town", with its "succulent" burgers, entrees and a bread basket "worth paying for" – and, indeed, they do charge; service matches the kitchen's "high competency", and a market annex sells "superb" desserts and savories.

The Palm *Steak*   25 | 21 | 25 | $69

Dupont Circle | 1225 19th St. NW (bet. M & N Sts.) | 202-293-9091
Tysons Corner | 1750 Tysons Blvd. (Rte. 123) | McLean, VA | 703-917-0200
www.thepalm.com

The "famous, rich and powerful" crowd these "classic", "clubby" steakhouse chain spots near Dupont Circle and in Tysons Corner, famed for their "superb" chops, "excellent" wine and "outstanding" service; "you never know who you might see" at the next table (or gazing down from the wall in "caricature" form), just "don't expect to hear your own thoughts" above the "noise", and bring a "full" wallet.

Panache Restaurant ⊠ *Mediterranean*   21 | 20 | 19 | $45

Golden Triangle | 1725 Desales St. NW (bet. Connecticut Ave. & 17th St.) | 202-293-7760
Tysons Corner | Pinnacle Towers S. | 1753 Pinnacle Dr. (Chain Bridge Rd.) | McLean, VA | 703-748-1919
www.panacherestaurant.com

Glamorous and grown-up, these stylish Med spots in the Golden Triangle and Tysons Corner boast "generous", "varied" tapas selections, suited to "share with friends" at the "chic", "hopping" bars backed by "awesome" staffers – or there's a full menu for a "cozy dinner for two"; "nice" servers, upscale prices and an "interesting" red-and-white color scheme rule at both locations.

Panjshir *Afghan*   ▽ 25 | 19 | 25 | $28

Falls Church | 924 W. Broad St. (West St.), VA | 703-536-4566 | www.panjshirrestaurant.com

Far-flung fans "schlep to Falls Church just to eat" at this "outstanding" Afghan stalwart, many of them praising "the most amazing *kadu* (pumpkin)"; a "lovely and welcoming" staff brightens the simple, traditionally decorated storefront, and "nice prices" seal the deal.

Paolo's *Californian/Italian*   21 | 19 | 21 | $36

Georgetown | 1303 Wisconsin Ave. NW (N St.) | 202-333-7353 ◐
Reston | Reston Town Ctr. | 11898 Market St. (Reston Pkwy.), VA | 703-318-8920
www.paolosristorante.com

A "reliably good" range of "well-prepared" pizza, pasta and mains make these "sleek" Cal-Ital spots in Georgetown and Reston Town

Center solid "standbys", but it's the standout "perfect" salads and "addicting" free "breadsticks and olive tapenade" that keep many "coming back"; "friendly personnel", moderate prices and "awesome" happy hours are added draws.

NEW Park Tavern *American*

- | - | - | M

Southeast | Canal Park | 202 M St. SE (2nd St.) | 202-554-0005 | www.parktaverndc.com

This new American watering hole takes full advantage of its setting in the Capitol Riverfront district's Canal Park, with plenty of outdoor seating among the park's sculptures and greenery; huge windows and a living wall garden also bring the outside into the large dining and bar space, where a tavern menu (appetizers, flatbreads, seafood and meats) complements fancy cocktails, beer and wine.

Parkway Deli *Deli*

22 | 11 | 19 | $19

Silver Spring | Rock Creek Shopping Ctr. | 8317 Grubb Rd. (Blaine Dr.), MD | 301-587-1427 | www.theparkwaydeli.com

"Where else can you find a tongue sandwich" inside the Beltway? ask lovers of this "low-priced" Jewish deli in Silver Spring, with "huge" "classic" sandwiches and other "traditional" noshes delivered by an "efficient" staff; a few kvetch it "comes up short" "if you're from NYC", and critique the "tacky" decor, but most say it's still "good after all these years" – and, hey, you "can't beat the [free] pickle bar!"

Pasha Cafe *Mediterranean*

∇ 23 | 17 | 24 | $29

Cherrydale | 3911 N. Fairfax Blvd. (Pollard St.) | Arlington, VA | 703-528-1111 | www.pashacafe.com

Boosters applaud "excellent food in an unlikely location" at this Mediterranean in a Cherrydale strip mall, which gets props for its Greek salads and pita sandwiches; the "casual", wood-accented digs are served by "friendly" staffers who "don't rush" customers, and "prices are just right" for a "neighborhood" restaurant.

Passage to India *Indian*

24 | 22 | 23 | $38

Bethesda | 4931 Cordell Ave. (bet. Norfolk Ave. & Old Georgetown Rd.), MD | 301-656-3373 | www.passagetoindia.info

"Entering the mosiac tile door" of this "upscale" Bethesda Indian, one senses its "authenticity", and indeed, its "divided-by-region" menu presents "perfectly spiced" dishes "rarely seen" elsewhere; for most who have booked passage, "gracious" treatment in a setting appointed with "colonial elegance" further "justifies the price."

PassionFish *American/Seafood*

26 | 24 | 24 | $52

Reston | Reston Town Ctr. | 11960 Democracy Dr. (Explorer St.), VA | 703-230-3474 | www.passionfishreston.com

"Downtown flair and finesse" pervade this seafood-focused American "showplace" in Reston, where "fresh, delicious, well-seasoned" choices "aren't just a rehash of classic fish dishes" (look for "Asian influences" and "amazing" sushi); even if "it ain't cheap", service is "top-notch", and its "Miami-like" bi-level space is "open, airy and always inviting", and consequently favored as a "date location" or "high-end after-work dinner."

	FOOD	DECOR	SERVICE	COST

Pasta Mia 🖉Ⓜ⌷ *Italian* · 26 | 14 | 16 | $27

Adams Morgan | 1790 Columbia Rd. NW (18th St.) | 202-328-9114
"Beautiful Bolognese and ravishing ravioli" in "portions that will last
you all week" is the rich reward for the "pain" of waiting in the "club-
style line" outside this dinner-only Adams Morgan Italian "institution"
and abiding by its rigid rules (e.g. "cash only", "no substitutions");
with its "impersonal" service and humble "red-and-white checker-
board tablecloths", it's maybe "not for first dates", but "terrific"
prices keep the hordes "coming back."

Paul *Bakery* · 22 | 19 | 18 | $19

Penn Quarter | 801 Pennsylvania Ave. (bet. 7th & 9th Sts.) | 202-524-4500
Golden Triangle | 1000 Connecticut Ave. NW (K St.) | 202-524-4860
NEW Foggy Bottom | 2000 Pennsylvania Ave. NW (I St.) | 202-524-4655
Georgetown | 1078 Wisconsin Ave. NW (bet. Grace & M Sts.) |
202-524-4630
NEW McLean | Tysons Galleria | 2001 International Dr.
(Tysons Blvd.), VA | 571-447-5600
www.paul-usa.com
"Ooh-la-la", it's "like being in a Parisian cafe" – "even the cashiers
say '*merci*'" – aver fans of this "authentic" French bakery import that
fills "baguette sandwich cravings" and leaves "no time to diet" with
its "buttery", "rich" pastries; if some say it's "not cheap" for what it
is and complain of "disorganized" service, dedicated Francophiles
"bliss" out with the "beautiful bread" on the "comfy" sofas and chairs.

Peacock Cafe *American* · 22 | 20 | 22 | $36

Georgetown | 3251 Prospect St. NW (bet. Potomac St. &
Wisconsin Ave.) | 202-625-2740 | www.peacockcafe.com
A "Georgetown institution" for "girls' night outings" or "ladies' lunch",
this "consistent" performer satisfies with its midpriced, "tasty"
American dishes and solid wine selection, with over a dozen by the
glass, served by a "fine" crew; there's good "people-watching" too,
in the "trendy", industrial-lite digs (and outside, weather permitting).

Pearl Dive Oyster Palace *Seafood* · 26 | 23 | 23 | $42

Logan Circle | 1612 14th St. NW (bet. Corcoran & Q Sts.) |
202-319-1612 | www.pearldivedc.com
This "skyrocketing" new "superstar" from the Black Restaurant
Group, near Logan Circle, is crewed by an "outstanding" staff that
serves up "superb" oysters and other "fabulous" seafood-centric
fare with a "distinctly Gulf Coast focus", like "rich and satisfying"
gumbos; with its crumbling "New England"–boardwalk look, it's a
"very cool place to hang your hat", and though pricey, "if they took
reservations", some "would probably spend all their money here";
P.S. the upstairs bar is a "fun" place to wait and play bocce.

Peking Duck Restaurant Ⓜ *Chinese* · 28 | 18 | 23 | $35

Greater Alexandria | 7531 Richmond Hwy. (Woodlawn Trail) |
Alexandria, VA | 703-768-2774 | www.pekingduck.com
No canard, "authentic barely begins to describe" this venerable but
unassuming-looking Peking duck specialist "all the way out" near

Fort Belvoir in Greater Alexandria, where the roasted fowl is sliced "in front of you" just "like in Peking" (er, Beijing); if that doesn't sound ducky, ask the "superb" staff for "suggestions" (hint: "delicious" soups), and have no fear of the bill – it won't bite.

Peking Gourmet Inn *Chinese*

25 | 17 | 22 | $35

Falls Church | Culmore Shopping Ctr. | 6029 Leesburg Pike (Glen Carlyn Rd.), VA | 703-671-8088 | www.pekinggourmet.com

"Duck in early to avoid huge crowds" clamoring for this "premier" Pekingese purveyor's signature bird, "crisp", "delicate" and "beautifully served tableside" by real "pros" in a sprawling, "old-fashioned" space in Falls Church; if a few feel it's "overpriced", most say it's "worth it" – heck, even Democrats agree that "there's more to this restaurant than the pictures of ex-presidents" ("Bush I and Bush II") on the wall.

Perrys ◐ *Asian*

22 | 22 | 22 | $45

Adams Morgan | 1811 Columbia Rd. NW (Biltmore St.) | 202-234-6218 | www.perrysadamsmorgan.com

"A delightful trip" away from Adams Morgan beckons diners up the stairs at this neighborhood destination where "prompt" servers tend a "warmly decorated" room, ferrying contemporary Asian fare and sushi (a recent switch from an American menu outdates the Food rating); there's a "totally different feel" on the "fabulous" roof deck, with its "little lights" and cityscape views, while "Sunday brunch will literally pull you" up out of your seat (there's a boisterous drag show).

Persimmon *American*

- | - | - | M

Bethesda | 7003 Wisconsin Ave. (bet. Leland & Walsh Sts.), MD | 301-654-9860 | www.persimmonrestaurant.com

This well-regarded Bethesda New American bistro was recently rebooted with a cheaper, more casual approach to its menu, though it still includes old favorites; it also added a skylight, larger front windows and white walls, giving it a brighter look, which is punctuated by pops of color from oversize canvases of fruits and vegetables.

Pesce ⌧Ⓜ *Seafood*

26 | 17 | 23 | $50

Dupont Circle | 2002 P St. NW (bet. Hopkins & 20th Sts.) | 202-466-3474 | www.pescedc.com

Regine Palladin's "firm hand on the tiller" keeps her Dupont Circle seafooder on its "excellent, creative", "fin-tastic" course; the simple, airy sliver of a space is a "delightful retreat from Washington's bustle", in which servers provide "reliable advice" about the "best available" "fish you've never heard of" on the chalkboard menu – in short, for the "quality", it's a relative "bargain."

Pete's New Haven Style Apizza *Pizza*

22 | 14 | 17 | $20

Columbia Heights | 1400 Irving St. NW (14th St.) | 202-332-7383
Upper NW | 4940 Wisconsin Ave. NW (Fessenden St.) | 202-237-7383
Clarendon | 3017 Clarendon Blvd. (bet. Garfield & Highland Sts.), VA | 703-527-7383
www.petesapizza.com

New Haven–style 'za – "the way God intended", with "slightly scorched" bottoms – keeps this inexpensive, "gourmet" pizzeria mini-chain "swarming with kids", though more grown-up palates also report "fantastic" salads, market-driven antipasti, pastas and brews; folks order at the counter and are served at tables by staffers who "move things along" in the "light and airy" spaces.

Petits Plats *French*   ▽ 22 | 18 | 21 | $48

Woodley Park | 2653 Connecticut Ave. NW (bet. Calvert St. & Woodley Rd.) | 202-518-0018 | www.petitsplats.com

This "adorable" bistro in a converted Woodley Park house takes diners "back to France" with its "cravable" mussels, steak frites and the like (there's also sandwiches on "fresh" baguettes for a take-out lunch); relax by one of the fireplaces, bask in attention from a "wonderful" owner who "takes good care of his clientele" and appreciate prices that are "decent" given the sizable quality of the *plats*.

P.F. Chang's China Bistro *Chinese*   23 | 23 | 22 | $30

Chevy Chase | Shops at Wisconsin Pl. | 5046 Wisconsin Ave. (Williard Ave.), MD | 301-654-4350

White Flint | White Flint Mall | 11301 Rockville Pike (Edson Ln.) | Rockville, MD | 301-230-6933

Ballston | Arlington Gateway | 901 N. Glebe Rd. (Fairfax Dr.) | Arlington, VA | 703-527-0955

Fairfax | Fairfax Corner | 4250 Fairfax Corner Ave. (Monument Dr.), VA | 703-266-2414

Tysons Corner | Tysons Galleria | 1716 International Dr. (bet. Galleria Dr. & Tysons Blvd.) | McLean, VA | 703-734-8996

Sterling | Dulles Town Ctr. | 21078 Dulles Town Circle (Nokes Blvd.), VA | 703-421-5540

www.pfchangs.com

"Tantalizing" "twists" on Chinese food (including the "famous", "addictive" lettuce wrap) in a "classy", "cool" Asian-inspired setting, plus "agreeable" service and "affordable" tabs add up to an "unbeatable combination" at this "upscale" Chinese chain; while maybe "not for the purist", it's a "regular favorite" for many, including families, groups and those who appreciate the "awesome" gluten-free items, though few relish the sometimes "horrendous" waits.

Phillips *Seafood*   20 | 19 | 20 | $39

SW | 900 Water St. SW (9th St.) | 202-488-8515 | www.phillipsseafood.com

See review in the Baltimore Directory.

Pho 14 *Vietnamese*   25 | 17 | 22 | $15

🆕 **Adams Morgan** | 1769 Columbia Rd. NW (bet. Adams Mill & Ontario Rds.) | 202-986-2288

🆕 **Golden Triangle** | 4201 Connecticut Ave. NW (Van Ness St.) | 202-686-6275

Columbia Heights | 1436 Park Rd. NW (bet. 14th St. & Hiatt Pl.) | 202-986-2326

www.dcpho14.com

Whether it's the "best pho in Columbia Heights" or "in the District" (or "this side of the Pacific"), many agree there's an "extra little bit of something" that sets apart this "neighborhood place" – even the veggie pho "has really complex flavors"; "quick and polite" servers deliver "super-value" namesake soups plus "out-of-this-world" banh mi and other traditional eats in a simple storefront nook.

Pho DC *Vietnamese*   ▽ 24 | 21 | 21 | $22

Chinatown | 608 H St. NW (bet. 6th & 7th Sts.) | 202-506-2888 | www.phodc.com

This slim spot in Chinatown serves a variety of "tasty", "inexpensive" Vietnamese specialties, but regulars say that a "large" bowl of "fabulous, steaming pho is the way to go"; the "attentive" staff gets to "know" regulars who frequent the "stylish, little" brick-walled space, complete with a mod wall of color-changing LED lights.

Pho 75 ⊅ *Vietnamese*   24 | 8 | 16 | $13

Langley Park | 1510 University Blvd. E. (bet. New Hampshire Ave. & Riggs Rd.), MD | 301-434-7844
Rockville | 771 Hungerford Dr. (bet. Gude Dr. & Park Rd.), MD | 301-309-8873
Clarendon | 1721 Wilson Blvd. (Quinn St.), VA | 703-525-7355
Falls Church | 3103 Graham Rd. (Woodley Ln.), VA | 703-204-1490
Herndon | 382 Elden St. (Herndon Pkwy.), VA | 703-471-4145
www.pho75.tumblr.com

"A big bowl of steaming-hot love" with "many options for extras" stars on the menu at these local Vietnamese "standard-bearers"; despite decor that makes "elementary school cafeterias look like the Four Seasons", service is "fast" and it's "cheap, cheap, cheap"; P.S. cash only and most locations close at 8 PM nightly.

Pie-Tanza *Pizza*   23 | 16 | 20 | $21

Arlington | Lee Harrison Shopping Ctr. | 2503 N. Harrison St. (bet. Lee Hwy. & 26th St.), VA | 703-237-0200
Falls Church | Falls Plaza Shopping Ctr. | 1216 W. Broad St. (Gordon Rd.), VA | 703-237-0977
www.pie-tanza.com

"Put on Sinatra" to get in the mood for these "cozy", "family-friendly" pizzerias in Falls Church and Arlington that wow "all ages" with thin-crust, wood-fired wonders (they also serve "other Italian favorites"); add in low prices, "extremely nice" servers and open kitchens that allow patrons to see all the pie-making action, and regulars say they "couldn't ask for more out of a small neighborhood" joint.

The Pig *American/Eclectic*   – | – | – | M

Logan Circle | 1320 14th St. NW (bet. North St. & Rhode Island Ave.) | 202-290-2821 | www.thepigdc.com

Pork, unsurprisingly, is the focus at this Logan Circle American-Eclectic spot with a snout-to-corkscrew-tail bent, where the kitchen turns out midpriced fodder such as boar spoonbread; the lofty space has a rustic feel thanks to plenty of repurposed barn lumber.

Ping by Charlie Chiang's *Asian*   23 | 22 | 22 | $28

Shirlington | Village at Shirlington | 4060 Campbell Ave. (Randolph St.) | Arlington, VA | 703-671-4900 | www.charliechiangs.com

This "sleek", "sexy" Asian restaurant/lounge with a "hip clientele" in Shirlington gets buzzy at its "awesome happy hour" on account of its "great drinks list" ("the craft-beer menu puts most bars to shame") and impresses with its "creative" Chinese-leaning fare, plus sushi; "accommodating" staffers love "what they do and it shows", plus the bill "won't chokeslam your wallet."

Ping Pong Dim Sum *Asian* ___21___ ___22___ ___19___ ___$34___

Chinatown | 900 Seventh St. NW (bet. I & K Sts.) | 202-506-3740
Dupont Circle | 1 Dupont Circle NW (bet. New Hampshire Ave. & P St.) | 202-293-1268
www.pingpongdimsum.us

"Ultramodern" settings filled with moody dark lacquer are the first clue that these Dupont Circle and Chinatown Asian venues are "not your normal" dim sum houses, offering instead "creative", "tapas-style" takes on traditional nibbles alongside "gigantic" cocktails ("if you can move past the wonderful teas"); a few call it "kinda pricey" and complain of "uncomfortable" backless seats and "inconsistent" service, but the "urban-chic" vibe keeps most happy, especially "groups."

Piola *Italian/Pizza* ▽ ___21___ ___19___ ___18___ ___$24___

NEW **U Street Corridor** | 2208 14th St. NW (W St.) | 202-986-8729
Rosslyn | 1550 Wilson Blvd. (bet. Oak & Pierce Sts.), VA | 703-528-1502
www.piola.it

Regulars "recommend that you stick with what it does best" and opt for the "fantastic" "thin, crusty" pizza baked in a brick oven with "quality" ingredients at this Italian chain direct from The Boot in Rosslyn (with a new location in DC); service is solid, and a "lively" atmosphere plays well for either "commuter's happy hour" or dine-in, when regulars recommend taking a gander at the month's art installation; P.S. there's a patio too.

Pizzeria Da Marco *Pizza* ▽ ___23___ ___20___ ___22___ ___$25___

Bethesda | 8008 Woodmont Ave. (bet. Cordell & St. Elmo Aves.), MD | 301-654-6083 | www.pizzeriadamarco.net

"No, pizzas are not sliced", and yes, crusts are "charred" and centers a bit "soggy" when they're "authentic" Neapolitans like the "delicious" rounds baked in this Bethesda Italian's imported oven; servers who "really like" their patrons make both the "open, airy" brick-walled room and the "lovely" terrace feel "inviting", and moderate prices, especially the "great-deal" happy hour, make folks positively pie-eyed.

Pizzeria Orso Ⓜ *Pizza* ___22___ ___17___ ___18___ ___$27___

Falls Church | 400 S. Maple Ave. (Tinner Hill St.), VA | 703-226-3460 | www.pizzeriaorso.com

You'll want to "check out the small plates" whipped up by chef Will Artley, who also turns out authentic "cracker-thin" Neapolitan "brick-oven" pizzas at this "casual", sunny Falls Church Italian-influenced kitchen; though a few find service "wanting", this place is "kid-friendly" and "popular" with "parents who like to drink" (Italian margarita, anybody?).

	FOOD	DECOR	SERVICE	COST

Pizzeria Paradiso *Pizza*   23 | 17 | 19 | $26

Dupont Circle | 2003 P St. NW (20th St.) | 202-223-1245
Georgetown | 3282 M St. NW (bet. Potomac & 33rd Sts.) | 202-337-1245
Old Town | 124 King St. (bet. Lee & Union Sts.) | Alexandria, VA |
703-837-1245
www.eatyourpizza.com

These midpriced "pizza nirvanas" in Dupont Circle, Georgetown and
Old Town Alexandria are "delicious enough for serious foodies but still
casual enough for an outing with family and friends"; service is generally "ok" in the "pleasant", "cosmopolitan" brick-walled settings,
and if they tend to get "crowded" and "loud" at times, "beer geeks"
recommend the "ameliorating" powers of the "impressive" brew list.

P.J. Clarke's ● *Pub Food*   18 | 19 | 19 | $38

Downtown | 1600 K St. NW (16th St.) | 202-463-6610 |
www.pjclarkes.com

"Knowledgeable bartenders and an enthusiastic young wait staff"
are on the team of this "road version" of an NYC-based "burgers-
and-beer" joint, strategically located near the White House; some
sniff the "solid but not great" food means there are "better places to
drop your bar-food dollars", but the clubby, dark-walled environs offer a "chill atmosphere" in which to "meet for drinks"; P.S. there's a
more limited version of the menu upstairs at Sidecar.

Plaka Grill *Greek*   24 | 13 | 19 | $18

Vienna | 110 Lawyers Rd. NW (Lawyers Rd.), VA | 703-319-3131 |
www.plakagrill.com

It's "worth a trip to the suburbs" of Vienna for "soulful", "value"-
priced Hellenic cooking, including some of "the best gyros around"
("stuffed with fries!") and hummus that "must be whipped by the
goddess Hestia herself"; a picturesque mural of a Greek street
scene provides a bit of color to the "tiny", "not-fancy" cafe setting
that's serviced by "fast and friendly" help.

Plume ⓩⓂ *American*   26 | 28 | 29 | $109

Downtown | The Jefferson | 1200 16th St. NW (M St.) |
202-448-3227 | www.plumedc.com

"Not just a feather in the [Hotel] Jefferson's cap but a full plume"
enthuse guests who exalt this "impeccably dressed restaurant with
a gracious and elegant personality" crafting "superb", classically
grounded New American food inspired by Thomas Jefferson's gus-
tatory interests; there's also an "unbelievable" cellar that would
have impressed the oenophilic founding father himself, but as so
much "marble and gilt" signify, "expect to open up the wallet."

Policy Ⓜ *American*   22 | 19 | 19 | $35

U Street Corridor | 1904 14th St. NW (T St.) | 202-387-7654 |
www.policydc.com

"Interesting and tasty" midpriced New American small plates plus
"innovative" cocktails and craft beer draw the "hipster" 14th Street
NW crowd to this "urban destination" with a "fab interior" sporting
diner-esque red booths on the lower level, a "graffiti-glam" lounge

upstairs and several outdoor spaces; a few report being "under-whelmed" by the service, but most find the staff "friendly" and agree that it's a "great place to go with friends."

Pollo Campero Central American
19 | 12 | 17 | $11

Columbia Heights | 3229 14th St. NW (bet. Kenyon St. & Park Rd.) | 202-745-0078
Gaithersburg | Lakeforest Mall | 701 Russell Ave. (Odendhal Ave.), MD | 240-403-0135
Takoma Park | International Mall Shopping Ctr. | 1355 University Blvd. E. (New Hampshire Ave.), MD | 301-408-0555
Wheaton | 11420 Georgia Ave. (Blueridge Ave.), MD | 301-942-6868
Falls Church | 5852 Columbia Pike (Moncure Ave.), VA | 703-820-8400
Herndon | 496 Elden St. (Grant St.), VA | 703-904-7500
Manassas | 7913 Sudley Rd. (Lomond Dr.), VA | 703-368-1824
www.campero.com

"Fill up on a budget" at this Latin American "fast-food" franchise specializing in "crisp", "juicy" poultry dispensed with efficiency along with "a large selection" of sides; ok, so maybe the bright-yellow-and-orange interiors are a bit "sterile", and it may "not win any gas-tronomical awards", but legions of "locals looking for a chicken fix" attest that "once you start eating", it's "tough to stop."

Pork Barrel BBQ Restaurant BBQ
∇ 19 | 17 | 16 | $19

Del Ray | 2312 Mount Vernon Ave. (bet. Del Rey & Oxford Aves.) | Alexandria, VA | 703-822-5699 | www.porkbarrelbbq.com
Two former Senate staffers-turned-national BBQ champs run this Del Ray smoker dispensing "good Southern BBQ with some very tasty sides", though service and kitchen bumps lead some to bark it needs to "get its act together"; still, the price is right, even if the setup is "quirky" – the bar is full-service, but for food you "order at the counter and then find a table" in the "retro" room.

Poste Moderne
20 | 22 | 20 | $50

Brasserie American/French
Penn Quarter | Hotel Monaco DC | 555 Eighth St. NW (bet. E & F Sts.) | 202-783-6060 | www.postebrasserie.com
Hotel Monaco's French–New American "hidden enclave" reveals a "gorgeous" courtyard patio "perfect for summer canoodling" and a "trendy" yet "quiet" dining room; its latest chef, Dennis Marron (ex The Grille), puts a "thoughtful", "sustainable" spin on seasonal menus and, yes, it's "pretty pricey", but "good" service and "subtle mixology" help ease the sting, and there are "values" at lunch.

Posto Italian
23 | 20 | 22 | $46

Logan Circle | 1515 14th St. NW (bet. P & Q Sts.) | 202-332-8613 | www.postodc.com
Before saying 'bravo' next door at Studio Theatre, practice saying "*buono*" at this "delicious" but "pricey" Italian near Logan Circle, a spin-off of Penn Quarter's Tosca; the "open, bright" "contemporary" digs "can get noisy", but "quality" service and a pre-theater menu help keep it a before-curtain "favorite."

	FOOD	DECOR	SERVICE	COST

Praline *Bakery/French* — 23 | 16 | 20 | $38

Bethesda | The Shops at Sumner Pl. | 4611 Sangamore Rd. (Sentinel Dr.), MD | 301-229-8180 | www.praline-bakery.com

Its "suburban shopping-center" setting "might mislead", but "just try to stop the flakes from flying" when you bite into what are arguably the "best croissants in Greater DC" say fans of this "little slice of Paris" in Bethesda that, while not cheap, will "save you airfare" overseas; upstairs from the bakery/cafe, "bistro classics" are well served in a sunny setting, but better yet is a rendezvous in the "lovely", "easygoing" rooftop patio.

Present Restaurant *Vietnamese* — 26 | 23 | 25 | $32

Falls Church | 6678 Arlington Blvd. (Annandale Rd.), VA | 703-531-1881 | www.presentcuisine.com

"Sleeping Duck on the Golden Pond" and other "poetic names" "lyrically" describe the "creative" dishes at this "surprising" Vietnamese "oasis" that brings "upscale" dining at a "reasonable cost" to an "unlikely" location in a Falls Church strip mall; step inside and walk past the "fountain" to an "elegant" dining room where "attentive" waiters are always happy to "explain" the menu.

Pret A Manger *Sandwiches* — 19 | 13 | 18 | $14

Chinatown | 1155 F St. NW (bet. 11th & 12th Sts.) | 202-464-2791
Downtown | 1399 New York Ave. (14th St.) | 202-393-0533
Downtown | 1432 K St. NW (15th St.) | 202-559-8000 ☒
Golden Triangle | 1828 L St. NW (bet. 18th & 19th Sts.) | 202-689-1982 ☒
Golden Triangle | 1701 K St. (17th St.) | 202-857-7945
Golden Triangle | 1825 I St. NW (bet. 18th & 19th Sts.) | 202-403-2992 ☒
Capitol Hill | Union Station | 50 Massachusetts Ave. NE (F St.) | 202-289-0186
www.pret.com

"Why can't American fast food be this tasty?" ask fanciers of this British import making waves for its "always fresh" "grab-and-go" sandwiches, salads and soups (plus "delish" cookies); though "somewhat expensive for a sandwich", most agree it's "worth it", citing "convenience", "friendly" counter service and "nice" metal-trimmed interiors.

Prime Rib ☒ *Steak* — 28 | 26 | 28 | $71

Golden Triangle | 2020 K St. NW (bet. 20th & 21st Sts.) | 202-466-8811 | www.theprimerib.com
See review in the Baltimore Directory.

Primi Piatti ☒ *Italian* — 19 | 16 | 20 | $52

Foggy Bottom | 2013 I St. NW (20th St.) | 202-223-3600 | www.primipiatti.com

This Foggy Bottom Italian trattoria's owner occasionally performs "remarkable table-to-table magic tricks", but some in the audience feel there's a bit of "pizzazz missing" from the "solid", "genuinely good" fare that nonetheless "never disappoints"; it's "inviting" inside among mirrors and marble, and "pleasant" on the patio, even if it's on the "pricey" side.

Proof *American*

24 | 23 | 23 | $56

Penn Quarter | 775 G St. NW (bet. 7th & 8th Sts.) | 202-737-7663 | www.proofdc.com

"Find your own 'proof'" of this Penn Quarter New American's virtues via its "wonderfully original" food paired with "amazing" wines in "noisy", "sexy" and "dark" modern rusticity ("good for a date on which you want to lean in to 'hear better'", not so good to "read the menu"), where "power brokers and tourists collide"; "knowledge-able" servers and "savvy wine" pros "impress the 1%", while its $14 lunch special (entree plus a glass of wine) pleases the proletariat.

NEW Protein Bar *Health Food*

- | - | - | I

Penn Quarter | 398 Seventh St. NW (D St.) | 202-621-9574
Ballston | 800 N. Glebe Rd. (Wilson Blvd.) | Arlington, VA | 571-970-1573 🛱
Golden Triangle | 1011 19th St. NW (K St.) | 202-887-0100
www.theproteinbar.com

Protein-focused eats on the cheap (and on the go) is the m.o. of this Chicago-based chain with outlets in DC and Ballston; bodybuild-ers, health-conscious types and the gluten-averse are muscling their way into the streamlined industrial digs for all-day breakfast, burrito alternatives, chili, salads and quinoa bowls plus a variety of blended drinks.

Pulpo *Spanish*

- | - | - | M

Cleveland Park | 3407 Connecticut Ave. NW (bet. McComb & Ordway Sts.) | 202-450-6875 | www.pulpodc.com

This ambitious Spanish taperia in Cleveland Park serves a midpriced menu that runs the gamut from Iberian wine-bar classics to bites of newfangled molecular gastronomy; the interior aesthetic is loftlike and dimly lit, with exposed brick and an open kitchen overlooking several communal tables.

Pupatella Pizzeria 🛱 Ⓜ *Pizza*

26 | 15 | 19 | $19

Arlington | 5104 Wilson Blvd. (Edison St.), VA | 571-312-7230 | www.pupatella.com

"Incredibly authentic", "mighty good" pizza with a "perfectly charred" crust and "just the right balance of toppings" earns this "friendly" Arlington Neapolitan pie-and-fry (it also serves rice balls and cro-quettes) the top pizza rating in Greater DC; the "arty", graffitied space doubled in size post-Survey and added table service (possibly outdat-ing its Decor and Service ratings), and the prices are easy to stomach; P.S. the original Ballston food truck operates at special events.

Queen Vic *British*

▽ 23 | 21 | 21 | $23

Atlas District | 1206 H St. NE (bet. 12th & 13th Sts.) | 202-396-2001 | www.thequeenvicdc.com

"Quick-witted" publicans pull "superb" drafts and dish up "melt-in-your-mouth" Sunday roast, fish 'n' chips and other inexpensive forms of "traditional" British "comfort" at this Atlas District tavern; an "Old English" vibe pervades the dark-wood digs, and there's an at-tached tuck shop selling imported staples like McVitie's and Ribena.

FOOD | DECOR | SERVICE | COST

Quench *American*

`-` | `-` | `-` | `M`

Rockville | Traville Village Ctr. | 9712 Traville Gateway Dr.
(Shady Grove Rd.), MD | 301-424-8650 | www.quenchnation.com
This sleek entry in Rockville's Traville Village Center slakes MoCo
thirsts with craft cocktails and muddles in moderately priced, contemporary American bar bites, sandwiches and mains; the loungey
digs are decidedly more urbane, with faux-animal skin rugs and cut-
off logs serving as rustic tables.

Rabieng *Thai*

`25` | `17` | `22` | `$30`

Falls Church | Glen Forest Shopping Ctr. | 5892 Leesburg Pike
(Glen Forest Dr.), VA | 703-671-4222 | www.rabieng.com
Duangrat's "baby brother", this midpriced Falls Church Siamese
is around the corner in humbler yet "cozy" digs and does its elder
proud with "delicious" Northern Thai specialties and weekend Thai
dim sum; "thoughtful waiters who warn" patrons about spicing levels establish a "relaxed" environment for sampling unusual dishes,
so the only "problem is trying something new – because you want to
get what you had the last time."

NEW Radius Pizza *Pizza*

`-` | `-` | `-` | `I`

Mt. Pleasant | 3155 Mt. Pleasant St. NW (Lamont St.) | 202-234-0202 |
www.radiuspizza.com
This Mt. Pleasant pizzeria got a new lease on life thanks to a local
couple, who revived the shuttered space and revamped the affordable menu, tweaking the original pizza recipe and adding more
family-style pastas and appetizers; the simple setting remains much
as it was, with the addition of a decorative map of the neighborhood
on the wall, while a well-stocked bar mixing craft cocktails has am-
plified the bar scene.

Rail Stop Ⓜ *American*

∇ `23` | `19` | `20` | `$48`

The Plains | 6478 Main St. (bet. Bragg St. & Loudoun Ave.), VA |
540-253-5644 | www.railstoprestaurant.com
For "great food in horse country", this "tiny", "country-casual"
American in The Plains fits the bill with a "homespun" menu that
does the chef "proud"; it's "pricey", but that doesn't stop enthusiasts from declaring it a "real treat" with "friendly" service; P.S. don't
miss the patio or the toy train that circles above diners' heads.

Raku *Asian*

`23` | `18` | `20` | `$34`

Dupont Circle | 1900 Q St. NW (19th St.) | 202-265-7258
Bethesda | 7240 Woodmont Ave. (bet. Bethesda Ave. & Elm St.), MD |
301-718-8681
www.rakuasiandining.com
With "sushi down to a science" and a "great variety" of other
Japanese, Chinese and Thai bites "done with aplomb", these
"friendly", "go-to" Asian spots in Bethesda and Dupont Circle make
for a "quick, solidly good, inexpensive meal"; sensitive ears cite
"deafening" noise in the consistently "crowded" contemporary environs that are hung with brightly colored paper umbrellas, so outside
seating is a "nice plus."

NEW Range ◐ American

‒ | ‒ | ‒ | E

Chevy Chase | Chevy Chase Pavilion | 5335 Wisconsin Ave. NW (Western Ave.) | 202-803-8020 | www.voltrange.com

Bryan Voltaggio (Frederick's Volt, etc.) recently planted his flag inside the Beltway with this sprawling Chevy Chase enterprise, where long marble bars, polished wood tables and informal groupings of low-backed booths provide a relaxed yet elegant backdrop for a contemporary American menu, which has a fittingly wide range of food choices and price points; there's also plenty to look at, what with multiple open kitchens and hearth stations – not to mention all the eye candy sipping state-of-the art drinks at the bar.

Rangoli Indian

▽ 24 | 23 | 24 | $27

South Riding | South Riding Market Sq. | 24995 Riding Plaza (Riding Center Dr.), VA | 703-957-4900 | www.rangolirestaurant.us

The "superb" Indian specialties at this sunny-yellow South Riding venue come at a "great price", especially at its "wonderful" lunch buffet; service gets a thumbs-up too, and the overall positive experience has frequenters saying it "should be at the top of everyone's list."

NEW Rappahannock Oyster Bar Ⓜ Seafood

‒ | ‒ | ‒ | M

NoMa | Union Mkt. | 1309 Fifth St. NE (Neal Pl.) | 202-544-4702 | www.rroysters.com

The counter perches at this Chesapeake oyster farmer's new bivalve bar in Union Market are always filled with slurpers chilling out with its raw-bar selections or warming up with crab cakes and chowder; a smattering of small plates rounds out its food offerings, and there's beer, wine and cocktails for liquid refreshment; P.S. it also has a communal table and patio seating.

Rasika ⧄ Indian

28 | 25 | 26 | $51

Penn Quarter | 633 D St. NW (bet. 6th & 7th Sts.) | 202-637-1222
West End | 1190 New Hampshire Ave. NW (M St.) | 202-466-2500
www.rasikarestaurant.com

"Only superlatives" describe the "mind-blowing" "modern Indian" food that gives diners a "mouthgasm" at this "wildly popular", "classy" Penn Quarter destination (and its newer cosmopolitan West End sister) that has diners "salivating" for dishes like its crispy spinach; "luxurious" appointments, "knowledgeable" servers and a sommelier "savant" create a "sophisticated" environment that further makes it a "bargain for the quality" – translation: "plan early" for a reservation at Penn Quarter (West End is roomier) or "eat at the bar."

Ravi Kabob House ⧓ Pakistani

25 | 8 | 14 | $18

Arlington | 250 N. Glebe Rd. (Pershing Dr.), VA | 703-816-0222 Ⓜ
Arlington | 305 N. Glebe Rd. (Pershing Dr.), VA | 703-522-6666 ◐
www.ravikabobusa.com

"Mouthwatering", "wonderfully tasty" kebabs with "all the fixin's" rave devotees of these Greater Arlington Pakistani joints practically across the street from one another; "decor and ambiance are nonexistent", and service is only fair, but no one argues as it's so "cheap", with "quality" that's "much higher than the cost"; P.S. cash only.

Ray's The Classics *Steak*   25 | 19 | 22 | $43

Silver Spring | 8606 Colesville Rd. (Georgia Ave.), MD | 301-588-7297 | www.raystheclassics.com

"Any cut will satisfy" at Michael 'Ray' Landrum's Silver Spring chophouse where "steaks of the highest quality" put the "big boys to shame on price" and are accompanied by "delicious" sides and "bargain" wines; service is generally "attentive", and though the "fancy" white tablecloths are traditional, the decor feels "more gender-neutral than most" steakhouses; P.S. "burgers in the bar" are even more of a "deal."

Ray's The Steaks *Steak*   27 | 18 | 22 | $46

Courthouse | Navy League Bldg. | 2300 Wilson Blvd. (Adams St.) | Arlington, VA | 703-841-7297 | www.raysthesteaks.com

"No-frills deliciousness" sums up Mike 'Ray' Landrum's Courthouse beefeteria that "rays-es the bar on great steaks" at "bargain-basement prices" – the "breathtaking" hunks are served with two sides along with "affordable" wines in "sparse" white surroundings by "knowledgeable", "efficient" servers; "why pay for decor and snootiness at 'fine' steakhouses?" ask acolytes who appreciate "not being nickeled, dimed and dollared", saying this may be the "best restaurant idea in history"; P.S. for those without reservations, there's now an overflow space next door under the moniker Retro Ray's.

Ray's To The Third *American/Steak*   25 | 14 | 22 | $31

Courthouse | 1650 Wilson Blvd. (bet. Pierce & Quinn Sts.) | Arlington, VA | 703-974-7171 | www.raystothethird.com

"Ray's a toast" – with a glass from the "superior-for-a-neighborhood-place" wine selection – to Michael 'Ray' Landrum's "bistro version" in Courthouse that features steak frites "done very well" at prices that "can't be beat"; its unassuming premises are also home to his Ray's Hell Burger menu (now that that concept has closed) as well as "excellent" shrimp and chicken, and decadent shakes.

NEW Red Apron Butchery *American*   – | – | – | I

NoMa | Union Mkt. | 1309 Fifth St. NE (bet. Neal Pl. & Penn St.) | 202-524-6807 Ⓜ
Merrifield | Mosaic District | 8298 Glass Alley (bet. District Ave. & Eskridge Rd.), VA | 703-676-3550
www.redapronbutchery.com

Eco-conscious, whole-animal butchery is the hallmark of this affordable meat market and dining spot in Merrifield's Mosaic District and DC's Union Market (the latter is closed Monday and Tuesday); craft beer and wine accompanies meaty sandwiches, charcuterie and all manner of housemade salumi to eat in or take home.

NEW The Red Hen Ⓜ *Italian*   – | – | – | M

Bloomingdale | 1822 First St. NW (Seaton Pl.) | 202-525-3021 | www.theredhendc.com

This midpriced modern Italian arrival in burgeoning Bloomingdale offers creative cooking (unusual handmade pastas, items from a

| | FOOD | DECOR | SERVICE | COST |

wood grill, appetizers that do duty as small plates) plus cocktails and wines; natural light floods the high-ceilinged room with a raw, rustic feel courtesy of exposed brick and aged wood, plus there's an open kitchen and a centerpiece bar topped with embossed orange leather.

Red Hook

| 25 | 12 | 20 | $20 |

Lobster Pound *New England/Seafood*

Location varies; see website | 202-341-6263 | www.redhooklobsterdc.com

"People actually chase these food trucks" to "cure the urge" for a "succulent", "chunky" lobster roll offered "Maine-style with mayo or Connecticut-style with butter" ("the toughest call of the day"), with a whoopie pie to follow; "lines can be very long", making it hard for some folks to "justify the cost", while "longtime fans" advise: check its whereabouts online and "go early."

Red Hot & Blue *BBQ*

| 22 | 18 | 20 | $21 |

Gaithersburg | Crabbs Branch Plaza | 16811 Crabbs Branch Way (Shady Grove Rd.), MD | 301-948-7333

Greater Alexandria | 6482 Lansdowne Ctr. (Beulah St.) | Alexandria, VA | 703-550-6465

Rosslyn | 1600 Wilson Blvd. (Pierce St.), VA | 703-276-7427

Fairfax | 4150 Chain Bridge Rd. (Judicial Dr.), VA | 703-218-6989

Falls Church | Tower Sq. | 169 Hillwood Ave. (Douglass Ave.), VA | 703-538-6466

Herndon | 2403 Centreville Rd. (Sunrise Valley Dr.), VA | 703-870-7345

Manassas | 8366 Sudley Rd. (Rixlew Ln.), VA | 703-367-7100

Leesburg | Bellewood Commons | 541 E. Market St. (Sycolin Rd.), VA | 703-669-4242

www.redhotandblue.com

If you're "hard up for Memphis-style barbecue", this "trustworthy" chain will "scratch" the "itch" say boosters who praise "finger-licking" mains like "must-try" pulled pork and "catfish that makes a Delta-lover happy"; interiors are "nothing fancy", but service is "timely" and tabs are "inexpensive", so it's a "super place" to "get messy."

RedRocks *Pizza*

| 21 | 18 | 20 | $22 |

Columbia Heights | 1036 Park Rd. (11th St.) | 202-506-1402

Old Town | 904 King St. (bet. Alfred & Patrick Sts.) | Alexandria, VA | 703-717-9873

NEW **Arlington** | 2501 Ninth Rd. S. (Columbia Pike), VA | 703-920-0706

www.redrocksdc.com

"Tasty artisanal pizzas in the Neapolitan style" and an "excellent" beer and cocktail menu draw admirers to this inexpensive eatery with "welcoming" service; the Columbia Heights branch sports a "pleasure" of a patio and a "go-to" brunch, while the more spacious Old Town location features an open kitchen and the industrial-looking Arlington entry has a big bar.

Redwood *American*

| 19 | 22 | 18 | $42 |

Bethesda | Bethesda Row | 7121 Bethesda Ln. (bet. Bethesda Ave. & Elm St.), MD | 301-656-5515 | www.redwoodbethesda.com

"Wonderful for alfresco dining" on the "shaded" patio, this "solid" American "respite" in Bethesda attracts a ladies' lunch crowd that also enjoys sipping vino and "sitting by the big open windows" in the "contemporary" redwood-accented dining room; some find it "a bit pricey" and service "slow at times", but most "can't stay away" because it's just so darn "pleasant."

The Regent *Thai*

∇ 24 | 20 | 21 | $29

Dupont Circle | 1910 18th St. NW (bet. Florida Ave. & T St.) | 202-232-1781 | www.regentthai.com

This "flavorful" midpriced Thai in Dupont Circle with "terrific presentation" is favored for its "dark", "chic" atmosphere and "interesting" mixed drinks; those who like to linger also note that with "warm", "friendly" service, there's "no rush" to get you out.

Renato at River Falls *Italian*

22 | 17 | 20 | $47

Potomac | 10120 River Rd. (Falls Rd.), MD | 301-365-1900 | www.riverfallsseafood.com

Something of a "local club" for its tony Potomac neighbors, this "intimate" suburban ristorante "consistently" does Italian fare "well and with the best ingredients", including seafood from the co-owned fish market next door; its "friendly" staff facilitates the mealtime gatherings that make this place a "highlight" of the area's social scene, to whom it's "pricey" but "worth it."

Ren's Ramen ⊟ *Japanese/Noodle Shop*

∇ 24 | 11 | 14 | $15

Wheaton | 11403 Amherst Ave. (University Blvd.), MD | 301-693-0806 | www.rens-ramen.com

Forget about the much-maligned dorm-room staple – the "soul-satisfying", "authentic" Japanese ramen of this "one-dish Wheaton powerhouse" may be "the best soup you have ever had" with its "amazing pork-based broth" (or veggie broth option); but "be prepared to wait" at peak times, since "crowding tends to slow things down" in this "small", minimally decorated spot; P.S. cash only.

Restaurant Eve ⊠Ⓜ *American*

27 | 25 | 26 | $86

Old Town | 110 S. Pitt St. (bet. King & Prince Sts.) | Alexandria, VA | 703-706-0450 | www.restauranteve.com

"You don't just dine" at Cathal Armstrong's "pitch-perfect" Old Town New American, you get a taste of "perfection" as you are "cosseted" in "plush" banquettes in the "romantic" tasting room, where "personalized" multicourse menus evince the chef's "passion" and "attention to detail"; or head to the connecting bistro and bar to "savor the delicious food" on the cheap – it offers à la carte choices and, at lunch, there's a two-course "bargain" prix fixe for around $15.

Ricciuti's *Italian*

24 | 21 | 22 | $32

Olney | 3308 Olney Sandy Spring Rd. (Georgia Ave.), MD | 301-570-3388 | www.ricciutis.com

A "gem of a place" in a "warm, cozy old house", this Italian spot charms Olneyites with "foodie" sensibilities with its "wonderful", seasonal small and large plates plus brick-oven pizzas; a staff that's "willing to please" ensures that diners "never feel rushed", setting a "peaceful" tone for many a "date night."

| | FOOD | DECOR | SERVICE | COST |

Rice *Thai*

22 | 19 | 20 | $33

Logan Circle | 1608 14th St. (bet. Corcoran & Q Sts.) | 202-234-2400 | www.ricerestaurant.com

"Terrific Thai classics" meet with "a twist of art and experimentation" at this midpriced Logan Circle "date spot" where every dish "impresses"; low lighting and an exposed-brick and earth-toned interior lend a "cool NYC vibe", though "friendly" service "with a big smile" runs warm; P.S. while its sibling, DC Noodles, is temporarily closed, its menu is served here daily at lunch and Thursday–Sunday at dinner.

Rice Paper *Vietnamese*

‒ | ‒ | ‒ | I

Falls Church | Eden Ctr. | 6775 Wilson Blvd. (bet. Arlington & Roosevelt Blvds.), VA | 703-538-3888 | www.ricepaper-tasteofvietnam.com

A stylish, glitzy setting belies the serious, traditional cookery at this Falls Church Vietnamese in Eden Center; its inexpensive menu of multiregional classics intrigues experts as well as beginners, and features hard-to-find broken-rice dishes.

Ripple *American*

23 | 20 | 23 | $49

Cleveland Park | 3417 Connecticut Ave. (Ordway St.) | 202-244-7995 | www.rippledc.com

"Relax with a wonderful glass of wine" and "serious" cheese and charcuterie plus "innovative" small and large plates at this colorful, vibrant Cleveland Park New American restaurant and wine bar, where the "farm-to-table concept is truly experienced" at a "fairly reasonable price (by Washington standards)"; staffers are "extremely knowledgeable" about "the origins of every item of food", and a recent expansion could improve the Decor rating.

Ris *American*

25 | 22 | 24 | $57

West End | 2275 L St. NW (23rd St.) | 202-730-2500 | www.risdc.com

If only the "government was run as well as" Ris Lacoste's West End New American bistro sigh surveyors, citing "gold-star" service and a "polished kitchen" turning out "exciting" "market-fresh" dishes in a "sophisticated", "modern" setting; various deals offer a way around high prices, so whether headed for Kennedy Center, meeting "friends and family" or hanging at the bar, it suits the whole neighborhood.

River Falls Tavern *American*

‒ | ‒ | ‒ | E

Potomac | 10128 River Rd. (Falls Rd.), MD | 301-299-0481 | www.thetavernatriverfalls.com

Tony Potomac locals gather at this American tavern from the talents behind nearby Renato, serving crab cakes along with burgers and other comfort fare in a trim dining room decorated with area photographs and kaleidoscopic wall treatments; meanwhile, its granite-topped bar offers a low-key backdrop for meet-ups with friends.

Rocklands *BBQ*

22 | 14 | 18 | $19

Glover Park | 2418 Wisconsin Ave. NW (Calvert St.) | 202-333-2558

Rockville | Wintergreen Plaza | 891 Rockville Pike (Edmonston Dr.), MD | 240-268-1120

(continued)

Rocklands

Greater Alexandria | 25 S. Quaker Ln. (Duke St.) | Alexandria, VA | 703-778-9663

Arlington | 3471 Washington Blvd. (Lincoln St.), VA | 703-528-9663

www.rocklands.com

Though proponents can't agree if "finger-licking BBQ is the order of the day" or the "flavorful" "side dishes are the real stars", they do swear "no one walks away hungry" from this "smoky and delicious" area franchise; service is "just fine" in the "low-key" settings with "roadhouse decor" ("a roll of paper towels on each table"), and with "right-on" prices they also do a "tremendous take-out business."

Rogue 24 🗷 Ⓜ *American*   23 | 25 | 25 | $145

Mt. Vernon Square/Convention Center | 922 N St. (bet. 9th & 10th Sts.) | 202-408-9724 | www.rogue24.com

RJ Cooper "swings for the fences" at his Mt. Vernon New American where everything is a "real adventure" – from the hidden "back-alley entrance", to the showpiece "open kitchen smack in the middle" of the "wonderfully industrial" room, to the "imaginative" multicourse tasting menus coordinated by a "knowledgeable" staff and paired with a "variety of drinks" (4-, 16- or 24-course options only), "not just wine"; accordingly, the "entertaining" experience is priced like "dinner and a show", though wallet-watchers note the lounge (and tiny new SpiritsBar) has à la carte options in addition to prix fixe.

Rolls 'N Rice *Japanese*   ∇ 22 | 20 | 19 | $16

Rockville | 1701 Rockville Pike (bet. Halpine Rd. & Rollins Ave.), MD | 301-770-4030 | www.rollsnrice.com

"Cheap and cheerful" sushi, Japanese mains and even some Korean dishes strike Rockville regulars as ideal for a "quick bite" in a "bright", "family-friendly" environment; most find the counter staff "friendly" and the overall experience "convenient."

Roof Terrace at the   16 | 20 | 17 | $51
Kennedy Center *American*

Foggy Bottom | Kennedy Ctr. | 2700 F St. NW (bet. Rock Creek & Potomac Pkwy.) | 202-416-8555 | www.roofterracerestaurant.com

"It's all about the view" and "super-convenient" pre-event dining at this "elegant", white-tablecloth New American atop the Kennedy Center; besides an "inspired" brunch, the food is merely "acceptable" (and "expensive" to boot), but don't worry about missing your show since "fast" service is "geared for meeting curtain deadlines."

Room 11 *Eclectic*   ∇ 26 | 23 | 25 | $36

Columbia Heights | 3234 11th St. NW (Lamont St.) | 202-332-3234 | www.room11dc.com

Columbia Heights has the number on what "may be the perfect restaurant" concept: take a "cozy" zinc bar, add a large patio and serve "excellent, inventive" Eclectic small plates paired with "fabulous" wines; with its "Brooklyn"-"hipster" vibe and "tremendous bang for the buck", no wonder it expanded next door to alleviate "waits."

	FOOD	DECOR	SERVICE	COST

Rosa Mexicano *Mexican*   23 | 23 | 21 | $39

Chevy Chase | 5225 Wisconsin Ave. NW (bet. Ingomar & Jenifer Sts.) | 202-777-9959
Penn Quarter | 575 Seventh St. NW (bet. E & F Sts.) | 202-783-5522
National Harbor | 153 Waterfront St. (American Way), MD | 301-567-1005
www.rosamexicano.com

"Traditional dishes with a modern twist" are the hallmark of this "upscale Mexican" chain whose favorites include "killer" tableside guacamole and "outstanding" pomegranate margaritas; "fast" service keeps things rosy in the colorful, contemporary settings, so even if some feel the midpriced fare is "steep", the majority "loves" it.

Roti Mediterranean Grill *Mediterranean*   22 | 15 | 19 | $13

Downtown | 1311 F St. NW (bet. 13th & 14th Sts.) | 202-499-4145 ⊠
Golden Triangle | 1629 K St. NW (bet. 16th & 17th Sts.) | 202-499-2091 ⊠
Foggy Bottom | 2221 I St. NW (bet. 22nd & 23rd Sts.) | 202-499-2095
World Bank | 1747 Pennsylvania Ave. NW (bet. 17th & 18th Sts.) | 202-466-7684 ⊠
NoMa | 1275 First St. NE (bet. N & M Sts.) | 202-618-6969 ⊠
SW | L'Enfant Plaza | 955 L'Enfant Plaza SW (10th St.) | 202-618-6965 ⊠
NEW **Bethesda** | 10231 Westlake Dr. (Democracy Blvd.), MD | 301-327-1734
NEW **College Park** | 8150 Baltimore Ave. (Navahoe St.), MD | 301-569-2033
Courthouse | 1501 Wilson Blvd. (Oak St.) | Arlington, VA | 571-257-3295
www.roti.com

Dubbed the "Mediterranean version of Chipotle" by admirers, this chain fills a niche with "healthy, cheap and filling" pita-centered sandwiches, salads and platters that customers design themselves in industrial Aegean (orange-and-blue-tiled) settings; its "fast service despite the long lines" attracts office workers and others "in a rush", who rely on it for a "quick lunch."

Royal Mile Pub ● *Scottish*   23 | 20 | 22 | $25

Wheaton | 2407 Price Ave. (bet. Elkin St. & Georgia Ave.), MD | 301-946-4511 | www.royalmilepub.net

"Hours can go by" easily at this "cozy" Scottish pub in Wheaton known for its reasonable rates (though new ownership after a temporary closure may outdate the Food rating); aye, it's a "great place to drink" too, thanks to the "international" ale selection, one of the "best scotch lists" in the area and occasional live music.

RT's *Cajun/Creole*   26 | 16 | 24 | $39

Greater Alexandria | 3804 Mt. Vernon Ave. (Glebe Rd.) | Alexandria, VA | 703-684-6010 | www.rtsrestaurant.net

Long a "favorite" for those "craving New Orleans" flavors in Greater Alexandria, this Cajun-Creole classic has a "deft touch" in the kitchen, whipping up "outstanding" dishes such as its "famous" Jack Daniel's shrimp; yes, perhaps the old-time-saloon look "needs a shake-up", but the bayou brigade wouldn't change anything about the "excellent" food, "fine" service or reasonable tabs.

	FOOD	DECOR	SERVICE	COST

Ruan Thai *Thai*

27 | 15 | 21 | $22

Wheaton | 11407 Amherst Ave. (University Blvd.), MD | 301-942-0075 | www.ruanthaiwheaton.com

"Everything is just so good" on the menu – notably "not-to-be-missed" deep-fried watercress – at this Wheatonite known for its "real" Thai cuisine "priced well"; "fast", "friendly" service keeps the "bustling" scene and "very busy carry-out" operation under control, so who cares if the digs are "sparse", since you "don't go for the ambiance."

Russia House ◐ *Russian*

21 | 20 | 20 | $45

Dupont Circle | 1800 Connecticut Ave. NW (bet. Bancroft Pl. & Florida Ave.) | 202-234-9433 | www.russiahouselounge.com

"Na zdorovie!" toasts the "beautiful crowd" reveling in the "decadency of the czars" at this Russian retreat occupying an "opulent" yet "cozy" four-story townhouse in Dupont Circle; the food is "well prepared" if "expensive", but comrades claim it's really all about the "stunning" vodka collection and "choice" caviar dropped off by a "knowledgeable" staff to backdrop intimate "conversation post-dinner."

Russia House Restaurant *Russian*

27 | 23 | 25 | $51

Herndon | 790 Station St. (bet. Elden St. & Park Ave.), VA | 703-787-8880 | www.russiahouserestaurant.com

"Someone in the kitchen truly knows how to cook" say fans of this high-end Herndon spot's "superb" French-influenced Russian specialties that naturally don't come cheap; cocktails get a boost from the "welcoming" owners' "excellent stash of Russian vodka" ("flavored shots" work too), enhancing the "unique charm" of a "delightful" meal in formal surroundings.

Rustico ◐ *American*

22 | 21 | 20 | $30

Greater Alexandria | 827 Slaters Ln. (Potomac Greens Dr.) | Alexandria, VA | 703-224-5051
Ballston | Liberty Ctr. | 4075 Wilson Blvd. (bet. Quincy & Randolph Sts.) | Arlington, VA | 571-384-1820
www.rusticorestaurant.com

"They're passionate about beer" at these "value"-priced "neighborhood haunts" in Alexandria and Ballston, where "small-batch and hard-to-find" brews whet the appetite for "tasty" wood-fired pizza and seasonal "upscale" American "tavern fare"; a "knowledgeable", "low-key" staff creates a "relaxed" atmosphere at both locations, while Alexandria has a "funkier vibe", and Ballston is "bigger" with "lots of tables in the bar."

Rustik Tavern *Eclectic*

▽ 23 | 20 | 23 | $20

Bloomingdale | 84 T St. NW (First St.) | 202-290-2936 | www.rustikdc.com

"Delicious" wood-fired pizzas (you'll hear the "squeaky wheel that fires" the oven) and a whole range of Eclectic-American fare beckons "local foodies" to this "always welcoming", "fairly priced" Bloomingdale spot that's "cozy on the inside" (exposed brick, an eye-catching mural) with a "relaxing" outdoor patio; the whole place is under the radar, but a small cadre says the "real secret" is the weekend brunch.

Ruth's Chris Steak House *Steak*

26 | 24 | 26 | $67

Penn Quarter | 724 Ninth St. NW (bet. G & H Sts.) | 202-393-4488
Dupont Circle | 1801 Connecticut Ave. NW (S St.) | 202-797-0033
Bethesda | 7315 Wisconsin Ave. (Elm St.), MD | 301-652-7877
Crystal City | Crystal Park | 2231 Crystal Dr. (23rd St.) | Arlington, VA |
703-979-7275
Fairfax | 4100 Monument Corner Dr. (Monument Dr.), VA | 703-266-1004
Vienna | 8521 Leesburg Pike (Spring Hill Rd.), VA | 703-848-4290
www.ruthschris.com

You always "know what you're getting" at this eminently "reliable",
"classy" steakhouse chain: "superior" chops smothered in "buttery
excellence" that "melt in your mouth" after "sizzling" all the way to
the table via "unobtrusive", "top-of-the-line" servers; in short, go
for a "truly prime" time – just "bring your wallet."

Sabai Sabai Simply Thai *Thai*

26 | 20 | 21 | $27

Germantown | 19847 Century Blvd. (Middlebrook Rd.), MD |
301-528-1400 | www.sabaisimplythai.com

"Sensational, traditional" Thai cuisine employing "fresh ingredients
with just enough spice" is the hallmark of this midpriced Germantown
Siamese, but it also appeals for its "interesting mix of street food",
reflected in photos of Thai street life that dot the walls; a "tasteful"
interior of stone and earth tones heightens the "soothing" experience, as does an unexpectedly "worthwhile wine list."

Sakana ☒ *Japanese*

▽ 23 | 14 | 17 | $29

Dupont Circle | 2026 P St. NW (bet. Hopkins & 21st Sts.) | 202-887-0900

"Like the smart girl next door" ("not the 'it girl' of the moment"), this
Dupont Circle Japanese spot is an understated "gem" delivering
"quality" sushi and other dishes that are "consistently very good
without being showy"; "best-value" prices and adept service make
up for a "plain" space that "hustles" on weekend nights.

Sakoontra *Thai*

23 | 20 | 20 | $23

Fairfax | Costco Plaza | 12300 Costco Plaza (Ox Rd.), VA |
703-818-8886 | www.sakoontra.com

This "classic" "neighborhood" Thai in Fairfax impresses with affordable standards and house specialties (both the 'yum watercress'
salad and the namesake duck come recommended); the contemporary space is aswirl with eye-popping colors and includes playful
touches (the centerpiece is a parked tuk-tuk), and "quick", "efficient"
service plays well in the chain-heavy Costco Plaza.

Sakuramen Ⓜ *Noodle Shop*

– | – | – | I

Adams Morgan | 2441 18th St. NW (bet. Columbia & Kalorama Rds.) |
202-656-5285 | www.sakuramen.net

Amid the bar-heavy Adams Morgan scene, this noodle shop is a
welcome addition, serving wallet-friendly Asian fusion ramens
(even letting diners customize their own brothy bowl), perfect for
soaking up booze; tucked away in a basement, the compact digs
feature a communal table and an arresting mural of guardian spirit
Shoki on the wall.

Samantha's *Pan-Latin*
24 | 17 | 22 | $29

Silver Spring | 631 E. University Blvd. (Piney Branch Rd.), MD | 301-445-7300 | www.samanthasrestaurant.net

This "delightful" Pan-Latin in Silver Spring might look "like a hole-in-the-wall", but it's "nicer" inside, with white tablecloths and mood lighting, and the midpriced food is "out of this world" say "repeat customers"; "veteran" servers "know the menu well", and despite the "tight" parking, it's "worth it if you're in the neighborhood."

Scion Restaurant *American*
∇ 19 | 17 | 20 | $32

Dupont Circle | 2100 P St. NW (21st St.) | 202-833-8899
NEW **Silver Spring** | 1200 East-West Hwy. (Blair Mill Rd.), MD | 301-585-8878
www.scionrestaurant.com

"Bring your hangover" to this New American "neighborhood staple" in Dupont Circle (or its glossy new Silver Spring branch) for the bottomless liquid brunch that draws a "young" crowd at "the crack of noon" on Sunday – though it's also "worth a stop" at other days and times for a "nice mix" of "basics and more adventurous dishes"; other niceties include a "kind" staff, "reasonable" tabs and a year-round patio.

Sea Catch 🗷 *Seafood*
23 | 22 | 21 | $48

Georgetown | Canal Sq. | 1054 31st St. NW (bet. M & South Sts.) | 202-337-8855 | www.seacatchrestaurant.com

"Oyster happy hour rules" ($1 bivalves and half-priced wine) at this Georgetown seafooder where the mollusks are accompanied by a geographic "guide" from "aim-to-please" servers who also traffic in other aquatic "delights" like "delicious" grilled fish and "perfect" crab cakes; for most, a "romantic dinner" on the porch overlooking the C&O Canal, or fireside in winter, is worth the costly tabs.

Sea Pearl *American/Californian*
23 | 25 | 23 | $40

Merrifield | Merrifield Town Ctr. | 8191 Strawberry Ln. (Gallows Rd.), VA | 703-372-5161 | www.seapearlrestaurant.com

An "elegant and peaceful" "ocean oasis" (maritime hues, capiz-shell curtains, waveform wall) awaits at this Merrifield Cal-American where "personalized" hospitality hooks diners on seafood prepared with "Asian flavors that satisfy rather than overwhelm"; it's "not cheap", but there's a "lower-priced menu" for weeknight happy hour at the bar or in the lounge.

Sei *Asian*
26 | 25 | 22 | $51

Penn Quarter | 444 Seventh St. NW (bet. D & E Sts.) | 202-783-7007 | www.seirestaurant.com

"Extra flavor, sex and sizzle" dress up the "exceptional", "playful" sushi and "inventive" Asian-fusion small plates at this "sleek and shiny" Penn Quarter beauty queen where white-on-white surroundings "feel more like South Beach than DC"; costs can add up, but happy-hour specials keep it manageable, and "excellent" service makes it a lock for "date night" or pre-theater noshes before Woolly Mammoth or Shakespeare shows.

	FOOD	DECOR	SERVICE	COST

Senart's Oyster & Chop House *Seafood/Steak*

24 | 23 | 21 | $37

Capitol Hill | 520 Eighth St. SE (bet. E & G Sts.) | 202-544-1168 | www.senartsdc.com

A "charming", "modern version of an old-time East Coast oyster house" centered on a 50-ft. marble bar, this "upscale" American seafooder on Capitol Hill wins accolades for "high-quality" surf 'n' turf and a "top-shelf" raw bar happy hour from 4–6:30 PM daily; the bartenders "know what they're doing", which makes for a "lively" atmosphere, and "prices are low" for what you get.

Sequoia *American*

17 | 24 | 18 | $46

Georgetown | Washington Harbour | 3000 K St. NW (Thomas Jefferson St.) | 202-944-4200 | www.arkrestaurants.com

With a "stunning waterfront" setting on the Potomac in Georgetown, this American venue proves "lovely at sunset" from the "cruise-ship" interior or the multilevel outdoor terrace with a "vibrant" bar scene; service is solid, but if the "expensive", "marginal" fare doesn't float your boat, most insist it's still worth going for "drinks", "excellent" people-watching and the "outta-this-world" view.

Serendipity 3 *American/Dessert*

21 | 21 | 18 | $28

Georgetown | 3150 M St. NW (Wisconsin Ave.) | 202-333-5193 | www.serendipity3dc.com

"Save room for dessert" at this "just plain fun" American "fantasyland" in Georgetown, where signature frozen hot chocolate follows "above-average" "artery-clogging" favorites like burgers and fries, at middling prices; service is "friendly", though you'll still "wait to order, wait for ice cream, wait for the check", but while you do there's plenty to ogle, like "Tiffany lamps galore" and knickknacks "your crazy aunt stole."

Sergio Ristorante Italiano 🛇 *Italian*

▽ 27 | 19 | 25 | $33

Silver Spring | DoubleTree by Hilton Hotel – Silver Spring | 8727 Colesville Rd. (bet. Fenton & Spring Sts.), MD | 301-585-1040 | www.hilton.com

A "very loyal customer base" says there's "no better bargain in these down economic times" than an "authentic" Italian meal in the Silver Spring DoubleTree by Hilton's basement in this "homey" but "windowless" space; that's where chef-owner Sergio Toni can be found not only preparing the "wonderful" food, but also "seating guests and singing Italian tunes" alongside his "experienced" staff.

Sette Osteria *Italian*

21 | 17 | 17 | $37

Dupont Circle | 1666 Connecticut Ave. NW (R St.) | 202-483-3070 | www.setteosteria.com

"Reliable", "better-than-most" pizzas, pastas and more are the draws at this "popular" midpriced Dupont Circle "cafe-type" Italian where "waiters in a hurry" "cater to after-work and weekend" crowds; in nice weather, outdoor seats are in demand, while inside the "large", window-walled space, wood tables and terra-cotta tiles add rusticity.

	FOOD	DECOR	SERVICE	COST

701 *American*
23 | 24 | 24 | $54

Penn Quarter | 701 Pennsylvania Ave. NW (7th St.) | 202-393-0701 | www.701restaurant.com

"Classy with a hip feel to it", this "adventurous" New American in Penn Quarter is prized for "civilized" business lunches (a "professional" staff serves the "widely spaced" tables) and dinners that feel "like special occasions, even in jeans" ("candlelight" dots the "suave" setting); extras include "good-value" pre-theater and bar menus, "easy jazz" Thursday–Saturday and a "lovely" terrace with a view of the Navy Memorial.

Seven Seas *Chinese/Japanese*
22 | 14 | 19 | $23

College Park | 8503 Baltimore Ave. (Quebec St.), MD | 301-345-5808 | www.sevenseascp.com

Rockville | Federal Plaza | 1776 E. Jefferson St. (bet. California Cir. & Montrose Rd.), MD | 301-770-5020 | www.sevenseasrestaurant.com

This "good-value" Chinese-Japanese duo in College Park and Rockville specializes in "fresh seafood live from the tanks" and other "consistently good" fare; the "nothing-fancy" setups are "adequate", and the staff "treats you right"; P.S. College Park has a "cheap" lunch buffet.

1789 *American*
26 | 25 | 26 | $70

Georgetown | 1226 36th St. NW (Prospect St.) | 202-965-1789 | www.1789restaurant.com

"White gloves and pearls" might suit this "distinguished" Georgetown "classic" with a "refined", "historic" townhouse setting and "expertly prepared" "farm-to-table" New American cooking that together make it a "special place to impress or luxuriate"; politicians and parents visiting their kids at the university mean that the "people-watching" (and "eavesdropping") is as good as the food, while a "personable" staff makes diners feel so like "landed gentry" that it's "worth every penny" of its very contemporary prices.

Seventh Hill Pizza Ⓜ *Pizza*
25 | 14 | 20 | $19

Capitol Hill | 327 Seventh St. SE (Pennsylvania Ave.) | 202-544-1911 | www.montmartredc.com

Kids have "a great time" at this family-friendly Capitol Hill wood-fired-oven pizzeria, a bargain offshoot of Gallic bistro Montmartre next door, while more mature crustafarians go in for "artisanal" toppings ("goat cheese and tapenade", "brilliant") and "interesting" beers; the bright, airy space was recently expanded, possibly outdating the Decor rating.

Shake Shack *Burgers*
21 | 15 | 17 | $15

Dupont Circle | 1216 18th St. NW (Jefferson Pl.) | 202-683-9922

SW | Nationals Park | 1500 S. Capitol St. SE (Potomac Ave.) | no phone 🅢 Ⓜ
www.shakeshack.com

"You may have to wait", but the "addictive" burgers and "life-changing" 'concretes' ("milkshakes on steroids") are "worth it" say fans of this "friendly" counter-serve NYC import from Danny Meyer; a few dissenters dis "meh" crinkle-cut fries and "kinda pricey" tabs, but that doesn't stop the masses from shacking up at the wood-heavy Dupont Circle stop or Nationals Park stand (open during games only).

Shamshiry *Persian*　▽ 27 | 14 | 19 | $22

Tysons Corner | 8607 Westwood Center Dr. (Leesburg Pike) | Vienna, VA | 703-448-8883 | www.shamshiry.com

"Patrons speaking Farsi" and "totally enjoying themselves" signal that you're "in for a treat" at this "hard-to-find" eatery in a Tysons Corner office park, serving "delicious", "authentic" Persian cuisine – you can't go wrong with the "excellent" kebabs and rice dishes – in a utilitarian setting with solid service; plus portions are "great for the price" (folks "always have leftovers").

Shophouse Southeast　22 | 16 | 19 | $12
Asian Kitchen *SE Asian*

Dupont Circle | 1516 Connecticut Ave. NW (bet. Dupont Circle & Q St.) | 202-232-4141 | www.shophousekitchen.com

Southeast Asian–inspired "assembly-line fast food" (Chipotle's next "great concept") is available at this Dupont Circle joint, where "flavorful" meals of rice/noodle bowls with "spicy" sauces are served up "cheap", "quick and with a smile"; "daunting" crowds can feel "like vultures hovering" to nab your seat in the narrow, wood-lined space, but early-adopters "overlook" these obstacles; P.S. additional DC branches are in the works.

Sichuan Jin River *Chinese*　▽ 25 | 15 | 19 | $19

Rockville | 410 Hungerford Dr. (Beall Ave.), MD | 240-403-7351 | www.scjinriver.com

"Go with a big group" to sample the "massive" menu of "stunningly authentic" Sichuan fare at this Rockville strip-mall joint – and "don't be afraid to tell the waiters 'spicy'" for the "real experience"; the egg-noodle-hued digs are unassuming, but solid service and a low price further enamor fans.

Siroc *Italian*　24 | 20 | 23 | $50

Downtown | 915 15th St. NW (bet. I & K Sts.) | 202-628-2220 | www.sirocrestaurant.com

"Everything works" – from "business lunch" to "date night" – at this spendy Downtown Italian with an "elegant yet relaxed" interior and an outdoor cafe overlooking McPherson Square, offering "delicately handmade" pasta, "extensive" seafood and "excellent" wines; add in a "terrific", "no-attitude" staff, and even though it's seemingly "tucked away where no one will notice", it should be no surprise that "many have."

NEW Slate Wine　- | - | - | M
Bar + Bistro *American/Italian*

Glover Park | 2404 Wisconsin Ave. NW (bet. Calvert St. & Hall Pl.) | 202-333-4304 | www.slatewinebar.com

This new Glover Park wine bar and bistro showcases vino from small-production, sustainably run wineries from around the world, paired with moderately priced American and Italian small plates and entrees; the urban-rustic space has exposed brick and ductwork, plus a collection of carved bottle openers in light boxes on the wall.

Smith & Wollensky *Steak*

| 25 | 22 | 24 | $65 |

Golden Triangle | 1112 19th St. NW (bet. L & M Sts.) | 202-466-1100 | www.smithandwollensky.com

"Awesome" steaks and "strong" drinks draw carnivores to this "reliable" chain link with a "macho", "old-school" vibe in the Golden Triangle; servers that "go the extra mile" boost egos ("you'll feel like royalty"), but of course it's always "better if on someone else's tab."

Smith Commons *American*

| ∇ 22 | 25 | 21 | $35 |

Atlas District | 1245 H St. NE (bet. 12th & 13th Sts.) | 202-396-0038 | www.smithcommonsdc.com

A "gorgeous" triplex in a onetime carpet warehouse in the Atlas District is a chicly rough-hewn backdrop to a "good selection of small-brewery beers", "delicious" (if "hefty"-priced) cocktails and "inventive" New American plates; an "always-relaxed vibe" and "amazing bartenders" help make it a "highlight of H Street."

Smoke & Barrel ❶ *American/BBQ*

| ∇ 20 | 19 | 19 | $23 |

Adams Morgan | 2471 18th St. NW (bet. Columbia & Kalorama Rds.) | 202-319-9353 | www.smokeandbarreldc.com

"Pretty decent BBQ for a city that doesn't do it well" is the judgment on this "friendly" Adams Morgan eatery, whose rough-hewn digs offer a pleasant "oasis" from the neighborhood's "post-college mess" of a scene; but where it really has fans over a barrel is with its "killer" beer list (think "rare smoked" brews) and "magical" meatless 'cue options.

NEW Smoke BBQ *BBQ*

| - | - | - | I |

Bethesda | 4858 Cordell Ave. (bet. Norfolk & Woodmont Aves.), MD | 301-656-2011 | www.smokebbqbethesda.com

At this new Bethesda BBQ specialist, carnivores dig into spice-rubbed smoked meats dressed with their choice of sauces and paired with a smart list of craft brews; whether diners do their finger lickin' in the no-frills space or take it home, it's easy on the wallet.

Social Reform 🖾 *American*

| - | - | - | E |

Penn Quarter | 401 Ninth St. NW (D St.) | 202-393-1300 | www.socialreformbar.com

A makeover and rebranding of the Penn Quarter's Caucus Room has resulted in a more democratic (albeit still bipartisan) venue, given its somewhat lower-priced New American menu featuring small plates, burgers and sandwiches and plenty of meat (heavy hitters can still order premium beef cuts); the new look is airy and open, with a polished wood bar and a bistro-style dining area, and there's also a darker rear dining room with high-backed booths and group-sized tables.

Society Fair *American*

| ∇ 24 | 26 | 25 | $33 |

Old Town | 277 S. Washington St. (Duke St.) | Alexandria, VA | 703-683-3247 | www.societyfair.net

An "amazing concept" from Cathal Armstrong (Restaurant Eve), this "wonderful, sparkly" Victorian-themed American gourmet market/

eatery in Old Town tended by "attentive" staffers lets diners go shopping, then "sit down and have a nice wine" paired with cheese, charcuterie or other light fare in the wine room, or pick something from the bakery/cafe; prices are moderate, and for a "special treat", chef demos and classes in the showcase kitchen evolve into prix fixe dinners.

Sonoma Restaurant & Wine Bar *American* | 21 | 20 | 20 | $40 |

Capitol Hill | 223 Pennsylvania Ave. SE (bet. 2nd & 3rd Sts.) | 202-544-8088 | www.sonomadc.com

Uncorking "great" vino to complement its "tempting" New American small and large plates, this California-inspired venue is favored for "lunch on the Hill", with its solid service and moderate tabs; the narrow, brick-walled dining room sports a looong bar, and there's a "super-chill" lounge upstairs, and though it might "not pass muster in its namesake wine town", it's certainly "worth crossing the street for."

Sorriso *Italian* | ∇ 22 | 19 | 24 | $34 |

Cleveland Park | 3518 Connecticut Ave. NW (bet. Ordway & Porter Sts.) | 202-537-4800

"Spot-on" service with a "smile" is the specialty of this "family-run" Cleveland Park Italian whose "cozy", sunny storefront space "has real personality" swear its coterie; for some, the Treviso-style pizza is "the best part" of the "homestyle" menu, while wine from the family vineyards "is an absolute have-to-have" – all told, given the "attractive prices", there are very few frowns.

The Source ⊠ *Asian* | 27 | 24 | 24 | $68 |

Penn Quarter | Newseum | 575 Pennsylvania Ave. NW (6th St.) | 202-637-6100 | www.wolfgangpuck.com

"Brilliant East-meets-West fare" is the lead story (with a sidebar on "outstanding" bar bites) at this "hip" Wolfgang Puck destination adjacent to Penn Quarter's Newseum, sporting a "sleek" multilevel setting; "friendly but not intrusive" servers are another reason why subscribers place it in the "expensive-but-worth-it" column.

Sou'Wester *American* | 21 | 23 | 21 | $49 |

SW | Mandarin Oriental | 1330 Maryland Ave. SW (12th St.) | 202-787-6990 | www.mandarinoriental.com

"Ask for a window table", and take in the "lovely view" at this American resident of the Mandarin Oriental, serving "creative", "classy" interpretations of Southern-accented down-home favorites that make for "luxurious breakfasts" and "yummy lunches"; it's a bit "expensive", but "terrific" help monitors the "swanky" earth-toned, wood-paneled dining room (there's also a terrace), keeping the vibe "casual."

Spices *Asian* | 21 | 16 | 20 | $29 |

Cleveland Park | 3333 Connecticut Ave. NW (bet. Macomb & Ordway Sts.) | 202-686-3833 | www.spicesdc.com

"When you can't decide what kind of Asian food to get", this Cleveland Park "neighborhood place" does it "all well" (including "tasty" sushi) at a "more than right" price; the orange-and-gray Zen setting is also a "great spot for large groups" on account of many communal tables and "quick" service from "sweet and endearing" servers.

Spice Xing *Indian*

22 | 22 | 22 | $28

Rockville | Rockville Town Sq. | 100 Gibbs St. (Middle Ln.), MD | 301-610-0303 | www.spicexing.com

"Inventive" Indian with international accents adds "creative fusion" to subcontinental staples and "tapas-style" plates at this Rockville spot – and at fair prices, particularly for the "bargain" lunch buffet; "conscientious" service complements the "lovely", colorful space complete with a billowy, variegated silk ceiling, and for a change of pace, "curryoke" (curry plus karaoke) happens most Friday nights.

Standard ●Ⓜ *BBQ*

- | - | - | I

Logan Circle | 1801 14th St. NW (S St.) | no phone | www.standarddc.com

Hopping when the weather's nice, this mostly outdoor BBQ/beer garden smack on a trendy stretch of 14th Street NW adds foodie-friendly twists to its thrifty lineup, with unusual cuts and local vegetable offerings, capped with German and American craft beers; the game plan changes at the owners' inspiration (feel like barbecued pig's head? – it just might be available); P.S. closed in winter.

Star & Shamrock ● *Deli/Pub Food*

19 | 17 | 20 | $20

Atlas District | 1341 H St. NE (bet. 14th St. & Linden Ct.) | 202-388-3833 | www.starandshamrock.com

"A New York deli" walks into an "Irish pub" – it's no joke at this Atlas District "marriage" of "two culinary cultures" serving "nothing-fancy" grub, like 'paddy melts' and bagel pizza, that makes "perfect drunk food", plus "unique beer choices"; what's more, the price is right, the service is solid and the woody, taverny digs are cozy.

Station 4 *American*

21 | 24 | 18 | $40

SW Waterfront | 1101 Fourth St. SW (bet. I & M Sts.) | 202-488-0987 | www.station4dc.com

A "sexy, Miami-inspired setting" injects "a much-needed infusion of swank" into the Southwest Waterfront at this New American with a "tasty" menu of "creative" entrees and pizzas; yes, it "can get pricey", but the service is "pleasant", and most are just jazzed there's finally "a decent restaurant within easy walking distance of Arena Stage."

Sticky Rice *Asian/Eclectic*

23 | 19 | 19 | $26

Atlas District | 1224 H St. NE (bet. 12th & 13th Sts.) | 202-397-7655 | www.stickyricedc.com

An "odd" but "delicious" mix of "sushi and tater tots" plus noodle dishes and "interesting" cocktails keeps this inexpensive Atlas District Asian-Eclectic "hopping" with a "young, hip" throng, especially on weekends; a few say the help can be "friendly but a little too cool", but it remains "quirky and fun" on account of the nightly happenings, e.g. karaoke, speed bingo and such.

Stoney's ● *Pub Food*

▽ 18 | 13 | 18 | $21

Logan Circle | 1433 P St. NW (bet. 14th & 15th Sts.) | 202-234-1818

"Stick with the basics and you can't go wrong" at Logan Circle's "great local dive", a narrow, tin-ceilinged space that's a "pleasant" place to "enjoy time out with friends" over low-tabbed bar food (some say the "best grilled-cheese sandwich in DC") and a "surprisingly nice" selection of microbrews; it's also perfectly situated to grab a bite "before heading to nearby Studio Theatre."

Sugo Cicchetti *Italian/Pizza*

| - | - | - | M |

Potomac | Potomac Park | 12505 Park Potomac Ave. (Seven Locks Rd.), MD | 240-386-8080 | www.eatsugo.com

The Cava team's Italian-inspired taperia/pizzeria outlet in Potomac boasts an open industrial design, with a touch of luncheonette informality in its overstuffed red-leather booths; a wood-fired pizza oven sends out interestingly topped pies, while pastas, charcuterie and hot and cold *cicchetti* (small plates) provide plenty of options for moderately priced sampling and sharing – plus cotton candy for dessert.

Sunflower Vegetarian Restaurant *Asian/Vegetarian*

| 25 | 17 | 25 | $18 |

Falls Church | 6304 Leesburg Pike (Arlington Blvd.), VA | 703-237-3888
Vienna | 2531 Chain Bridge Rd. (Nutley St.), VA | 703-319-3888
www.crystalsunflower.com

Even "strict carnivores" may "forget they're in a vegetarian place" thanks to the "delicious" Asian-inspired fare with "lots of flavor" that shines "without emptying your billfold" at these eateries in Falls Church and Vienna; the "cheerful" decor is "cute if you like sunflowers", and the "family-friendly" service is "polite."

Surfside *Californian/Mexican*

| 21 | 13 | 14 | $21 |

Glover Park | 2444 Wisconsin Ave. NW (bet. Calvert St. & Hall Pl.) | 202-337-0004 | www.surfsidedc.com

Like a "seaside taco shack", this Glover Park Cal-Mex serves "spicy" fish tacos and other "exciting" eats to a company of "hipsters", "neighborhood singles" and families with "kids"; "cafeteria-style" service means "you're your own waiter, which can get hectic" in the narrow, "crowded" industrial room, so decamp to the rooftop with an icy margarita – "awesome on a hot summer day"; P.S. for food on the run, check online for the taco truck's location.

Sushi Damo *Japanese*

| 25 | 23 | 21 | $38 |

Rockville | Rockville Town Sq. | 36 Maryland Ave. (bet. Jefferson St. & Montgomery Ave.), MD | 301-340-8010 | www.sushidamo.com

"Sushi nirvana" is reached in Rockville at this NYC Japanese import via "layer upon layer of flavors" in the "beautifully presented", "innovative takes on old favorites" that appeal to the purist and modern-minded alike (there are cooked items too); factor in "ultrachic" yet "comfortable" digs and a "personable", "sincere" crew, and it's deemed "worth" the "not-cheap" price.

Sushiko *Japanese*

| 24 | 18 | 21 | $45 |

Glover Park | 2309 Wisconsin Ave. NW (Calvert St.) | 202-333-4187
Chevy Chase | 5455 Wisconsin Ave. (Wisconsin Circle), MD | 301-961-1644
www.sushikorestaurant.com

"Serious sushi eaters" consider this "pricey" Glover Park and Chevy Chase Japanese pair "essential" for its "very-high-quality" raw fish plus "inventive" East-meets-West small plates inspiringly paired with "outstanding" Burgundy wines; the DC original looks "rather plain", while Maryland's "hip", "modern" setting boasts a "vibrant bar scene" – and both keep attracting crowds on account of "attentive" service and "delicious" specials.

Sushi Taro ☒ *Japanese*   26 | 22 | 24 | $65

Dupont Circle | 1503 17th St. NW (P St.) | 202-462-8999 | www.sushitaro.com

For "divine" "classical sushi", piscine purists head to this "memorable" Dupont Circle Japanese where chefs who "know their stuff" present an "outstanding" omakase procession at the counter, while "exquisite" servers ferry "finely crafted" "traditional" dishes in a multicourse kaiseki to tables; "simple", "serene" surroundings contribute to a "calm" vibe despite "high" prices; P.S. bento box lunches offer a "real deal."

Sweet Ginger *Asian*   25 | 19 | 25 | $27

Vienna | Danor Plaza | 120 Branch Rd. SE (Maple Ave.), VA | 703-319-3922

Vienna's "beloved" Asian sweetheart attracts suitors with "wonderful sushi" and other "delicious" "comfort food" from China, Malaysia, Thailand et al., delivered by an "attentive" staff; although these charms are hidden in a "strip mall", her black, white and red dress is thoroughly modern, and everything comes together at a "decent price" that makes you want to commit.

Sweetgreen *Health Food*   22 | 15 | 18 | $13

Capitol Hill | 221 Pennsylvania Ave. SE (bet. 2nd & 3rd Sts.) | 202-547-9338

Dupont Circle | 1512 Connecticut Ave. NW (bet. Dupont Circle & Q St.) | 202-387-9338

Foggy Bottom | 2221 I St. NW (bet. 22nd & 23rd Sts.) | 202-507-8357

Georgetown | 3333 M St. NW (bet. 33rd & 34th Sts.) | 202-337-9338

Mt. Vernon Square/Convention Center | 1065 Fifth St. NW (L St.) | 202-289-4674

Logan Circle | 1471 P St. NW (bet. 14th & 15th Sts.) | 202-234-7336

NEW U Street Corridor | 1325 W St. NW (13th St.) | 202-506-2956

Bethesda | 4831 Bethesda Ave. (bet. Arlington Rd. & Woodmont Ave.), MD | 301-654-7336

Ballston | 4075 Wilson Blvd. (Randolph St.) | Arlington, VA | 703-522-2016

Reston | Reston Town Ctr. | 11935 Democracy Dr. (bet. Explore & Library Sts.), VA | 571-203-0082

www.sweetgreen.com

Additional locations throughout the DC area

Feel "virtuous" "stuffing your face" at this eco-chic, "Nouvelle salad bar" chain sourcing organic, local components for "creative pre-fab salads" or bowls "made to your specifications", plus soups and "amazing" frozen yogurts; there's almost "always a line", but there's also a "quick turnaround", so while some call it "a little pricey for some greens", most judge "the 'I-saved-the-world' vibe" "worth it."

Sweetwater Tavern *Southwestern*

| 26 | 23 | 24 | $29 |

Merrifield | 3066 Gatehouse Plaza (Rte. 50), VA | 703-645-8100
Centreville | 14250 Sweetwater Ln. (Multiplex Dr.), VA | 703-449-1100
Sterling | 45980 Waterview Plaza (Loudon Tech Dr.), VA | 571-434-6500
www.greatamericanrestaurants.com

"Always crowded", this "cowboy-themed" Southwestern micro-brewery chain in NoVa "never disappoints" – whether for "splendid" eats like the "beyond-delicious" rolls and "to-die-for" drunken rib-eye or the "awesome" fresh-brewed beer and root beer; the only bitter notes are sounded by some who cite "ear-shattering" noise and the no-reservations policy ("call ahead . . . way ahead"), though "prompt" service and "reasonable" prices more than make up for it.

NEW Taan Noodles *Asian/Noodle Shop*

| – | – | – | M |

Adams Morgan | 1817 Columbia Rd. NW (bet. Biltmore St. & Mintwood Pl.) | 202-450-2416 | www.taandc.com

Ramen is the star at this Adams Morgan noodle house newcomer, which serves brothy bowls with modern toppings like duck confit and charred corn alongside Asian small plates, sake and Eastern-influenced cocktails; low lighting casts a date-night spell over the rustic high-tops downstairs, while the second floor has a lounge vibe.

Tabaq Bistro ❶ *Mediterranean*

| ∇ 20 | 22 | 20 | $32 |

U Street Corridor | 1336 U St. NW (bet. 13th & 14th Sts.) | 202-265-0965 | www.tabaqdc.com

The "awesome" 360-degree view of DC's skyline from the roof deck of this U Street Med is a "favorite" backdrop for brunch or cocktails that "get the job done", while downstairs is "sexy" and "chill"; some say the food is "average" and "a bit pricey", and service can swing from "on point" to "inattentive", but the venue works for parties or a "night on the town" when "ambiance" matters.

Tabard Inn *American*

| 25 | 23 | 22 | $47 |

Dupont Circle | Hotel Tabard Inn | 1739 N St. NW (bet. 17th & 18th Sts.) | 202-331-8528 | www.tabardinn.com

"DC's (not-so-well-kept) secret treasure" tucked in a "quaint" inn off Dupont Circle "keeps earning its reputation" with "innovative" New American cooking and a "warm", "knowledgeable" staff that's there to help explain the seasonally changing menu and "excellent" wine list; a true "romantic's place", it's a perfect "rendezvous" for dinner in the "intimate" main room, "cozy" drinks by the fire or a "wonderful" reservation-worthy brunch in the "hidden" garden – and for all that, it's "still not a wallet-buster."

NEW Table *European*

| – | – | – | E |

Shaw | 903 N. St. NW (bet. 9th & 10th Sts.) | 202-588-5200 | www.tabledc.com

Expect handwritten, ever-changing menus of contemporary European-style food and drink at this buzzing, upscale farm-to-table newcomer in Shaw from Frederik de Pue (Azur); the raw, artfully restrained setting features an open kitchen where diners can interact with the chefs, plus sidewalk seats and a roof deck.

Tachibana *Japanese*

24 | 14 | 20 | $37

McLean | 6715 Lowell Ave. (Emerson Ave.), VA | 703-847-1771 | www.tachibana.us

Regulars flock to the sushi counter at this well-"established" McLean Japanese for the "quality" fin fare at "quite reasonable" prices; a "caring" staff tends to customers who acknowledge the "tired" interior "is simply not the point", as evidenced by the fact that it's often "crowded."

Tackle Box *Seafood*

18 | 13 | 15 | $23

Georgetown | 3245 M St. NW (bet. Potomac St. & Wisconsin Ave.) | 202-337-8269 | www.tackleboxrestaurant.com

Lured by "fresh fish served quickly" and on the "cheap", seafood-seekers catch what they're craving at this "airy", industrial "sea shack" in Georgetown, ordering "fast-food" style, plonking their trays on communal "indoor picnic" tables and digging into lobster rolls that are "worth it, even if they leave you longing for seconds"; they also offer full lobster-pot dinners to go, and there are drinks and snacks upstairs at Crackle Bar.

NEW Tacos El Chilango 🗷 *Mexican*

- | - | - | I

Courthouse | 14th St. N. (Fairfax Dr.) | Arlington, VA | 571-236-0355
U Street Corridor | 1119 V St. NW (bet. 11th & 12th Sts.) | 202-986-3030
www.tacoselchilango.com

Real-deal tacos at bargain-bin prices come to the U Street NW corridor by way of Mexico City at this nuevo brick-and-mortar outpost of a popular Arlington food truck (the latter is usually parked on 14th Street just off Route 50), which also serves south-of-the-border sodas and agua frescas; since the get-go, fans have been clamoring for seats in the small but colorful storefront and out on the back patio.

NEW Takeateasy *Pan-Latin*

- | - | - | M

Golden Triangle | 1990 M St. NW (bet. 19th & 20 Sts.) | 202-290-2440 | www.takeateasydc.com

Late-night weekend hours and moderate tabs make it easy indeed to score a bite at this Golden Triangle bistro recently launched by Fast Gourmet vets, which dishes out Latin American sandwiches (e.g. *chivito*), tapas and entrees; a full bar, happy-hour deals and dimly lit, contemporary digs make it a natural after-work drinks stop for the area's white-collar crowd.

Tako Grill *Japanese*

24 | 18 | 20 | $33

Bethesda | 7756 Wisconsin Ave. (Norfolk Ave.), MD | 301-652-7030 | www.takogrill.com

The "consistently high standard" of sushi, robatayaki and other cooked specialties appeals to supporters of this longtime midpriced Bethesda Japanese that also boasts a "strong sake selection"; the "pleasant" contemporary space is "large" enough that "you can usually get a table anytime" and promptly relax in the hands of "friendly", "efficient" servers; P.S. some nonpurists "love the brown-rice sushi" option.

	FOOD	DECOR	SERVICE	COST

Tallula/EatBar ● *American* | 24 | 20 | 22 | $40 |

Clarendon | 2761 Washington Blvd. (Daniel St.), VA | 703-778-5051 |
www.tallularestaurant.com

There's "funky decor but serious food" at these side-by-side
Clarendon New Americans, where "creativity in the kitchen" means
"an exciting mix of flavors" whether you're in the mood for the
higher-priced seasonal offerings in the formal main dining room or
just wanna "share some appetizers" in the relaxed gastropub; both
sides can get a bit "noisy" but offer the same "accommodating" service and "excellent", "affordable" wine menu.

Tandoori Nights *Indian* | 24 | 22 | 21 | $30 |

Bethesda | 7236 Woodmont Ave. (bet. Bethesda Ave. & Elm St.), MD |
301-656-4002
Gaithersburg | 106 Market St. (Kentlands Blvd.), MD |
301-947-4007
www.tandoorinightsmd.com

Sign up for "North Indian Food 101" at these tandoori night schools
where "tasty" subcontinental fare "prepared for American tastes"
runs "lighter than the more traditional styles"; the "modern" dining
rooms render a "trendy" backdrop for "attentive" service, and moderate tabs seal the deal.

Taqueria Distrito | ▽ 22 | 11 | 17 | $13 |
Federal *Mexican*

Columbia Heights | 3463 14th St. NW (Oak St.) | 202-276-7331
Petworth | 805 Kennedy St. NW (8th St.) | 202-545-6990
www.taqueriadf.com

The "fantastic" "street tacos" might be "the best you'll find north of
the Rio Grande" at these "tiny" Columbia Heights and Petworth
"joints" where photos of Latin movie stars and "obligatory fútbol
paraphernalia" make amigos feel like they're "in Mexico"; sí, the service is only "ok", but with prices as sweet as the "multiple" aguas
frescas, most "look forward to going back."

Taqueria La Placita ⊅ *Mexican* | - | - | - | I |

Hyattsville | 5020 Edmonston Rd. (Farragut St.), MD |
301-277-4477

Suburban Maryland may seem like it's south of the border thanks to
the many authentic taco versions at this inexpensive Mexican joint
in Hyattsville; the small, bright room is decorated with a massive
mural and interesting artifacts from home.

ᴺᴱᵂ Taqueria Nacional *Mexican* | - | - | - | I |

U Street Corridor | 1409 T St. NW (14th St.) | 202-299-1122 |
www.taquerianacional.com

Ann Cashion's cult-fave taco/breakfast counter-serve joint recently
relocated to the happening 14th Street NW corridor, where it was
reborn as this sit-down restaurant (though there's still no table service); fans will find all the affordable Mexican favorites, along with
frozen margaritas and beer, in a transporting setting that evokes a
small-town cafe south of the border.

Taqueria Poblano *Mexican* | 22 | 15 | 20 | $21 |

Del Ray | 2400 Mt. Vernon Ave. (Oxford Ave.) | Alexandria, VA |
703-548-8226
Arlington | 2401 Columbia Pike (Adams St.), VA | 703-271-8979
Arlington | Harrison Shopping Ctr. | 2503 N. Harrison St. (Lee Hwy.), VA |
703-237-8250
www.taqueriapoblano.com

"Swimmingly good" fish tacos are the lure at these "sunny"
Californian-inspired Mexican joints in Arlington and Del Ray that also
draw accolades for "good" salsa that hits the table "almost immedi-
ately" and "zippy" 'ritas ("no margarita mix here"); "efficient", family-
friendly service and "low prices" please an "enthusiastic crowd."

Tara Thai *Thai* | 20 | 19 | 19 | $25 |

Upper NW | Spring Valley Shopping Ctr. | 4849 Massachusetts Ave. NW
(49th St.) | 202-363-4141
Bethesda | 4828 Bethesda Ave. (bet. Arlington Rd. & Hagar Ln.), MD |
301-657-0488
Gaithersburg | Rio Entertainment Ctr. | 9811 Washingtonian Blvd.
(Rio Blvd.), MD | 301-947-8330
Hyattsville | 5501 Baltimore Ave. (Jefferson St.), MD |
301-277-7888
Rockville | Montrose Crossing | 12071 Rockville Pike (Bou Ave.), MD |
301-231-9899
Falls Church | Idylwood Plaza | 7501 Leesburg Pike (Pimmit Dr.), VA |
703-506-9788
Herndon | Worldgate Ctr. | 13021 Worldgate Dr. (Centreville Rd.), VA |
703-481-8999
Vienna | 226 Maple Ave. W. (bet. Courthouse Rd. & Pleasant St.), VA |
703-255-2467
www.tarathai.com

A "cute" "undersea vibe" sets a "relaxing" tone at this chainlet serving "reliably good" "standard-issue" Thai with a "focus on fish" for
"relatively cheap; service is "efficient", especially at lunch, and many
count it as an "around-the-corner" "favorite."

NEW Tash House | - | - | - | I |
of Kabob *Mideastern*

Capitol Hill | 524 Eighth St. SE (bet. E & G Sts.) | 202-733-1133
On a thoroughfare packed with international restaurants on
Capitol Hill, this newcomer distinguishes itself with its Middle
Eastern menu of fire-grilled meats and kebabs along with salads
and traditional sides like baba ghanoush and homemade hummus; a casually stylish cafe setting, patio and inexpensive prices
are additional draws.

Taste of Burma Ⓜ *Burmese* | ∇ 26 | 19 | 20 | $20 |

Sterling | Countryside Shopping Ctr. | 126 Edds Ln. (Cromwell Rd.), VA |
703-444-8510 | www.tasteofburma.com
Families enjoy "trying new things out" on the "exotic" 100-item menu
at this Sterling Burmese that knows "how to do spicy right"; golden
embroidered panels jazz up the otherwise simple digs, and the "relaxed" service and modest tabs solidify it as a "neighborhood favorite."

Taste of Morocco *Moroccan* ∇ 23 | 20 | 23 | $36

Clarendon | 3211 N. Washington Blvd. (Wilson Blvd.), VA | 703-527-7468 | www.atasteofmorocco.com

There's no end to the "old-school, authentic" Moroccan experience at this "breath of fresh air in Clarendon" that offers the option of a traditional multicourse dinner capped with mint tea and has a belly dancer Wednesday–Sunday; the "sincere", "generous" staff, Mediterranean-tinged setting and moderate prices are further pluses.

Taste of Saigon *Vietnamese* 22 | 21 | 22 | $28

Rockville | Rockville Town Sq. | 20 Maryland Ave. (bet. Beall Ave. & Middle Ln.), MD | 301-424-7222 | www.tasteofsaigon.com

"Not your usual pho joint", this "good-value" Vietnamese venue in Rockville brings a French influence to bear on the "consistently excellent", "authentic dishes of Saigon"; service is "extraordinarily friendly", and the atmosphere is "airy" and "attractive", adding up to a "pleasant" experience.

Tasting Room ⑤ *American* 27 | 23 | 26 | $48

Frederick | 101 N. Market St. (Church St.), MD | 240-379-7772 | www.tastetr.com

Floor-to-ceiling windows bordering a "bright, contemporary interior" mean this "sophisticated" Frederick "favorite" is literally "a place to see and be seen" while partaking of "wonderful", "well-executed" New American fare, "superb martinis" and an "extensive" wine list; it's a "splurge" and can be "crowded", but with "exceptional" service, it's suited to a "special occasion."

NEW Tavern 64 – | – | – | M
Regional Kitchen ● *American*

Reston | Hyatt Regency Reston | 1800 Presidents St. (Market St.), VA | 703-925-8250 | www.reston.hyatt.com

This new American dining and drinking option at Reston Town Center's Hyatt Regency provides guests and locals alike with a spacious, casual setting outfitted with leather chairs and banquettes as well as several large communal tables for big groups; the kitchen's midpriced regional fare features many ingredients sourced from local producers, while the bar pours local microbrews and specialty cocktails made with liquor from nearby distilleries.

Tavira *Portuguese* 25 | 20 | 24 | $47

Chevy Chase | Chevy Chase Bank Bldg. | 8401 Connecticut Ave. (Chevy Chase Lake Dr.), MD | 301-652-8684 | www.tavirarestaurant.com

"So what" if it's in the "basement of a bank" – where else to keep a "neighborhood treasure" ask acolytes of this "wonderful" Portuguese "hideaway" in Chevy Chase, where "magicians with fish" and meat make "outstanding" dishes appear from the kitchen; the "attentive" staff suggests Med wines for a "white-tablecloth" meal in an "old-world" setting complete with "high" prices (bargain-hunters suggest the three-course daily prix fixe).

	FOOD	DECOR	SERVICE	COST

NEW Taylor Charles
Steak & Ice *Sandwiches*

-	-	-	I

Atlas District | 1320 H St. NE (bet. 13th & 14th Sts.) |
202-388-6880 | www.steakandice.com

The Taylor Gourmet hoagie whizzes turn their focus to their native
Philly cheesesteak at this new, inexpensive H Street NE counter joint
wit' an industrial look; besides offering creative takes on the canon-
ical sandwich (one rendition features broccoli rabe), they also delve
into water ices, gelato, frozen custard and even the occasional salad.

Taylor Gourmet *Deli/Italian*

22	16	17	$14

Atlas District | 1116 H St. NE (bet. 11th & 12th Sts.) | 202-684-7001
Dupont Circle | 1200 19th St. NW (M St.) | 202-775-2005
NEW Golden Triangle | 624 E St. NW (7th St.) | 202-652-0145
Mt. Vernon Square/Convention Center | 485 K St. NW (bet. 4th &
5th Sts.) | 202-289-8001
Logan Circle | 1908 14th St. NW (bet. T & U Sts.) | 202-588-7117
Bethesda | 7280 Woodmont Ave. (bet. Elm St. & Hampden Ln.), MD |
301-951-9001
NEW Merrifield | 2905 District Ave. (bet. Merrifield Town Ctr. &
Strawberry Ln.), VA | 703-462-9970
www.taylorgourmet.com

With "fresh", "zesty" ingredients piled high on "perfect seeded"
bread, expats from the City of Brotherly Love feel like they've re-
turned "home" at these Philly-inspired delis where the "criminally
good" Italian-style hoagies are made to order by "friendly" crews;
low tabs match the "simple" industrial setups.

Teaism *Tearoom*

20	16	17	$17

Penn Quarter | Lexington Market Sq. | 400 Eighth St. NW (D St.) |
202-638-6010
Dupont Circle | 2009 R St. NW (Connecticut Ave.) | 202-667-3827
Golden Triangle | 800 Connecticut Ave. NW (H St.) |
202-835-2233 Ⓜ
Greater Alexandria | 682 N. St. Asaph St. (bet. Pendleton &
Wythe Sts.) | Alexandria, VA | 703-684-7777
www.teaism.com

"Linger over your tea" at this "quick", "casual" chain-coffee-shop
"alternative" serving "wonderful" leafy brews alongside "tasty"
"Eastern-flavored" bento boxes and sandwiches plus salty oat
cookies that "can improve any dreary day"; "inexpensive" tabs and
"tasteful" "Zen" decor contribute to the sense of "serenity", which
you can even take home (they have "nice tea-related gifts").

NEW Teddy & The Bully Bar *American*

-	-	-	M

Golden Triangle | 1200 19th St. NW (M St.) | 202 872-8700 |
www.teddyandthebullybar.net

Similar to its sibling Lincoln, this tribute to Theodore Roosevelt in
the Golden Triangle, draws inspiration from a former president's
persona for its midpriced American menu, drinks and decor; look for
game, house-baked breads, steak and a raw bar (Teddy loved oysters) plus a full range of classic cocktails served against a contemporary yet classic backdrop.

Ted's Bulletin *American* `23` `23` `21` `$26`

Capitol Hill | 505 Eighth St. SE (bet. E & G Sts.) | 202-544-8337 | www.tedsbulletin.com

This retro Capitol Hill "throwback" puts "twists" on its midpriced American "favorites" in an upscale luncheonette setting with authentic "art deco" details and "classic B&W movies" screened on the wall; fans warn the "only downside is long wait times", but say you'll be "delighted" once installed at the counter stools or comfy booths.

Tel'Veh Café & Wine Bar ● *Mediterranean* `-` `-` `-` `M`

Mt. Vernon Square/Convention Center | 401 Massachusetts Ave. NW (4th St.) | 202-241-9696

In the burgeoning Convention Center area is this Mediterranean from the team behind Agora, serving midpriced eats alongside a 300-label wine list; full-height windows flood the wavy, nautical-chic space with light during the day, while the rope-lined bar fills with punched-out office workers come evening.

Tempo *French/Italian* `24` `20` `23` `$36`

Greater Alexandria | 4231 Duke St. (Gordon St.) | Alexandria, VA | 703-370-7900 | www.temporestaurant.com

"You'd never believe it's a converted gas station" say advocates who appreciate this "upscale" "neighborhood treasure" in Alexandria for its "excellent" French-Italian fare and "bargain" wines; service comes "with a personal touch" in the white, airy, art-filled space, and the "reasonable" prices are often lower than what you pay at the pump.

Thai at Silver Spring *Thai* `24` `18` `21` `$22`

Silver Spring | Downtown Silver Spring | 921 Ellsworth Dr. (bet. Fenton St. & Georgia Ave.), MD | 301-650-0666 | www.thaiatsilverspring.com

With a "convenient location" in the Downtown Silver Spring complex, inexpensive tabs and a "sophisticated" look, this "consistent, delicious" Thai eatery is an attractive option; "fast" service is "accommodating" of children and suitable "if you are in a hurry to see a movie" at the nearby multiplex.

Thai Basil *Thai* `26` `15` `21` `$21`

Chantilly | Chantilly Park Shopping Ctr. | 14511 Lee Jackson Memorial Hwy. (Airline Pkwy.), VA | 703-631-8277 | www.thaibasilchantilly.com

Chef-owner Nonkgran Daks' Thai dishes are an "unexpectedly excellent" surprise given the "unremarkable" setting in a Chantilly shopping center, where this "diamond in the rough" is "always busy" (especially at lunch), and the popular cooking classes are always booked; with solid service and "bargain" prices, for those sweet on Siam, it's "nirvana."

T.H.A.I. in Shirlington *Thai* `25` `22` `23` `$24`

Shirlington | Village at Shirlington | 4029 Campbell Ave. (Randolph St.) | Arlington, VA | 703-931-3203 | www.thaiinshirlington.com

"Consistently Thai-rific" cuisine "that's not dumbed down for Western palates" gets Shirlington tongues wagging "tasty, spicy, nicey" at this area "go-to" sporting a "subdued" Eastern-accented space; "fair" prices, especially at lunch when service is suitably "speedy", please wallet-watchers.

Thaiphoon *Thai*   21 | 18 | 19 | $24

Dupont Circle | 2011 S St. NW (bet. Connecticut Ave. & 20th St.) | 202-667-3505

Pentagon City | 1301 S. Joyce St. (Army Navy Dr.) | Arlington, VA | 703-413-8200

www.thaiphoon.com

Locals are "happy with the quality" of the "traditional" Thai eats at this Pentagon City and Dupont Circle duo, with nine-to-fivers especially appreciative of the "fast lunch service"; "extraordinarily reasonable" prices mean the "modern" environs "can get packed" (especially on weekends at the S Street locale).

Thai Square *Thai*   26 | 14 | 20 | $25

Arlington | 3217 Columbia Pike (Highland St.), VA | 703-685-7040 | www.thaisquarerestaurant.com

"Enjoy the spices and the prices" at this "authentic", "consistently excellent" Thai in Arlington, where the dishes may be "simple", but the taste is "complex"; if a few fret that there's "not much to look at" in the "cozy", "rather minimal" space, most prefer to focus on the "cheerful" service or opt for takeout.

Thai Tanic *Thai*   23 | 17 | 18 | $23

Columbia Heights | 3462 14th St. NW (bet. Meridian Pl. & Newton St.) | 202-387-0882

Logan Circle | 1326 14th St. NW (bet. N St. & Rhode Island Ave.) | 202-588-1795

www.thaitanic.us

All aboard these "good, cheap and fast" Siamese twins in Logan Circle and Columbia Heights for "flavor-packed" fare, notably some "fire-hot" specialties begging to be cooled down with a "mean mai tai"; "efficient" crews keep everything running shipshape in the "sleek", "colorful" quarters as well as offer an "always dependable" delivery service.

Thunder Burger & Bar ❶ *Burgers*   24 | 21 | 20 | $22

Georgetown | 3056 M St. NW (bet. 31st & Thomas Jefferson Sts.) | 202-333-2888 | www.thunderburger.com

"Gourmet" "build-your-own" burgers with "creative" toppings and "tip-top" fries impress at this Georgetown spot whose "funky", glitzy rock-themed interior looks like something off of "VH1"; prices and service are perfectly solid – more striking, perhaps, is the "truly exceptional" draft beer list and happy hour.

Todd Gray's Watershed *American/Seafood*   ▽ 23 | 19 | 23 | $49

NoMa | Hilton Garden Inn | 1225 First St. NE (bet. M & N Sts.) | 202-534-1350 | www.toddgrayswatershed.com

Todd Gray's "gourmet touch" is on display in the "casual" seafood with a "Southern twist" at this Hilton venue in NoMa, though a recent chef change may outdate the Food rating; a few label the setting "corporate", but many area workers enjoy eating, drinking and "chatting with the bartenders" in the bar/lounge and find its spacious courtyard a "summer treat."

Toki Underground *Noodle Shop/Taiwanese*   26 | 22 | 24 | $22

Atlas District | 1234 H St. NE (bet. 12th & 13th Sts.) | 202-388-3086 | www.tokiunderground.com

"Come hungry, leave sloshy-full" of the "modern takes" on Taiwanese "comfort food", like "out-of-this-world" steamed dumplings, dished by this Atlas District "heavy-metal ramen shop"; it's a wallet-friendly "cool scene" (with a decorative skateboard ramp on the ceiling) where the "out-of-control" waits for its few seats after ordering at the counter are deemed part of the "unique" experience.

Tonic *American*   17 | 17 | 16 | $23

Foggy Bottom | Quigley's Pharmacy | 2036 G St. NW (21st St.) | 202-296-0211

Mt. Pleasant | 3155 Mt. Pleasant St. NW (bet. Irving & Lamont Sts.) | 202-986-7661 ●

www.tonicrestaurant.com

You've "got to have the tater tots" at this American duo slinging "decent" "upscale comfort" fare washed down by plenty of suds at bargain rates; service is fair for places that are "always crowded", and a "welcoming" vibe pleases "State Department types, Fed bankers and GWU students" at the three-story Foggy Bottom location, while the bi-level Mt. Pleasant branch acts as a "neighborhood *Cheers.*"

Tono Sushi *Japanese/Thai*   ▽ 22 | 15 | 24 | $25

Woodley Park | 2605 Connecticut Ave. NW (bet. Calvert St. & Woodley Rd.) | 202-332-7300 | www.tonosushi.com

"Affordable", "creative" sushi is the name of the game at this Woodley Parker that also offers cooked Japanese and Thai standards to locals and "name-tagged convention-goers" from nearby hotels; the setting is simple (brick walls, sushi counter), but a "friendly" staff will even keep "young children entertained", and the daily $1 sushi happy hour has acolytes professing their "love."

NEW Tony & Joe's Seafood Place *Seafood*   – | – | – | E

Georgetown | Washington Harbour | 3000 K St. NW (30th St.) | 202-944-4545 | www.tonyandjoes.com

Ringed by tall windows, with cascading water features, nautical wood and an upscale seafood menu featuring a few updated Chesapeake classics, this newly recommissioned Washington Harbour behemoth has been netting crowds since it was relaunched following a complete overhaul; the sweeping outdoor patio by a lovely fountain plaza provides Potomac River vistas along with cocktails, noshing and people-watching.

Tony Cheng's *Chinese*   22 | 17 | 19 | $27

Chinatown | 619 H St. NW (bet. 6th & 7th Sts.) | 202-842-8669 | www.tonychengrestaurant.com

A Chinatown "institution", this Asian triple play offers diners three options: upstairs, a "complex" Chinese menu, plus "quality" daily dim sum (although carts roll only on the weekends), and downstairs, an "authentic", "way-to-go" Mongolian BBQ buffet; service is professional in accord with the (some say "dated") white-tablecloth look, though tabs are positively Formican.

Tosca 🖫 *Italian*   27 | 24 | 26 | $68

Penn Quarter | 1112 F St. NW (bet. 11th & 12th Sts.) | 202-367-1990 | www.toscadc.com

"Fine dining gets no finer" say fans, than at this "sophisticated" Penn Quarter Italian where the "flawless", uniformed waiters deliver near-"perfect" food as "ex-senators and lobbyists swap business cards" in the "elegant" neutral-toned setting; it's a perfect place for observing "how Washington really works", and the relatively "affordable" pre-theater dinner menu is ideal "for those not on an expense account."

Toscana Café *Deli/Italian*   ▽ 25 | 20 | 25 | $42

Capitol Hill | 601 Second St. NE (F St.) | 202-525-2693 | www.toscanacafedc.com

Chef-owner Daniele Catalani evokes his native Tuscany in a "rustic" Capitol Hill townhouse, hidden behind Union Station, where "outstanding" housemade pastas, pizza and focaccia sandwiches are doled out in a first-floor counter-serve at lunch, while in the evening "fabulous" dinners are set in the trim upstairs dining room; relatively "reasonable" prices, "fast" service and an outdoor patio are highlights of this "funky" trattoria.

Town Hall ◑ *American*   ▽ 23 | 19 | 22 | $27

Glover Park | 2340 Wisconsin Ave. NW (bet. Calvert St. & Hall Pl.) | 202-333-5640 | www.townhalldc.com

Glover Park's young set gravitates to this all-American neighborhood "mecca" for "food, drinks and good times"; the rustic, art-filled dining room is suited to downing midpriced quality fare like grilled cheese, burgers and salads – and there's a breezy garden patio and sundeck that's ideal for a "cool cocktail."

NEW Trademark *American*   - | - | - | M

Greater Alexandria | Westin Alexandria | 2080 Jamieson Ave. (bet. Dulany St. & Mill Rd.) | Alexandria, VA | 703-253-8640 | www.trademarkdrinkandeat.com

This newly patented hotel eatery in Alexandria's Carlyle District serves a midpriced menu of American comfort classics like mac 'n' cheese and beer-can chicken; the smart-looking space has a lounge atmosphere courtesy of a serious bar pouring creative cocktails, with photos of famous inventors adorning the walls, a nod to the nearby U.S. Patent & Trademark Office.

Trummer's On Main 🅼 *American*   24 | 26 | 24 | $71

Clifton | 7134 Main St. (bet. Chapel St. & Clifton Creek Dr.), VA | 703-266-1623 | www.trummersonmain.com

Take a "culinary journey" to "bucolic" Clifton, VA, for "dive" wines and a "memorable", "inspired" New American menu, now under the direction of new chef Austin Fausett (ex Central), who has added southern, seasonal and modernist touches; the "beautiful, bright", "richly" appointed main dining room and buzzing bar, overseen by a "top-notch" staff, make for a "perfect" evening that's "pricey but worth every cent."

Tryst ● *Coffeehouse*

| 21 | 22 | 19 | $17 |

Adams Morgan | 2459 18th St. NW (bet. Columbia & Kalorama Rds.) | 202-232-5500 | www.trystdc.com

"Thick-rimmed glasses" and "laptops" are the must-have accessories at Adams Morgan's "packed" answer to a "Berkeley" coffeehouse, where "comfy", "unhomologous" furniture and "great" music (recorded by day, live some nights) invite "hipsters" to "hang out" nursing a latte or noshing on "reasonably priced" "sandwiches and sweets"; "friendly" service matches the "relaxed" groove – speaking of which, wine, beer and cocktails offer further opportunities to "chill."

Tuscarora Mill *American*

| 25 | 25 | 25 | $45 |

Leesburg | Market Station | 203 Harrison St. SE (Loudoun St.), VA | 703-771-9300 | www.tuskies.com

Set in a restored old mill and affectionately known as 'Tuskie's' by its tony "horse-country" clientele, this longtime Leesburger features "superb", "creative" American fare complemented by Virginia wines and served in a "romantic" dining room, "rustic" bar or garden room; "polished" service matches the "expensive" price tag (the cafe menu is cheaper), providing grist for those who claim it's the area's "finest white-tablecloth restaurant."

Tutto Bene *Italian/S American*

| ▽ 23 | 18 | 20 | $27 |

Ballston | 501 N. Randolph St. (5th Rd.) | Arlington, VA | 703-522-1005 | www.tuttobeneitalian.com

Few know that this "old-school Italian banquet hall" in Ballston, frequented by an "older crowd", lives a double life on the weekends when it serves "authentic" food from the Bolivian Highlands (the popular *salteñas,* which resemble baked empanadas, are available daily); service is solid and fare midpriced, so everything is, indeed, *tutto bene.*

2941 Restaurant ⊠ *American*

| 27 | 27 | 26 | $70 |

Falls Church | 2941 Fairview Park Dr. (I-495), VA | 703-270-1500 | www.2941.com

This "French-meets-American" "oasis" "hidden" in a Falls Church office park boasts a "casually elegant" look (recently updated, possibly outdating its Decor rating) to match chef Bertrand Chemel's ambitious bistro menu, which includes a large number of offerings like small plates and pastas at "reasonable" prices; longtime loyalists say the "focused" staff and "stunning" setting – with floor-to-ceiling windows showcasing "beautifully landscaped" grounds – remain as some of the "2,941 reasons to love this place."

2100 Prime *American*

| 24 | 23 | 22 | $56 |

Dupont Circle | The Fairfax at Embassy Row Hotel | 2100 Massachusetts Ave. NW (21st St.) | 202-835-2100 | www.2100prime.com

Formerly home of the "classic" Jockey Club, this storied Dupont Circle hotel dining room now features an "excellent" slate of "elegant

[American] comfort" food served with "attention to detail"; "prime" pricing goes with the "upscale" private-club vibe that emanates from its wood-paneled walls and equestrian-themed art.

Twisted Vines Bottleshop & Bistro *Eclectic*

▽ 20 | 21 | 23 | $26

Arlington | 2803 Columbia Pike (Walter Reed Dr.), VA | 571-482-8581 | www.twisted-vines.com

They're "helpful about explaining" Cabs and Chards at this triple threat in South Arlington – part "great little wine bar", part bottle shop with an "eclectic selection" and part bistro with a "small" menu of "interesting" cheeses, charcuterie, entrees and flatbreads; a mod yet "cozy atmosphere" with window seats and a sinuous bar, combined with "fun" tasting events, have area oenophiles "thrilled."

2 Amys *Pizza*

25 | 17 | 20 | $25

Cleveland Park | 3715 Macomb St. NW (Wisconsin Ave.) | 202-885-5700 | www.2amyspizza.com

"Dough my god, the crust!" gush groupies wowed by the "ambrosial" DOC-certified Neapolitan pies at this "popular" Cleveland Park pizzeria (some tout the "exceptional" small plates too); the scene inside the "sunny", white-tiled premises can be "mayhem" – it's a "yuppies-with-kids" magnet – but once the "friendly" staff delivers the "excellent-for-the-price" food, most "everyone is happy" – especially after swigging one of the "treasures on tap" or something from the quieter wine bar's "adventurous selection."

Ulah Bistro ◐ *American*

20 | 20 | 20 | $31

U Street Corridor | 1214 U St. NW (bet. 12th & 13th Sts.) | 202-234-0123 | www.ulahbistro.com

The "tasty", "reliable" menu at this "rustic-chic" bi-level U Street American bistro trades on its "variety" – both in its offerings (pizza, sandwiches, pastas, chops, pub grub and more) and its "good range of prices"; the "easygoing" crowd also appreciates a "low-key" vibe from the "friendly" staff and the flowing "libations."

Uncle Julio's *Tex-Mex*

21 | 19 | 20 | $26

Bethesda | 4870 Bethesda Ave. (Arlington Rd.), MD | 301-656-2981
Gaithersburg | 231 Rio Blvd. (Washingtonian Blvd.), MD | 240-632-2150
Ballston | 4301 N. Fairfax Dr. (Taylor St.) | Arlington, VA | 703-528-3131
Fairfax | 4251 Fairfax Corner Ave. (Monument Dr.), VA | 703-266-7760
Reston | Reston Town Ctr. | 1827 Library St. (Democracy Dr.), VA | 703-904-0703
Woodbridge | Stonebridge At Potomac Town Ctr. | 14900 Potomac Town Pl. (Potomac Town Ctr.), VA | 703-763-7322 www.unclejulios.com

Believers say *"bueno"* to "absolutely huge portions" of this Dallas-based chain's midpriced "Texican" grub, with the "endless" chips and salsa scooping up *mucho* praise, along with the "obligatory 'swirl'" (a drink of layered frozen margarita and sangria), all served "quick" in a colorful hacienda-style setting; that parents can bring children and "never feel nervous about them being too loud" has some quipping it's the "Chuck E. Cheese's of Mexican" eateries.

	FOOD	DECOR	SERVICE	COST

Unum *American*

| | – | – | – | E |

Georgetown | 2917 M St. NW (bet. 29th & 30th Sts.) | 202-621-6959 | www.unumdc.com

Culinary and political worlds meet at this singular spot in Georgetown owned by chef Phillip Blane and his wife, Laura Schiller (Barbara Boxer's chief of staff), where high-end, creative takes on America's many culinary traditions are presented within intimate, modern rusticity; there's also an inviting bar with cheese and charcuterie to pair smartly with cocktails, craft beer and international wines.

Urbana *French/Italian*

| | 21 | 22 | 21 | $44 |

Dupont Circle | Hotel Palomar | 2121 P St. NW (bet. 21st & 22nd Sts.) | 202-956-6650 | www.urbanadc.com

Step down into a "sexy", "cool" enclave for "consistently good" French-Italian fare in Dupont Circle's Hotel Palomar, where a "young" crowd gives it a "local hangout" vibe; bar noshes and "friendly" bartenders keep happy hour "frenetic", but dinner can be great for an intimate "date", thanks in part to "perfectly selected" "wine pairings."

Urban Bar-B-Que Company *BBQ*

| | 24 | 16 | 19 | $18 |

Rockville | 2007 Chapman Ave. (Twinbrook Pkwy.), MD | 240-290-4827
Rockville | Rock Creek Village Ctr. | 5566 Norbeck Rd. (Bauer Dr.), MD | 301-460-0050 ●
Sandy Springs | 805 Olney Sandy Spring Rd. (Skymeadow Way), MD | 301-570-3663 ●
Silver Spring | Hillandale Shopping Ctr. | 10163 New Hampshire Ave. (Powder Mill Rd.), MD | 301-434-7427
Ashburn | Ashburn Village Shopping Ctr. | 44050 Ashburn Village Shopping Ctr. (Christiana Dr.), VA | 703-858-7226
www.urbanbbqco.com

Be prepared to "get dirty" digging into the "juicy", "tender", "smoky" meat at these "down-to-earth" BBQ havens guaranteed to "fatten you up" on the "cheap"; "takeout is big" at the counter-serve operations, while other locations boast table service and bars, but all of them are "friendly" and plastered with "kitschy" bumper stickers and the like.

Vapiano *Italian*

| | 20 | 20 | 17 | $20 |

Chinatown | 625 H St. NW (bet. 6th & 7th Sts.) | 202-621-7636
Golden Triangle | 1800 M St. NW (18th St.) | 202-640-1868
Bethesda | 4900 Hampden Ln. (Woodmont Ave.), MD | 301-215-7013
Ballston | 4401 Wilson Blvd. (Glebe Rd.) | Arlington, VA | 703-528-3113
Reston | Reston Town Ctr. | 1875 Explorer St. (bet. Freedom Dr. & Market St.), VA | 571-281-2893
Sterling | Dulles Town Ctr. | 21100 Dulles Town Circle (Nokes Blvd.), VA | 703-574-4740
www.vapiano.com

"A swanky cafeteria with made-to-order food", this Italian chain does things differently with a card system for "DIY" ordering ("convenient for large groups", although a few find it "complicates dining")

and "solid" pasta, pizza and salad stations staffed with "delightful" chefs; so what if you "bus your own table", "the price is right", and many "love" the "fresh potted herbs" throughout the space.

Vaso's Kitchen 🗷 *Greek* `26` `17` `24` `$30`

Old Town | 1225 Powhatan St. (Bashford Ln.) | Alexandria, VA | 703-548-2747

The "historic BBQ pig" neon sign on the roof of this Old Town "gem" offers no clues as to the "excellent" Greek and Italian "comfort food" within; expect to be treated "with real warmth" in the "cute, little" dining room or the "nice" patio, so with "moderate" prices ("rare in this area"), it's a "must-try."

NEW Vendetta *Italian* `-` `-` `-` `M`

Atlas District | 1212 H St. NE (12th St.) | 202-399-3201 | www.vendettadc.com

Nightlife impresario Joe Englert's new Italian bar/restaurant offers plenty of wine and beer together with mix-and-match pastas (choice of sauce and noodle shape) for a casual, booze-fueled evening out in the Atlas District; the bi-level space sports playful touches like Vespas, vintage Italian advertising posters, paparazzi-style cameras and two 25-ft. bocce courts abutting the tables (*attento!*).

Vermilion *American* `26` `22` `24` `$51`

Old Town | 1120 King St. (bet. Fayette & Henry Sts.) | Alexandria, VA | 703-684-9669 | www.vermilionrestaurant.com

Old Town's "farm-to-table" "jewel" glimmers with a "constantly changing" menu of "wonderfully prepared" New American fare, offered in a "hip", "chic" atmosphere ("romantic" dining room or "lively" bar) where "foodies" rave over the "awesome" tasting menu with wine pairings served by a "fabulous" staff; "terrific lunch deals" and happy-hour specials satisfy those who worry that "prices are a bit high."

Vidalia *Southern* `26` `24` `25` `$63`

Golden Triangle | 1990 M St. NW (bet. 19th & 20th Sts.) | 202-659-1990 | www.vidaliadc.com

"Southern roots" sprout "undeniably cosmopolitan" blossoms on the "inspired" New American menu at this fine-dining "favorite" in Golden Triangle, where the "impeccable" staff makes each meal "an event in itself"; hidden underground, the "comfortably" "elegant" setting is "just right" for "intimate moments" and "special events", with "witty" cocktails and happy-hour specials in the lounge; P.S. for around $20, the three-course lunch is a "fantastic deal."

Village Bistro *European* ∇ `26` `20` `24` `$38`

Courthouse | Colonial Vill. | 1723 Wilson Blvd. (bet. Quinn & Rhodes Sts.) | Arlington, VA | 703-522-0284 | www.villagebistro.com

A wide range of "European-style" cuisine that's "excellent for the price" has long been the draw at this Arlington Courthouse "gem" with a French-leaning wine list and "small-town" feel; the "friendli-est" staff tends to a cozy, tin-ceilinged bistro-style room "crowded" with everyone from "groups" to "dates."

Villa Mozart ☒ *Italian* `26` `21` `25` `$49`

Fairfax | 4009 Chain Bridge Rd. (Main St.), VA | 703-691-4747 |
www.villamozartrestaurant.com

Chef-owner Andrea Pace brings a "delicate balance" of "inventive",
"delicious" Northern Italian flavors to his "classically elegant" Fairfax
ristorante where the "polished" service and "formal yet not intimi-
dating" grayscale environs say "special event"; the "small, quiet"
space (perfect for eavesdroppers) encourages reservations, and the
prix fixe menus are a welcome option for those who cry "expensive."

Vinifera Wine Bar & Bistro *American* ▽ `23` `22` `22` `$45`

Reston | Westin Reston Heights | 11750 Sunrise Valley Dr.
(Reston Pkwy.), VA | 703-234-3550 | www.viniferabistro.com

"Tucked away" in the Westin Reston Heights, this New American
harbors a "vast" vino vault to go with its "ambitious" seasonal menu
that includes small plates with "big flavor"; the "soothing", glam environment, including a nightclubby lounge and a patio with fire pits,
"invites you to get cozy", as do "accommodating" staffers.

Vinoteca ● *Eclectic* `22` `21` `21` `$35`

U Street Corridor | 1940 11th St. NW (U St.) | 202-332-9463 |
www.vinotecadc.com

It's "fun to eat, drink and socialize" at this "hip" U Street wine bar/
bistro with "knowledgeable" servers uncorking "lovely" vintages to
match its "tasty" Eclectic "nosh"; pops of red punctuate the "chic",
"romantic" interior, and with bocce on the "back patio", "how could
you go wrong?"

NEW Vino Volo *Italian* `–` `–` `–` `M`

Bethesda | 7243-7247 Woodmont Ave. (Elm St.), MD | 301-656-0916 |
www.vinovolobethesdarow.com

This modern wine bar – with outlets at many major U.S. airports, including Dulles and Baltimore's BWI – recently touched down in
Bethesda with its first non-airport venue; the rustic, wine country atmosphere is an appropriate backdrop for wine flights and its midpriced
menu of Italian small plates; P.S. there's also a wine shop.

Virtue Feed & Grain Ⓜ *American* `–` `–` `–` `M`

Old Town | 106 S. Union St. (bet. King & Prince Sts.) | Alexandria, VA |
571-970-3669 | www.virtuefeedandgrain.com

The rustic-meets-urban confines of this 18th-century granary in Old
Town now houses a more casual American bar and grill following the
departure of original owner Cathal Armstrong; new owners have installed a more approachable menu featuring bar food, burgers and
such that should keep the bar lively and fuel the competitive buzz
upstairs in the game room.

Volt Ⓜ *American* `28` `26` `28` `$104`

Frederick | Houck Mansion | 228 N. Market St. (bet. 2nd & 3rd Sts.), MD |
301-696-8658 | www.voltrestaurant.com

An "evening in foodie heaven" awaits at this true "dining destination" in a "beautiful", contemporized 1890s mansion in Frederick,

where chef/co-owner Bryan Voltaggio "evokes a sense of wonder" with his "exotically scrumptious" New American meals based on seasonal ingredients; choose from several prix fixe options for dinner, including a "well-choreographed" 21-course "culinary adventure", then let the "incredibly friendly", "top-notch" servers take it from there; "is it expensive? yes – is it really worth it? yes."

NEW Wagshal's *American* | - | - | - | M |

Upper NW | 3201 New Mexico Ave. NW (Macomb St.) | 202-363-0884 Ex. 3 | www.wagshals.com

From a beloved, homegrown grocery chain comes this new Upper NW multitasker that's part market, part restaurant; the market side includes a deli, bakery, produce and seafood departments plus ready-to-eat meals, while the company's famous brisket sandwiches, along with burgers, pastas and the like, are available at its indoor/outdoor American eatery; P.S. Wagshal's other stores remain open.

Westend Bistro *American* | 22 | 21 | 22 | $57 |

West End | Ritz-Carlton, Washington DC | 1190 22nd St. NW (M St.) | 202-974-4900 | www.westendbistrodc.com

While this New American bistro in the West End Ritz-Carlton and chef Eric Ripart have parted ways post-Survey, not much else has changed: its "lovely combinations" of "seasonal" food "awaken the taste buds" and are ferried by a pro crew in a "sleek" and "lively" setting; true, a vocal minority complains it's "overpriced", but most say it "doesn't disappoint" and praise "wonderful" cocktails and happy-hour deals that make the bar a "highlight" for the "ultracool" crowd.

We the Pizza ☒ *Pizza* | 22 | 15 | 17 | $16 |

Capitol Hill | 305 Pennsylania Ave. SE (bet. 3rd & 4th Sts.) | 202-544-4008 | www.wethepizza.com

Spike Mendelsohn's "superb" take on NY-style pizza "could lead to consensus between even the most contentious political opponents" say partisans of his cheap, "no-frills but cute" joint on Capitol Hill (next to his Good Stuff Eatery); beyond slices and pies, wings, salads and "incredible" jerked sodas are also a draw, so though it's "crowdy" ("all interns, all the time"), most keep "coming back for more."

Wildfire *Seafood/Steak* | 22 | 21 | 22 | $42 |

Tysons Corner | Tysons Galleria | 1714 International Dr. (Tysons Blvd.) | McLean, VA | 703-442-9110 | www.wildfirerestaurant.com

You almost expect to rub shoulders with "gentlemen in three-piece suits and fedoras" in the "dark", "sophisticated" expanses of this "pricey" Chicago-born surf 'n' turfer with a "1940s" supper club vibe at the Tysons Galleria; "consistent" staffers ferry "large" portions of "delicious" eats and "perfect" martinis through the "bustle" to guys and dolls who call it a "great date place."

Wild Tomato *American* | 22 | 13 | 17 | $28 |

Cabin John | 7945 MacArthur Blvd. (79th St.), MD | 301-229-0680 | www.wildtomatorestaurant.com

An "oasis in a food desert", this "sorely needed" Cabin John bistro turns out "enjoyable" pizza and other "all-American" "genuine comfort" fare that will "satisfy almost anyone" – and for a "reasonable price"; despite the "informal", "plain" setting, it's often "jammed", though the "young" servers are nevertheless "attentive."

NEW Wildwood Kitchen *Mediterranean* — — — E

Bethesda | Wildwood Shopping Ctr. | 10307 Old Georgetown Rd. (Cheshire Dr.), MD | 301-571-1700 | www.wildwoodkitchenrw.com
The latest venture from Robert Wiedmaier (Marcel's, Brabo, Brasserie Beck) is this sophisticated, upscale eatery in Bethesda's Wildwood Shopping Center, which specializes in light and healthy Mediterranean fare; a see-and-be-seen crowd settles into a warm space that evokes the outdoors with nature photography, raw wood and chandeliers that evoke tree branches.

William Jeffrey's Tavern ● *American* ▽ 20 | 22 | 18 | $25

Arlington | 2301 Columbia Pike (bet. Barton & Wayne Sts.), VA | 703-746-6333 | www.williamjeffreystavern.com
This "welcoming" American, a "nice addition to the 'Pike'" in South Arlington, satisfies with a "creative, affordable" tavern menu and an "extensive" craft-beer list; "classy" digs that are part prohibition (speakeasy murals, tin ceilings), part exhibition (flat-screen TVs, communal high-tops) leave most declaring it "a winner."

Willow ⊠ *American* 24 | 22 | 22 | $50

Ballston | 4301 N. Fairfax Dr. (bet. Taylor & Utah Sts.) | Arlington, VA | 703-465-8800 | www.willowva.com
"Culinary art", in the form of contemporary Americana, awaits at this "fine-dining" bastion in Ballston's "concrete jungle", where "attentive" servers suggest "excellent wine pairings" to accompany the "beautifully presented" seasonal dishes; a "grown-up" crowd appreciates the "relaxed", "elegant" atmosphere (mood lighting, jewel tones, mahogany), a patio with "real trees" (though not willows) and a "clubby" bar serving small plates.

Wine Kitchen Ⓜ *American* 26 | 24 | 25 | $34

Frederick | 50 Carroll Creek Way (Market St.), MD | 301-663-6968
Leesburg | 7 S. King St. (Market St.), VA | 703-777-9463
www.thewinekitchen.com
These New American wine bars "tickle the taste buds" with flights from their "dynamic" vino selection and "phenomenal" "matching" fare, featuring "unusual combinations that work" in Leesburg and Frederick, the latter of which does small plates; the urbanely countrified premises are patrolled by a "friendly" staff, and "reasonable" prices seal the deal.

Wings To Go *Chicken* 25 | 16 | 22 | $18

Capitol Hill | 3502 12th St. NE (Monroe St.) | 202-529-7619 | www.wingstogodc.com
There's "no atmosphere, but who cares" with such "excellent" wings and so "many different types of sauces" at this Capitol Hill take-out "staple for the college kids and neighborhood folks", which also serves pizza and subs; bonus: the "not-expensive" fare comes "quick" and "friendly."

Woodlands Restaurant *Indian/Vegetarian* 24 | 15 | 20 | $20

Hyattsville | 8046 New Hampshire Ave. (Lebanon St.), MD | 301-434-4202 | www.woodlandsrestaurants.com

"Authentic and delicious" South Indian vegetarian fare is the "main attraction" at this subcontinental survivor that's also valued by the Hyattsville hoi polloi for its "cheap, cheap, cheap" prices, especially during its "excellent" lunch buffet; if the storefront space is "without a lot of ambiance", it's made up for by "very friendly" service.

NEW Woodward Table *American* - | - | - | E

Downtown | Woodward Bldg. | 1426 H St. NW (15th St.) | 202-347-5355 | www.woodwardtable.com

Restaurateur Jeffrey Buben (Bistro Bis, Vidalia) is behind this American bistro in the Woodward Building Downtown serving expensive regional classics in a sit-down dining room and cheaper breakfast and lunch at a casual eat-in/take-out annex called WTF (short for, er, Woodward Takeout Food); the main restaurant has a spacious, modern feel with wraparound streetscape views and an open kitchen, while the express area is decked out in white and cherry-red tiles.

Woo Lae Oak *Korean* 23 | 21 | 18 | $36

Tysons Corner | 8240 Leesburg Pike (Chain Bridge Rd.) | Vienna, VA | 703-827-7300 | www.woolaeoak.com

Most give "two thumbs-up" to this "upscale Korean" banquet hall-style restaurant in Tysons Corner, serving "premium-quality" barbecue (plus other standards and sushi) in a "vibrant", "elegant" setting that's a "marriage of modern and traditional" Asian decor; "rooftop parking" is another perk beyond the "attentive" service and moderate prices.

Woomi Garden ● *Korean* 20 | 15 | 19 | $27

Wheaton | 2423 Hickerson Dr. (bet. Elkin St. & Georgia Ave.), MD | 301-933-0100 | www.woomigarden.com

"Get an education" in bibimbop, bulgogi and other Korean staples at this no-frills Wheaton emissary known for its lunch buffet "bargain", pricier "grill-your-own" barbecue and even sushi from a small Japanese menu; "pleasant" service helps keep it "jammed", so if you hate crowds, chill out with a cold sake, or come on the "later" side of dinner.

X.O. Taste *Chinese* 24 | 14 | 17 | $24

Germantown | Middlebrook Village Shopping Ctr. | 11542 Middlebrook Rd. (Frederick Rd.), MD | 240-686-3560
Falls Church | 6124 Arlington Blvd. (Patrick Henry Dr.), VA | 703-536-1630 ●

Falls Church and Germantown locals challenge their palates with "outstanding" Hong Kong-style choices from a menu as "huge" as the portions at this Cantonese twosome; there's not "much to look at" (aside from the lobster tanks), but with service so "friendly" you trust their suggestions, you're in for "one of the best Chinese meals" around.

| | FOOD | DECOR | SERVICE | COST |

Yama *Japanese*
25 | 18 | 23 | $27

Vienna | Jade Plaza | 328 Maple Ave. W. (Nutley St.), VA | 703-242-7703 | www.sushiyamava.com

"Sit at the bar" and "watch the artistry" unfold at what's an "amazing sushi place for a Vienna strip mall" and that delivers "yummy" Japanese fare of all stripes (tempura, katsu, noodles) in a minimalist space; it's a "value for the money", servers are "warm and responsive" and "reservations on weekends" are suggested.

Yamazato *Japanese*
25 | 18 | 22 | $29

Greater Alexandria | Beauregard Sq. | 6303 Little River Tpke. (Beauregard St.) | Alexandria, VA | 703-914-8877 | www.yamazato.net

A "perfect balance between modern Western style and [traditional] Japanese spirit" can be found at this "always consistent" sushi spot in Alexandria known for its "fresh, innovative" take on raw fish, "superb" cooked Japanese fare and even a few "delicious" Thai dishes, all at a "great price"; "trendy" green-and-orange decor and an "über-friendly" staff help keep it on rotation as a local "favorite."

Yechon ● *Japanese/Korean*
22 | 16 | 18 | $23

Annandale | 4121 Hummer Rd. (Little River Tpke.), VA | 703-914-4646

"They've got it all" at this budget Annandale Japanese-Korean, from "authentic" barbecue "prepared at your table" to "good" sushi, and "the best part might be" the "little dishes you get before you even order" (aka banchan); a low-frills, "hustle-bustle ambiance" requires patience "if you arrive at the peak time", but service from the traditionally dressed staff is "quick"; P.S. the 24/7 hours are "an added plus."

🆕 Yo! Sushi *Japanese*
- | - | - | I

Capitol Hill | Union Station | 50 Massachusetts Ave. NE (1st St.) | 202-408-1716 | www.yosushi.com

Sushi and other affordable Japanese dishes zoom by diners who snatch them off a conveyor belt (*kaiten*) as they pass at this international chain restaurant in Union Station, a quick system suited to on-the-go Capitol Hill staffers and travelers; a riot of urban Tokyo and DC images adorns the walls of the futuristic, red, orange and white space.

Yosaku *Japanese*
21 | 14 | 23 | $29

Upper NW | 4712 Wisconsin Ave. NW (bet. Chesapeake & Ellicott Sts.) | 202-363-4453 | www.yosakusushi.com

The "staff treats everyone like a returning customer" at this Tenleytown "old favorite" dating from "before there was sushi in the grocery store"; it's traditionally "nondescript", but offers a "huge value" on "traditional" and "creative" raw fish and other Japanese dishes, in particular the "bargain" lunch and "deal" of a happy hour.

Yuan Fu *Chinese/Vegan*
25 | 16 | 23 | $20

Rockville | 798 Rockville Pike (Wootton Pkwy.), MD | 301-762-5937 | www.yuanfuvegetarian.com

Converts report they went in "skeptical" and "came out a true believer" thanks to an "incredible menu" of "mock meats" that'll make "you wonder 'how'd they do it?'" at this reasonably priced Chinese vegan haven in Rockville; it "doesn't look like much from the outside", and inside it's "tight quarters", but the "warm" service has habitués feeling "like family."

NEW Yuzu *Japanese*

| - | - | - | M |

Bethesda | 7345 Wisconsin Ave. (bet. Montgomery Ave. & Waverly St.), MD | 301-656-234 | www.yuzubethesda.com

Chef-owner Yoshihisa Ota (a former part-owner of Kushi) unveils jewellike sushi and moderately priced traditional Japanese small plates at his Bethesda newcomer; its spare surroundings include seating at a hand-hewn maple chef's table for those who want to partake of the special omakase menu.

Yves Bistro *French*

| 25 | 21 | 21 | $27 |

Old Town | 235 Swamp Fox Rd. (Eisenhower Ave.) | Alexandria, VA | 703-329-1010 | www.yvesbistrova.com

For a "warm", "down-to-earth" French dining experience, this "charming" peach-colored bistro/cafe in Old Town (across from the Eisenhower Avenue Metro stop and AMC cinema) has connoisseurs raving about its "excellent" "home-cooked" provincial fare; it's an "outstanding value" for the "quality", from breakfast through dinner, and the "friendly" owner "seems to be working at all times."

Zaytinya *Mediterranean/Mideastern*

| 26 | 24 | 22 | $43 |

Penn Quarter | Pepco Bldg. | 701 Ninth St. NW (bet. G & H Sts.) | 202-638-0800 | www.zaytinya.com

"Who can resist" the "wonders" of chef José Andrés' "unbelievably tasty" Eastern Mediterranean meze, especially when paired with "phenomenal" regional wines in a "beautiful, light, airy" setting close to everything in the Penn Quarter; the city's "enduring" "love affair" with this "crazy, loud" stunner means reservations are "highly recommended", but once your "culinary tour" is booked, a "helpful staff" will be your "guide" – just beware: it's "hard to keep the bill down with so many tempting small plates."

Zeffirelli Ristorante *Italian*

| 24 | 21 | 25 | $43 |

Herndon | 728 Pine St. (Station St.), VA | 703-318-7000 | www.zeffirelliristorante.com

"It's hard to resist" the "wonderful" signature veal chop say long-time customers who look to this Herndon Italian mainstay as a setting for a "special occasion" or "romantic evening", with its "pleasant" candlelit setting; it's expensive, but the "extensive" wine list and "warm", family-owned atmosphere make it a comfortable fit, time and again.

Zengo *Asian/Pan-Latin*

| 22 | 23 | 20 | $41 |

Chinatown | Gallery Pl. | 781 Seventh St. NW (bet. F & H Sts.) | 202-393-2929 | www.richardsandoval.com

This Chinatown outpost of Richard Sandoval's Asian-Latin fusion concept is "always buzzing" with groups of "adventuresome" friends sampling "creative", if "somewhat pricey", small plates ferried by a professional crew; the "sexy", "Vegasy vibe" appeals to PYTs who take full advantage of the "terrific", "heavy-on-the-booze" cocktails and "great" happy hour.

Zentan *Asian*

22 | 22 | 20 | $43

Downtown | Donovan Hse. | 1155 14th St. NW (Thomas Cir.) | 202-379-4366 | www.zentanrestaurant.com

"Trendsetting cocktails" draw a "wild, fun" bar crowd to this "hip" Downtown hotel resto-lounge, now managed by the Kimpton brand, where diners feast on Asian fusion fare and "fresh, innovative" sushi from chef Jennifer Nguyen, whose post-Survey arrival may outdate the Food rating; it's "pricey", and service is just "ok", but most find it "delightful" chilling in the "sleek", sexy "black-lacquered" interior (the restaurant is also responsible for nibbles at the hotel's stunning rooftop lounge, DNV).

Zest *American*

21 | 18 | 22 | $32

Capitol Hill | 735 Eighth St. SE (bet. G & I Sts.) | 202-544-7171 | www.zestbistro.com

"Easy to miss" on Capitol Hill's Barracks Row, this "solid", "moderately" priced New American bistro charms neighborhood denizens with its "tasty sandwiches", Tuesday nights' half-off wine bottles ("just have a ride ready") and a "cheerful" staff; a "nice mix of couples, groups and families" fills the "small but bustling" brick-walled space, although it's "lovely to sit outside on a fine day."

Zorba's Cafe ● *Greek*

23 | 16 | 20 | $20

Dupont Circle | 1612 20th St. NW (bet. Hillyer Pl. & Q St.) | 202-387-8555 | www.zorbascafe.com

This "cheap Greek stays the same" say Dupont Circle denizens who appreciate the perennial nature of the bi-level blue-and-white "hole-in-the-wall" where you "order at the counter" and "lug your pungent kebabs or salty-good salad" outside for "people-watching" and Hellenic "background music" or upstairs for "nice views"; solid service aids in its forte: a "quick, casual meal."

WASHINGTON, DC
INDEXES*

LOCATION MAPS

---

* These lists include low vote places that do not qualify for top lists.

Special Features

Listings cover the best in each category and include names, locations and Food ratings. Multi-location restaurants' features may vary by branch.

ADDITIONS

(Properties added since the last edition of the book)

AGB | **Georgetown** ⌐⌐

Ambar | **Cap Hill** ⌐⌐

Ancora | **Foggy Bottom** ⌐⌐

&pizza | **multi.** ⌐⌐

Aroma Espresso | **Bethesda** ⌐⌐

Astro | **D'town** ⌐⌐

Azur | **Penn Qtr** ⌐⌐

Beau Thai | **multi.** ⌐⌐

Bench | **Gaith'burg** ⌐⌐

Beuchert's | **Cap Hill** ⌐⌐

Black Whiskey | **Logan Cir** ⌐⌐

Bóveda | **West End** ⌐⌐

Brickside | **Bethesda** ⌐⌐

B Too | **Logan Cir** ⌐⌐

Bub & Pops | **Dupont Cir** ⌐⌐

Bungalow | **Sterling** ⌐⌐

Carving Room | **Chinatown** ⌐⌐

Chupacabra | **Atlas Dist** ⌐⌐

Crossroads | **World Bank** ⌐⌐

Daikaya Izakaya | **Chinatown** ⌐⌐

Daikaya Ramen | **Chinatown** ⌐⌐

Decanter | **D'town** ⌐⌐

Del Campo | **Penn Qtr** ⌐⌐

DGS Deli | **Dupont Cir** ⌐⌐

East Dumpling | **Rockville** ⌐⌐

Edgar | **Gldn Triangle** ⌐⌐

Etto | **Logan Cir** ⌐⌐

Farmers Fishers | **Georgetown** ⌐⌐

Fat Shorty's | **Clarendon** ⌐⌐

Fuego Cocina | **Clarendon** ⌐⌐

GBD | **Dupont Cir** ⌐⌐

Ghibellina | **Logan Cir** ⌐⌐

Grill Room | **Georgetown** ⌐⌐

Gryphon | **Dupont Cir** ⌐⌐

Hikari | **Atlas Dist** ⌐⌐

Izakaya Seki | **U St** ⌐⌐

Jardenea | **West End** ⌐⌐

Kadhai | **Bethesda** ⌐⌐

La Tagliatella | **Clarendon** ⌐⌐

Le Diplomate | **Logan Cir** ⌐⌐

Le Grenier | **Atlas Dist** ⌐⌐

Little Ricky's | **Brookland** ⌐⌐

Malgudi | **Glover Pk** ⌐⌐

Malmaison | **Georgetown** ⌐⌐

Mari Vanna | **Gldn Triangle** ⌐⌐

Masala Exp. | **Arlington** ⌐⌐

Mi Cocina | **Chevy Chase** ⌐⌐

Mi Cuba | **Columbia Hts** ⌐⌐

Monty's Steak | **Springfield** ⌐⌐

Mothership | **Columbia Hts** ⌐⌐

MXDC | **D'town** ⌐⌐

Ninnella | **Cap Hill** ⌐⌐

NoPa | **Penn Qtr** ⌐⌐

Park Tavern | **Southeast** ⌐⌐

Protein Bar | **multi.** ⌐⌐

Radius Pizza | **Mt. Pleasant** ⌐⌐

Range | **Chevy Chase** ⌐⌐

Rappahannock | **NoMa** ⌐⌐

Red Apron | **multi.** ⌐⌐

Red Hen | **Bloomingdale** ⌐⌐

Slate | **Glover Pk** ⌐⌐

Smoke BBQ | **Bethesda** ⌐⌐

Taan Noodles | **Adams Mor** ⌐⌐

Table | **Shaw** ⌐⌐

Tacos El Chilango | **U St** ⌐⌐

Takeateasy | **Gldn Triangle** ⌐⌐

Taqueria Nacional | **U St** ⌐⌐

Tash House | **Cap Hill** ⌐⌐

Tavern 64 | **Reston** ⌐⌐

Taylor Charles | **Atlas Dist** ⌐⌐

Teddy/The Bully Bar | **Gldn Triangle** ⌐⌐

Tony & Joe's | **Georgetown** ⌐⌐

Trademark | **Alexandria** ⌐⌐

Vendetta | **Atlas Dist** ⌐

Vino Volo | **Bethesda** ⌐

Wagshal's | **Upper NW** ⌐

Wildwood Kit. | **Bethesda** ⌐

Woodward Table | **D'town** ⌐

Yo! Sushi | **Cap Hill** ⌐

Yuzu | **Bethesda** ⌐

BREAKFAST

(See also Hotel Dining)

Bayou Bakery | **Arlington** 22

Ben's Chili | **U St** 22

Bob & Edith's | **Arlington** 20

Bread Line | **World Bank** 23

Dean & DeLuca | **Georgetown** 23

Diner | **Adams Mor** 21

Double T | **Frederick** 20

Family Meal | **Frederick** ⌐

Florida Ave. Grill | **Shaw** 22

NEW GBD | **Dupont Cir** ⌐

Hamilton | **D'town** 20

Johnny's Half Shell | **Cap Hill** 21

Le Pain Quotidien | **multi.** 21

Mark's Kit. | **Takoma Pk** 21

McCormick/Schmick's | **multi.** 23

Mosaic Cuisine | **White Flint** 23

Northside | **Clarendon** 22

Old Ebbitt | **D'town** 23

Open City | **Woodley Pk** 21

Parkway Deli | **Silver Spring** 22

Paul | **Penn Qtr** 22

Pho 75 | **multi.** 24

Teaism | **multi.** 20

NEW Woodward Table | **D'town** ⌐

BRUNCH

Acacia Bistro | **Frederick** 24

Al Dente | **Upper NW** ⌐

Ardeo/Bardeo | **Cleve Pk** 22

NEW Beuchert's | **Cap Hill** ⌐

Birch/Barley | **Logan Cir** 24

Bistro Bis | **Cap Hill** 26

Black Mkt. | **Garrett Pk** 26

BlackSalt | **Palisades** 27

Blue Duck | **West End** 27

Bombay Club | **Gldn Triangle** 25

Blvd. Woodgrill | **Clarendon** 20

B. Smith's | **Cap Hill** 22

NEW B Too | **Logan Cir** ⌐

Café Bonaparte | **Georgetown** 23

Cafe Deluxe | **multi.** 20

Café Saint-Ex | **Logan Cir** 20

Carlyle | **Arlington** 25

Cashion's Eat | **Adams Mor** 25

Chef Geoff's | **multi.** 21

Clyde's | **multi.** 22

Co Co. Sala | **Penn Qtr** 24

Cork | **Logan Cir** 25

Crème | **U St** 21

Dutch's Daughter | **Frederick** 25

Eatonville | **U St** 23

Estadio | **Logan Cir** 25

Et Voila | **Palisades** 25

Evening Star | **Alexandria** 23

Eventide | **Clarendon** 23

NEW Farmers Fishers | **Georgetown** ⌐

Filomena | **Georgetown** 24

Firestone's | **Frederick** 26

Fortune | **Falls Ch** 22

Founding Farmers | **multi.** 24

Georgia Brown | **D'town** 22

Graffiato | **Chinatown** 24

Green Pig | **Clarendon** ⌐

Hank's Oyster | **Dupont Cir** 24

Howard Theatre | **Shaw** ⌐

Jackie's | **Silver Spring** 23

J&G Steak | **D'town** 24

Kellari Taverna | **Gldn Triangle** 23

NEW Le Diplomate | **Logan Cir** ⌐

Leopold's Kafe | **Georgetown** 23

Liberty Tav. | **Clarendon** 24

Magnolias/Mill | **Purcellville** 25

Masa 14 | **Logan Cir** 23

Matchbox | **multi.**	23	Bombay Club | **Gldn Triangle**	25
Matisse | **Upper NW**	23	Bond 45 | **Nat'l Harbor**	22
Medium Rare | **Cleve Pk**	22	Bourbon Steak | **Georgetown**	25
Mike's | **Springfield**	26	Brass. Beck | **D'town**	25
Mintwood | **Adams Mor**	–	B. Smith's | **Cap Hill**	22
Nage | **Scott Cir**	21	**NEW** Bungalow | **Sterling**	–
Napoleon Bistro | **Adams Mor**	24	Busara | **multi.**	22
Old Angler's | **Potomac**	20	Café du Parc | **D'town**	21
Old Ebbitt | **D'town**	23	Café Dupont | **Dupont Cir**	21
Open City | **Woodley Pk**	21	Cafe Milano | **Georgetown**	22
Palena | **Cleve Pk**	27	Capital Grille | **multi.**	26
Pearl Dive | **Logan Cir**	26	Carlyle | **Arlington**	25
Perrys | **Adams Mor**	22	Carmine's | **Penn Qtr**	20
Ping Pong | **multi.**	21	Ceiba | **D'town**	24
Poste Moderne | **Penn Qtr**	20	Central Michel | **Penn Qtr**	26
Praline | **Bethesda**	23	Cesco Osteria | **Bethesda**	19
Ris | **West End**	25	C.F. Folks | **Dupont Cir**	24
Roof Terr. | **Foggy Bottom**	16	Charlie Palmer | **Cap Hill**	26
Room 11 | **Columbia Hts**	26	Chef Geoff's | **multi.**	21
Sequoia | **Georgetown**	17	Chima | **Vienna**	26
Source | **Penn Qtr**	27	Circle Bistro | **West End**	20
Tabard Inn | **Dupont Cir**	25	CityZen | **SW**	27
NEW Table | **Shaw**	–	Clyde's | **multi.**	22
		Corduroy | **Mt. Vernon Sq**	28
BUSINESS DINING		**NEW** Crossroads | **World Bank**	–
Acadiana | **Mt. Vernon Sq**	24	DC Coast | **D'town**	23
Acqua al 2 | **Cap Hill**	24	Degrees | **Georgetown**	22
Addie's | **White Flint**	25	Del Frisco's | **Penn Qtr**	–
NEW Ambar | **Cap Hill**	–	**NEW** DGS Deli | **Dupont Cir**	–
NEW Ancora | **Foggy Bottom**	–	District Commons | **Foggy Bottom**	22
Artie's | **Fairfax**	25	**NEW** Edgar | **Gldn Triangle**	–
Assaggi | **McLean**	23	8407 Kit. | **Silver Spring**	24
NEW Azur | **Penn Qtr**	–	El Manantial | **Reston**	24
Bamian | **Falls Ch**	26	Equinox | **Gldn Triangle**	25
Bazin's/Church | **Vienna**	26	Family Meal | **Frederick**	–
Bibiana | **D'town**	25	**NEW** Farmers Fishers | **Georgetown**	–
Bistro Bis | **Cap Hill**	26	15 Ria | **Scott Cir**	22
BlackSalt | **Palisades**	27	Fiola | **Penn Qtr**	27
Black's Bar | **Bethesda**	24	Fogo de Chão | **Penn Qtr**	27
BLT Steak | **Gldn Triangle**	25		
Blue Duck | **West End**	27		
Bobby Van's | **D'town**	23		

Foti's | **Culpeper**	27
Founding Farmers | **multi.**	24
NEW Fuego Cocina | **Clarendon**	–
Georgia Brown | **D'town**	22
NEW Grill Room | **Georgetown**	–
Hamilton | **D'town**	20
Harry's | **Arlington**	21
Härth | **McLean**	23
Heritage India | **Dupont Cir**	22
Hill Country | **Penn Qtr**	21
Il Fornaio | **Reston**	25
I Ricchi | **Dupont Cir**	24
Jackson's | **Reston**	23
Jackson 20 | **Alexandria**	21
J&G Steak | **D'town**	24
NEW Jardenea | **West End**	–
Johnny's Half Shell | **Cap Hill**	21
Juniper | **West End**	24
Kazan | **McLean**	25
Kaz Sushi | **World Bank**	25
Kellari Taverna | **Gldn Triangle**	23
Lafayette Rm. | **Gldn Triangle**	27
La Ferme | **Chevy Chase**	24
Landini Bros. | **Alexandria**	25
La Taberna | **World Bank**	26
NEW La Tagliatella | **Clarendon**	–
NEW Le Diplomate | **Logan Cir**	–
Lia's | **Chevy Chase**	21
Magnolias/Mill | **Purcellville**	25
NEW Malgudi | **Glover Pk**	–
Maple Ave | **Vienna**	–
Marcel's | **West End**	28
NEW Mari Vanna | **Gldn Triangle**	–
NEW Masala Exp. | **Arlington**	–
Matchbox | **Rockville**	23
McCormick/Schmick's | **multi.**	23
Mike's | **Springfield**	26
Mio | **D'town**	26
Monocle | **Cap Hill**	21
Morton's | **multi.**	26
Nage | **Scott Cir**	21
NEW Ninnella | **Cap Hill**	–
NEW NoPa | **Penn Qtr**	–
Nostos | **Vienna**	26
Occidental | **D'town**	23
Oceanaire | **D'town**	24
Old Ebbitt | **D'town**	23
Osteria Elisir | **Penn Qtr**	26
Oval Rm. | **Gldn Triangle**	26
Oyamel | **Penn Qtr**	25
Ozzie's Corner | **Fairfax**	24
Palena | **Cleve Pk**	27
Palm | **multi.**	25
PassionFish | **Reston**	26
Persimmon | **Bethesda**	–
P.J. Clarke's | **D'town**	18
Plume | **D'town**	26
Poste Moderne | **Penn Qtr**	20
Posto | **Logan Cir**	23
Prime Rib | **Gldn Triangle**	28
Primi Piatti | **Foggy Bottom**	19
Proof | **Penn Qtr**	24
NEW Range | **Chevy Chase**	–
Rasika | **West End**	28
Ray's/Steaks | **Arlington**	27
Redwood | **Bethesda**	19
Restaurant Eve | **Alexandria**	27
Ris | **West End**	25
Rosa Mexicano | **multi.**	23
Ruth's Chris | **multi.**	26
Sergio Rist. | **Silver Spring**	27
701 | **Penn Qtr**	23
Smith/Wollensky | **Gldn Triangle**	25
Sonoma | **Cap Hill**	21
Source | **Penn Qtr**	27
Sou'Wester | **SW**	21
Tabard Inn | **Dupont Cir**	25
Thai Basil | **Chantilly**	26
Todd Gray's Watershed | **NoMa**	23
Tosca | **Penn Qtr**	27
NEW Trademark | **Alexandria**	–
2941 | **Falls Ch**	27

2100 Prime | **Dupont Cir**	24
Unum | **Georgetown**	-
Urbana | **Dupont Cir**	21
Vidalia | **Gldn Triangle**	26
Vinifera | **Reston**	23
NEW Vino Volo | **Bethesda**	-
Westend Bistro | **West End**	22
Wildfire | **McLean**	22
NEW Wildwood Kit. | **Bethesda**	-
Willow | **Arlington**	24
NEW Woodward Table | **D'town**	-
Woo Lae Oak | **Vienna**	23
Zaytinya | **Penn Qtr**	26
Zentan | **D'town**	22

CELEBRITY CHEFS

José Andrés

Jaleo | **multi.**	24
Minibar | **Penn Qtr**	28
Oyamel | **Penn Qtr**	25
Zaytinya | **Penn Qtr**	26

Cathal Armstrong

Eamonn's | **multi.**	23
Majestic | **Alexandria**	24
Restaurant Eve | **Alexandria**	27
Society Fair | **Alexandria**	24

Jeffrey Buben

Bistro Bis | **Cap Hill**	26
Vidalia | **Gldn Triangle**	26
NEW Woodward Table | **D'town**	-

Yannick Cam

Bistro Provence | **Bethesda**	26

Ann Cashion

Cashion's Eat | **Adams Mor**	25
Johnny's Half Shell | **Cap Hill**	21
NEW Taqueria Nacional | **U St**	-

RJ Cooper

Rogue 24 | **Mt. Vernon Sq**	23

Frederik de Pue

NEW Azur | **Penn Qtr**	-
NEW Table | **Shaw**	-

Roberto Donna

Al Dente | **Upper NW**	-

Bobby Flay

Bobby's Burger | **multi.**	22

Todd Gray

Equinox | **Gldn Triangle**	25
Todd Gray's Watershed | **NoMa**	23

Mike Isabella

Bandolero | **Georgetown**	-
Graffiato | **Chinatown**	24

Ris Lacoste

Ris | **West End**	25

Spike Mendelsohn

Good Stuff | **multi.**	23
We the Pizza | **Cap Hill**	22

Michael Mina

Bourbon Steak | **Georgetown**	25

Johnny Monis

Komi | **Dupont Cir**	28
Little Serow | **Dupont Cir**	28

Andrea Pace

NEW Brickside | **Bethesda**	-
Villa Mozart | **Fairfax**	26

Guillermo Pernot

Cuba Libre | **Penn Qtr**	20

Nora Pouillon

Nora | **Dupont Cir**	26

Wolfgang Puck

Source | **Penn Qtr**	27

Francesco Ricchi

Cesco Osteria | **Bethesda**	19

Michel Richard

Central Michel | **Penn Qtr**	26

Frank Ruta

Palena | **Cleve Pk**	27

Richard Sandoval

El Centro | **Logan Cir**	21
Masa 14 | **Logan Cir**	23
Zengo | **Chinatown**	22

Art Smith

Art & Soul | **Cap Hill**	23

Fabio Trabocchi

    Fiola | **Penn Qtr** — 27

Mark Vidal

    Boqueria | **Dupont Cir** — ⌐

Bryan Voltaggio

    Family Meal | **Frederick** — ⌐

    Lunchbox | **Frederick** — 24

    NEW Range | **Chevy Chase** — ⌐

    Volt | **Frederick** — 28

Jean-Georges Vongerichten

    J&G Steak | **D'town** — 24

Antoine Westermann

    Café du Parc | **D'town** — 21

Robert Wiedmaier

    Brabo | **Alexandria** — 26

    Brass. Beck | **D'town** — 25

    Marcel's | **West End** — 28

    Mussel B&G | **Bethesda** — 20

    NEW Wildwood Kit. | — ⌐
    Bethesda

Eric Ziebold

    CityZen | **SW** — 27

CHILD-FRIENDLY

(Alternatives to the usual fast-food places; * children's menu available)

NEW &pizza | **Atlas Dist** — ⌐

Artie's* | **Fairfax** — 25

Arucola* | **Chevy Chase** — 20

Austin Grill* | **multi.** — 18

Black Mkt.* | **Garrett Pk** — 26

Buzz | **Alexandria** — 22

Cactus Cantina* | **Cleve Pk** — 21

Cafe Deluxe* | **multi.** — 20

Cafe Pizzaiolo* | **multi.** — 24

Calif. Tortilla* | **multi.** — 22

Carlyle* | **Arlington** — 25

Carmine's* | **Penn Qtr** — 20

Chef Geoff's* | **multi.** — 21

Clyde's* | **multi.** — 22

Coastal Flats* | **Fairfax** — 24

Comet Ping Pong | **Upper NW** — 20

Double T* | **Frederick** — 20

Eamonn's* | **Alexandria** — 23

Elevation Burger | **Falls Ch** — 21

El Golfo* | **Silver Spring** — 23

Ella's Pizza* | **Penn Qtr** — 21

Filomena | **Georgetown** — 24

Firefly* | **Dupont Cir** — 23

Five Guys* | **multi.** — 24

Founding Farmers | **Potomac** — 24

Guardado's* | **Bethesda** — 23

Haven | **Bethesda** — ⌐

Jaleo | **multi.** — 24

Kabob Palace | **Arlington** — 26

Lebanese Tav.* | **multi.** — 23

Legal Sea Foods* | **multi.** — 23

Lia's* | **Chevy Chase** — 21

Maggiano's* | **multi.** — 23

Majestic* | **Alexandria** — 24

Mark's Kit.* | **Takoma Pk** — 21

Matchbox* | **multi.** — 23

Mike's* | **Springfield** — 26

Minerva | **multi.** — 23

Mi Rancho | **multi.** — 22

Old Glory* | **Georgetown** — 19

Open City* | **Woodley Pk** — 21

Pete's Apizza* | **multi.** — 22

P.F. Chang's* | **multi.** — 23

Pizzeria Orso* | **Falls Ch** — 22

Pizzeria Paradiso | **multi.** — 23

Rabieng | **Falls Ch** — 25

Red Hot/Blue* | **multi.** — 22

Samantha's | **Silver Spring** — 24

Serendipity 3 | **Georgetown** — 21

Sugo Cicchetti | **Potomac** — ⌐

Surfside* | **Glover Pk** — 21

Sweetwater Tav.* | **multi.** — 26

Taqueria Poblano* | **multi.** — 22

Tara Thai* | **multi.** — 20

Taste/Saigon | **Rockville** — 22

2 Amys | **Cleve Pk** — 25

Uncle Julio's* | **multi.** — 21

Virtue | **Alexandria** — ⌐

Wild Tomato | **Cabin John**	22
NEW Yo! Sushi | **Cap Hill**	–

DESSERT SPECIALISTS

Acadiana | **Mt. Vernon Sq**	24
Al Tiramisu | **Dupont Cir**	25
NEW Aroma Espresso | **Bethesda**	–
Bastille | **Alexandria**	24
Bayou Bakery | **Arlington**	22
Birch/Barley | **Logan Cir**	24
Black Mkt. | **Garrett Pk**	26
BlackSalt | **Palisades**	27
Blue Duck | **West End**	27
Bread Line | **World Bank**	23
Buzz | **multi.**	22
Café Bonaparte | **Georgetown**	23
Café Saint-Ex | **Logan Cir**	20
Carlyle | **Arlington**	25
Central Michel | **Penn Qtr**	26
Cheesecake Factory | **multi.**	24
CityZen | **SW**	27
Co Co. Sala | **Penn Qtr**	24
Dangerously Delicious | **Atlas Dist**	21
NEW Decanter | **D'town**	–
District Commons | **Foggy Bottom**	22
Equinox | **Gldn Triangle**	25
Et Voila | **Palisades**	25
Fiola | **Penn Qtr**	27
Good Stuff | **Cap Hill**	23
Green Pig | **Clarendon**	–
Haven | **Bethesda**	–
Inn/Little Washington | **Washington**	29
Jaleo | **multi.**	24
J&G Steak | **D'town**	24
Johnny's Half Shell | **Cap Hill**	21
Juniper | **West End**	24
L'Auberge/Jaques' | **Grt Falls**	28
Leopold's Kafe | **Georgetown**	23
Le Pain Quotidien | **multi.**	21

Liberty Tav. | **Clarendon**	24
Majestic | **Alexandria**	24
Marcel's | **West End**	28
Napoleon Bistro | **Adams Mor**	24
Northside | **Clarendon**	22
Obelisk | **Dupont Cir**	28
Palena | **Cleve Pk**	27
Paul | **Penn Qtr**	22
Praline | **Bethesda**	23
NEW Range | **Chevy Chase**	–
Restaurant Eve | **Alexandria**	27
Ripple | **Cleve Pk**	23
Ris | **West End**	25
Serendipity 3 | **Georgetown**	21
1789 | **Georgetown**	26
Society Fair | **Alexandria**	24
Sweetgreen | **multi.**	22
Tabard Inn | **Dupont Cir**	25
Ted's Bulletin | **Cap Hill**	23
2941 | **Falls Ch**	27
2 Amys | **Cleve Pk**	25
Willow | **Arlington**	24
Zaytinya | **Penn Qtr**	26

ENTERTAINMENT

(Call for days and times of performances)

Banana Café | **Cap Hill**	19
Bayou | **West End**	20
Bombay Club | **Gldn Triangle**	25
Café Saint-Ex | **Logan Cir**	20
Comet Ping Pong | **Upper NW**	20
Da Domenico | **McLean**	23
Dukem | **U St**	24
Evening Star | **Alexandria**	23
Georgia Brown | **D'town**	22
Hamilton | **D'town**	20
Hill Country | **Penn Qtr**	21
Howard Theatre | **Shaw**	–
Las Tapas | **Alexandria**	24
Napoleon Bistro | **Adams Mor**	24
Neyla | **Georgetown**	24
Perrys | **Adams Mor**	22

701 | **Penn Qtr** 23

Sticky Rice | **Atlas Dist** 23

Taste/Morocco | **Clarendon** 23

FIREPLACES

Al Tiramisu | **Dupont Cir** 25

Bistro Bis | **Cap Hill** 26

Bistro D'Oc | **Penn Qtr** 23

Blue Rock | **Sperryville** 24

Bodega | **Georgetown** 23

Brixton | **U St** ‑

Chart House | **Alexandria** 23

Chef Geoff's | **Vienna** 21

Circle Bistro | **West End** 20

Clyde's | **multi.** 22

Columbia Firehse. | **Alexandria** 23

Comus Inn | **Dickerson** 20

Dutch's Daughter | **Frederick** 25

Eamonn's | **Alexandria** 23

Equinox | **Gldn Triangle** 25

15 Ria | **Scott Cir** 22

Fogo de Chão | **Penn Qtr** 27

Foti's | **Culpeper** 27

Fyve | **Arlington** 24

Geranio | **Alexandria** 25

Grace's | **Nat'l Harbor** 25

Hunter's Head | **Upperville** 23

Il Fornaio | **Reston** 25

Inn/Little Washington | **Washington** 29

I Ricchi | **Dupont Cir** 24

Irish Whiskey | **Dupont Cir** ‑

Isabella's | **Frederick** 26

La Chaumière | **Georgetown** 26

L'Auberge/Jaques' | **Grt Falls** 28

L'Auberge Provençale | **Boyce** 26

Lia's | **Chevy Chase** 21

Lightfoot | **Leesburg** 26

Little Fountain | **Adams Mor** 23

Magnolias/Mill | **Purcellville** 25

Matchbox | **U St** 23

Matisse | **Upper NW** 23

Morrison-Clark | **D'town** 24

Mrs. K's | **Silver Spring** 23

NEW NoPa | **Penn Qtr** ‑

Old Angler's | **Potomac** 20

Oya | **Penn Qtr** 24

Paolo's | **Georgetown** 21

Petits Plats | **Woodley Pk** 22

Pizzeria Da Marco | **Bethesda** 23

Pizzeria Orso | **Falls Ch** 22

Plume | **D'town** 26

Redwood | **Bethesda** 19

Restaurant Eve | **Alexandria** 27

Rolls 'N Rice | **Rockville** 22

Rustico | **Alexandria** 22

Sea Catch | **Georgetown** 23

1789 | **Georgetown** 26

Tabard Inn | **Dupont Cir** 25

Tavira | **Chevy Chase** 25

Trummer's | **Clifton** 24

Tuscarora Mill | **Leesburg** 25

2941 | **Falls Ch** 27

Vapiano | **multi.** 20

William Jeffrey's | **Arlington** 20

Wine Kit. | **Frederick** 26

Woo Lae Oak | **Vienna** 23

Zaytinya | **Penn Qtr** 26

FOOD TRUCKS

CapMac | **Location Varies** 23

El Floridano | **Location Varies** ‑

Kangaroo/PORC | **Location Varies** ‑

Red Hook | **Location Varies** 25

NEW Tacos El Chilango | **Arlington** ‑

HISTORIC PLACES

(Year opened; * building)

1750 | Hunter's Head* | **Upperville** 23

1753 | L'Auberge Provençale* | **Boyce** 26

1786 | Virtue* | **Alexandria** ‑

1800 | Black Mkt.* | **Garrett Pk** 26

1800 | Corduroy* | **Mt. Vernon Sq** 28

1800	Restaurant Eve*	Alexandria	27
1829	Ashby Inn*	Paris	27
1841	Poste Moderne*	Penn Qtr	20
1860	Old Angler's*	Potomac	20
1862	Comus Inn*	Dickerson	20
1864	Morrison-Clark*	D'town	24
1869	Trummer's*	Clifton	24
1872	Brewer's Alley*	Frederick	22
1876	District ChopHse.*	Penn Qtr	21
1880	Beuchert's*	Cap Hill	–
1883	Columbia Firehse.*	Alexandria	23
1885	Monocle*	Cap Hill	21
1887	Tabard Inn*	Dupont Cir	25
1887	Woodward Table*	D'town	–
1888	Lightfoot*	Leesburg	26
1890	Inn/Little Washington*	Washington	29
1890	La Bergerie*	Alexandria	26
1890	Nora*	Dupont Cir	26
1890	Volt*	Frederick	28
1897	Irish Inn/Glen Echo*	Glen Echo	20
1900	Standard*	Logan Cir	–
1904	Occidental*	D'town	23
1905	Magnolias/Mill*	Purcellville	25
1907	Liberty Tav.*	Clarendon	24
1908	B. Smith's*	Cap Hill	22
1909	Ben's Chili*	U St	22
1912	Zeffirelli Rist.*	Herndon	24
1913	Boundary Stone*	Bloomingdale	24
1920	Matchbox*	Cap Hill	23
1921	Firestone's*	Frederick	26
1925	Eventide*	Clarendon	23
1930	Mrs. K's	Silver Spring	23
1932	Degrees*	Georgetown	22
1932	Majestic*	Alexandria	24
1933	Martin's Tav.	Georgetown	20
1940	Graffiato*	Chinatown	24
1944	Florida Ave. Grill	Shaw	22
1946	Lyon Hall*	Clarendon	24
1950	Lost Dog*	Arlington	23
1962	1789	Georgetown	26

HOTEL DINING

Ashby Inn		
Ashby Inn	Paris	27
Blue Rock Inn		
Blue Rock	Sperryville	24
Capella Hotel		
NEW Grill Room	Georgetown	–
Donovan Hse.		
Zentan	D'town	22
DoubleTree DC		
15 Ria	Scott Cir	22
DoubleTree Silver Spring		
Sergio Rist.	Silver Spring	27
Dupont Circle Hotel		
Café Dupont	Dupont Cir	21
Fairfax at Embassy Row		
2100 Prime	Dupont Cir	24
Fairmont Hotel		
Juniper	West End	24
Four Seasons Hotel DC		
Bourbon Steak	Georgetown	25
Gaylord National Hotel		
Old Hickory	Nat'l Harbor	26
George, Hotel		
Bistro Bis	Cap Hill	26
Georgetown Hill Inn		
Cafe Divan	Glover Pk	24
George Washington Univ. Inn		
Notti Bianche	Foggy Bottom	22
Graham Georgetown Hotel		
NEW AGB	Georgetown	–

Hay-Adams
Lafayette Rm. | **Gldn Triangle**   27

Hilton Garden Inn
Todd Gray's Watershed | 23
NoMa

Hilton McLean Tysons Corner
Härth | **McLean**   23

Hyatt Regency
Morton's | **Bethesda**   26

Hyatt Regency Reston
NEW Tavern 64 | **Reston**   ⎯

Inn at Little Washington
Inn/Little Washington | 29
Washington

Jefferson
Plume | **D'town**   26

L'Auberge Provençale
L'Auberge Provençale | **Boyce**   26

Liaison Capitol Hill
Art & Soul | **Cap Hill**   23

Lorien Hotel & Spa
Brabo | **Alexandria**   26

Mandarin Oriental
CityZen | **SW**   27
Sou'Wester | **SW**   21

Marriott Embassy Row
Nage | **Scott Cir**   21

Marriott Gaithersburg
NEW Bench | **Gaith'burg**   ⎯

Mayflower Renaissance Hotel
NEW Edgar | **Gldn Triangle**   ⎯

Melrose Georgetown Hotel
NEW Jardenea | **West End**   ⎯

Monaco Alexandria, Hotel
Jackson 20 | **Alexandria**   21

Monaco DC, Hotel
Poste Moderne | **Penn Qtr**   20

Morrison-Clark Inn
Morrison-Clark | **D'town**   24

Morrison Hse.
Grille | **Alexandria**   25

One Washington Circle Hotel
Circle Bistro | **West End**   20

Palomar, Hotel
Urbana | **Dupont Cir**   21

Park Hyatt
Blue Duck | **West End**   27

Ritz-Carlton DC
Westend Bistro | **West End**   22

Ritz-Carlton Georgetown
Degrees | **Georgetown**   22

Ritz-Carlton Pentagon City
Fyve | **Arlington**   24

River Inn
Dish/Drinks | **Foggy Bottom**   21

St. Regis
NEW Decanter | **D'town**   ⎯

Tabard Inn
Tabard Inn | **Dupont Cir**   25

Westin Alexandria
NEW Trademark | **Alexandria**   ⎯

Westin Georgetown
NEW Bóveda | **West End**   ⎯

Westin Reston Heights
Vinifera | **Reston**   23

W Hotel
J&G Steak | **D'town**   24

Willard InterContinental Hotel
Café du Parc | **D'town**   21

LATE DINING

(Weekday closing hour)
Amsterdam Falafel | varies | 25
Adams Mor

NEW Azur | varies | **Penn Qtr**   ⎯

Bar Pilar | 1:30 AM | **U St**   23

Ben's Chili | 2 AM | **U St**   22

Biergarten Haus | 12 AM | 17
Atlas Dist

Bistro Bohem | 12 AM | **Shaw**   ⎯

Bistro Français | 3 AM | 21
Georgetown

Bistro La Bonne | 12 AM | **U St**   21

Bistrot du Coin | 12 AM | Dupont Cir — 22

Bistrot Lepic | 12 AM | Georgetown — 24

Black & Orange | 5 AM | multi. — 25

Blackfinn Amer. | 1 AM | multi. — 18

Bob & Edith's | 24 hrs. | Arlington — 20

BonChon | 12 AM | Fairfax — 26

Boundary Rd. | 2 AM | Atlas Dist — -

Bourbon | 1:30 AM | multi. — 21

NEW Bóveda | 12 AM | West End — -

NEW Brickside | 1 AM | Bethesda — -

Brixton | 1:30 AM | U St — -

NEW Bungalow | 1:30 AM | Sterling — -

Busboys/Poets | 12 AM | multi. — 22

Cafe Nola | varies | Frederick — 24

Café Saint-Ex | 1:30 AM | Logan Cir — 20

NEW Carving Room | 12 AM | Chinatown — -

Chef Geoff's | 12 AM | multi. — 21

Circa | varies | multi. — 20

Clyde's | varies | multi. — 22

Co Co. Sala | varies | Penn Qtr — 24

Columbia Firehse. | 1:30 AM | Alexandria — 23

Dangerously Delicious | varies | Atlas Dist — 21

Daniel O'Connell's | 1 AM | Alexandria — 20

Del Frisco's | 12 AM | Penn Qtr — -

Diner | 24 hrs. | Adams Mor — 21

District Kit. | 12 AM | Woodley Pk — 24

Dukem | 1 AM | U St — 24

Eat First | 2 AM | Chinatown — 22

El Centro | 2 AM | Logan Cir — 21

El Chucho | 3 AM | Columbia Hts — -

El Tamarindo | 2 AM | Adams Mor — 21

Eventide | 1 AM | Clarendon — 23

Fire Works | varies | Arlington — 24

Fujimar | varies | D'town — -

Full Kee (DC) | varies | Chinatown — 23

Full Kee (VA) | varies | Falls Ch — 22

NEW GBD | 2 AM | Dupont Cir — -

Graffiato | varies | Chinatown — 24

NEW Gryphon | varies | Dupont Cir — -

Hamilton | 24 hrs. | D'town — 20

Hard Times | varies | multi. — 22

Hill Country | 2 AM | Penn Qtr — 21

Honey Pig | 24 hrs. | multi. — 23

Horace/Dickie's | 2 AM | Atlas Dist — 22

Irish Whiskey | 2 AM | Dupont Cir — -

Jack Rose | 2 AM | Adams Mor — 20

Jackson's | 12 AM | Reston — 23

Kabob N Karahi | 12 AM | Silver Spring — 26

Kangaroo/PORC | 2 AM | Columbia Hts — -

NEW Le Grenier | 12 AM | Atlas Dist — -

Lia's | 12 AM | Chevy Chase — 21

Liberty Tav. | 2 AM | Clarendon — 24

Lincoln | varies | D'town — 20

Local 16 | 2 AM | U St — 17

Lost Society | 1 AM | U St — 18

Lyon Hall | 2 AM | Clarendon — 24

Madhatter | 2 AM | Dupont Cir — 18

Mandu | varies | multi. — 23

Maple | 12 AM | Columbia Hts — -

Martin's Tav. | 1:30 AM | Georgetown — 20

Marvin | 2 AM | U St — 23

Masa 14 | 1 AM | Logan Cir — 23

Matchbox | 12:30 AM | Cap Hill — 23

Meridian | 12 AM | Columbia Hts — 20

Mezè | 1:30 AM | Adams Mor — 24

New Kam | 12 AM | Wheaton — 25

Old Ebbitt | 1 AM | **D'town** 23

Old Glory | 1 AM | **Georgetown** 19

Open City | 1:30 AM | **Woodley Pk** 21

Ozzie's Corner | 12 AM | **Fairfax** 24

Perrys | 1 AM | **Adams Mor** 22

P.J. Clarke's | 1 AM | **D'town** 18

🆕 Range | 12 AM | **Chevy Chase** ⁻

Ravi Kabob | 1 AM | **Arlington** 25

Royal Mile | 12 AM | **Wheaton** 23

Russia Hse. | 1:30 AM | **Dupont Cir** 21

Rustico | 12 AM | **multi.** 22

Smoke/Barrel | 2 AM | **Adams Mor** 20

Standard | 1 AM | **Logan Cir** ⁻

Star/Shamrock | 12 AM | **Atlas Dist** 19

Stoney's | 12:45 AM | **Logan Cir** 18

Tabaq Bistro | 12 AM | **U St** 20

Tallula/EatBar | 12 AM | **Clarendon** 24

🆕 Tavern 64 | 12 AM | **Reston** ⁻

Tel'Veh | 12 AM | **Mt. Vernon Sq** ⁻

Thunder Burger | varies | **Georgetown** 24

Tonic | 12 AM | **Mt. Pleasant** 17

Town Hall | 2 AM | **Glover Pk** 23

Tryst | 1:30 AM | **Adams Mor** 21

Ulah Bistro | 2 AM | **U St** 20

Urban BBQ | 12 AM | **multi.** 24

Vinoteca | 12 AM | **U St** 22

William Jeffrey's | 1 AM | **Arlington** 20

Woomi Gdn. | 4 AM | **Wheaton** 20

X.O. Taste | 2 AM | **Falls Ch** 24

Yechon | 24 hrs. | **Annandale** 22

MEET FOR A DRINK

Acacia Bistro | **Frederick** 24

Acadiana | **Mt. Vernon Sq** 24

🆕 Ambar | **Cap Hill** ⁻

🆕 Ancora | **Foggy Bottom** ⁻

Ardeo/Bardeo | **Cleve Pk** 22

Art & Soul | **Cap Hill** 23

Artie's | **Fairfax** 25

🆕 Azur | **Penn Qtr** ⁻

Bandolero | **Georgetown** ⁻

Bar Pilar | **U St** 23

Bastille | **Alexandria** 24

Bayou | **West End** 20

Bazin's/Church | **Vienna** 26

Belga Café | **Cap Hill** 25

🆕 Bench | **Gaith'burg** ⁻

🆕 Beuchert's | **Cap Hill** ⁻

Bezu | **Potomac** 24

Bibiana | **D'town** 25

Biergarten Haus | **Atlas Dist** 17

Big Bear Cafe | **Bloomingdale** ⁻

Birch/Barley | **Logan Cir** 24

Bistro Bohem | **Shaw** ⁻

Bistrot du Coin | **Dupont Cir** 22

Black's Bar | **Bethesda** 24

BLT Steak | **Gldn Triangle** 25

Blue Duck | **West End** 27

Boqueria | **Dupont Cir** ⁻

Boundary Rd. | **Atlas Dist** ⁻

Boundary Stone | **Bloomingdale** 24

Bourbon Steak | **Georgetown** 25

🆕 Bóveda | **West End** ⁻

Brass. Beck | **D'town** 25

🆕 Brickside | **Bethesda** ⁻

Brixton | **U St** ⁻

🆕 Bungalow | **Sterling** ⁻

Busboys/Poets | **multi.** 22

Buzz | **Arlington** 22

Café Saint-Ex | **Logan Cir** 20

Capital Grille | **multi.** 26

Carlyle | **Arlington** 25

Ceiba | **D'town** 24

Central Michel | **Penn Qtr** 26

Chasin' Tails | **Arlington** ⁻

Chef Geoff's | **multi.**	21
Chez Billy | **Petworth**	–
CityZen | **SW**	27
Clyde's | **multi.**	22
Co Co. Sala | **Penn Qtr**	24
Columbia Firehse. | **Alexandria**	23
Cork | **Logan Cir**	25
NEW Crossroads | **World Bank**	–
NEW Daikaya Izakaya | **Chinatown**	–
DC Coast | **D'town**	23
NEW DGS Deli | **Dupont Cir**	–
Dickson Wine | **U St**	21
Dogfish Head | **Falls Ch**	21
Eamonn's | **Arlington**	23
Eatonville | **U St**	23
NEW Edgar | **Gldn Triangle**	–
8407 Kit. | **Silver Spring**	24
El Centro | **Logan Cir**	21
El Chucho | **Columbia Hts**	–
Estadio | **Logan Cir**	25
Evening Star | **Alexandria**	23
Eventide | **Clarendon**	23
Evo Bistro | **McLean**	22
NEW Farmers Fishers | **Georgetown**	–
Fiola | **Penn Qtr**	27
Firefly | **Dupont Cir**	23
Fire Works | **multi.**	24
Founding Farmers | **multi.**	24
NEW Fuego Cocina | **Clarendon**	–
NEW GBD | **Dupont Cir**	–
Graffiato | **Chinatown**	24
Granville Moore's | **Atlas Dist**	24
NEW Gryphon | **Dupont Cir**	–
Hamilton | **D'town**	20
Hank's Oyster | **multi.**	24
Harry's | **Arlington**	21
Härth | **McLean**	23
NEW Hikari | **Atlas Dist**	–
Hill Country | **Penn Qtr**	21
Jackie's | **Silver Spring**	23
Jack Rose | **Adams Mor**	20
Jackson's | **Reston**	23
Jackson 20 | **Alexandria**	21
Jaleo | **multi.**	24
J&G Steak | **D'town**	24
NEW Jardenea | **West End**	–
Johnny's Half Shell | **Cap Hill**	21
Kangaroo/PORC | **Columbia Hts**	–
Kellari Taverna | **Gldn Triangle**	23
Kushi | **Mt. Vernon Sq**	25
Landini Bros. | **Alexandria**	25
La Taberna | **World Bank**	26
NEW La Tagliatella | **Clarendon**	–
Lauriol Plaza | **Dupont Cir**	21
NEW Le Diplomate | **Logan Cir**	–
NEW Le Grenier | **Atlas Dist**	–
Lia's | **Chevy Chase**	21
Liberty Tav. | **Clarendon**	24
Lincoln | **D'town**	20
Lyon Hall | **Clarendon**	24
Mad Fox Brew | **Falls Ch**	20
Majestic | **Alexandria**	24
Mandu | **multi.**	23
Maple | **Columbia Hts**	–
NEW Mari Vanna | **Gldn Triangle**	–
Martin's Tav. | **Georgetown**	20
Masa 14 | **Logan Cir**	23
Matchbox | **multi.**	23
Mezè | **Adams Mor**	24
Mike's | **Springfield**	26
Mio | **D'town**	26
Monocle | **Cap Hill**	21
Nage | **Scott Cir**	21
New Heights | **Woodley Pk**	22
1905 | **Shaw**	21
NEW NoPa | **Penn Qtr**	–
Northside | **Clarendon**	22
Old Ebbitt | **D'town**	23
Osteria Elisir | **Penn Qtr**	26
Oya | **Penn Qtr**	24
Oyamel | **Penn Qtr**	25

Pearl Dive	**Logan Cir**	26
Perrys	**Adams Mor**	22
Ping Pong	**multi.**	21
Plume	**D'town**	26
Policy	**U St**	22
Poste Moderne	**Penn Qtr**	20
Proof	**Penn Qtr**	24
Quench	**Rockville**	‒
NEW Radius Pizza	**Mt. Pleasant**	‒
NEW Range	**Chevy Chase**	‒
Rasika	**multi.**	28
NEW Red Hen	**Bloomingdale**	‒
Restaurant Eve	**Alexandria**	27
Ripple	**Cleve Pk**	23
Ris	**West End**	25
Room 11	**Columbia Hts**	26
Rosa Mexicano	**multi.**	23
Roti	**Bethesda**	22
Russia Hse.	**Dupont Cir**	21
Rustico	**multi.**	22
Rustik Tav.	**Bloomingdale**	23
Sei	**Penn Qtr**	26
701	**Penn Qtr**	23
NEW Slate	**Glover Pk**	‒
Smith Commons	**Atlas Dist**	22
Source	**Penn Qtr**	27
Sushi Damo	**Rockville**	25
Tabard Inn	**Dupont Cir**	25
NEW Table	**Shaw**	‒
NEW Takeateasy	**Gldn Triangle**	‒
Tallula/EatBar	**Clarendon**	24
Tandoori Nights	**Gaith'burg**	24
Tasting Rm.	**Frederick**	27
NEW Trademark	**Alexandria**	‒
Tryst	**Adams Mor**	21
Tuscarora Mill	**Leesburg**	25
Twisted Vines	**Arlington**	20
2 Amys	**Cleve Pk**	25
Unum	**Georgetown**	‒
Vermilion	**Alexandria**	26
Vidalia	**Gldn Triangle**	26

Vinifera	**Reston**	23
NEW Vino Volo	**Bethesda**	‒
Virtue	**Alexandria**	‒
Westend Bistro	**West End**	22
Wildfire	**McLean**	22
NEW Wildwood Kit.	**Bethesda**	‒
Willow	**Arlington**	24
NEW Woodward Table	**D'town**	‒
Zaytinya	**Penn Qtr**	26
Zengo	**Chinatown**	22
Zentan	**D'town**	22

OUTDOOR DINING

Addie's	**White Flint**	25
Ashby Inn	**Paris**	27
Austin Grill	**Penn Qtr**	18
Bastille	**Alexandria**	24
Biergarten Haus	**Atlas Dist**	17
Bistro Bis	**Cap Hill**	26
Bistro Provence	**Bethesda**	26
Blue Duck	**West End**	27
Bombay Club	**Gldn Triangle**	25
Bourbon Steak	**Georgetown**	25
Café du Parc	**D'town**	21
Cashion's Eat	**Adams Mor**	25
Cava Mezze	**Cap Hill**	25
Comus Inn	**Dickerson**	20
NEW Del Campo	**Penn Qtr**	‒
El Centro	**Logan Cir**	21
Equinox	**Gldn Triangle**	25
NEW Farmers Fishers	**Georgetown**	‒
NEW Grill Room	**Georgetown**	‒
Hank's Oyster	**Dupont Cir**	24
J&G Steak	**D'town**	24
Juniper	**West End**	24
La Taberna	**World Bank**	26
L'Auberge/Jaques'	**Grt Falls**	28
L'Auberge Provençale	**Boyce**	26
NEW Le Diplomate	**Logan Cir**	‒
Lucky Corner	**Frederick**	28
Magnolias/Mill	**Purcellville**	25

Marcel's | **West End**	28
Mezè | **Adams Mor**	24
Mintwood | **Adams Mor**	-
Monocacy Cross. | **Frederick**	28
Occidental | **D'town**	23
Old Angler's | **Potomac**	20
Open City | **Woodley Pk**	21
Oro Pomodoro | **Rockville**	21
Oval Rm. | **Gldn Triangle**	26
Palena | **Cleve Pk**	27
Paolo's | **multi.**	21
NEW Park Tavern | **Southeast**	-
Ping Pong | **Dupont Cir**	21
Pizzeria Paradiso | **Dupont Cir**	23
Poste Moderne | **Penn Qtr**	20
Rail Stop | **Plains**	23
Raku | **multi.**	23
Red Hot/Blue | **Falls Ch**	22
Redwood | **Bethesda**	19
Renato/River Falls | **Potomac**	22
Ris | **West End**	25
Siroc | **D'town**	24
Source | **Penn Qtr**	27
Standard | **Logan Cir**	-
Tabard Inn | **Dupont Cir**	25
NEW Table | **Shaw**	-
NEW Tony & Joe's | **Georgetown**	-
2 Amys | **Cleve Pk**	25
NEW Woodward Table | **D'town**	-
Zaytinya | **Penn Qtr**	26

PEOPLE-WATCHING

NEW Ambar | **Cap Hill**	-
NEW Ancora | **Foggy Bottom**	-
NEW Azur | **Penn Qtr**	-
Bandolero | **Georgetown**	-
Bibiana | **D'town**	25
Big Bear Cafe | **Bloomingdale**	-
Bistro Bis | **Cap Hill**	26
Bistrot Lepic | **Georgetown**	24
BlackSalt | **Palisades**	27
Black's Bar | **Bethesda**	24

BLT Steak | **Gldn Triangle**	25
Boqueria | **Dupont Cir**	-
Blvd. Woodgrill | **Clarendon**	20
Boundary Rd. | **Atlas Dist**	-
Bourbon Steak | **Georgetown**	25
NEW Bóveda | **West End**	-
Brass. Beck | **D'town**	25
Bread Line | **World Bank**	23
NEW Brickside | **Bethesda**	-
Brixton | **U St**	-
NEW Bungalow | **Sterling**	-
Café Saint-Ex | **Logan Cir**	20
Carlyle | **Arlington**	25
Carmine's | **Penn Qtr**	20
NEW Carving Room | **Chinatown**	-
Cava Mezze Grill | **multi.**	22
Central Michel | **Penn Qtr**	26
Charlie Palmer | **Cap Hill**	26
Chef Geoff's | **Rockville**	21
Chez Billy | **Petworth**	-
Circa | **multi.**	20
Co Co. Sala | **Penn Qtr**	24
Commissary | **Logan Cir**	19
Cork | **Logan Cir**	25
NEW Daikaya Ramen | **Chinatown**	-
Del Frisco's | **Penn Qtr**	-
NEW DGS Deli | **Dupont Cir**	-
Eamonn's | **Arlington**	23
NEW Edgar | **Gldn Triangle**	-
El Chucho | **Columbia Hts**	-
Equinox | **Gldn Triangle**	25
Estadio | **Logan Cir**	25
NEW Farmers Fishers | **Georgetown**	-
Fiola | **Penn Qtr**	27
NEW Fuego Cocina | **Clarendon**	-
Graffiato | **Chinatown**	24
NEW Gryphon | **Dupont Cir**	-
Hill Country | **Penn Qtr**	21
Jack Rose | **Adams Mor**	20
Jaleo | **multi.**	24

J&G Steak | **D'town**	24
Johnny's Half Shell | **Cap Hill**	21
Kangaroo/PORC | **Columbia Hts**	–
Lafayette Rm. | **Gldn Triangle**	27
Landini Bros. | **Alexandria**	25
Lauriol Plaza | **Dupont Cir**	21
NEW Le Diplomate | **Logan Cir**	–
NEW Le Grenier | **Atlas Dist**	–
Lincoln | **D'town**	20
Marcel's | **West End**	28
NEW Mari Vanna | **Gldn Triangle**	–
Martin's Tav. | **Georgetown**	20
Matchbox | **U St**	23
Mike's | **Springfield**	26
Monocle | **Cap Hill**	21
Mussel B&G | **Bethesda**	20
NEW NoPa | **Penn Qtr**	–
Nora | **Dupont Cir**	26
Osteria Elisir | **Penn Qtr**	26
Oval Rm. | **Gldn Triangle**	26
Oyamel | **Penn Qtr**	25
Palm | **multi.**	25
Poste Moderne | **Penn Qtr**	20
NEW Range | **Chevy Chase**	–
Rasika | **West End**	28
NEW Red Hen | **Bloomingdale**	–
Sakuramen | **Adams Mor**	–
Sequoia | **Georgetown**	17
Sonoma | **Cap Hill**	21
Source | **Penn Qtr**	27
Standard | **Logan Cir**	–
Sugo Cicchetti | **Potomac**	–
NEW Table | **Shaw**	–
NEW Takeateasy | **Gldn Triangle**	–
Tryst | **Adams Mor**	21
Vidalia | **Gldn Triangle**	26
NEW Vino Volo | **Bethesda**	–
NEW Wildwood Kit. | **Bethesda**	–
NEW Woodward Table | **D'town**	–
Zaytinya | **Penn Qtr**	26

POWER SCENES

Acadiana | **Mt. Vernon Sq**	24
Acqua al 2 | **Cap Hill**	24
Ardeo/Bardeo | **Cleve Pk**	22
Art & Soul | **Cap Hill**	23
Bazin's/Church | **Vienna**	26
Ben's Chili | **U St**	22
Bibiana | **D'town**	25
Bistro Bis | **Cap Hill**	26
BLT Steak | **Gldn Triangle**	25
Bobby Van's | **D'town**	23
Bombay Club | **Gldn Triangle**	25
Bourbon Steak | **Georgetown**	25
Brass. Beck | **D'town**	25
Cafe Milano | **Georgetown**	22
Capital Grille | **multi.**	26
Central Michel | **Penn Qtr**	26
C.F. Folks | **Dupont Cir**	24
Charlie Palmer | **Cap Hill**	26
Chef Geoff's | **multi.**	21
CityZen | **SW**	27
Clyde's | **multi.**	22
Columbia Firehse. | **Alexandria**	23
Corduroy | **Mt. Vernon Sq**	28
DC Coast | **D'town**	23
Del Frisco's | **Penn Qtr**	–
District Commons | **Foggy Bottom**	22
Equinox | **Gldn Triangle**	25
Evo Bistro | **McLean**	22
Fiola | **Penn Qtr**	27
Founding Farmers | **World Bank**	24
Fyve | **Arlington**	24
Georgia Brown | **D'town**	22
NEW Grill Room | **Georgetown**	–
Hamilton | **D'town**	20
Hill Country | **Penn Qtr**	21
Hunan Dynasty | **Cap Hill**	20
Inn/Little Washington | **Washington**	29
I Ricchi | **Dupont Cir**	24

J&G Steak | **D'town**	24
Johnny's Half Shell | **Cap Hill**	21
Lafayette Rm. | **Gldn Triangle**	27
Landini Bros. | **Alexandria**	25
La Taberna | **World Bank**	26
🆕 Le Diplomate | **Logan Cir**	–
Marcel's | **West End**	28
Martin's Tav. | **Georgetown**	20
Mintwood | **Adams Mor**	–
Monocle | **Cap Hill**	21
Morton's | **multi.**	26
🆕 NoPa | **Penn Qtr**	–
Nora | **Dupont Cir**	26
Occidental | **D'town**	23
Oceanaire | **D'town**	24
Old Ebbitt | **D'town**	23
Osteria Elisir | **Penn Qtr**	26
Oval Rm. | **Gldn Triangle**	26
Palena | **Cleve Pk**	27
Palm | **multi.**	25
Peking Gourmet | **Falls Ch**	25
Plume | **D'town**	26
Prime Rib | **Gldn Triangle**	28
Proof | **Penn Qtr**	24
🆕 Range | **Chevy Chase**	–
Rasika | **West End**	28
Renato/River Falls | **Potomac**	22
Restaurant Eve | **Alexandria**	27
701 | **Penn Qtr**	23
1789 | **Georgetown**	26
Sonoma | **Cap Hill**	21
Source | **Penn Qtr**	27
Tosca | **Penn Qtr**	27
Tuscarora Mill | **Leesburg**	25
2941 | **Falls Ch**	27
Vidalia | **Gldn Triangle**	26
Volt | **Frederick**	28
Westend Bistro | **West End**	22
Willow | **Arlington**	24
🆕 Woodward Table | **D'town**	–
Zaytinya | **Penn Qtr**	26

PRIVATE ROOMS

(Restaurants charge less at off
times; call for capacity)

Afghan | **Alexandria**	23
🆕 Ancora | **Foggy Bottom**	–
Birch/Barley | **Logan Cir**	24
Bistro Bis | **Cap Hill**	26
Bistro D'Oc | **Penn Qtr**	23
Bistrot Lepic | **Georgetown**	24
Brass. Beck | **D'town**	25
B. Smith's | **Cap Hill**	22
🆕 Bungalow | **Sterling**	–
Cafe Milano | **Georgetown**	22
Carmine's | **Penn Qtr**	20
Ceiba | **D'town**	24
Central Michel | **Penn Qtr**	26
Charlie Palmer | **Cap Hill**	26
Chef Geoff's | **multi.**	21
Chima | **Vienna**	26
CityZen | **SW**	27
Clyde's | **multi.**	22
Corduroy | **Mt. Vernon Sq**	28
DC Coast | **D'town**	23
Duangrat's | **Falls Ch**	26
Dutch's Daughter | **Frederick**	25
Equinox | **Gldn Triangle**	25
Fiola | **Penn Qtr**	27
Fleming's Steak | **McLean**	25
Geranio | **Alexandria**	25
🆕 Grill Room | **Georgetown**	–
Irish Inn/Glen Echo | **Glen Echo**	20
Johnny's Half Shell | **Cap Hill**	21
La Chaumière | **Georgetown**	26
La Ferme | **Chevy Chase**	24
La Taberna | **World Bank**	26
Lebanese Tav. | **Woodley Pk**	23
Lightfoot | **Leesburg**	26
Marcel's | **West End**	28
Matisse | **Upper NW**	23
Monocle | **Cap Hill**	21
Morton's | **multi.**	26
🆕 NoPa | **Penn Qtr**	–

Nora | **Dupont Cir**	26
Occidental | **D'town**	23
Old Angler's | **Potomac**	20
Oval Rm. | **Gldn Triangle**	26
Oya | **Penn Qtr**	24
Palm | **multi.**	25
Pizzeria Da Marco | **Bethesda**	23
NEW Range | **Chevy Chase**	–
Rasika | **Penn Qtr**	28
Sequoia | **Georgetown**	17
701 | **Penn Qtr**	23
1789 | **Georgetown**	26
Smith/Wollensky | **Gldn Triangle**	25
Tosca | **Penn Qtr**	27
2941 | **Falls Ch**	27
Vidalia | **Gldn Triangle**	26
Wildfire | **McLean**	22
NEW Woodward Table | **D'town**	–
Woo Lae Oak | **Vienna**	23
Zengo | **Chinatown**	22

PRIX FIXE MENUS

(Call for prices and times)

Bastille | **Alexandria**	24
Bistro Français | **Georgetown**	21
BlackSalt | **Palisades**	27
Bombay Club | **Gldn Triangle**	25
Charlie Palmer | **Cap Hill**	26
Chef Geoff's | **multi.**	21
Corduroy | **Mt. Vernon Sq**	28
Dino | **Cleve Pk**	24
Eola | **Dupont Cir**	25
Inn/Little Washington | **Washington**	29
J&G Steak | **D'town**	24
La Bergerie | **Alexandria**	26
La Taberna | **World Bank**	26
L'Auberge/Jaques' | **Grt Falls**	28
Lia's | **Chevy Chase**	21
Makoto | **Palisades**	27
Mannequin Pis | **Olney**	23
Marcel's | **West End**	28

Masala Art | **Upper NW**	25
Matisse | **Upper NW**	23
Medium Rare | **Cleve Pk**	22
Me Jana | **Arlington**	24
Nora | **Dupont Cir**	26
Obelisk | **Dupont Cir**	28
Palena | **Cleve Pk**	27
PassionFish | **Reston**	26
Ray's/Classics | **Silver Spring**	25
Restaurant Eve | **Alexandria**	27
Rogue 24 | **Mt. Vernon Sq**	23
Source | **Penn Qtr**	27
Tosca | **Penn Qtr**	27

QUIET CONVERSATION

NEW Ancora | **Foggy Bottom**	–
Ashby Inn | **Paris**	27
Bastille | **Alexandria**	24
Benjarong | **Rockville**	23
Bistro L'Hermitage | **Woodbridge**	26
Blue Rock | **Sperryville**	24
Bombay Club | **Gldn Triangle**	25
Bourbon Steak | **Georgetown**	25
Café Renaissance | **Vienna**	26
Ching Ching | **Georgetown**	20
CityZen | **SW**	27
Corduroy | **Mt. Vernon Sq**	28
NEW Crossroads | **World Bank**	–
Degrees | **Georgetown**	22
NEW Edgar | **Gldn Triangle**	–
El Manantial | **Reston**	24
Eola | **Dupont Cir**	25
Equinox | **Gldn Triangle**	25
Eventide | **Clarendon**	23
15 Ria | **Scott Cir**	22
Fiola | **Penn Qtr**	27
NEW Grill Room | **Georgetown**	–
Guardado's | **Bethesda**	23
Heritage India | **multi.**	22
Il Canale | **Georgetown**	22
Indique | **multi.**	23

Inn/Little Washington | **Washington**	29
NEW Izakaya Seki | **U St**	–
J&G Steak | **D'town**	24
NEW Jardenea | **West End**	–
Juniper | **West End**	24
Kellari Taverna | **Gldn Triangle**	23
Komi | **Dupont Cir**	28
La Bergerie | **Alexandria**	26
La Chaumière | **Georgetown**	26
Lafayette Rm. | **Gldn Triangle**	27
La Ferme | **Chevy Chase**	24
La Taberna | **World Bank**	26
L'Auberge Provençale | **Boyce**	26
Liberty Tav. | **Clarendon**	24
Makoto | **Palisades**	27
NEW Malgudi | **Glover Pk**	–
Masala Art | **Upper NW**	25
Matisse | **Upper NW**	23
Minh's | **Arlington**	24
New Heights | **Woodley Pk**	22
Newton's | **Bethesda**	22
NEW Ninnella | **Cap Hill**	–
Nora | **Dupont Cir**	26
Obelisk | **Dupont Cir**	28
Oceanaire | **D'town**	24
Orchard | **Frederick**	25
Osteria Elisir | **Penn Qtr**	26
Oval Rm. | **Gldn Triangle**	26
Palena | **Cleve Pk**	27
Passage to India | **Bethesda**	24
Pesce | **Dupont Cir**	26
Plume | **D'town**	26
Restaurant Eve | **Alexandria**	27
Ris | **West End**	25
Russia House Rest. | **Herndon**	27
Sea Catch | **Georgetown**	23
Sergio Rist. | **Silver Spring**	27
701 | **Penn Qtr**	23
1789 | **Georgetown**	26
Source | **Penn Qtr**	27
Sou'Wester | **SW**	21

Sushi Taro | **Dupont Cir**	26
Sweet Ginger | **Vienna**	25
NEW Table | **Shaw**	–
Todd Gray's Watershed | **NoMa**	23
Tosca | **Penn Qtr**	27
2941 | **Falls Ch**	27
2100 Prime | **Dupont Cir**	24
Villa Mozart | **Fairfax**	26
Westend Bistro | **West End**	22
Woo Lae Oak | **Vienna**	23
Zentan | **D'town**	22

ROMANTIC PLACES

Acqua al 2 | **Cap Hill**	24
Agora | **Dupont Cir**	23
Al Tiramisu | **Dupont Cir**	25
NEW Ambar | **Cap Hill**	–
Ashby Inn | **Paris**	27
Atlas Rm. | **Atlas Dist**	25
NEW Azur | **Penn Qtr**	–
Bangkok 54 | **Arlington**	25
Bar Pilar | **U St**	23
Bezu | **Potomac**	24
Big Bear Cafe | **Bloomingdale**	–
Birch/Barley | **Logan Cir**	24
Bistro Bohem | **Shaw**	–
Bistro Cacao | **Cap Hill**	23
Bistro L'Hermitage | **Woodbridge**	26
Bistro Provence | **Bethesda**	26
Bistrot Lepic | **Georgetown**	24
Blue Rock | **Sperryville**	24
Bodega | **Georgetown**	23
Bombay Club | **Gldn Triangle**	25
NEW Bóveda | **West End**	–
Brabo | **Alexandria**	26
Brixton | **U St**	–
Busara | **McLean**	22
Busboys/Poets | **Arlington**	22
Café Bonaparte | **Georgetown**	23
Café Renaissance | **Vienna**	26
Casa Oaxaca | **Adams Mor**	22

Cashion's Eat	**Adams Mor**	25	Le Refuge	**Alexandria**	26
Cava Mezze	**multi.**	25	Little Fountain	**Adams Mor**	23
Chez Billy	**Petworth**	–	Little Serow	**Dupont Cir**	28
Circle Bistro	**West End**	20	NEW Mari Vanna	**Gldn Triangle**	–
CityZen	**SW**	27	Marrakesh P	**Dupont Cir**	23
Co Co. Sala	**Penn Qtr**	24	Marvin	**U St**	23
Comus Inn	**Dickerson**	20	Mezè	**Adams Mor**	24
Corduroy	**Mt. Vernon Sq**	28	Mintwood	**Adams Mor**	–
Cork	**Logan Cir**	25	Montmartre	**Cap Hill**	25
Cuba Libre	**Penn Qtr**	20	New Heights	**Woodley Pk**	22
Dickson Wine	**U St**	21	Newton's	**Bethesda**	22
District Kit.	**Woodley Pk**	24	Neyla	**Georgetown**	24
Dolce Vita	**Fairfax**	25	1905	**Shaw**	21
8407 Kit.	**Silver Spring**	24	NEW Ninnella	**Cap Hill**	–
El Centro	**Logan Cir**	21	NEW NoPa	**Penn Qtr**	–
Estadio	**Logan Cir**	25	Nora	**Dupont Cir**	26
Eventide	**Clarendon**	23	Obelisk	**Dupont Cir**	28
Ezmè	**Dupont Cir**	22	Old Angler's	**Potomac**	20
Fiola	**Penn Qtr**	27	Oya	**Penn Qtr**	24
Firefly	**Dupont Cir**	23	Palena	**Cleve Pk**	27
Floriana Rest.	**Dupont Cir**	24	Paul	**Georgetown**	22
Fontaine Caffe	**Alexandria**	25	Plume	**D'town**	26
Foti's	**Culpeper**	27	Present	**Falls Ch**	26
Grapeseed	**Bethesda**	23	Proof	**Penn Qtr**	24
Heritage India	**Glover Pk**	22	Rasika	**multi.**	28
Himalayan Heritage	**Adams Mor**	21	NEW Red Hen	**Bloomingdale**	–
Il Canale	**Georgetown**	22	Restaurant Eve	**Alexandria**	27
Indique	**multi.**	23	Ripple	**Cleve Pk**	23
Inn/Little Washington	**Washington**	29	Room 11	**Columbia Hts**	26
			Rustico	**Arlington**	22
NEW Izakaya Seki	**U St**	–	Sea Pearl	**Merrifield**	23
Jack Rose	**Adams Mor**	20	Sei	**Penn Qtr**	26
J&G Steak	**D'town**	24	701	**Penn Qtr**	23
Juniper	**West End**	24	1789	**Georgetown**	26
Komi	**Dupont Cir**	28	Source	**Penn Qtr**	27
La Bergerie	**Alexandria**	26	Tabard Inn	**Dupont Cir**	25
La Canela	**Rockville**	23	NEW Table	**Shaw**	–
La Chaumière	**Georgetown**	26	Tallula/EatBar	**Clarendon**	24
La Ferme	**Chevy Chase**	24	NEW Taqueria Nacional	**U St**	–
La Taberna	**World Bank**	26	Trummer's	**Clifton**	24
L'Auberge/Jaques'	**Grt Falls**	28	2941	**Falls Ch**	27
L'Auberge Provençale	**Boyce**	26		

Unum | **Georgetown**	⁻⌋
Vermilion | **Alexandria**	26⌋
Zentan | **D'town**	22⌋

SINGLES SCENES

Asia Bistro/Zen | **Arlington**	21⌋
Austin Grill | **multi.**	18⌋
Bar Pilar | **U St**	23⌋
Birch/Barley | **Logan Cir**	24⌋
Blackfinn Amer. | **Bethesda**	18⌋
BLT Steak | **Gldn Triangle**	25⌋
Bourbon | **multi.**	21⌋
Brass. Beck | **D'town**	25⌋
Cafe Deluxe | **multi.**	20⌋
Cafe Milano | **Georgetown**	22⌋
Café Saint-Ex | **Logan Cir**	20⌋
Central Michel | **Penn Qtr**	26⌋
Chef Geoff's | **multi.**	21⌋
Circa | **multi.**	20⌋
Clyde's | **multi.**	22⌋
Columbia Firehse. | **Alexandria**	23⌋
Dogfish Head | **Falls Ch**	21⌋
NEW Gryphon | **Dupont Cir**	⁻⌋
Indique | **Chevy Chase**	23⌋
Jackson's | **Reston**	23⌋
Kramerbooks | **Dupont Cir**	19⌋
Liberty Tav. | **Clarendon**	24⌋
Local 16 | **U St**	17⌋
Madhatter | **Dupont Cir**	18⌋
Marvin | **U St**	23⌋
Masa 14 | **Logan Cir**	23⌋
Matchbox | **U St**	23⌋
Mio | **D'town**	26⌋
NEW Mothership | **Columbia Hts**	⁻⌋
Neyla | **Georgetown**	24⌋
Old Ebbitt | **D'town**	23⌋
Oya | **Penn Qtr**	24⌋
Oyamel | **Penn Qtr**	25⌋
NEW Park Tavern | **Southeast**	⁻⌋
Perrys | **Adams Mor**	22⌋
Room 11 | **Columbia Hts**	26⌋
Rustico | **multi.**	22⌋

Sequoia | **Georgetown**	17⌋
Standard | **Logan Cir**	⁻⌋
Star/Shamrock | **Atlas Dist**	19⌋
Tabaq Bistro | **U St**	20⌋
Tasting Rm. | **Frederick**	27⌋
NEW Tony & Joe's | **Georgetown**	⁻⌋
Zaytinya | **Penn Qtr**	26⌋
Zengo | **Chinatown**	22⌋

SLEEPERS

(Good food, but little known)

Adam Express | **Mt. Pleasant**	25⌋
Blue Rock | **Sperryville**	24⌋
Cosmopolitan Grill | **Alexandria**	27⌋
Eola | **Dupont Cir**	25⌋
Fast Gourmet | **U St**	27⌋
Fontaine Caffe | **Alexandria**	25⌋
Fyve | **Arlington**	24⌋
Grille | **Alexandria**	25⌋
Hama Sushi | **Herndon**	25⌋
Huong Viet | **Falls Ch**	25⌋
India Palace | **Germantown**	26⌋
Juniper | **West End**	24⌋
Kabob N Karahi | **Silver Spring**	26⌋
La Caraqueña | **Falls Ch**	25⌋
Lafayette Rm. | **Gldn Triangle**	27⌋
Las Canteras | **Adams Mor**	24⌋
L'Auberge Provençale | **Boyce**	26⌋
Lighthouse Tofu | **Rockville**	24⌋
Morrison-Clark | **D'town**	24⌋
Myanmar | **Falls Ch**	24⌋
Napoleon Bistro | **Adams Mor**	24⌋
New Kam | **Wheaton**	25⌋
Old Hickory | **Nat'l Harbor**	26⌋
Panjshir | **Falls Ch**	25⌋
Pho DC | **Chinatown**	24⌋
Rangoli | **S Riding**	24⌋
Regent | **Dupont Cir**	24⌋
Ren's | **Wheaton**	24⌋
Room 11 | **Columbia Hts**	26⌋
Senart's Oyster | **Cap Hill**	24⌋
Sergio Rist. | **Silver Spring**	27⌋

Shamshiry	**Vienna**	27
Sichuan Jin River	**Rockville**	25
Sweet Ginger	**Vienna**	25
Taste/Burma	**Sterling**	26
Toscana Café	**Cap Hill**	25
Village Bistro	**Arlington**	26

TRANSPORTING EXPERIENCES

Biergarten Haus	**Atlas Dist**	17
Bombay Club	**Gldn Triangle**	25
Brass. Beck	**D'town**	25
Ching Ching	**Georgetown**	20
Cuba Libre	**Penn Qtr**	20
NEW Daikaya Izakaya	**Chinatown**	–
NEW Daikaya Ramen	**Chinatown**	–
Freddy's Lobster	**Bethesda**	19
Heritage India	**Glover Pk**	22
Hill Country	**Penn Qtr**	21
Honey Pig	**Annandale**	23
Hunter's Head	**Upperville**	23
NEW Izakaya Seki	**U St**	–
Kazan	**McLean**	25
Kushi	**Mt. Vernon Sq**	25
La Taberna	**World Bank**	26
L'Auberge/Jaques'	**Grt Falls**	28
NEW Le Diplomate	**Logan Cir**	–
Makoto	**Palisades**	27
NEW Mari Vanna	**Gldn Triangle**	–
Marrakesh P	**Dupont Cir**	23
Martin's Tav.	**Georgetown**	20
Neyla	**Georgetown**	24
Oya	**Penn Qtr**	24
Russia Hse.	**Dupont Cir**	21
Sushi Taro	**Dupont Cir**	26
NEW Taqueria Nacional	**U St**	–

TRENDY

Alegria	**Vienna**	–
NEW Ambar	**Cap Hill**	–
American Ice	**U St**	19

NEW Aroma Espresso	**Bethesda**	–
Art & Soul	**Cap Hill**	23
NEW Astro	**D'town**	–
Atlas Rm.	**Atlas Dist**	25
NEW Azur	**Penn Qtr**	–
Bandolero	**Georgetown**	–
Bayou Bakery	**Arlington**	22
NEW Beau Thai	**multi.**	–
NEW Beuchert's	**Cap Hill**	–
Bibiana	**D'town**	25
Birch/Barley	**Logan Cir**	24
Bistro Bis	**Cap Hill**	26
Bistro Bohem	**Shaw**	–
Bistrot du Coin	**Dupont Cir**	22
Black's Bar	**Bethesda**	24
Boqueria	**Dupont Cir**	–
Boundary Rd.	**Atlas Dist**	–
Brass. Beck	**D'town**	25
Bread Line	**World Bank**	23
NEW Brickside	**Bethesda**	–
Brixton	**U St**	–
NEW Bungalow	**Sterling**	–
Busboys/Poets	**multi.**	22
Cafe Milano	**Georgetown**	22
Café Saint-Ex	**Logan Cir**	20
Cashion's Eat	**Adams Mor**	25
Cava Mezze Grill	**multi.**	22
Central Michel	**Penn Qtr**	26
Chef Geoff's	**Rockville**	21
Chez Billy	**Petworth**	–
Circa	**multi.**	20
CityZen	**SW**	27
Co Co. Sala	**Penn Qtr**	24
Cork	**Logan Cir**	25
Curry Mantra	**Falls Ch**	23
NEW Daikaya Ramen	**Chinatown**	–
Del Frisco's	**Penn Qtr**	–
NEW DGS Deli	**Dupont Cir**	–
Dickson Wine	**U St**	21
District of Pi	**Penn Qtr**	23

Eamonn's | **Arlington**	23
NEW East Dumpling | **Rockville**	–
Eatonville | **U St**	23
El Centro | **Logan Cir**	21
El Chucho | **Columbia Hts**	–
Estadio | **Logan Cir**	25
Ethiopic | **Atlas Dist**	24
Evening Star | **Alexandria**	23
Family Meal | **Frederick**	–
Fast Gourmet | **U St**	27
Fiola | **Penn Qtr**	27
Founding Farmers | **multi.**	24
NEW Fuego Cocina | **Clarendon**	–
Fuel Pizza Cafe | **multi.**	–
Fujimar | **D'town**	–
Good Stuff | **multi.**	23
Graffiato | **Chinatown**	24
Granville Moore's | **Atlas Dist**	24
Green Pig | **Clarendon**	–
Hank's Oyster | **Dupont Cir**	24
Haven | **Bethesda**	–
Hill Country | **Penn Qtr**	21
Honey Pig | **Annandale**	23
NEW Izakaya Seki | **U St**	–
Jackie's | **Silver Spring**	23
Jack Rose | **Adams Mor**	20
Jaleo | **multi.**	24
J&G Steak | **D'town**	24
Johnny's Half Shell | **Cap Hill**	21
Kangaroo/PORC | **Columbia Hts**	–
Komi | **Dupont Cir**	28
Kushi | **Mt. Vernon Sq**	25
Lauriol Plaza | **Dupont Cir**	21
NEW Le Diplomate | **Logan Cir**	–
NEW Le Grenier | **Atlas Dist**	–
Leopold's Kafe | **Georgetown**	23
Lincoln | **D'town**	20
Little Serow | **Dupont Cir**	28
Local 16 | **U St**	17
Luke's Lobster | **Georgetown**	23
Mandu | **multi.**	23
NEW Mari Vanna | **Gldn Triangle**	–
Marvin | **U St**	23
Masa 14 | **Logan Cir**	23
Matchbox | **multi.**	23
NEW Mi Cuba | **Columbia Hts**	–
Minibar | **Penn Qtr**	28
Mio | **D'town**	26
Mussel B&G | **Bethesda**	20
1905 | **Shaw**	21
Oya | **Penn Qtr**	24
Oyamel | **Penn Qtr**	25
Palena | **Cleve Pk**	27
NEW Park Tavern | **Southeast**	–
Pearl Dive | **Logan Cir**	26
Perrys | **Adams Mor**	22
Pete's Apizza | **multi.**	22
Pho 14 | **multi.**	25
Policy | **U St**	22
Proof | **Penn Qtr**	24
Pupatella Pizzeria | **Arlington**	26
NEW Radius Pizza | **Mt. Pleasant**	–
NEW Range | **Chevy Chase**	–
Rasika | **multi.**	28
NEW Red Apron | **multi.**	–
NEW Red Hen | **Bloomingdale**	–
Red Hook | **Location Varies**	25
Renato/River Falls | **Potomac**	22
Ren's | **Wheaton**	24
Restaurant Eve | **Alexandria**	27
Ripple | **Cleve Pk**	23
Rogue 24 | **Mt. Vernon Sq**	23
Room 11 | **Columbia Hts**	26
Ruan Thai | **Wheaton**	27
Russia Hse. | **Dupont Cir**	21
Sei | **Penn Qtr**	26
Society Fair | **Alexandria**	24
Source | **Penn Qtr**	27
Standard | **Logan Cir**	–
Stoney's | **Logan Cir**	18
Sugo Cicchetti | **Potomac**	–
Sushi Damo | **Rockville**	25

Tabard Inn	**Dupont Cir**	25
NEW Table	**Shaw**	-
NEW Takeateasy	**Gldn Triangle**	-
Tallula/EatBar	**Clarendon**	24
NEW Tash House	**Cap Hill**	-
NEW Taylor Charles	**Atlas Dist**	-
Taylor Gourmet	**multi.**	22
Thunder Burger	**Georgetown**	24
Toki	**Atlas Dist**	26
2 Amys	**Cleve Pk**	25
Vermilion	**Alexandria**	26
Vinoteca	**U St**	22
NEW Vino Volo	**Bethesda**	-
Volt	**Frederick**	28
We the Pizza	**Cap Hill**	22
NEW Wildwood Kit.	**Bethesda**	-
Zaytinya	**Penn Qtr**	26
Zengo	**Chinatown**	22
Zentan	**D'town**	22

VALET PARKING

Acadiana	**Mt. Vernon Sq**	24
Acre 121	**Columbia Hts**	21
Al Tiramisu	**Dupont Cir**	25
Ardeo/Bardeo	**Cleve Pk**	22
Art & Soul	**Cap Hill**	23
Assaggi	**Bethesda**	23
NEW Bench	**Gaith'burg**	-
Bibiana	**D'town**	25
Biergarten Haus	**Atlas Dist**	17
BLT Steak	**Gldn Triangle**	25
Blue Duck	**West End**	27
Bobby Van's	**D'town**	23
Bombay Club	**Gldn Triangle**	25
Bond 45	**Nat'l Harbor**	22
Bourbon Steak	**Georgetown**	25
Brabo	**Alexandria**	26
Brass. Beck	**D'town**	25
Brass. Monte Carlo	**Bethesda**	22
NEW B Too	**Logan Cir**	-
Café du Parc	**D'town**	21

Café Dupont	**Dupont Cir**	21
Calif. Tortilla	**Cleve Pk**	22
Capital Grille	**multi.**	26
Carmine's	**Penn Qtr**	20
Cashion's Eat	**Adams Mor**	25
Cava Mezze	**Cap Hill**	25
Ceiba	**D'town**	24
Central Michel	**Penn Qtr**	26
Cesco Osteria	**Bethesda**	19
Charlie Palmer	**Cap Hill**	26
Cheesecake Factory	**multi.**	24
Chef Geoff's	**multi.**	21
Chima	**Vienna**	26
Circle Bistro	**West End**	20
CityZen	**SW**	27
Clyde's	**multi.**	22
Co Co. Sala	**Penn Qtr**	24
Cuba Libre	**Penn Qtr**	20
Curry Mantra	**Falls Ch**	23
DC Coast	**D'town**	23
NEW Decanter	**D'town**	-
Degrees	**Georgetown**	22
Dish/Drinks	**Foggy Bottom**	21
District ChopHse.	**Penn Qtr**	21
District Commons	**Foggy Bottom**	22
NEW Edgar	**Gldn Triangle**	-
Estadio	**Logan Cir**	25
15 Ria	**Scott Cir**	22
Finemondo	**D'town**	20
Fiola	**Penn Qtr**	27
Fleming's Steak	**McLean**	25
Fogo de Chão	**Penn Qtr**	27
Georgia Brown	**D'town**	22
Graffiato	**Chinatown**	24
Grapeseed	**Bethesda**	23
Grille	**Alexandria**	25
Grill/Ipanema	**Adams Mor**	24
NEW Grill Room	**Georgetown**	-
NEW Gryphon	**Dupont Cir**	-
Härth	**McLean**	23
Hee Been	**Alexandria**	23

Heritage India	**Glover Pk**	22	Pesce	**Dupont Cir**	26
Howard Theatre	**Shaw**	-_	Petits Plats	**Woodley Pk**	22
Inn/Little Washington	**Washington**	29	P.J. Clarke's	**D'town**	18
I Ricchi	**Dupont Cir**	24	Plume	**D'town**	26
Irish Inn/Glen Echo	**Glen Echo**	20	Policy	**U St**	22
J&G Steak	**D'town**	24	Poste Moderne	**Penn Qtr**	20
NEW Jardenea	**West End**	-_	Prime Rib	**Gldn Triangle**	28
Juniper	**West End**	24	Primi Piatti	**Foggy Bottom**	19
Lafayette Rm.	**Gldn Triangle**	27	Proof	**Penn Qtr**	24
NEW Le Diplomate	**Logan Cir**	-_	**NEW** Range	**Chevy Chase**	-_
Lia's	**Chevy Chase**	21	Rasika	**Penn Qtr**	28
Local 16	**U St**	17	**NEW** Red Hen	**Bloomingdale**	-_
Lyon Hall	**Clarendon**	24	Rosa Mexicano	**Penn Qtr**	23
Maggiano's	**McLean**	23	Ruth's Chris	**multi.**	26
Marcel's	**West End**	28	Sei	**Penn Qtr**	26
Masa 14	**Logan Cir**	23	Sette Osteria	**Dupont Cir**	21
Matchbox	**Rockville**	23	701	**Penn Qtr**	23
Matisse	**Upper NW**	23	1789	**Georgetown**	26
McCormick/Schmick's	**multi.**	23	Siroc	**D'town**	24
Minibar	**Penn Qtr**	28	Smith/Wollensky	**Gldn Triangle**	25
Mintwood	**Adams Mor**	-_	Source	**Penn Qtr**	27
Mio	**D'town**	26	Sou'Wester	**SW**	21
Mon Ami Gabi	**Bethesda**	22	Sushiko	**Glover Pk**	24
Morrison-Clark	**D'town**	24	Tabaq Bistro	**U St**	20
Morton's	**multi.**	26	Tabard Inn	**Dupont Cir**	25
Nage	**Scott Cir**	21	**NEW** Table	**Shaw**	-_
New Heights	**Woodley Pk**	22	Thai Sq.	**Arlington**	26
Newton's	**Bethesda**	22	Todd Gray's Watershed	**NoMa**	23
Neyla	**Georgetown**	24	Tosca	**Penn Qtr**	27
NEW NoPa	**Penn Qtr**	-_	**NEW** Trademark	**Alexandria**	-_
Nora	**Dupont Cir**	26	2941	**Falls Ch**	27
Notti Bianche	**Foggy Bottom**	22	2100 Prime	**Dupont Cir**	24
Occidental	**D'town**	23	Ulah Bistro	**U St**	20
Oceanaire	**D'town**	24	Urbana	**Dupont Cir**	21
Old Ebbitt	**D'town**	23	Vidalia	**Gldn Triangle**	26
Osteria Elisir	**Penn Qtr**	26	Vinifera	**Reston**	23
Oval Rm.	**Gldn Triangle**	26	**NEW** Vino Volo	**Bethesda**	-_
Oya	**Penn Qtr**	24	Westend Bistro	**West End**	22
Palm	**multi.**	25	Wildfire	**McLean**	22
Panache	**McLean**	21	**NEW** Woodward Table	**D'town**	-_
Passage to India	**Bethesda**	24	Woo Lae Oak	**Vienna**	23

| Zaytinya | **Penn Qtr** | 26 |
| Zengo | **Chinatown** | 22 |

VIEWS

Acre 121	**Columbia Hts**	21
NEW Ancora	**Foggy Bottom**	-J
Ashby Inn	**Paris**	27
NEW Black Whiskey	**Logan Cir**	-J
Blue Rock	**Sperryville**	24
Charlie Palmer	**Cap Hill**	26
Clyde's	**Rockville**	22
District Commons	**Foggy Bottom**	22
NEW Farmers Fishers	**Georgetown**	-J
Guapo's	**Gaith'burg**	22
Inn/Little Washington	**Washington**	29
J&G Steak	**D'town**	24
Lafayette Rm.	**Gldn Triangle**	27
L'Auberge/Jaques'	**Grt Falls**	28
NEW Le Diplomate	**Logan Cir**	-J
1905	**Shaw**	21
NEW NoPa	**Penn Qtr**	-J
Perrys	**Adams Mor**	22
Phillips	**SW**	20
Rogue 24	**Mt. Vernon Sq**	23
Rosa Mexicano	**Nat'l Harbor**	23
Roti	**World Bank**	22
Ruth's Chris	**Arlington**	26
Sea Catch	**Georgetown**	23
Sequoia	**Georgetown**	17
701	**Penn Qtr**	23
Source	**Penn Qtr**	27
NEW Table	**Shaw**	-J
NEW Tony & Joe's	**Georgetown**	-J
2941	**Falls Ch**	27
Virtue	**Alexandria**	-J
NEW Woodward Table	**D'town**	-J

WINE BARS

| Acacia Bistro | **Upper NW** | 20 |
| A La Lucia | **Alexandria** | 23 |

Al Crostino	**U St**	23
Ardeo/Bardeo	**Cleve Pk**	22
Asia Bistro/Zen	**Arlington**	21
Bazin's/Church	**Vienna**	26
Bistro Cacao	**Cap Hill**	23
Bistro D'Oc	**Penn Qtr**	23
Bistrot Lepic	**Georgetown**	24
Cava Mezze	**Rockville**	25
Cork	**Logan Cir**	25
Curious Grape	**Arlington**	-J
Dickson Wine	**U St**	21
Dolce Veloce	**Fairfax**	-J
Estadio	**Logan Cir**	25
NEW Etto	**Logan Cir**	-J
Evo Bistro	**McLean**	22
Ezmè	**Dupont Cir**	22
Fleming's Steak	**McLean**	25
Grapeseed	**Bethesda**	23
Iron Bridge Wine	**Warrenton**	25
NEW Jardenea	**West End**	-J
Liberty Tree	**Atlas Dist**	23
Lincoln	**D'town**	20
Local 16	**U St**	17
Lost Society	**U St**	18
Luna Grill	**multi.**	19
Mad Fox Brew	**Falls Ch**	20
Madhatter	**Dupont Cir**	18
Mamma Lucia	**multi.**	22
Mandalay	**Silver Spring**	23
Maple	**Columbia Hts**	-J
Matchbox	**U St**	23
Mrs. K's	**Silver Spring**	23
Northside	**Clarendon**	22
Oakville Grille	**Bethesda**	21
Pearl Dive	**Logan Cir**	26
Proof	**Penn Qtr**	24
Redwood	**Bethesda**	19
Ripple	**Cleve Pk**	23
Room 11	**Columbia Hts**	26
Serendipity 3	**Georgetown**	21
701	**Penn Qtr**	23

NEW Slate | **Glover Pk**	-
Sonoma | **Cap Hill**	21
NEW Table | **Shaw**	-
Twisted Vines | **Arlington**	20
Urbana | **Dupont Cir**	21
Vidalia | **Gldn Triangle**	26
Vinifera | **Reston**	23
Vinoteca | **U St**	22
NEW Vino Volo | **Bethesda**	-
Wine Kit. | **multi.**	26

WINNING WINE LISTS

Acqua al 2 | **Cap Hill**	24
Al Dente | **Upper NW**	-
Al Tiramisu | **Dupont Cir**	25
NEW Ambar | **Cap Hill**	-
NEW Ancora | **Foggy Bottom**	-
Ashby Inn | **Paris**	27
NEW Azur | **Penn Qtr**	-
Bastille | **Alexandria**	24
Bibiana | **D'town**	25
Birch/Barley | **Logan Cir**	24
Bistro Bis | **Cap Hill**	26
Bistro L'Hermitage | **Woodbridge**	26
Bistro Provence | **Bethesda**	26
Bistrot Lepic | **Georgetown**	24
BlackSalt | **Palisades**	27
BLT Steak | **Gldn Triangle**	25
Blue Duck | **West End**	27
Bond 45 | **Nat'l Harbor**	22
Boqueria | **Dupont Cir**	-
Blvd. Woodgrill | **Clarendon**	20
Bourbon Steak | **Georgetown**	25
Brabo | **Alexandria**	26
Brass. Beck | **D'town**	25
Buck's Fishing | **Upper NW**	20
Café du Parc | **D'town**	21
Cafe Milano | **Georgetown**	22
Café Renaissance | **Vienna**	26
Capital Grille | **multi.**	26
Carlyle | **Arlington**	25

Cashion's Eat | **Adams Mor**	25
Central Michel | **Penn Qtr**	26
Cesco Osteria | **Bethesda**	19
Charlie Palmer | **Cap Hill**	26
Circa | **Dupont Cir**	20
CityZen | **SW**	27
Corduroy | **Mt. Vernon Sq**	28
Cork | **Logan Cir**	25
Curious Grape | **Arlington**	-
NEW DGS Deli | **Dupont Cir**	-
Dickson Wine | **U St**	21
Dino | **Cleve Pk**	24
District Commons | **Foggy Bottom**	22
District Kit. | **Woodley Pk**	24
Dolce Vita | **Fairfax**	25
Eola | **Dupont Cir**	25
Equinox | **Gldn Triangle**	25
Estadio | **Logan Cir**	25
Et Voila | **Palisades**	25
Evening Star | **Alexandria**	23
Eventide | **Clarendon**	23
Evo Bistro | **McLean**	22
Fiola | **Penn Qtr**	27
Fleming's Steak | **McLean**	25
Floriana Rest. | **Dupont Cir**	24
Food Wine | **Bethesda**	22
Foti's | **Culpeper**	27
Graffiato | **Chinatown**	24
Grapeseed | **Bethesda**	23
NEW Grill Room | **Georgetown**	-
Harry's | **Arlington**	21
Il Canale | **Georgetown**	22
Il Pizzico | **Rockville**	27
Inn/Little Washington | **Washington**	29
I Ricchi | **Dupont Cir**	24
Irish Whiskey | **Dupont Cir**	-
Jack Rose | **Adams Mor**	20
Jackson 20 | **Alexandria**	21
Jaleo | **multi.**	24
J&G Steak | **D'town**	24

Johnny's Half Shell | **Cap Hill**	21
Kaz Sushi | **World Bank**	25
Kellari Taverna | **Gldn Triangle**	23
Komi | **Dupont Cir**	28
Kushi | **Mt. Vernon Sq**	25
La Chaumière | **Georgetown**	26
Landini Bros. | **Alexandria**	25
La Taberna | **World Bank**	26
L'Auberge/Jaques' | **Grt Falls**	28
L'Auberge Provençale | **Boyce**	26
NEW Le Diplomate | **Logan Cir**	–
Leopold's Kafe | **Georgetown**	23
Maple | **Columbia Hts**	–
Marcel's | **West End**	28
Medium Rare | **Cleve Pk**	22
Menomale | **Brookland**	–
Minibar | **Penn Qtr**	28
Mintwood | **Adams Mor**	–
Mon Ami Gabi | **multi.**	22
Mrs. K's | **Silver Spring**	23
Mussel B&G | **Bethesda**	20
New Heights | **Woodley Pk**	22
NEW NoPa | **Penn Qtr**	–
Nora | **Dupont Cir**	26
Northside | **Clarendon**	22
Nostos | **Vienna**	26
Oakville Grille | **Bethesda**	21
Obelisk | **Dupont Cir**	28
Occidental | **D'town**	23
Old Ebbitt | **D'town**	23
Osteria Elisir | **Penn Qtr**	26
Oval Rm. | **Gldn Triangle**	26
Oya | **Penn Qtr**	24
Palena | **Cleve Pk**	27
Palm | **multi.**	25
PassionFish | **Reston**	26
Persimmon | **Bethesda**	–
Pesce | **Dupont Cir**	26
Ping | **Arlington**	23
Pizzeria Da Marco | **Bethesda**	23
Plume | **D'town**	26

Posto | **Logan Cir**	23
Prime Rib | **Gldn Triangle**	28
Proof | **Penn Qtr**	24
NEW Range | **Chevy Chase**	–
Rasika | **multi.**	28
Ray's/Classics | **Silver Spring**	25
Ray's/Steaks | **Arlington**	27
Ray's/Third | **Arlington**	25
NEW Red Hen | **Bloomingdale**	–
Redwood | **Bethesda**	19
Restaurant Eve | **Alexandria**	27
Ripple | **Cleve Pk**	23
Ris | **West End**	25
Rogue 24 | **Mt. Vernon Sq**	23
Room 11 | **Columbia Hts**	26
Sabai | **Germantown**	26
NEW Slate | **Glover Pk**	–
Smith/Wollensky | **Gldn Triangle**	25
Society Fair | **Alexandria**	24
Sonoma | **Cap Hill**	21
Sorriso | **Cleve Pk**	22
Source | **Penn Qtr**	27
Sushiko | **multi.**	24
Tabard Inn | **Dupont Cir**	25
NEW Table | **Shaw**	–
Tallula/EatBar | **Clarendon**	24
Tasting Rm. | **Frederick**	27
Tavira | **Chevy Chase**	25
Tel'Veh | **Mt. Vernon Sq**	–
Tosca | **Penn Qtr**	27
Toscana Café | **Cap Hill**	25
Trummer's | **Clifton**	24
Tuscarora Mill | **Leesburg**	25
2941 | **Falls Ch**	27
2100 Prime | **Dupont Cir**	24
Twisted Vines | **Arlington**	20
2 Amys | **Cleve Pk**	25
Vidalia | **Gldn Triangle**	26
Vinifera | **Reston**	23
Vinoteca | **U St**	22
Volt | **Frederick**	28

WASHINGTON, DC

SPECIAL FEATURES

Cuisines

Includes names, locations and Food ratings.

AFGHAN

Afghan	**Alexandria**	23
Afghan Kabob Hse.	**Arlington**	23
Afghan Kabob Rest.	**Springfield**	25
Bamian	**Falls Ch**	26
Faryab	**Bethesda**	24
Food Corner Kabob	**multi.**	25
Kabob Palace	**Arlington**	26
Panjshir	**Falls Ch**	25

AMERICAN

Acacia Bistro	**Frederick**	24
Addie's	**White Flint**	25
NEW AGB	**Georgetown**	–
Ardeo/Bardeo	**Cleve Pk**	22
NEW Aroma Espresso	**Bethesda**	–
Art & Soul	**Cap Hill**	23
Artie's	**Fairfax**	25
Ashby Inn	**Paris**	27
Bar Pilar	**U St**	23
Bazin's/Church	**Vienna**	26
NEW Bench	**Gaith'burg**	–
Ben's Chili	**U St**	22
NEW Beuchert's	**Cap Hill**	–
Bezu	**Potomac**	24
Big Bear Cafe	**Bloomingdale**	–
Birch/Barley	**Logan Cir**	24
Blackfinn Amer.	**multi.**	18
Black Mkt.	**Garrett Pk**	26
BlackSalt	**Palisades**	27
Black's Bar	**Bethesda**	24
NEW Black Whiskey	**Logan Cir**	–
Blue Duck	**West End**	27
Blue Ridge	**multi.**	24
Blue Rock	**Sperryville**	24
Blvd. Woodgrill	**Clarendon**	20
Boxcar Tav.	**Cap Hill**	21
NEW Brickside	**Bethesda**	–
Brixton	**U St**	–
Buck's Fishing	**Upper NW**	20

NEW Bungalow	**Sterling**	–
Busboys/Poets	**Mt. Vernon Sq**	22
Cafe Deluxe	**multi.**	20
Cafe Nola	**Frederick**	24
CapMac	**Location Varies**	23
Carlyle	**Arlington**	25
Cashion's Eat	**Adams Mor**	25
Cedar Rest.	**Penn Qtr**	23
Central Michel	**Penn Qtr**	26
Cheesecake Factory	**multi.**	24
Chef Geoff's	**multi.**	21
Chesapeake Rm.	**Cap Hill**	20
Chop't	**multi.**	21
Circa	**multi.**	20
Circle Bistro	**West End**	20
CityZen	**SW**	27
Clyde's	**multi.**	22
Co Co. Sala	**Penn Qtr**	24
Columbia Firehse.	**Alexandria**	23
Commissary	**Logan Cir**	19
Comus Inn	**Dickerson**	20
Corduroy	**Mt. Vernon Sq**	28
Cork	**Logan Cir**	25
Counter	**Reston**	21
Dangerously Delicious	**Atlas Dist**	21
DC Coast	**D'town**	23
Del Frisco's	**Penn Qtr**	–
Dish/Drinks	**Foggy Bottom**	21
District Commons	**Foggy Bottom**	22
District Kit.	**Woodley Pk**	24
Dutch's Daughter	**Frederick**	25
NEW Edgar	**Gldn Triangle**	–
Eggspectation	**multi.**	21
8407 Kit.	**Silver Spring**	24
Eola	**Dupont Cir**	25
Equinox	**Gldn Triangle**	25
Evening Star	**Alexandria**	23
Eventide	**Clarendon**	23

Persimmon | **Bethesda**	⌐⌐
Pig | **Logan Cir**	⌐⌐
P.J. Clarke's | **D'town**	18
Plume | **D'town**	26
Policy | **U St**	22
Poste Moderne | **Penn Qtr**	20
Proof | **Penn Qtr**	24
Quench | **Rockville**	⌐⌐
Rail Stop | **Plains**	23
NEW Range | **Chevy Chase**	⌐⌐
Ray's/Steaks | **Arlington**	27
Ray's/Third | **Arlington**	25
NEW Red Apron | **multi.**	⌐⌐
Redwood | **Bethesda**	19
Restaurant Eve | **Alexandria**	27
Ripple | **Cleve Pk**	23
Ris | **West End**	25
River Falls Tav. | **Potomac**	⌐⌐
Rogue 24 | **Mt. Vernon Sq**	23
Roof Terr. | **Foggy Bottom**	16
Rustico | **multi.**	22
Scion | **multi.**	19
Sequoia | **Georgetown**	17
Serendipity 3 | **Georgetown**	21
701 | **Penn Qtr**	23
1789 | **Georgetown**	26
NEW Slate | **Glover Pk**	⌐⌐
Smith Commons | **Atlas Dist**	22
Social Reform | **Penn Qtr**	⌐⌐
Society Fair | **Alexandria**	24
Sonoma | **Cap Hill**	21
Station 4 | **SW Waterfront**	21
Tabard Inn | **Dupont Cir**	25
Tallula/EatBar | **Clarendon**	24
Tasting Rm. | **Frederick**	27
NEW Tavern 64 | **Reston**	⌐⌐
Ted's Bulletin | **Cap Hill**	23
Todd Gray's Watershed | **NoMa**	23
Tonic | **multi.**	17
Town Hall | **Glover Pk**	23
NEW Trademark | **Alexandria**	⌐⌐
Trummer's | **Clifton**	24
Tuscarora Mill | **Leesburg**	25
2941 | **Falls Ch**	27
2100 Prime | **Dupont Cir**	24
Ulah Bistro | **U St**	20
Unum | **Georgetown**	⌐⌐
Vermilion | **Alexandria**	26
Vidalia | **Gldn Triangle**	26
Vinifera | **Reston**	23
Virtue | **Alexandria**	⌐⌐
Volt | **Frederick**	28
NEW Wagshal's | **Upper NW**	⌐⌐
Westend Bistro | **West End**	22
Wild Tomato | **Cabin John**	22
William Jeffrey's | **Arlington**	20
Willow | **Arlington**	24
Wine Kit. | **multi.**	26
NEW Woodward Table | **D'town**	⌐⌐
Zest | **Cap Hill**	21

ASIAN

Adam Express | **Mt. Pleasant**	25
Asia Bistro/Zen | **Arlington**	21
Asian Bistro | **multi.**	25
Asian Spice | **Chinatown**	23
Banana Leaves | **Dupont Cir**	⌐⌐
Batik | **Gaith'burg**	22
Cafe Asia | **multi.**	21
Ching Ching | **Georgetown**	20
Fujimar | **D'town**	⌐⌐
Grace's | **Nat'l Harbor**	25
Masa 14 | **Logan Cir**	23
Nooshi | **Cap Hill**	21
Oya | **Penn Qtr**	24
Perrys | **Adams Mor**	22
Sei | **Penn Qtr**	26
Shophouse | **Dupont Cir**	22
Source | **Penn Qtr**	27
Sticky Rice | **Atlas Dist**	23
Sunflower Veg. | **multi.**	25
Sweet Ginger | **Vienna**	25

Zengo | **Chinatown** `22`

Zentan | **D'town** `22`

AUSTRIAN

Leopold's Kafe | **Georgetown** `23`

BAKERIES

NEW Astro | **D'town** `-`

Bread Line | **World Bank** `23`

Buzz | **multi.** `22`

Dangerously Delicious | **multi.** `21`

NEW Farmers Fishers | **Georgetown** `-`

NEW GBD | **Dupont Cir** `-`

Il Fornaio | **Reston** `25`

Leopold's Kafe | **Georgetown** `23`

Le Pain Quotidien | **multi.** `21`

Paul | **multi.** `22`

Praline | **Bethesda** `23`

BARBECUE

Acre 121 | **Columbia Hts** `21`

American Ice | **U St** `19`

Harry's | **Arlington** `21`

Hill Country | **Penn Qtr** `21`

Kangaroo/PORC | **multi.** `-`

Old Glory | **Georgetown** `19`

Pork Barrel | **Alexandria** `19`

Red Hot/Blue | **multi.** `22`

Rocklands | **multi.** `22`

Smoke/Barrel | **Adams Mor** `20`

NEW Smoke BBQ | **Bethesda** `-`

Standard | **Logan Cir** `-`

Urban BBQ | **multi.** `24`

BELGIAN

Belga Café | **Cap Hill** `25`

Brabo | **Alexandria** `26`

Brass. Beck | **D'town** `25`

NEW B Too | **Logan Cir** `-`

Et Voila | **Palisades** `25`

NEW Fat Shorty's | **Clarendon** `-`

Granville Moore's | **Atlas Dist** `24`

Le Pain Quotidien | **multi.** `21`

Mannequin Pis | **Olney** `23`

Marcel's | **West End** `28`

Marvin | **U St** `23`

Mussel B&G | **Bethesda** `20`

BRAZILIAN

Chima | **Vienna** `26`

NEW Del Campo | **Penn Qtr** `-`

Fogo de Chão | **Penn Qtr** `27`

Grill/Ipanema | **Adams Mor** `24`

BRITISH

Brixton | **U St** `-`

Hunter's Head | **Upperville** `23`

Queen Vic | **Atlas Dist** `23`

BURGERS

BGR | **multi.** `22`

Big Board | **Atlas Dist** `-`

Black & Orange | **multi.** `25`

Bobby's Burger | **multi.** `22`

Burger Tap | **Foggy Bottom** `21`

Clyde's | **multi.** `22`

Counter | **Reston** `21`

Elevation Burger | **multi.** `21`

Five Guys | **multi.** `24`

Good Stuff | **multi.** `23`

Harry's | **Arlington** `21`

Palena | **Cleve Pk** `27`

Ray's/Third | **Arlington** `25`

Red Hot/Blue | **multi.** `22`

Thunder Burger | **Georgetown** `24`

NEW Woodward Table | **D'town** `-`

BURMESE

Burma | **Chinatown** `22`

Burma Rd. | **Gaith'burg** `22`

Mandalay | **Silver Spring** `23`

Myanmar | **Falls Ch** `24`

Taste/Burma | **Sterling** `26`

CAJUN

Acadiana | **Mt. Vernon Sq** `24`

Bayou | **West End** `20`

Cajun Experience | **Leesburg** `23`

Chasin' Tails | **Arlington** ⌐|

Hot 'N Juicy | **Woodley Pk** 20⌐

RT's | **Alexandria** 26⌐

CALIFORNIAN

Paolo's | **multi.** 21⌐

Sea Pearl | **Merrifield** 23⌐

Surfside | **Glover Pk** 21⌐

CAVIAR

NEW Azur | **Penn Qtr** ⌐|

NEW Mari Vanna | **Gldn Triangle** ⌐|

Russia Hse. | **Dupont Cir** 21⌐

CENTRAL AMERICAN

Pollo Campero | **Columbia Hts** 19⌐

CHICKEN

NEW Astro | **D'town** ⌐|

Chicken/Run | **Bethesda** 24⌐

Crisp/Juicy | **multi.** 24⌐

Don Pollo | **multi.** 23⌐

El Pollo | **multi.** 26⌐

NEW GBD | **Dupont Cir** ⌐|

Nando's | **multi.** 22⌐

Pollo Campero | **multi.** 19⌐

Wings To Go | **Cap Hill** 25⌐

CHINESE

(* dim sum specialist)

A&J* | **multi.** 25⌐

Burma Rd. | **Gaith'burg** 22⌐

China Bistro | **Rockville** 24⌐

China Gdn.* | **Rosslyn** 22⌐

China Jade | **Rockville** 25⌐

China Star | **Fairfax** 24⌐

Chinatown Express | **Chinatown** 23⌐

City Lights | **multi.** 19⌐

NEW East Dumpling | **Rockville** ⌐|

East Pearl | **Rockville** ⌐|

Eat First | **Chinatown** 22⌐

Fortune | **Falls Ch** 22⌐

Full Kee (DC) | **Chinatown** 23⌐

Full Kee (VA) | **Falls Ch** 22⌐

Full Key | **Wheaton** 25⌐

Fu Shing | **Bethesda** 22⌐

Good Fortune* | **Wheaton** 22⌐

Hollywood E.* | **Wheaton** 24⌐

Hong Kong Palace | **Falls Ch** 27⌐

Hunan Dynasty | **Cap Hill** 20⌐

Joe's Noodle Hse. | **Rockville** 23⌐

Mala Tang | **Arlington** 22⌐

Mark's Duck Hse.* | **Falls Ch** 25⌐

Meiwah | **multi.** 21⌐

Michael's Noodles | **Rockville** 22⌐

New Fortune* | **Gaith'burg** 23⌐

New Kam | **Wheaton** 25⌐

100 Degree | **Fairfax** 24⌐

Oriental E.* | **Silver Spring** 23⌐

Peking Duck | **Alexandria** 28⌐

Peking Gourmet | **Falls Ch** 25⌐

P.F. Chang's | **multi.** 23⌐

Ping | **Arlington** 23⌐

Ping Pong* | **multi.** 21⌐

Seven Seas | **multi.** 22⌐

Sichuan Jin River | **Rockville** 25⌐

Tony Cheng's | **Chinatown** 22⌐

X.O. Taste | **multi.** 24⌐

Yuan Fu | **Rockville** 25⌐

COFFEEHOUSES

NEW Aroma Espresso | **Bethesda** ⌐|

Buzz | **multi.** 22⌐

Café Bonaparte | **Georgetown** 23⌐

Northside | **Clarendon** 22⌐

Tryst | **Adams Mor** 21⌐

CONTEMPORARY LOUISIANA

Acadiana | **Mt. Vernon Sq** 24⌐

CONTINENTAL

Café Renaissance | **Vienna** 26⌐

CREOLE

Acadiana | **Mt. Vernon Sq** 24⌐

Bayou | **West End** 20⌐

Cajun Experience | **Leesburg** 23⌐

Chasin' Tails | **Arlington** ⌐|

Hot 'N Juicy | **Woodley Pk** 20⌐

RT's | **Alexandria** 26⌐

CUBAN

Banana Café | **Cap Hill**	19
Cuba de Ayer | **Burtonsville**	25
Cuba Libre | **Penn Qtr**	20
Cubano's | **Silver Spring**	23
La Limeña | **Rockville**	23
NEW Little Ricky's | **Brookland**	-
NEW Mi Cuba | **Columbia Hts**	-

CZECH

Bistro Bohem | **Shaw**	-

DELIS

Chutzpah | **Fairfax**	23
NEW DGS Deli | **Dupont Cir**	-
Parkway Deli | **Silver Spring**	22
Star/Shamrock | **Atlas Dist**	19
Taylor Gourmet | **multi.**	22
Toscana Café | **Cap Hill**	25
NEW Wagshal's | **Upper NW**	-

DINERS

Ben's Chili | **U St**	22
Bob & Edith's | **Arlington**	20
Diner | **Adams Mor**	21
Double T | **Frederick**	20
Family Meal | **Frederick**	-
Florida Ave. Grill | **Shaw**	22
Luna Grill | **multi.**	19
Open City | **Woodley Pk**	21

EASTERN EUROPEAN

NEW Ambar | **Cap Hill**	-
Cosmopolitan Grill | **Alexandria**	27
Domku | **Petworth**	22

ECLECTIC

Atlas Rm. | **Atlas Dist**	25
Boundary Rd. | **Atlas Dist**	-
Busboys/Poets | **multi.**	22
Café Saint-Ex | **Logan Cir**	20
NEW Carving Room | **Chinatown**	-
C.F. Folks | **Dupont Cir**	24
Co Co. Sala | **Penn Qtr**	24
NEW Crossroads | **World Bank**	-

Curious Grape | **Arlington**	-
Dean & DeLuca | **Georgetown**	23
Dickson Wine | **U St**	21
NEW Gryphon | **Dupont Cir**	-
Little Fountain | **Adams Mor**	23
Maple Ave | **Vienna**	-
Mark's Kit. | **Takoma Pk**	21
Minibar | **Penn Qtr**	28
Mosaic Cuisine | **White Flint**	23
El Floridano | **Location Varies**	-
Orchard | **Frederick**	25
Pig | **Logan Cir**	-
Room 11 | **Columbia Hts**	26
Rustik Tav. | **Bloomingdale**	23
Sticky Rice | **Atlas Dist**	23
Twisted Vines | **Arlington**	20
Vinoteca | **U St**	22
NEW Vino Volo | **Bethesda**	-

ETHIOPIAN

Dukem | **U St**	24
Etete | **U St**	24
Ethiopic | **Atlas Dist**	24
LacoMelza | **Silver Spring**	-
Meskerem | **Adams Mor**	22

EUROPEAN

NEW Azur | **Penn Qtr**	-
It's About Thyme | **Culpeper**	25
NEW Table | **Shaw**	-
Village Bistro | **Arlington**	26

FRENCH

Bastille | **Alexandria**	24
Bezu | **Potomac**	24
Bistro Bis | **Cap Hill**	26
Bistro Provence | **Bethesda**	26
Brabo | **Alexandria**	26
Brass. Monte Carlo | **Bethesda**	22
Chez Billy | **Petworth**	-
Degrees | **Georgetown**	22
Et Voila | **Palisades**	25
Grille | **Alexandria**	25
La Bergerie | **Alexandria**	26

La Chaumière | **Georgetown** 26

La Ferme | **Chevy Chase** 24

La Fourchette | **Adams Mor** 23

L'Auberge/Jaques' | **Grt Falls** 28

L'Auberge Provençale | **Boyce** 26

Lavandou | **Cleve Pk** 23

NEW Le Diplomate | **Logan Cir** ⌐

NEW Malmaison | **Georgetown** ⌐

Marcel's | **West End** 28

Matisse | **Upper NW** 23

Mosaic Cuisine | **White Flint** 23

Paul | **multi.** 22

Poste Moderne | **Penn Qtr** 20

Russia House Rest. | **Herndon** 27

Tempo | **Alexandria** 24

Urbana | **Dupont Cir** 21

FRENCH (BISTRO)

Bistro Cacao | **Cap Hill** 23

Bistro D'Oc | **Penn Qtr** 23

Bistro Français | **Georgetown** 21

Bistro La Bonne | **U St** 21

Bistro L'Hermitage | **Woodbridge** 26

Bistrot du Coin | **Dupont Cir** 22

Bistrot Lepic | **Georgetown** 24

Bistro Vivant | **McLean** ⌐

Brass. Beck | **D'town** 25

Café Bonaparte | **Georgetown** 23

Café du Parc | **D'town** 21

Café Dupont | **Dupont Cir** 21

Central Michel | **Penn Qtr** 26

Fontaine Caffe | **Alexandria** 25

La Côte d'Or | **Arlington** 24

Le Chat Noir | **Upper NW** 20

NEW Le Grenier | **Atlas Dist** ⌐

Le Refuge | **Alexandria** 26

Le Zinc | **Cleve Pk** 22

Lyon Hall | **Clarendon** 24

Mon Ami Gabi | **multi.** 22

Montmartre | **Cap Hill** 25

Napoleon Bistro | **Adams Mor** 24

Petits Plats | **Woodley Pk** 22

Praline | **Bethesda** 23

Yves Bistro | **Alexandria** 25

GASTROPUBS

Birch/Barley | Amer. | **Logan Cir** 24

NEW Black Whiskey | Amer. | ⌐
Logan Cir

Boundary Rd. | Eclectic | ⌐
Atlas Dist

NEW Brickside | Amer. | ⌐
Bethesda

Granville Moore's | Amer./Belgian | **Atlas Dist** 24

NEW Gryphon | Amer. | ⌐
Dupont Cir

Queen Vic | British | **Atlas Dist** 23

GERMAN

Biergarten Haus | **Atlas Dist** 17

Lyon Hall | **Clarendon** 24

GREEK

Athens Grill | **Gaith'burg** 26

Cava Mezze | **multi.** 25

Cava Mezze Grill | **multi.** 22

Kellari Taverna | **Gldn Triangle** 23

Mourayo | **Dupont Cir** 25

Mykonos Grill | **Rockville** 23

Nostos | **Vienna** 26

Plaka Grill | **Vienna** 24

Vaso's Kit. | **Alexandria** 26

Zorba's Cafe | **Dupont Cir** 23

HEALTH FOOD
(See also Vegetarian)

Juice Joint | **D'town** 23

NEW Protein Bar | **multi.** ⌐

Sweetgreen | **multi.** 22

HOT DOGS

DC-3 | **Cap Hill** 18

INDIAN

Aditi | **multi.** 23

Amma Veg. | **Vienna** 22

Angeethi | **multi.** 23

Aroma | **multi.**	23
Bombay Bistro | **Rockville**	24
Bombay Club | **Gldn Triangle**	25
Bombay Tandoor | **Vienna**	26
Curry Mantra | **multi.**	23
Delhi Club | **Clarendon**	24
Delhi Dhaba | **Arlington**	20
Haandi | **Falls Ch**	24
Heritage India | **multi.**	22
Himalayan Heritage | **multi.**	21
India Palace | **Germantown**	26
Indique | **multi.**	23
Jaipur | **Fairfax**	25
Kabob N Karahi | **Silver Spring**	26
NEW Kadhai | **Bethesda**	-
NEW Malgudi | **Glover Pk**	-
Masala Art | **Upper NW**	25
NEW Masala Exp. | **Arlington**	-
Merzi | **Penn Qtr**	20
Minerva | **multi.**	23
Passage to India | **Bethesda**	24
Rangoli | **S Riding**	24
Rasika | **multi.**	28
Spice Xing | **Rockville**	22
Tandoori Nights | **multi.**	24
Woodlands Rest. | **Hyattsville**	24

IRISH

Daniel O'Connell's | **Alexandria**	20
Eamonn's | **multi.**	23
Irish Inn/Glen Echo | **Glen Echo**	20
Irish Whiskey | **Dupont Cir**	-
Star/Shamrock | **Atlas Dist**	19

ITALIAN

(N=Northern; S=Southern)

Acqua al 2 | **Cap Hill**	24
Agrodolce | **Germantown**	23
A La Lucia | **Alexandria**	23
Al Crostino | **U St**	23
Al Dente | **Upper NW**	-
Al Tiramisu | **Dupont Cir**	25
Amici Miei | **Potomac**	21
NEW Ancora | **Foggy Bottom**	-

Argia's | **Falls Ch**	21
Arucola | **Chevy Chase**	20
Assaggi | **multi.**	23
Bibiana | **D'town**	25
Bond 45 | **Nat'l Harbor**	22
Cafe Milano | **Georgetown**	22
Cafe Pizzaiolo | S | **multi.**	24
Capri | **McLean**	23
Carmine's | S | **Penn Qtr**	20
Cesco Osteria | **Bethesda**	19
Da Domenico | **McLean**	23
Dino | **Cleve Pk**	24
Dolce Veloce | **Fairfax**	-
Dolce Vita | **Fairfax**	25
NEW Etto | **Logan Cir**	-
Filomena | **Georgetown**	24
Finemondo | **D'town**	20
Fiola | **Penn Qtr**	27
Floriana Rest. | **Dupont Cir**	24
Fontina Grille | **Rockville**	20
Geranio | N | **Alexandria**	25
NEW Ghibellina | N | **Logan Cir**	-
Graffiato | **Chinatown**	24
Il Canale | **Georgetown**	22
Il Fornaio | **Reston**	25
Il Pizzico | **Rockville**	27
Il Porto | **Alexandria**	24
I Ricchi | N | **Dupont Cir**	24
Kora | **Arlington**	17
Landini Bros. | N | **Alexandria**	25
NEW La Tagliatella | **Clarendon**	-
La Tomate | **Dupont Cir**	19
Ledo Pizza | N | **multi.**	23
Lia's | **Chevy Chase**	21
Maggiano's | **multi.**	23
Mamma Lucia | **multi.**	22
Maple | **Columbia Hts**	-
NEW Ninnella | **Cap Hill**	-
Notti Bianche | **Foggy Bottom**	22
Obelisk | **Dupont Cir**	28
Olazzo | **multi.**	24

Original Ledo | **College Pk**	24
Oro Pomodoro | **Rockville**	21
Osteria Elisir | **Penn Qtr**	26
Ozzie's Corner | **Fairfax**	24
Pacci's Tratt. | **Silver Spring**	23
Paolo's | **multi.**	21
Pasta Mia | **Adams Mor**	26
Piola | **Rosslyn**	21
Pizzeria Orso | **Falls Ch**	22
Posto | **Logan Cir**	23
Primi Piatti | **Foggy Bottom**	19
NEW Red Hen | **Bloomingdale**	–
RedRocks | **multi.**	21
Renato/River Falls | **Potomac**	22
Ricciuti's | **Olney**	24
Sergio Rist. | **Silver Spring**	27
Sette Osteria | **Dupont Cir**	21
Siroc | **D'town**	24
NEW Slate | **Glover Pk**	–
Sorriso | **Cleve Pk**	22
Sugo Cicchetti | **Potomac**	–
Taylor Gourmet | **multi.**	22
Tempo | N | **Alexandria**	24
Tosca | N | **Penn Qtr**	27
Toscana Café | **Cap Hill**	25
Tutto Bene | N | **Arlington**	23
2 Amys | **Cleve Pk**	25
Urbana | **Dupont Cir**	21
Vapiano | **multi.**	20
NEW Vendetta | **Atlas Dist**	–
Villa Mozart | N | **Fairfax**	26
NEW Vino Volo | **Bethesda**	–
Zeffirelli Rist. | **Herndon**	24

JAMAICAN

Negril | **multi.**	24

JAPANESE

(* sushi specialist)

NEW Daikaya Izakaya | **Chinatown**	–
NEW Daikaya Ramen | **Chinatown**	–
Hama Sushi* | **Herndon**	25
NEW Hikari* | **Atlas Dist**	–
Hinode* | **multi.**	20
Hooked* | **Sterling**	20
NEW Izakaya Seki | **U St**	–
Kaz Sushi* | **World Bank**	25
Kobe | **Leesburg**	27
Kotobuki* | **Palisades**	25
Kushi* | **Mt. Vernon Sq**	25
Makoto | **Palisades**	27
Matuba | **Bethesda**	23
Murasaki* | **Upper NW**	23
Niwano Hana* | **Rockville**	26
Nooshi* | **Gldn Triangle**	21
Ping* | **Arlington**	23
Raku* | **multi.**	23
Ren's | **Wheaton**	24
Rolls 'N Rice* | **Rockville**	22
Sakana | **Dupont Cir**	23
Seven Seas | **multi.**	22
Spices* | **Cleve Pk**	21
Sushi Damo* | **Rockville**	25
Sushiko* | **multi.**	24
Sushi Taro* | **Dupont Cir**	26
Tachibana* | **McLean**	24
Tako Grill* | **Bethesda**	24
Tono Sushi* | **Woodley Pk**	22
Woomi Gdn.* | **Wheaton**	20
Yama* | **Vienna**	25
Yamazato* | **Alexandria**	25
Yechon | **Annandale**	22
NEW Yo! Sushi* | **Cap Hill**	–
Yosaku* | **Upper NW**	21
NEW Yuzu | **Bethesda**	–

JEWISH

Chutzpah | **Fairfax**	23
NEW DGS Deli | **Dupont Cir**	–
Parkway Deli | **Silver Spring**	22
Star/Shamrock | **Atlas Dist**	19

KOREAN

(* barbecue specialist)

BonChon | **multi.**	26
Hee Been* | **Alexandria**	23
Honey Pig* | **multi.**	23
Lighthouse Tofu | **Rockville**	24
Mandu | **multi.**	23
Woo Lae Oak* | **Vienna**	23
Woomi Gdn.* | **Wheaton**	20
Yechon | **Annandale**	22

LAOTIAN

Bangkok Golden | **Falls Ch**	24

LEBANESE

Layalina | **Arlington**	24
Lebanese Tav. | **multi.**	23
Me Jana | **Arlington**	24
Neyla | **Georgetown**	24

MALAYSIAN

Malaysia Kopitiam | **Dupont Cir**	23

MEDITERRANEAN

Acacia Bistro | **Upper NW**	20
Agora | **Dupont Cir**	23
Bistro LaZeez | **Bethesda**	22
Brass. Monte Carlo | **Bethesda**	22
Café Olé | **Upper NW**	20
Cava Mezze | **multi.**	25
Cava Mezze Grill | **multi.**	22
NEW Decanter | **D'town**	-
El Manantial | **Reston**	24
Evo Bistro | **McLean**	22
Komi | **Dupont Cir**	28
Matisse | **Upper NW**	23
Neyla | **Georgetown**	24
Panache | **multi.**	21
Pasha Cafe | **Arlington**	23
Roti | **multi.**	22
Tabaq Bistro | **U St**	20
Tavira | **Chevy Chase**	25
Tel'Veh | **Mt. Vernon Sq**	-
NEW Wildwood Kit. | **Bethesda**	-
Zaytinya | **Penn Qtr**	26

MEXICAN

Alegria | **Vienna**	-
Azucar | **Silver Spring**	24
Bandolero | **Georgetown**	-
Cacique | **Frederick**	24
Casa Oaxaca | **Adams Mor**	22
NEW Chupacabra | **Atlas Dist**	-
El Centro | **Logan Cir**	21
El Chucho | **Columbia Hts**	-
El Tamarindo | **Adams Mor**	21
NEW Fuego Cocina | **Clarendon**	-
Guajillo | **Arlington**	21
Lauriol Plaza | **Dupont Cir**	21
NEW MXDC | **D'town**	-
Oyamel | **Penn Qtr**	25
Rosa Mexicano | **multi.**	23
Surfside | **Glover Pk**	21
NEW Tacos El Chilango | **multi.**	-
Taqueria Distrito | **multi.**	22
Taqueria La Placita | **Hyattsville**	-
NEW Taqueria Nacional | **U St**	-
Taqueria Poblano | **multi.**	22

MIDDLE EASTERN

Amsterdam Falafel | **Adams Mor**	25
Bistro LaZeez | **Bethesda**	22
Mezè | **Adams Mor**	24
NEW Tash House | **Cap Hill**	-
Zaytinya | **Penn Qtr**	26

MONGOLIAN

Tony Cheng's | **Chinatown**	22

MOROCCAN

Marrakesh P | **Dupont Cir**	23
Taste/Morocco | **Clarendon**	23

NEPALESE

Himalayan Heritage | **multi.**	21

NEW ENGLAND

Ford's Fish | **multi.**	26
Red Hook | **Location Varies**	25

NEW ZEALAND

Cassatt's Café	**Arlington**	20

NOODLE SHOPS

Bob's Noodle	**Rockville**	22
Chinatown Express	**Chinatown**	23
NEW Daikaya Ramen	**Chinatown**	–
Full Key	**Wheaton**	25
Pho 75	**multi.**	24
Ren's	**Wheaton**	24
Sakuramen	**Adams Mor**	–
NEW Taan Noodles	**Adams Mor**	–
Toki	**Atlas Dist**	26

NUEVO LATINO

Ceiba	**D'town**	24
Masa 14	**Logan Cir**	23
Mio	**D'town**	26

PAKISTANI

Kabob N Karahi	**Silver Spring**	26
Kabob Palace	**Arlington**	26
Ravi Kabob	**Arlington**	25

PAN-LATIN

Azucar	**Silver Spring**	24
NEW Bóveda	**West End**	–
NEW Chupacabra	**Atlas Dist**	–
El Golfo	**Silver Spring**	23
Fast Gourmet	**U St**	27
Fujimar	**D'town**	–
Guardado's	**Bethesda**	23
Lauriol Plaza	**Dupont Cir**	21
Masa 14	**Logan Cir**	23
Pollo Campero	**multi.**	19
Samantha's	**Silver Spring**	24
NEW Takeateasy	**Gldn Triangle**	–
Zengo	**Chinatown**	22

PERSIAN

Kabob Bazaar	**multi.**	25
Moby Dick	**multi.**	23
Shamshiry	**Vienna**	27

PERUVIAN

Chicken/Run	**Bethesda**	24
Crisp/Juicy	**multi.**	24
Don Pollo	**multi.**	23
El Chalan	**Foggy Bottom**	22
El Pollo	**multi.**	26
La Canela	**Rockville**	23
La Limeña	**Rockville**	23
Las Canteras	**Adams Mor**	24

PIZZA

Agrodolce	**Germantown**	23
Al Dente	**Upper NW**	–
NEW &pizza	**multi.**	–
Cafe Pizzaiolo	**multi.**	24
Coal Fire	**multi.**	22
Comet Ping Pong	**Upper NW**	20
District of Pi	**Penn Qtr**	23
Dolce Vita	**Fairfax**	25
Ella's Pizza	**Penn Qtr**	21
NEW Etto	**Logan Cir**	–
Faccia Luna	**multi.**	23
Fire Works	**multi.**	24
Fontina Grille	**Rockville**	20
Fuel Pizza Cafe	**multi.**	–
Graffiato	**Chinatown**	24
Haven	**Bethesda**	–
Il Canale	**Georgetown**	22
NEW La Tagliatella	**Clarendon**	–
Ledo Pizza	**multi.**	23
Liberty Tree	**Atlas Dist**	23
Local 16	**U St**	17
Mad Fox Brew	**Falls Ch**	20
Mamma Lucia	**multi.**	22
Matchbox	**multi.**	23
Mellow Mushroom	**Adams Mor**	25
Menomale	**Brookland**	–
Mia's Pizzas	**Bethesda**	25
Original Ledo	**College Pk**	24
Oro Pomodoro	**Rockville**	21
Pacci's Neapolitan	**Silver Spring**	23
Pete's Apizza	**multi.**	22

Pie-Tanza | **multi.**	23
Piola | **multi.**	21
Pizzeria Da Marco | **Bethesda**	23
Pizzeria Orso | **Falls Ch**	22
Pizzeria Paradiso | **multi.**	23
Posto | **Logan Cir**	23
Pupatella Pizzeria | **Arlington**	26
NEW Radius Pizza | **Mt. Pleasant**	–
RedRocks | **multi.**	21
Ricciuti's | **Olney**	24
Rustik Tav. | **Bloomingdale**	23
Sette Osteria | **Dupont Cir**	21
Seventh Hill | **Cap Hill**	25
Sorriso | **Cleve Pk**	22
Sugo Cicchetti | **Potomac**	–
2 Amys | **Cleve Pk**	25
Vapiano | **multi.**	20
We the Pizza | **Cap Hill**	22

PORTUGUESE

Nando's | **multi.**	22
Tavira | **Chevy Chase**	25

PUB FOOD

Biergarten Haus | **Atlas Dist**	17
Boundary Stone | **Bloomingdale**	24
Bourbon | **multi.**	21
Brewer's Alley | **Frederick**	22
NEW Brickside | **Bethesda**	–
Clyde's | **multi.**	22
Daniel O'Connell's | **Alexandria**	20
Dogfish Head | **multi.**	21
Franklin's | **Hyattsville**	21
NEW Gryphon | **Dupont Cir**	–
Hunter's Head | **Upperville**	23
Irish Whiskey | **Dupont Cir**	–
Liberty Tav. | **Clarendon**	24
Lost Dog | **multi.**	23
Madhatter | **Dupont Cir**	18
Meridian | **Columbia Hts**	20
P.J. Clarke's | **D'town**	18
Royal Mile | **Wheaton**	23

Star/Shamrock | **Atlas Dist**	19
Stoney's | **Logan Cir**	18

PUERTO RICAN

Banana Café | **Cap Hill**	19

RUSSIAN

NEW Mari Vanna | **Gldn Triangle**	–
Russia Hse. | **Dupont Cir**	21
Russia House Rest. | **Herndon**	27

SANDWICHES

(See also Delis)

Banh Mi DC | **Falls Ch**	21
Bread Line | **World Bank**	23
NEW Bub & Pops | **Dupont Cir**	–
Buzz | **multi.**	22
NEW Carving Room | **Chinatown**	–
C.F. Folks | **Dupont Cir**	24
Chutzpah | **Fairfax**	23
Coal Fire | **Gaith'burg**	22
NEW DGS Deli | **Dupont Cir**	–
Faccia Luna | **multi.**	23
Fast Gourmet | **U St**	27
Lunchbox | **Frederick**	24
El Floridano | **Location Varies**	–
Pie-Tanza | **multi.**	23
Pret A Manger | **multi.**	19
NEW Red Apron | **multi.**	–
Sweetgreen | **Mt. Vernon Sq**	22
NEW Takeateasy | **Gldn Triangle**	–
NEW Taylor Charles | **Atlas Dist**	–
NEW Wagshal's | **Upper NW**	–

SCANDINAVIAN

Domku | **Petworth**	22

SCOTTISH

Royal Mile | **Wheaton**	23

SEAFOOD

Adam Express | **Mt. Pleasant**	25
NEW Azur | **Penn Qtr**	–
BlackSalt | **Palisades**	27
Bobby Van's | **D'town**	23
Chart House | **Alexandria**	23

Chasin' Tails | **Arlington**	-ᴵ
Chesapeake Rm. | **Cap Hill**	20
Coastal Flats | **multi.**	24
DC Coast | **D'town**	23
Dutch's Daughter | **Frederick**	25
NEW Farmers Fishers | **Georgetown**	-ᴵ
Fishnet | **College Pk**	24
Ford's Fish | **multi.**	26
Freddy's Lobster | **Bethesda**	19
Grillfish | **West End**	20
NEW Grill Room | **Georgetown**	-ᴵ
Hank's Oyster | **multi.**	24
Hooked | **Sterling**	20
Horace/Dickie's | **multi.**	22
Jackson's | **Reston**	23
Johnny's Half Shell | **Cap Hill**	21
Kellari Taverna | **Gldn Triangle**	23
Legal Sea Foods | **multi.**	23
Luke's Lobster | **multi.**	23
M&S Grill | **multi.**	22
McCormick/Schmick's | **multi.**	23
Mussel B&G | **Bethesda**	20
Nage | **Scott Cir**	21
Nick's Chophse. | **Rockville**	21
Occidental | **D'town**	23
Oceanaire | **D'town**	24
Palm | **McLean**	25
PassionFish | **Reston**	26
Pearl Dive | **Logan Cir**	26
Perrys | **Adams Mor**	22
Pesce | **Dupont Cir**	26
Phillips | **SW**	20
Prime Rib | **Gldn Triangle**	28
NEW Rappahannock | **NoMa**	-ᴵ
Ray's/Classics | **Silver Spring**	25
Red Hook | **Location Varies**	25
Sea Catch | **Georgetown**	23
Sea Pearl | **Merrifield**	23
Senart's Oyster | **Cap Hill**	24
Seven Seas | **Rockville**	22
Surfside | **Glover Pk**	21
Tackle Box | **Georgetown**	18
Todd Gray's Watershed | **NoMa**	23
NEW Tony & Joe's | **Georgetown**	-ᴵ
Wildfire | **McLean**	22

SMALL PLATES

(See also Spanish tapas specialist)

Acacia Bistro | Italian | **Upper NW**	20
Al Dente | Italian | **Upper NW**	-ᴵ
NEW Ambar | E Euro. | **Cap Hill**	-ᴵ
Asia Bistro/Zen | Asian | **Arlington**	21
Bandolero | Mex. | **Georgetown**	-ᴵ
Bistro Vivant | French | **McLean**	-ᴵ
Café du Parc | French | **D'town**	21
Café Olé | Med. | **Upper NW**	20
NEW Carving Room | Eclectic | **Chinatown**	-ᴵ
Cava Mezze | Greek | **Cap Hill**	25
Co Co. Sala | Eclectic | **Penn Qtr**	24
Cork | Amer. | **Logan Cir**	25
NEW Crossroads | Eclectic | **World Bank**	-ᴵ
Fiola | Italian | **Penn Qtr**	27
NEW Ghibellina | Italian | **Logan Cir**	-ᴵ
Graffiato | Italian | **Chinatown**	24
Indique | Indian | **multi.**	23
Iron Bridge Wine | Amer. | **Warrenton**	25
Kaz Sushi | Japanese | **World Bank**	25
Lincoln | Amer. | **D'town**	20
Maple | Italian | **Columbia Hts**	-ᴵ
Mezè | Turkish | **Adams Mor**	24
Mintwood | Amer. | **Adams Mor**	-ᴵ
Oyamel | Mex. | **Penn Qtr**	25
Policy | Amer. | **U St**	22
Raku | Asian | **multi.**	23
Rasika | Indian | **multi.**	28
Room 11 | Eclectic | **Columbia Hts**	26
Sei | Asian | **Penn Qtr**	26

NEW Slate | Amer./Italian | -| Glover Pk

Source | Amer. | **Penn Qtr** 27|

Sugo Cicchetti | Italian | **Potomac** -|

Sushiko | Japanese | **multi.** 24|

Tabaq Bistro | Med. | **U St** 20|

Tallula/EatBar | Amer. | 24| **Clarendon**

Tandoori Nights | Indian | 24| **Gaith'burg**

Tel'Veh | Med. | **Mt. Vernon Sq** -|

2941 | Amer. | **Falls Ch** 27|

Vinifera | Amer. | **Reston** 23|

NEW Vino Volo | Italian | -| **Bethesda**

NEW Yuzu | Japanese | -| **Bethesda**

Zaytinya | Mideast. | **Penn Qtr** 26|

Zengo | Asian/Pan-Latin | 22| **Chinatown**

SOUL FOOD

Florida Ave. Grill | **Shaw** 22|

Oohh's & Aahh's | **U St** 23|

SOUTH AMERICAN

El Mariachi | **Rockville** 25|

La Caraqueña | **Falls Ch** 25|

Tutto Bene | **Arlington** 23|

SOUTHERN

Acadiana | **Mt. Vernon Sq** 24|

Acre 121 | **Columbia Hts** 21|

Art & Soul | **Cap Hill** 23|

Bayou Bakery | **Arlington** 22|

B. Smith's | **Cap Hill** 22|

Carolina Kit. | **Hyattsville** 25|

Crème | **U St** 21|

Eatonville | **U St** 23|

Evening Star | **Alexandria** 23|

Florida Ave. Grill | **Shaw** 22|

Georgia Brown | **D'town** 22|

Howard Theatre | **Shaw** -|

Oohh's & Aahh's | **U St** 23|

Sou'Wester | **SW** 21|

Vidalia | **Gldn Triangle** 26|

SOUTHWESTERN

Sweetwater Tav. | **multi.** 26|

SPANISH

(* tapas specialist)

Bodega* | **Georgetown** 23|

Boqueria* | **Dupont Cir** -|

Cacique | **Frederick** 24|

Estadio* | **Logan Cir** 25|

Guardado's | **Bethesda** 23|

Isabella's* | **Frederick** 26|

Jaleo* | **multi.** 24|

Las Tapas* | **Alexandria** 24|

La Taberna* | **World Bank** 26|

La Tasca* | **multi.** 21|

Pulpo* | **Cleve Pk** -|

STEAKHOUSES

BLT Steak | **Gldn Triangle** 25|

Bobby Van's | **D'town** 23|

Bond 45 | **Nat'l Harbor** 22|

Bourbon Steak | **Georgetown** 25|

Capital Grille | **multi.** 26|

Charlie Palmer | **Cap Hill** 26|

Del Frisco's | **Penn Qtr** -|

District ChopHse. | **Penn Qtr** 21|

Fleming's Steak | **McLean** 25|

Fogo de Chão | **Penn Qtr** 27|

Grillmarx | **Olney** 22|

NEW Grill Room | **Georgetown** -|

J&G Steak | **D'town** 24|

Lost Society | **U St** 18|

M&S Grill | **multi.** 22|

Medium Rare | **Cleve Pk** 22|

NEW Monty's Steak | **Springfield** -|

Morton's | **multi.** 26|

Nick's Chophse. | **Rockville** 21|

Occidental | **D'town** 23|

Old Hickory | **Nat'l Harbor** 26|

Palm | **multi.** 25|

Prime Rib | **Gldn Triangle** 28|

Ray's/Classics	**Silver Spring**	25
Ray's/Steaks	**Arlington**	27
Ray's/Third	**Arlington**	25
Ruth's Chris	**multi.**	26
Senart's Oyster	**Cap Hill**	24
Smith/Wollensky	**Gldn Triangle**	25
Wildfire	**McLean**	22

SYRIAN

Layalina	**Arlington**	24

TAIWANESE

Bob's Noodle	**Rockville**	22
Toki	**Atlas Dist**	26

TEAHOUSES

Ching Ching	**Georgetown**	20
Teaism	**multi.**	20

TEX-MEX

Austin Grill	**multi.**	18
Cactus Cantina	**Cleve Pk**	21
Calif. Tortilla	**multi.**	22
El Mariachi	**Rockville**	25
Guapo's	**multi.**	22
NEW Mi Cocina	**Chevy Chase**	-
Mi Rancho	**multi.**	22
Uncle Julio's	**multi.**	21

THAI

Bangkok 54	**Arlington**	25
Bangkok Golden	**multi.**	24
Bangkok Joe's	**Georgetown**	23
NEW Beau Thai	**multi.**	-
Benjarong	**Rockville**	23
Busara	**multi.**	22
Crystal Thai	**Arlington**	23
Duangrat's	**Falls Ch**	26
Elephant Jumps	**Falls Ch**	26
Haad Thai	**D'town**	21
Little Serow	**Dupont Cir**	28
Mai Thai	**multi.**	23
Nava Thai	**Wheaton**	26
Rabieng	**Falls Ch**	25
Regent	**Dupont Cir**	24

Rice	**Logan Cir**	22
Ruan Thai	**Wheaton**	27
Sabai	**Germantown**	26
Sakoontra	**Fairfax**	23
Sushiko	**Chevy Chase**	24
Tara Thai	**multi.**	20
Thai/Silver Spring	**Silver Spring**	24
Thai Basil	**Chantilly**	26
T.H.A.I.	**Arlington**	25
Thaiphoon	**multi.**	21
Thai Sq.	**Arlington**	26
Thai Tanic	**multi.**	23
Tono Sushi	**Woodley Pk**	22

TURKISH

Agora	**Dupont Cir**	23
Cafe Divan	**Glover Pk**	24
Ezmè	**Dupont Cir**	22
Kazan	**McLean**	25

VEGETARIAN

(* vegan)

Amma Veg.	**Vienna**	22
Amsterdam Falafel	**Adams Mor**	25
Luna Grill*	**multi.**	19
Mandalay	**Silver Spring**	23
Sunflower Veg.	**multi.**	25
Woodlands Rest.	**Hyattsville**	24
Yuan Fu*	**Rockville**	25

VIETNAMESE

Banh Mi DC	**Falls Ch**	21
Four Sisters	**Merrifield**	25
Huong Viet	**Falls Ch**	25
Lucky Corner	**Frederick**	28
Minh's	**Arlington**	24
Nam-Viet	**multi.**	21
Pho 14	**multi.**	25
Pho DC	**Chinatown**	24
Pho 75	**multi.**	24
Present	**Falls Ch**	26
Rice Paper	**Falls Ch**	-
Taste/Saigon	**Rockville**	22

Locations

Includes names, cuisines and Food ratings.

Washington, DC

ADAMS MORGAN

Amsterdam Falafel	*Mideast.*	25
Bourbon	*Pub*	21
Casa Oaxaca	*Mex.*	22
Cashion's Eat	*Amer.*	25
Diner	*Diner*	21
El Tamarindo	*Mex.*	21
Grill/Ipanema	*Brazilian*	24
Himalayan Heritage	*Indian/Nepalese*	21
Jack Rose	*Amer.*	20
La Fourchette	*French*	23
Las Canteras	*Peruvian*	24
Little Fountain	*Eclectic*	23
Mellow Mushroom	*Pizza*	25
Meskerem	*Ethiopian*	22
Mezè	*Mideast.*	24
Mintwood	*Amer.*	-
Napoleon Bistro	*French*	24
Pasta Mia	*Italian*	26
Perrys	*Asian*	22
Pho 14	*Viet.*	25
Sakuramen	*Noodle Shop*	-
Smoke/Barrel	*Amer./BBQ*	20
NEW Taan Noodles	*Asian/Noodle Shop*	-
Tryst	*Coffee*	21

ATLAS DISTRICT

NEW &pizza	*Pizza*	-
Atlas Rm.	*Eclectic*	25
Biergarten Haus	*German*	17
Big Board	*Burgers*	-
Boundary Rd.	*Eclectic*	-
NEW Chupacabra	*Pan-Latin*	-
Dangerously Delicious	*Amer./Bakery*	21
Ethiopic	*Ethiopian*	24

Granville Moore's	*Amer./Belgian*	24
NEW Hikari	*Japanese*	-
Horace/Dickie's	*Seafood*	22
NEW Le Grenier	*French*	-
Liberty Tree	*Amer./Pizza*	23
Queen Vic	*British*	23
Smith Commons	*Amer.*	22
Star/Shamrock	*Deli/Pub*	19
Sticky Rice	*Asian/Eclectic*	23
NEW Taylor Charles	*Sandwiches*	-
Taylor Gourmet	*Deli/Italian*	22
Toki	*Noodle Shop/Taiwanese*	26
NEW Vendetta	*Italian*	-

BLOOMINGDALE

Big Bear Cafe	*Amer.*	-
Boundary Stone	*Pub*	24
NEW Red Hen	*Italian*	-
Rustik Tav.	*Amer./Eclectic*	23

BROOKLAND

NEW Little Ricky's	*Cuban*	-
Menomale	*Pizza*	-

CAPITOL HILL

Acqua al 2	*Italian*	24
Aditi	*Indian*	23
NEW Ambar	*E Euro.*	-
Art & Soul	*Southern*	23
Banana Café	*Cuban/Puerto Rican*	19
Belga Café	*Belgian*	25
NEW Beuchert's	*Amer.*	-
Bistro Bis	*French*	26
Bistro Cacao	*French*	23
Boxcar Tav.	*Amer.*	21
B. Smith's	*Southern*	22
Cava Mezze	*Greek*	25
Charlie Palmer	*Steak*	26
Chesapeake Rm.	*Amer./Seafood*	20

Chop't | *Amer.*	21
Dangerously Delicious | *Amer./Bakery*	21
DC-3 | *Hot Dogs*	18
Good Stuff | *Burgers*	23
Hank's Oyster | *Amer./Seafood*	24
Hunan Dynasty | *Chinese*	20
Johnny's Half Shell | *Amer./Seafood*	21
Ledo Pizza | *Pizza*	23
Le Pain Quotidien | *Bakery/Belgian*	21
Matchbox | *Amer.*	23
Monocle | *Amer.*	21
Montmartre | *French*	25
NEW Ninnella | *Italian*	-
Nooshi | *Asian*	21
Pret A Manger | *Sandwiches*	19
Senart's Oyster | *Seafood/Steak*	24
Seventh Hill | *Pizza*	25
Sonoma | *Amer.*	21
Sweetgreen | *Health*	22
NEW Tash House | *Mideastern*	-
Ted's Bulletin | *Amer.*	23
Toscana Café | *Deli/Italian*	25
We the Pizza | *Pizza*	22
Wings To Go | *Chicken*	25
NEW Yo! Sushi | *Japanese*	-
Zest | *Amer.*	21

CHEVY CHASE

Arucola | *Italian*	20
Le Pain Quotidien | *Bakery/Belgian*	21
NEW Mi Cocina | *Mex.*	-
NEW Range | *Amer.*	-
Rosa Mexicano | *Mex.*	23

CHINATOWN/ PENN QUARTER

(Including Gallery Place)

Asian Spice | *Asian*	23
Austin Grill | *Tex-Mex*	18
NEW Azur | *Seafood*	-
Bistro D'Oc | *French*	23

Burma | *Burmese*	22
Calif. Tortilla | *Tex-Mex*	22
Capital Grille | *Steak*	26
Carmine's | *Italian*	20
NEW Carving Room | *Sandwiches*	-
Cedar Rest. | *Amer.*	23
Central Michel | *Amer./French*	26
Chinatown Express | *Chinese*	23
Chop't | *Amer.*	21
Clyde's | *Amer.*	22
Co Co. Sala | *Eclectic*	24
Cuba Libre | *Cuban*	20
NEW Daikaya Izakaya | *Japanese*	-
NEW Daikaya Ramen | *Noodles*	-
Dangerously Delicious | *Amer./Bakery*	21
NEW Del Campo | *Pan-Latin*	-
Del Frisco's | *Steak*	-
District ChopHse. | *Steak*	21
District of Pi | *Pizza*	23
Eat First | *Chinese*	22
Ella's Pizza | *Pizza*	21
Fiola | *Italian*	27
Five Guys | *Burgers*	24
Fogo de Chão | *Brazilian/Steak*	27
Fuel Pizza Cafe | *Amer./Pizza*	-
Full Kee (DC) | *Chinese*	23
Graffiato | *Italian/Pizza*	24
Hill Country | *BBQ*	21
Jaleo | *Spanish*	24
La Tasca | *Spanish*	21
Legal Sea Foods | *Seafood*	23
Luke's Lobster | *Seafood*	23
Matchbox | *Amer.*	23
McCormick/Schmick's | *Seafood*	23
Merzi | *Indian*	20
Minibar | *Eclectic*	28
Nando's | *Chicken*	22
NEW NoPa | *Amer.*	-
Osteria Elisir | *Italian*	26
Oya | *Asian*	24
Oyamel | *Mex.*	25

Paul	*Bakery*	22
Pho DC	*Viet.*	24
Ping Pong	*Asian*	21
Poste Moderne	*Amer./French*	20
Pret A Manger	*Sandwiches*	19
Proof	*Amer.*	24
NEW Protein Bar	*Health*	-
Rasika	*Indian*	28
Rosa Mexicano	*Mex.*	23
Ruth's Chris	*Steak*	26
Sei	*Asian*	26
701	*Amer.*	23
Social Reform	*Amer.*	-
Source	*Asian*	27
Teaism	*Tea*	20
Tony Cheng's	*Chinese*	22
Tosca	*Italian*	27
Vapiano	*Italian*	20
Zaytinya	*Med./Mideast.*	26
Zengo	*Asian/Pan-Latin*	22

CLEVELAND PARK/ WOODLEY PARK

Ardeo/Bardeo	*Amer./Wine*	22
Cactus Cantina	*Tex-Mex*	21
Cafe Deluxe	*Amer.*	20
Calif. Tortilla	*Tex-Mex*	22
Dino	*Italian*	24
District Kit.	*Amer.*	24
Hot 'N Juicy	*Cajun/Creole*	20
Indique	*Indian*	23
Lavandou	*French*	23
Lebanese Tav.	*Lebanese*	23
Le Zinc	*French*	22
Medium Rare	*Steak*	22
Nam-Viet	*Viet.*	21
New Heights	*Amer.*	22
Open City	*Diner*	21
Palena	*Amer.*	27
Petits Plats	*French*	22
Pulpo	*Spanish*	-
Ripple	*Amer.*	23
Sorriso	*Italian*	22

Spices	*Asian*	21
Tono Sushi	*Japanese/Thai*	22
2 Amys	*Pizza*	25

DOWNTOWN

NEW Astro	*Bakery/Chicken*	-
Bibiana	*Italian*	25
Blackfinn Amer.	*Amer.*	18
Bobby Van's	*Steak*	23
Brass. Beck	*Belgian/French*	25
Café du Parc	*French*	21
Ceiba	*Nuevo Latino*	24
Chef Geoff's	*Amer.*	21
Chop't	*Amer.*	21
DC Coast	*Amer.*	23
NEW Decanter	*Med.*	-
Finemondo	*Italian*	20
Fuel Pizza Cafe	*Amer./Pizza*	-
Fujimar	*Asian/Pan-Latin*	-
Georgia Brown	*Southern*	22
Haad Thai	*Thai*	21
Hamilton	*Amer.*	20
J&G Steak	*Amer./Steak*	24
Juice Joint	*Health*	23
Lincoln	*Amer.*	20
M&S Grill	*Seafood/Steak*	22
Mio	*Nuevo Latino*	26
Morrison-Clark	*Amer.*	24
NEW MXDC	*Mex.*	-
Occidental	*Seafood/Steak*	23
Oceanaire	*Seafood*	24
Old Ebbitt	*Amer.*	23
P.J. Clarke's	*Pub*	18
Plume	*Amer.*	26
Pret A Manger	*Sandwiches*	19
Roti	*Med.*	22
Siroc	*Italian*	24
NEW Woodward Table	*Amer.*	-
Zentan	*Asian*	22

DUPONT CIRCLE

Agora	*Turkish*	23
Al Tiramisu	*Italian*	25

Banana Leaves	*Asian*	–	Palm	*Steak*	25
BGR	*Burgers*	22	Pesce	*Seafood*	26
Bistrot du Coin	*French*	22	Ping Pong	*Asian*	21
Black & Orange	*Burgers*	25	Pizzeria Paradiso	*Pizza*	23
Boqueria	*Spanish*	–	Raku	*Asian*	23
NEW Bub & Pops	*Sandwiches*	–	Regent	*Thai*	24
Café Dupont	*French*	21	Russia Hse.	*Russian*	21
C.F. Folks	*Eclectic*	24	Ruth's Chris	*Steak*	26
Chop't	*Amer.*	21	Sakana	*Japanese*	23
Circa	*Amer.*	20	Scion	*Amer.*	19
City Lights	*Chinese*	19	Sette Osteria	*Italian*	21
NEW DGS Deli	*Jewish*	–	Shake Shack	*Burgers*	21
Eola	*Amer.*	25	Shophouse	*SE Asian*	22
Ezmè	*Turkish*	22	Sushi Taro	*Japanese*	26
Firefly	*Amer.*	23	Sweetgreen	*Health*	22
Floriana Rest.	*Italian*	24	Tabard Inn	*Amer.*	25
Food Corner Kabob	*Afghan*	25	Taylor Gourmet	*Deli/Italian*	22
NEW GBD	*Bakery/Chicken*	–	Teaism	*Tea*	20
NEW Gryphon	*Amer.*	–	Thaiphoon	*Thai*	21
Hank's Oyster	*Amer./Seafood*	24	2100 Prime	*Amer.*	24
Heritage India	*Indian*	22	Urbana	*French/Italian*	21
I Ricchi	*Italian*	24	Zorba's Cafe	*Greek*	23
Irish Whiskey	*Pub*	–		

Komi | *Amer./Med.* | 28

Kramerbooks	*Amer.*	19
La Tomate	*Italian*	19
Lauriol Plaza	*Mex.*	21
Le Pain Quotidien	*Bakery/Belgian*	21
Levante's	*Mideast.*	21
Little Serow	*Thai*	28
Luna Grill	*Diner/Veg.*	19
Madhatter	*Amer./Pub*	18
Mai Thai	*Thai*	23
Malaysia Kopitiam	*Malaysian*	23
Mandu	*Korean*	23
Marrakesh P	*Moroccan*	23
Moby Dick	*Persian*	23
Mourayo	*Greek*	25
Nando's	*Chicken*	22
Nora	*Amer.*	26
Obelisk	*Italian*	28

FOGGY BOTTOM/ WORLD BANK

NEW Ancora	*Italian*	–
Aroma	*Indian*	23
Bread Line	*Bakery/Sandwiches*	23
Burger Tap	*Burgers*	21
Circa	*Amer.*	20
NEW Crossroads	*Eclectic*	–
Dish/Drinks	*Amer.*	21
District Commons	*Amer.*	22
El Chalan	*Peruvian*	22
Founding Farmers	*Amer.*	24
Heritage India	*Indian*	22
Kaz Sushi	*Japanese*	25
La Taberna	*Spanish*	26
Notti Bianche	*Italian*	22
Paul	*Bakery*	22
Primi Piatti	*Italian*	19
Roof Terr.	*Amer.*	16

Roti | *Med.*	22
Sweetgreen | *Health*	22
Tonic | *Amer.*	17

GEORGETOWN

NEW AGB | *Amer.*	-
Bandolero | *Mex.*	-
Bangkok Joe's | *Thai*	23
Bistro Français | *French*	21
Bistrot Lepic | *French*	24
Bodega | *Spanish*	23
Bourbon Steak | *Steak*	25
Café Bonaparte | *French*	23
Cafe Milano | *Italian*	22
Ching Ching | *Tea*	20
Clyde's | *Amer.*	22
Dean & DeLuca | *Eclectic*	23
Degrees | *French*	22
NEW Farmers Fishers | *Amer.*	-
Filomena | *Italian*	24
Five Guys | *Burgers*	24
NEW Grill Room | *Amer.*	-
Il Canale | *Italian/Pizza*	22
La Chaumière | *French*	26
Ledo Pizza | *Pizza*	23
Leopold's Kafe | *Austrian*	23
Le Pain Quotidien | *Bakery/Belgian*	21
Luke's Lobster | *Seafood*	23
Mai Thai | *Thai*	23
NEW Malmaison | *French*	-
Martin's Tav. | *Amer.*	20
Moby Dick | *Persian*	23
Morton's | *Steak*	26
Neyla | *Lebanese*	24
Old Glory | *BBQ*	19
Paolo's | *Cal./Italian*	21
Paul | *Bakery*	22
Peacock Cafe | *Amer.*	22
Pizzeria Paradiso | *Pizza*	23
Sea Catch | *Seafood*	23
Sequoia | *Amer.*	17

Serendipity 3 | *Amer./Dessert*	21
1789 | *Amer.*	26
Sweetgreen | *Health*	22
Tackle Box | *Seafood*	18
Thunder Burger | *Burgers*	24
NEW Tony & Joe's | *Seafood*	-
Unum | *Amer.*	-

GLOVER PARK

Bourbon | *Pub*	21
Cafe Divan | *Turkish*	24
Heritage India | *Indian*	22
NEW Malgudi | *Indian*	-
Rocklands | *BBQ*	22
NEW Slate | *Amer./Italian*	-
Surfside | *Cal./Mex.*	21
Sushiko | *Japanese*	24
Town Hall | *Amer.*	23

GOLDEN TRIANGLE

BLT Steak | *Steak*	25
Bombay Club | *Indian*	25
Cafe Asia | *Asian*	21
Chop't | *Amer.*	21
NEW Edgar | *Amer.*	-
Equinox | *Amer.*	25
Kellari Taverna | *Greek*	23
Lafayette Rm. | *Amer.*	27
NEW Mari Vanna | *Russian*	-
McCormick/Schmick's | *Seafood*	23
Morton's | *Steak*	26
Nooshi | *Asian*	21
Oval Rm. | *Amer.*	26
Panache | *Med.*	21
Paul | *Bakery*	22
Pho 14 | *Viet.*	25
Pret A Manger | *Sandwiches*	19
Prime Rib | *Steak*	28
NEW Protein Bar | *Health*	-
Roti | *Med.*	22
Smith/Wollensky | *Steak*	25
NEW Takeateasy | *Pan-Latin*	-
Taylor Gourmet | *Deli/Italian*	22

Teaism	*Tea*	20
NEW Teddy/The Bully Bar	*Amer.*	–
Vapiano	*Italian*	20
Vidalia	*Southern*	26

MT. PLEASANT

Adam Express	*Asian/Seafood*	25
NEW Beau Thai	*Thai*	–
NEW Radius Pizza	*Pizza*	–
Tonic	*Amer.*	17

MT. VERNON SQUARE/ CONVENTION CENTER

Acadiana	*Cajun/Creole*	24
Busboys/Poets	*Amer./Eclectic*	22
Corduroy	*Amer.*	28
Kushi	*Japanese*	25
Mandu	*Korean*	23
Rogue 24	*Amer.*	23
Sweetgreen	*Health*	22
Taylor Gourmet	*Deli/Italian*	22
Tel'Veh	*Med.*	–

NOMA

NEW Rappahannock	*Seafood*	–
NEW Red Apron	*Amer.*	–
Roti	*Med.*	22
Todd Gray's Watershed	*Amer./Seafood*	23

PALISADES

BlackSalt	*Amer./Seafood*	27
Et Voila	*Belgian/French*	25
Kotobuki	*Japanese*	25
Makoto	*Japanese*	27

PETWORTH/ BRIGHTWOOD/ COLUMBIA HEIGHTS

Acre 121	*BBQ/Southern*	21
Cava Mezze Grill	*Greek*	22
Chez Billy	*French*	–
Domku	*E Euro./Scan.*	22
El Chucho	*Mex.*	–
Kangaroo/PORC	*BBQ*	–

Maple	*Italian*	–
Meridian	*Pub*	20
NEW Mi Cuba	*Cuban*	–
NEW Mothership	*Amer.*	–
Pete's Apizza	*Pizza*	22
Pho 14	*Viet.*	25
Pollo Campero	*Central Amer.*	19
RedRocks	*Pizza*	21
Room 11	*Eclectic*	26
Taqueria Distrito	*Mex.*	22
Thai Tanic	*Thai*	23

SCOTT CIRCLE/ LOGAN CIRCLE

Birch/Barley	*Amer.*	24
NEW Black Whiskey	*Amer.*	–
NEW B Too	*Belgian*	–
Café Saint-Ex	*Eclectic*	20
Commissary	*Amer.*	19
Cork	*Amer.*	25
El Centro	*Mex.*	21
Estadio	*Spanish*	25
NEW Etto	*Italian/Pizza*	–
15 Ria	*Amer.*	22
NEW Ghibellina	*Italian*	–
NEW Le Diplomate	*French*	–
Logan Tav.	*Amer.*	20
Masa 14	*Asian/Pan-Latin*	23
Nage	*Amer./Seafood*	21
Pearl Dive	*Seafood*	26
Pig	*Amer./Eclectic*	–
Posto	*Italian*	23
Rice	*Thai*	22
Standard	*BBQ*	–
Stoney's	*Pub*	18
Sweetgreen	*Health*	22
Taylor Gourmet	*Deli/Italian*	22
Thai Tanic	*Thai*	23

SHAW

NEW Beau Thai	*Thai*	–
Bistro Bohem	*Czech/Euro.*	–
Florida Ave. Grill	*Diner*	22

Howard Theatre	*Southern*	-
1905	*Amer.*	21
NEW Table	*Euro.*	-

SOUTHEAST

| NEW Park Tavern | *Amer.* | - |

SW/SW WATERFRONT

CityZen	*Amer.*	27
Mitsitam	*Amer.*	23
Phillips	*Seafood*	20
Roti	*Med.*	22
Shake Shack	*Burgers*	21
Sou'Wester	*Amer.*	21
Station 4	*Amer.*	21

TAKOMA

| Horace/Dickie's | *Seafood* | 22 |

UPPER NW

Acacia Bistro	*Med.*	20
Al Dente	*Italian/Pizza*	-
Buck's Fishing	*Amer.*	20
Café Olé	*Med.*	20
Cava Mezze Grill	*Greek*	22
Chef Geoff's	*Amer.*	21
Comet Ping Pong	*Pizza*	20
Crisp/Juicy	*Chicken/Peruvian*	24
Guapo's	*Tex-Mex*	22
Le Chat Noir	*French*	20
Le Pain Quotidien	*Bakery/Belgian*	21
Maggiano's	*Italian*	23
Masala Art	*Indian*	25
Matisse	*French/Med.*	23
Murasaki	*Japanese*	23
Pete's Apizza	*Pizza*	22
Tara Thai	*Thai*	20
NEW Wagshal's	*Amer.*	-
Yosaku	*Japanese*	21

U STREET CORRIDOR

Al Crostino	*Italian*	23
American Ice	*BBQ*	19
NEW &pizza	*Pizza*	-

Bar Pilar	*Amer.*	23
Ben's Chili	*Diner*	22
Bistro La Bonne	*French*	21
Black & Orange	*Burgers*	25
Brixton	*Amer./British*	-
Busboys/Poets	*Amer./Eclectic*	22
Crème	*Southern*	21
Dickson Wine	*Eclectic*	21
Dukem	*Ethiopian*	24
Eatonville	*Southern*	23
Etete	*Ethiopian*	24
Fast Gourmet	*Pan-Latin*	27
NEW Izakaya Seki	*Japanese*	-
Local 16	*Amer./Pizza*	17
Lost Society	*Amer./Steak*	18
Marvin	*Amer./Belgian*	23
Matchbox	*Amer.*	23
Negril	*Jamaican*	24
Oohh's & Aahh's	*Southern*	23
Piola	*Italian/Pizza*	21
Policy	*Amer.*	22
Sweetgreen	*Health*	22
Tabaq Bistro	*Med.*	20
NEW Tacos El Chilango	*Mex.*	-
NEW Taqueria Nacional	*Mex.*	-
Ulah Bistro	*Amer.*	20
Vinoteca	*Eclectic*	22

WEST END

Bayou	*Cajun/Creole*	20
Blue Duck	*Amer.*	27
Bobby's Burger	*Burgers*	22
NEW Bóveda	*Pan-Latin*	-
Circle Bistro	*Amer.*	20
Grillfish	*Seafood*	20
NEW Jardenea	*Amer.*	-
Juniper	*Amer.*	24
Marcel's	*Belgian/French*	28
Meiwah	*Chinese*	21
Rasika	*Indian*	28
Ris	*Amer.*	25
Westend Bistro	*Amer.*	22

Nearby Maryland

BETHESDA/CHEVY CHASE

NEW Aroma Espresso	*Coffee*	-
Assaggi	*Italian*	23
BGR	*Burgers*	22
Bistro LaZeez	*Mideast.*	22
Bistro Provence	*French*	26
Blackfinn Amer.	*Amer.*	18
Black's Bar	*Amer.*	24
Brass. Monte Carlo	*French/Med.*	22
NEW Brickside	*Amer.*	-
Cafe Deluxe	*Amer.*	20
Calif. Tortilla	*Tex-Mex*	22
Capital Grille	*Steak*	26
Cava Mezze Grill	*Greek*	22
Cesco Osteria	*Italian*	19
Cheesecake Factory	*Amer.*	24
Chicken/Run	*Chicken/Peruvian*	24
Chop't	*Amer.*	21
City Lights	*Chinese*	19
Clyde's	*Amer.*	22
Don Pollo	*Chicken/Peruvian*	23
Faryab	*Afghan*	24
Five Guys	*Burgers*	24
Food Wine	*Amer.*	22
Freddy's Lobster	*Seafood*	19
Fu Shing	*Chinese*	22
Grapeseed	*Amer.*	23
Guapo's	*Tex-Mex*	22
Guardado's	*Pan-Latin/Spanish*	23
Hard Times	*Amer.*	22
Haven	*Pizza*	-
Himalayan Heritage	*Indian/Nepalese*	21
Hinode	*Japanese*	20
Indique	*Indian*	23
Jaleo	*Spanish*	24
Kabob Bazaar	*Persian*	25
NEW Kadhai	*Indian*	-
La Ferme	*French*	24
Lebanese Tav.	*Lebanese*	23
Ledo Pizza	*Pizza*	23
Legal Sea Foods	*Seafood*	23
Le Pain Quotidien	*Bakery/Belgian*	21
Lia's	*Amer./Italian*	21
Luke's Lobster	*Seafood*	23
Mamma Lucia	*Italian*	22
Matuba	*Japanese*	23
Meiwah	*Chinese*	21
Mia's Pizzas	*Pizza*	25
Moby Dick	*Persian*	23
Mon Ami Gabi	*French*	22
Morton's	*Steak*	26
Mussel B&G	*Belgian*	20
Nando's	*Chicken*	22
Newton's	*Amer.*	22
Oakville Grille	*Amer.*	21
Olazzo	*Italian*	24
Passage to India	*Indian*	24
Persimmon	*Amer.*	-
P.F. Chang's	*Chinese*	23
Pizzeria Da Marco	*Pizza*	23
Praline	*Bakery/French*	23
Raku	*Asian*	23
Redwood	*Amer.*	19
Roti	*Med.*	22
Ruth's Chris	*Steak*	26
NEW Smoke BBQ	*BBQ*	-
Sushiko	*Japanese*	24
Sweetgreen	*Health*	22
Tako Grill	*Japanese*	24
Tandoori Nights	*Indian*	24
Tara Thai	*Thai*	20
Tavira	*Portug.*	25
Taylor Gourmet	*Deli/Italian*	22
Uncle Julio's	*Tex-Mex*	21
Vapiano	*Italian*	20
NEW Vino Volo	*Italian*	-
NEW Wildwood Kit.	*Med.*	-
NEW Yuzu	*Japanese*	-

WASHINGTON, DC

LOCATIONS

FREDERICK

Acacia Bistro | *Amer.*	24
Brewer's Alley | *Pub*	22
Cacique | *Mex./Spanish*	24
Cafe Nola | *Amer.*	24
Coal Fire | *Pizza*	22
Double T | *Diner*	20
Dutch's Daughter | *Amer.*	25
Elevation Burger | *Burgers*	21
Family Meal | *Amer./Diner*	-
Firestone's | *Amer.*	26
Five Guys | *Burgers*	24
Hinode | *Japanese*	20
Isabella's | *Spanish*	26
Lucky Corner | *Viet.*	28
Lunchbox | *Amer.*	24
Mamma Lucia | *Italian*	22
Monocacy Cross. | *Amer.*	28
Orchard | *Eclectic*	25
Tasting Rm. | *Amer.*	27
Volt | *Amer.*	28
Wine Kit. | *Amer.*	26

GAITHERSBURG/
DICKERSON/
GERMANTOWN/
OLNEY/SHADY GROVE

Agrodolce | *Italian*	23
Athens Grill | *Greek*	26
Batik | *Asian*	22
NEW Bench | *Amer.*	-
Burma Rd. | *Burmese/Chinese*	22
Cafe Deluxe | *Amer.*	20
Calif. Tortilla | *Tex-Mex*	22
Coal Fire | *Pizza*	22
Comus Inn | *Amer.*	20
Crisp/Juicy | *Chicken/Peruvian*	24
Dogfish Head | *Pub*	21
El Pollo | *Chicken/Peruvian*	26
Grillmarx | *Steak*	22
Guapo's | *Tex-Mex*	22
Hard Times | *Amer.*	22
India Palace | *Indian*	26

Mamma Lucia | *Italian*	22
Mannequin Pis | *Belgian*	23
Minerva | *Indian*	23
Mi Rancho | *Tex-Mex*	22
Moby Dick | *Persian*	23
Nando's | *Chicken*	22
New Fortune | *Chinese*	23
Pollo Campero | *Central Amer.*	19
Red Hot/Blue | *BBQ*	22
Ricciuti's | *Italian*	24
Sabai | *Thai*	26
Tandoori Nights | *Indian*	24
Tara Thai | *Thai*	20
Uncle Julio's | *Tex-Mex*	21
X.O. Taste | *Chinese*	24

NATIONAL HARBOR/
FORT WASHINGTON

Bangkok Golden | *Thai*	24
Bond 45 | *Italian*	22
Elevation Burger | *Burgers*	21
Grace's | *Asian*	25
Nando's | *Chicken*	22
Old Hickory | *Steak*	26
Rosa Mexicano | *Mex.*	23

POTOMAC/
GLEN ECHO/
CABIN JOHN

Amici Miei | *Italian*	21
Bezu | *Amer./French*	24
Calif. Tortilla | *Tex-Mex*	22
Founding Farmers | *Amer.*	24
Irish Inn/Glen Echo | *Irish*	20
Old Angler's | *Amer.*	20
Renato/River Falls | *Italian*	22
River Falls Tav. | *Amer.*	-
Sugo Cicchetti | *Italian/Pizza*	-
Wild Tomato | *Amer.*	22

PRINCE GEORGE'S
COUNTY

Bobby's Burger | *Burgers*	22
Busboys/Poets | *Amer./Eclectic*	22

Carolina Kit.	*Southern*	25
Cuba de Ayer	*Cuban*	25
Elevation Burger	*Burgers*	21
Fishnet	*Seafood*	24
Franklin's	*Pub*	21
Hard Times	*Amer.*	22
Mamma Lucia	*Italian*	22
Original Ledo	*Italian/Pizza*	24
Pho 75	*Viet.*	24
Roti	*Med.*	22
Seven Seas	*Chinese/Japanese*	22
Taqueria La Placita	*Mex.*	-
Tara Thai	*Thai*	20
Woodlands Rest.	*Indian/Veg.*	24

ROCKVILLE/ GARRETT PARK/ WHITE FLINT

A&J	*Chinese*	25
Addie's	*Amer.*	25
Benjarong	*Thai*	23
Black Mkt.	*Amer.*	26
Bob's Noodle	*Taiwanese*	22
Bombay Bistro	*Indian*	24
Calif. Tortilla	*Tex-Mex*	22
Cava Mezze	*Greek*	25
Cheesecake Factory	*Amer.*	24
Chef Geoff's	*Amer.*	21
China Bistro	*Chinese*	24
China Jade	*Chinese*	25
Clyde's	*Amer.*	22
Crisp/Juicy	*Chicken/Peruvian*	24
Don Pollo	*Chicken/Peruvian*	23
NEW East Dumpling	*Chinese*	-
East Pearl	*Chinese*	-
Elevation Burger	*Burgers*	21
El Mariachi	*S Amer./Tex-Mex*	25
First Watch	*Amer.*	21
Fontina Grille	*Italian*	20
Hard Times	*Amer.*	22
Hinode	*Japanese*	20
Il Pizzico	*Italian*	27
Joe's Noodle Hse.	*Chinese*	23

La Canela	*Peruvian*	23
La Limeña	*Cuban/Peruvian*	23
La Tasca	*Spanish*	21
Lebanese Tav.	*Lebanese*	23
Lighthouse Tofu	*Korean*	24
Mamma Lucia	*Italian*	22
Matchbox	*Amer.*	23
Michael's Noodles	*Chinese*	22
Mi Rancho	*Tex-Mex*	22
Moby Dick	*Persian*	23
Mosaic Cuisine	*Eclectic*	23
Mykonos Grill	*Greek*	23
Nick's Chophse.	*Steak*	21
Niwano Hana	*Japanese*	26
Oro Pomodoro	*Italian/Pizza*	21
P.F. Chang's	*Chinese*	23
Pho 75	*Viet.*	24
Quench	*Amer.*	-
Rocklands	*BBQ*	22
Rolls 'N Rice	*Japanese*	22
Seven Seas	*Chinese/Japanese*	22
Sichuan Jin River	*Chinese*	25
Spice Xing	*Indian*	22
Sushi Damo	*Japanese*	25
Tara Thai	*Thai*	20
Taste/Saigon	*Viet.*	22
Urban BBQ	*BBQ*	24
Yuan Fu	*Chinese/Vegan*	25

SANDY SPRINGS

Urban BBQ	*BBQ*	24

SILVER SPRING/ TAKOMA PARK/ WHEATON

Austin Grill	*Tex-Mex*	18
Azucar	*Mex./Pan-Latin*	24
Calif. Tortilla	*Tex-Mex*	22
Crisp/Juicy	*Chicken/Peruvian*	24
Cubano's	*Cuban*	23
Eggspectation	*Amer.*	21
8407 Kit.	*Amer.*	24
Elevation Burger	*Burgers*	21

El Golfo	*Pan-Latin*	23
El Pollo	*Chicken/Peruvian*	26
Full Key	*Chinese*	25
Good Fortune	*Chinese*	22
Hollywood E.	*Chinese*	24
Jackie's	*Amer.*	23
Kabob N Karahi	*Indian/Pakistani*	26
LacoMelza	*Ethiopian*	-
Lebanese Tav.	*Lebanese*	23
Ledo Pizza	*Pizza*	23
Mamma Lucia	*Italian*	22
Mandalay	*Burmese*	23
Mark's Kit.	*Eclectic*	21
Mi Rancho	*Tex-Mex*	22
Moby Dick	*Persian*	23
Mrs. K's	*Amer.*	23
Nando's	*Chicken*	22
Nava Thai	*Thai*	26
Negril	*Jamaican*	24
New Kam	*Chinese*	25
Olazzo	*Italian*	24
Oriental E.	*Chinese*	23
Pacci's Neapolitan	*Pizza*	23
Pacci's Tratt.	*Italian*	23
Parkway Deli	*Deli*	22
Pollo Campero	*Central Amer.*	19
Ray's/Classics	*Steak*	25
Ren's	*Japanese/Noodle Shop*	24
Royal Mile	*Scottish*	23
Ruan Thai	*Thai*	27
Samantha's	*Pan-Latin*	24
Scion	*Amer.*	19
Sergio Rist.	*Italian*	27
Thai/Silver Spring	*Thai*	24
Urban BBQ	*BBQ*	24
Woomi Gdn.	*Korean*	20

Nearby Virginia

ALEXANDRIA

Aditi	*Indian*	23
Afghan	*Afghan*	23

Buzz	*Coffee*	22
Cafe Pizzaiolo	*Italian/Pizza*	24
Calif. Tortilla	*Tex-Mex*	22
Clyde's	*Amer.*	22
Cosmopolitan Grill	*E Euro.*	27
Evening Star	*Southern*	23
Five Guys	*Burgers*	24
Hee Been	*Korean*	23
Il Porto	*Italian*	24
Peking Duck	*Chinese*	28
Pork Barrel	*BBQ*	19
Red Hot/Blue	*BBQ*	22
Rocklands	*BBQ*	22
RT's	*Cajun/Creole*	26
Rustico	*Amer.*	22
Taqueria Poblano	*Mex.*	22
Teaism	*Tea*	20
Tempo	*French/Italian*	24
NEW Trademark	*Amer.*	-
Yamazato	*Japanese*	25

ALEXANDRIA (OLD TOWN)

A La Lucia	*Italian*	23
Asian Bistro	*Asian*	25
Austin Grill	*Tex-Mex*	18
Bastille	*French*	24
BGR	*Burgers*	22
Brabo	*Belgian/French*	26
Chart House	*Seafood*	23
Columbia Firehse.	*Amer.*	23
Daniel O'Connell's	*Pub*	20
Eamonn's	*Irish*	23
Faccia Luna	*Pizza*	23
Five Guys	*Burgers*	24
Fontaine Caffe	*French*	25
Gadsby's Tavern	*Amer.*	21
Geranio	*Italian*	25
Grille	*Amer./French*	25
Hank's Oyster	*Amer./Seafood*	24
Hard Times	*Amer.*	22
Jackson 20	*Amer.*	21
La Bergerie	*French*	26

Landini Bros. | *Italian*	25
Las Tapas | *Spanish*	24
La Tasca | *Spanish*	21
Le Pain Quotidien | *Bakery/Belgian*	21
Le Refuge | *French*	26
Mai Thai | *Thai*	23
Majestic | *Amer.*	24
Nando's | *Chicken*	22
Pizzeria Paradiso | *Pizza*	23
RedRocks | *Pizza*	21
Restaurant Eve | *Amer.*	27
Society Fair | *Amer.*	24
Vaso's Kit. | *Greek*	26
Vermilion | *Amer.*	26
Virtue | *Amer.*	–
Yves Bistro | *French*	25

ARLINGTON

Afghan Kabob Hse. | *Afghan*	23
Aroma | *Indian*	23
Asia Bistro/Zen | *Asian*	21
Bangkok 54 | *Thai*	25
Bayou Bakery | *Southern*	22
BGR | *Burgers*	22
Bob & Edith's | *Diner*	20
Busboys/Poets | *Amer./Eclectic*	22
Buzz | *Coffee*	22
Cafe Asia | *Asian*	21
Cafe Pizzaiolo | *Italian/Pizza*	24
Calif. Tortilla | *Tex-Mex*	22
Carlyle | *Amer.*	25
Cassatt's Café | *New Zealand*	20
Chasin' Tails | *Cajun/Creole*	–
China Gdn. | *Chinese*	22
Chop't | *Amer.*	21
Crisp/Juicy | *Chicken/Peruvian*	24
Crystal Thai | *Thai*	23
Curious Grape | *Eclectic*	–
Delhi Dhaba | *Indian*	20
Eamonn's | *Irish*	23
Elevation Burger | *Burgers*	21
El Pollo | *Chicken/Peruvian*	26

Farrah Olivia | *Amer.*	23
Fire Works | *Pizza*	24
Fyve | *Amer.*	24
Good Stuff | *Burgers*	23
Guajillo | *Mex.*	21
Guapo's | *Tex-Mex*	22
Harry's | *BBQ/Burgers*	21
Jaleo | *Spanish*	24
Kabob Palace | *Mideast.*	26
Kora | *Italian*	17
La Côte d'Or | *French*	24
Layalina | *Lebanese/Syrian*	24
Lebanese Tav. | *Lebanese*	23
Ledo Pizza | *Pizza*	23
Legal Sea Foods | *Seafood*	23
Lost Dog | *Pub*	23
Luna Grill | *Diner/Veg.*	19
Mala Tang | *Chinese*	22
NEW Masala Exp. | *Indian*	–
McCormick/Schmick's | *Seafood*	23
Me Jana | *Lebanese*	24
Minh's | *Viet.*	24
Moby Dick | *Persian*	23
Morton's | *Steak*	26
Nando's | *Chicken*	22
Pasha Cafe | *Med.*	23
P.F. Chang's | *Chinese*	23
Pie-Tanza | *Pizza*	23
Ping | *Asian*	23
Piola | *Italian/Pizza*	21
NEW Protein Bar | *Health*	–
Pupatella Pizzeria | *Pizza*	26
Ravi Kabob | *Pakistani*	25
Ray's/Steaks | *Steak*	27
Ray's/Third | *Amer./Steak*	25
Red Hot/Blue | *BBQ*	22
RedRocks | *Pizza*	21
Rocklands | *BBQ*	22
Roti | *Med.*	22
Rustico | *Amer.*	22
Ruth's Chris | *Steak*	26

WASHINGTON, DC

LOCATIONS

Sweetgreen | *Health*	22
NEW Tacos El Chilango | *Mex.*	–
Taqueria Poblano | *Mex.*	22
T.H.A.I. | *Thai*	25
Thaiphoon | *Thai*	21
Thai Sq. | *Thai*	26
Tutto Bene | *Italian/S Amer.*	23
Twisted Vines | *Eclectic*	20
Uncle Julio's | *Tex-Mex*	21
Vapiano | *Italian*	20
Village Bistro | *Euro.*	26
William Jeffrey's | *Amer.*	20
Willow | *Amer.*	24

CLARENDON

BGR | *Burgers*	22
Blvd. Woodgrill | *Amer.*	20
Cava Mezze | *Greek*	25
Cheesecake Factory | *Amer.*	24
Circa | *Amer.*	20
Delhi Club | *Indian*	24
Eventide | *Amer.*	23
Faccia Luna | *Pizza*	23
NEW Fat Shorty's | *Belgian*	–
NEW Fuego Cocina | *Mex.*	–
Green Pig | *Amer.*	–
Hard Times | *Amer.*	22
Kabob Bazaar | *Persian*	25
NEW La Tagliatella | *Italian*	–
La Tasca | *Spanish*	21
Le Pain Quotidien | *Bakery/Belgian*	21
Liberty Tav. | *Amer.*	24
Lyon Hall | *French/German*	24
Nam-Viet | *Viet.*	21
Northside | *Coffee*	22
Pete's Apizza | *Pizza*	22
Pho 75 | *Viet.*	24
Tallula/EatBar | *Amer.*	24
Taste/Morocco | *Moroccan*	23

FAIRFAX

Artie's | *Amer.*	25
Asian Bistro | *Asian*	25

Bangkok Golden | *Thai*	24
BonChon | *Korean*	26
Calif. Tortilla | *Tex-Mex*	22
Cheesecake Factory | *Amer.*	24
China Star | *Chinese*	24
Chutzpah | *Deli*	23
Coastal Flats | *Seafood*	24
Curry Mantra | *Indian*	23
Dogfish Head | *Pub*	21
Dolce Veloce | *Italian*	–
Dolce Vita | *Italian*	25
Elevation Burger | *Burgers*	21
First Watch | *Amer.*	21
Guapo's | *Tex-Mex*	22
Hard Times | *Amer.*	22
Jaipur | *Indian*	25
Lost Dog | *Pub*	23
Matchbox | *Amer.*	23
Minerva | *Indian*	23
Moby Dick | *Persian*	23
100 Degree | *Chinese*	24
Ozzie's Corner | *Italian*	24
P.F. Chang's | *Chinese*	23
NEW Red Apron | *Amer.*	–
Red Hot/Blue | *BBQ*	22
Ruth's Chris | *Steak*	26
Sakoontra | *Thai*	23
Uncle Julio's | *Tex-Mex*	21
Villa Mozart | *Italian*	26

FALLS CHURCH

Argia's | *Italian*	21
Bamian | *Afghan*	26
Bangkok Golden | *Thai*	24
Banh Mi DC | *Viet.*	21
Crisp/Juicy | *Chicken/Peruvian*	24
Curry Mantra | *Indian*	23
Dogfish Head | *Pub*	21
Duangrat's | *Thai*	26
Elephant Jumps | *Thai*	26
Elevation Burger | *Burgers*	21
Fortune | *Chinese*	22

Full Kee (VA)	*Chinese*	22
Haandi	*Indian*	24
Hong Kong Palace	*Chinese*	27
Huong Viet	*Viet.*	25
La Caraqueña	*S Amer.*	25
Ledo Pizza	*Pizza*	23
Mad Fox Brew	*Amer.*	20
Mark's Duck Hse.	*Chinese*	25
Myanmar	*Burmese*	24
Panjshir	*Afghan*	25
Peking Gourmet	*Chinese*	25
Pho 75	*Viet.*	24
Pie-Tanza	*Pizza*	23
Pizzeria Orso	*Pizza*	22
Pollo Campero	*Central Amer.*	19
Present	*Viet.*	26
Rabieng	*Thai*	25
Red Hot/Blue	*BBQ*	22
Rice Paper	*Viet.*	–
Sunflower Veg.	*Asian/Veg.*	25
Tara Thai	*Thai*	20
2941	*Amer.*	27
X.O. Taste	*Chinese*	24

GREAT FALLS

L'Auberge/Jaques'	*French*	28

MCLEAN

Assaggi	*Italian*	23
Bistro Vivant	*French*	–
Capri	*Italian*	23
Elevation Burger	*Burgers*	21
Evo Bistro	*Med.*	22
Kazan	*Turkish*	25
Lost Dog	*Pub*	23
Moby Dick	*Persian*	23
Paul	*Bakery*	22
Tachibana	*Japanese*	24

RESTON/HERNDON

Angeethi	*Indian*	23
Busara	*Thai*	22
Clyde's	*Amer.*	22

Counter	*Burgers*	21
El Manantial	*Med.*	24
Five Guys	*Burgers*	24
Hama Sushi	*Japanese*	25
Il Fornaio	*Italian*	25
Jackson's	*Amer.*	23
Ledo Pizza	*Pizza*	23
M&S Grill	*Seafood/Steak*	22
McCormick/Schmick's	*Seafood*	23
Minerva	*Indian*	23
Mon Ami Gabi	*French*	22
Morton's	*Steak*	26
Paolo's	*Cal./Italian*	21
PassionFish	*Amer./Seafood*	26
Pho 75	*Viet.*	24
Pollo Campero	*Central Amer.*	19
Red Hot/Blue	*BBQ*	22
Russia House Rest.	*Russian*	27
Sweetgreen	*Health*	22
Tara Thai	*Thai*	20
NEW Tavern 64	*Amer.*	–
Uncle Julio's	*Tex-Mex*	21
Vapiano	*Italian*	20
Vinifera	*Amer.*	23
Zeffirelli Rist.	*Italian*	24

SPRINGFIELD/ ANNANDALE

A&J	*Chinese*	25
Afghan Kabob Rest.	*Afghan*	25
Austin Grill	*Tex-Mex*	18
BGR	*Burgers*	22
Five Guys	*Burgers*	24
Food Corner Kabob	*Afghan*	25
Hard Times	*Amer.*	22
Honey Pig	*Korean*	23
Mike's	*Amer.*	26
NEW Monty's Steak	*Steak*	–
Yechon	*Japanese/Korean*	22

TYSONS CORNER

Bombay Tandoor	*Indian*	26
Busara	*Thai*	22

Cafe Deluxe	*Amer.*	20
Capital Grille	*Steak*	26
Cava Mezze Grill	*Greek*	22
Cheesecake Factory	*Amer.*	24
Chef Geoff's	*Amer.*	21
Chima	*Brazilian*	26
Clyde's	*Amer.*	22
Coastal Flats	*Seafood*	24
Da Domenico	*Italian*	23
Fleming's Steak	*Steak*	25
Food Corner Kabob	*Afghan*	25
Härth	*Amer.*	23
Lebanese Tav.	*Lebanese*	23
Legal Sea Foods	*Seafood*	23
Maggiano's	*Italian*	23
McCormick/Schmick's	*Seafood*	23
Nostos	*Greek*	26
Palm	*Steak*	25
Panache	*Med.*	21
P.F. Chang's	*Chinese*	23
Shamshiry	*Persian*	27
Wildfire	*Seafood/Steak*	22
Woo Lae Oak	*Korean*	23

VIENNA/OAKTON/ MERRIFIELD

Alegria	*Mex.*	-
Amma Veg.	*Indian*	22
Bazin's/Church	*Amer.*	26
Café Renaissance	*Continental*	26
Cava Mezze Grill	*Greek*	22
Four Sisters	*Viet.*	25
Maple Ave	*Eclectic*	-
Plaka Grill	*Greek*	24
Ruth's Chris	*Steak*	26
Sea Pearl	*Amer./Cal.*	23
Sunflower Veg.	*Asian/Veg.*	25
Sweet Ginger	*Asian*	25
Sweetwater Tav.	*SW*	26
Tara Thai	*Thai*	20
Taylor Gourmet	*Deli/Italian*	22
Yama	*Japanese*	25

Exurban Virginia

BROADLANDS

| Clyde's | *Amer.* | 22 |

CENTREVILLE/ MANASSAS/ PRINCE WILLIAM COUNTY

Bistro L'Hermitage	*French*	26
Bobby's Burger	*Burgers*	22
BonChon	*Korean*	26
Cheesecake Factory	*Amer.*	24
El Pollo	*Chicken/Peruvian*	26
Five Guys	*Burgers*	24
Food Corner Kabob	*Afghan*	25
Hard Times	*Amer.*	22
Honey Pig	*Korean*	23
Nando's	*Chicken*	22
Pollo Campero	*Central Amer.*	19
Red Hot/Blue	*BBQ*	22
Sweetwater Tav.	*SW*	26
Uncle Julio's	*Tex-Mex*	21

CHANTILLY

Eggspectation	*Amer.*	21
First Watch	*Amer.*	21
Ford's Fish	*New Eng./Seafood*	26
Minerva	*Indian*	23
Thai Basil	*Thai*	26

CLIFTON

| Trummer's | *Amer.* | 24 |

LEESBURG/ LANSDOWNE

Angeethi	*Indian*	23
Blue Ridge	*Amer.*	24
Cajun Experience	*Cajun/Creole*	23
Eggspectation	*Amer.*	21
Fire Works	*Pizza*	24
Kobe	*Japanese*	27
Lightfoot	*Amer.*	26
Red Hot/Blue	*BBQ*	22
Tuscarora Mill	*Amer.*	25
Wine Kit.	*Amer.*	26

PURCELLVILLE

Magnolias/Mill | *Amer.* 25

STERLING/ASHBURN/ SOUTH RIDING

Blue Ridge | *Amer.* 24

NEW Bungalow | *Amer.* -

Cheesecake Factory | *Amer.* 24

Ford's Fish | *New Eng./Seafood* 26

Hooked | *Seafood* 20

P.F. Chang's | *Chinese* 23

Rangoli | *Indian* 24

Sweetwater Tav. | *SW* 26

Taste/Burma | *Burmese* 26

Urban BBQ | *BBQ* 24

Vapiano | *Italian* 20

Virginia Countryside

Ashby Inn | *Amer.* 27

Blue Rock | *Amer.* 24

Foti's | *Amer.* 27

Hunter's Head | *British* 23

Inn/Little Washington | *Amer.* 29

Iron Bridge Wine | *Amer.* 25

It's About Thyme | *Amer./Euro.* 25

L'Auberge Provençale | *French* 26

Rail Stop | *Amer.* 23

WASHINGTON, DC

LOCATIONS

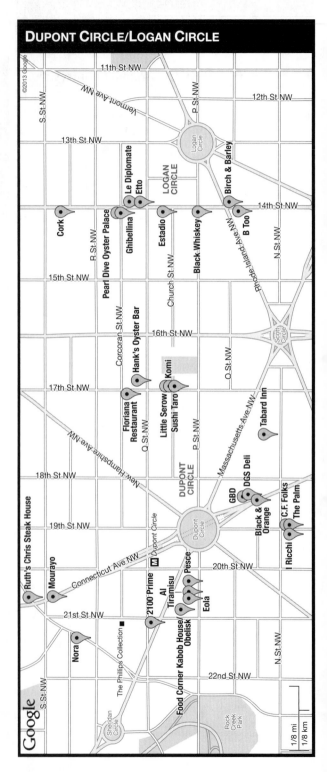

DUPONT CIRCLE/LOGAN CIRCLE

GOLDEN TRIANGLE/WEST END

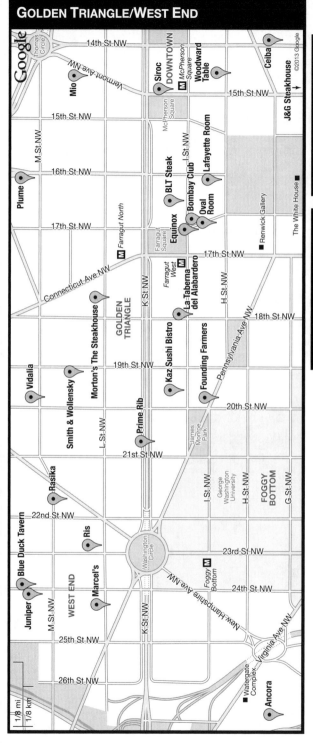

14th St NW
Thomas Circle
Vermont Ave NW
Mio
Siroc
DOWNTOWN
McPherson Square
Woodward Table
Ceiba
J&G Steakhouse
15th St NW
15th St NW
Plume
M St NW
16th St NW
16th St NW
BLT Steak
Bombay Club
Lafayette Room
L St NW
Oval Room
17th St NW
Equinox
Renwick Gallery
The White House
Farragut North
17th St NW
Farragut Square
Connecticut Ave NW
Farragut West
La Taberna del Alabardero
H St NW
GOLDEN TRIANGLE
K St NW
18th St NW
Morton's The Steakhouse
Kaz Sushi Bistro
Founding Farmers
Pennsylvania Ave NW
19th St NW
Vidalia
Smith & Wollensky
20th St NW
Prime Rib
L St NW
James Monroe Park
21st St NW
I St NW
George Washington University
FOGGY BOTTOM
G St NW
Rasika
22nd St NW
Blue Duck Tavern
Ris
Washington Circle
23rd St NW
M
Foggy Bottom
New Hampshire Ave NW
24th St NW
Juniper
Marcel's
WEST END
M St NW
K St NW
25th St NW
Watergate Complex
Virginia Ave NW
26th St NW
Ancora

1/8 mi
1/8 km

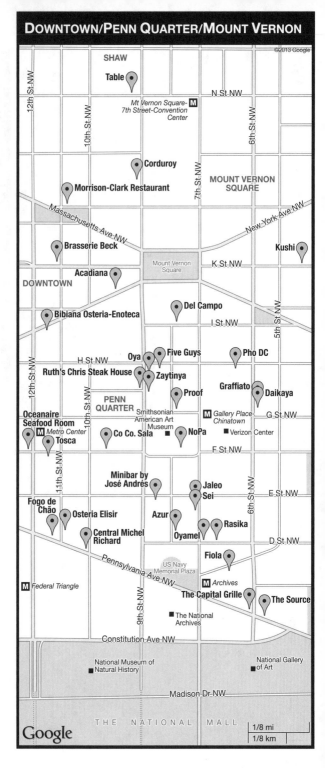

DOWNTOWN/PENN QUARTER/MOUNT VERNON

©2013 Google

SHAW

Table

12th St NW

10th St NW

N St NW

Mt Vernon Square-
7th Street-Convention
Center

Corduroy

MOUNT VERNON
SQUARE

Morrison-Clark Restaurant

7th St NW

6th St NW

Massachusetts Ave NW

New York Ave NW

Brasserie Beck

Kushi

Mount Vernon
Square

K St NW

Acadiana

DOWNTOWN

Del Campo

5th St NW

Bibiana Osteria-Enoteca

I St NW

12th St NW

Oya   Five Guys

Pho DC

H St NW

Ruth's Chris Steak House   Zaytinya

Graffiato

Proof

Daikaya

PENN
QUARTER

10th St NW

Smithsonian
American Art
Museum

Gallery Place-
Chinatown

G St NW

Oceanaire
Seafood Room

Co Co. Sala

NoPa

Verizon Center

Metro Center

Tosca

F St NW

11th St NW

Minibar by
José Andrés

Jaleo

Sei

E St NW

Fogo de
Chão

Osteria Elisir

Azur

Rasika

6th St NW

Central Michel
Richard

Oyamel

D St NW

Pennsylvania Ave NW

US Navy
Memorial Plaza

Fiola

Federal Triangle

Archives

9th St NW

The Capital Grille

The Source

The National
Archives

Constitution Ave NW

National Museum of
Natural History

National Gallery
of Art

Madison Dr NW

THE   NATIONAL   MALL

Google

1/8 mi
1/8 km

GEORGETOWN

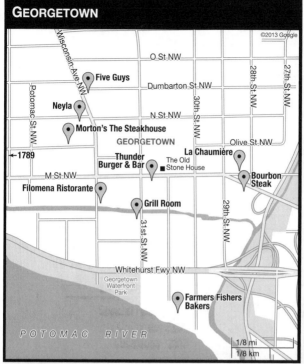

©2013 Google

O St NW

Wisconsin Ave NW

● Five Guys

Dumbarton St NW

Potomac St NW

28th St NW

27th St NW

30th St NW

Neyla ●

N St NW

● Morton's The Steakhouse

GEORGETOWN

Olive St NW

←1789

● La Chaumière

Thunder
Burger & Bar ■ The Old
Stone House

Bourbon
Steak ●

M St NW

29th St NW

Filomena Ristorante ●

● Grill Room

31st St NW

Whitehurst Fwy NW

Georgetown
Waterfront
Park

● Farmers Fishers
Bakers

P O T O M A C   R I V E R

1/8 mi
1/8 km

CAPITOL HILL

A St SE

10th St SE

➤ Bistro Bis
➤ Charlie Palmer Steak

Independence Ave SE

● Acqua al 2

North Carolina Ave SE

8th St SE

9th St SE

C St SE

Seward
Square

Beuchert's
Saloon ●

● Montmartre/
Seventh Hill Pizza

5th St SE

Hank's
Oyster Bar

South Carolina Ave SE

4th St SE

M Eastern
Market

Market
Park

D St SE

D St SE

E St SE

CAPITOL HILL

6th St SE

7th St SE

E St SE

11th St SE

Marion Park

● Belga Café
● Senart's Oyster &
Chop House

G St SE

1/8 mi
1/8 km

Google

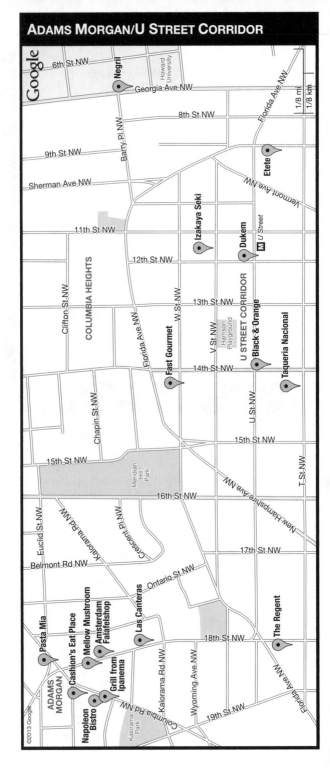

Google

6th St NW

Negril

Howard University

Georgia Ave NW

8th St NW

Florida Ave NW

1/8 mi

1/8 km

9th St NW

Barry Pl NW

Etete

Sherman Ave NW

Vermont Ave NW

11th St NW

Izakaya Seki

Dukem

M U Street

12th St NW

U Street

COLUMBIA HEIGHTS

Clifton St NW

13th St NW

W St NW

Florida Ave NW

V St NW

Harrison Playground

Black & Orange

U STREET CORRIDOR

Fast Gourmet

14th St NW

Taqueria Nacional

Chapin St NW

U St NW

15th St NW

15th St NW

Meridian Hill Park

T St NW

16th St NW

New Hampshire Ave NW

Euclid St NW

Kalorama Rd NW

Crescent Pl NW

17th St NW

Belmont Rd NW

Ontario St NW

Las Canteras

The Regent

Pasta Mia

Mellow Mushroom

Amsterdam Falafelshop

18th St NW

Cashion's Eat Place

Florida Ave NW

Grill from Ipanema

Kalorama Rd NW

Wyoming Ave NW

Napoleon Bistro

ADAMS MORGAN

Columbia Rd NW

Kalorama Park

19th St NW

©2013 Google

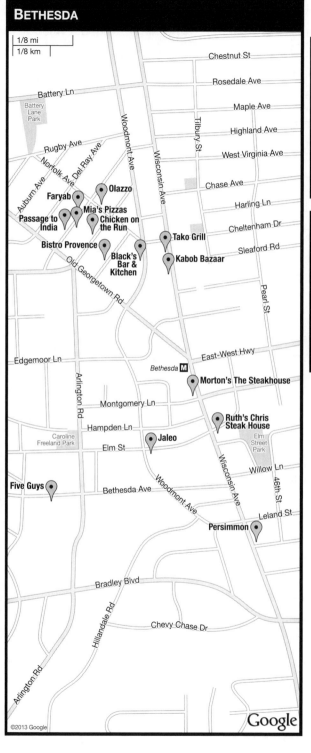

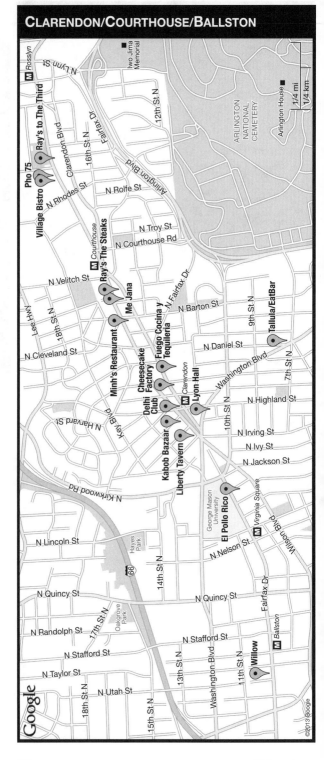

CLARENDON/COURTHOUSE/BALLSTON

Iwo Jima Memorial

Arlington House

ARLINGTON NATIONAL CEMETERY

1/4 mi
1/4 km

Rosslyn

N Lynn St

Ray's to The Third

Pho 75

Village Bistro

N Rhodes St

Clarendon Blvd

16th St N

Fairfax Dr

N Rolfe St

Arlington Blvd

12th St N

N Troy St

N Courthouse Rd

Courthouse

Ray's The Steaks

N Velitch St

Me Jana

N Fairfax Dr

N Barton St

9th St N

Tallula/EatBar

Lee Hwy

18th St N

Minh's Restaurant

Fuego Cocina y Tequileria

N Daniel St

Washington Blvd

7th St N

N Cleveland St

Cheesecake Factory

Delhi Club

Clarendon

Lyon Hall

N Highland St

Key Blvd

Kabob Bazaar

10th St N

N Irving St

N Harvard St

Liberty Tavern

N Ivy St

N Jackson St

N Kirkwood Rd

George Mason University

El Pollo Rico

Virginia Square

N Lincoln St

Hayes Park

N Nelson St

Wilson Blvd

66

N Quincy St

N Quincy St

Fairfax Dr

N Randolph St

17th St N

Oakgrove Park

N Stafford St

Ballston

N Stafford St

13th St N

Willow

N Taylor St

Washington Blvd

11th St N

N Utah St

18th St N

15th St N

Google

©2013 Google

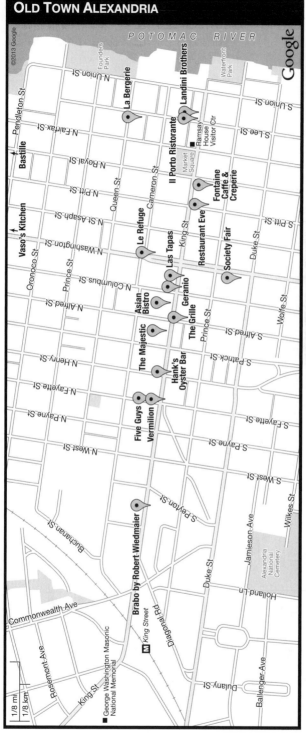

OLD TOWN ALEXANDRIA

POTOMAC RIVER

©2013 Google

Google

Founders Park

Waterfront Park

N Union St

S Union St

Pendleton St

La Bergerie

Landini Brothers

N Fairfax St

S Lee St

Bastille

N Royal St

Il Porto Ristorante

Ramsay House Visitor Ctr

Market Square

Vaso's Kitchen

N Pitt St

Queen St

Cameron St

Fontaine Caffe & Creperie

S Pitt St

N Asaph St

Le Refuge

Restaurant Eve

Oronoco St

N Washington St

King St

Society Fair

Duke St

Prince St

Las Tapas

N Columbus St

Geranio

Wolfe St

N Alfred St

Asian Bistro

The Grille

S Alfred St

Prince St

S Patrick St

The Majestic

N Henry St

Hank's Oyster Bar

N Fayette St

S Fayette St

Five Guys

Vermilion

N Payne St

S Payne St

N West St

S West St

Wilkes St

Jamieson Ave

Brabo by Robert Wiedmaier

S Peyton St

Alexandria National Cemetery

Holland Ln

Buchanan St

Commonwealth Ave

King Street

Diagonal Rd

Ballenger Ave

Rosemont Ave

M King St

George Washington Masonic National Memorial

Dulany St

King St

1/8 mi
1/8 km

Visit zagat.com

253

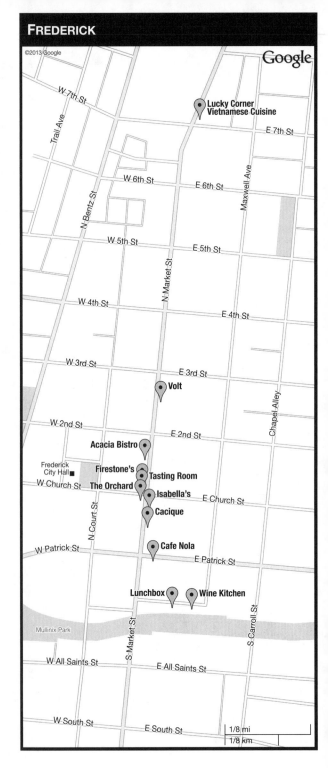

©2013 Google

Google

W 7th St

Trail Ave

Lucky Corner
Vietnamese Cuisine

E 7th St

Maxwell Ave

N Bentz St

W 6th St

E 6th St

W 5th St

E 5th St

N Market St

W 4th St

E 4th St

W 3rd St

E 3rd St

Volt

W 2nd St

E 2nd St

Chapel Alley

Acacia Bistro

Frederick
City Hall

Firestone's

Tasting Room

W Church St

The Orchard

Isabella's

E Church St

Cacique

N Court St

W Patrick St

Cafe Nola

E Patrick St

Lunchbox

Wine Kitchen

S Market St

S Carroll St

Mullinix Park

W All Saints St

E All Saints St

W South St

E South St

1/8 mi

1/8 km

BALTIMORE, ANNAPOLIS AND THE EASTERN SHORE

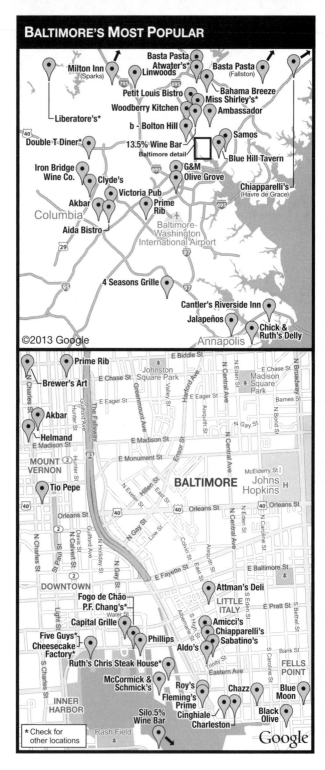

BALTIMORE'S MOST POPULAR

Milton Inn (Sparks)
Atwater's*
Basta Pasta
Linwoods
Basta Pasta (Fallston)
Petit Louis Bistro
Bahama Breeze
Miss Shirley's*
Woodberry Kitchen
Ambassador
Liberatore's*
b - Bolton Hill
Double T Diner*
Samos
13.5% Wine Bar
Baltimore detail
Blue Hill Tavern
Iron Bridge Wine Co.
G&M
Olive Grove
Clyde's
Chiapparelli's (Havre de Grace)
Victoria Pub
Akbar
Prime Rib
Aida Bistro
Columbia
Baltimore-Washington International Airport
4 Seasons Grille
Cantler's Riverside Inn
Jalapeños
Chick & Ruth's Delly
Annapolis
©2013 Google

Prime Rib
Brewer's Art
Johnston Square Park
Madison Square Park
Akbar
Helmand
MOUNT VERNON
BALTIMORE
Johns Hopkins
Tio Pepe
DOWNTOWN
Attman's Deli
Fogo de Chão
P.F. Chang's*
LITTLE ITALY
Capital Grille
Amicci's
Chiapparelli's
Five Guys*
Phillips
Sabatino's
Cheesecake Factory*
Aldo's
Ruth's Chris Steak House*
FELLS POINT
McCormick & Schmick's
Roy's
Chazz
Blue Moon
Fleming's Prime
INNER HARBOR
Silo.5% Wine Bar
Cinghiale
Charleston
Black Olive
Rash Field

*Check for other locations

Google

Baltimore's Most Popular

All restaurants are in the Baltimore area unless otherwise noted (A=Annapolis and E=Eastern Shore). When a restaurant has locations both inside and out of the city limits, we include the notation BA as well.

1. Woodberry Kitchen | *American*
2. Double T Diner/A/BA | *Diner*
3. Prime Rib | *Steak*
4. Charleston | *American*
5. G&M | *Seafood*
6. Miss Shirley's/A/BA | *American*
7. 4 Seasons Grille | *Eclectic/Med.*
8. Tio Pepe | *Continental/Spanish*
9. Cinghiale | *Italian*
10. Sabatino's | *Italian*
11. Brewer's Art | *American*
12. Liberatore's | *Italian*
13. Petit Louis Bistro | *French*
14. Clyde's | *American*
15. Chiapparelli's | *Italian*
16. 13.5% Wine Bar/Silo | *American*
17. Linwoods | *American*
18. Helmand | *Afghan*
19. Aldo's | *Italian*
20. Black Olive | *Greek/Seafood*
21. Jalapeños/A | *Mexican/Spanish*
22. Blue Moon Cafe | *American*
23. Phillips | *Seafood*
24. Atwater's | *Bakery*
25. Iron Bridge Wine Co. | *Amer.*
26. Samos | *Greek*
27. Attman's Delicatessen | *Deli*
28. Amicci's | *Italian*
29. Akbar | *Indian*
30. Blue Hill Tavern | *American*
31. Cantler's Riverside/A | *Crab Hse.*
32. Victoria Gastro Pub | *Eclectic*
33. Olive Grove | *Italian*
34. Chick & Ruth's Delly/A | *Diner*
35. b – Bolton Hill Bistro | *Amer.*
36. Basta Pasta | *Italian*
37. Ambassador Dining | *Indian*
38. Chazz: A Bronx Orig. | *Ital./Pizza*
39. Aida Bistro & Wine Bar | *Italian*
40. Milton Inn | *American*

MOST POPULAR CHAINS

1. Cheesecake/A/BA | *Amer.*
2. Five Guys/A/BA | *Burgers*
3. P.F. Chang's/A/BA | *Chinese*
4. Ruth's Chris/A/BA/E | *Steak*
5. Fogo de Chão | *Braz./Steak*
6. Bahama Breeze | *Caribbean*
7. Capital Grille | *Steak*
8. Roy's | *Hawaiian*
9. McCormick/Schmick | *Seafood*
10. Fleming's Prime | *Steak*

KEY NEWCOMERS

Our editors' picks among this year's arrivals.

Admiral's Cup | *American*
Birroteca | *Italian/Pizza*
David's 1st & 10 | *American*
Fleet Street Kitchen | *American*
Johnny's | *Californian*

Liv2eat | *American*
Maggie's Farm | *American*
McFaul's IronHorse Tavern | *Amer.*
Ouzo Bay | *Greek/Seafood*
Verde Pizza Napolitano | *Pizza*

Top Food

| 29 | Charleston | *American* |

| 28 | Di Pasquale's | *Italian* |

Samos | *Greek*
Vin 909/A | *American*
Bartlett Pear Inn/E | *American*
Prime Rib | *Steak*
Tersiguel's | *French*
Out of the Fire/E | *Amer./Eclec.*
Sushi King | *Japanese*
Milton Inn | *American*
Aldo's | *Italian*
Lewnes' Steak/A | *Steak*
Scossa/E | *Italian*

| 27 | Koco's | *Pub Food* |

Osteria 177/A | *Italian*
Mekong Delta | *Viet.*
R & R Taqueria | *Mexican*
Linwoods | *American*
Peter's Inn | *American*
Salt | *American*

Bon Fresco | *Sandwiches*
Black Olive | *Greek/Seafood*
Woodberry Kitchen | *American*
Broom's Bloom | *Ice Cream*
Chicken Rico | *Peruvian*
Johnny Rad's | *Pizza*
Iggies | *Pizza*
Joss Cafe/A/BA | *Japanese*
Ava's/E | *Italian/Pizza*
Sushi Sono | *Japanese*
Les Folies/A | *French*
Kobe | *Japanese*
Antrim 1844 | *Amer./French*
Attman's Deli | *Deli*
Matthew's Pizza | *Pizza*
Helmand | *Afghan*
Roy's | *Hawaiian*
Jack's Bistro | *Eclectic*
Fogo de Chão | *Brazilian/Steak*
Chaps Pit Beef | *BBQ*

Top Decor

| 29 | Charleston |

| 27 | Antrim 1844 |

Pazo
Wit & Wisdom
Elkridge Furnace Inn

| 26 | Milton Inn |

Mr. Rain's Fun House
Linwoods
Cinghiale
Woodberry Kitchen

Aldo's
Ambassador Dining
Prime Rib
Scossa/E
Kali's Court
Oregon Grille

| 25 | Reynolds Tavern/A |

Severn Inn/A
Blue Hill Tavern
Vin 909/A

Top Service

| 28 | Charleston |

Tersiguel's
Prime Rib

| 27 | Bartlett Pear Inn/E |

Aldo's
Antrim 1844
Scossa/E
Linwoods
Elkridge Furnace Inn
Fogo de Chão

| 26 | Roy's |

Lewnes' Steak/A
Vin 909/A
Milton Inn
Out of the Fire/E
Capital Grille
Ruth's Chris/A/BA/E
Mari Luna Latin Grill
Morton's
Jalapeños/A

Excludes places with low votes, unless otherwise indicated

TOPS BY CUISINE

AMERICAN (NEW)

29 Charleston
28 Vin 909/A
   Bartlett Pear Inn/E
   Out of the Fire/E
   Milton Inn

AMERICAN (TRAD.)

26 Miss Shirley's/A/BA
25 Friendly Farm
   Harry Browne's/A
24 Stanford Grill
   Open Door

BURGERS

24 Five Guys/A/BA
22 Kooper's Chowhound
   Bobby's Burger Palace
   Gino's Burgers & Chicken
   BGR, The Burger Joint

CHINESE

26 Red Pearl
   Szechuan House
25 Grace's Fortune
   David Chu's
23 Hunan Manor

CRAB HOUSES

26 Faidley's
25 Costas Inn
24 Harris Crab/E
   Cantler's Riverside/A
23 Gunning's Seafood

FRENCH

28 Tersiguel's
27 Les Folies/A
   Antrim 1844
26 Petit Louis
25 Café Normandie/A

GREEK

28 Samos
27 Black Olive
25 Paul's Homewood/A
24 Olive Room▽
23 Ikaros

INDIAN

25 Ambassador Dining
24 Akbar
23 House of India

ITALIAN

28 Di Pasquale's
   Aldo's
   Scossa/E
27 Osteria 177/A
   Ava's/E

JAPANESE

28 Sushi King
27 Joss Cafe/A/BA
   Sushi Sono
   Kobe
26 Sushi Hana

MEXICAN/SPANISH

27 R & R Taqueria
   Jalapeños/A
26 Tio Pepe
25 Mari Luna Latin Grill
24 Mari Luna Mexican Grill

PIZZA

27 Johnny Rad's
   Iggies
   Ava's/E
   Matthew's Pizza
24 Joe Squared

PUB FOOD

27 Koco's
   Johnny Rad's
24 Hamilton Tavern
   Galway Bay/A
23 McCabe's

SEAFOOD

27 Black Olive
26 Jerry's Seafood
   Faidley's
   Seaside Restaurant
   Catonsville Gourmet

STEAKHOUSES

28 Prime Rib
   Lewnes' Steak/A
26 Capital Grille
   Ruth's Chris/A/BA/E
   Morton's

THAI

26 Thai Arroy
25 Lemongrass/A
23 Bân Thai

TOPS BY SPECIAL FEATURE

BREAKFAST
26 Miss Shirley's/A/BA
25 Blue Moon
  Main Ingredient/A
  Goldberg's
24 Open Door

BRUNCH
26 b – Bolton Hill Bistro
  Orchard Mkt.
24 Harryman Hse.
23 City Cafe
22 Gertrude's

BUSINESS DINING
29 Charleston
28 Lewnes' Steak/A
27 Linwoods
  Roy's
26 Capital Grille

HOTEL DINING
28 Bartlett Pear Inn/E
27 Antrim 1844
26 Ruth's Chris (Pier 5)
  Morton's (Sheraton Inner Harbor)
25 Salter's/E (Robert Morris)

LIVE ENTERTAINMENT
28 Prime Rib
26 Sotto Sopra
24 Joe Squared
  Germano's Trattoria
23 Jesse Wong's Asean

MEET FOR A DRINK
28 Out of the Fire/E
  Lewnes' Steak/A
26 Cinghiale
24 Victoria Gastro Pub
23 B&O

OUTDOORS
25 Kali's Court
  Ambassador Dining
24 Wine Mkt.
22 Gertrude's
  13.5% Wine/Silo (Locust Pt.)

POWER SCENES
29 Charleston
28 Prime Rib
  Lewnes' Steak/A
27 Linwoods
  Woodberry Kitchen

QUICK BITES
28 Samos
27 R & R Taqueria
  Bon Fresco
  Attman's Deli
26 Faidley's

ROMANTIC
29 Charleston
28 Milton Inn
27 Antrim 1844
25 Kali's Court
  Ambassador Dining

TRENDY
28 Out of the Fire/E
27 Osteria 177/A
24 Chazz
22 13.5% Wine Bar/Silo
19 Bond St. Social

VIEWS
24 Olive Room▽
23 Carrol's Creek/A
  Wit & Wisdom
22 Rusty Scupper
  Waterfront Kitchen

WATERSIDE
24 Cantler's Riverside/A
23 Carrol's Creek/A
  Wit & Wisdom
22 Rusty Scupper
  Waterfront Kitchen

WORTH A TRIP
28 Lewnes' Steak/A (Eastport)
27 Broom's Bloom (Bel Air)
  Antrim 1844 (Westminster)
26 O'Learys/A (Eastport)
25 Salter's/E (Oxford)

TOPS BY LOCATION

ANNAPOLIS

- 28 Vin 909
- 27 Osteria 177
- Joss Cafe
- Les Folies
- Jalapeños

CANTON

- 27 Jack's Bistro
- 26 Mama's on the Half Shell
- 25 Blue Hill Tavern
- 24 Five Guys
- 22 Langermann's

COLUMBIA

- 28 Sushi King
- 27 Bon Fresco
- Sushi Sono
- 26 Red Pearl
- 25 Iron Bridge Wine Co.

EASTERN SHORE

- 28 Bartlett Pear Inn
- Out of the Fire
- Scossa
- 27 Ava's
- 26 Ruth's Chris

EASTPORT

- 28 Lewnes' Steak
- 26 Ruth's Chris
- O'Learys Seafood
- 23 Carrol's Creek
- 22 Boatyard Bar & Gril

FELLS POINT

- 27 Peter's Inn
- Salt
- Black Olive
- Johnny Rad's
- 25 Kali's Court

HAMPDEN

- 25 Grano Pasta Bar
- 24 Corner BYOB
- 23 McCabe's
- Alchemy
- 22 13.5% Wine Bar

HARBOR EAST

- 29 Charleston
- 27 Roy's
- 26 Cinghiale
- 25 Pazo
- Fleming's Prime

INNER HARBOR

- 27 Fogo de Chão
- 26 Capital Grille
- Ruth's Chris
- Morton's
- Miss Shirley's

LITTLE ITALY

- 28 Aldo's
- 26 La Tavola
- La Scala
- 25 Da Mimmo
- 24 Amicci's

LUTHERVILLE/TIMONIUM

- 26 Sushi Hana
- Szechuan House
- 24 Liberatore's
- Edo Sushi
- 23 BlueStone

MT. VERNON

- 28 Prime Rib
- 27 Joss Cafe
- Helmand
- 26 Sotto Sopra
- Tio Pepe

SOUTH BALTIMORE

- 26 Thai Arroy
- 24 Bluegrass
- 23 Regi's
- Mr. Rain's Fun House
- 22 Blue Agave

TOWSON

- 26 Sushi Hana
- Orchard Mkt.
- 25 Atwater's
- 24 Five Guys
- Pho Dat Thanh

Best Buys

In order of rating.

1. Broom's Bloom
2. Ann's Dari Creme
3. R & R Taqueria
4. Bon Fresco
5. Greg's Bagels
6. Gino's Burgers & Chicken
7. Sofi's Crepes/A/BA
8. Five Guys/A/BA
9. Chaps Pit Beef
10. Grilled Cheese & Co.
11. Goldberg's
12. Chicken Rico
13. First Watch
14. Matthew's Pizza
15. Andy Nelson's BBQ
16. Di Pasquale's
17. Big Bad Wolf's House of BBQ
18. Atwater's
19. Negril
20. Baugher's
21. Attman's Delicatessen
22. Sip & Bite Restaurant
23. Chick & Ruth's Delly/A
24. Open Door
25. BGR, The Burger Joint
26. Iggies
27. An Loi
28. Nando's Peri-Peri/A/BA
29. Dangerously Delicious Pies
30. Pho Dat Thanh

OTHER GOOD VALUES

Akbar
Ale Mary's
Artifact Coffee
Bagby Pizza Co.
Blue Moon Cafe
Breakfast Shoppe
Coal Fire
Corner BYOB
Dizz
Faidley's
49 West/A
Golden West Cafe
Grano Pasta Bar
Hamilton Tavern
House of India
Joe Squared
Johnny Rad's
Level/A
Nacho Mama's
One World Cafe
Orchard Mkt.
Piedigrotta Bakery
Samos
Spice & Dice
Suburban House
Talara
Teavolve
Towson Diner
Verde Pizza Napolitano
Woman's Industrial Kitchen

BALTIMORE, ANNAPOLIS AND THE EASTERN SHORE RESTAURANT DIRECTORY

Baltimore

Adam's Eve *American*

FOOD	DECOR	SERVICE	COST
-	-	-	I

Canton | 3328 Foster Ave. (Highland Ave.) | 443-619-0856 | www.adamsevegastropub.com

At this cheerful Canton gastropub, the New American farm-to-table menu of burgers, steaks and salads is courtesy of Mark Littleton, who helped launch Annabel Lee Tavern; the vintage posters of '70s bands, free popcorn in the bar, local drafts and Maryland wines are aimed at an after-work crowd and grown-ups from the neighborhood in search of a sedate repast.

NEW Admiral's Cup ● *American*

FOOD	DECOR	SERVICE	COST
-	-	-	M

Fells Point | 1647 Thames St. (Broadway) | 410-534-5555 | www.theadmiralscup.com

This historic Fells Point tavern was revamped and relaunched by the Kali's Restaurant Group as a grown-up spot for mingling over drinks (lots of local brews on tap) and casual American eats, including plenty of seafood; the deep-blue interior combines sailcloth banquettes, tin ceilings and reclaimed floors, plus there are plenty of TVs for sports fans as well as live music Wednesday–Sunday nights.

Aida Bistro & Wine Bar ⊠ *Italian*

FOOD	DECOR	SERVICE	COST
24	21	23	$44

Columbia | 6741 Columbia Gateway Dr. (Rte. 175) | 410-953-0500 | www.aidabistro.com

"Real homemade pasta" and "innovative" Italian small and large plates – plus a "top-notch" "wine-on-tap program" – make this bistro/wine bar with a "wide-open" contemporary setting in an "unexpected" business-park locale a Howard County favorite; if it strikes some as "a bit pricey", the owners "make it seem like you're eating at their house", and hard-core fans are willing to splurge on the chef's table to watch the cooking action.

Akbar *Indian*

FOOD	DECOR	SERVICE	COST
24	18	22	$25

Mt. Vernon | 823 N. Charles St. (bet. Madison & Read Sts.) | 410-539-0944
Columbia | Columbia Mktpl. | 9400 Snowden River Pkwy.
(bet. Carved Stone Way & Rustling Leaf) | 410-381-3600
www.akbar-restaurant.com

"Authentic" Indian dishes "fit for the raja" can be piled high at the "excellent-value" lunch buffets or served by the "attentive but not hovering" staffs at these subcontinental survivors occupying an "underground lair" in Mt. Vernon and a strip mall in Columbia; if the decor's somewhat "dated", few mind.

Alchemy Ⓜ *American*

FOOD	DECOR	SERVICE	COST
23	21	22	$40

Hampden | 1011 W. 36th St. (bet. Hickory & Roland Aves.) |
410-366-1163 | www.alchemyon36.com

Ever-present chef Michael Matassa's "inspired", moderately priced New American offerings are well paired with wine by the sommelier, his wife Debi, at this Hampdenite "right on the 'Avenue'"; the "enthusiastic and helpful" staff ably plays upstairs/downstairs in the bi-level space that's "snug" but "sleek."

	FOOD	DECOR	SERVICE	COST

Aldo's *Italian*
28 | 26 | 27 | $57

Little Italy | 306 S. High St. (Fawn St.) | 410-727-0700 |
www.aldositaly.com

"Splendid" "old-world Italian" cuisine is "served with class" by tuxedoed waiters at this venerable Little Italy "gem" that's "worth all the hype" (and the liras) thanks to chef-owners Aldo and Sergio Vitale, who "make you feel Italian"; a light-filled atrium is the centerpiece of the "serene", "elegant" dining room, which many deem the perfect place "to entertain clients, take a romantic date or just spoil yourself."

NEW Ale House Columbia *American*
- | - | - | I

Columbia | 6480 Dobbin Center Way (Dobbin Rd.) | 443-546-3640 |
www.thealehousecolumbia.com

While the focal point may be the lengthy beer list (several dozen on tap, more by the bottle), this new Columbia watering hole is also becoming known for its family-friendly atmosphere and affordable, wide-ranging American menu; the sprawling space encompasses several bars and dining areas, all in a contemporary style and loaded with TVs, and there's a large patio to boot.

Ale Mary's ● *Pub Food*
22 | 19 | 22 | $23

Fells Point | 1939 Fleet St. (Washington St.) | 410-276-2044 |
www.alemarys.com

There are "enough photos of nuns to make any lapsed Catholic feel guilty (or at least giggle)" mixed in with other "campy" religious ephemera at this late-night, "laid-back" "neighborhood" watering hole in Fells Point; the taps are loaded with "prime" suds and helmed by "personable" bartenders, and the cheap eats provide a "fun twist on classic pub fare" (multiple styles of tater tots, Krispy Kreme bread pudding).

Alewife ● *American*
22 | 20 | 21 | $30

Downtown West | 21 N. Eutaw St. (Fayette St.) | 410-545-5112 |
www.alewifebaltimore.com

A "monstrously delicious" "smoke burger" tops the midpriced American menu (though a recent chef change may put the Food rating in question) at this Downtown West gastropub housed in an "intriguingly" reimagined 1800s bank that retains a whiff of gaslight in its coffered ceilings and ye olde floors; it's also known for its "phenomenal" beer offerings, including 40 craft brews on tap, and a solid staff that's adept at getting ticket-holders to the nearby Hippodrome by curtain time.

Ambassador Dining Room *Indian*
25 | 26 | 25 | $41

Homewood | Ambassador Apts. | 3811 Canterbury Rd. (bet. 39th St. & University Pkwy.) | 410-366-1484 | www.ambassadordining.com

A Homewood apartment building hides this "delicious" "time machine" to "colonial India" that's "romantic" whether dining in the "gorgeous" garden in warm weather or in the "quiet and dignified" wood-beamed interior with fireplaces blazing in season; "thoughtful and timely" service contributes to the "expensive but worth it" designation, and free valet parking is a nice extra.

Amicci's *Italian*   24 | 19 | 23 | $29

Little Italy | 231 S. High St. (bet. Fawn & Stiles Sts.) | 410-528-1096 | www.amiccis.com

There's "plenty of cheese and sauce to go around" at this "reason-ably" priced, "family-friendly" Little Italy longtimer in a "simple" space decorated with movie posters; thanks to the "attentive" staff and "huge" servings – like the "big-as-your-head" *pane rotundo,* a bread bowl stuffed with shrimp – "you won't go home hungry."

Andy Nelson's BBQ ⊠ *BBQ*   26 | 14 | 22 | $15

Cockeysville | 11007 York Rd. (Wight Ave.) | 410-527-1226 | www.andynelsonsbbq.com

If you miss the "pig on the roof", follow your nose to this "venerable" Cockeysville "hole-in-the-wall", where "succulent" pulled pork "drenched" in "special sauce" "tastes as good as it smells"; besides, "you can't beat the price" or the sides with "kick"; P.S. check out the pigskin "memorabilia" from the eponymous Baltimore Colts safety.

An Loi *Vietnamese*   23 | 13 | 19 | $16

Columbia | 7104 Minstrel Way (Snowden River Pkwy.) | 410-381-3188

"Soul-warming" pho noodle soup bowls over connoisseurs at this "delicious" Columbia Vietnamese that also throws in some Korean fusion dishes for good measure; some "don't think much of its plain decor and strip-mall location", but it's always "packed at lunch" on account of "prompt" service and "cheap" tabs.

Annabel Lee Tavern ⊘🄳 *American*   26 | 24 | 23 | $27

Highlandtown | 601 S. Clinton St. (Fleet St.) | 410-522-2929 | www.annabelleetavern.com

This Edgar Allen Poe–themed tavern on the edge of Highlandtown near Canton is a favorite local "haunt" with its "killer" New American menu and moderate tabs; while the small place gets "crowded" and "enthusiastically noisy", Poe fans can sip "clever" cocktails and "read the writing on the walls – literally" (they're covered in excerpts), prompting one reviewer to quoth "I will dine here evermore."

Ann's Dari Creme *Hot Dogs*   25 | 14 | 25 | $10

Glen Burnie | 7918 Ritchie Hwy. (Americana Circle) | 410-761-1231

"They don't make them" like this "kitschy" red, white and blue "Ritchie Highway landmark" anymore, a roadside stand beloved by several generations for its "top-notch deep-fried hot dog subs" and "scrumptious shakes" served by a "witty" staff that "never writes anything down and always gets your order right"; there are a few stools inside, but better to "eat in your car" or at a picnic table.

Antrim 1844's Smokehouse Restaurant *American/French*   27 | 27 | 27 | $89

Westminster | Antrim 1844 | 30 Trevanion Rd. (Rte. 140) | 410-756-6812 | www.antrim1844.com

"A night of luxury" awaits at this "historic" inn just outside Westminster, where the "romantic" experience may start with "hand-passed hors d'oeuvres" "elegantly served" in the drawing room before moving to the dining room for a multicourse French-inspired New American feast that's "as stellar as the starlit sky" – best viewed via a "delightful" stroll through the formal gardens after dinner; it will add considerably to the "splurge", but "stay overnight for the full, unforgettable experience."

Artifact Coffee *Coffeehouse* `- | - | - | I`

Clipper Mill | 1500 Union Ave. (Buena Vista Ave.) | 410-449-2287 | www.artifactcoffee.com

Expanding on Woodberry Kitchen's passion for caffeine is this rustic coffeehouse in a reclaimed stone factory building near Clipper Mill; a simple American menu of housemade pastries in the morning as well as local and seasonal lunches and a prix fixe–only dinner share the philosophy, though not the high prices, of the parental unit.

Attman's Delicatessen *Deli* `27 | 12 | 20 | $16`

East Baltimore | 1019 E. Lombard St. (Exeter St.) | 410-563-2666 | www.attmansdeli.com

The "best corned beef this side of Brooklyn" and "fabulous" pickles straight out of the barrel star at this "fantastic old-fashioned deli" in East Baltimore; ok, the decor ("what decor?") "doesn't cut the mustard", and there's "always a line", but the "efficient" counter help who "shout your order" and provide "running commentary" really "keep it moving", and it's "reasonably priced" to boot.

Atwater's *Bakery* `25 | 16 | 21 | $16`

Bare Hills | 1407 Clarkview Rd. (Falls Rd.) | 410-296-0373 🗷
Bare Hills | 1425 Clarkview Rd. (Falls Rd.) | 410-821-6021 🗷
York Road Corridor | Belvedere Square Mkt. | 529 E. Belvedere Ave. (York Rd.) | 410-323-2396
Catonsville | 815 Frederick Rd. (bet. Mellor & Newburg Aves.) | 410-747-4120
Towson | 798 Kenilworth Dr. (West Rd.) | 410-938-8775
www.atwaters.biz

Daily choices of "homemade" soups at Ned Atwater's bakery/cafe empire are "innovative takes on classic comfort", while breads and "artisan" sandwiches, though "a tad pricey", are "made with love" from "locally grown" ingredients; there's a "pared-down" aesthetic across the chain, but each staff is "sweet and helpful."

Azul 17 *Mexican* `23 | 22 | 22 | $33`

Columbia | Columbia Mktpl. | 9400 Snowden River Pkwy. (bet. Carved Stone & Rustling Leaf) | 410-309-9717

This "upscale Mexican" in Columbia "rocks the guac" with tableside preparation by a "congenial" staff and a "contemporary" look that makes you feel "like you're in a cool club in the city"; a "margarita for every mood" and weekend DJs help make it a "girls' night out favorite."

b – A Bolton Hill Bistro 🅼 *American* `26 | 21 | 24 | $39`

Downtown North | 1501 Bolton St. (Mosher St.) | 410-383-8600 | www.b-bistro.com

"One of Bolton Hill's most valuable assets" is this "cute and quirky" corner bistro with big picture windows, "a real neighborhood" spot

| | FOOD | DECOR | SERVICE | COST |

that nevertheless "outperforms trendier places" with its "creative" American dishes made with "lovely locally sourced ingredients" (though a recent chef change may outdate the Food rating); just be prepared to sit "elbow-to-elbow" or grab a table "outside in summer."

Bagby Pizza Company *Pizza*

23 | 18 | 21 | $18

Harbor East | 1006 Fleet St. (bet. Central Ave. & Exeter St.) | 410-605-0444 | www.bagbypizza.com

"Crispy", "cracker-thin" pizza loaded with an "abundance" of "novel ingredients" is this Harbor East spot's bag; the "casual" distressed-wood-and-brick look, "young", "friendly" staff and "reasonable" tabs are an alternative to many of the "upscale" area's more formal options.

Bahama Breeze *Caribbean*

23 | 23 | 22 | $27

Towson | 100 E. Joppa Rd. (Virginia Ave.) | 410-821-7090 | www.bahamabreeze.com

A "mini vacation" awaits just outside Towson Town Center at this "jumping" Caribbean chain outpost that "exceeds expectations" by dishing up "tasty" eats with "a tropical twist" within "colorful", "beach"-y environs; service is suitably "attentive", and with moderate prices, open-air seating and live music on weekends, it promises a "fun night out with friends or family."

B&O American
Brasserie *American*

23 | 24 | 22 | $43

Downtown | Hotel Monaco | 2 N. Charles St. (bet. Baltimore St. & Wilkes Ln.) | 443-692-6172 | www.bandorestaurant.com

At the Hotel Monaco's "historic" beaux arts digs Downtown, this "lively" American turns out "innovative", seasonal small plates, brick-oven items and mains; the space is "very *Mad Men*", with a "chic" crowd downing "creative" drinks in the lounge and, overlooking the action from the mezzanine, a "swanky" dining room.

Bân Thai ⊠ *Thai*

23 | 16 | 20 | $23

Mt. Vernon | 340 N. Charles St. (bet. Mulberry & Pleasant Sts.) | 410-727-7971 | www.banthai.us

The "always reliable" Thai standards at this North Charles Street storefront are "like grandma would have made if she were from Chiang Mai"; though some describe the ambiance as a "glorified take-out place", a majority praises it as a "good lunch option" for its "super-cheap prices" and "gracious" service.

Basta Pasta *Italian*

21 | 19 | 22 | $27

Fallston | 2745 Fallston Rd. (Baldwin Mill Rd.) | 410-692-5200
Timonium | 60 W. Timonium Rd. (Greenspring Dr.) | 410-308-0838
www.bastapastamd.com

Service is "on point" at these "suburban red-sauce joints" plating up "consistent" Italian eats in Fallston and Timonium; the "casual" strip-mall digs are "nice" enough, but the main appeal is the "decent" tab, made even more of a "value" given that the "huge" portion sizes have many "bringing leftovers home."

	FOOD	DECOR	SERVICE	COST

Baugher's *American*

20 | 13 | 23 | $15

Westminster | 289 W. Main St. (New Windsor Rd.) | 410-848-7413 | www.baughers.com

"Down-home, country-style" cooking is just "like grandma used to make" at this "timeless" Westminster all-American restaurant where much of the produce comes from the family's nearby orchard (and is also for sale at the adjacent farm stand); sure, it's "nothing fancy", but the "simple", "homey" digs get a boost from "cheerful" servers, and the "old-timey food" is matched by "old-timey prices"; P.S. for dessert: "homemade ice cream and pie."

Bertha's ● *Seafood*

22 | 18 | 21 | $28

Fells Point | 734 S. Broadway (Lancaster St.) | 410-327-5795 | www.berthas.com

A "must when visiting Baltimore" insist fans of this Fells Point "institution" famous for its "sweet, huge mussels" served with "out-of-this-world" dipping sauces by "friendly" staffers; other midpriced offerings are just "so-so", and if the decor looks like it "hasn't changed since Millard Fillmore occupied the White House", most call that "character", deeming it a "warm, cheery place" to "hang out", especially Tuesday–Saturday, when the bar has live music.

BGR, The Burger Joint *Burgers*

22 | 15 | 17 | $15

Columbia | Columbia Crossing | 6250 Columbia Crossing Circle (Dobbin Rd.) | 443-319-5542 | www.bgrtheburgerjoint.com

See review in the Washington, DC, Directory.

Big Bad Wolf's House of Barbeque *BBQ*

26 | 12 | 23 | $15

Northeast Baltimore | 5713 Harford Rd. (White Ave.) | 410-444-6422

"Not at all big and bad", this "little" yellow-brick smokehouse in Hamilton 'cues up some of the "best barbecue in Baltimore" with its "first-class" ribs, pulled pork and "amazing Eastern Shore"–style chicken; the staff is "friendly", but since "there isn't much seating" in the "modest" environs, "get your food to go"; P.S. they cater.

NEW Birroteca *Italian/Pizza*

– | – | – | M

Hampden | 1520 Clipper Rd. (Ash St.) | 443-708-1934 | www.bmorebirroteca.com

A sudsy riff on the enoteca, this freshly brewed Hampdenite serves as a showcase for locally brewed beer, backed up by thin-crust pizzas with seasonal toppings and other midpriced Italian offerings; the rustic refurbished setting in an old stone mill is often packed with hipsters sampling the goods before hauling home growlers.

Bistro Blanc *American*

26 | 22 | 23 | $42

Glenelg | 3800 Ten Oaks Rd. (bet. Ivory & Triadelphia Rds.) | 410-489-7907 | www.bistroblancmd.com

"Out in the boonies" between Baltimore and the District (in Glenelg) lies this "high-class" "hideaway" that's part wine shop, wine bar and "pricey" New American restaurant, with a "fabulous" selection of vintages, some proffered by "knowledgeable" servers, others by an Enomatic dispenser; not to be outdone, chef-owner Marc Dixon "cooks up a storm", concocting "gorgeous" small and large plates that are "fun" to share "with friends" amid the racks of wine.

Bistro Rx *American* ▽ 25 | 23 | 22 | $33

Highlandtown | 2901 E. Baltimore St. (Linwood Ave.) | 410-276-0820 | www.bistrorx.net

The "ambitious" New American menu at this "friendly" Patterson Park corner spot includes a "good mix of reasonably priced sandwiches and more expensive entrees" along with "great-value wines and cocktails"; exposed-brick walls belie its past as a pharmacy, but it's still a panacea for "locals" who prize it as an "awesome" brunch spot, especially at its sidewalk tables.

Black Olive *Greek/Seafood* 27 | 22 | 23 | $54

Fells Point | 814 S. Bond St. (Shakespeare St.) | 410-276-7141 | www.theblackolive.com

"Swimmingly fresh" fish is whisked from the ice display to be "prepared simply and beautifully" in the "delectable Greek style" before being filleted tableside at this "authentic" Fells Point Hellenic seafood specialist; "knowledgeable" servers and an "elegant, relaxed atmosphere" help make it a "perennial favorite" for those "willing to pay" the "heavy price tag"; P.S. nearby Olive Room has rooftop dining.

Blue Agave Restaurante y Tequileria ● *Mexican* 22 | 21 | 21 | $31

South Baltimore | 1032 Light St. (bet. Cross & Poultney Sts.) | 410-576-3938 | www.blueagaverestaurant.com

This "*muy* fun" Federal Hill Mexican eatery and tequila bar has an exposed-brick setting with classic ceramic-tiled tabletops, though a post-Survey ownership change may outdate Food and Service ratings; for partying types, there's plenty of top-shelf tequila (more than 130 labels), "amazing 'ritas" (including frozen varieties) and "extended happy-hour pricing."

Bluegrass Ⓜ *American* 24 | 22 | 23 | $39

South Baltimore | 1500 S. Hanover St. (Fort Ave.) | 410-244-5101 | www.bluegrasstavern.com

"Homemade charcuterie" and a mix of "classic" and more "adventurous" Southern-accented American fare make this midpriced Federal Hill venue "a great neighborhood find" – especially in warm weather when "they throw open the doors and windows" of the rustic, blue-green space; the entire staff is "fantastic", but the bartenders are especially "terrific" say those sweet on sour mash, who dub it a "bourbon-lover's heaven."

Blue Hill Tavern *American* 25 | 25 | 23 | $39

Canton | 938 S. Conkling St. (Dillon St.) | 443-388-9363 | www.bluehilltavern.com

"Beautiful people and great food intersect" at this midpriced Canton resto-lounge offering "innovative", "well-prepared" New American fare in an "urban-chic" interior or outside; "warm", "solicitous" servers add to the "grown-up atmosphere", and though the "bar scene can get loud", it's still a "local favorite"; P.S. free valet parking offered.

	FOOD	DECOR	SERVICE	COST

Blue Moon Cafe *American*

25 | 19 | 21 | $22

Fells Point | 1621 Aliceanna St. (bet. Bethel St. & B'way) | 410-522-3940 | www.bluemoonbaltimore.com

"Eccentric, eclectic, exciting" sums up this "funky" Fells Point American "favorite" known for its "unique" breakfast and lunch items (e.g. "amazing" Cap'n Crunch French toast") and "off-the-wall" decor; "great prices" "guarantee looong waits on weekends" when "crowds can be as large as the portions", but just "accept" it, as everything's served with "flair" and perfect "after a night out drinking"; P.S. open 24 hours Friday and Saturday (7 AM–3 PM otherwise).

BlueStone *Seafood*

23 | 22 | 23 | $36

Timonium | 11 W. Aylesbury Rd. (Business Park Dr.) | 410-561-1100 | www.bluestoneonline.net

Timonium "locals flock" to this "upscale, trendy"-looking New American seafood specialist for its "above-average" fish preparations that are a relative "value"; a "wide range of selections from full dinners to light fare", and an "inviting bar" with a "swingin' happy hour" please all comers, as does "considerate" service.

Bobby's Burger Palace ❷ *Burgers*

22 | 19 | 19 | $16

NEW **Hanover** | Maryland Live! Casino | 7002 Arundel Mills Circle (Arundel Mills Blvd.) | 443-661-4147 | www.bobbysburgerpalace.com
See review in the Washington, DC, Directory.

Bond Street Social ❷ *Eclectic*

19 | 25 | 21 | $35

Fells Point | 901 S. Bond St. (Thames St.) | 443-449-6234 | www.bondstreetsocial.com

This "terrific" Fells Point "hangout" is a magnet for the "young and hip" on account of its "stunning, modern yet inviting" wood-and-steel decor and harbor views, though to sensitive ears it's possibly "the noisiest place on Earth"; an Eclectic array of gently priced, "tasty" tapas and mains are washed down by huge 'social' drinks (80-oz. jars) served by a "great" crew.

Bon Fresco ⬛ *Sandwiches*

27 | 14 | 22 | $11

Columbia | 6945 Oakland Mills Rd. (Snowden River Pkwy.) | 410-290-3434
Once a "well-kept secret", this "inexpensive" Columbia sandwich shop is now "bumping" with "weekday lunch" crowds, thanks to owner Gerald Koh's "crusty and chewy", "beyond-fresh" housemade bread, the bedrock for sandwiches "lovingly" filled with "top-notch" fixin's (and also served alongside "dreamy" soups); the "friendly" staff keeps things moving in the "narrow", no-frills digs.

Breakfast Shoppe *American*

▽ 25 | 18 | 22 | $14

Severna Park | Park Plaza Shopping Ctr. | 552 Ritchie Hwy. (McKinsey Rd.) | 410-544-8599 | www.thebreakfastshoppe.com

"Excellent" American eats – including "some updates on classic breakfast dishes" like the meal-in-a-skillet backpackers pie – are the wares on offer at this Severna Park strip-maller outfitted with curvy banquettes and greenery; though waits can be "daunting" at peak times, a "friendly" staff and budget prices keep most shoppers happy.

	FOOD	DECOR	SERVICE	COST

Brewer's Art *American* | 25 | 24 | 23 | $33 |

Mt. Vernon | 1106 N. Charles St. (bet. Biddle & Chase Sts.) |
410-547-6925 | www.thebrewersart.com

It's easy to "fill up on beer" because the "housemade" Belgian-style brews are "affordable and delicious" at this "bohemian bourgeois paradise" in Mt. Vernon – but foodies say the "sophisticated" New American eats are equally "outstanding"; set in an *"Age of Innocence"*-era townhouse, the "incredibly atmospheric" upstairs encompasses an "elegant" dining room and "boisterous" bar, while the "dungeon-like" downstairs lounge lures local art students.

Broom's Bloom Dairy Ⓜ *Ice Cream* | 27 | 20 | 25 | $10 |

Bel Air | 1700 S. Fountain Green Rd./Rte. 543 (Rte. 136) |
410-399-2697 | www.bbdairy.com

Its "awesome" "homemade" ice cream is best enjoyed "with a view of the cows who contributed" at this "friendly", family-owned "country" cafe in "idyllic" rural Harford County that's ranked as Greater Baltimore's No. 1 Bang for the Buck; in addition to the "relaxing farm atmosphere", "simple" soups and sandwiches give many I-95 drivers "the energy to continue on" their road trips.

NEW The Bun Shop ● *Eclectic* | - | - | - | I |

Mt. Vernon | 239 W. Read St. (Tyson St.) | 410-989-2033

The objective of this new Mt. Vernon specialist – to serve street-food-style buns from various cultures – is novel, and further distinguishing it from the cafe crowd is a 3 AM closing time, Vietnamese coffee and a BYO policy; live music and literary events occasionally transform the loftlike space, with its collection of vintage furniture and glass terrariums, into a neighborhood salon.

Caesar's Den *Italian* | 23 | 19 | 24 | $40 |

Little Italy | 223 S. High St. (bet. Fawn & Stiles Sts.) | 410-547-0820 |
www.caesarsden.com

The "old-school" service at this Little Italy "classic" is a "throwback to another time" that's bolstered by "generous portions" of "well-prepared standards"; the tabs aren't au courant either, so even though the "subdued" setting is "nothing flashy", it's still a "nice evening out."

Cafe Bretton Ⓜ *French* | ▽ 27 | 23 | 26 | $47 |

Severna Park | 849 Baltimore-Annapolis Blvd. (Smith Rd.) |
410-647-8222 | www.cafe-bretton.com

"Out of the way" in Severna Park, this "quaint" bistro matching "high-quality" "classic French fare" with a "complete" wine list "feels like a romantic château in Provence" (with prices to match); the staff ensures "a good time", especially if sitting on the verdant back patio with a "view of the garden", the source for many ingredients.

Café de Paris ⓈⓂ *French* | 24 | 21 | 23 | $41 |

Columbia | 8808 Centre Park Dr. (Rte. 108) | 410-997-3904 |
www.cafedepariscolumbia.com

For "a taste of France in the suburbs", gourmands head to this white-tablecloths-and-red-banquettes "gem hidden" in a Columbia "office park" for "delicious" "French country cooking" along with a "fantastic" selection of wines (there's also a separate crêperie); the "unpretentious" staff is headed by the "solicitous" owner Erik Rochard, who "treats you like family" and occasionally entertains on his flute.

Café Gia *Italian*   22 | 23 | 22 | $33

Little Italy | 410 S. High St. (Eastern Ave.) | 410-685-6727 | www.cafegias.com

Reminiscent of a "corner bistro in Rome", this Little Italy ristorante is festooned with "welcoming" murals on the facade that carry into the "art deco" interior where "mama's cooking" gets "an updated twist"; "personalized service" and fair prices complete the "homey" effect.

Cafe Hon *American*   16 | 18 | 17 | $23

Hampden | 1002 W. 36th St. (Roland Ave.) | 410-243-1230 | www.cafehon.com

A "landmark" of "Baltimore quirk", this Hampdenite "marches on" following a "trademark dispute" over the word 'hon' and a subsequent "Gordon Ramsay makeover" that tweaked the menu of "dependable", "affordable" American "comfort food" and modded up the decor; some find "more big hair than great fare", declaring "meh, hon", but "out-of-town visitors" and local supporters still "love" going "for the camp of it."

Café Troia *Italian*   23 | 21 | 23 | $45

Towson | 31 W. Allegheny Ave. (Washington Ave.) | 410-337-0133 | www.cafetroia.com

"Inspired", "authentic" Italian cuisine and a "superior wine list" make this "comfortable" but "upscale", ochre-hued spot in Towson a "longtime favorite" for well-heeled suburbanites; service is "professional", but "be prepared to hand over your wallet" – unless it's Sunday, which is half-price wine night.

Cafe Zen *Chinese*   22 | 15 | 20 | $23

York Road Corridor | 438 E. Belvedere Ave. (York Rd.) | 410-532-0022 | www.cafezen.us

The "diverse menu" of "Chinese food with imagination" ("don't miss the string bean rolls") has made this "spare" but contemporary eatery a "North Baltimore mainstay"; "low" prices and "cordial" service make it an "excellent" dining option before or after shopping at nearby Belvedere Square, though "carryout" works too.

The Capital Grille *Steak*   26 | 25 | 26 | $62

Inner Harbor | 500 E. Pratt St. (Gay St.) | 443-703-4064 | www.thecapitalgrille.com

See review in the Washington, DC, Directory.

Carlyle Club *Indian*   ▽ 21 | 22 | 23 | $37

Homewood | The Carlyle | 500 W. University Pkwy. (bet. 39th & 40th Sts.) | 410-243-5454 | www.carlyleclub.com

This "hidden" Indian "gem" (a sibling of Homewood's Ambassador), "nestled" just off the Johns Hopkins Homewood campus, specializes in coastal subcontinental cuisine that's "delicious", if pricey, and deftly served by a "great" staff; the "peaceful and intimate" space is "surprisingly romantic", with booths for two making it "ideal for dates."

Carolina Kitchen *Southern*
25 | 23 | 23 | $24

Largo | 800 Shoppers Way (Harry S. Truman Dr.) | 301-350-2929 | www.thecarolinakitchen.com

Southern "home cooking" "just like at grandma's (except here the furniture and dishes actually match)" is the word on these Largo-Hyattsville comfort stations; they're "inviting" places, with polished wood and homey touches, offering "good value" that a local might visit "every Friday night."

Catonsville Gourmet *Seafood*
26 | 20 | 23 | $35

Catonsville | 829 Frederick Rd. (bet. Mellor & Newburg Aves.) | 410-788-0005 | www.catonsvillegourmet.com

"Not to be missed if you're in the western suburbs", this "fantastic find" in Catonsville nets fans with its "wonderful", "expertly prepared" seafood with occasional Asian touches; while the "noise level" is often high in the "classy"-"casual", nautically minded digs, BYO "helps to keep costs down" (the "knowledgeable" staff is happy to provide the "essentials"); P.S. no reservations means occasional "waits", but the in-house fish market is a "quick" take-out option.

Cazbar ● *Turkish*
24 | 21 | 21 | $29

Mt. Vernon | 316 N. Charles St. (bet. Pleasant & Saratoga Sts.) | 410-528-1222 | www.cazbar.pro

A "delectable magic carpet ride" – woven from "elegantly spiced" kebabs, "dreamy" mezes and "Turkish coffee to die for" – is in store at this "cool", "dimly" lit Ottoman "hideaway" in Mt. Vernon tended by an "informed" staff; weekend belly dancers and DJs add to "value", and you can get your puff on in the upstairs hookah lounge.

Chaps Pit Beef *BBQ*
27 | 10 | 23 | $12

East Baltimore | 5801 Pulaski Hwy. (Erdman Ave.) | 410-483-2379 | www.chapspitbeef.com

"Meat paired with meat with a side of meat" makes for "carnivore heaven" at this "East Bawlmer" pit-beef stand that's famous for its "smoked deliciousness on a bun" – and where "the only green thing may be relish"; service is solid, and prices are low, but "prepare for lines" and the fact that it's located "in the parking lot of a strip club."

Charleston ☒ *American*
29 | 28 | 28 | $99

Harbor East | 1000 Lancaster St. (Exeter St.) | 410-332-7373 | www.charlestonrestaurant.com

Cindy Wolf remains "at the top of her game", applying "world-class technique" to "Lowcountry" cuisine to create "phenomenal" New American masterpieces at her Harbor East "destination", which ranks as "Baltimore's best restaurant" with its No. 1 ratings for Food, Decor and Service; "no detail goes unnoticed" by the "superlative" staffers, who "spoil" guests with selections from co-owner Tony Foreman's "epic" wine list in a "stunningly beautiful" space; just "be prepared" for the multicourse menu's "sticker shock" – for many, it's a "once-every-few-years kind of place."

	FOOD	DECOR	SERVICE	COST

Chazz: A Bronx Original *Italian/Pizza*   24 | 25 | 23 | $32

Harbor East | 1415 Aliceanna St. (Eden St.) | 410-522-5511 |
www.chazzbronxoriginal.com

"Welcome to the Bronx", or as close as you can get to it in Harbor
East, says the "authentic" decor (subway tiles, old-timey photo murals) at actor Chazz Palminteri's Arthur Avenue–Italian theme park
that's "loads of fun"; the "excellent" menu, including "awesome"
coal-fired pizza, is overseen by the Vitale family of Aldo's, prompting
even "New Yorkers" to praise the food and "courteous" service.

Cheesecake Factory *American*   24 | 22 | 22 | $30

Inner Harbor | Harborplace Pratt Street Pavilion | 201 E. Pratt St.
(Light St.) | 410-234-3990
Hanover | Arundel Mills | 7002 Arundel Mills Circle (Arundel Mills Blvd.) |
410-579-5867 ◐
Columbia | Mall in Columbia | 10300 Little Patuxent Pkwy.
(Wincopin Circle) | 410-997-9311
Towson | Towson Town Ctr. | 825 Dulaney Valley Rd. (Fairmount Ave.) |
410-337-7411
www.thecheesecakefactory.com

"Folks need 15 minutes" just to "pore over" the "book"-length menu at
this "perennial favorite" (indeed, it's ranked the Most Popular chain in
Baltimore) that has lots of fans thanks to "scrumptious", midpriced
American eats in "insanely large" portion sizes, including the "sinfully
rich" signature cheesecakes; service is "prompt and courteous", and
the "loud", "brassy", glitzy setting makes for a "lively" meal, though tables are tightly packed, and "eternal" waits "require patience."

Chef Paolino *Italian/Pizza*   21 | 17 | 18 | $17

Catonsville | 726 Frederick Rd. (Ingleside Ave.) | 410-747-4949 |
www.chefpaolinoscafe.com

A "go-to" for Catonsville locals when they just "don't feel like cooking", this "quick and easy", kid-friendly cafe fits the bill inexpensively,
with a "variety" of solid Italian fare and "traditional NYC-style" pizza;
the staff is "polite", but service is "minimal" – i.e. you order at the
front counter of the modest space decorated with murals of Italy.

NEW The Chesapeake ◐ *American*   – | – | – | E

Downtown North | 1701 N. Charles St. (Lanvale St.) | 410-547-2760 |
www.thechesapeakebaltimore.com

One of Baltimore's landmark restaurants has been reborn after decades lying fallow, as new owners have dusted off this grand old
Downtown North space and completely updated it with leather banquettes, a large marble bar and other elegant touches; the upscale
American offerings include cheese and charcuterie boards and raw
bar items in addition to heartier entrees.

Chiapparelli's *Italian*   24 | 21 | 23 | $34

Little Italy | 237 S. High St. (Fawn St.) | 410-837-0309
Havre de Grace | 400 N. Union Ave. (Franklin St.) | 410-939-5440
www.chiapparellis.com

You "can't go wrong with old-time Italian" fare at this "moderately
priced" "Little Italy classic" that debuted in 1940 (and its Havre de

Grace grandkid), where "authentic" pastas and meat dishes win raves, but the "memorable" signature salad is what will really "make you salivate"; the "outdated", "old-world" trappings and "pure Bawlmer" service make it feel like "nothing ever changes" – but that's "part of its charm."

Chicken Rico *Chicken/Peruvian*   27 | 11 | 18 | $13

Highlandtown | 3728 Eastern Ave. (bet. Dean & Eaton Sts.) | 410-522-2950 | www.chickenricobaltimore.com

The "fall-off-the-bone-juicy" charcoal chicken slow-roasted Peruvian-style at this "low-frills" Highlandtown counter-serve has "budget-conscious" diners "addicted"; "mounds" of "very authentic" yuca, plantains, rice and beans available on the side plus "fast" service prompt some to warn "psst, keep this place a secret."

Chiyo Sushi Ⓜ *Japanese*   ▽ 26 | 17 | 23 | $29

Mt. Washington | 1619 Sulgrave Ave. (Kelly Ave.) | 410-466-1000 | www.chiyosushi.com

Other sushi spots "may have more style", but for "seriously delicious" rolls in a dizzying variety of "innovative" combinations, maki mavens head to this Mt. Washington Japanese "hole-in-the-wall" – and if you eat there often enough you might "get a roll named after you"; welcoming servers and gentle prices seal the deal.

Christopher Daniel *American*   23 | 19 | 21 | $40

Timonium | Padonia Park Shopping Ctr. | 106 W. Padonia Rd. (Broad Ave.) | 410-308-1800 | www.christopher-daniel.com

"An above-par neighborhood restaurant", this "gem" "by the fairgrounds" in Timonium features a New American menu full of "fresh, inventive twists" paired with "carefully selected" wines; "professional" service befits the "white-tablecloth", if "plain-Jane", setting and "big price", though thrifty types point to the attached martini bar, which has a smaller but equally "delicious" menu that's "cheaper."

Ciao Bella *Italian*   22 | 20 | 22 | $38

Little Italy | 236 S. High St. (bet. Fawn & Stiles Sts.) | 410-685-7733 | www.cbella.com

"Almost a caricature of a Little Italy restaurant", but that's just as it should be say fans of this ristorante purveying "wonderful, slow-cooked" eats that are "heavy on the red sauce", amid suitably "authentic", old-school decor; a "friendly" staff and "nice bar area" have longtime loyalists saying they "would go back any day."

Cinghiale *Italian*   26 | 26 | 26 | $58

Harbor East | 822 Lancaster St. (Exeter St.) | 410-547-8282 | www.cgeno.com

Cindy Wolf and Tony Foreman hit "on all cylinders" with this Harbor East Italian (across the street from their Charleston), which has an "exquisite baronial" dining room on one side and a "rustic" enoteca on the other, both offering a "consistently exceptional", daily changing menu (including "excellent" housemade charcuterie) and a "deep" wine list; "attentive, knowledgeable" service is de rigueur, and though it costs "big bucks", think of it as a chance to "wear your Armani suit."

	FOOD	DECOR	SERVICE	COST

City Cafe *American*
23 | 20 | 21 | $33

Mt. Vernon | 1001 Cathedral St. (Eager St.) | 410-539-4252 | www.citycafebaltimore.com

"A little bit of everything" is brewing at this Mt. Vernon cafe-plus – from morning cuppas in the front cafe to "imaginative" American fare, including small plates, in the "sleek", "modern" dining room; "funky" servers tend to the "young, smart" crowd that gathers at all hours, though it's especially "great" pre-theater.

Clementine Ⓜ *American*
25 | 21 | 23 | $32

Northeast Baltimore | 5402 Harford Rd. (Gibbons Ave.) | 410-444-1497 | www.bmoreclementine.com

This Lauraville "gem" serves "inventive, delicious comfort food", in-cluding "on-point" housemade charcuterie, at moderate tabs; owner Winston Blick oversees the "cordial" service, resulting in a "pleas-ant, homey" feel in the cozy bistro setting with pressed-tin ceilings.

Clyde's ❶ *American*
22 | 23 | 22 | $33

Columbia | 10221 Wincopin Circle (Little Patuxent Pkwy.) | 410-730-2829 | www.clydes.com

See review in the Washington, DC, Directory.

Coal Fire *Pizza*
22 | 18 | 20 | $21

Ellicott City | 5725 Richards Valley Rd. (Waterloo Rd.) | 410-480-2625
Gambrills | S. Main Chapel Way (Brandermill Blvd.) | 410-721-2625
www.coalfireonline.com

"Charred-to-perfection" crusts, three "delicious" sauce options and a "great variety" of toppings earn raves from zealous 'zapporters of this "decently priced" pizzeria mini-chain; many say service is "un-even" ("excellent" vs. "poor"), but there's "warmth" in the simple copper-and-yellow digs, and "kids" love to watch the pizza-makers through the partially open kitchens.

Corner BYOB *Continental*
24 | 17 | 21 | $41

Hampden | 850 W. 36th St. (Elm Ave.) | 443-869-5075 | www.cornerbyob.com

At this "intimate" and "funky" corner spot, Hampdenites sample a "creative" Continental menu, which on a typical evening may in-clude "big and little game meats" like "kangaroo" and "frogs' legs" as well as the Belgian chef's "authentic" moules frites; the staff is "welcoming", and it's got a "banging" wine list – you BYO from the nearby wine shop, which helps keep tabs manageable.

Costas Inn Crab House ❶ *Crab House*
25 | 16 | 23 | $34

Dundalk | 4100 N. Point Blvd. (New Battle Grove Rd.) | 410-477-1975 | www.costasinn.com

The "fattest" steamed Gulf crustaceans (reservable in advance – a big time-saver) along with "awesome" crab cakes have made this "friendly" Dundalk crab house a "neighborhood" favorite for four de-cades; "reasonable prices" go hand in hand with the "bright lights", drop ceiling and "brown-paper tablecloths" (or there's always carry-out); P.S. crab cakes and lump meat are available by mail order.

	FOOD	DECOR	SERVICE	COST

Crème ⓜ Southern

| 21 | 16 | 19 | $31 |

Mt. Vernon | 518 N. Charles St. (Hamilton St.) | 443-869-3382 | www.crloungebalt.com

See review in the Washington, DC, Directory.

Crêpe du Jour French

| 21 | 18 | 21 | $26 |

Mt. Washington | 1609 Sulgrave Ave. (bet. Kelly Ave. & Newbury St.) | 410-542-9000 | www.crepedujour.com

Crêpes "savory and sweet" are the main attraction at this "adorable" blue-awninged "mini France" in Mt. Washington, though a few also praise the more "solid bistro fare"; "fine" service and "reasonable" tabs have most folks saying *oui* for "lunch or dessert" here.

Da Mimmo Italian

| 25 | 20 | 22 | $56 |

Little Italy | 217 S. High St. (Stiles St.) | 410-727-6876 | www.damimmo.com

"As good as it gets this side of Pisa", this "old-school" and "upscale Little Italy jewel" has long been known for its "outstanding" "classic" dishes like the "don't-miss" veal chop; "pricey", *sì*, but it's "worth every penny" to its "well-heeled" clientele, especially those impressed by a display of celebrity photos, a live piano player and a parking lot.

Dangerously Delicious Pies American/Bakery

| 21 | 13 | 18 | $15 |

Canton | 2839 O'Donnell St. (Linwood Ave.) | 410-522-7437 | www.dangerouspies.com

See review in the Washington, DC, Directory.

David Chu's China Bistro Chinese/Kosher

| 25 | 19 | 21 | $22 |

Pikesville | 7105 Reisterstown Rd. (bet. Glengyle Ave. & Seven Mile Ln.) | 410-602-5008

"You don't have to sacrifice good taste" for kosher Chinese at this "small" and "friendly" Pikesville strip place where "delicious" dishes (sans pork and shellfish) "satisfy" not only "kosher dietary laws" but "palates of all kinds"; since you "get your money's worth", it's a "favorite family" spot, so best to "call ahead"; P.S. closed Friday for dinner and all day Saturday.

NEW David's 1st & 10 Sports Bar American

| - | - | - | I |

Hampden | 3626 Falls Rd. (36th St.) | 410-662-7779

The everywhere-you-look TVs tuned to multiple games (including some niche sports) tell only half the story at this new Hampden bar/restaurant; even the sports-averse will note that, besides the basics, its bar stocks a deep selection of bourbon and a carefully edited wine list, and the food goes beyond the standard pub grub with a selection of updated American classics.

Della Notte Italian

| 24 | 24 | 24 | $44 |

Little Italy | 801 Eastern Ave. (President St.) | 410-837-5500 | www.dellanotte.com

There's "sexy curb appeal" at this Little Italy palazzo that takes up a whole block, leading on to a "gorgeous", "over-the-top Roman"-style

	FOOD	DECOR	SERVICE	COST

interior festooned with marble, colonnades and vaulted ceilings that's perhaps only matched in scale by the "expansive", "excellent" Italian menu and 1,400-bottle wine list; it's "priced well" given that live piano on weekends plus free parking add to the "lovely" experience.

Dempsey's Brew Pub *Pub Food*   — | — | — | M

Camden Yards | Oriole Park at Camden Yards | 555 Russel St. (Hwy. 395) | 410-843-7901 | www.dempseysbaltimore.com

Named for the famed Orioles catcher, this Camden Yards prospect covers the bases with a basic menu of midpriced pub food, including crab cakes, wings, nachos and bacon on a stick, washed down by proprietary beers brewed on-site; the old warehouse environs are festooned with baseball memorabilia, but if you want to ogle any of it on game days around game time, you must have a ticket.

Di Pasquale's Marketplace ⊠ *Italian*   28 | 15 | 22 | $16

East Baltimore | 3700 Gough St. (Dean St.) | 410-276-6787 | www.dipasquales.com

"Bring your appetite" to this "old-fashioned" East Baltimore specialty store where Europhiles shop for "Italian staples" or sit in the cafe area for a quick meal of "homemade" soups and "big, fat" sandwiches heaped with "made-fresh-daily" mozzarella; staffers "make you feel at home", and though there is "no decor" to speak of, the "wonderful aromas" provide ambiance; P.S. closes at 6 PM.

The Dizz ◑ *American*   19 | 16 | 20 | $20

Hampden | 300 W. 30th St. (Remington Ave.) | 443-869-5864 | www.thedizzbaltimore.com

"Baltimore in a bar" say adoptees of this "homey" Hampdenite with "mismatched" decor, a "mixed bag of patrons" and servers who "treat you like family"; the "big plates" of "well-made" American pub "standards" – burgers, wings and a few "fancy" specials – come at prices that are "hard to beat."

🆕 Dooby's ◑ *Coffeehouse*   — | — | — | I

Mt. Vernon | 802 N. Charles St. (Madison St.) | no phone | www.doobyscoffee.com

This big, ambitious Mt. Vernon coffeehouse (about to open at press time) will keep late hours and serve plenty of coffee, microbrews and wine plus sandwiches, small plates and pastries to folks relaxing in Eames-style chairs at communal tables and at a marble-topped bar; the owners' smaller space around the corner on Madison Street will host pop-up restaurants and shops.

Double T Diner *Diner*   20 | 16 | 21 | $18

Bel Air | 543 Market Place Dr. (Veterans Memorial Hwy.) | 410-836-5591
White Marsh | 10741 Pulaski Hwy. (Ebenezer Rd.) | 410-344-1020 ◑
Catonsville | 6300 Baltimore National Pike (Rolling Rd.) | 410-744-4151 ◑
Ellicott City | 10055 Baltimore National Pike (Centennial Ln.) | 410-750-3300
Perry Hall | Joppa Corners | 4140 E. Joppa Rd. (Belair Rd.) | 410-248-0160 ◑

(continued)

(continued)

Double T Diner

Pasadena | 1 Mountain Rd. (Ritchie Hwy.) | 410-766-9669 ●
www.doubletdiner.com

For "sinful" breakfasts or "a quick bite anytime", eaters of "all ages" flock to this "always busy", "subtly Greek", retro-looking Maryland diner chain; the menu is "novel"-length, and the "tasty" grub and "phenomenal" desserts – served "lickety-split" by "courteous" staffers – are a "great value for the money"; P.S. some locations are open 24/7.

Du-Claw ● *Pub Food*

| 21 | 20 | 20 | $24 |

Bel Air | 16 Bel Air S. Pkwy. (bet. Tollgate Rd. & Veterans Memorial Hwy.) | 410-515-3222
Bowie | Bowie Town Ctr. | 4000 Town Center Blvd. (bet. Collington Rd. & Emerald Way) | 301-809-6943
Hanover | Arundel Mills | 7000 Arundel Mills Circle (Arundel Mills Blvd.) | 410-799-1166
www.duclaw.com

"Crispy" wings, "go-to" burgers and other pub grub standards provide an inexpensive, "dependable" accompaniment to the "awesome" selection of beer at this microbrewery mini-chain; service is "energetic", and the "homey" spaces are "relaxing", plus there are occasional "fun" beer-release events.

Dukem *Ethiopian*

| 24 | 15 | 19 | $25 |

Mt. Vernon | 1100 Maryland Ave. (Chase St.) | 410-385-0318 | www.dukemrestaurant.com
See review in the Washington, DC, Directory.

Earth, Wood & Fire Ⓜ *Pizza*

| - | - | - | I |

Bare Hills | 1407 Clarkview Rd. (Falls Rd.) | 410-825-3473 | www.earthwoodfire.com

A coal-burning oven that can crisp a pizza in just four minutes flat cranks out pies – with both traditional and creative toppings – at this inexpensive Bare Hills parlor; the modern-industrial decor of the former machine-parts factory provides an inviting backdrop for noshing and sampling from a well-edited selection of craft beers and wines.

Edo Sushi *Japanese*

| 24 | 20 | 23 | $29 |

Inner Harbor | Harborplace Pratt Street Pavilion | 201 E. Pratt St. (Light St.) | 410-843-9804
Timonium | Padonia Village Shopping Ctr. | 53 E. Padonia Rd. (bet. York Rd. & Hillbrook Ct.) | 410-667-9200

Edo Mae Sushi *Japanese*

Owings Mills | Boulevard Corporate Ctr. | 10995 Owings Mills Blvd. (Boulevard Circle) | 410-356-6818

Edo Sushi II *Japanese*

Owings Mills | Garrison Forest Plaza | 10347 Reisterstown Rd. (Rosewood Ln.) | 410-363-7720
www.edosushimd.com

"Dynamite!" say raw-raw supporters of this "local favorite" chain of sushi specialists, whose "fun chefs" craft "inventive rolls" that are

	FOOD	DECOR	SERVICE	COST

"always super-fresh" and priced to move; service is "pleasant" and "polite", and the traditional blond-wood settings are "inviting" (the more contemporary Harborplace outpost commands a "wonderful view" of the water).

Eggspectation *American*   21 | 20 | 21 | $22

Ellicott City | Columbia Corporate Park 100 | 6010 University Blvd. (Waterloo Rd.) | 410-750-3115 | www.eggspectations.com
See review in the Washington, DC, Directory.

Elevation Burger *Burgers*   21 | 13 | 18 | $12

Bowie | 10201 Martin Luther King Jr. Blvd. (Lottsford Vista Rd.) | 301-262-7585 | www.elevationburger.com
See review in the Washington, DC, Directory.

Elkridge Furnace Inn Ⓜ *American*   25 | 27 | 27 | $49

Elkridge | 5745 Furnace Ave. (Race Rd.) | 410-379-9336 | www.elkridgefurnaceinn.com

"An elegance rarely seen in Elkridge" is the draw at this 18th-century inn offering a "plush, Colonial" backdrop for an "excellent" New American repast that may include a few "unusual offerings" like game in season; service is "impeccable", and though it's "expensive", true "romantics" aver "that's how you tell someone you care."

Facci *Italian/Pizza*   24 | 21 | 21 | $30

Laurel | Montpelier Shopping Ctr. | 7530 Montpelier Rd. (Johns Hopkins Rd.) | 301-604-5555 | www.faccirestaurant.com

"Wildly popular" in Laurel, this "progressive Italian" features a "diverse, modern" menu that includes "fantastic" brick-oven pizza, washed down by "impressive" wines, some dispensed by an Enomatic machine; "parking can be a challenge", but the "casual-classy" atmosphere, "pleasant" service and "reasonable" prices make it worth fighting for a space.

Faidley's Seafood Ⓢ *Seafood*   26 | 10 | 18 | $21

Downtown West | Lexington Mkt. | 203 N. Paca St. (Lexington St.) | 410-727-4898 | www.faidleyscrabcakes.com

"True crab cake pilgrims" come from afar for the "incredible", "softball-sized" delicacies "jam-packed with big chunks" of lump meat at this "real Baltimore experience" in the "historic", circa-1886 Lexington Market on the "gritty" Westside; service is "quick", prices are "low" and there are "no frills" (and no chairs – you stand up to eat at communal tables); P.S. fans swear by an "unsurpassed raw bar" and oyster shuckers that are "the best in the business."

First Watch *American*   21 | 16 | 22 | $14

NEW **Timonium** | Timonium Square | 2159 York Rd. (Gerard Ave.) | 410-308-3447
Pikesville | 1431 Reisterstown Rd. (bet. Old Court Rd. & Walker Ave.) | 410-602-1595
www.firstwatch.com
See review in the Washington, DC, Directory.

	FOOD	DECOR	SERVICE	COST

Five Guys *Burgers* | 24 | 14 | 21 | $12

Inner Harbor | Harborplace Pratt Street Pavilion | 201 E Pratt St. (Light St.) | 410-244-7175
Canton | 3600 Boston St. (Conkling St.) | 410-522-1580
White Marsh | Nottingham Square Shopping Ctr. | 5272 Campbell Blvd. (Philadelphia Rd.) | 410-933-1017
Bowie | Bowie Town Ctr. | 3851 Town Center Blvd. (Evergreen Pkwy.) | 301-464-9633
Hanover | Shops at Arundel Preserve | 7690 Dorchester Blvd. (Arundel Mills Blvd.) | 410-799-3933
Glen Burnie | Glen Burnie Mall Shopping Ctr. | 6711 Ritchie Hwy. (bet. Holsum Way & Ordnance Rd.) | 410-590-3933
Cockeysville | Yorktowne Plaza Shopping Ctr. | 10015 York Rd. (bet. Cranbrook & Halesworth Rds.) | 410-667-0818
Towson | 936 York Rd. (Fairmount Ave.) | 410-321-4963
Westminster | 140 Village Shopping Ctr. | 596 Jermor Ln. (Malcolm Dr.) | 410-751-9969
www.fiveguys.com
See review in the Washington, DC, Directory.

NEW Fleet Street Kitchen 🗷 *American* | - | - | - | VE

Harbor East | 1012 Fleet St. (Central Ave.) | 410-244-5830 | www.fleetstreetkitchen.com

The team behind Bagby Pizza and Ten Ten also helms this Harbor East New American entry that makes use of seasonal, local ingredients – including some from the owner's Baltimore County farm; the bi-level interior is elegant (white linens, high ceilings) yet warm (exposed bricks, wrought iron), and though the prices may augur special occasions, a burger and a glass of wine at the bar is an affordable treat.

Fleming's Prime Steakhouse & Wine Bar *Steak* | 25 | 24 | 25 | $61

Harbor East | 720 Aliceanna St. (President St.) | 410-332-1666 | www.flemingssteakhouse.com
See review in the Washington, DC, Directory.

Fogo de Chão *Brazilian/Steak* | 27 | 24 | 27 | $61

Inner Harbor | 600 E. Pratt St. (bet. Gay St. & Market Pl.) | 410-528-9292 | www.fogodechao.com
See review in the Washington, DC, Directory.

Food Market ● *American* | - | - | - | M

Hampden | 1017 W. 36th St. (Roland Ave.) | 410-366-0606 | www.thefoodmarketbaltimore.com

From the open kitchen of a former Hampden grocery store made famous in John Waters' film *Pecker*, Chad Gauss dishes up traditional Americana with a twist; the sleek interior with rustic overtones, plus a bar pouring cool cocktails until late, make it a favorite on the 'Avenue.'

Fork & Wrench ● *American* | - | - | - | M

Canton | 2322 Boston St. (Wagner St.) | 443-759-9360 | www.theforkandwrench.com

The setting for this New American gastropub in Canton is designed to evoke early 20th-century industry, with distressed zinc-covered tables, retro fixtures and vintage tools throughout its many dark nooks; the midpriced, oft-changing farm-to-table menu is likewise period themed – presented in categories like 'jars', 'flock and field' and 'herd and pen' – as is the cocktail list (how about an Aviation?).

4 Seasons Grille *Eclectic/Mediterranean*   25 | 24 | 24 | $40

Gambrills | 2630 Chapel Lake Dr. (Crain Hwy.) | 410-451-5141 | www.4seasonsgrille.com

A "bright little surprise" in a Gambrills strip mall, this midpriced Mediterranean-Eclectic bistro "delivers" with its "excellent", "healthy"-feeling cuisine and "wonderful" service; it's "warm and inviting" and "just dark enough" for an "awesome" date night, and there's a "popular" bar that's a "great place to meet friends."

Friendly Farm *American*   25 | 16 | 24 | $25

Upperco | 17434 Foreston Rd. (Mt. Carmel Rd.) | 410-239-7400 | www.friendlyfarm.net

"Only real Hoovers leave" this "old-fashioned dining hall" on a "picturesque" North Baltimore County farm "without a doggy bag" of "1950s"-inspired Americana reminiscent of "Sunday dinner at grandma's" (e.g. "excellent" fried chicken, "out-of-this-world" sugar biscuits); the "service lives up to the name", and those waiting in weekend lines can visit the gift shop or feed the ducks.

G&M *Seafood*   24 | 16 | 20 | $29

Linthicum | 804 N. Hammonds Ferry Rd. (Nursery Rd.) | 410-636-1777 | www.gandmcrabcakes.com

"Bigger-than-your-head" crab cakes with "lots of lump meat" are the reason travelers "take cabs from BWI" during layovers to visit this "affordable" Linthicum "mecca", where the lengthy menu has Italian and Greek eats, but the crustacean creations are the "real star"; the simple, white-tablecloth setting is "pleasant" enough, and service is "old-school", but really, it's all about "one thing" here.

Garry's   20 | 14 | 19 | $22
Grill & Catering *American*

Severna Park | 553 Baltimore Annapolis Blvd. (McKinsey Rd.) | 410-544-0499 | www.garrysgrill.com

"Homestyle cooking" "with a twist" makes this "casual" American fixture "hidden" in a Severna Park strip mall a "decent" "neighborhood" option for a "nice, reasonable meal", especially at "breakfast"; the upscale-diner setup gets a boost from the "friendly" service.

Germano's Trattoria *Italian*   24 | 21 | 23 | $35

Little Italy | 300 S. High St. (Fawn St.) | 410-752-4515 | www.germanostrattoria.com

Owner Germano Fabiani "oversees all" at his long-standing Little Italy mainstay, ensuring "excellent" service as diners sup on the "extremely good" midpriced Tuscan fare; "fantastic belle époque art posters" (yes, they're originals) are the highlight of the old-school interior, though the musically minded "love" the upstairs cabaret, "a gem" that features performances by local and far-flung acts Thursday–Sunday.

	FOOD	DECOR	SERVICE	COST

Gertrude's Ⓜ *Chesapeake*   22 | 25 | 23 | $37

Charles Village | Baltimore Museum of Art | 10 Art Museum Dr. (bet. Charles St. & Wyman Park Dr.) | 410-889-3399 | www.gertrudesbaltimore.com

"Manet and Cezanne would have stopped painting" to enjoy an alfresco meal "at the edge of the sculpture garden" or inside this "oasis" within the Baltimore Museum of Art say admirers of John Shields' "sassy, Southern", "Chesapeake Bay–oriented" menu presented by "knowledgeable" servers; prices are moderate, and $12 entrees on Tuesdays are "a great touch."

Gino's Burgers & Chicken *Burgers*   22 | 20 | 21 | $12

Perry Hall | 5001 Honeygo Center Dr. (Honeygo Blvd.) | 410-870-2746
Towson | 8600 Lasalle Road (bet. Joppa Rd. & Putty Hill Ave.) | 410-583-0000
www.ginosgiant.com

"Nostalgia" reigns for those who remember the original Gino's drive-up, founded by two former Baltimore Colts in the '50s, when they visit these "popular" sit-down retro revivals in Towson and Perry Hall; longtime loyalists say the "tasty" burgers and "fantastic" shakes are "almost as good as the original", the service "lives up to the food" and the prices are still fairly vintage.

Goldberg's New York Bagels *Bakery/Jewish*   25 | 9 | 16 | $11

Timonium | 31 E. Padonia Rd. (York Rd.) | 410-891-8559
Pikesville | 1500 Reisterstown Rd. (Old Court Rd.) | 410-415-7001
www.goldbergsbagels.com

You can "skip the trip to NYC" in favor of this "real-deal" Pikesville bakery/deli (with a newer Timonium branch) that "isn't much to look at" but "sure knows how to bake bagels", not to mention make all manner of other "kosher Jewish delights" like blintzes and rugalach; "service could be improved" – still, it's "fast" and the prices are right; P.S. serves breakfast and lunch only, except Saturdays, when Pikesville is dinner only and Timonium is closed.

Golden West Cafe ● *Eclectic/New Mexican*   21 | 19 | 16 | $21

Hampden | 1105 West 36th St. (bet. Falls Rd. & Hickory Ave.) | 410-889-8891 | www.goldenwestcafe.com

"Tasty" New Mexican dishes (including "magical" Frito pie) come in portions "way too big for one person" at this "funky", "retro" Hampden "roadhouse", but if that's not your thing it also offers "vegetarian" options and a passel of Eclectic comfort grub and other "hangover" helpers; it's "inexpensive" too, though some say beware the "too-cool" "hipster" staffers who sometimes "take forever" – the place is "nicknamed 'Golden Wait' for a reason."

Grace Garden Ⓢ *Chinese*   ▽ 28 | 9 | 20 | $22

Odenton | 1690 Annapolis Rd. (Reece Rd.) | 410-672-3581 | www.gracegardenchinese.com

"Authentic wonders" come from this "unassuming" Odenton Chinese, where a husband-and-wife team "takes great pride" in introducing such "un-localized" treats as "flavorful" tea-smoked duck and noodles "made from ground fish", most at an "unbelievable bargain"; ignore the "hole-in-the-wall" surrounds and focus on the "rare" fare that'll make you say "we don't need no stinkin' chop suey" (though they do have a full Westernized Chinese menu too).

Grace's Fortune *Chinese*
25 | 24 | 25 | $30

Bowie | 15500 Annapolis Rd. (Scarlet Oak Terr.) | 301-805-1108 | www.gracesrestaurants.com

"Wonderful" Chinese cookery "right down to the soy sauce" is the way the cookie crumbles at Grace Tang's Bowie bastion that's been "a family favorite for many years"; it "isn't cheap" exactly, but there's plenty of value in the "superb" service and "exotic" decor, which features hand-carved wood furnishings and a koi pond.

Grano Emporio *Italian*
▽ 25 | 18 | 22 | $34

(aka Big Grano)

Hampden | 3547 Chestnut Ave. (36th St.) | 443-438-7521 | www.granopastabar.com

The "lovely" owner and "happy" staff "define warmth" at this "cute and cozy" midpriced Italian spot "at the edge of 'hon'-dom", er Hampden, and better yet, the "home-cooked" pasta and such is "outstanding"; add in a wine bar and a "wonderful" deck, and it's a "gem", if somewhat "undiscovered."

Grano Pasta Bar 🗷 *Italian*
25 | 14 | 22 | $22

(aka Little Grano)

Hampden | 1031 W. 36th St. (Hickory Ave.) | 443-869-3429 | www.granopastabar.com

Providing a "laid-back pasta break" in Hampden is this "homey" spot that offers a simple "mix-and-match" menu of "delicious, hearty" pastas and sauces; service is "great", and low prices are abetted by a BYO policy, and though it's "tiny" one can "usually snag" a seat inside or on the sidewalk.

Great Sage Ⓜ *Vegan*
24 | 21 | 24 | $25

Clarksville | Clarksville Square Dr. | 5809 Clarksville Square Dr. (Clarksville Pike) | 443-535-9400 | www.greatsage.com

"Even a carnivore" will feel "satisfied" after a meal at this colorfully decorated vegan bastion in Clarksville, where there's a "delicious" dish for everyone, including "gluten-, soy-, peanut-free" choices and the "occasional raw" option; the staff is "accommodating" – "special orders delight them" – and the prices are easy to digest, leaving money for shopping at the other co-owned 'mindful' businesses in the strip (market, pet store, home-goods store).

Greg's Bagels Ⓜ⇗ *Bakery*
24 | 14 | 22 | $10

York Road Corridor | Belvedere Sq. | 519 E. Belvedere Ave. (York Rd.) | 410-323-9463

"Always-there" owner Greg Novik is "the key" to the long-running "success" of this Belvedere Square bakery that weathered the area's decline and rebirth; "friendly" staffers serve "fresh", "interesting" bagels, an "amazing selection of smoked fish" and possibly "the largest choice of spreads in Baltimore", at affordable prices in a no-frills cafe with a checkered floor; P.S. it's cash only and closes by 3 PM weekdays.

Greystone Grill *Steak*

FOOD	DECOR	SERVICE	COST
19	20	19	$42

Ellicott City | MDG Corporate Ctr. | 8850 Columbia 100 Pkwy. (bet. Centre Park Rd. & Executive Park Dr.) | 410-715-4739 | www.greystonegrill.com

Located in an Ellicott City office park, this value-priced steakhouse specializes in "well-prepared, filling" fare fit for a "nice dinner", where "everyone finds something they like"; although some call the whole experience "ho-hum", restaurant-wide WiFi and a private wine vault equipped with audio-visual equipment make the stone-and-wood-accented setting "recommended" for a "business meeting."

Grilled Cheese & Co. *Sandwiches*

FOOD	DECOR	SERVICE	COST
22	16	20	$12

Federal Hill | 1036 Light St. (bet. Cross & Poultney Sts.) | 410-244-6333
Catonsville | 500 Edmondson Ave. (Harlem Ln.) | 410-747-2610
Eldersburg | 577 Johnsville Rd. (Sykesville Rd.) | 443-920-3238
www.ilovegrilledcheese.com

With an "updated" take on the "comfort classic", this "feel-good" chainlet puts "grilled cheese on steroids", offering "inventive" versions stuffed with everything from crab to crumbled meatballs; though there's "limited seating" in the simple, earth-toned digs, the "fast food"–style counter service is "friendly" and the tabs "reasonable."

Gunning's Seafood *Seafood*

FOOD	DECOR	SERVICE	COST
23	16	21	$29

Hanover | 7304 Parkway Dr. (Race Rd.) | 410-712-9404
Glen Burnie | Burwood Shopping Plaza | 7089 Baltimore Annapolis Blvd. (Furnace Branch Rd.) | 410-691-2722
www.gunningsonline.com

"Bring your mallet" to this midpriced seafooder in Hanover (with a newer location in Glen Burnie), where you'll crack open "awesome" steamed Chesapeake Bay crustaceans, gobble "superior" crab cakes and down pitchers of beer "to extinguish the spice"; there's "nothing fancy" about the setting, but with "attentive" servers and specials available "nowhere else", coming here is a "tradition."

Hamilton Tavern *Pub Food*

FOOD	DECOR	SERVICE	COST
24	21	21	$23

Northeast Baltimore | 5517 Harford Rd. (Hamilton Ave.) | 410-426-1930 | www.hamiltontavern.com

"Tasty farm-to-table versions of pub standards" make up the "always changing" menu at this affordable Harford Road tavern where folks rave about the "fabulous" burgers (worth a "cross-town" trip) and "thoughtful" microbrew selection; tin ceilings, exposed brick and lots of wood give it a "cozy" vibe, and staffers reinforce the "unpretentious" feel, all the more reason you'll "wish you lived next door."

Harryman House Grill *American*

FOOD	DECOR	SERVICE	COST
24	23	23	$36

Reisterstown | 340 Main St. (bet. Resisters & West Sts.) | 410-833-8850 | www.harrymanhouse.com

Fittingly located near "Antiques Row" in Reisterstown, this "quaint" old house has long provided a "cherished" backdrop for well-heeled "family gatherings" and "romantic dates" in its sprawling environs, which include a circa-1791 log cabin room ("dark" and "charming") and a newer high-ceilinged great room and adjacent porch (bright and airy); "creative" New American entrees and more casual "standards like burgers" share the midpriced menu and are served with aplomb.

Havana Road Cuban Café *Cuban*   21 | 18 | 20 | $26

Towson | 8 W. Pennsylvania Ave. (bet. Washington Ave. & York Rd.) | 410-494-8222 | www.havanaroad.com

"Authentic" offerings like pork sandwiches and ropa vieja from Marta Inés Quintana's "Cuban heaven" in Towson are enthusiastically compared to their "South Florida" compadres, and her sauces are so "tasty" they're sold at local stores; BYO mellows already "reasonable" tabs, another reason guests have had "many happy returns" to the "small, attractive spot" decorated with pictures of Old Havana.

Heavy Seas Alehouse ● *American*   ▽ 19 | 21 | 21 | $41

Harbor East | Tack Factory Bldg. | 1300 Bank St. (Central Ave.) | 410-522-0850 | www.heavyseasalehouse.com

"Stupendous" locally brewed ale gets showcased at this rustic 19th-century tack factory dressed in the "original brick and timber" in Harbor East; "quite tasty" is the word on the raw bar and American gastropub menu designed by chef/co-owner Matt Seeber (a Tom Colicchio protégé), and of course the able-bodied deckhands can suggest beer pairings as well as high-end rum.

Helmand *Afghan*   27 | 21 | 23 | $32

Mt. Vernon | 806 N. Charles St. (bet. Madison & Read Sts.) | 410-752-0311 | www.helmand.com

Diners make a "culinary expedition" to this midpriced Mt. Vernon "landmark" for "consistently amazing" Afghani fare (baked pumpkin is "especially recommended") served by "gracious" staffers justifiably "proud" of the cuisine; add an "elegant" space enriched with "attractive tapestries" and fans call it a "work of art."

Henninger's Tavern 🅿Ⓜ *American*   ▽ 25 | 22 | 24 | $35

Fells Point | 1812 Bank St. (bet. Ann & Wolfe Sts.) | 410-342-2172 | www.henningerstavern.com

On a "quiet street" in Fells Point is this "hidden gem" serving "expert" New American fare in a "rustic old pub" whose "every inch" is filled with "kitschy" "photos, paintings and oddities"; tabs are moderate, and the couple who runs it keeps things "friendly" and "always fun."

Hersh's Pizza *Pizza*   - | - | - | I

South Baltimore | 1843 Light St. (E. Wells St.) | 443-438-4948 | www.hershspizza.com

The siblings behind this inexpensive pizzeria in South Baltimore take pride in their ingredient-driven philosophy, expressed in pie toppings like housemade sausage and house-pickled hot peppers (they also serve Italian small plates) washed down by craft cocktails and microbrews; surreal, larger-than-life photo-realistic grayscale murals are a conversation piece in the speakeasy-feeling digs; P.S. closed Tuesdays.

	FOOD	DECOR	SERVICE	COST

Honey Pig Gooldaegee
Korean BBQ ⏺ *Korean* — 23 | 13 | 17 | $24

Ellicott City | 10045 Baltimore National Pike (Centennial Ln.) | 410-696-2426 | www.eathoneypig.com
See review in the Washington, DC, Directory.

House of India *Indian* — 23 | 17 | 20 | $22

Columbia | 9350 Snowden River Pkwy. (bet. Carved Stone & Rustling Leaf) | 410-381-3844 | www.houseofindiainc.com
It may be located in a "modest" storefront in a Snowden River Parkway strip mall, but this North Indian option is "worth a second glance" for "big, bold flavors" and "generous portions" at "low prices", plus an "excellent" lunch buffet; "very attentive" servers make sure water glasses are "never empty", much to the relief of its fans (it can be "very spicy" if so desired).

Hunan Manor *Chinese* — 23 | 20 | 21 | $23

Columbia | 7091 Deepage Dr. (Carved Stone) | 410-381-1134 | www.hunanmanorrestaurant.com
For more than 20 years, this "solid" Columbia "standby" has been serving up "generous" portions of "better-than-average" Chinese food in a "pleasant" setting surrounded by "large fish tanks"; "many a work lunch" has been hosted here because there are "tons of tables" (read: "never a wait"), prices are "competitive" and servers are "so quick" – plus they have "awesome carryout."

Iggies Ⓜ *Pizza* — 27 | 17 | 19 | $18

Mt. Vernon | 818 N. Calvert St. (Read St.) | 410-528-0818 | www.iggiespizza.com
"Crisp-crust" pizzas with "inventive toppings" (duck, leeks, squash) and "creative salads" delight the "highfalutin foodies" who visit this affordable Mt. Vernon BYO, whether it's "before Centerstage" or on a "casual" "night out"; the colorful "warehouse-chic" interior is set up "cafeteria-style", so "you provide most of the service"; P.S. closed Monday and Tuesday.

Ikaros *Greek* — 23 | 17 | 22 | $28

Greektown | 4901 Eastern Ave. (Oldham St.) | 410-633-3750 | www.ikarosrestaurant.com
This Greektown stalwart boasts a decades-long reputation for "solid Greek classics" that are "reasonably priced" and delivered by staffers who "bend over backward" to please; a post-Survey move to larger digs that are more contemporary and nightclub-esque outdates the Decor rating, while it added items from a charcoal rotisserie and brick oven, plus there's now a late-night taverna menu available at the huge square bar.

Iron Bridge Wine Company *American* — 25 | 23 | 23 | $41

Columbia | 10435 State Rte. 108 (Centennial Ln.) | 410-997-3456 | www.ironbridgewines.com
A "treat to your senses" awaits at this "pricey" but "worth-the-cash" New American (with locations in the Columbia "farmlands" and

Warrenton, VA) presenting a "seasonal menu" that's "ever evolving" and "consistently delicious"; however, oenophiles say the real star is the "amazing wine collection", and the "charming" servers are "expert at recommending pairings", making for a "jovial" mood in "cozy, intimate" settings "among the wine racks."

Jack's Bistro ☒ *Eclectic* | 27 | 19 | 24 | $36 |

Canton | 3123 Elliott St. (S. Robinson St.) | 410-878-6542 | www.jacksbistro.net

Behold "crazy decadence" at this "quirky" Canton bistro "tucked away in a row house", in such "outlandish" Eclectic creations as "chocolate mac 'n' cheese", plus sous vide and other "daring" dishes; "creative cocktails", moderate prices and a "super-friendly staff" help make the simple cafe's "sardine-can seating" worthwhile; P.S. closed Monday and Tuesday; late-night menu till 1 AM otherwise.

Jerry's Seafood *Seafood* | 26 | 18 | 23 | $45 |

Bowie | 15211 Major Lansdale Blvd. (off Northview Dr.) | 301-805-2284

Lanham | Seabrook Station | 9364 Lanham Severn Rd. (94th Ave.) | 301-577-0333 ☒

www.jerrysseafood.com

The "amazing" crab bombs truly are "the bomb" at these "expensive" Bowie and Lanham eateries known for their "excellent", "all-meat" crab specialties and other well-prepared seafood; service is "respectful" and "unhurried" in the "cozy", simple settings that sport a vibe "the whole family can enjoy."

Jesse Wong's Asean Bistro *Pan-Asian* | 23 | 20 | 22 | $28 |

Columbia | 8775 Centre Park Dr. (Old Annapolis Rd.) | 410-772-5300 | www.aseanbistro.com

"Consistently good" offerings on a "varied" Pan-Asian menu "draw lots of regulars" to this midpriced Columbia spot where "attentive" servers tend to eat-in and carry-out customers; the "tranquil", "tastefully" wood-accented environs are made even more "lovely" by a muted piano player weeknights and a weekend jazz ensemble.

Jesse Wong's Kitchen *Asian* | 20 | 21 | 18 | $29 |

Hunt Valley | Hunt Valley Towne Ctr. | 118 Shawan Rd. (bet. McCormick & York Rds.) | 410-329-1088 | www.jessewongskitchen.com

Chef Wong's "very good Asian fusion" wins kudos in Hunt Valley for a "pretty" interior featuring a glass-enclosed kitchen that's worth watching; the "upscale" cuisine and competent service are backed by a "weekend pianist" and attractive lunchtime bargains.

Jimmy's *Diner* | 20 | 13 | 20 | $18 |

Fells Point | 801 S. Broadway (Lancaster St.) | 410-327-3273

Enjoy an "old-time breakfast" alongside "night-shift workers" in the early morning or "candidates" at election time at this "classic diner" in Fells Point, with proletariat prices and "timely" service; so it's a "working-class place" in "a neighborhood that's no longer working class" – that means you can still "get a beer with your French toast"; P.S. hours are 5 AM to 7 PM.

	FOOD	DECOR	SERVICE	COST

Joe Squared   *Italian/Pizza*   24 | 16 | 21 | $21

Downtown | Power Plant Live | 30 Market Pl. (Water St.) | 410-962-5566 ●
Downtown North | 133 W. North Ave. (Howard St.) | 410-545-0444
www.joesquared.com

"Pizza with an attitude" – "thin and crackly" crust topped with "spaghetti and meatballs", for instance – shares the fair-priced menu with an extensive list of "delicious", "interesting" risottos plus "rums from around the world" at this "gritty" Downtown North "art-school hangout" (and its offshoot at Power Plant Live); service is "attentive yet laid-back", and if the pies are "square", the "bohemian" clientele and "live music" most nights are not.

Johnny Rad's ● *Pizza*   27 | 21 | 22 | $20

Fells Point | 2108 Eastern Ave. (S. Duncan St.) | 443-759-6464 | www.johnnyrads.com

Perhaps the "raddest pub in Baltimore", this "surprisingly friendly" "punk-rock skateboard bar" near Patterson Park peddles nice-priced, "excellent" "artisanal pizza", plus "inventive" grub like fried edamame, and an "awesome beer selection" in "cool digs" decked out with Skee-Ball and other vintage arcade games; early-afternoon tipplers just "wish they'd open up earlier in the day."

NEW Johnny's Ⓜ *Californian*   - | - | - | M

Roland Park | Roland Park Shopping Ctr. | 4800 Roland Ave (bet. Elmhurst & Upland Rds.) | 410-773-0777 | www.johnnysdownstairs.com

Tony Foreman and Cindy Wolf (Charleston, Pazo) are behind this upscale diner in Roland Park dispensing Californian fare peppered with Asian and Central American flavors, and washed down with domestic wines and spirits plus plenty of upscale coffee; staffers in starched white shirts work two distinct areas: a light-filled coffee bar and a subterranean dining area with deep leather banquettes surrounding nickel-clad tables.

John Steven, Ltd. ● *Seafood*   ▽ 20 | 18 | 21 | $25

Fells Point | 1800 Thames St. (Ann St.) | 410-327-5561 | www.johnstevenstavern.com

This "cozy little" tavern in Fells Point provides a "funky" dose of "local color" with its long history in the neighborhood, allowing regulars to "go back time and again" for "consistent", fairly priced seafood ("great" steamed shrimp), backed by solid service; for "maximum" character, "eat at the bar", though the sidewalk patio is pleasant too.

Josef's Country Inn   *Continental*   25 | 23 | 25 | $38

Fallston | 2410 Pleasantville Rd. (Fallston Rd.) | 410-877-7800 | www.josefscountryinn.com

A mostly "older crowd, all dressed up", sits down to "special dinners" in the "elegant", "old-style" dining room of this time-honored "true country inn" in Fallston to partake of "superb", "classic" Continental cuisine served by an "excellent" staff; the "lively" bar area suits "young professionals" for "simpler meals" and, of course, "good German beer on tap."

	FOOD	DECOR	SERVICE	COST

Joss Cafe & Sushi Bar *Japanese*   `27` `20` `23` `$33`
Mt. Vernon | 413 N. Charles St. (bet. Franklin & Mulberry Sts.) |
410-244-6988 | www.josssushi.com
See review in the Annapolis Directory.

Kali's Court *Mediterranean/Seafood*   `25` `26` `24` `$56`
Fells Point | 1606 Thames St. (Bond St.) | 410-276-4700 |
www.kaliscourt.com

The "stunning setting" of velvet and dark wood at this seafood-slanted Med in Fells Point, entered through a "beautiful garden" (open for seating in warm months), is "predictably wonderful" for a "romantic tête-à-tête"; the "artful" "gourmet" dishes are "carefully prepared", and delivered by servers who "read their tables well", abetting a "dining rather than eating experience" that "justifies" the high tab.

Kali's Mezze *Mediterranean*   `25` `22` `22` `$36`
Fells Point | 1606 Thames St. (Bond St.) | 410-563-7600 |
www.kalismezze.com

Regulars "never get tired" of this Fells Pointer serving up a "diverse" and "delectable" slate of Greek-inspired Mediterranean tapas in a contemporary space full of curvy lines; a "fun atmosphere", midrange prices and "helpful" service make this next-door sibling of Kali's Court a good choice for "a cozy date" or group gathering (order the "deliciously fruity" sangria to share).

The Kings Contrivance *American*   `24` `24` `25` `$50`
Columbia | 10150 Shaker Dr. (bet. Rtes. 29 & 32) | 410-995-0500 |
www.thekingscontrivance.com

"Set your GPS" and "step back into the past" to this "tucked-away little treasure" in a "beautiful old mansion" in Columbia; "delightful" service and "consistently excellent" American fare contribute to an "old-fashioned-in-a-good-way" dining experience that "mom would dig", and if it's "slightly expensive", it's "well worth it."

Kloby's Smokehouse *BBQ*   `21` `16` `20` `$19`
Laurel | Montpelier Liquors | 7500 Montpelier Rd. (Johns Hopkins Rd.) |
301-362-1510 | www.klobysbbq.com

The "mouthwatering" barbecue at this "casual", "rustic" orange-hued joint tucked into a Laurel strip mall includes the curious 'jar-b-que', brainchild of chef/co-owner Steve Klobosits, wherein "all the good stuff" – hand-pulled pork, beans and slaw – is layered in a mason jar; the meats are matched by a "spectacular draft beer selection", "good bourbon too", "friendly people" and easy prices.

Kobe Japanese Steak & Seafood House *Japanese*   `27` `24` `25` `$41`
White Marsh | White Marsh Mall | 8165 Honeygo Blvd. (Campbell Blvd.) |
410-931-8900
Largo | 860 Capital Centre Blvd. (Lottsford Rd.) | 301-333-5555
www.kobejs.com

Chefs "dazzle" diners at this Japanese teppanyaki/sushi palace in Largo (there are also branches in White Marsh and Leesburg, VA, which were not surveyed), with an "intriguing" culinary show featur-

ing fireworks and "games with the food" that provides "entertainment" for diners seated at communal grill tables, watching their
"delicious" multicourse meals being prepared; it works well for
"group gatherings", when the "amount of food" (doggy bags rou-
tinely provided) and the "experience" "make the cost moot."

Koco's ⊠ Ⓜ *Pub Food*

| 27 | 15 | 24 | $28 |

Northeast Baltimore | 4301 Harford Rd. (bet. Overland & Weaver Aves.) |
410-426-3519 | www.kocospub.com

Take "a quirky jaunt to the tropics, Baltimore-style", at this
Lauraville pub where a "really friendly" staff doles out some of the
"best" jumbo lump crab cakes around, plus classic bar food, in
"Jimmy Buffett"-esque, "delicious"-margarita-fueled digs; in keeping with the "unpretentious" setting, tabs are "reasonable" – especially on Thursday's crab cake night, when the joint is "humming."

Kooper's North *American*

| 22 | 17 | 21 | $21 |

NEW **Lutherville** | 12240 Tullamore Rd. (W. Padonia Rd.) |
410-853-7324 | www.koopersnorth.com

Kooper's Tavern ◑ *American*

Fells Point | 1702 Thames St. (B'way) | 410-563-5423 | www.koopers.com

Kooper's Chowhound Food Truck ⊠ *Burgers*

Location varies; see website | 410-563-5423 |
www.kooperschowhound.com

"Fantastic" burgers, including Angus, Kobe, lamb and black bean varieties, star on the American "comfort" menu at this "casual, cozy"
Fells Point tavern (and newer Lutherville branch) named for the
owner's pup; the feel is "always friendly", as are the prices, and
hopsheads note an "awesome beer selection" in the bar where "cute
dog photos" dot the walls; P.S. its related food truck takes a limited
menu out and about (check website for schedule).

La Famiglia *Italian*

| 22 | 22 | 23 | $43 |

Homewood | 105 W. 39th St. (bet. Canterbury Rd. & University Pkwy.) |
443-449-5555 | www.lafamigliabaltimore.com

"Delicious" "simple Italian dishes" and "attentive" service led by
proprietor Dino Zeytinoglu, who "works the crowd", have JHU types
and other locals feeling "at home" in this "relaxing", contemporary
Homewood space with a "cozy roaring fireplace in winter" (there's a
"great" terrace in warmer months); it's costly, but there's "something for everybody" here, even if it's just "drinks and dessert."

Langermann's *Southern*

| 22 | 21 | 22 | $33 |

Canton | 2400 Boston St. (Hudson St.) | 410-534-3287
NEW **Federal Hill** | 1542 Light St. (Randall St.) | 410-528-1200 ◑
www.langermanns.com

"Lowcountry" cuisine is elevated to "haute Southern" at Neal
Langermann's "upbeat" "hot spot" set amid warehouse-chic digs in
Canton (there's also a newer Federal Hill location); the staff "aims
to please", as do easygoing tabs, which get even easier during the
weeknight happy hour and "filling" Sunday brunch (entree charge
includes access to a buffet of sides).

	FOOD	DECOR	SERVICE	COST

La Scala *Italian*
26 | 23 | 25 | $42

Little Italy | 1012 Eastern Ave. (bet. Central Ave. & Exeter St.) | 410-783-9209 | www.lascaladining.com

"Special-occasion" dining and an "indoor bocce ball" court meet with "incredible atmosphere" under one roof at this Little Italy destination where high-end, "delectable" Sicilian fare and an "extensive" wine list are served by a "flawless", "long-tenured" team; upstairs, away from the fray, the mood is "romantic", while for the true sports-minded, an "active bar scene" attracts the "requisite beautiful people."

La Tavola *Italian*
26 | 22 | 25 | $41

Little Italy | 248 Albemarle St. (Fawn St.) | 410-685-1859 | www.la-tavola.com

Still somewhat "undiscovered" despite its longevity (and large exterior mural), this "exquisite" Little Italy ristorante purveys "authentic" Italian fare with "delicate" sauces that "will knock your socks off" at tabs that are deemed fair for the quality; servers "make dining a pleasurable adventure" in the roomy, toned-down setting.

The Laurrapin ⓜ *American*
∇ 26 | 24 | 25 | $34

Havre de Grace | 209 N. Washington St. (Pennington Ave.) | 410-939-4956 | www.laurrapin.com

"New York quality" at "half the price" is the hallmark at this "wonderful" Havre de Grace meeting place turning out "excellent" organic, locally sourced Californian-accented New American fare in a "funky", multicolored and muraled space; in keeping with its "pub-style" aesthetic, "fantastic", "personable" bartenders pour a "nice" selection of drinks, and live local music on weekends further adds to the good times.

Lebanese Taverna *Lebanese*
23 | 20 | 21 | $29

Harbor East | 719 S. President St. (Lancaster St.) | 410-244-5533 | www.lebanesetaverna.com

See review in the Washington, DC, Directory.

Ledo Pizza *Pizza*
23 | 15 | 20 | $17

Lanham | 9454 Lanham Severn Rd. (94th Ave.) | 301-577-5550 | www.ledopizza.com

See review in the Washington, DC, Directory.

Liberatore's *Italian*
24 | 22 | 23 | $33

Bel Air | 562 Baltimore Pike (Veterans Memorial Hwy.) | 410-838-9100 ◗
Timonium | Timonium Corporate Ctr. | 9515 Deereco Rd. (Padonia Rd.) | 410-561-3300 ◗
Perry Hall | Honeygo Village Ctr. | 5005 Honeygo Center Dr. (Honeygo Blvd.) | 410-529-4567 ◗
Eldersburg | Freedom Village Shopping Ctr. | 6300 Georgetown Blvd. (Liberty Rd.) | 410-781-4114
Westminster | 140 Village Shopping Ctr. | 521 Jermor Ln. (Rte. 97) | 410-876-2121 ⓜ
www.liberatores.com

"If you don't feel like going to Little Italy", these extended family-owned ristorantes around Greater Baltimore are "mainstays" for a "low-key" Italian meal, cooking up "old-fashioned", "seriously good grub" in "family-friendly" settings with "upbeat flair" and "solid", "attentive" service; half-price wine specials add to the "value."

Linwoods *American*

| 27 | 26 | 27 | $56 |

Owings Mills | 25 Crossroads Dr. (bet. McDonogh & Reisterstown Rds.) | 410-356-3030 | www.linwoods.com

Chef-owner Linwood Dame brings "interesting nuances" to his "impeccable" "modern" American cuisine at this "serene" spot in Owings Mills that's been "charming" "sophisticated" diners for around a quarter-century; a "contemporary, elegant" room with an open grill, patrolled by a "first-rate" staff, enhances an experience that's worthy of a "special occasion" or any time "you're feeling plush."

Little Spice ⓈＩ *Thai*

| ▽ 25 | 17 | 24 | $25 |

Hanover | 1350 Dorsey Rd. (Ridge Rd.) | 410-859-0100 | www.littlespicethairestaurant.co

Conjuring the "wonderful street food you would find in Thailand" ("upsized" for America "of course"), this Hanover spot between BWI and the Arundel Mills Mall serves "outstanding" Thai fare in "minimalist" digs for a "reasonable" price; "excellent" service comes from a "friendly" staff willing to "adjust the heat level either up or down."

NEW Liv2eat *American*

| - | - | - | E |

Federal Hill | 1444 Light St. (bet. Brickhead St. & Fort Ave.) | 443-449-7129 | www.liv2eat.com

Run by a married couple, this Federal Hill newcomer offers diners a smartly edited menu of upscale New American offerings driven by what's available at the market; the casual but elegant row-house interior gives way to a serene courtyard in the back, a prime spot for Sunday brunch.

NEW Maggie's Farm Ⓜ *American*

| - | - | - | M |

Northeast Baltimore | 4341 Harford Rd. (Montebello Terr.) | 410-254-2376 | www.maggiesfarmmd.com

Andrew Weinzirl has put his stamp on more than just the sign outside this Lauraville New American (formerly the highly regarded Chameleon Cafe) after taking over from his former employer; renamed for the famous Bob Dylan song, this incarnation may seem familiar in its intimate interior and farm-to-table philosophy, but a new emphasis on creative small plates shifts the focus from a special-occasion destination to a more casual neighborhood dining option.

Mama's on the Half Shell *Seafood*

| 26 | 22 | 23 | $32 |

Canton | 2901 O'Donnell St. (S. Linwood Ave.) | 410-276-3160 | www.mamasmd.com

"Butter, cream and deep-fried batter rule the menu" at this "reasonably priced" Canton Square tavern offering "large portions" of "exceptional", "guilty-pleasure seafood", plus an "amazing" oyster selection and "freshly squeezed orange crush"; it's "popular (read: noisy and crowded)", but the service is "timely", and there are plenty of places to perch among the "pictures and artifacts from the city's past" – at the "lively bar downstairs" or "cozy tables upstairs" – or on the sidewalk in the summer.

Mamma Lucia *Italian*   22 | 16 | 21 | $23

Elkridge | Gateway Overlook | 6630 Marie Curie Dr. (Lark Brown Rd.) | 410-872-4894 | www.mammaluciarestaurants.com
See review in the Washington, DC, Directory.

M&S Grill *Seafood/Steak*   22 | 21 | 21 | $38

Inner Harbor | Harborplace Pratt Street Pavilion | 201 E. Pratt St. (South St.) | 410-547-9333 | www.mandsgrill.com
See review in the Washington, DC, Directory.

Mango Grove *Indian*   ∇ 24 | 20 | 21 | $20

Columbia | 8865 Stanford Blvd. (Dobbin Rd.) | 410-884-3426 | www.themangogrove.net
Vegetarian and vegan "mouths water just thinking about" the "extensive" buffet at this "friendly" and affordable Indian oasis in Columbia that also throws a few bones to "die-hard meat eaters" with a separate Indo-Chinese menu under the banner Mirchi Wok; followers also approve of the "large" space's "snazzy" decor featuring table linens and orange and plum accents.

Manor Tavern ❶ *American*   24 | 23 | 23 | $35

Monkton | 15819 Old York Rd. (Hess Rd.) | 410-771-8155 | www.themanortavern.com
This longtime "special-occasion" spot nestled "in the middle of horse country" in Monkton features a "delightful" menu of mid-priced Americana, much of it made from "locally grown and sourced ingredients"; adding to its charms are "competent" service and a "pleasant" setting composed of an equine-themed dining room, lounge and banquet facilities.

Marie Louise Bistro ❶ *French/Mediterranean*   22 | 21 | 19 | $32

Mt. Vernon | 904 N. Charles St. (Read St.) | 410-385-9946 | www.marielouisebistrocatering.com
A "relaxing" place to linger near the Walters Art Museum is this French-Med Mt. Vernonite with an "attractive" European-cafe look to its tiled floor, marble-topped tables and chandeliers suspended from the high ceiling (upstairs, there's a bar area); the "reasonably priced" bistro fare and "gorgeous desserts" are served with aplomb by a "cheerful" staff, making it a "neighborhood gem."

Mari Luna Latin Grill *Mexican/Pan-Latin*   25 | 22 | 26 | $28

Pikesville | 1010 Reisterstown Rd. (Sherwood Ave.) | 410-653-5151 | www.mariluna.com
Offering a "nice change of pace" for Pikesville is Jaime Luna's "popular" Pan-Latin counterpart to his Mexican grill down the road, where "terrific" eats (including popovers "to die for") are washed down by gallons of "tasty" sangria in a "beautiful" gold-and-red setting that features a huge picture-window view of the kitchen; like its sibling, it boasts "wonderful", "professional" service and "fair" prices.

Mari Luna Mexican
Grill *Mexican/Pan-Latin*

24 | 16 | 22 | $23

Pikesville | 102 Reisterstown Rd. (Colonial Rd.) | 410-486-9910

Mari Luna Bistro *Mexican/Pan-Latin*
Mt. Vernon | 1225 Cathedral St. (Preston St.) | 410-637-8013
www.mariluna.com

"Unpretentious" but "wonderful" say compadres of chef-owner Jaime Luna's Pikesville flagship Mexican and its "fantastic", "inexpensive" south-of-the-border classics ported by an "extremely friendly" staff to a "bustling", "brightly colored" dining space; the newer Mt. Vernon bistro is a perfect spot to grab some guac or a drink "before a show at the BSO."

NEW Marquee Lounge *American*

- | - | - | M

Highlandtown | Creative Alliance | 3134 Eastern Ave. (East Ave.) | 410-276-1651 | www.creativealliance.org

Originally born out of a creative alliance between Clementine and the theater housing it, this New American has been relaunched under the sole aegis of the theater; founding chef Jeremy Price remains, cranking out midpriced inventive dishes for those with or without tickets to the show; P.S. open for dinner and drinks Thursday–Saturday and brunch on weekends.

NEW Martick's *American*

- | - | - | E

Downtown West | 214 W. Mulberry St. (bet. Park Ave. & Tyler St.)

Downtown West's beloved, long-running French restaurant closed a few years ago, but it will live on in spirit when this space reopens (imminent at press time) as a New American resto-lounge, run by family members of the legendary late owner Morris 'Mo' Martick; like the original, it will be accessed speakeasy-style by a rap at the door, which leads on to an updated version of the vintage interior, where small plates will be washed down with pricey craft cocktails.

Matsuri *Japanese*

▽ 24 | 19 | 21 | $25

South Baltimore | 1105 S. Charles St. (Cross St.) | 410-752-8561 | www.matsuri.us

A "young", "upbeat crowd" claims this Federal Hill sushi spot as a "local" go-to for "first-rate", "decently" priced raw and cooked Japanese eats served at a "good tempo"; the "traditional" setting includes "limited" seating downstairs, supplemented by a more spacious room upstairs (also available for private parties) and sidewalk tables; P.S. check out the weeknight happy-hour "deals."

Matthew's Pizza *Pizza*

27 | 15 | 23 | $16

Highlandtown | 3131 Eastern Ave. (S. East Ave.) | 410-276-8755 | www.matthewspizza.com

"Crust, sauce and cheese are in perfect harmony" at this "insanely good" deep-dish purveyor (they also offer thin crust) in Highlandtown, which many consider the "birthplace of pizza in Baltimore" because it opened in 1943; the "friendly" staff, modest tabs and "small" storefront that's "quirkily" decorated with vivid fauvist murals of Italy all

	FOOD	DECOR	SERVICE	COST

offer a "trip back to simpler times"; P.S. it's "convenient" before or after a show at Creative Alliance.

McCabe's ● *Pub Food*
| 23 | 16 | 22 | $28 |

Hampden | 3845 Falls Rd. (bet. 40th St. & Kelly Pl.) | 410-467-1000 | www.mccabeshampden.com

"Perfect for a good burger or crab cake", this midpriced Hampden pub is a "true neighborhood place", drawing a "local crowd" with "reliable comfort food" in "quaint" wood-and-brick-accented environs; the "nice folks" who staff it contribute to the overall "charming" vibe.

McCormick & Schmick's *Seafood*
| 23 | 22 | 23 | $45 |

Inner Harbor | Pier 5 Hotel | 711 Eastern Ave. (President St.) | 410-234-1300 | www.mccormickandschmicks.com
See review in the Washington, DC, Directory.

NEW McFaul's IronHorse
Tavern ● *American*
| - | - | - | M |

Parkville | 2260 Cromwell Bridge Rd. (Lock Raven Dr.) | 410-828-1625 | www.mcfaulsironhorsetavern.com

New twists on American and regional classics and raw-bar offerings rub shoulders with gussied-up pub fare on the menu of this Parkville newcomer aiming to please exurbanites and urban explorers alike with its moderate prices and local ingredients; longtime fans of the location's past life as Sanders' Corners will recognize the covered porch overlooking the Loch Raven Reservoir, though its bar and dining rooms have been updated with a clean, contemporary look.

Meet 27 *American*
| ▽ 21 | 15 | 21 | $24 |

Charles Village | 127 W. 27th St. (Howard St.) | 410-585-8121 | www.meet27.com

"Picky eaters, the wheat-free, vegans" and even carnivores too have no reason to fear at this Charles Village noshery whose "affordable" New American menu, with South Asian and Caribbean influences, "caters to diet-sensitives" – "and does it well"; reclaimed-wood tables and colorful murals painted by local students provide a modicum of ambiance, and "BYO is a plus."

Mekong Delta Cafe ⓜ⇗ *Vietnamese*
| 27 | 14 | 22 | $19 |

Downtown West | 105 W. Saratoga St. (Cathedral St.) | 410-244-8677
For "phenomenal pho" and other "authentic" Vietnamese "delicacies", this "mom-and-pop" "gem" in an "easy-to-miss" location in Downtown West is "worth the occasional wait" for "limited" seating amid "plain-Jane decor"; the family that runs it is "sweet and lovely", and while prices are "low", remember: it's cash only.

Metropolitan Coffeehouse &
Wine Bar *American*
| ▽ 23 | 18 | 20 | $27 |

South Baltimore | 902 S. Charles St. (bet. Henrietta & Wheeling Sts.) | 410-234-0235 | www.metrobalto.com
South Baltimore is home to this "cool, little" multitasker that's "convenient" for "early coffee", "a biz lunch" or "meeting up with friends" to nosh on "beautifully prepared" and moderately priced

New American fare; it also boasts a "diverse" wine list and a "good variety of brews", which means the exposed-brick-walled space can get "noisy" (upstairs, which is only open for dinner, is quieter).

Michael's Café ● *American*   23 | 19 | 22 | $33

Timonium | 2119 York Rd. (bet. Gerard Ave. & Greenmeadow Dr.) | 410-252-2022 | www.michaelscafe.com

Appealing to an "interesting mix of good ol' boys" and "professional types", this sprawling, multipart Timonium American bar and grill is a go-to "meeting spot" for locals, with its seafood-slanted "comfort food at its best" in an "inviting" "modern" space arrayed with sports memorabilia; prices are moderate, service "always smiles" and, no surprise, there's a "vibrant bar scene" too.

Miguel's Cocina y Cantina *Mexican*   ▽ 20 | 24 | 20 | $28

Locust Point | Silo Point | 1200 Steuart St. (Clement St.) | 443-438-3139 | www.miguelsbaltimore.com

Industrial swank meets Día de los Muertos in this "fascinating" room in a "totally awesome" location – Locust Point's luxury Silo Point condo conversion – where floor-to-ceiling windows are offset by colorful skulls and skeletons; like the decor, the "upscale Mexican" eats offer a "fresh take" on "old standards", while solid service adds value to already affordable tabs.

Milton Inn *American*   28 | 26 | 26 | $59

Sparks | 14833 York Rd. (Quaker Bottom Rd.) | 410-771-4366 | www.miltoninn.com

Dripping with "ambiance", this circa-1740 fieldstone inn is an "enduring treasure" in Sparks, with "cozy fireplaces, oil paintings and white tablecloths" spread over multiple rooms that provide suitably "elegant" backdrops for its "sophisticated" American cuisine; service is "impeccable", and while a typical experience is "pricey", the lounge menu offers "lesser-priced" options.

Minato *Japanese*   ▽ 24 | 22 | 24 | $23

Mt. Vernon | 1013 N. Charles St. (Eager St.) | 410-332-0332 | www.minatosushibar.com

If it's "not the most authentic Japanese in the city", this Mt. Vernon purveyor may be one of the "hippest", with "cute", colorful, contemporary decor and "creative" sushi that attract happy-hour crowds for cocktails and rolls at bargain prices; tempura, rice bowls and noodles (plus Vietnamese pho) are also served, and in a "speedy" manner.

Miss Shirley's *American*   26 | 21 | 23 | $24

Inner Harbor | 750 E. Pratt St. (President St.) | 410-528-5373
Roland Park | 513 W. Cold Spring Ln. (Kittery Ln.) | 410-889-5272

Miss Shirley's Food Truck *American*

Location varies; see website | no phone
www.missshirleys.com

"Down-home cooking at its best" cheer fans of this "always crowded" daytime mini-chain where the "extensive" menu of "dangerously delish" American fare features many a "Chesapeake" or "Southern" "twist"; yes, there's often "a wait" (no reservations) in "funky", colorful digs, but tabs are fair, and staffers are "super", so most ultimately leave "stuffed and happy"; P.S. check online for time and location info for its food truck.

NEW Moonshine Tavern ❶ *Creole/Southern*   - | - | - | M

Canton | 2300 Boston St. (Leakin St.) | 410-327-6455 |
www.bmoreshine.com

A menu of white lightning–based cocktails (available by the mason jar) hauls a young crowd into this new, rough-hewn Canton bar/restaurant, while the updated Southern and Creole food, including po' boy sandwiches, shrimp 'n' grits and beignets, lends an air of respectability to the mix; if hooch isn't your bag, there are plenty of craft beers and regular liquors to wet your whistle too.

Morton's The Steakhouse *Steak*   26 | 24 | 26 | $71

Inner Harbor | Sheraton Inner Harbor Hotel | 300 S. Charles St. (Conway St.) | 410-547-8255 | www.mortons.com
See review in the Washington, DC, Directory.

Mr. Bill's Terrace Inn Ⓜ *Crab House*   ▽ 26 | 13 | 21 | $40

Essex | 200 Eastern Blvd. (Helena Ave.) | 410-687-5996
Hard-shell fans can "wait as long as an hour-plus" to get their mallets on what they claim are "the best steamed crabs in the Baltimore area" at this "quintessential" crab house in Essex ("grab a beer at the bar and be patient"); authenticity comes at a "high cost", but for "laid-back crab pickin'" with a "warm, fuzzy" neighborhood feel, this place is a "little gem."

Mr. Rain's Fun House Ⓜ *American*   23 | 26 | 23 | $45

South Baltimore | American Visionary Art Museum | 800 Key Hwy. (Covington St.) | 443-524-7379 | www.mrrainsfunhouse.com
The "fun and funky" environs of this "clever", "inventive" New American spot are fitting given its setting within the American Visionary Art Museum, where the "charming and wacky artwork carries into the restaurant"; though a few find it "a little pricey", most consider the "outside-the-box" experience with "lovely" service to be "worth it."

NEW My Thai *Thai*   - | - | - | M

Harbor East | Tack Factory Bldg. | 1300 Bank St. (bet. Central Ave. & Eden St.) | 410-327-0023 | www.mythaibaltimore.com
Following a fire, this Thai relocated from Mt. Vernon to new Harbor East digs in a former tack factory and bolstered its classic menu with the addition of adventurous Asian street fare like skewered tongue and sautéed silkworms; diners can watch the food fly at the industrial-looking grill bar or settle into the contemporary dining room for a more traditional repast.

Nacho Mama's ❶ *Mexican*   22 | 22 | 21 | $22

Canton | 2911 O'Donnell St. (bet. Curley St. & Linwood Ave.) |
410-675-0898 | www.nachomamascanton.com
"Hubcap margaritas" (as in four drinks' worth of margarita served in a hubcap) wash down "off-the-hook" grub like "don't-miss" "Mexican

meatloaf" and "gold-standard" wings at this "crowded" "cheap-eats" cantina in Canton; the atmosphere is "friendly" and "quirky" (there's an Elvis motif) with a dash of "Bawlmer flair" – Natty Boh served only in a can, Journey "on the juke every night."

NEW Nando's Peri-Peri *Chicken* | 22 | 19 | 19 | $17 |

Charles Village | 421 W. Baltimore St. (Paca St.) | 443-681-3675
Gambrills | 1403 Main Chapel Way (Brandermill Blvd.) | 443-302-6225
www.nandosperiperi.com
See review in the Washington, DC, Directory.

Negril ⊠ *Jamaican* | 24 | 13 | 20 | $15 |

Laurel | Laurel Shopping Ctr. | 331 Montrose Ave. (Baltimore Ave.) | 301-498-0808
Mitchellville | Mitchellville Plaza | 12116 Central Ave. (Enterprise Rd.) | 301-249-9101
www.negrileats.com
See review in the Washington, DC, Directory.

Oceanaire Seafood Room *Seafood* | 24 | 23 | 24 | $58 |

Harbor East | 801 Aliceanna St. (President St.) | 443-872-0000 | www.theoceanaire.com
See review in the Washington, DC, Directory.

Of Love & Regret ◗ *American* | - | - | - | M |

Canton | 1028 S. Conkling St. (O'Donnell St.) | 410-327-0760 | www.ofloveandregret.com
This Brewers Hill gastropub delivers a midpriced, inventive American menu that's designed to soak up plenty of craft beer, appropriately enough since it's owned by Stillwater Artisanal Ales' brewer Brian Strumke; thirsts are quenched by a wall of taps gushing artisanal suds plus wine and iced coffee in the tin-ceilinged and brick-walled space.

Olive Grove Restaurant *Italian* | 24 | 20 | 22 | $27 |

Linthicum | 705 N. Hammonds Ferry Rd. (bet. Evelyn Ave. & Nursery Rd.) | 410-636-1385 | www.olivegroverestaurant.com
Likened to "Olive Garden" ("endless salad and breadsticks!") but with a "personal, hometown touch", this Linthicum spot is "well attended" thanks to its "large portions" of "solid, straightforward Italian" cooking plus "great, big crab cakes", all at "respectable prices"; the simple, spacious setting and "professional", "courteous" staff help make it a lock for "family" outings, and "large parties" note there's a "banquet hall" on-site.

Olive Room *Greek* | ∇ 24 | 20 | 22 | $44 |

Fells Point | Inn at The Black Olive | 803 S. Caroline St. (Lancaster St.) | 443-681-6316 | www.theblackolive.com
"Small but elegant", this Greek entry perched above the Inn at the Black Olive in Fells Point offers "high-quality" fare like its more well-known big sister (Black Olive); the vibe is "laid-back", with solid service, and while decor indoors is "sparse", the harbor view from the rooftop terrace is "fantastic."

	FOOD	DECOR	SERVICE	COST

One-Eyed Mike's ● *Pub Food* ▽ 23 | 18 | 23 | $27

Fells Point | 708 S. Bond St. (bet. Aliceanna & Lancaster Sts.) | 410-327-0445 | www.oneeyedmikes.com

Walls lined "with Grand Marnier bottles" (bought by and stored on-site for "members") set the mood at this "off-the-beaten-path" Fells Point "neighborhood" tavern, where the "dark and intimate" bar could be "a setting for a film noir" if the "friendly bartenders" didn't make it such a "fun and happy place"; "surprisingly good" upscale pub food at fair prices works for a "casual lunch or dinner."

One World Cafe *Vegetarian* 22 | 16 | 19 | $19

Homewood | 100 W. University Pkwy. (Canterbury Rd.) | 410-235-5777

There are some "pleasant culinary surprises" on the "interesting" vegetarian menu at this affordable Homewood catch-all that's part cafe, bar, coffeehouse, juice bar and, above all, "hangout for Johns Hopkins students and professors"; some say the basic decor (local art on the walls) could use an "upgrade", but it's "comfy" and the staff is "laid-back", making it "conducive to unhurried dining."

Open Door Café *American* 24 | 24 | 23 | $19

Bel Air | 528 Baltimore Pike/Rte. 1 (Rte. 24) | 410-838-4393 | www.theopendoorcafe.com

Inside this "charming" Bel Air bistro/coffeehouse "tucked unassumingly" into a strip mall, trompe l'oeil murals ensconce patrons amid a "French country" auberge while they dine on "delicious" American classics with "a bit of a gourmet flair"; other reasons to open the door: "pleasant" service, "value" prices and an "excellent" breakfast menu.

Orchard Market & Café Ⓜ *Persian* 26 | 21 | 26 | $25

Towson | 8815 Orchard Tree Ln. (Joppa Rd.) | 410-339-7700 | www.orchardmarketandcafe.com

"Hidden away" "behind a furniture store" in Towson, this "tiny" Persian prepares a "mouthwatering" blend of "authentic" and "modern flavors"; "artful" decor with a Middle Eastern bent and "gracious", "warm" service add up to a "total gem" worthy of "celebrations" that "don't [cost] an arm and a leg" ("BYO helps").

Oregon Grille *Seafood/Steak* 25 | 26 | 25 | $61

Hunt Valley | 1201 Shawan Rd. (Beaver Dam Rd.) | 410-771-0505 | www.theoregongrille.com

Located "nicely away from the city" in Hunt Valley "horse country", this "romantic retreat" is known for its "exquisite" steaks and seafood (at "high-but-worth-it" prices), accompanied by "just-as-it-should-be" service; "proper linens", "equestrian" decor, wood-burning fireplaces and piano music in the background complete the thoroughbred picture; P.S. jackets required in the main dining room.

NEW Ouzo Bay *Greek/Seafood* - | - | - | E

Harbor East | 1000 Lancaster St. (bet. Central Ave. & Exeter St.) | 443-708-5818 | www.ouzobay.com

This upscale Greek newcomer on the water in Harbor East takes pride in its wild-caught whole fish flown in daily, grilled with a minimum of fuss and served in a modern setting bathed in electric-blue light; while the tab may be all business, the mood is not, especially on weekends when the lounge cues up house music and people-watching becomes an art form.

Pabu *Japanese*

─ | ─ | ─ | E

Harbor East | Four Seasons Baltimore | 200 International Dr. (Aliceanna St.) | 410-223-1460 | www.michaelmina.net

Celebrity chef Michael Mina takes on Japanese cuisine (with partner Ken Tominaga) at this high-end izakaya in Harbor East's Four Seasons (but accessed via a separate entrance on Aliceanna Street) that serves classic dishes from a robata grill and a sushi bar, washed down by a world-class sake selection; the rough-wood tables, bamboo ceiling and privacy panels keep things casual even though there's a sleek sheen to everything.

Pappas *American/Seafood*

23 | 16 | 21 | $26

Glen Burnie | 6713 Ritchie Hwy. (Americana Circle) | 410-766-3713
Parkville | 1725 Taylor Ave. (Oakleigh Rd.) | 410-661-4357
www.pappascrabcakes.com

A "packed parking lot" and "lots of locals" are a sure sign this "bargain" American seafooder pleases Parkville denizens with its signature "primo" crab cakes with "little filler and great flavor" (there's also a Glen Burnie branch with a "sports bar atmosphere"); if there's "not much to say" about the decor, diners talk up the merits of the "folksy atmosphere" and "friendly" service from "old-fashioned waitresses."

Pasta Plus Ⓜ *Italian*

26 | 17 | 24 | $32

Laurel | Center Plaza | 209 Gorman Ave. (bet. Rtes. 1 & 198) | 301-498-5100 | www.pastaplusrestaurant.com

There's "always a line" at this "family-owned" Italian "diamond hidden in the rough" of a "moribund" Laurel strip mall, but carb zealots have no reservations (literally) about standing by for "generous" portions of "perfect" housemade pastas, "great" pizza and other "hearty" fare; folks are "tightly packed" in the simple, white-tablecloth space, but service is "attentive" and the prices "reasonable"; P.S. to avoid a wait, eat in or carry out at the adjacent market, which is open daily.

Patrick's *American*

▽ 22 | 18 | 23 | $28

Cockeysville | Cranbrook Shopping Ctr. | 550 Cranbrook Rd. (Gelding Dr.) | 410-683-0604 | www.patricksrestaurant.com

For "steady", "dependable" American eats (think steaks, fish and crab cakes), this Cockeysville local "favorite" is a "go-to" with a "comfortable atmosphere" and "happy", "pleasant" servers, which adds up to a "great value"; with separate sports bar, martini lounge and fine-dining areas, it's conducive to "everyday" dining or "special occasions."

Pazo *Mediterranean*

25 | 27 | 24 | $48

Harbor East | 1425 Aliceanna St. (Spring St.) | 410-534-7296 | www.pazorestaurant.com

A former machine shop in Harbor East hosts Tony Foreman and Cindy Wolf's visually "stunning" "industrial-chic" destination for "scrumptious" Med tapas and entrees delivered by "attentive" pros;

a few warn that "small plates equal big bucks", and the noise level on weekend nights can be "deafening", but most of the "trendy", "people-watching" crowd is down with the "sizzling-hot scene."

Peerce's Ⓜ *American*
(aka The Grille at Peerce's)

▽ 21 | 20 | 20 | $44

Phoenix | 12460 Dulaney Valley Rd. (Loch Raven Dr.) | 410-252-7111 | www.thegrilleatpeerces.com

This "fine old place" in Phoenix offers "really tasty" American tavern fare on a menu that varies from "simple to fancy" amid "pleasant surroundings" that include a "warm fireplace" and horse-and-hound prints; it's expensive, but service is solid, and longtime loyalists say it's "worth" a visit for the "pretty drive" by the Loch Raven Reservoir.

Peppermill *American*

23 | 18 | 24 | $28

Lutherville | Heaver Plaza | 1301 York Rd. (Greenridge Rd.) | 410-583-1107 | www.pepmill.com

"Huge portions" of "excellent" American fare are served by a staff that "knows how to treat guests" at this white-tablecloth Lutherville "institution" with a "very loyal following" among a "lovely, older clientele"; what's more, as "times are changing", "others are discovering" that their elders know a "bang for the buck" when they find it.

Peter's Inn 🅩Ⓜ *American*

27 | 17 | 22 | $35

Fells Point | 504 S. Ann St. (Eastern Ave.) | 410-675-7313 | www.petersinn.com

"What looks like (and once was) a dive bar is merely a front" for this Fells Point "foodie destination" with a "magic kitchen" plating up "farmer's market–inspired" New American "gourmet" "treats" served by a "friendly", "tattooed" staff; the "almost too hip" scene unfolds in "funky", "cramped quarters", so "go early" or "get in line", because they don't take reservations.

Petit Louis Bistro *French*

26 | 23 | 25 | $46

Roland Park | 4800 Roland Ave. (Upland Rd.) | 410-366-9393 | www.petitlouis.com

Like an "upbeat Paris bistro" set down in Roland Park, this "buzzing little place" delivers "dependably delicious" traditional French "favorites" via "impressively coordinated" service in a "cozy" storefront; it's "pricey", though "more reasonable" at lunch, and one diner's "thrum of happy people" is another's "din" amid "closely arranged" tables, but *c'est la vie*, as this "classique" remains "wildly popular."

P.F. Chang's China Bistro *Chinese*

23 | 23 | 22 | $30

Inner Harbor | Market Pl. | 600 E. Pratt St. (Market Pl.) | 410-649-2750
White Marsh | White Marsh Mall | 8342 Honeygo Blvd. (White Marsh Blvd.) | 410-931-2433
Columbia | Mall in Columbia | 10300 Little Patuxent Pkwy. (Mall Access Rd.) | 410-730-5344
Towson | Towson Town Ctr. | 825 Dulaney Valley Rd. (Fairmount Ave.) | 410-372-5250
www.pfchangs.com
See review in the Washington, DC, Directory.

	FOOD	DECOR	SERVICE	COST

Phillips *Seafood* | 20 | 19 | 20 | $39 |

Inner Harbor | 601 E. Pratt St. (Pratt St.) | 410-685-6600 |
www.phillipsseafood.com

Sure they're "touristy, but who cares?" demand defenders of these
tanker-sized seafooders in Baltimore's Inner Harbor and DC – after
all, they both sport "spectacular" water views, and their crab cakes
are "just about the best"; if a few "serious seafood eaters" judge it a
bit "assembly line" for their taste, less picky palates savor the midpriced tabs and "respectable" service.

Pho Dat Thanh *Vietnamese* | 24 | 14 | 19 | $16 |

Columbia | Columbia Mktpl. | 9400 Snowden River Pkwy.
(bet. Carved Stone Way & Rustling Leaf) | 410-381-3839
Towson | 510 York Rd. (bet. Pennsylvania & Shealy Aves.) |
410-296-9118
www.phodatthanh.com

"For a slurping good time", pho-natics count on this "unfussy" twosome in Columbia and Towson for "huge", "rich" bowls of "excellent"
broth as well as a "large menu of non-pho options" at attractively
"small prices"; less attractive, perhaps, are the "unfussy", "unremarkable" surroundings, leading some to "recommend takeout",
though the in-house service is solid.

Pho Nam ⊉ *Vietnamese* | ▽ 27 | 14 | 23 | $11 |

Catonsville | Westview | 6477 Baltimore National Pike (Rolling Rd.) |
410-455-6000

What some claim is the "best pho by far" is ladled out along with a
"limited" menu of other Vietnamese fare at this "hole-in-the-wall"
noodle shop in a Catonsville strip mall; "super-fast" service "just
wants to make you happy", and if decor is "lacking", it doesn't dis-
tract from that "aromatic broth" that will "cure what ails you";
P.S. it's cash only, but you won't need much.

Piedigrotta Bakery *Bakery/Italian* | ▽ 28 | 20 | 26 | $26 |

Harbor East | 1300 Bank St. (Eden St.) | 410-522-6900 |
www.piedigrottabakery.com

A few conflicted sorts "hate the calories" but still love the "amazing
sweets" ("pastries! pastries! pastries!") as well as "large portions"
of gently priced, "home-cooked Italian" fare at this lesser-known
Harbor East bakery-plus; the setting is small and no-frills, but a
"relaxed atmosphere" and "excellent" service make patrons feel like
they've "arrived home."

Plug Ugly's | - | - | - | M |
Publick House ❶ *Pub Food*

Canton | 2908 O'Donnell St. (S. Linwood Ave.) | 410-563-8459 |
www.pluguglyspub.com

Named for a 19th-century Baltimore street gang, this pub on
O'Donnell Square sports a nostalgic, wood-paneled tavern look and
trades in midpriced pub classics plus shellfish-packed steam pots
and local beers; the two-story space has an outdoor deck, a great place
to sip a signature 'pirate juice' – fruit-steeped rum made at the bar.

	FOOD	DECOR	SERVICE	COST

Pollo Campero *Central American*

19 | 12 | 17 | $11

Laurel | 833 S. Washington Blvd. (Archer St.) | 301-776-7590 | www.campero.com

See review in the Washington, DC, Directory.

Portalli's *Italian*

22 | 20 | 23 | $38

Ellicott City | 8085 Main St. (Maryland Ave.) | 410-720-2330 | www.portallisec.com

Ellicott City's "historic district" is home to this neighborhood boîte where "well-executed" Italian "standbys" and more "creative" choices share space on an "easy", midpriced menu; service is "attentive but not pushy", and live piano on weekends "sets the mood" in the "relaxing", "romantic" dark-leather and white-tablecloth digs.

Porters *American*

▽ 22 | 19 | 22 | $27

South Baltimore | 1032 Riverside Ave. (Cross St.) | 410-332-7345 | www.portersfederalhill.com

This "comfortable" and "homey" Fed Hill "neighborhood bar" offers "tasty" midpriced New American "gastropub" grub, "great beers on tap" and "plenty of TVs to catch the game" while you munch; the "good" service is in line with the "relaxed atmosphere."

Prime Rib *Steak*

28 | 26 | 28 | $71

Mt. Vernon | 1101 N. Calvert St. (Chase St.) | 410-539-1804
NEW **Hanover** | Maryland Live! Casino | 7002 Arundel Mills Circle (Arundel Mills Blvd.) | 443-445-2970
www.theprimerib.com

Do as they do in *Mad Men* – "dress up and have a martini" – at this "classic" Mt. Vernon steakhouse (with branches in DC and Maryland Live! Casino) that's operating at the "top of its game", delivering "fantastic" "slabs of meat" and "masterful seafood"; from the "1940s supper-club vibe" to the "sublime" tuxedoed service, it's a "perfect evening out"; P.S. business-casual dress is recommended.

R & R Taqueria *Mexican*

27 | 7 | 23 | $10

Elkridge | 7894 Washington Blvd. (Waterloo Rd.) | 410-799-0001
Perry Hall | 5005 Honeygo Center Dr. (Scott Moore Way) | 410-870-0185
www.rrtaqueria.com

Possibly "the best food you'll ever eat in a gas station" is pumped out at this "awesome", "authentic" Mexican fast-fooder in an Elkridge Shell station (there's also a branch in Perry Hall) known for its "exemplary selection of tacos" and more, "made fresh in front of you" by folks who "really care"; the "decor is barstools at a counter", but it's "worth" the *muy bajo* prices.

Ra Sushi Bar Restaurant *Japanese*

24 | 24 | 21 | $31

Harbor East | 1390 Lancaster St. (Spring St.) | 410-522-3200 | www.rasushi.com

"Flashy" nightclub-esque decor – and "blaring music" to go with it – makes this "trendy" chain link in Harbor East a "favorite happy-hour spot" for "pretty" "young" things; while it may not be a venue for "sushi snobs", admirers assert that the "creative" rolls are equal to the "happening scene", the staff is "helpful" and prices are "affordable."

	FOOD	DECOR	SERVICE	COST

Red Hot & Blue *BBQ*   22 | 18 | 20 | $21

Laurel | 677 Main St. (7th St.) | 301-953-1943 | www.redhotandblue.com
See review in the Washington, DC, Directory.

Red Pearl *Chinese*   26 | 21 | 23 | $23

Columbia | 10215 Wincopin Circle (Little Patuxent Pkwy.) |
410-715-6530 | www.redpearlrestaurant.com
Dim sum "as good as in Hong Kong" is the main draw (especially "on
weekends when the carts are rolling") at this "authentic" Chinese
spot near Lake Kittamaqundi in Columbia, but "genuine Sichuan" as
well as Cantonese dishes round out the budget-friendly menu; the
"friendly, smart" staff patrols a "modern" space that feels airy on
account of its blond-wood accents, high ceilings and large windows.

Regions Ⓜ *Eclectic*   ▽ 23 | 19 | 22 | $44

Catonsville | 803 Frederick Rd. (Mellor Ave.) | 410-788-0075 |
www.regionsrestaurant.com
"Interesting" Eclectic small and large plates based on different
regions – e.g. Maryland, Cajun country, France, Italy, Asia – meet on
the "limited but excellent" monthly changing menu of this "upscale"
relative of nearby Catonsville Gourmet; exposed-brick and earth-
toned walls with stenciled accents create a "cozy" yet contemporary
space, while solid service and BYO with a small corkage fee bring
value to the bill.

Regi's *American*   23 | 19 | 24 | $31

South Baltimore | 1002 Light St. (Hamburg St.) | 410-539-7344 |
www.regisamericanbistro.com
This "cornerstone" bistro in Federal Hill serves up "interesting"
American eats, many made with herbs "grown on the roof"; after a fire
in 2012, most of the "cozy" interior's details – fireplace, hardwood
floors – remain but have been buffed up (possibly outdating the Decor
rating), which should ensure it will remain a "neighborhood gem."

Rocket to Venus ❶ *Eclectic*   20 | 19 | 17 | $23

Hampden | 3360 Chestnut Ave. (34th St.) | 410-235-7887 |
www.rockettovenus.com
A "hipster crowd" frequents this "quirky" Hampden watering hole,
bellying up to the 40-ft. copper horseshoe bar for the "excellent options on tap" or sliding into black-and-teal retro-style booths to
chow down on "interesting" Eclectic menu offerings like the deep-
fried PB&J; it gets "packed", especially on weekends, but the staff is
"nice" enough, and the prices are "definitely right."

Roy's *Hawaiian*   27 | 25 | 26 | $53

Harbor East | 720 Aliceanna St. (President St.) | 410-659-0099 |
www.roysrestaurant.com
From the "top-notch", "imaginative" Hawaiian fusion cuisine to the
staff that treats each diner like a "big kahuna", "you would never
know" this Harbor East spot is part of "a chain" (from celeb chef Roy
Yamaguchi); the "upscale"-casual digs feature a lively open kitchen
and a bar slinging "potent" drinks, which promotes a "chatty, up-

	FOOD	DECOR	SERVICE	COST

tempo" vibe, and though "fat wallets" are helpful, it's "cheaper than a trip to Hawaii."

Rusty Scupper *Seafood*

22	25	22	$47

South Baltimore | 402 Key Hwy. (Light St.) | 410-727-3678 | www.selectrestaurants.com

The "truly awesome view" of the Inner Harbor has beckoned diners for over 30 years to this South Baltimore seafooder perched right on the water, where "well-prepared" takes on "traditional favorites" are delivered by capable servers in a vast glass box of a room; while some call it "a tourist destination", others say go "if you have some-one to impress" – either way, remember that "location, location, location" "comes at a price."

Ruth's Chris Steak House *Steak*

26	24	26	$67

Business District | Power Plant Live | 600 Water St. (bet. Gay St. & Market Pl.) | 410-783-0033
Inner Harbor | Pier 5 | 711 Eastern Ave. (S. President St.) | 410-230-0033
Pikesville | 1777 Reisterstown Rd. (Hooks Ln.) | 410-837-0033
www.ruthschris.com

See review in the Washington, DC, Directory.

Sabatino's ● *Italian*

24	19	24	$35

Little Italy | 901 Fawn St. (High St.) | 410-727-9414 | www.sabatinos.com

Everything from the 'Bookmaker' salads to the "homemade" pastas is "generously" heaped up in a way that's "more grandmother's kitchen than posh" at this eminently "reliable" "red-sauce" "land-mark" in Little Italy; a staff with "personality", plus friendly tabs and an "old-fashioned" setting make diners "feel like family", and late hours are nice too.

Salt ☒ *American*

27	23	25	$46

Fells Point | 2127 E. Pratt St. (Collington St.) | 410-276-5480 | www.salttavern.com

It's "destination-quality" gush adoptees of this "sophisticated" New American eatery on a quiet corner near Patterson Park, thanks to an "original" menu that's full of "surprises" bolstered by "thoughtful" draft beers and a "well-composed" wine list; though it's "on the pricey side", and parking can be a "challenge" ("bring the smallest car you own"), most agree "kind", "knowledgeable" service and "chic"-meets-"relaxed" exposed-brick surrounds work well for a "comfortable night out" or an "occasion."

Sammy's Trattoria *Italian*

21	20	20	$42

Mt. Vernon | 1200 N. Charles St. (Biddle St.) | 410-837-9999 | www.sammystrattoria.com

"Skip Little Italy" and head to Mt. Vernon say fans of the "big por-tions" of "solid" Italian fare at this "reliable" trattoria; it's "on the ex-pensive side", but the high-vaulted-ceilinged space is "tastefully appointed", and the staff is "fast and attentive before shows" at the nearby Meyerhoff or Lyric theaters, taking a more "leisurely" (some say "slow") approach afterward.

	FOOD	DECOR	SERVICE	COST

Samos ☒⇨ Greek
28 | 16 | 24 | $21

Greektown | 600 Oldham St. (Fleet St.) | 410-675-5292 |
www.samosrestaurant.com

"As close to the real thing as you can get" say ardent admirers of the "phenomenal" food "like yia-yia used to make" at this Greektown elder statesman where even the "salad dressing has a huge following"; the wait is often "long" since there are no reservations and only "limited seating" in the "underwhelming", mural-bedecked space, but it's "stupidly cheap" and "so very worth it"; P.S. it's cash only and BYO.

San Sushi Japanese
∇ 26 | 15 | 21 | $29

Cockeysville | 9832 York Rd. (bet. Galloway Ave. & Padonia Rd.) |
410-453-0140 | www.timoniumrestaurant.com

"They don't skimp on the size of the rolls" at this "excellent", mid-priced Japanese BYO in a Cockeysville strip mall, a "locals'" favorite for "tasty" sushi from servers who "learn your name" if you're a regular; "little ones" are entertained by the aquarium in the otherwise simple, traditional digs.

San Sushi Too/
Thai One On Japanese/Thai
∇ 21 | 16 | 20 | $26

Towson | 10 W. Pennsylvania Ave. (bet. Washington Ave. & York Rd.) |
410-825-0908 | www.towsonrestaurant.com

Sushi San/Thai Jai Dee Japanese/Thai

Canton | 2748 Lighthouse Point (Boston St.) | 410-534-8888 |
www.sushisanbaltimore.com

In a stalemate between whether to do Japanese or Thai, these dual-menu "neighborhood staples" in Towson and Canton act as tie-breakers with their "interesting" sushi, cooked Japanese fare and "great pad Thai" and the like; "kind" service distracts from rather "informal" surroundings, and wallet-watchers note it's "a steal."

Sascha's 527 ☒ American
24 | 24 | 22 | $30

Mt. Vernon | 527 N. Charles St. (bet. Centre & Hamilton Sts.) |
410-539-8880 | www.saschas.com

A "culinary surprise" say diners of this "moderately priced" Mt. Vernon New American offering an "inventive" menu featuring "quality ingredients and a good mix of options"; the "colorful", "gorgeously designed" dining room feels like a "movie set", and service is "attentive without being overbearing", plus it's a "convenient stop" before or after visiting the Walters Art Museum or Peabody Conservatory; P.S. its express cafe at Centerstage operates when there's a show.

Schultz's Crab House Crab House
∇ 27 | 20 | 26 | $27

Essex | 1732 Old Eastern Ave. (Walkern Rd.) | 410-687-1020

"Locals who know their Maryland seafood" hit this circa-1969 "Essex tradition" for "flavorful" offerings including "meaty" crabs and what some claim are "the best lump crab cakes"; "old"-time decor (knotty pine walls, trophy fish) makes it a "sentimental favorite", while "always accommodating" staffers and "reasonable prices" are more contemporary perks.

	FOOD	DECOR	SERVICE	COST

Seaside Restaurant & Crab House *Seafood*

26 | 17 | 24 | $34

Glen Burnie | 224 Crain Hwy. N. (New Jersey Ave.) | 410-760-2200 | www.theseasiderestaurant.com

"Crabs, crabs, crabs, that's what it's all about" – the "best steamed crabs", "exquisite crab cakes", soft-shell crab sandwiches "that are worth every penny" and a crab dip that's "like a spoonful of heaven" – at this "friendly" crustacean station in Glen Burnie; the nautically trimmed, sports bar–esque digs have a "down-home feel", and while it "ain't cheap", you won't shell out that much either.

Shin Chon *Korean*

∇ 22 | 19 | 19 | $34

Ellicott City | Golden Triangle Shopping Ctr. | 8801 Baltimore National Pike (Ridge Rd.) | 410-461-3280

"Delicious" Korean BBQ – "how can you go wrong?" ask enthusiasts who roll up their sleeves and grill their own "interesting" vittles right on each table under kitchen-grade vents at this midpriced Ellicott City strip-maller; some report a bit of a "language barrier" and say service is of the "leave you alone unless you ask for something" variety, but to devotees, that's all part of the charm.

NEW Shiso Tavern Ⓜ *Asian*

- | - | - | M

Canton | 2933 O'Donnell St. (bet. Curley & Potomac Sts.) | 410-276-8800 | www.shisotavern.com

The capacious bar, as well as its Blue Hill Tavern parentage, give this bright and airy Canton hangout cred in a neighborhood known for its after-work singles scene; along with specialty cocktails (and bottomless spirits during weekend brunch), it offers midpriced Asian fare including wok dishes, fusion plates and a large selection of sushi rolls, both classic and trendy.

Sip & Bite Restaurant ● *Diner*

19 | 12 | 20 | $14

Fells Point | 2200 Boston St. (Van Lill St.) | 410-675-7077 | www.sipandbite.com

"Classic Bawlmer, hon" servers "get the job done with no fluff" at this "classic" all-nighter in Fells Point, where the "honest diner food" "isn't creative", but "it's exactly what you want", and at a "very good bang for your buck"; the "old-fashioned neighborhood" experience plays out in a remodeled retro setting with red-checked trim and pop art on the walls.

Sofi's Crepes *Crêpes*

24 | 14 | 21 | $12

Downtown North | 1723 N. Charles St. (bet. Lafayette Ave. & Lanvale St.) | 410-727-7732
NEW Fells Point | 1627 Thames St. (B'way) | 410-563-0471
York Road Corridor | Belvedere Sq. | 5911 York Rd. (Belvedere Ave.) | 410-727-5737
Owings Mills | Valley Village Shopping Ctr. | 9123 Reisterstown Rd. (Old Craddock Rd.) | 410-356-4191
www.sofiscrepes.com

"Sweet and savory" crêpes "for every palate", with "quirky names" like "Kevin Bacon", are made "before your eyes" and served "piping hot" at this "cute" chainlet of crêperies that cater to pancake-thin wallets; there's often a "wait" in the "snug" but "friendly" counter-service spaces, so some suggest getting your "yummy" "light lunch or snack" to go.

Sotto Sopra *Italian*

26 | 25 | 25 | $47

Mt. Vernon | 405 N. Charles St. (bet. Franklin & Mulberry Sts.) | 410-625-0534 | www.sottosopra.us

It's the "Maserati of Italian restaurants" purr paesani about this "elegant and sexy" Northern Italian in a "tastefully" theatrical room with sweeping curtains and "colorful murals", housed in a Mt. Vernon townhouse, which provides "divine" cuisine prepared with "an artist's touch"; "attentive" but "not invasive" service and once-monthly Sunday dinners featuring live opera also rev motors.

Spice & Dice *Thai*

▽ 29 | 15 | 21 | $18

Towson | 1220 E. Joppa Rd. (bet. Edgeclift Rd. & Mylander Ln.) | 410-494-8777 | www.thaispiceanddice.com

The "authentic" Thai tastes "will set your mouth on fire" in the "first-rate" fare at this Towson BYO sibling of Little Spice, though the spice averse note with relief that there are five heat levels to choose from; service is "efficient", and if some feel the "quirky", colorful room "resembles a kindergarten classroom" (it's in a comic book/gamer shop), live jazz on Thursday adds a grown-up touch; P.S. extensive gluten-free/vegan options available.

Stanford Grill *American*

24 | 24 | 23 | $41

Columbia | 8900 Stanford Blvd. (Dobbin Rd.) | 410-312-0445 | www.thestanfordgrill.com

"Terrific steaks" hot off the grill and "mouthwatering" rotisserie chicken are standouts on a menu full of "moderately innovative twists" on "typical American fare" at this Columbia locals' spot; "responsive" servers cruise the cozy warren of booths, and though it's "a bit pricey", live jazz most nights adds value (even if it's "noisy").

Stang of Siam *Thai*

▽ 23 | 23 | 17 | $27

Mt. Vernon | 200 E. Preston St. (bet. Calvert & Hunter Sts.) | 443-453-9142 | www.stangofsiam.com

The owners of The Regent in DC bring "much-needed" Thai to Mt. Vernon with this fair-priced "gem" on a "quiet corner", which "displays creativity" with the "ancient cuisine"; "artful decor" – chocolate-brown walls with elaborate teak carvings and Buddha statues – and "pretty" cocktails compensate for "very sweet servers" who a few say can seem "overwhelmed" at peak times.

Stone Mill Bakery & Cafe ⊠ *Bakery*

24 | 15 | 19 | $22

Brooklandville | Green Spring Station | 10751 Falls Rd. (Greenspring Valley Rd.) | 410-821-1358
NEW **Pikesville** | Stevenson Village Shopping Ctr. | 10423 Stevenson Rd. (Old Valley Rd.) | 443-660-7390
www.stonemillbakery.com

A "higher-end clientele" (think "ladies who lunch") flocks to this "friendly" bakery/cafe within Brooklandville's posh Green Spring

Station for "amazing" "fresh-baked" breads, "lovely" sandwiches and "to-die-for" brownies and other sweets served in a bright, arched-windowed space or on an outdoor patio; true, you may "pay for the privilege", but it "never disappoints"; P.S. there's a new, smaller Pikesville branch.

Suburban House *Deli*
19 | 13 | 17 | $20

Pikesville | 1700 Reisterstown Rd. (Naylors Ln.) | 410-484-7775 | www.suburbanhousedeli.com

"Everything you order is big" at this "classic old-timey Jewish deli" in Pikesville, known for its "tasty" sandwiches, bagels and smoked fish at "reasonable prices"; there's "no real atmosphere" in the simple digs, but the booths are "comfortable", there's "conversation worth overhearing" and the service is "fast"; P.S. it closes at 8 PM.

Sullivan's Steakhouse *Steak*
25 | 25 | 25 | $60

Inner Harbor | 1 E. Pratt St. (Light St.) | 410-962-5503 | www.sullivanssteakhouse.com

Satisfy the urge to "splurge" at this "enjoyable" Inner Harbor link in a national chain, a Chicago-style steakhouse known for its chops "done to perfection", "equally good" classic sides and "fancy cocktails" brought by "attentive" servers in a spacious, retro wood-paneled setting; a bar scene at happy hour contributes to a "lively" atmosphere.

Sushi Hana *Japanese*
26 | 20 | 23 | $31

Mt. Washington | Lake Falls Shopping Ctr. | 6080 Falls Rd. (Lake Ave.) | 410-377-4228
Timonium | Yorkridge Shopping Ctr. | 6 W. Ridgely Rd. (York Rd.) | 410-560-7090
Towson | 6 E. Pennsylvania Ave. (York Rd.) | 410-823-0372
www.sushihanabaltimore.com

For some of the "best sushi and sashimi around", including an "expansive" selection of "specialty rolls" "filled with melt-in-your-mouth goodness", plus "reliable and tasty" cooked Japanese fare, area raw-fish fans "love" these upscale, "cozy" and "casual" settings in Towson, Mt. Washington and Timonium; bonus: prices are moderate and servers "attentive."

Sushi King ☒ *Japanese*
28 | 20 | 24 | $32

Columbia | 6490 Dobbin Rd. (Rte. 175) | 410-997-1269 | www.sushikingmd.com

An "insiders' jewel", this "decently" priced Columbia Japanese "hidden" near the MVA "isn't flashy" but "completely rocks" for "consistently terrific" sushi "masterpieces" created by veritable "artists" and delivered by "courteous" servers in "traditional garb"; "seating is packed", so regulars suggest calling ahead, "even on weekdays."

Sushi Sono ☒ *Japanese*
27 | 22 | 25 | $38

Columbia | 10215 Wincopin Circle (Little Patuxent Pkwy.) | 410-997-6131 | www.sushisonomd.com

It's easy to become "addicted" to the "first-rate" raw fish (and cooked fare) at this "romantic" yet "casual" Columbia Japanese with "attractive" traditional decor framed by a "scenic view" of Lake Kittamaqundi; "expect a wait at peak hours", "delightful" service and a final bill that's "not that bad" given the "reverence for the art of sushi" on display here.

Szechuan House ● *Chinese*   26 | 16 | 23 | $20

Lutherville | 1427 York Rd. (Seminary Ave.) | 410-825-8181

This Lutherville dine-in/carryout is "a cut above" the "typical" with its "extensive" menu offering "delicious" "real" Chinese dishes you don't often see alongside Americanized "standards"; you "don't go there for the decor", but "impossibly fast" service, "large portions" and prices "from the '60s" add up to one of the "best values around."

Tabrizi's ⬛Ⓜ *Mediterranean/Mideastern*   ▽ 21 | 24 | 21 | $40

South Baltimore | Harborview | 500 Harborview Dr. (Key Hwy.) | 410-727-3663 | www.tabrizis.com

"Sit outside on a pleasant evening and enjoy" one of the city's "best water views" from this window-lined Med-Mideasterner offering "great" midpriced fare and a "nice, affordable wine list" via "helpful" service; as the setting in South Baltimore's Harborview enclave "can't be beat", Saturdays are often booked for weddings, so call ahead.

Talara ● *Nuevo Latino*   24 | 23 | 22 | $32

Harbor East | 615 S. President St. (Fleet St.) | 410-528-9883 | www.talarabaltimore.com

A "Miami vibe" pulses in Harbor East at this "trendy" Nuevo Latino cantina offering an "amazing selection of ceviche" and "lots of tasty small bites" at "not-too-pricey" tabs; neon and contemporary art add to an "energetic" mood that's all about the "can't-beat" happy hour, though service remains "accommodating" throughout; P.S. Monday night salsa dancing with free lessons is "a plus."

Tapas Adela ● *Spanish*   23 | 23 | 22 | $35

Fells Point | 814 S. Broadway (Shakespeare St.) | 410-534-6262 | www.tapasadela.com

"Stylish" like its elder siblings (Kali's, Meli, Mezze), this Spaniard keeps pace with fairly priced tapas that "burst with flavor", shuttled by "accommodating" servers; a prime location "in the heart of Fells Point" and sexy, Gothic decor pull in "beautiful people" for "date night", or "larger parties" at the communal white-marble table, and in season, the garden has a "great vibe."

Tapas Teatro ●Ⓜ *Eclectic/Mediterranean*   24 | 21 | 20 | $32

Downtown North | 1711 N. Charles St. (bet. Lafayette Ave. & Lanvale St.) | 410-332-0110 | www.tapasteatro.com

It feels "fun and adventurous" splicing together a meal out of the "innovative", midpriced Eclectic-Med tapas at this "popular", "energetic" Downtown North night spot next to the Charles Theatre; when movie fans "crush" into the dimly lit interior featuring exposed brick and "tiny tables", some say the otherwise-"skilled" service can "suffer", but most love "staying up late discussing" films "over a pitcher" of sangria – and "lovely" outside seating is a quieter option.

	FOOD	DECOR	SERVICE	COST

Tark's Grill *American*
21 | 21 | 22 | $39

Brooklandville | Green Spring Station | 2360 W. Joppa Rd. (Falls Rd.) | 410-583-8275 | www.tarksgrill.com

With a "classic" menu of "predictably fine" American fare and a "well-trained" staff, this "casual, upscale" "neighborhood gathering spot" for "ladies" who lunch and "business" types alike is a "solid option" in Brooklandville's tony Green Spring Station; vintage photos highlighting the area's sporting history create a clubby feel.

Teavolve *American/Tearoom*
23 | 21 | 19 | $21

Harbor East | Eden Luxury Apartments | 1401 Aliceanna St. (Eden St.) | 410-522-1907 | www.teavolve.com

Leaf-steepers are buzzing over the "best assortment of tea in the city" (plus coffee and cocktails) at this "adorable" Harbor East tearoom/cafe that bolsters its beverage selection with "simply good, light" New American food; the prices are sweet, service is capable and the mellow vibe and free WiFi make for "a lovely space to linger."

Ten Ten *American*
∇ 25 | 26 | 24 | $47

Harbor East | Bagby Bldg. | 1010 Fleet St. (S. Exeter St.) | 410-244-6867 | www.bagbys1010.com

This "secret little place" "nestled" down a pedestrian alley, in Harbor East's Bagby Building, lures a "diverse clientele" with its "remarkable" "farm-to-table" New American dishes and "actually reasonable" wine list; it's expensive, but the "modern" industrial interior – exposed brick, reclaimed wood – is quite "comfortable", and the staff is "well trained", leading guests to gush "wow, what a find."

Tersiguel's *French*
28 | 25 | 28 | $59

Ellicott City | 8293 Main St. (Forrest St.) | 410-465-4004 | www.tersiguels.com

"Exquisite" French country "creations" comprised of "prime ingredients", including produce from the family farm, plus a "refined but not stuffy" "white-napkin" ambiance and "attentive, unobtrusive" service have Ellicott City diners calling this "romantic" special-occasioner "a favorite for years"; it's "expensive", *oui*, but "a great treat when you want to play grown-up" (and prix fixe menus "help with the cost").

Thai ⓜ *Thai*
∇ 24 | 14 | 22 | $25

Charles Village | 3316-18 Greenmount Ave. (bet. 33rd St. & Venable Ave.) | 410-889-6002

"You really get your money's worth" at this "pleasant little surprise" in Charles Village, a plainly named Thai mainstay known for its "excellent", well-priced fare; the "quiet" setting is "cozy enough for a romantic meal" and still "kitschy enough for a fun gathering", while solid service and parking out back are further pluses.

Thai Arroy ⓜ *Thai*
26 | 16 | 23 | $21

South Baltimore | 1019 Light St. (bet. Cross & Hamburg Sts.) | 410-385-8587 | www.thaiarroy.com

Regular waits "speak to the quality and deliciousness" of the "authentic" Thai fare at this small South Baltimore spot; so the "decor could be nicer" – just focus on food that "couldn't be finer" brought by a "fast", "friendly" crew at "bargain" prices, and you'll know why regulars return "again and again"; P.S. BYO is "a welcome treat."

Thames Street Oyster House *Seafood*   ▽ 24 | 21 | 23 | $43

Fells Point | 1728 Thames St. (S. Ann St.) | 443-449-7726 |
www.thamesstreetoysterhouse.com

"Just-out-of-the-sea seafood" is reeled into this brass-and-wood-trimmed oyster house dripping with "tons of charm and character", situated "right off the water" in Fells Point; the menu features "mighty tasty" Eastern coastal fare of every stripe (try a "Baltimore oyster shooter", complete with a splash of Natty Boh), the wine list "pairs perfectly" and service "provides guidance"; P.S. upstairs window seats afford a "harbor view."

13.5% Wine Bar *American*   22 | 23 | 22 | $31

Hampden | 1117 W. 36th St. (bet. Falls Rd. & Hickory Ave.) |
410-889-1064 | www.13.5winebar.com

Silo.5% Wine Bar ●Ⓜ *American*

Locust Point | Silo Point | 1200 Steuart St. (Clement St.) | 443-438-4044 |
www.silo.5winebar.com

"Raise a glass" (or two, or three) say cork dorks who frequent this "hip" Hampden wine bar with a "funky" but "stylish" orange-accented lounge sporting a wall of wine and a long bar; "tasty" pizzas and New American "nibbles" please, but the main draw is vino "at every price point" and a "knowledgeable" staff that "looks great serving it"; P.S. sibling Silo.5% mimics the "cool" vibe, albeit in a green shade, in Silo Point, with an emphasis on seafood.

Tidewater Grille *American*   22 | 23 | 22 | $29

Havre de Grace | 300 Franklin St. (St John St.) | 410-939-3313 |
www.thetidewatergrille.com

You "can't beat the decor" – a "picturesque" view of "water, boats and wildlife" via floor-to-ceiling windows and patio tables – at this "pleasant destination" on the Susquehanna River in Havre de Grace; both "budgets and taste buds" are well served by the variety on the "consistently good" American surf 'n' turf menu brought by a "friendly" team.

Timbuktu *Seafood*   23 | 15 | 20 | $32

Hanover | 1726 Dorsey Rd. (Coca Cola Dr.) | 410-796-0733 |
www.timbukturestaurant.com

"Crab cakes are the real draw" at this "raucous" Hanover seafooder where "an undemanding but hungry" army of eaters goes gaga for "hearty" patties made with "golf-ball-size chunks of crab and very little filler"; "don't count on ambiance" in the cavernous space, but prices are "reasonable", and the "friendly" service "keeps pace."

Tio Pepe *Continental/Spanish*   26 | 23 | 25 | $52

Mt. Vernon | 10 E. Franklin St. (bet. Charles & St. Paul Sts.) |
410-539-4675 | www.coloquio.com

If this "immutable" special-occasion "staple" in Mt. Vernon is "favored by people nostalgic for the Nixon administration", well, longtime faithfuls explain it truly is "as great as it was years ago" – from the "outstanding", "authentic" Spanish-Continental fare to the "potent" sangria; a "superb" crew works the "wonderfully cozy", white-washed subterranean setting (just make sure to bring mucho dinero).

Townhouse Kitchen & Bar ● American | - | - | - | M |

Harbor East | 1350 Lancaster St. (S. Spring St.) | 443-268-0323 | www.townhousebaltimore.com

It's BYOB – as in 'be your own bartender' – at this Harbor East gastropub, where a handful of communal tables are outfitted with personalized beer and vodka taps billed by the ounce (mixers provided); a casual New American menu with international influences complements the beverages within the industrial-chic digs lined with leather sofas and furry pillows.

Towson Diner ● Diner | 21 | 16 | 21 | $18 |

Towson | 718 York Rd. (Lambourne Rd.) | 410-321-0407 | www.towsondiner.net

Sporting a menu as thick as a "small-town" "phone book", this "low-priced" 24/7 diner in Towson dishes "huge portions of comfort food", including "breakfast around the clock" and Greek specialties; "pleasant" staffers work the "old-fashioned" room with jukeboxes and a dessert case that makes some "weak in the knees."

Trattoria Alberto Ⓢ Italian | ▽ 28 | 20 | 26 | $63 |

Glen Burnie | 1660 Crain Hwy. S. (bet. Hospital Dr. & Rte. 100) | 410-761-0922 | www.trattoriaalberto.com

Specials evoking "a trattoria on the Adriatic" and other "delectable" fare are purveyed in this "relaxing", white-tablecloth Northern Italian stalwart consigned to an unlikely storefront setting in Glen Burnie; "personable", "professional" service rounds out the "old-style" experience, though the "steep" tabs should come as no surprise.

Umi Sake Asian | ▽ 28 | 21 | 25 | $27 |

Cockeysville | 9726 York Rd. (Padonia Rd.) | 410-667-6586 | www.umisake.com

Considered a "gem amid the clutter of York Road" in Cockeysville's "quintessential suburbia", this "reasonably priced" Pan-Asian "go-to" garners waves of praise for "excellent" offerings, starring "creative" sushi; a team that "makes you feel special" works the simple, "modern" space with separate dining and lounge areas.

NEW Verde Pizza Napolitano Ⓜ Pizza | - | - | - | M |

Canton | 641 S. Montford Ave. (Foster Ave.) | 410-522-1000 | www.verdepizza.com

The husband-and-wife team behind this new Canton pizzeria takes pains to establish its Neapolitan authenticity, kneading crust made from imported flour for pies crisped in 90 seconds and washed down with Italian microbrews or Chianti (besides pizza, it offers traditional antipasti and salads); the airy space is bathed in light, reflected by white penny-tile floors and a white marble-topped bar, and the rough-hewn wood tables are packed with families early on, yielding to a more mature crowd later.

Victoria Gastro Pub ◑ *Eclectic*　　24 | 22 | 22 | $32

Columbia | 8201 Snowden River Pkwy. (Waterloo Rd.) | 410-750-1880 | www.victoriagastropub.com

A "beer-lover's dream", this Columbia "after-office crowd"-pleaser pairs "wonderful" draft selections and an "epic" bottle list with Eclectic "gourmet" gastropub fare (the signature poutine is "decadence in a dish"); "friendly" servers and the "fabulous" Euro-style setting deliver "first-date classy" at prices that "won't bankrupt you."

Vino Rosina ⊠ *American*　　▽ 22 | 24 | 19 | $36

Harbor East | Bagby Bldg. | 507 S. Exeter St. (Fleet St.) | 410-528-8600 | www.vinorosina.com

With a "modern, sleek" setting, this Harbor East wine bar in the Bagby Building draws in the "almost-40 crowd" for "tasty" New American eats and a happy hour that delivers "super food and drink specials" plus "ambiance" to boot; service is solid, and if a few find the experience "uneven", the recent return of original toque (and *Top Chef* contendor) Jesse Sandlin may smooth any rough edges.

Waterfront Kitchen ⓜ *American*　　22 | 24 | 21 | $43

Fells Point | 1417 Thames St. (Block St.) | 443-681-5310 | www.waterfrontkitchen.com

This aptly named Fells Pointer is truly a "place to discover", with its "stunning" space featuring "one of the loveliest views of the harbor", offset by soothing neutrals; against this backdrop, diners tuck into a menu of "delicious", if "a little pricey", New American fare (made partly with produce grown nearby by at-risk youth) brought by a team that "seems to enjoy your good fortune in discovering this place."

NEW Willow ◑ *Tex-Mex*　　- | - | - | M

Fells Point | 811 S. Broadway (Lancaster St.) | 443-835-4086 | www.willowbaltimore.com

Mixology fans are drawn to this hip new Fells Point resto-bar by cocktails made with fresh-squeezed fruit and artisanal liquors, which are downed at one of the communal tables or in the cushy upstairs lounge; meanwhile, a mod Tex-Mex menu turns the attention to food.

Wine Market ⓜ *American*　　24 | 21 | 23 | $40

Locust Point | 921 E. Fort Ave. (Lawrence St.) | 410-244-6166 | www.the-wine-market.com

The "excellent wines to complement" the "creative" seasonal dishes are no surprise at this midpriced Locust Point New American where an attached wine shop provides guests with "access to hundreds" of bottles at retail price plus a $9 corkage fee ($18 if you BYO); expect an "energetic urban atmosphere" in the warehouse setting tended by a "genial" staff that can handle a corkscrew.

Wit & Wisdom *American*　　23 | 27 | 24 | $56

Harbor East | Four Seasons Baltimore | 200 International Dr. (Aliceanna St.) | 410-576-5800 | www.witandwisdombaltimore.com

"Not your typical hotel restaurant", this "divine" New American at the Four Seasons brings to Baltimore the "creativity, flavor and attention to detail" that celeb chefrateur Michael Mina is known for; the "chic" setting features a "huge" bar and panoramic views of the Inner Harbor through grand windows, and while service is highly professional, you're paying for the "high-profile atmosphere."

Woman's Industrial Kitchen *American/Tearoom*

▽ 24 | 18 | 23 | $15

(aka Woman's Industrial Exchange)

Mt. Vernon | 333 N. Charles St. (Pleasant St.) | 410-244-6450 | www.womansindustrialkitchen.com

A "wonderful old slice of Baltimore", this circa-1880 Mt. Vernon tearoom "harks back to the past" with classic American gems gracing its inexpensive lunch-only menu; the black-and-white linoleum tiles recall its former glory, and though the staff may be "on the young side" these days (for "those who recall" its "grandmotherly waitresses" from years past), it sure is "friendly"; P.S. the attached shop sells items handmade by area women.

Woodberry Kitchen *American*

27 | 26 | 25 | $49

Clipper Mill | 2010 Clipper Park Rd. (Clipper Mill Rd.) | 410-464-8000 | www.woodberrykitchen.com

"A smash" since it opened and still "wildly popular" (in fact, it's Baltimore's Most Popular restaurant), this Clipper Mill New American in a "rebuilt old factory" hosts a "hip", "boisterous" crowd happily devouring the "complex" farm-to-table "amazingness" ferried by "friendly, smart" servers who "aim to please"; some find it "a bit pricey", but its huge fan base deems it "worth the trip many times over" – which is why it's "oh so hard to get into" ("reserve way in advance").

NEW The Yard ● *American*

- | - | - | M

Inner Harbor | Marriott Inner Harbor | 110 S. Eutaw St. (Lombard St.) | 410-209-2853 | www.marriott.com

This casual American eatery serving three square meals a day to guests of the Marriott Inner Harbor Hotel has been rebooted with an eye on becoming more than a hotel restaurant; its new look features murals of local landmarks like the Hippodrome and the Domino Sugars sign, which are a fitting backdrop for its wide-ranging new menu featuring close-to-home specialties like Maryland rockfish, Chesapeake blue crab and beef and produce from area farms.

Ze Mean Bean Café *E European*

23 | 20 | 20 | $29

Fells Point | 1739 Fleet St. (bet. Ann & Regester Sts.) | 410-675-5999 | www.zemeanbean.com

"Slavs hankering for a taste of the homeland can't go wrong" at this "value"-priced Eastern European bistro in Fells Point, with "excellent" pierogi and the like, plus a jazz-inflected weekend brunch; an "intimate", "richly decorated" interior ("the fireplace rocks" on cold winter days) and "pleasant" service have ze-alots wondering "what's not to like?"

Annapolis

	FOOD	DECOR	SERVICE	COST

NEW Annapolis Smokehouse *BBQ* — — — M

Annapolis | Bay Ridge Shopping Ctr. | 107 Hillsmere Dr. (Bay Ridge Rd.) | 410-571-5073 | www.annapolissmokehouse.com

This contemporary-looking new BBQ eatery in a Hillsmere strip mall offers a wide range of options, which include Texas brisket, Memphis pulled pork and St. Louis–style ribs along with the usual sides plus a bunch of creative apps, soups, salads and sandwiches; diners can wash it all down with microbrews and wine, which also wet the whistle for live music on Thursday evenings.

Boatyard Bar & Grill *Pub Food* 22 21 22 $26

Eastport | 400 Fourth St. (Severn Ave.) | 410-216-6206 | www.boatyardbarandgrill.com

"Nautical types" (including "families") weigh anchor at this "casual", "affordable" Eastport "watering hole" for "reliably good" pub eats and "great raw bar" selections; the "galleylike" wood interior feels "like you're on a yacht", especially if it appears to pitch and roll after a few too many in the "rowdy" bar; P.S. there's occasional live music, and boat races on TV.

Café Normandie *French* 25 22 23 $39

Annapolis | 185 Main St. (Conduit St.) | 410-263-3382 | www.cafenormandie.com

"Vive la France!" say boosters of the "scrumptious" "country French cuisine" at this Gallic "sanctuary" in Annapolis, known for favorites like "wonderful" crêpes and omelets at prices that won't break the bank; servers "aim to please", and it's "cozy", with a fireplace providing "added comfort" in the colder months.

Cantler's Riverside Inn *Crab House* 24 16 20 $34

Annapolis | 458 Forest Beach Rd. (Browns Woods Rd.) | 410-757-1311 | www.cantlers.com

"Don't wear your nice clothes" to "hammer away" at "superb" crabs on the "brown-paper"-covered communal picnic tables at this "friendly" "old-school crab house" in Annapolis, which also floats boats with a few "landlubber" items; if there's a wait – a guarantee "when the weather's nice" – "occupy yourself with some cold ones" and the "lovely view of the creek" from the deck; P.S. "cost varies" based on what you get (crabs can get "pricey").

Carpaccio *Italian* 25 24 23 $39

Annapolis | Park Pl. | 1 Park Pl. (West St.) | 410-268-6569 | www.carpacciotuscankitchen.com

"Tuscany at its most terrific" is how some describe this "upscale" Italian anchor to Annapolis' Park Place complex, serving "consistently excellent" fare, not least of which is the complimentary pizza bread (*molto bene*); the "amiable" staff, "sophisticated" setting and "pleasant" patio with a fountain are further pluses, and happy-hour deals are a way around pricey tabs.

FOOD | DECOR | SERVICE | COST

Carrol's Creek Cafe *Seafood*

23 | 23 | 23 | $44

Eastport | 410 Severn Ave. (bet. 4th & 5th Sts.) | 410-263-8102 | www.carrolscreek.com

"Get a table by the window" to fully exploit the "yacht-club atmosphere" at this "elegant" Eastport seafooder with a "primo" waterfront location "overlooking Spa Creek" and the boats bobbing at the dock; the pricey but "classic Chesapeake fare", served by an "impeccable" crew, "won't let you down" – but while the crab cakes may have "little filler", the restaurant itself is "loaded with tourists" during "high season."

Cheesecake Factory *American*

24 | 22 | 22 | $30

Annapolis | Annapolis Mall | 1872 Annapolis Mall Rd. (Jennifer Rd.) | 410-224-0565 | www.thecheesecakefactory.com
See review in the Baltimore Directory.

Chick & Ruth's Delly ◐ *Diner*

22 | 16 | 21 | $16

Annapolis | 165 Main St. (Conduit St.) | 410-269-6737 | www.chickandruths.com

"Come hungry" and "squeeze into" a booth at this longtime Annapolis diner "landmark" for "obscene" portions of "inexpensive" "greasy-spoon breakfast" favorites and "mile-high sandwiches" "honoring politicians who visit often"; "outstanding kitsch" decor is complemented by "down-home fun" (magic tricks performed by the owner, 110-oz. "milkshake challenge") and a side of "patriotism" (the "Pledge of Allegiance" is recited every morning).

Chop House *Steak*

25 | 24 | 25 | $47

Annapolis | Annapolis Towne Ctr. | 1915 Towne Centre Blvd. (Harker Pl.) | 410-224-4344 | www.thechophouserestaurant.com

You may "want to get a second job" so you can dine more often at this "high-quality" modern steakhouse dressed in plush leather and masculine earth tones at Annapolis Towne Centre; an "accommodating" staff presides over a sometimes-"lively" crowd of diners, but tipplers maintain the real action is at the bar with the "exceptional" bartenders, especially during the "heavenly" happy hour.

Crush Kitchen & Winehouse *American*

23 | 25 | 23 | $33

Annapolis | 114 West St. (Lafayette Ave.) | 410-216-9444 | www.crushwinehouse.com

A "breath of fresh air" on Annapolis' West Street, this lounge-style wine bar offers a "wide variety" of mostly Italian bottles (and "many by the glass" too) that pair well with its "limited", midpriced menu of "interesting" American small plates; staffers can suggest "perfectly matched" vintages, or grape apes can sample pours from the Enomatic dispenser.

Double T Diner ◐ *Diner*

20 | 16 | 21 | $18

Annapolis | 12 Defense St. (Cedar Ave.) | 410-571-9070 | www.doubletdiner.com
See review in the Baltimore Directory.

Five Guys *Burgers*

24 | 14 | 21 | $12

Annapolis | Annapolis Mall | 1046 Annapolis Mall Rd. (Jennifer Rd.) | 410-573-0581
Annapolis | Village Greens | 509 S. Cherry Grove Ave. (Forest Dr.) | 410-216-7971
Edgewater | 3059 Solomons Island Rd. (bet. Mayo & Wards Rds.) | 410-956-8212
www.fiveguys.com
See review in the Washington, DC, Directory.

49 West ● *Coffeehouse*

22 | 20 | 20 | $24

Annapolis | 49 West St. (Cathedral St.) | 410-626-9796 | www.49westcoffeehouse.com
This "quintessential coffee shop" – with "eccentric" servers, local art and bookshelves – is a "dash of hip" in Annapolis, offering affordable American bites along with caffeine, beer and wine; there's always a "different vibe depending on the time of day", so "park your laptop" in the afternoon, and return for live music most evenings.

Galway Bay ● *Pub Food*

24 | 22 | 24 | $30

Annapolis | 63 Maryland Ave. (State Circle) | 410-263-8333 | www.galwaybaymd.com
A "pleasantly varied" menu at this "convivial" Annapolis pub "goes well beyond the always-excellent corned beef and cabbage" to lesser-known "authentic" Gaelic grub, plus American standards and gluten-free choices; the interior is "like stepping into an old tavern in Ireland", an illusion abetted by the "unhurried", mostly Irish staff, the "beer-on-tap selection" and the "must-try" Irish coffee.

Harry Browne's *American*

25 | 23 | 24 | $48

Annapolis | 66 State Circle (bet. East St. & Maryland Ave.) | 410-263-4332 | www.harrybrownes.com
With its "view of the State House", this "expensive" Annapolis American has long been a "hangout" for the "'in' crowd" and a "good place to spot a legislator" in the "classy" art deco dining room or upstairs bar; its "diverse" menu of "delicious food, expertly prepared", and a "great wine selection" also help make it a "favorite."

Jalapeños ● *Mexican/Spanish*

27 | 23 | 26 | $34

Annapolis | Forest Plaza | 85 Forest Dr. (Forest Dr.) | 410-266-7580 | www.jalapenosonline.com
This Spanish-Mexican "jewel" in Annapolis presents a "lovingly prepared" blend of the two cuisines via an "outstanding" tapas menu, plus "terrific" sangria and "great" margaritas that flow during happy hour; the "on-site" owner ensures a "welcoming" atmosphere and, with the frescoed and wrought-iron interior, plus live music on Thursdays, you'll be "transported to Spain" (and/or south of the border).

Joss Cafe & Sushi Bar *Japanese*

27 | 20 | 23 | $33

Annapolis | 195 Main St. (Church Circle) | 410-263-4688 | www.josssushi.com
The sushi chefs who "greet you as you enter" ('*irasshai!*') also slice "fresh, delicious" fish at these conventionally dressed Japanese

spots in Annapolis and Baltimore's Mt. Vernon; sushistas also appreciate the "hard-working" staffs and moderate tabs.

Lebanese Taverna *Lebanese*

23 | 20 | 21 | $29

Annapolis | Annapolis Harbour Ctr. | 2478 Solomons Island Rd. (Aris T. Allen Blvd.) | 410-897-1111 | www.lebanesetaverna.com
See review in the Washington, DC, Directory.

Lemongrass *Thai*

25 | 20 | 22 | $25

Annapolis | 167 West St. (Colonial Ave.) | 410-280-0086
Annapolis | Gateway Village Shopping Ctr. | 2625 Housely Rd. (bet. General Hwy. & Rte. 450) | 410-224-8424
Crofton | 2225 Defense Hwy. (Patuxent River Rd.) | 410-721-1111
www.kapowgroup.com
Combining local flavors with "Thai style" – think "crab-fried rice" and "Chesapeake pad Thai" – is the signature at these Annapolis and Crofton Siamese triplets that also dish "delicious" "authentic" staples spiced from "conservative American" all the way to "make you sweat"; "light" and "airy", "low-key" settings, solid service and "good values" round out these "well-worth-it" neighborhood "mainstays"; P.S. Crofton is separately owned.

Les Folies Brasserie *French*

27 | 22 | 25 | $51

Annapolis | 2552 Riva Rd. (Aris T. Allen Blvd.) | 410-573-0970 | www.lesfoliesbrasserie.com
Long a "go-to place for special celebrations" or "quiet, romantic" dinners, this "wonderfully authentic" French bastion in Annapolis delivers "delicious" and "well-executed", if "expensive", takes on Gallic "standards"; "absolutely charming" touches include fresh flowers and a "personable maitre d'" who ensures service that makes everyone "feel like a regular", thus sealing the deal.

Level *American*

24 | 24 | 24 | $35

Annapolis | 69 West St. (Calvert St.) | 410-268-0003 | www.levelsmallplateslounge.com
It's easy to "support" local growers and have "fun" with your "friends" at this "happening" and "chic, urban lounge" in Annapolis, where servers who "really make a connection" sling "excellent" New American "tapaslike" plates "packed with flavor"; "super bartenders" mix "phenomenal" "crafted cocktails" too, so even though it's already affordable, some suggest "go at happy hour" for food and drink specials.

Lewnes' Steakhouse *Steak*

28 | 23 | 26 | $66

Eastport | 401 Fourth St. (Severn Ave.) | 410-263-1617 | www.lewnessteakhouse.com
A "go-to for best impressions", this venerable "locally owned, locally run" Eastport steakhouse "easily competes with the famous names" say those who rave about its "invariably excellent" cuts, sides "meant to be shared" and "extensive" wine list; "retro booths" and "low lights" encourage "private conversation", and "knowledgeable" servers "go out of their way" to please, so although it's "pricey", remember, "you get what you pay for."

Luna Blu *Italian*
22 | 19 | 23 | $35

Annapolis | 36 West St. (Calvert St.) | 410-267-9950 |
www.lunabluofannapolis.com

This "eager-to-please" spot in Annapolis "makes you feel like you've come home to mama's kitchen", given the "good, basic" Southern Italian food, "friendly" service plus fresh-cut flowers and murals of Naples on the walls; a four-course prix fixe dinner option appeals to those with "more pinch in their pockets", and the mix-and-match "create-your-own pasta" special is "a great option" at lunch.

Main Ingredient Café *American*
25 | 17 | 22 | $28

Annapolis | 914 Bay Ridge Rd. (Georgetown Rd.) | 410-626-0388 |
www.themainingredient.com

With a "deceiving" "strip-mall location" "just outside Annapolis", this New American bakery/cafe wows with "home-cooked fare" exhibiting flashes of "excellence", particularly their "to-die-for" breakfast items and soups; it's "priced right" too, making the earth-toned storefront with "sunny window" booths served by a "welcoming staff" "popular with locals"; P.S. check out the "outrageous" desserts.

Miss Shirley's *American*
26 | 21 | 23 | $24

Annapolis | 1 Park Pl. (West St.) | 410-268-5171 | www.missshirleys.com
See review in the Baltimore Directory.

Nando's Peri-Peri *Chicken*
22 | 19 | 19 | $17

Annapolis | Annapolis Mall | 2002 Annapolis Mall Rd. (Jennifer Rd.) |
410-224-0585 | www.nandosperiperi.com
See review in the Washington, DC, Directory.

O'Learys Seafood *Seafood*
26 | 21 | 25 | $52

Eastport | 310 Third St. (Severn Ave.) | 410-263-0884 |
www.olearysseafood.com

A "charming house" in Eastport is host to this "long-standing favorite" for what some say is the "best seafood in Annapolis"; the fare has a "surprising" "inventiveness", and while it's "not cheap", "superb" service and an "intimate" timber-framed setting, adorned with the owner's colorful abstract artwork, leave diners feeling "pampered."

Osteria 177 *Italian*
27 | 24 | 25 | $51

Annapolis | 177 Main St. (Conduit St.) | 410-267-7700 |
www.osteria177.com

"Outstanding" Northern Italian cuisine paired with "broad-ranging" wines and "delicious" seasonal cocktails are the main attractions at this "delightful surprise in the heart of Annapolis"; "expensive", *sì*, but the "polished" staff "truly knows the meaning of the word" 'service', making it a lock for "special occasions."

Paladar *Caribbean/Pan-Latin*
23 | 24 | 23 | $31

Annapolis | Annapolis Towne Ctr. | 1905 Towne Centre Blvd. (Tower Pl.) |
410-897-1022 | www.paladarlatinkitchen.com

A "vibrant" atmosphere, supported by solid service, is the backdrop for the "flavorful" Latin menu with a notable "Caribbean influence" at this midpriced chain in the Annapolis Town Centre; starring "spectacular" rum-flight options and "devilishly delicious" mojitios that bring out the "inner dancer", happy hour at the "lively" bar is a "great value" and "perfect" for "drinks with coworkers" or "girls' night out."

Paul's Homewood Café *American/Greek* | 25 | 19 | 24 | $35 |

Annapolis | 919 West St. (Taylor Ave.) | 410-267-7891 | www.paulscafe-annapolis.com

It's "easy to miss" this cafe off the tourist track in Annapolis, but "the hardest part" after finding it "is deciding what to eat" since everything's "a treat" on its menu of "excellent" American and Greek "homestyle" cooking; add in "decent" prices, "attentive" service and an "attractive", "modern" setting, and no wonder it's a "local favorite."

P.F. Chang's China Bistro *Chinese* | 23 | 23 | 22 | $30 |

Annapolis | Annapolis Towne Ctr. | 307 Sail Pl. (Forest Dr.) | 410-573-2990 | www.pfchangs.com

See review in the Washington, DC, Directory.

Red Hot & Blue *BBQ* | 22 | 18 | 20 | $21 |

Annapolis | 200 Old Mill Bottom Rd. S. (Ferguson Rd.) | 410-626-7427 | www.redhotandblue.com

See review in the Washington, DC, Directory.

Reynolds Tavern | 23 | 25 | 23 | $35 |
Restaurant *American/British*

Annapolis | Reynolds Tavern | 7 Church Circle (Franklin St.) | 410-295-9555 | www.reynoldstavern.org

"Step back in time" to "Colonial Annapolis" at this "historic" inn serving a "varied" American menu, though it's perhaps better known for its "unmatched" "British-style afternoon tea" (make reservations); the "friendly owners" and "refined" atmosphere that pervades the "quaint", "cozy" rooms allow patrons "to pause, reflect" and "recover from life's vicissitudes"; P.S. the basement tavern is "quite good too."

The Rockfish ● *American* | ∇ 20 | 22 | 22 | $44 |

Eastport | 400 Sixth St. (Severn Ave.) | 410-267-1800 | www.rockfishmd.com

A "welcoming" stop "after sailing on the bay", this Eastporter across the bridge from the Annapolis City Dock offers solid if pricey seafood-centric American fare along with "a bit of local flavor"; the airy space is enhanced by a "knowledgeable" staff, live music Tuesday–Saturday and "outgoing patrons" fishing for dates at the "popular bar."

Ruth's Chris Steak House *Steak* | 26 | 24 | 26 | $67 |

Eastport | 301 Severn Ave. (3rd St.) | 410-990-0033 | www.ruthschris.com

See review in the Washington, DC, Directory.

Severn Inn *American* | 22 | 25 | 22 | $44 |

Annapolis | 1993 Baltimore Annapolis Blvd. (Ritchie Hwy.) | 410-349-4000 | www.severninn.com

"The view is the big attraction" at this American seafooder with plenty of deck seating overlooking the Severn River and the Naval Academy, though the "delicious" fare (including "one of the best" Sunday brunches in Annapolis) is also available inside, where there's a "nautical" feel; service is "attentive", but tabs can get "pricey", so frugal locals suggest "go for a drink with out-of-town guests."

Sofi's Crepes *Crêpes*
24 | 14 | 21 | $12

Annapolis | 1 Craig St. (bet. Dock & Prince George Sts.) | 410-990-0929 | www.sofiscrepes.com
See review in the Baltimore Directory.

Tsunami ● *Asian*
25 | 22 | 23 | $36

Annapolis | 51 West St. (bet. Calvert St. & Church Circle) | 410-990-9868 | www.kapowgroup.com
Take a seat at the window for a "great view" of "hipsters inside and out" of this "trendy" Annapolis Asian fusion drink-and-eatery plating "fantastic" midpriced sushi and the like in a "modern" milieu, supported by "personable" service and "creative bartending"; just "don't go for a quiet romantic dinner" on the "very crowded" weekends.

Vin 909 Ⓜ *American*
28 | 25 | 26 | $32

Eastport | 909 Bay Ridge Ave. (Chesapeake Ave.) | 410-990-1846 | www.vin909.com
"Off the beaten path" in Eastport, this vin-centric venue appeals to locals and visitors alike with its "great-value" offering of "fabulous", "refined" New American fare and an "outstanding" wine selection; "exceptional" service and an "intimate", contemporary "cottage" setting create a "calming" backdrop "suitable for quiet conversation."

NEW West *American*
- | - | - | E

Annapolis | Loews Annapolis Hotel | 126 West St. (Lafayette Ave.) | 410-295-3232 | www.loewshotels.com
The Loews Hotel sets a local course with this new modern American restaurant that pays tribute to the Chesapeake area via an upscale menu of regional fare, which includes plenty of cooked seafood and an extensive raw bar; distinguishing it from typical hotel dining rooms are rustic beams and reclaimed wood, while a sleek bar and a covered terrace also work to draw local folks as well as staying guests.

Wild Orchid Café *American*
23 | 21 | 23 | $42

Annapolis | 200 Westgate Circle (Spa Rd.) | 410-268-8009 | www.thewildorchidcafe.com
A "modern", "minimalist" setting is the backdrop at this New American on Westgate Circle, where "ingenuity" is evident in the "unique" seasonal menu focusing on local produce, meat and seafood ("which shows clearly in the prices"); factor in "personable" service, and it's "where Annapolis adults go for peaceful fine dining."

Yellowfin *American*
23 | 22 | 21 | $36

Edgewater | 2840 Solomons Island Rd. (Old S. River Rd.) | 410-573-1333 | www.yellowfinrestaurant.com
"Come by land or by sea, dressed up or down" for "lovely sunsets over the South River" at this seafood-leaning American in Edgewater; the extensive menu offers many "good" options (even sushi), but what this place is really known for is its "worst-kept secret" of a happy hour (from 11:30 AM to 7 PM daily) and "can't-be-beat" Sunday brunch.

	FOOD	DECOR	SERVICE	COST

Eastern Shore

Ava's *Italian/Pizza*　　　　　　27 | 20 | 24 | $28

St. Michaels | 409 S. Talbot St. (bet. Grace & Thompson Sts.) |
410-745-3081 | www.avaspizzeria.com

"High-end pizzas" and other "always delicious" choices (e.g. wasabi
oysters, meatball sliders) pair with "serious wine" at this "reasonably
priced" Italian "jewel" in St. Michaels; "personable" service is another
asset, and if the brick-walled quarters get a bit "cozy" for some, a
fireplace-enhanced patio provides a "pleasant" alternative.

Banning's Tavern *American*　　　∇ 22 | 20 | 23 | $29

Easton | Avalon Theatre | 42 E. Dover St. (Harrison St.) | 410-822-1733 |
www.banningstavern.com

An "old-fashioned pub" ambiance, "great beer deals" and a "friendly"
staff endow this Easton tavern with a convivial glow; and "hearty
portions" of "good, honest" American eats at moderate prices
also make it a "perfect" fueling spot when attending a show at the
adjacent Avalon Theatre.

Bartlett Pear Inn Restaurant *American*　28 | 25 | 27 | $58

Easton | Bartlett Pear Inn | 28 S. Harrison St. (South Ln. & South St.) |
410-770-3300 | www.bartlettpearinn.com

"Extraordinary doesn't begin to describe this culinary temple" rave
pear-amours of the "beautifully prepared" New American dishes
presented by a "superb" staff at this "charming" and "gorgeous"
Easton inn that dates to the late 18th century; prices place it "high
on the romance and special-occasion scale", though the chef's tasting menu is a "relative bargain", and the bar offers a more casual approach; P.S. closed Monday and Tuesday.

Bistro Poplar *French*　　　　　　∇ 28 | 25 | 28 | $41

Cambridge | 535 Poplar St. (High St.) | 410-228-4884 |
www.bistropoplar.com

"Every flavor is spot-on" at this "pleasantly authentic" French bistro
in Cambridge that offers "a refreshing" breath of "fine dining" on the
Eastern Shore; with über-"friendly" service and a "lovely" Gallic atmosphere, it's a "great value"; P.S. closed Tuesday and Wednesday.

NEW Blackthorn Irish Pub *Pub Food*　– | – | – | M

St. Michaels | 209 S. Talbot St. (Carpenter St.) | 410-745-8011

This fun-loving Irish pub in St. Michaels provides patrons with live
music, theme nights and other special events; a party vibe pervades
the heavily muraled ground-floor bar, where Gaelic snacks are
washed down with black & tans and whiskey drams, while quieter
meals can be had upstairs.

Brasserie Brightwell ◐ *American/French*　21 | 23 | 18 | $34

Easton | 206 N. Washington St. (Harisson St.) | 410-819-3838 |
www.brasseriebrightwell.com

French and American "food with flair" – including "a wide variety of
petits plats" plus items from a raw bar and wood-fire grill – is served

up at this "friendly" Easton brasserie whose "garage-chic" setting gets a lot of adaptive reuse out of its bay doors that open to a "sprawling patio" and outside bar; the "joie de vivre" is further expressed by an "ample" selection of wine and beer, all "reasonably" priced.

Harris Crab House *Crab House*
24 | 18 | 21 | $33

Grasonville | 433 Kent Narrows Way N. (Rte. 50, exit 42) | 410-827-9500 | www.harriscrabhouse.com

"Amazing" crabs, "oysters galore" and other "excellent" catch are ferried by an "honest", hard-working staff, an ample "reward for driving" by land or sea to this midpriced "old-time crab house" in Grasonville; the huge, "shabby-chic" setting may feel like a "cafeteria" to some, but on a nice day there's "nothing better" than a brown-papered picnic table with a "commanding view of Kent Narrows."

Kentmorr *Crab House*
∇ 25 | 18 | 22 | $33

Stevensville | 910 Kentmorr Rd. (Lane Ave.) | 410-643-2263 | www.kentmorr.com

An "extensive" menu of "fantastic" seafood-focused American fare draws crab-lovers and others "off the beaten path", by car and boat, to this "casual", midpriced Kent Island "bay-front spot" that recalls the Eastern Shore "years ago"; the service is "warm and friendly", and its "cool" tiki bar, with hammocks on the beach, gives new meaning to "relaxing" "by the water."

Mason's Ⓢ *American*
26 | 24 | 25 | $49

Easton | 22 S. Harrison St. (South Ln.) | 410-822-3204 | www.masonsgourmet.com

As a purveyor of "delectable" New American edibles, this "classic" in an old home in Easton's "historic district" has foodies "dreaming"; a staff that goes the "extra mile" patrols the multitude of rooms that leavens their "traditional character" with "an upbeat contemporary atmosphere", and though the experience can be pricey, "they never skimp on the portions"; P.S. "alfresco dining is a plus" in fine weather.

The Narrows *Seafood*
25 | 21 | 23 | $42

Grasonville | 3023 Kent Narrows Way S. (Rte. 50, exit 41/42) | 410-827-8113 | www.thenarrowsrestaurant.com

"Those delicious creatures that inhabit the bay" take the form of "buttery" crab cakes "full of giant lumps" and "to-die-for" crab soup at this "expensive", "open and airy" "touch of fine dining" in Kent Narrows; the other seafood offerings are "fabulous" too, and "spectacular" waterfront views are supported by "impeccable" service.

Out of the Fire Ⓢ Ⓜ *American/Eclectic*
28 | 24 | 26 | $42

Easton | 22 Goldsborough St. (Washington St.) | 410-770-4777 | www.outofthefire.com

"Sit at the bar and watch the action" in the kitchen at this "superb" Easton American-Eclectic where "amazing chefs" who really "get the magic of fresh, local ingredients" "artfully plate" "great things" cooked via the showpiece open hearth; it's not cheap for such an "informal" vibe, but service is "attentive" and the space is "inviting" with a "warm" "Tuscan" palette.

	FOOD	DECOR	SERVICE	COST

Pope's Tavern *American* ▽ 27 | 25 | 28 | $44

Oxford | Oxford Inn | 504 S. Morris St. (Oxford Rd.) | 410-226-5220 | www.oxfordinn.net

A circa-1880 Oxford inn is the romantic setting for this high-end "Eastern shore favorite" offering "superbly prepared" New American selections in a best-of-both-worlds setting: "cozy in winter, airy in summer"; a mix of "locals" and "visitors" appreciates the "first-rate" service and complimentary "Popemobile" (i.e. a British cab) that shuttles diners from the dock or other locales within town; P.S. closed Tuesday and Wednesday.

Rustico *Italian* ▽ 25 | 23 | 23 | $37

Stevensville | 401 Love Point Rd. (Rte. 8) | 410-643-9444 | www.rusticoonline.com

This "terrific" "little gem" in Stevensville "does not disappoint" Eastern Shore residents with its "delicious", midpriced menu of "awesome pasta" and other traditional Southern Italian fare served in "huge portions" indoors or "alfresco on a summer's day"; a "comfy" rustico atmosphere, capable service and an "excellent wine list" are also inducements, and the four-course prix fixe dinner gets special mention.

Ruth's Chris Steak House *Steak* 26 | 24 | 26 | $67

Berlin | GlenRiddle Golf Clubhse. | 11501 Maid at Arms Ln. (off Rte. 50) | 888-632-4747 | www.ruthschris.com

See review in the Washington, DC, Directory.

Salter's Tavern *American/Seafood* 25 | 23 | 23 | $54

Oxford | Robert Morris Inn | 314 N. Morris St. (Strand) | 410-226-5111 | www.robertmorrisinn.com

"Every meal hits the mark" at this Oxfordian in a "picturesque" circa-1710 inn, where chef Mark Salter brings a British sensibility to crab cakes and other Chesapeake classics, which are "smoothly" served by a "dedicated" staff; the "dark" and "cozy" space, with its open-hearth fireplace, has the "quaint elegance of Colonial times", while the patio and porch, with a view of the ferry, are "bliss on a summer's eve"; P.S. the casual taproom is significantly cheaper.

Scossa *Italian* 28 | 26 | 27 | $52

Easton | 8 N. Washington St. (Dover St.) | 410-822-2202 | www.scossarestaurant.com

This "sophisticated" "surprise for the Eastern Shore" in Easton comprises "exceptional", "authentic" Northern Italian fare "you'll dream about for weeks" with "a great wine list to support it", a "delightful, chic" interior (plus "lovely" terrace) and "superb" service; it can be "expensive", yes, but it's an all-around "fabulous dining experience."

Theo's Steakhouse Ⓜ *Steak* - | - | - | E

St. Michaels | 407 S. Talbot St. (Grace St.) | 407-754-2106 | www.theossteakhouse.com

The lean, meat-focused menu at this St. Michaels steakhouse may not be big, but it includes all the usual suspects plus a few pricey, limited-availability prime cuts (sourced from a butcher shop two blocks away); classic and not-so-classic apps and sides round out the offerings in the sleek, caramel-hued space; P.S. closed Monday and Tuesday.

208 Talbot  *American*

St. Michaels | 208 N. Talbot St. (bet. Dodson Ave. & North St.) | 410-745-3838 | www.208talbot.com

Shore star chef David Clark lures well-heeled types to this reinvigorated sequel to what was once a foodie and weekender destination on St. Michaels' main drag; longtime fans may recognize some edgy New American–Chesapeake items from his erstwhile restaurant Julia's in Centreville while dining in the tavern setting that's dressed in exposed bricks and dove-gray walls; P.S. closed Monday and Tuesday.

BALTIMORE & ENVIRONS INDEXES*

---

* These lists include low vote places that do not qualify for top lists.

Special Features

Listings cover the best in each category and include names, locations and Food ratings. Multi-location restaurants' features may vary by branch.

ADDITIONS

(Properties added since the last edition of the book)

Admiral's Cup | **Fells Pt** — —
Ale Hse. | **Columbia** — —
Annapolis Smokehouse & Tavern | — —
  Annap
Birroteca | **Hampden** — —
Blackthorn | **E Shore** — —
Bun Shop | **Mt. Vernon** — —
Chesapeake | **D'town N** — —
David's | **Hampden** — —
Dooby's | **Mt. Vernon** — —
Fleet St. Kit. | **Harbor E** — —
Johnny's | **Roland Pk** — —
Liv2eat | **Fed Hill** — —
Maggie's Farm | **NE Balt** — —
Marquee | **Hi'town** — —
Martick's | **D'town W** — —
McFaul's | **Parkville** — —
Moonshine Tav. | **Canton** — —
My Thai | **Harbor E** — —
Ouzo Bay | **Harbor E** — —
Shiso Tavern | **Canton** — —
Verde Pizza | **Canton** — —
West | **Annap** — —
Willow | **Fells Pt** — —
Yard | **Inner Harbor** — —

BREAKFAST

(See also Hotel Dining)

Artifact Coffee | **Clipper Mill** — —
Baugher's | **Westminster** 20
Blue Moon | **Fells Pt** 25
Breakfast Shoppe | **Severna Pk** 25
Chick/Ruth's | **Annap** 22
Double T | **multi.** 20
Goldberg's | **Pikesville** 25
Jimmy's | **Fells Pt** 20
NEW Johnny's | **Roland Pk** — —
Main Ingredient | **Annap** 25
Miss Shirley's | **multi.** 26
Open Door | **Bel Air** 24
Stone Mill | **Brook'ville** 24

BRUNCH

Ambassador | **Homewood** 25
b | **D'town N** 26

Bertha's | **Fells Pt** 22
Carrol's Creek | **Annap** 23
City Cafe | **Mt. Vernon** 23
Clyde's | **Columbia** 22
Gertrude's | **Charles Vill** 22
Harryman Hse. | **Reist'town** 24
Jesse Wong's Asean | **Columbia** 23
Jesse Wong's Kit. | **Hunt Valley** 20
NEW Liv2eat | **Fed Hill** — —
Main Ingredient | **Annap** 25
Orchard Mkt. | **Towson** 26
Regi's | **S Balt** 23
NEW Shiso Tavern | **Canton** — —
Woman's | **Mt. Vernon** 24
Ze Mean Bean | **Fells Pt** 23

BUSINESS DINING

Capital Grille | **Inner Harbor** 26
Carpaccio | **Annap** 25
Charleston | **Harbor E** 29
Cinghiale | **Harbor E** 26
Clyde's | **Columbia** 22
NEW Fleet St. Kit. | **Harbor E** — —
Fleming's Steak | **Harbor E** 25
Greystone Grill | **Ellicott City** 19
Harry Browne | **Annap** 25
NEW Johnny's | **Roland Pk** — —
La Famiglia | **Homewood** 22
Lewnes' Steak | **Annap** 28
Linwoods | **Owings Mills** 27
Morton's | **Inner Harbor** 26
Oceanaire | **Harbor E** 24
NEW Ouzo Bay | **Harbor E** — —
Roy's | **Harbor E** 27
Ruth's Chris | **Inner Harbor** 26
Sullivan's Steak | **Inner Harbor** 25

BYO

Andy Nelson's | **Cockeysville** 26
Atwater's | **multi.** 25
Blue Moon | **Fells Pt** 25
NEW Bun Shop | **Mt. Vernon** — —
Catonsville Gourm. | 26
  Catonsville
Corner BYOB | **Hampden** 24
Dangerously Delicious | **Canton** 21
Edo Sushi | **Owings Mills** 24
Grano Pasta | **Hampden** 25

Havana Rd. | **Towson**	21
Iggies | **Mt. Vernon**	27
Mari Luna Mex. | **Pikesville**	24
Meet 27 | **Charles Vill**	21
Mekong Delta | **D'town W**	27
Orchard Mkt. | **Towson**	26
R & R | **Elkridge**	27
Regions | **Catonsville**	23
Samos | **Gr'town**	28
Sofi's Crepes | **York Rd Corr**	24
Spice & Dice | **Towson**	29
Sushi Hana | **Timonium**	26
Thai Arroy | **S Balt**	26

CHILD-FRIENDLY

(Alternatives to the usual fast-food places; * children's menu available)

🆕 Ale Hse.* | **Columbia**	–
Ann's Dari* | **Glen Burnie**	25
b* | **D'town N**	26
Baugher's* | **Westminster**	20
Broom's Bloom | **Bel Air**	27
Cafe Hon | **Hampden**	16
Chick/Ruth's* | **Annap**	22
Clyde's* | **Columbia**	22
Double T* | **multi.**	20
Five Guys* | **multi.**	24
Friendly Farm* | **Upperco**	25
Grilled Cheese/Co.* | **multi.**	22
Hunan Manor | **Columbia**	23
🆕 Johnny's* | **Roland Pk**	–
Open Door* | **Bel Air**	24
P.F. Chang's* | **Columbia**	23
Red Hot/Blue* | **Laurel**	22
🆕 Verde Pizza | **Canton**	–
Woodberry Kit.* | **Clipper Mill**	27

DESSERT SPECIALISTS

Baugher's | **Westminster**	20
Broom's Bloom | **Bel Air**	27
Cafe Hon | **Hampden**	16
Cheesecake Factory | **Inner Harbor**	24
Chick/Ruth's | **Annap**	22
City Cafe | **Mt. Vernon**	23
Crêpe du Jour | **Mt. Wash**	21
Dangerously Delicious | **Canton**	21
🆕 Fleet St. Kit. | **Harbor E**	–
Gunning's | **multi.**	23
Main Ingredient | **Annap**	25
🆕 Ouzo Bay | **Harbor E**	–
Paul's Homewood | **Annap**	25
Prime Rib | **Hanover**	28

Stone Mill | **Brook'ville**	24
Teavolve | **Harbor E**	23
Wit/Wisdom | **Harbor E**	23

ENTERTAINMENT

(Call for days and times of performances)

🆕 Annapolis Smokehouse & Tavern | **Annap**	–
Bertha's | **Fells Pt**	22
Boatyard B&G | **Annap**	22
49 West | **Annap**	22
Germano's | **Little Italy**	24
Gertrude's | **Charles Vill**	22
Jesse Wong's Asean | **Columbia**	23
Joe Squared | **D'town N**	24
Prime Rib | **multi.**	28
Reynolds Tav. | **Annap**	23
Rockfish | **Annap**	20
Sotto Sopra | **Mt. Vernon**	26
Tabrizi's | **S Balt**	21
Ze Mean Bean | **Fells Pt**	23

FIREPLACES

Ambassador | **Homewood**	25
Antrim 1844 | **Westminster**	27
Bartlett Pear | **E Shore**	28
Bond St. | **Fells Pt**	19
Cafe Bretton | **Severna Pk**	27
Café Normandie | **Annap**	25
Ciao Bella | **Little Italy**	22
Da Mimmo | **Little Italy**	25
Elkridge Furnace | **Elkridge**	25
Harry Browne | **Annap**	25
Harryman Hse. | **Reist'town**	24
Iron Bridge Wine | **Columbia**	25
Jalapeños | **Annap**	27
Kentmorr | **E Shore**	25
Kings Contrivance | **Columbia**	24
Langermann's | **Canton**	22
Manor Tav. | **Monkton**	24
Mason's | **E Shore**	26
🆕 McFaul's | **Parkville**	–
Milton Inn | **Sparks**	28
🆕 Moonshine Tav. | **Canton**	–
Oregon Grille | **Hunt Valley**	25
Pappas | **Parkville**	23
Patrick's | **Cockeysville**	22
Peerce's | **Phoenix**	21
Petit Louis | **Roland Pk**	26
Regi's | **S Balt**	23
Salter's Tav. | **E Shore**	25
Sammy's Tratt. | **Mt. Vernon**	21

Stanford Grill | **Columbia** 24

Tabrizi's | **S Balt** 21

Ava's | **E Shore** -

Ze Mean Bean | **Fells Pt** 23

HISTORIC PLACES

(Year opened; * building)

1710 | Salter's Tav.* | **E Shore** 25

1740 | Milton Inn* | **Sparks** 28

1744 | Elkridge Furnace* | 25
Elkridge

1747 | Reynolds Tav.* | **Annap** 23

1772 | Faidley's* | **D'town W** 26

1799 | Peter's Inn* | **Fells Pt** 27

1820 | Bertha's* | **Fells Pt** 22

1844 | Antrim 1844* | 27
Westminster

1850 | Martick's* | **D'town W** -

1865 | Henninger's* | **Fells Pt** 25

1880 | Pope's Tav.* | **E Shore** 27

1880 | Woman's* | **Mt. Vernon** 24

1886 | Mason's* | **E Shore** 26

1890 | Lewnes' Steak* | **Annap** 28

1890 | Petit Louis* | **Roland Pk** 26

1896 | Chiapparelli's* | 24
Havre de Grace

1900 | Kings Contrivance* | 24
Columbia

1900 | Luna Blu* | **Annap** 22

1900 | Regions* | **Catonsville** 23

1905 | Annabel Lee* | **Hi'town** 26

1905 | Brewer's Art* | **Mt. Vernon** 25

1914 | Di Pasquale's | **E Balt** 28

1915 | Attman's Deli | **E Balt** 27

1920 | Hamilton Tav.* | **NE Balt** 24

1920 | Josef's* | **Fallston** 25

1940 | Chiapparelli's | **Little Italy** 24

1943 | Matthew's Pizza | **Hi'town** 27

1948 | Baugher's | **Westminster** 20

1949 | Cantler's Riverside* | 24
Annap

1949 | Paul's Homewood | **Annap** 25

1951 | Ann's Dari | **Glen Burnie** 25

1952 | Jimmy's | **Fells Pt** 20

1955 | Sabatino's | **Little Italy** 24

1958 | Kentmorr* | **E Shore** 25

1959 | Friendly Farm | **Upperco** 25

HOTEL DINING

Antrim 1844
Antrim 1844 | **Westminster** 27

Bartlett Pear Inn
Bartlett Pear | **E Shore** 28

Four Seasons Baltimore
Pabu | **Harbor E** -
Wit/Wisdom | **Harbor E** 23

Inn at Black Olive
Olive Rm. | **Fells Pt** 24

Loews Annapolis Hotel
NEW West | **Annap** -

Marriott Inner Harbor
NEW Yard | **Inner Harbor** -

Monaco
B&O | **D'town** 23

Oxford Inn
Pope's Tav. | **E Shore** 27

Pier 5
Ruth's Chris | **Inner Harbor** 26
McCormick/Schmick's | 23
Inner Harbor

Reynolds Tavern
Reynolds Tav. | **Annap** 23

Robert Morris Inn
Salter's Tav. | **E Shore** 25

Sheraton Inner Harbor
Morton's | **Inner Harbor** 26

LATE DINING

(Weekday closing hour)

NEW Admiral's Cup | 2 AM | -
Fells Pt

Ale Mary's | 2 AM | **Fells Pt** 22

Alewife | 1 AM | **D'town W** 22

Annabel Lee | 12:30 AM | 26
Hi'town

NEW Annapolis Smokehouse & -
Tavern | 12 AM | **Annap**

Bertha's | 2 AM | **Fells Pt** 22

Blue Agave | 2 AM | **S Balt** 22

Bobby's Burger | 12 AM | 22
Hanover

Bond St. | 2 AM | **Fells Pt** 19

Brass. Brightwell | 12 AM | 21
E Shore

NEW Bun Shop | 3 AM | -
Mt. Vernon

Cazbar | 12 AM | **Mt. Vernon** 24

Clyde's | 12 AM | **Columbia** 22

Costas Inn | 1 AM | **Dundalk** 25

Dizz | 2AM | **Hampden** 19

Double T | varies | **multi.** 20

Du-Claw | 12 AM | **multi.** 21

Food Market | 2 AM | **Hampden** -

Fork & Wrench | 2 AM | **Canton** -

49 West | 12 AM | **Annap** 22

Golden West | 1 AM | 21
Hampden

Heavy Seas | 12 AM | **Harbor E**	19
Honey Pig | 24 hrs. | **Ellicott City**	23
Jalapeños | 12 AM | **Annap**	27
Joe Squared | 12 AM | **D'town**	24
Johnny Rad's | 2 AM | **Fells Pt**	27
John Steven | 2 AM | **Fells Pt**	20
Kooper's | 2 AM | **Fells Pt**	22
Langermann's | 12 AM | **Fed Hill**	22
Liberatore's | varies | **multi.**	24
Manor Tav. | varies | **Monkton**	24
McCabe's | 12 AM | **Hampden**	23
NEW McFaul's | 2 AM | **Parkville**	-
Michael's Café | 2 AM | **Timonium**	23
NEW Moonshine Tav. | 12 AM | **Canton**	-
Nacho Mama's | 2 AM | **Canton**	22
Of Love/Regret | 2 AM | **Canton**	-
One-Eyed Mike | 2 AM | **Fells Pt**	23
Plug Ugly's | 2 AM | **Canton**	-
Rocket/Venus | 2 AM | **Hampden**	20
Rockfish | varies | **Annap**	20
Sabatino's | varies | **Little Italy**	24
Sip & Bite | 24 hrs. | **Fells Pt**	19
Szechuan Hse. | 12 AM | **Lutherville**	26
Talara | 12 AM | **Harbor E**	24
Tapas Adela | 12 AM | **Fells Pt**	23
Tapas Teatro | 12 AM | **D'town N**	24
13.5%/Silo | varies | **Locust Pt**	22
Townhouse | 2 AM | **Harbor E**	-
Towson Diner | 24 hrs. | **Towson**	21
Tsunami | 1 AM | **Annap**	25
Victoria | 2 AM | **Columbia**	24
NEW Willow | 2 AM | **Fells Pt**	-
NEW Yard | 12 AM | **Inner Harbor**	-

MEET FOR A DRINK

NEW Admiral's Cup | **Fells Pt**	-
Aida | **Columbia**	24
Annabel Lee | **Hi'town**	26
Azul 17 | **Columbia**	23
B&O | **D'town**	23
Banning's | **E Shore**	22
NEW Birroteca | **Hampden**	-
Bistro Rx | **Hi'town**	25
Bond St. | **Fells Pt**	19
Brass. Brightwell | **E Shore**	21

Brewer's Art | **Mt. Vernon**	25
Café de Paris | **Columbia**	24
Capital Grille | **Inner Harbor**	26
Carpaccio | **Annap**	25
Chazz | **Harbor E**	24
Cinghiale | **Harbor E**	26
City Cafe | **Mt. Vernon**	23
Clyde's | **Columbia**	22
NEW David's | **Hampden**	-
Earth/Wood/Fire | **Bare Hills**	-
Food Market | **Hampden**	-
Fork & Wrench | **Canton**	-
Galway Bay | **Annap**	24
Heavy Seas | **Harbor E**	19
Henninger's | **Fells Pt**	25
Iron Bridge Wine | **Columbia**	25
NEW Johnny's | **Roland Pk**	-
John Steven | **Fells Pt**	20
Lewnes' Steak | **Annap**	28
Liberatore's | **multi.**	24
Manor Tav. | **Monkton**	24
NEW McFaul's | **Parkville**	-
Of Love/Regret | **Canton**	-
One-Eyed Mike | **Fells Pt**	23
Out of the Fire | **E Shore**	28
NEW Ouzo Bay | **Harbor E**	-
Pazo | **Harbor E**	25
Porters | **S Balt**	22
Prime Rib | **Hanover**	28
Rocket/Venus | **Hampden**	20
NEW Shiso Tavern | **Canton**	-
Talara | **Harbor E**	24
Tark's Grill | **Brook'ville**	21
Teavolve | **Harbor E**	23
Thames St. | **Fells Pt**	24
13.5%/Silo | **Hampden**	22
Townhouse | **Harbor E**	-
Victoria | **Columbia**	24
Vino Rosina | **Harbor E**	22
Wine Mkt. | **Locust Pt**	24
Wit/Wisdom | **Harbor E**	23

OUTDOOR DINING

Ambassador | **Homewood**	25
b | **D'town N**	26
Bartlett Pear | **E Shore**	28
Blue Hill Tav. | **Canton**	25
Carlyle Club | **Homewood**	21
Carrol's Creek | **Annap**	23
Charleston | **Harbor E**	29
Cinghiale | **Harbor E**	26
Crêpe du Jour | **Mt. Wash**	21

Gertrude's | **Charles Vill**	22
Harris Crab | **E Shore**	24
Kali's Ct. | **Fells Pt**	25
Kentmorr | **E Shore**	25
Linwoods | **Owings Mills**	27
Mari Luna Latin | **Pikesville**	25
Mason's | **E Shore**	26
McCormick/Schmick's | **Inner Harbor**	23
Milton Inn | **Sparks**	28
Mr. Rain's Fun Hse. | **S Balt**	23
Oceanaire | **Harbor E**	24
Oregon Grille | **Hunt Valley**	25
Peter's Inn | **Fells Pt**	27
Plug Ugly's | **Canton**	-
Reynolds Tav. | **Annap**	23
Sotto Sopra | **Mt. Vernon**	26
Tabrizi's | **S Balt**	21
Tapas Teatro | **D'town N**	24
Tark's Grill | **Brook'ville**	21
Tersiguel's | **Ellicott City**	28
13.5%/Silo | **Locust Pt**	22
Wine Mkt. | **Locust Pt**	24

PEOPLE-WATCHING

NEW Birroteca | **Hampden**	-
Chick/Ruth's | **Annap**	22
Dempsey's Brew | **Camden Yds**	-
Faidley's | **D'town W**	26
Food Market | **Hampden**	-
Harry Browne | **Annap**	25
Honey Pig | **Ellicott City**	23
Jimmy's | **Fells Pt**	20
NEW McFaul's | **Parkville**	-
NEW Ouzo Bay | **Harbor E**	-
Pazo | **Harbor E**	25
Sabatino's | **Little Italy**	24
Victoria | **Columbia**	24

POWER SCENES

Banning's | **E Shore**	22
Capital Grille | **Inner Harbor**	26
Charleston | **Harbor E**	29
NEW Fleet St. Kit. | **Harbor E**	-
Harry Browne | **Annap**	25
Lewnes' Steak | **Annap**	28
Linwoods | **Owings Mills**	27
Miss Shirley's | **multi.**	26
NEW Ouzo Bay | **Harbor E**	-
Prime Rib | **multi.**	28
Woodberry Kit. | **Clipper Mill**	27

PRIVATE ROOMS

(Restaurants charge less at off times; call for capacity)

Antrim 1844 | **Westminster**	27
Broom's Bloom | **Bel Air**	27
Cafe Hon | **Hampden**	16
Capital Grille | **Inner Harbor**	26
Charleston | **Harbor E**	29
Cinghiale | **Harbor E**	26
Clyde's | **Columbia**	22
Elkridge Furnace | **Elkridge**	25
Fleming's Steak | **Harbor E**	25
Greystone Grill | **Ellicott City**	19
Harry Browne | **Annap**	25
Ikaros | **Gr'town**	23
Kali's Mezze | **Fells Pt**	25
Kings Contrivance | **Columbia**	24
La Famiglia | **Homewood**	22
Lewnes' Steak | **Annap**	28
Milton Inn | **Sparks**	28
Morton's | **Inner Harbor**	26
O'Learys | **Annap**	26
Oregon Grille | **Hunt Valley**	25
Pabu | **Harbor E**	-
Pazo | **Harbor E**	25
Portalli's | **Ellicott City**	22
Sabatino's | **Little Italy**	24
Tersiguel's | **Ellicott City**	28

PRIX FIXE MENUS

(Call for prices and times)

Antrim 1844 | **Westminster**	27
Café de Paris | **Columbia**	24
Charleston | **Harbor E**	29
Jesse Wong's Kit. | **Hunt Valley**	20
Luna Blu | **Annap**	22
Milton Inn | **Sparks**	28
Petit Louis | **Roland Pk**	26
Tabrizi's | **S Balt**	21
Tersiguel's | **Ellicott City**	28
Wild Orchid | **Annap**	23

QUIET CONVERSATION

Ambassador | **Homewood**	25
Bân Thai | **Mt. Vernon**	23
NEW Fleet St. Kit. | **Harbor E**	-
Great Sage | **Clarksville**	24
Havana Rd. | **Towson**	21
NEW Johnny's | **Roland Pk**	-
Little Spice | **Hanover**	25
NEW Liv2eat | **Fed Hill**	-

Mari Luna Mex. | **Mt. Vernon** 24
Meet 27 | **Charles Vill** 21
Pabu | **Harbor E** -
Paul's Homewood | **Annap** 25
Teavolve | **Harbor E** 23
Woman's | **Mt. Vernon** 24

ROMANTIC PLACES

Aldo's | **Little Italy** 28
Ambassador | **Homewood** 25
Antrim 1844 | **Westminster** 27
Charleston | **Harbor E** 29
Elkridge Furnace | **Elkridge** 25
NEW Fleet St. Kit. | **Harbor E** -
Kali's Ct. | **Fells Pt** 25
Linwoods | **Owings Mills** 27
NEW Liv2eat | **Fed Hill** -
Milton Inn | **Sparks** 28
Narrows | **E Shore** 25
NEW Ouzo Bay | **Harbor E** -
Paul's Homewood | **Annap** 25
Petit Louis | **Roland Pk** 26
Pope's Tav. | **E Shore** 27
Scossa | **E Shore** 28
Sotto Sopra | **Mt. Vernon** 26
Tersiguel's | **Ellicott City** 28

SINGLES SCENES

NEW Admiral's Cup | **Fells Pt** -
B&O | **D'town** 23
NEW Birroteca | **Hampden** -
Brewer's Art | **Mt. Vernon** 25
NEW David's | **Hampden** -
Liberatore's | **multi.** 24
Mama's/Shell | **Canton** 26
NEW McFaul's | **Parkville** -
NEW Ouzo Bay | **Harbor E** -
Pazo | **Harbor E** 25
NEW Shiso Tavern | **Canton** -
Sullivan's Steak | **Inner Harbor** 25
Tsunami | **Annap** 25

SLEEPERS

(Good food, but little known)
Bistro Poplar | **E Shore** 28
Bistro Rx | **Hi'town** 25
Breakfast Shoppe | **Severna Pk** 25
Cafe Bretton | **Severna Pk** 27
Chiyo Sushi | **Mt. Wash** 26
Grace Gdn. | **Odenton** 28
Grano Emporio | **Hampden** 25
Henninger's | **Fells Pt** 25
Kentmorr | **E Shore** 25

Laurrapin | **Havre de Grace** 26
Little Spice | **Hanover** 25
Mr. Bill's | **Essex** 26
Pho Nam | **Catonsville** 27
Piedigrotta | **Harbor E** 28
Pope's Tav. | **E Shore** 27
Rustico | **E Shore** 25
San Sushi | **Cockeysville** 26
Schultz's Crab | **Essex** 27
Spice & Dice | **Towson** 29
Tratt. Alberto | **Glen Burnie** 28
Umi Sake | **Cockeysville** 28

TRENDY

Alchemy | **Hampden** 23
NEW Birroteca | **Hampden** -
Bistro Blanc | **Glenelg** 26
Bond St. | **Fells Pt** 19
Brewer's Art | **Mt. Vernon** 25
Chazz | **Harbor E** 24
Corner BYOB | **Hampden** 24
Food Market | **Hampden** -
Fork & Wrench | **Canton** -
Heavy Seas | **Harbor E** 19
Honey Pig | **Ellicott City** 23
NEW Johnny's | **Roland Pk** -
Of Love/Regret | **Canton** -
Olive Rm. | **Fells Pt** 24
Osteria 177 | **Annap** 27
Out of the Fire | **E Shore** 28
Pabu | **Harbor E** -
Pazo | **Harbor E** 25
Rocket/Venus | **Hampden** 20
Talara | **Harbor E** 24
13.5%/Silo | **Hampden** 22

VALET PARKING

Aldo's | **Little Italy** 28
NEW Ale Hse. | **Columbia** -
Ambassador | **Homewood** 25
Bagby Pizza | **Harbor E** 23
Bahama Breeze | **Towson** 23
B&O | **D'town** 23
Black Olive | **Fells Pt** 27
Bluegrass | **S Balt** 24
Blue Hill Tav. | **Canton** 25
Caesar's Den | **Little Italy** 23
Café Troia | **Towson** 23
Capital Grille | **Inner Harbor** 26
Carpaccio | **Annap** 25
Charleston | **Harbor E** 29
Chazz | **Harbor E** 24

BALTIMORE AREA

SPECIAL FEATURES

Visit zagat.com

335

Cheesecake Factory | **multi.** 24]
Chiapparelli's | **Little Italy** 24]
Ciao Bella | **Little Italy** 22]
Cinghiale | **Harbor E** 26]
City Cafe | **Mt. Vernon** 23]
Crêpe du Jour | **Mt. Wash** 21]
Facci | **Laurel** 24]
NEW Fleet St. Kit. | **Harbor E** -]
Fleming's Steak | **Harbor E** 25]
Germano's | **Little Italy** 24]
Harry Browne | **Annap** 25]
Kali's Ct. | **Fells Pt** 25]
Kali's Mezze | **Fells Pt** 25]
La Famiglia | **Homewood** 22]
Langermann's | **multi.** 22]
La Scala | **Little Italy** 26]
La Tavola | **Little Italy** 26]
Lebanese Tav. | **Harbor E** 23]
NEW Liv2eat | **Fed Hill** -]
Mari Luna Latin | **Pikesville** 25]
McCormick/Schmick's | **Inner Harbor** 23]
NEW McFaul's | **Parkville** -]
NEW Moonshine Tav. | **Canton** -]
Morton's | **Inner Harbor** 26]
Oceanaire | **Harbor E** 24]
Osteria 177 | **Annap** 27]
NEW Ouzo Bay | **Harbor E** -]
Pabu | **Harbor E** -]
Paladar | **Annap** 23]
Pazo | **Harbor E** 25]
P.F. Chang's | **Annap** 23]
Phillips | **Inner Harbor** 20]
Portalli's | **Ellicott City** 22]
Prime Rib | **Mt. Vernon** 28]
Regi's | **S Balt** 23]
Roy's | **Harbor E** 27]
Ruth's Chris | **multi.** 26]
Sabatino's | **Little Italy** 24]
Sammy's Tratt. | **Mt. Vernon** 21]
Sotto Sopra | **Mt. Vernon** 26]
Sullivan's Steak | **Inner Harbor** 25]
Talara | **Harbor E** 24]
Tapas Adela | **Fells Pt** 23]
Ten Ten | **Harbor E** 25]
Townhouse | **Harbor E** -]
NEW Verde Pizza | **Canton** -]
NEW West | **Annap** -]
Wit/Wisdom | **Harbor E** 23]
Woodberry Kit. | **Clipper Mill** 27]
Yellowfin | **Annap** 23]

VIEWS

Antrim 1844 | **Westminster** 27]
Broom's Bloom | **Bel Air** 27]
Cantler's Riverside | **Annap** 24]
Carrol's Creek | **Annap** 23]
Cheesecake Factory | **Inner Harbor** 24]
Clyde's | **Columbia** 22]
Friendly Farm | **Upperco** 25]
Harris Crab | **E Shore** 24]
Kentmorr | **E Shore** 25]
Mango Grove | **Columbia** 24]
McCormick/Schmick's | **Inner Harbor** 23]
Narrows | **E Shore** 25]
Olive Rm. | **Fells Pt** 24]
NEW Ouzo Bay | **Harbor E** -]
Pabu | **Harbor E** -]
Pope's Tav. | **E Shore** 27]
Red Pearl | **Columbia** 26]
Salter's Tav. | **E Shore** 25]
Severn Inn | **Annap** 22]
Sushi Sono | **Columbia** 27]
Tabrizi's | **S Balt** 21]
13.5%/Silo | **Locust Pt** 22]
Waterfront Kit. | **Fells Pt** 22]
NEW Willow | **Fells Pt** -]
Wit/Wisdom | **Harbor E** 23]
Yellowfin | **Annap** 23]

WINNING WINE LISTS

Antrim 1844 | **Westminster** 27]
Bistro Blanc | **Glenelg** 26]
Café de Paris | **Columbia** 24]
Capital Grille | **Inner Harbor** 26]
Charleston | **Harbor E** 29]
Cinghiale | **Harbor E** 26]
Della Notte | **Little Italy** 24]
NEW Fleet St. Kit. | **Harbor E** -]
Fleming's Steak | **Harbor E** 25]
Iron Bridge Wine | **Columbia** 25]
NEW Johnny's | **Roland Pk** -]
Oregon Grille | **Hunt Valley** 25]
Out of the Fire | **E Shore** 28]
NEW Ouzo Bay | **Harbor E** -]
Pazo | **Harbor E** 25]
Petit Louis | **Roland Pk** 26]
Prime Rib | **Hanover** 28]
Tersiguel's | **Ellicott City** 28]
13.5%/Silo | **multi.** 22]
Vino Rosina | **Harbor E** 22]
Wine Mkt. | **Locust Pt** 24]

BALTIMORE AREA

SPECIAL FEATURES

Cuisines

Includes names, locations and Food ratings.

AFGHAN

Helmand | **Mt. Vernon** — 27

AMERICAN

Adam's Eve | **Canton** — -
🆕 Admiral's Cup | **Fells Pt** — -
Alchemy | **Hampden** — 23
🆕 Ale Hse. | **Columbia** — -
Ale Mary's | **Fells Pt** — 22
Alewife | **D'town W** — 22
Annabel Lee | **Hi'town** — 26
Ann's Dari | **Glen Burnie** — 25
Antrim 1844 | **Westminster** — 27
Artifact Coffee | **Clipper Mill** — -
Attman's Deli | **E Balt** — 27
b | **D'town N** — 26
B&O | **D'town** — 23
Banning's | **E Shore** — 22
Bartlett Pear | **E Shore** — 28
Baugher's | **Westminster** — 20
Bistro Blanc | **Glenelg** — 26
Bistro Rx | **Hi'town** — 25
Bluegrass | **S Balt** — 24
Blue Hill Tav. | **Canton** — 25
Blue Moon | **Fells Pt** — 25
BlueStone | **Timonium** — 23
Brass. Brightwell | **E Shore** — 21
Breakfast Shoppe | **Severna Pk** — 25
Brewer's Art | **Mt. Vernon** — 25
Cafe Hon | **Hampden** — 16
Charleston | **Harbor E** — 29
Cheesecake Factory | **multi.** — 24
🆕 Chesapeake | **D'town N** — -
Christopher Daniel | **Timonium** — 23
City Cafe | **Mt. Vernon** — 23
Clementine | **NE Balt** — 25
Clyde's | **Columbia** — 22
Crush | **Annap** — 23
Dangerously Delicious | **Canton** — 21
🆕 David's | **Hampden** — -
Dizz | **Hampden** — 19
Eggspectation | **Ellicott City** — 21
Elkridge Furnace | **Elkridge** — 25
First Watch | **multi.** — 21
🆕 Fleet St. Kit. | **Harbor E** — -
Food Market | **Hampden** — -
Fork & Wrench | **Canton** — -
49 West | **Annap** — 22

Friendly Farm | **Upperco** — 25
Garry's | **Severna Pk** — 20
Greystone Grill | **Ellicott City** — 19
Harry Browne | **Annap** — 25
Harryman Hse. | **Reist'town** — 24
Heavy Seas | **Harbor E** — 19
Henninger's | **Fells Pt** — 25
Iron Bridge Wine | **Columbia** — 25
Kentmorr | **E Shore** — 25
Kings Contrivance | **Columbia** — 24
Kooper's | **multi.** — 22
Laurrapin | **Havre de Grace** — 26
Level | **Annap** — 24
Linwoods | **Owings Mills** — 27
🆕 Liv2eat | **Fed Hill** — -
🆕 Maggie's Farm | **NE Balt** — -
Main Ingredient | **Annap** — 25
Manor Tav. | **Monkton** — 24
🆕 Marquee | **Hi'town** — -
🆕 Martick's | **D'town W** — -
Mason's | **E Shore** — 26
🆕 McFaul's | **Parkville** — -
Meet 27 | **Charles Vill** — 21
Metropolitan Coffee | **S Balt** — 23
Michael's Café | **Timonium** — 23
Milton Inn | **Sparks** — 28
Miss Shirley's | **multi.** — 26
Mr. Rain's Fun Hse. | **S Balt** — 23
Of Love/Regret | **Canton** — -
Olive Grove | **Linthicum** — 24
One-Eyed Mike | **Fells Pt** — 23
Open Door | **Bel Air** — 24
Oregon Grille | **Hunt Valley** — 25
Out of the Fire | **E Shore** — 28
Paladar | **Annap** — 23
Pappas | **multi.** — 23
Patrick's | **Cockeysville** — 22
Paul's Homewood | **Annap** — 25
Peerce's | **Phoenix** — 21
Peppermill | **Lutherville** — 23
Peter's Inn | **Fells Pt** — 27
Pope's Tav. | **E Shore** — 27
Porters | **S Balt** — 22
Regi's | **S Balt** — 23
Reynolds Tav. | **Annap** — 23
Rockfish | **Annap** — 20
Salt | **Fells Pt** — 27
Sascha's 527 | **Mt. Vernon** — 24

Severn Inn | **Annap**	22
Stanford Grill | **Columbia**	24
Tark's Grill | **Brook'ville**	21
Teavolve | **Harbor E**	23
Ten Ten | **Harbor E**	25
13.5%/Silo | **multi.**	22
Tidewater | **Havre de Grace**	22
Townhouse | **Harbor E**	-
208 Talbot | **E Shore**	-
Vin 909 | **Annap**	28
Vino Rosina | **Harbor E**	22
Waterfront Kit. | **Fells Pt**	22
NEW West | **Annap**	-
Wild Orchid | **Annap**	23
Wine Mkt. | **Locust Pt**	24
Wit/Wisdom | **Harbor E**	23
Woman's | **Mt. Vernon**	24
Woodberry Kit. | **Clipper Mill**	27
NEW Yard | **Inner Harbor**	-
Yellowfin | **Annap**	23

ASIAN

Jesse Wong's Asean | **Columbia**	23
Jesse Wong's Kit. | **Hunt Valley**	20
NEW Shiso Tavern | **Canton**	-
Tsunami | **Annap**	25

BAKERIES

Atwater's | **multi.**	25
Bon Fresco | **Columbia**	27
NEW Bun Shop | **Mt. Vernon**	-
Dangerously Delicious | **Canton**	21
Goldberg's | **multi.**	25
Greg's Bagels | **York Rd Corr**	24
Main Ingredient | **Annap**	25
Piedigrotta | **Harbor E**	28
Stone Mill | **multi.**	24

BARBECUE

Andy Nelson's | **Cockeysville**	26
NEW Annapolis Smokehouse & Tavern | **Annap**	-
Big Bad Wolf | **NE Balt**	26
Chaps Pit Beef | **E Balt**	27
Kloby's Smokehse. | **Laurel**	21
Red Hot/Blue | **multi.**	22

BRAZILIAN

Fogo de Chão | **Inner Harbor**	27

BRITISH

Reynolds Tav. | **Annap**	23

BURGERS

BGR | **Columbia**	22
Bobby's Burger | **Hanover**	22
Clyde's | **Columbia**	22
Elevation Burger | **Bowie**	21
Five Guys | **multi.**	24
Gino's | **multi.**	22
Hamilton Tav. | **NE Balt**	24
Kooper's | **Location Varies**	22
Linwoods | **Owings Mills**	27
Red Hot/Blue | **multi.**	22

CALIFORNIAN

NEW Johnny's | **Roland Pk**	-

CARIBBEAN

Bahama Breeze | **Towson**	23
Paladar | **Annap**	23

CENTRAL AMERICAN

Pollo Campero | **Laurel**	19

CHESAPEAKE

Gertrude's | **Charles Vill**	22
Narrows | **E Shore**	25
Salter's Tav. | **E Shore**	25

CHICKEN

Chicken Rico | **Hi'town**	27
Gino's | **multi.**	22
Nando's | **multi.**	22

CHINESE

Cafe Zen | **York Rd Corr**	22
David Chu's | **Pikesville**	25
Grace Gdn. | **Odenton**	28
Grace's | **Bowie**	25
Hunan Manor | **Columbia**	23
P.F. Chang's | **multi.**	23
Red Pearl | **Columbia**	26
Szechuan Hse. | **Lutherville**	26

COFFEEHOUSES

Artifact Coffee | **Clipper Mill**	-
NEW Bun Shop | **Mt. Vernon**	-
City Cafe | **Mt. Vernon**	23
NEW Dooby's | **Mt. Vernon**	-
49 West | **Annap**	22
One World | **Homewood**	22

CONTINENTAL

Corner BYOB | **Hampden**	24
Josef's | **Fallston**	25
Tio Pepe | **Mt. Vernon**	26

CRAB HOUSES

Cantler's Riverside | **Annap**	24
Costas Inn | **Dundalk**	25
Faidley's | **D'town W**	26
Gunning's | **Hanover**	23
Harris Crab | **E Shore**	24
Kentmorr | **E Shore**	25
Mr. Bill's | **Essex**	26
Schultz's Crab | **Essex**	27

CREOLE

NEW Moonshine Tav. | **Canton**	–

CRÊPES

Crêpe du Jour | **Mt. Wash**	21
Sofi's Crepes | **multi.**	24

CUBAN

Havana Rd. | **Towson**	21

DELIS

Attman's Deli | **E Balt**	27
Chick/Ruth's | **Annap**	22
Suburban Hse. | **Pikesville**	19

DINERS

Cafe Hon | **Hampden**	16
Chick/Ruth's | **Annap**	22
Double T | **multi.**	20
Jimmy's | **Fells Pt**	20
Sip & Bite | **Fells Pt**	19
Towson Diner | **Towson**	21

EASTERN EUROPEAN

Ze Mean Bean | **Fells Pt**	23

ECLECTIC

Bond St. | **Fells Pt**	19
NEW Bun Shop | **Mt. Vernon**	–
Double T | **multi.**	20
4 Seasons | **Gambrills**	25
Golden West | **Hampden**	21
Great Sage | **Clarksville**	24
Jack's Bistro | **Canton**	27
NEW Maggie's Farm | **NE Balt**	–
Marie Louise | **Mt. Vernon**	22
Out of the Fire | **E Shore**	28
Regions | **Catonsville**	23
Rocket/Venus | **Hampden**	20
Tapas Teatro | **D'town N**	24
Tsunami | **Annap**	25
Victoria | **Columbia**	24

ETHIOPIAN

Dukem | **Mt. Vernon**	24

FRENCH

Antrim 1844 | **Westminster**	27
Cafe Bretton | **Severna Pk**	27
Les Folies | **Annap**	27
Marie Louise | **Mt. Vernon**	22
Sofi's Crepes | **multi.**	24
Tersiguel's | **Ellicott City**	28

FRENCH (BISTRO)

Bistro Poplar | **E Shore**	28
Brass. Brightwell | **E Shore**	21
Café de Paris | **Columbia**	24
Café Normandie | **Annap**	25
Crêpe du Jour | **Mt. Wash**	21
Petit Louis | **Roland Pk**	26

GASTROPUBS

Adam's Eve | Amer. | **Canton**	–
Alewife | Amer. | **D'town W**	22
Fork & Wrench | Amer. | **Canton**	–
Heavy Seas | Amer. | **Harbor E**	19
Porters | Amer. | **S Balt**	22
Victoria | Eclectic | **Columbia**	24

GREEK

Black Olive | **Fells Pt**	27
Ikaros | **Gr'town**	23
Olive Rm. | **Fells Pt**	24
NEW Ouzo Bay | **Harbor E**	–
Paul's Homewood | **Annap**	25
Samos | **Gr'town**	28

HAWAIIAN

Roy's | **Harbor E**	27

HOT DOGS

Ann's Dari | **Glen Burnie**	25
Five Guys | **Annap**	24

ICE CREAM PARLOR

Broom's Bloom | **Bel Air**	27

INDIAN

Akbar | **multi.**	24
Ambassador | **Homewood**	25
Carlyle Club | **Homewood**	21
House of India | **Columbia**	23
Mango Grove | **Columbia**	24

IRISH

NEW Blackthorn | **E Shore**	–
Galway Bay | **Annap**	24

ITALIAN

(N=Northern; S=Southern)

Aida | **Columbia**	24
Aldo's | S | **Little Italy**	28
Amicci's | **Little Italy**	24
Ava's | **E Shore**	27
Basta Pasta | **multi.**	21
NEW Birroteca | **Hampden**	-
Caesar's Den | S | **Little Italy**	23
Café Gia | S | **Little Italy**	22
Café Troia | **Towson**	23
Carpaccio | N | **Annap**	25
Chazz | **Harbor E**	24
Chef Paolino | **Catonsville**	21
Chiapparelli's | **multi.**	24
Ciao Bella | **Little Italy**	22
Cinghiale | **Harbor E**	26
Da Mimmo | **Little Italy**	25
Della Notte | **Little Italy**	24
Di Pasquale's | **E Balt**	28
Facci | **Laurel**	24
Germano's | **Little Italy**	24
Grano Emporio | **Hampden**	25
Grano Pasta | **Hampden**	25
Joe Squared | **multi.**	24
La Famiglia | **Homewood**	22
La Scala | S | **Little Italy**	26
La Tavola | **Little Italy**	26
Ledo Pizza | N | **Lanham**	23
Liberatore's | **multi.**	24
Luna Blu | **Annap**	22
Mamma Lucia | **Elkridge**	22
Olive Grove | **Linthicum**	24
Osteria 177 | **Annap**	27
Pasta Plus | **Laurel**	26
Piedigrotta | **Harbor E**	28
Portalli's | **Ellicott City**	22
Rustico | S | **E Shore**	25
Sabatino's | **Little Italy**	24
Sammy's Tratt. | S | **Mt. Vernon**	21
Scossa | N | **E Shore**	28
Sotto Sopra | N | **Mt. Vernon**	26
Tratt. Alberto | N | **Glen Burnie**	28

JAMAICAN

Negril | **multi.**	24

JAPANESE

(* sushi specialist)

Chiyo Sushi* | **Mt. Wash**	26
Edo Sushi* | **multi.**	24
Joss Cafe* | **multi.**	27
Kobe | **multi.**	27

Matsuri | **S Balt**	24
Minato* | **Mt. Vernon**	24
Pabu | **Harbor E**	-
Ra Sushi* | **Harbor E**	24
San Sushi* | **Cockeysville**	26
San Sushi/Thai* | **multi.**	21
Sushi Hana* | **multi.**	26
Sushi King* | **Columbia**	28
Sushi Sono* | **Columbia**	27
Umi Sake* | **Cockeysville**	28

JEWISH

Goldberg's | **multi.**	25
Suburban Hse. | **Pikesville**	19

KOREAN

(* barbecue specialist)

Honey Pig* | **Ellicott City**	23
Shin Chon* | **Ellicott City**	22

KOSHER/ KOSHER-STYLE

David Chu's | **Pikesville**	25
Goldberg's | **Pikesville**	25

LEBANESE

Lebanese Tav. | **multi.**	23

MEDITERRANEAN

4 Seasons | **Gambrills**	25
Kali's Ct. | **Fells Pt**	25
Kali's Mezze | **Fells Pt**	25
Marie Louise | **Mt. Vernon**	22
Pazo | **Harbor E**	25
Tabrizi's | **S Balt**	21
Tapas Teatro | **D'town N**	24

MEXICAN

Azul 17 | **Columbia**	23
Blue Agave | **S Balt**	22
Jalapeños | **Annap**	27
Mari Luna Latin | **Pikesville**	25
Mari Luna Mex. | **multi.**	24
Miguel's Cocina | **Locust Pt**	20
Nacho Mama's | **Canton**	22
R & R | **multi.**	27
NEW Willow | **Fells Pt**	-

MIDDLE EASTERN

Tabrizi's | **S Balt**	21

NEW MEXICAN

Golden West | **Hampden**	21

NUEVO LATINO

Talara | **Harbor E**	24

PAN-LATIN

Mari Luna Latin | **Pikesville**	25
Mari Luna Mex. | **Mt. Vernon**	24
Paladar | **Annap**	23

PERSIAN

Orchard Mkt. | **Towson**	26

PERUVIAN

Chicken Rico | **Hi'town**	27

PIZZA

Ava's | **E Shore**	27
Bagby Pizza | **Harbor E**	23
NEW Birroteca | **Hampden**	-
Chazz | **Harbor E**	24
Chef Paolino | **Catonsville**	21
Coal Fire | **multi.**	22
Earth/Wood/Fire | **Bare Hills**	-
Facci | **Laurel**	24
Hersh's Pizza | **S Balt**	-
Iggies | **Mt. Vernon**	27
Joe Squared | **D'town N**	24
Johnny Rad's | **Fells Pt**	27
Ledo Pizza | **Lanham**	23
Mamma Lucia | **Elkridge**	22
Matthew's Pizza | **Hi'town**	27
Pasta Plus | **Laurel**	26
NEW Verde Pizza | **Canton**	-

PORTUGUESE

Nando's | **multi.**	22

PUB FOOD

Ale Mary's | **Fells Pt**	22
NEW Blackthorn | **E Shore**	-
Boatyard B&G | **Annap**	22
Clyde's | **Columbia**	22
NEW David's | **Hampden**	-
Dempsey's Brew | **Camden Yds**	-
Du-Claw | **multi.**	21
Galway Bay | **Annap**	24
Hamilton Tav. | **NE Balt**	24
Johnny Rad's | **Fells Pt**	27
Koco's | **NE Balt**	27
McCabe's | **Hampden**	23
NEW McFaul's | **Parkville**	-
One-Eyed Mike | **Fells Pt**	23
Plug Ugly's | **Canton**	-

SANDWICHES

(See also Delis)

Attman's Deli | **E Balt**	27
Atwater's | **multi.**	25
Bon Fresco | **Columbia**	27
Broom's Bloom | **Bel Air**	27
Chick/Ruth's | **Annap**	22
Goldberg's | **Pikesville**	25
Greg's Bagels | **York Rd Corr**	24
Grilled Cheese/Co. | **multi.**	22
Stone Mill | **Brook'ville**	24

SEAFOOD

Bertha's | **Fells Pt**	22
Black Olive | **Fells Pt**	27
BlueStone | **Timonium**	23
Cantler's Riverside | **Annap**	24
Carrol's Creek | **Annap**	23
Catonsville Gourm. | **Catonsville**	26
Costas Inn | **Dundalk**	25
Faidley's | **D'town W**	26
G&M | **Linthicum**	24
Gertrude's | **Charles Vill**	22
Gunning's | **multi.**	23
Harris Crab | **E Shore**	24
Jerry's | **multi.**	26
John Steven | **Fells Pt**	20
Kali's Ct. | **Fells Pt**	25
Kentmorr | **E Shore**	25
Liberatore's | **Perry Hall**	24
Mama's/Shell | **Canton**	26
M&S Grill | **Inner Harbor**	22
McCormick/Schmick's | **Inner Harbor**	23
Michael's Café | **Timonium**	23
Mr. Bill's | **Essex**	26
Narrows | **E Shore**	25
Oceanaire | **Harbor E**	24
O'Learys | **Annap**	26
Oregon Grille | **Hunt Valley**	25
NEW Ouzo Bay | **Harbor E**	-
Pappas | **multi.**	23
Phillips | **Inner Harbor**	20
Prime Rib | **Mt. Vernon**	28
Rockfish | **Annap**	20
Rusty Scupper | **S Balt**	22
Salter's Tav. | **E Shore**	25
Schultz's Crab | **Essex**	27
Seaside Rest. | **Glen Burnie**	26
Severn Inn | **Annap**	22
Thames St. | **Fells Pt**	24
Timbuktu | **Hanover**	23

NEW West | **Annap** — |
Yellowfin | **Annap** 23

SMALL PLATES

(See also Spanish tapas specialist)
Aida | Italian | **Columbia** 24
Bond St. | Eclectic | **Fells Pt** 19
City Cafe | Amer. | **Mt. Vernon** 23
Crush | Amer. | **Annap** 23
Hersh's Pizza | Pizza | **S Balt** — |
Iron Bridge Wine | Amer. | 25
    Columbia
Kali's Mezze | Med. | **Fells Pt** 25
Level | Amer. | **Annap** 24
NEW Martick's | Amer. | — |
    D'town W
Pazo | Med. | **Harbor E** 25
Talara | Nuevo Latino | **Harbor E** 24
Tapas Teatro | Eclectic | 24
    D'town N

SOUTH AFRICAN

Nando's | **Charles Vill** 22

SOUTHERN

Carolina Kit. | **Largo** 25
Crème | **Mt. Vernon** 21
Langermann's | **multi.** 22
Miss Shirley's | **Annap** 26
NEW Moonshine Tav. | **Canton** — |

SPANISH

(* tapas specialist)
Jalapeños* | **Annap** 27
Tapas Adela* | **Fells Pt** 23
Tio Pepe | **Mt. Vernon** 26

STEAKHOUSES

Capital Grille | **Inner Harbor** 26
Chop Hse. | **Annap** 25
Fleming's Steak | **Harbor E** 25
Fogo de Chão | **Inner Harbor** 27

Greystone Grill | **Ellicott City** 19
Lewnes' Steak | **Annap** 28
M&S Grill | **Inner Harbor** 22
Morton's | **Inner Harbor** 26
Oregon Grille | **Hunt Valley** 25
Prime Rib | **multi.** 28
Ruth's Chris | **multi.** 26
Sullivan's Steak | **Inner Harbor** 25
Ava's | **E Shore** — |
Yellowfin | **Annap** 23

TEAHOUSE

Teavolve | **Harbor E** 23

TEX-MEX

NEW Willow | **Fells Pt** — |

THAI

Bân Thai | **Mt. Vernon** 23
Lemongrass | **Annap** 25
Little Spice | **Hanover** 25
NEW My Thai | **Harbor E** — |
San Sushi/Thai | **multi.** 21
Spice & Dice | **Towson** 29
Stang/Siam | **Mt. Vernon** 23
Thai | **Charles Vill** 24
Thai Arroy | **S Balt** 26

TURKISH

Cazbar | **Mt. Vernon** 24

VEGETARIAN

(* vegan)
Great Sage* | **Clarksville** 24
Mango Grove* | **Columbia** 24
One World* | **Homewood** 22

VIETNAMESE

An Loi | **Columbia** 23
Mekong Delta | **D'town W** 27
Pho Dat Thanh | **multi.** 24
Pho Nam | **Catonsville** 27

Locations

Includes names, cuisines and Food ratings.

Baltimore

BARE HILLS/ MT. WASHINGTON

Atwater's	Bakery	25
Chiyo Sushi	Japanese	26
Crêpe du Jour	French	21
Earth/Wood/Fire	Pizza	-
Sushi Hana	Japanese	26

BUSINESS DISTRICT/ CAMDEN YARDS/ CONVENTION CTR./ DOWNTOWN/ INNER HARBOR

B&O	Amer.	23
Capital Grille	Steak	26
Cheesecake Factory	Amer.	24
Dempsey's Brew	Pub	-
Edo Sushi	Japanese	24
Five Guys	Burgers	24
Fogo de Chão	Brazilian/Steak	27
Joe Squared	Italian/Pizza	24
M&S Grill	Seafood/Steak	22
McCormick/Schmick's	Seafood	23
Miss Shirley's	Amer.	26
Morton's	Steak	26
P.F. Chang's	Chinese	23
Phillips	Seafood	20
Ruth's Chris	Steak	26
Sullivan's Steak	Steak	25
NEW Yard	Amer.	-

CANTON

Adam's Eve	Amer.	-
Blue Hill Tav.	Amer.	25
Dangerously Delicious	Amer./Bakery	21
Five Guys	Burgers	24
Fork & Wrench	Amer.	-
Jack's Bistro	Eclectic	27
Langermann's	Southern	22
Mama's/Shell	Seafood	26
NEW Moonshine Tav.	Creole/Southern	-
Nacho Mama's	Mex.	22
Of Love/Regret	Amer.	-
Plug Ugly's	Pub	-
NEW Shiso Tavern	Asian	-

San Sushi/Thai	Japanese/Thai	21
NEW Verde Pizza	Pizza	-

CHARLES VILLAGE

Gertrude's	Chesapeake	22
Meet 27	Amer.	21
Nando's	Chicken	22
Thai	Thai	24

DOWNTOWN NORTH/ CHARLES ST./ MT. VERNON

Akbar	Indian	24
b	Amer.	26
Bân Thai	Thai	23
Brewer's Art	Amer.	25
NEW Bun Shop	Eclectic	-
Cazbar	Turkish	24
NEW Chesapeake	Amer.	-
City Cafe	Amer.	23
Crème	Southern	21
NEW Dooby's	Coffee	-
Dukem	Ethiopian	24
Helmand	Afghan	27
Iggies	Pizza	27
Joe Squared	Italian/Pizza	24
Joss Cafe	Japanese	27
Marie Louise	French/Med.	22
Mari Luna Mex.	Mex./Pan-Latin	24
Minato	Japanese	24
Prime Rib	Steak	28
Sammy's Tratt.	Italian	21
Sascha's 527	Amer.	24
Sofi's Crepes	Crêpes	24
Sotto Sopra	Italian	26
Stang/Siam	Thai	23
Tapas Teatro	Eclectic/Med.	24
Tio Pepe	Continental/Spanish	26
Woman's	Amer./Tea	24

EAST BALTIMORE

Attman's Deli	Deli	27
Chaps Pit Beef	BBQ	27
Di Pasquale's	Italian	28

FELLS POINT

NEW Admiral's Cup	Amer.	-
Ale Mary's	Pub	22
Bertha's	Seafood	22

Black Olive	*Greek/Seafood*	27
Blue Moon	*Amer.*	25
Bond St.	*Eclectic*	19
Henninger's	*Amer.*	25
Jimmy's	*Diner*	20
Johnny Rad's	*Pizza*	27
John Steven	*Seafood*	20
Kali's Ct.	*Med./Seafood*	25
Kali's Mezze	*Med.*	25
Kooper's	*Amer.*	22
Olive Rm.	*Greek*	24
One-Eyed Mike	*Pub*	23
Peter's Inn	*Amer.*	27
Salt	*Amer.*	27
Sip & Bite	*Diner*	19
Sofi's Crepes	*Crêpes*	24
Tapas Adela	*Spanish*	23
Thames St.	*Seafood*	24
Waterfront Kit.	*Amer.*	22
NEW Willow	*Tex-Mex*	-
Ze Mean Bean	*E Euro.*	23

HAMPDEN/
ROLAND PARK

(Including Clipper Mill)

Alchemy	*Amer.*	23
Artifact Coffee	*Coffee*	-
NEW Birroteca	*Italian/Pizza*	-
Cafe Hon	*Amer.*	16
Corner BYOB	*Continental*	24
NEW David's	*Amer.*	-
Dizz	*Amer.*	19
Food Market	*Amer.*	-
Golden West	*Eclectic/New Mex.*	21
Grano Emporio	*Italian*	25
Grano Pasta	*Italian*	25
NEW Johnny's	*Calif.*	-
McCabe's	*Pub*	23
Miss Shirley's	*Amer.*	26
Petit Louis	*French*	26
Rocket/Venus	*Eclectic*	20
13.5%/Silo	*Amer.*	22
Woodberry Kit.	*Amer.*	27

HARBOR EAST/
LITTLE ITALY

Aldo's	*Italian*	28
Amicci's	*Italian*	24
Bagby Pizza	*Pizza*	23
Caesar's Den	*Italian*	23
Café Gia	*Italian*	22
Charleston	*Amer.*	29
Chazz	*Italian/Pizza*	24

Chiapparelli's	*Italian*	24
Ciao Bella	*Italian*	22
Cinghiale	*Italian*	26
Da Mimmo	*Italian*	25
Della Notte	*Italian*	24
NEW Fleet St. Kit.	*Amer.*	-
Fleming's Steak	*Steak*	25
Germano's	*Italian*	24
Heavy Seas	*Amer.*	19
La Scala	*Italian*	26
La Tavola	*Italian*	26
Lebanese Tav.	*Lebanese*	23
NEW My Thai	*Thai*	-
Oceanaire	*Seafood*	24
NEW Ouzo Bay	*Greek/Seafood*	-
Pabu	*Japanese*	-
Pazo	*Med.*	25
Piedigrotta	*Bakery/Italian*	28
Ra Sushi	*Japanese*	24
Roy's	*Hawaiian*	27
Sabatino's	*Italian*	24
Talara	*Nuevo Latino*	24
Teavolve	*Amer./Tea*	23
Ten Ten	*Amer.*	25
Townhouse	*Amer.*	-
Vino Rosina	*Amer.*	22
Wit/Wisdom	*Amer.*	23

HIGHLANDTOWN/
GREEKTOWN

Annabel Lee	*Amer.*	26
Bistro Rx	*Amer.*	25
Chicken Rico	*Chicken/Peruvian*	27
Ikaros	*Greek*	23
NEW Marquee	*Amer.*	-
Matthew's Pizza	*Pizza*	27
Samos	*Greek*	28

HOMEWOOD

Ambassador	*Indian*	25
Carlyle Club	*Indian*	21
La Famiglia	*Italian*	22
One World	*Veg.*	22

LOCUST POINT

Miguel's Cocina	*Mex.*	20
13.5%/Silo	*Amer.*	22
Wine Mkt.	*Amer.*	24

NORTH BALTIMORE/
YORK ROAD CORRIDOR

Atwater's	*Bakery*	25
Cafe Zen	*Chinese*	22

Greg's Bagels | *Bakery* 24
Sofi's Crepes | *Crêpes* 24

SOUTH BALTIMORE

(Including Federal Hill)

Blue Agave | *Mex.* 22
Bluegrass | *Amer.* 24
Grilled Cheese/Co. | *Sandwiches* 22
Hersh's Pizza | *Pizza* -
Langermann's | *Southern* 22
NEW Liv2eat | *Amer.* -
Matsuri | *Japanese* 24
Metropolitan Coffee | *Amer.* 23
Mr. Rain's Fun Hse. | *Amer.* 23
Porters | *Amer.* 22
Regi's | *Amer.* 23
Rusty Scupper | *Seafood* 22
Tabrizi's | *Med./Mideast.* 21
Thai Arroy | *Thai* 26

WEST BALTIMORE

Alewife | *Amer.* 22
Faidley's | *Seafood* 26
NEW Martick's | *Amer.* -
Mekong Delta | *Viet.* 27

Outer Baltimore

ABERDEEN/
HARFORD COUNTY/
HAVRE DE GRACE

(Including White Marsh)

Basta Pasta | *Italian* 21
Broom's Bloom | *Ice Cream* 27
Chiapparelli's | *Italian* 24
Double T | *Diner* 20
Du-Claw | *Pub* 21
Five Guys | *Burgers* 24
Josef's | *Continental* 25
Kobe | *Japanese* 27
Laurrapin | *Amer.* 26
Liberatore's | *Italian* 24
Open Door | *Amer.* 24
P.F. Chang's | *Chinese* 23
Tidewater | *Amer.* 22

BOWIE/LAUREL

Du-Claw | *Pub* 21
Elevation Burger | *Burgers* 21
Facci | *Italian/Pizza* 24
Five Guys | *Burgers* 24
Grace's | *Chinese* 25
Jerry's | *Seafood* 26
Kloby's Smokehse. | *BBQ* 21

Negril | *Jamaican* 24
Pasta Plus | *Italian* 26
Pollo Campero | *Central Amer.* 19
Red Hot/Blue | *BBQ* 22

BROOKLANDVILLE

Stone Mill | *Bakery* 24
Tark's Grill | *Amer.* 21

BWI/ELKRIDGE/
HANOVER/LINTHICUM

Bobby's Burger | *Burgers* 22
Cheesecake Factory | *Amer.* 24
Du-Claw | *Pub* 21
Elkridge Furnace | *Amer.* 25
Five Guys | *Burgers* 24
G&M | *Seafood* 24
Gunning's | *Seafood* 23
Little Spice | *Thai* 25
Mamma Lucia | *Italian* 22
Olive Grove | *Italian* 24
Prime Rib | *Steak* 28
R & R | *Mex.* 27
Timbuktu | *Seafood* 23

CATONSVILLE/
WOODLAWN

Atwater's | *Bakery* 25
Catonsville Gourm. | *Seafood* 26
Chef Paolino | *Italian/Pizza* 21
Double T | *Diner* 20
Grilled Cheese/Co. | *Sandwiches* 22
Pho Nam | *Viet.* 27
Regions | *Eclectic* 23

CLARKSVILLE/
GLENELG

Bistro Blanc | *Amer.* 26
Great Sage | *Vegan* 24

COLUMBIA/
ELLICOTT CITY/
HIGHLAND

Aida | *Italian* 24
Akbar | *Indian* 24
NEW Ale Hse. | *Amer.* -
An Loi | *Viet.* 23
Azul 17 | *Mex.* 23
BGR | *Burgers* 22
Bon Fresco | *Sandwiches* 27
Café de Paris | *French* 24
Cheesecake Factory | *Amer.* 24
Clyde's | *Amer.* 22
Coal Fire | *Pizza* 22

Double T	*Diner*	20
Eggspectation	*Amer.*	21
Greystone Grill	*Steak*	19
Honey Pig	*Korean*	23
House of India	*Indian*	23
Hunan Manor	*Chinese*	23
Iron Bridge Wine	*Amer.*	25
Jesse Wong's Asean	*Pan-Asian*	23
Kings Contrivance	*Amer.*	24
Mango Grove	*Indian*	24
P.F. Chang's	*Chinese*	23
Pho Dat Thanh	*Viet.*	24
Portalli's	*Italian*	22
Red Pearl	*Chinese*	26
Shin Chon	*Korean*	22
Stanford Grill	*Amer.*	24
Sushi King	*Japanese*	28
Sushi Sono	*Japanese*	27
Tersiguel's	*French*	28
Victoria	*Eclectic*	24

ESSEX/DUNDALK

Costas Inn	*Crab*	25
Mr. Bill's	*Crab*	26
Schultz's Crab	*Crab*	27

GAMBRILLS

Coal Fire	*Pizza*	22
4 Seasons	*Eclectic/Med.*	25
Nando's	*Chicken*	22

GLEN BURNIE/ ODENTON/ SEVERNA PARK

Ann's Dari	*Hot Dogs*	25
Breakfast Shoppe	*Amer.*	25
Cafe Bretton	*French*	27
Five Guys	*Burgers*	24
Garry's	*Amer.*	20
Grace Gdn.	*Chinese*	28
Gunning's	*Seafood*	23
Pappas	*Amer./Seafood*	23
Seaside Rest.	*Seafood*	26
Tratt. Alberto	*Italian*	28

HUNT VALLEY/ NORTH BALTIMORE COUNTY

Friendly Farm	*Amer.*	25
Jesse Wong's Kit.	*Asian*	20
Manor Tav.	*Amer.*	24
Milton Inn	*Amer.*	28
Oregon Grille	*Seafood/Steak*	25
Peerce's	*Amer.*	21

LANHAM

Jerry's	*Seafood*	26
Ledo Pizza	*Pizza*	23

LARGO

Carolina Kit.	*Southern*	25
Kobe	*Japanese*	27

LUTHERVILLE/ COCKEYSVILLE/ TIMONIUM

Andy Nelson's	*BBQ*	26
Basta Pasta	*Italian*	21
BlueStone	*Seafood*	23
Christopher Daniel	*Amer.*	23
Edo Sushi	*Japanese*	24
First Watch	*Amer.*	21
Five Guys	*Burgers*	24
Goldberg's	*Bakery/Jewish*	25
Kooper's	*Amer.*	22
Liberatore's	*Italian*	24
Michael's Café	*Amer.*	23
Patrick's	*Amer.*	22
Peppermill	*Amer.*	23
San Sushi	*Japanese*	26
Sushi Hana	*Japanese*	26
Szechuan Hse.	*Chinese*	26
Umi Sake	*Asian*	28

MITCHELLVILLE

Negril	*Jamaican*	24

NORTHEAST BALTIMORE/ PERRY HALL

Big Bad Wolf	*BBQ*	26
Clementine	*Amer.*	25
Double T	*Diner*	20
Gino's	*Burgers*	22
Hamilton Tav.	*Pub*	24
Koco's	*Pub*	27
Liberatore's	*Italian*	24
NEW Maggie's Farm	*Eclectic*	-
R & R	*Mex.*	27

OWINGS MILLS/ REISTERSTOWN/ FINKSBURG

Edo Sushi	*Japanese*	24
Harryman Hse.	*Amer.*	24
Linwoods	*Amer.*	27
Sofi's Crepes	*Crêpes*	24

PARKVILLE

NEW McFaul's	*Amer.*	-
Pappas	*Amer./Seafood*	23

PASADENA

Double T	*Diner*	20

PIKESVILLE

David Chu's	*Chinese/Kosher*	25
First Watch	*Amer.*	21
Goldberg's	*Bakery/Jewish*	25
Mari Luna Latin	*Mex./Pan-Latin*	25
Mari Luna Mex.	*Mex./Pan-Latin*	24
Ruth's Chris	*Steak*	26
Stone Mill	*Bakery*	24
Suburban Hse.	*Deli*	19

TOWSON

Atwater's	*Bakery*	25
Bahama Breeze	*Carib.*	23
Café Troia	*Italian*	23
Cheesecake Factory	*Amer.*	24
Five Guys	*Burgers*	24
Gino's	*Burgers*	22
Havana Rd.	*Cuban*	21
Orchard Mkt.	*Persian*	26
P.F. Chang's	*Chinese*	23
Pho Dat Thanh	*Viet.*	24
San Sushi/Thai	*Japanese/Thai*	21
Spice & Dice	*Thai*	29
Sushi Hana	*Japanese*	26
Towson Diner	*Diner*	21

WESTMINSTER/ ELDERSBURG/ SYKESVILLE

Antrim 1844	*Amer./French*	27
Baugher's	*Amer.*	20
Five Guys	*Burgers*	24
Grilled Cheese/Co.	*Sandwiches*	22
Liberatore's	*Italian*	24

Annapolis/ Anne Arundel

NEW Annapolis Smokehouse & Tavern	*BBQ*	-
Boatyard B&G	*Pub*	22
Café Normandie	*French*	25
Cantler's Riverside	*Crab*	24
Carpaccio	*Italian*	25
Carrol's Creek	*Seafood*	23
Cheesecake Factory	*Amer.*	24
Chick/Ruth's	*Diner*	22
Chop Hse.	*Steak*	25
Crush	*Amer.*	23
Double T	*Diner*	20

Five Guys	*Burgers*	24
49 West	*Coffee*	22
Galway Bay	*Pub*	24
Harry Browne	*Amer.*	25
Jalapeños	*Mex./Spanish*	27
Joss Cafe	*Japanese*	27
Lebanese Tav.	*Lebanese*	23
Lemongrass	*Thai*	25
Les Folies	*French*	27
Level	*Amer.*	24
Lewnes' Steak	*Steak*	28
Luna Blu	*Italian*	22
Main Ingredient	*Amer.*	25
Miss Shirley's	*Amer.*	26
Nando's	*Chicken*	22
O'Learys	*Seafood*	26
Osteria 177	*Italian*	27
Paladar	*Carib./Pan-Latin*	23
Paul's Homewood	*Amer./Greek*	25
P.F. Chang's	*Chinese*	23
Red Hot/Blue	*BBQ*	22
Reynolds Tav.	*Amer./British*	23
Rockfish	*Amer.*	20
Ruth's Chris	*Steak*	26
Severn Inn	*Amer.*	22
Sofi's Crepes	*Crêpes*	24
Tsunami	*Asian*	25
Vin 909	*Amer.*	28
NEW West	*Amer.*	-
Wild Orchid	*Amer.*	23
Yellowfin	*Amer.*	23

Eastern Shore

Ava's	*Italian/Pizza*	27
Banning's	*Amer.*	22
Bartlett Pear	*Amer.*	28
Bistro Poplar	*French*	28
NEW Blackthorn	*Pub*	-
Brass. Brightwell	*Amer./French*	21
Harris Crab	*Crab*	24
Kentmorr	*Crab*	25
Mason's	*Amer.*	26
Narrows	*Seafood*	25
Out of the Fire	*Amer./Eclectic*	28
Pope's Tav.	*Amer.*	27
Rustico	*Italian*	25
Ruth's Chris	*Steak*	26
Salter's Tav.	*Amer./Seafood*	25
Scossa	*Italian*	28
Ava's	*Steak*	-
208 Talbot	*Amer.*	-